LODZ GHETTO

LODZ GHETTO

INSIDE A COMMUNITY UNDER SIEGE

Compiled and Edited by
Alan Adelson and Robert Lapides

WITH AN AFTERWORD BY GEOFFREY HARTMAN

ANNOTATIONS AND BIBLIOGRAPHICAL NOTES BY MAREK WEB

VIKING

VIKING
Published by the Penguin Group
Viking Penguin, a division of Penguin Books USA Inc.,
40 West 23rd Street, New York, New York 10010, U.S.A.
Penguin Books Ltd, 27 Wrights Lane, London W8 5TZ, England
Penguin Books Australia Ltd, Ringwood, Victoria, Australia
Penguin Books Canada Ltd, 2801 John Street, Markham, Ontario, Canada L3R 1B4
Penguin Books (N.Z.) Ltd, 182–190 Wairau Road, Auckland 10, New Zealand
Penguin Books Ltd, Registered Offices: Harmondsworth, Middlesex, England

First published in 1989 by Viking Penguin, a division of Penguin Books USA Inc.

1 3 5 7 9 10 8 6 4 2

Grateful acknowledgment is made for permission to reprint the following works: Material from the archives of Beit Lohamei Haghetaot, The Jewish Historical Institute of Warsaw, Yad Vashem, the Holocaust Martyrs' and Heroes' Remembrance Authority, and YIVO Institute for Jewish Research. Excerpts from *The Chronicle of the Lodz Ghetto,* by Lucjan Dobroszycki. By permission of the author and Yale University Press. Excerpt from *Kiddush Hashem.* © 1987, Yeshiva University Press. By permission of Ktav Publishers. Excerpt from *In These Nightmarish Days,* by Jozef Zelkowicz, which appears in *A Holocaust Reader,* edited by Lucy Dawidowicz. Published by Behrman House, Inc., 235 Watchung Ave., West Orange, NJ 07052. Used with permission. Excerpt from letter written by Felicia Weingarten. Excerpts from diary of Dawid Sierakowiak. Copyright Konrad Turowski. Excerpt from *Infiltration,* by Albert Speer, translated by Joachim Neugroschel. Reprinted with permission of Macmillan Publishing Company. Copyright © 1984 Macmillan Publishing Company, Inc. Excerpts from diary and memoirs of Irena Liebman. Photographs from the collection of Erhard Löcker Verlag, Copyright Erhard Löcker Verlag, Vienna.

LIBRARY OF CONGRESS CATALOGING IN PUBLICATION DATA
Lodz ghetto: inside a community under siege / compiled and edited by Alan Adelson and Robert Lapides; with annotations and bibliographical notes by Marek Web.
p. cm.
ISBN 0-670-82983-8
1. Jews—Poland—Lodz—Persecutions. 2. Holocaust, Jewish (1939–1945)—Poland—Lodz—Personal narratives. 3. Lodz (Poland)—Ethnic relations. I. Adelson, Alan.
II. Lapides, Robert. III. Web, Marek.
DS135.P62L6441354 1989
305.8′0094384—dc20 89-40167

Printed in the United States of America
Set in Granjon
Designed by Ann Gold

Page 526 constitutes a continuation of the copyright page.

"Listen and believe this, even though it happened here,
even though it seems so old, so distant and so strange."

—Jozef Zelkowicz

September 1942

CONTENTS

Color illustrations follow pages 130 and 386.

ACKNOWLEDGMENTS

The compilation of this volume has been a worldwide effort which innumerable individuals have assisted with their time, talents, and materials. Efforts to bring these writings and images to the light of print have gone on for fifty years and have involved many individuals not known to us today who hid, kept, reclaimed, transcribed, reproduced, and preserved these writings and pictures. Some may be alive today and will see the fruits of those efforts now for the first time.

For all of us involved, the physical production of this volume and with it the preservation and dissemination of the material is thanks enough. But the following institutions and individuals have contributed to the project in ways which the editors want to recognize and thank directly:

Lucjan Dobroszycki, whose life's work has been to bring the writings from the Lodz Ghetto to print, and whose constant guidance and unstinting sharing of material have been central to the compilation of this volume.

Yad Vashem, Beit Lohamei Haghetaot, Zydowski Instytut Historyczny, and YIVO, the Institute for Jewish Research, whose vast archives have contributed many of the texts and photographs presented here.

Erhard Löcker, of Löcker Verlag, Vienna, for permission to use the color photographs taken in the ghetto.

Archivists Schmuel Krakowski, Benjamin Anulik, Chana Abels, Chaya Levinson, and Marek Web.

Konrad Turowski and Bono Wiener for contributing materials in their private possession.

The New York chapter of the American Foundation for Polish/Jewish Studies, the Alfred Jurzykowski Foundation, the Joe and Emily Lowe Foundation, the Literature Program of the New York State Council on the Arts, the Samuel Bronfman Foundation, the S. H. and Helen R. Scheuer Family Foundation, and Jack Tramiel for financial support. The Borough of Manhattan Community College of the City University of New York, for supporting Robert Lapides' work on this project with a faculty fellowship.

Hedwig Heilbrun, for her help in annotating and explicating religious and cultural references. Molly M. Hoagland, for her research.

Harry and Ina Lapides, and Martin D. Payson, for their personal support.

Kathryn Taverna for her honest and able responses to the material and guidance in its selection.

Stephen Samuels for his extensive efforts in the development of *Lodz Ghetto,* both film and book.

Ellen Levine, for recognizing the value of the manuscript and guiding it to the publisher.

And Mindy H. Werner, our editor at Viking Penguin, who has managed the intricate process of producing this volume.

A COLLECTED CONSCIOUSNESS

Any moment now, the search will begin. If they find our hiding place, I will leave these notebooks in the dungeon. They might be our last trace.

—Jakub Poznanski, engineer

Son of man, go out into the streets. Soak in the unconscious terror of the new-born babies about to be slaughtered. Be strong. Keep your heart from breaking so you'll be able to describe, carefully and clearly, what happened in the ghetto during the first days of September in the year one thousand, nine hundred and forty two.

—Jozef Zelkowicz, journalist

I want to be able to record for posterity what I have seen. . . . I've been in contact with first-hand sources for a long time. I know many nuances, many details not known officially. And I deem it my duty to report them, if not in a finished, systematically researched work of history, then at least as source material for the objective historians who will come later.

—Jakub Szulman, physician

I can't write . . . I can't concentrate and describe it all chronologically. I am broken, I feel guilty, I am a murderer . . . I killed Mookha . . . how can a father desert his own child and run away?

—Anonymous

The authors of this volume had accurate foresight fifty years ago when they began these accounts of their lives in the progressing Holocaust. All too aware of how incredible their plight was, they knew that readers of the future would find the loss and torment unfathomable. That in time, people might forget, disbelieve, and deny the destruction. That generations to come might not learn of it. So, in these diaries and personal monographs, the writers beg for your understanding and command your attention, grasping for the solace of believing that humanity could eventually know exactly what had happened, and perhaps cure itself.

So the journalist Jozef Zelkowicz reaches through time, at the opening of a story about a mother's refusal to give up her child, with the words which we have brought to the cover of this book:

"Listen and believe this, even though it happened here, even though it seems so old, so distant and so strange."

These are the stories of the years of confinement which preceded mass death. They reveal physical and spiritual breakdown, strife within families, endurance, and surrender. People who want to understand why the Jews boarded the trains, people who have become hardened to the loss or who have disengaged from it, people who are unable to see heroes or martyrs in the slaughter, who see only victims—all such readers can enter and understand this volume.

From *then,* unmediated by time, it can give you access to those who were trapped, whether or not they knew it, in a scheme which would destroy nearly all the Jews of Europe.

In the last months of the Lodz Ghetto's existence, a young man, fully aware of the death which threatened him and his young sister, began a diary in the margins of a French novel, *Les Vrais Riches* (The Truly Rich). To ensure that his words would be recognized and saved, he wrote in four languages—Polish, English, Yiddish, and Hebrew. He railed at "the devouring Nazi beast," and he prayed the ghetto would be saved "at the last minute." His book was found at Auschwitz. The dream he devoutly expressed, to be able to tell the world what he endured in the ghetto, is fulfilled here with the first publication of his words.

We have gathered a community's consciousness through the vast written remnants of a society confronting annihilation but struggling to survive. Schoolchildren, a journalist, a theologian, a doctor, a policeman, an engineer, a soup kitchen worker, the community's appointed leader, the secret memoranda of its rulers, the notes and ruminations of a gifted intellectual—*"notes for the future."*

> September 8, 1939 . . . Lodz is occupied . . . the frightening news reaches us: Lodz has surrendered. German patrols are on Piotrkowska Street. Fear,

> surprise . . . surrendered without a fight? Maybe it's just a tactical maneuver. We'll see.
> —from the diary of Dawid Sierakowiak

Hope answers fear, despair can be countered with self-deception. It is in the Jewish tradition to wait and hope, adapting in order to ride out troubles, accommodating, "coping" in the belief that with resourcefulness, strength, and good fortune, you and your family will survive.

> What have we learned from the Torah? Hunger? One goes hungry. Beatings? One is beaten.
>
> We're the Chosen People. There's nothing we can do about it.
> —from the notebooks of Oskar Rosenfeld

Here you will follow Jewish spirits, denied truth about the genocide or news of the world at war, but groping to understand. Reading through the book chronologically, or using the index by authors to trace each voice *seriatim,* you will experience the progression of the war against the Jews as it advances through Europe's second-largest Jewish community.

The Jewish response to the Nazi attack brought forward a theological trait which had imbued the culture through many eras of persecution. It is characterized by the phrase *Kiddush Hashem,* In His Blessed Name. The belief holds that Jews killed in a time of persecution are martyrs to God, and it comes forward both intentionally and through inadvertent cultural influences in the writings from the Lodz Ghetto. Its most direct expression in this volume appears in *"Lekh Lekho* [Go Forth]," the epic work of ghetto poet Simcha Bunim Shayevitsh:

> But let us not weep, let us not
> Moan, and to spite all enemies,
> Let us smile, only smile, that they
> May be amazed at what Jews are capable of . . .
>
> And though beneath our steps lies death,
> Over our heads is the divine presence of God.
> So, child, go forth with a new sacrifice of self
> And with the old *"Ekhod,"* the oneness of God.
> *Shema Yisrael.* [Hear O Israel] The Lord is One.

A TRANSITIONAL MEASURE

The Jewish population of Lodz numbered at least a quarter of a million before the German invasion. It was prominent and prosperous—prosperity visible today in the overgrown but still beautiful Jewish cemetery which takes up more than a square mile of the city's northeast sector. Here stands the gold-domed tomb of the Jewish textile magnate I. K. Poznanski, whose factory employed thousands of workers and clothed much of Eastern Europe. The city's municipal offices are now housed in one of the three palaces Poznanski built for himself and his family.

Most of the wealthy Lodz Jews escaped entrapment before the Nazis invaded the city in September 1939. And many middle-class Jews also fled, east to Russia or west into free Europe. But more than 200,000 Jews, like young Sierakowiak's family, had no place to go and remained in their homes, hoping to ride out the storm. You will find in the schoolboy's early diary entries no vision of their impending deaths, his mother to be asphyxiated three years later in a gas van, his father to die of exhaustion in the ghetto soon afterward, and the diarist himself, a young man of nineteen, to succumb to tuberculosis just after that.

Following the Sierakowiak family through its last years, you cannot forget the diary's early scenes of confusion, with neighbors warning that everyone should flee to avoid being sent to work camps by the enemy. In retrospect, their worst fears seem so naïve.

While it is true that the Nazis' official Final Solution to the Jewish question was not promulgated until after the Wannsee Conference of January 20, 1942, assertions that the Germans at first only intended to *concentrate* the Jews are challenged by the December 10, 1939, top-secret memorandum here of Secret Service Brigadenführer Friedrich Übelhoer. He asserts that the establishment of the ghetto is only a *transitional* measure: "The final aim must be to burn out entirely this pestilent abscess."

The diaries published here of the Jews caught in that "transition" form a record which is utterly different from the recollections of survivors. Here there is no sense of knowing what is going to happen—little certainty among their subjects about the Nazis' plan. These accounts were not written with arrival at the death camp as their inevitable conclusion. Instead, we read of the instinctual struggle to hold on to human experience: family, art, education, sex, religion, hope. But also of the progressive loss of those values to grief, exhaustion, and starvation.

> Gangs of scruffy children, their yellow, wrinkled faces looking aged, walk tiredly through the streets. Sometimes one sees a fleeting smile on their

faces, hears singing from their bloodless lips. Sometimes they throw a snowball like children elsewhere.

No one can say what will happen tomorrow. What will happen to all of us. What all this is for. Why the ghetto? Will there be a tomorrow? Is it worth thinking about?

We are lepers, outcasts, common thieves, people without music, without earth, without beds, without a world. There is no other city like this in the world. Come here, people from the outside, from over there . . . where there are normal days and holidays, where there are dreams and desire and resistance. Come quickly. For when it is all over, we will be so thinned out and so miserable that we will no longer be able to enjoy the pleasure of seeing you again. —from the notebooks of Oskar Rosenfeld

The transport of "cultural" Jews from Prague brought Oskar Rosenfeld to the Lodz Ghetto in October 1941. His notebooks, translated and excerpted for publication here for the first time, show a ruminating, evaluative, intellectual man, searching his own knowledge of Jewish heritage to understand the holocaust burning away his people.

A translator of great books, a lover and critic of literature, art, and music, he grows, even in the ghetto. He plans a novella, "The Secret of the Ghetto." He finds himself swept away by the humble ghetto orchestra's inspired performance of a liberation motif in Beethoven. Never before in the concert halls of any European city, he realizes, has he been so thrilled.

He writes fragments of scenes he calls "Talkies." Many details in Rosenfeld's notebooks tease the understanding. Who is Henuschi, who so occupies the man's thoughts? His daughter? No, a woman. But he calls her "my golden child," then asks, in his thoughts, "Are you as gray as I am now?" They've been separated by the war. She went to London.

Is Henuschi still alive? How would she respond now to his reveries? Does she know of Oskar's fate?

Rosenfeld's taste for intrigue leads to furtive coding and transcription. He reports forbidden news of the progress of the war, news which he could have gained only from access to a clandestine radio. He calls Spain *Cervantes,* Russia is *Vanya,* England is *Insel.*

He has contact with Rumkowski, the Eldest of the Jews, goes directly to him for housing, receives a writer's job (as an official chronicler), nurtures the liaison in conversations, and then writes that Rumkowski has promised him protection from deportation—for as long as possible. He moves from image to thought, a writer's consciousness recording, interpreting, always against the condemned man's craving for freedom.

THE KING OF THE JEWS

Mordechai Chaim Rumkowski believed he was ruling a Jewish state. He embodies the paradox of Jewish leadership during the Holocaust and is perhaps the most controversial Jew in modern history. We see him reflected kaleidoscopically in nearly every one of this book's eighteen individual accounts.

In a preamble to the "Encyclopedia of the Ghetto," a never-completed background companion to the official day-to-day *Chronicle of the Lodz Ghetto,* the writers in Rumkowski's employ describe him as "born" for the position.

Historians have speculated that he was chosen by the Nazis because of his energy, his ability to speak German, or even because of his white hair. But we learn from Jakub Poznanski that when the Germans began seizing Jews off the streets for forced labor soon after the invasion, Rumkowski was noteworthy among the Jewish leaders who proposed for the sake of peace to *deliver* daily quotas of Jews to the Nazis. Is it forcing logic to wonder if Rumkowski's role in those first transactions signaled to the Nazis that he could be counted on to continue delivering Jews on command? Or even that this may have been what he intended to have them understand?

But one must also wonder from this first episode how Rumkowski could have continued to so underestimate the inevitable outcome of Faustian deals with the Nazis. Poznanski goes on to tell us that the Nazis promptly reneged on the arrangement, going right back to grabbing Jews violently off the streets again, and then even taking them out of their homes.

Rumkowski loved the ghetto, his dominion. On a visit to the Warsaw Ghetto in May 1941, he tried to point out the "creative" value of ghettoization, as he saw it—a partial fulfillment of the Zionist goals he embraced. He repeatedly told Jews in the ghetto that when the war was over he would be chosen to run a protectorate which the Nazis would establish to contain all the Jews of Europe.

But as much as he wanted to preserve the ghetto and its population, he found himself obliged to fulfill an unending series of deportation orders imposed on him by the Nazis: ten thousand, fifteen thousand, twenty thousand, ten thousand more. Finally, as the people had always rumored, the entire ghetto was gone.

Rumkowski bargained with the Germans to minimize the deportations. His realm was reduced gradually, and his goal with it: from saving a majority to at least a portion of the ghetto, and finally to what few souls he could rescue. He accepted responsibility for delivering the population. His transcribed speeches and preserved proclamations are here, berating the people for their gossip, for thinking they knew better than he, for being too smart for their own good, even, in the end, exhorting them: "Jews of the ghetto, come to your senses. Volunteer for the transports."

SLAVERY OR DEATH

You do not forget about the Nazis, although the masters appear only occasionally in these accounts. The whole ghetto serves them. In life under enslavement, the masters are presupposed.

The murderers do not hesitate to lie. The Nazis could not expect the Jews to walk knowingly and willingly to their deaths. Not at first. So they offered the hopeful prospect of a better life *outside* the ghetto, on Polish farms or at work camps in the Reich. They cut the ghetto off from the rest of the world. Except for the death camps themselves, it was the most hermetically sealed concentration of Jews in Europe. In Lodz, now renamed Litzmannstadt after a World War I German general who died battling to conquer the city, the Jews were separated, under threat of death, from contact with the Poles. The Germans built three bridges, paid for by the Jews, over thoroughfares used by the Poles and Germans. These streets were fenced on both sides to contain and isolate the Jews.

Ghetto children played daredevil games stepping through the barbed wire at the ghetto's perimeters into no-man's-land, then stepping back. A few individuals escaped from the ghetto. One pathetically dropped the Jewish star he had removed from his clothing as he reached into his pocket to purchase a train ticket in a neighboring town. He was brought back and publicly hanged. Many Jews were shot near the barbed wire as the Germans enforced the ghetto's isolation. "Going to the wire" became a euphemism for suicide in the ghetto. Dozens of ghetto dwellers chose to end their lives simply by approaching a fence within view of a German guardpost.

The strategies of enslavement and genocide merged conveniently. The Nazis worked them so hard and fed them so little, the Jews willingly boarded the trains, "if only to get out of this ghetto."

The Nazis set the provisioning level for the ghetto population at one half of the per-capita norm for inmates of German prisons. Hans Biebow, the German overseer, rightly assumed that the Jews would part with all their valuable possessions to stave off hunger, and thereafter they would have to earn their meager keep through slave labor in one of the ghetto industries—or perish.

But even labor in a ghetto workshop did not carry any assurance of survival. During the best of times in the ghetto—in mid-1940—the average person's daily intake has been estimated at about 1,800 calories, while the required level of nutrition for a working person is between 3,000 and 5,000 calories. At the end of 1941 the average ghetto Jew's nourishment was brought as low as 700 to 900 calories a day. For the human organism this meant progressive deterioration: in the beginning a feeling of gnawing hunger, followed by rapid weight loss, swelling, mental breakdown, total weakness, and increased susceptibility to disease. Death ravaged the ghetto daily. In 1942, of every 1,000 people in the ghetto population, 161 died from hunger, cold, or disease.

Deceptive postcards came back to the ghetto from deportees forced to write favorable reports about their destinations, and on at least one occasion an SS officer presented himself in the ghetto market to describe how well the deportees were being fed and housed in a newly developed work camp.

But rumors of the death camps kept coming back, and then there was talk of a site at Chelmno, in Kolo County, where the Jews of Lodz were being exterminated. Several traces of the emergence of the truth are found in the diaries here. Rumkowski, who was bound to fulfill the Nazi demands, saw these rumors as a direct threat to his power. He used all the force he could muster to suppress them. His speeches reflect this campaign. On January 3, 1942, when a rumor spread through the ghetto that the entire population was to be deported, Rumkowski stood before a select audience in the House of Culture and said: "And now I come to the plague known as gossip. Once again a gang of scoundrels is spreading rumors in the hope of disturbing the peace. Perhaps the authors of these panic-producing stories are lurking even here, in this audience. I would like to murder them! . . . The stories circulating today are one hundred percent false. . . . Bear in mind that at the heart of all my projects is the goal that honest people may sleep in peace. Nothing bad will happen to people of good will. . . . I give you my word of honor that no evil waits concealed in the wings of the new registration. . . . The authorities respect us because we constitute a center of productivity."

Two weeks later, Rumkowski was announcing: "We are now on the threshold of very bad times, and everyone needs to be aware of this. Only work can save us from the worst calamity."

With the first wave of deportations under way, Rumkowski began using the power of selection to enforce his policies: "Remember that when there is a demand for more deportees, I will put all the parasites on the lists."

But it was not just with those who were unemployed or on welfare that he fulfilled the early deportation quotas. Rumkowski placed on the first lists the politically outspoken resistance leaders he thought were behind the widespread labor unrest. With these deportations he consolidated his power beyond any further challenge.

Jews who survived the ghetto often consider Rumkowski a hateful tyrant with no scruples; others believe he saved their lives.

A communiqué from the Jewish underground on May 24, 1944, identifies the Lodz Ghetto as the longest-lasting concentration of Jews in Poland. By then, all other cities were *Judenrein*—Jew-clean. A dispute was going on at the highest levels of the Nazi regime, with Albert Speer arguing that Rumkowski's Jews should be kept to produce munitions, while Himmler confidently gives the order to carry out the Final Solution.

Unquestionably, Rumkowski succeeded in making the Jewish ghetto a remarkably profitable enterprise for the Germans. Within six months of its sealing off, the ghetto was self-sufficient. Hans Biebow's ghetto administration, which is generally considered to have hidden revenues from Berlin, reported a net profit from productivity and confiscations between November 1940 and August 1942 of 20 million Reichsmarks, after deducting 33 million for "maintenance" of the ghetto. In the following two years, from September 1942 to September 1944, the *Gettoverwaltung* reported a net profit of 26,211,485 Reichsmarks, after taking 43,232,813 for maintaining the Jews.

In addition to the tons of munitions, telecommunications equipment, uniforms, boots, lingerie, temporary housing, carpets, and all manner of other goods the Germans extracted from the Jewish laborers, Berlin had a net profit of 46,211,485 Reichsmarks from the ghetto, following its final liquidation. The Jews had certainly demonstrated to the Germans that they were not "parasites." The ghetto had worked instead as a giant war industry, arming its enemy.

A BACKGROUND TO THE COMPILATION OF THIS VOLUME

This book was engendered directly by the publication of its predecessor, *The Chronicle of the Lodz Ghetto,* edited by Lucjan Dobroszycki and Danuta Dabrowska for publication in Poland, then abridged by Dr. Dobroszycki to form the volume published in 1984 by Yale University Press.

At the Jewish Heritage Project, an organization committed to bringing literature related to Jewish history and culture to a wide audience, it was immediately apparent that the literary and photographic legacy of the Lodz Ghetto was unparalleled, and that the destruction of this single community could stand in many ways for the course of the Holocaust through all of European Jewry.

We began almost immediately to develop a film which would draw from the *Chronicle* and the thousands of photographs made in the ghetto.

But the *Chronicle,* written under the official sponsorship of the Rumkowski administration, and in an impersonal editorial voice, left much unexpressed. Dr. Dobroszycki urged a close examination of the private diaries and monographs of the ghetto dwellers. He progressively turned over to the project his lifetime's archive of ghetto materials—literally sheaves of ghetto writings. These became the core of this new volume.

A worldwide search followed. Every known diary was retrieved. Archives and libraries around the world were researched. Essential material was contributed from private sources. The largest gatherings of material came from the Jewish Historical Institute in Warsaw, the Lodz civic archives, and the two major Holocaust archives in Israel: Yad Vashem and the Ghetto Fighters' House (*Beit Lohamei Hagetoat*). In New York we used extensively the fine Nachman Zonabend Collection at YIVO, the Institute for Jewish Research.

Thirteen different translators were employed, working from original materials written in the ghetto's four languages: Polish, Yiddish, Hebrew, and German. Over ten thousand pages of material were translated during a three-year period, retaining the authors' original designations of dates and the writers' own underlining.

We gathered two thousand photographs for the project from many of the same sources.

The ghetto photographers, particularly Mendel Grossman and Henryk Ross, worked with a full awareness that they were recording the most tragic period in human history. They were motivated by the same drive as our authors, to preserve for people of the future an understanding of daily life and work in the ghetto. Grossman gave prints of his photographs to many people in the ghetto and left thousands more in carefully prepared albums and in the ghetto archives. He also catalogued meticulously the tiny contact prints from his 35-millimeter negatives, leaving our photo reproduction director, Mary Bachmann, with a difficult technical task of reclamation, but one which produced hundreds of images previously out of view.

We did not *discover* the remarkable color photographs which were shot in the ghetto; they came to us. Late in 1987, a representative of the Viennese publisher Erhard Löcker arrived in New York to show Lucjan Dobroszycki the contents of numerous contemporary snapshot packets. In them were astounding full-color photos of the ghetto.

Neither Dr. Dobroszycki nor anyone in his field had known such photographs existed. Color film was produced by AGFA in Germany as early as 1936, and a few color images from the Warsaw Ghetto were known to exist.

But here were hundreds of images of the Lodz Jews in their workshops, wearing yellow stars; here was Reichsführer Heinrich Himmler in his green BMW cabriolet, license plate "SS 1," conversing with Mordechai Chaim Rumkowski, the "Eldest" bowing his silver head within a protective circle of Nazi officers.

The Austrian publisher had bought these original color pictures in glass-mounted transparencies from an antiquarian book dealer who had purchased them from a source "not to be identified"—presumably the photographer or his family.

ENTER THE GHETTO

Every reader will struggle to reconcile the material which follows. I recall one moment in the five years I have spent with these ghetto writings which was very helpful:

I was filled with despair, conferring with Dr. Dobroszycki on how this overwhelming material should be presented. I poured out a litany of criticisms: of the ghetto dwellers' selfishness, of family members stealing food from their loved ones, of official corruption, extreme class stratification, the brutality of the Jewish police, the apparent deceptions of Rumkowski . . .

The scholar, a ghetto survivor who had spent more than forty years since the war bringing the Lodz writings to the light of print, quietly insisted that the ghetto's story was essentially life-affirming.

"We were pressed to the limit of human endurance, and beyond," he said, "and the society did not break down."

—Alan Adelson,
with Robert Lapides and Marek Web

LODZ GHETTO

ЛУИ ГЕЙЕРА

The second-largest Jewish population in Europe, the Jews of Lodz gather in 1912 before the Old Town Synagogue for the funeral of Elias Haim Meisel, Chief Rabbi of the Lodz *Kehillah.*

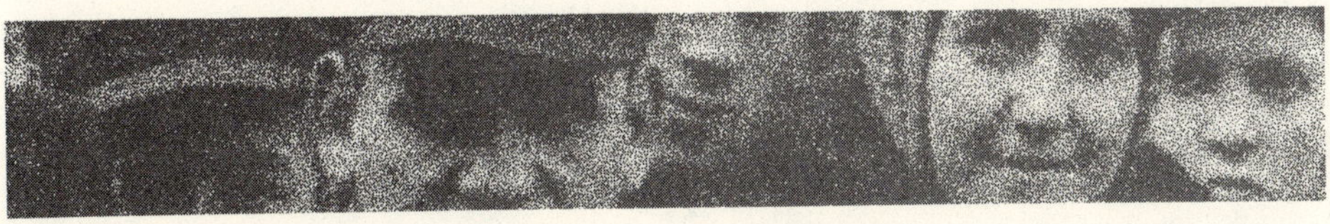

PROLOGUE

OSKAR ROSENFELD'S NOTEBOOKS

NOTEBOOK A

17 FEBRUARY 1942 PRIVATE DIARY

Transcribing what is present: very short, concrete phrases, everything sentimental pushed to the side, reading oneself, far from the world, alone in the room, not intended for other people—as a memory *for later.*

One was supposed to arrive neat, trim, well-groomed, quite *soigné* in Lodz; one finally knew where one was going. One thought it more than one knew, for the trip had gone through the grim landscapes of Poland, through autumn potato fields that stretched without break as far as the horizon.

Lodz, where it had been said a Council of Elders would be glad to receive its guests, had readied everything for them: places to live, food, work, even happiness. For, so it was said even before the departure, Jews would live "there" in freedom, follow their professions, be among themselves, and finally have peace. A rare bit of luck, for which one could thank the beloved Gestapo.

"We will hold out, we will outlive you, you cannot destroy us." (Rosenfeld)

The train stopped in an open field. The doors were ripped open. Exhausted, harrowed, their bags in their hands, on their backs, under their arms, more than a thousand people crawled down the exit planks into deep muck, mud, and water. It was autumn, Polish-Russian autumn. *Feldgraues* [Ger: field-greys; i.e., soldiers] drove us on. One—a blond, well-nourished youth, with a bristly reddish beard and reddish eyebrows—shouted, "Run, run, you Jewish pigs." Where had one landed? To whom did one belong? Who was there to help? Nothing, nothing. One could not orient oneself. The brain was empty, and one forgot that it was due to having eaten almost nothing for a day and a night.

A line formed. Through muck and mud it went, not knowing where. Curious people stood on the sides of a street in a neglected area with few houses. A few wagons, each with a gaunt horse, picked up the elderly and sick. Ragged people with exhausted pale faces trotted alongside. One saw carts, small wagons, pulled not by animals but by people, young and old. Grim clay huts—pathetic trees and bushes—lakes of muck, stinking garbage—countless creatures with backs bent over—next to them faces that had already gone beyond all pain, on which were written: We will hold out, we will outlive you, you cannot destroy us—impoverished stores, taverns, coffee houses, cigarette vendors, children offering things for sale, smells of things not seen in the West, young people in uniform with the Star of Zion on their arms, shrieking next to silence, above it all a foggy grey sky, across which birds like ravens flew every now and then. This was the outcast quarter of Lodz, the Litzmannstadt Ghetto.

What the doctor says: There is no reason to let oneself fall into moods that depress the spirit. Spirit is worth as much as health, and health is what is most important. We must hold our nerves together, avoid everything that can weaken the organism. For we have only *one* task: to survive the crisis and live. We must live and experience the moment in which we can say: it was worth bearing the difficulty and the misery . . . Next to this, everything is insignificant, petty, transitory. That moment will "make good on" even the hundreds of thousands who died before the end. The many things which we cannot give you patients you replace with strength of character, a capacity to bear misery, daily pride, and consciousness of your innocence. Somehow and sometime freedom will come. That is supported by our history and the eternal principle that has ruled the world until now: the triumph of righteousness over worthlessness. Clever, therefore: keeping silent, clenching one's teeth, being patient and ready for anything.

Mood: Let oneself wonder about the bleak, grey sky behind the gold, dirty blue houses and barracks full of snow, the withered trees with their withered branches covered in ice.

"Wagons, pulled not by animals but by people . . ." (Rosenfeld)

Details: Which groups or individuals are against the Eldest? How do they want to seize power? What do these people do? Are there political groups?

LES VRAIS RICHES

[A young man's diary, written in four languages in the margin of a French novel.]

JUNE 1944

In spite of all this, I am still dreaming; thank Heavens I am no realist, since to be a realist is to realize, and realizing the whole horror of our situation would have been more than any human being could endure. I go on dreaming, dreaming about survival and about getting fame in order to "tell" the world, to "tell and to protest." Both seem at the present moment remote and unbelievable, but who knows, maybe, perhaps. I dream about telling humanity, but would I be able to? Would Shakespeare be able? And I, who merely am a little proud of understanding Shakespeare?!

"We will succeed in drawing out all the valuables the Jews have accumulated and squirreled away." (Übelhoer's secret memorandum)

CHAPTER ONE

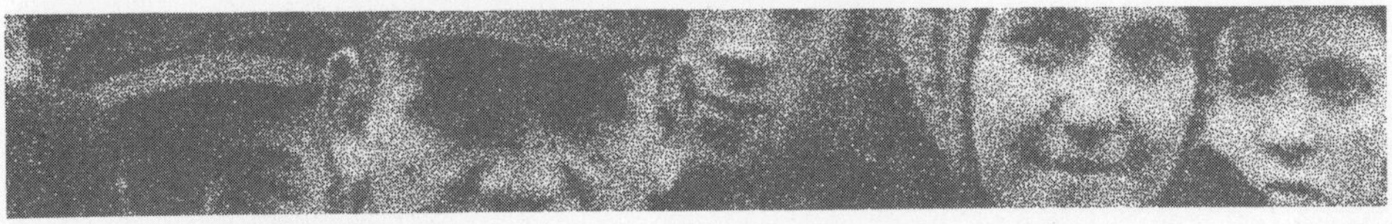

THE INITIAL TERROR

1939

DAWID SIERAKOWIAK'S DIARY

LODZ, AUGUST 24, 1939

Mobilization! We don't know if this is the real thing or not, but nearly every recruit is reporting. Many of our neighbors have already gone. . . . There's not the least hint of defeatism.

LODZ, AUGUST 26, 1939

Today I read Mayor [Jan] Kwapinski's appeal for volunteers to dig anti-aircraft ditches. Having gotten my parents' permission, I signed up immediately at the police station, as did all my schoolmates, and tomorrow morning I go to work. There are tens of thousands of volunteers. . . . Old Jews, young women, Chassidim, all citizens (except the Germans) are rushing to volunteer. The bloody Hun will not pass!

LODZ, AUGUST 28, 1939

My bones ache like everyone else's from yesterday's work. Fifty thousand people were out digging.

AUGUST 30, 1939
General mobilization! All reservists up to age 40 have been called.

LODZ, SEPTEMBER 1, 1939
The German army has crossed the Polish border in several places. Air raids on Polish towns such as Cracow, Czestochowa, Katowice, Grodno, etc., have begun. Things are boiling around the world. We're waiting for France and England to join the war; maybe even the United States. Meanwhile, we're repelling German attacks quite well. We had 3 alerts today, during which enemy planes were kept from approaching our town. I go to bed half dressed.

WEDNESDAY, SEPTEMBER 6, 1939—LODZ
Oh, God, what's going on here? Panic, departures en masse, defeatism. The city, abandoned by its institutions and by the police, awaits the imminent arrival of the German army in terror. What's happened? People are running nervously from place to place, anxiously carrying around their worn-out possessions. An aimless confusion. I was on duty till 1:00 am. I go to wake Rysio Wojcikowski for his turn. He is quite pessimistic, and he tells me that some kind of evacuation of the city is contemplated. He tells me that in his father's office everything is packed, and that they're getting ready to leave Lodz at any minute. I'm astonished. How? Where? I hear that the Germans are going to occupy Lodz any hour now. At home I meet our neighbor Mr. Grabinski, who has just returned from the city. He tells me of the great panic and frenzy seizing people. Throngs are leaving their homes on a dangerous migration to an uncertain future. There is crying and lamenting in the streets.

I go to bed, but at 5 am loud voices in the apartment wake me. Our neighbor Mr. Grodzenski, with his crying wife, is urging us to leave. Where? What for? Nobody knows. Run, run, run away as far as possible; move with care, stumble, forget everything—as long as you run from danger. My mother, my beloved, everlastingly sensitive mother, shows unusual composure as she consoles Mrs. Grodzenski, dissuading her from her ridiculous plans. Slowly, the contagion of mass hysteria, as well as the psychosis of crowds heading for slaughter, is eliminated. Father loses his head; he doesn't know what to do. Other neighbors come in, Jews, to seek counsel. They say that it's recommended that everyone able to bear arms leave the city, since the enemy will send them to work camps. They don't know what to do. The matter is considered and the decision is made to stay put. Whatever will be will be.

People are constantly on the move. Groups of men are heading toward Brzeziny to report for duty, while at the same time reservists and recruits are running away. Following them are women carrying bundles on their backs, filled with clothes, bedding and food. Even small children are running. All the leaders have left, so, for fun, we acted like we were the leaders, playing that role till noon.

Meanwhile, the situation is becoming ever more tense. Everyone has a different story to tell. Someone said that 150 English airplanes are waiting in Sieradz, another that the Germans have already occupied Zdunska Wola and are heading toward Lodz. The news gets stranger and more fantastic all the time.

Aunt Estera came to us with her children, and the house is filled with crying. Abek and Jankus ran away to Brzeziny. What is to be done? What can be accomplished? At 5 pm a kind of potato soup materialized: that's today's dinner. Other people might not even have that much. My father runs to our uncle, uncle back to father, but the decision remains the same: we will stay put and not run. In the afternoon a civilian patrol is organized in our neighborhood. My father signs up for it. In the evening Rysio Wojcikowski returns with his father. They've bought bicycles and are leaving once again. The roads are impossible.

I go to bed, expecting, for the first time, a good night's sleep. Unfortunately, there is no fear of air raids now. When you want to take over something, you don't destroy it. In the evening a column of Polish soldiers began arriving in town. They march quietly, in formation. It's hard to tell whether they're advancing or retreating. A little later some armored tanks left the city heading for the front.... What will tomorrow bring?

THURSDAY, SEPTEMBER 7, 1939

Today there was nothing new. Like everyone else I went outside this morning, did nothing but talk about what will happen. Will they, or won't they come? We dragged ourselves to Pabianicka Highway to watch the approaching Polish military column. So that's how a retreating army looks, rather like a regular army passing by. Can it be hoped that they won't come? Will there be another "Miracle on the Vistula River"? Will we live to see another Marne?* We sit together, boys and girls, trying to chase our worst thoughts away. It's no use. What will happen?

Our neighbor's brother came on horseback. He says the Germans are being pushed back and our columns are holding fast. The afternoon newspaper claims that the French are marching into Germany and that the Poles are holding fast. A militia is being organized. My father has signed up. Maybe now he'll regain his composure and calm down.

*Indicates end note.

In the evening we could hear the cannons boom and see a fiery glow in the south. Can it be so near? Some fellow claims that Lodz will be taken any moment now. I'm going home to bed, so I won't hear or see anything. Come what may! Maybe there'll be a miracle . . . Marne, oh Marne, if only it could happen again. Maybe a miracle is possible.

FRIDAY, SEPTEMBER 8, 1939—LODZ

Lodz is occupied. It's been quiet all day, too quiet. As I sit in the park in the afternoon, drawing a portrait of a girl I know, the frightening news reaches us: Lodz has surrendered. German patrols are on Piotrkowska Street. Fear, surprise . . . surrendered without a fight? Maybe it's just a tactical maneuver. We'll see. Meanwhile, conversations cease, the streets empty.

Mr. Grabinski returned from town and told everyone how the local Germans greeted their countrymen. The Grand Hotel, where the General Staff is to be headquartered, is decked with flowers. Civilians, including boys and girls, are jumping into passing military cars with a happy "Heil Hitler." One can hear loud German conversations on the streets. Whatever was hidden in the past, under the pretext of patriotism and civic-mindedness, now shows its true face.

SATURDAY, SEPTEMBER 9, 1939—LODZ

An announcement in Polish and German (German first) was posted this morning, advising calm while German units enter the city. It was signed "Civic Committee for the City of Lodz." A little later I went over to Pabianicka Highway to see the arriving army. A great number of vehicles, but the soldiers are nothing out of the ordinary. They differ from Polish soldiers only by the uniforms they wear, which are steel grey. Their expressions are boisterous—after all, they are the conquerors! A car of officers with Martian-like faces speeds by like lightning. The street is quiet, watching the passing army with indifference. It's quiet, all quiet. We get back to our neighborhood, sit on benches, talk, and joke. What the hell! Damn them.

SUNDAY, SEPTEMBER 10, 1939—LODZ

The first manifestation of the German presence: Jews were being seized to do digging. An elderly retired professor, a Christian who lives in no. 11, warned me about going into town. A decent man. What should I do now? Tomorrow is the first day of school; who knows what's happening to our beloved school. My friends are all going to attend, just to see what's going on. But I have to stay home. I must. My parents feel they don't want to lose me yet. Oh, my beloved school! Curse the times I complained about getting up early or about tests. If only those times could return!

LODZ, SEPTEMBER 12, 1939

Jews are being seized again, and beaten and robbed. The store where my father works was robbed, as the local Germans freely indulge their whims. People speak about the way Jews are treated at work: some are treated decently, but others are sadistically abused. Some Jews were ordered to stop working, to remove their clothes and stand facing the wall, at which point they were told they'd be shot. Shots were fired in their direction, and though nobody was killed, this was repeated a few times.

LODZ, SEPTEMBER 13, 1939

Erev Rosh Hashanah [Rosh Hashanah eve]. I haven't gone out and won't now that the sad holiday is approaching. It's no different from a sad ordinary day, when all one has is bread and (occasionally) herring. According to an order issued today, stores are to remain open tomorrow. What a blow to the Jews on Rosh Hashanah, the worst in ages! However, the synagogues are to be closed. There is no possibility of communal prayer for mercy. All basic personal freedoms are cancelled. Though I'm not old-fashioned (I've considered it my freedom to avoid prayer every year), this prohibition is painful, for I understand what faith means to the devout. It's an irreparable crime to take away someone's only happiness, his belief. The Jews will not forgive Hitler for this. Our vengeance will be awesome.

LODZ, SEPTEMBER 15, 1939

German agents remove Jews from all food lines, so that a poor Jew who has no maid is condemned to die of hunger.

LODZ, SEPTEMBER 16, 1939

Store-robbing continues. They get everything they can. Epsztajn's jewelry [and] watch store was completely emptied, and they scarcely got away alive.

SEPTEMBER 19, 1939

. . . listened to Hitler's speech about Danzig, ranting, raving, insulting, begging, ingratiating himself, but above all lying and lying. He lied that Poland started the war, he lied about the barbaric persecution of Germans in Poland and lied about his own, always peaceful, intentions.

LODZ, SEPTEMBER 20, 1939

The Germans have introduced the German mark alongside the Polish zloty (2 zlotys per mark) and the civic committee scrip. And a few anti-Semitic orders have been issued, namely that Jews cannot have more than 1000 marks and can draw only 250 marks per week from the bank. Stores are being robbed less often, but grabbing people for work continues.

LODZ, OCTOBER 3, 1939

People are gradually getting used to the new conditions and are returning to their jobs.

WEDNESDAY, OCTOBER 4, 1939—LODZ

I have not escaped the sad fate of my compatriots being seized to do work. Yesterday I took a shortcut to school, passing buildings covered with swastikas, many German cars, a lot of soldiers, and Lodz Germans wearing swastikas. I managed to evade them and, emboldened, took the same road today. A youth holding a big stick ran over, yelling in German: "Come, let's get to work! You're not allowed to go to school." I didn't resist, for no identification card would have been of any use there. He took me to a certain square where several Jews were already working, clearing the ground of leaves. He wanted me to jump over a high fence, but when he saw I wouldn't do it, he left me. The work on the square was supervised by a soldier, also with a big stick, who told me to fill some puddles with sand.

I've never been more humiliated than when I saw those passersby smiling and laughing at someone else's misfortune. Oh, you stupid, ignorant oafs, you simpletons! We don't need to feel ashamed; only our tormentors should. Enforced humiliation isn't humiliation. But the anger, the helpless fury of being forced to do this stupid, disgraceful task filled with provocation tore me apart. One thing is left: revenge!

After about a half hour of work, the soldier gathered all the Jews, some with their hats turned the wrong way (for the sport of it), lined us up, told one of us to put away the shovels, and dismissed the rest of us. It was supposed to be a show of magnanimity. I got to school halfway through the first class, my first lateness ever. The teachers can do nothing. "For reasons beyond the Jews' control."

This evening we found out that one of the Germans who live in our neighborhood is "eyeing" the Jews, "keeping watch" over them. This completely unnerved my poor anguished parents. Meanwhile, it was announced in school that students who do not pay at least some tuition will be barred from classes. What will happen to me? We will see.

LODZ, OCTOBER 6, 1939

Hitler called a meeting of the Reichstag, where he laughed at the former Polish government, rightly so, and where he gave his "final" offer for peace. His terms, given on the radio earlier this week, are unacceptable. He said that he is even ready to resolve the Jewish question, and ridiculed the British rule in Palestine.* At any rate, the speech brought nothing new.

LODZ, OCTOBER 8, 1939

Today the Jewish community council announced that it will provide 700 Jews for work. Will they now stop grabbing people on the street?

LODZ, OCTOBER 18, 1939

The Germans have set up a police station in our area and are going through apartments belonging to Jews, taking away radios, carpets, quilts, etc. They'll probably throw us out of our apartment soon.

LODZ, OCTOBER 19, 1939

No bread, no coal to be had.

LODZ, OCTOBER 20, 1939

An order was issued today forbidding Jews from trading in textiles, leather, and clothing. A Jew is not allowed to buy any of these, and he can sell these goods only to Christians. A shoemaker can buy leather for repairing heels and soles but not for making new shoes. It's true that this order hurts the black market in clothing; still, thousands of Jewish families are being brought to ruin.

LODZ, OCTOBER 22, 1939

Sunday, 11 a.m. A knock at the door. In comes a German officer, two policemen, and the super. The officer asks how many people live in the apartment, looks over the beds, asks about bedbugs, then if we have a radio—and finally leaves disappointed. He took radios from our neighbors (of course, they only go to Jews), as well as mattresses, quilts, carpets, etc. He found nothing of value in our place. Father was very frightened because he was praying in a *tallis* [prayer shawl], but the officer didn't notice. It's lucky, because people say that in such cases the Germans drive the Jews into the street and make them run until their *tallis* and *tefillin* [phylacteries] fall off. They took our neighbor Mr. Grabinski's only down quilt. Now it's 100% sure that they'll throw us out of our buildings.

OCTOBER 28, 1939

They ordered Mrs. Heller out of her apartment by 4 pm tomorrow; the administration gave her an empty apartment but only until she finds another one. Now we are all endangered.

LODZ, NOVEMBER 7, 1939

And so it's happened. Today's *Deutsche Lodscher Zeitung* announces the annexation of Lodz to Wartheland [the western part of Poland, annexed into the Reich] and, thus, to the Greater Reich. Of course, the appropriate orders have been issued, namely: Jews are not allowed to walk on Piotrkowska Street, since it's the main street; Jews and Poles are to yield always and everywhere to uniformed Germans; wearing four-cornered hats, uniforms, army coats, shiny buttons, and military belts is forbidden. Jewish bakeries are permitted to bake only bread. Jewish stores are to be marked "*Jüdisches Geschaft*" [Ger: Jewish business] next to a yellow Star of David inscribed with the word "*Jude*" [Ger: Jew]. It's a return to the yellow patches of the Middle Ages.

LODZ, NOVEMBER 8, 1939

Terrible things are going on in town. Jews are grabbed and ordered to report tomorrow to a designated area, to bring a shovel, food for 2 days, and 20 zlotys. What new idea is this? What kind of agony? Posters on street corners announce the annexation of Lodz to the Reich. A Nazi Youth Party was formed in the city: marching, singing, parades—one wants to stay home to keep from seeing all of this.

A meeting of "The Jewish Elders of Lodz" with the authorities was called for tomorrow. We'll see what comes of it.

LODZ, NOVEMBER 9, 1939

The Germans came to school yesterday and ordered that its Polish-Hebrew sign be taken down and the library made orderly.

The Jews who were grabbed for work and told to bring food and money were released after one day and their money taken from them. Those living on Piotrkowska Street can buy a pass for 5 zlotys per person. Everything is done for money. The community elders meeting with the authorities have not yet returned.

LODZ, NOVEMBER 10, 1939

There is talk that the Jewish elders were jailed and also that they were released. We were advised in school not to venture out tomorrow, the 11th of November, the traditional Polish national holiday. They hanged 3 criminals in Balut Market today—2 Poles for murder and a Jew for blackmarketeering, so it's rumored—to scare us. They're afraid of provocation. I am sure nothing will happen; nobody would dare attempt anything.

LODZ, NOVEMBER 11, 1939

It's quiet in town, though yesterday and today they arrested a lot of teachers, activists who fought for Polish independence (in 1918), policemen, etc. The daily *Dziennik Lodzki* is discontinued as of today. An order was issued that all signs must be written in German, correctly, since we are now part of the Reich! As of the 15th all Poles and Jews must give up their radios. We'll have no news after that. The Germans do whatever they want.

WEDNESDAY, NOVEMBER 15, 1939—LODZ

The synagogue was burned down. Barbaric methods for annihilating the world are being activated. They demanded 25 million zlotys in exchange for stopping the terror. The community didn't have it, so it didn't deliver. Something is wrong with the Germans. Since yesterday they've been engaged in terrible plunder, robbing wantonly, whatever they can: furniture, clothes, underwear, food. All Lodz German males, 18 to 45, are being mobilized today for *selbstschutz* [Ger: self-defense]. Since the regular army is leaving, someone has to stay and guard the city. We'll get the brunt of it. It's worse dealing with one Lodz German than a whole regiment from Germany.

THURSDAY, NOVEMBER 16, 1939—LODZ

We're returning to the Middle Ages. The yellow star is again part of the Jew's garb. An order was issued today that all Jews, regardless of age or gender, must wear a 10-centimeter armband—of "Jewish-yellow" color—on the right arm, directly below the armpit. In addition, Jews are to observe a curfew from 5 pm to 8 am.

FRIDAY, NOVEMBER 17, 1939—LODZ

The mood in town is depressed. It's hard getting used to the idea of being persecuted. The Germans are on the lookout for provocations from "yellow-armbanded Jews." There's a lot of opportunity now to ridicule and provoke. It'll be interesting to see how the Poles react. Will they join the German rabble?

The required armbands were prepared at home.

SATURDAY, NOVEMBER 18, 1939—LODZ

The Poles lower their eyes when they see Jews wearing yellow stars. Acquaintances console us that it will not be for long. Meanwhile, the Germans show complete indifference. The curfew for Poles and Germans has been changed: they may go out at 6 am (it was 5 am before), but now they can stay out till 8:30 pm (it was 8 before). We can stay locked in our homes from 5 pm. It doesn't matter. There will be better times!

LODZ, DECEMBER 6, 1939

The first Chanukah candle was lit. Father made a hole in a potato, poured in some oil, inserted a wick of braided cotton, and lit it. All our Jewish neighbors are waiting for a new Chanukah miracle. Maybe the fervent prayers of millions of Jews to be liberated will be answered! We have a buyer for our wardrobe and couch, who will give us 130 zlotys for both pieces. (They cost us 350 zlotys.) He is a German, a very decent man, known for his kindness toward Jews. Father is trying to secure a permit from the authorities allowing him to make the sale so that he can pay the rent.*

THURSDAY, DECEMBER 7, 1939—LODZ

The ZUS* administration gave its permission to sell the furniture. Father is still worried constantly; he gets upset very easily. I wish everything could finally be taken care of. Everyone is surprised that nothing's been heard about Hitler lately. There is speculation that he is dead or removed from power. There is news that Germany has suffered heavy defeats in the air and at sea.

LODZ, DECEMBER 8, 1939

The cupboard-wardrobe was finally sold and rent paid till Dec. 31. There are new rumors of all kinds, probably just gossip.

LODZ, DECEMBER 9, 1939

Today we heard about Jews being badly beaten on Reymont Square yesterday; even 3-year-old children were kicked. Jews are now living on messianic prophesies. A rabbi has said that on the 6th day of Chanukah a judgment, and liberation, will occur. Uncle says there are few Germans and not many soldiers on the streets. I'm annoyed by such talk, would prefer to hear nothing.

LODZ, DECEMBER 10, 1939

A great many of the large buildings in the city center have been "cleared" of Jews, and there's talk of sending a large number of Jews from Lodz to the Protectorate*—not a pleasant prospect.

LODZ, DECEMBER 11, 1939

Father came home with the news that starting today at 6 pm Jews will be deported from Lodz. All the neighbors packed bags, bundles, etc., and we did also, but nothing happened, and everyone eventually went to bed.

LODZ, DECEMBER 12, 1939

I saw a frightful sight. A Jew was being hit with a huge pole by a German. The Jew kept bending lower and lower without turning around, so as not to be hit from the front.

A new order was issued today: The yellow patches are to be removed, and 10 cm. yellow Stars of David are to be worn on the right chest and on the right side of the back.

LODZ, DECEMBER 13, 1939

There was more fear and anxiety when Dadek Hamer came to tell us that Jews are being driven into the empty market halls in Nowo-Zarzewska Street, to be sent into the Lublin district.

This evening we heard that the Jewish community administration has announced that the Jews must leave Lodz. Apparently, during the next four days, anyone can leave for any destination, except the Reich, and after that mass deportations will begin. The community administration will give the poor 50 zl. each and has started sending them out as of today. There is terrible panic in town, everyone has lost his head, but knapsacks and bundles are being packed.

LODZ, DECEMBER 14, 1939

Mass arrests continue into the third day: thousands of teachers, doctors, engineers with families (babies included) are driven into the empty market halls and then to German prisons. The same happens to old activists, former legionnaires, even ordinary rich men. Quite often, groups of important people are dispatched to their death.

It seems that Lodz is really going to be cleared of Jews. For the time being, only the poor are registering. They get 50 zl. per person and are literally thrown out of town: first transported by rail to Koluszki and from there let go.

LODZ, DECEMBER 15, 1939

It gets worse all the time. Last night some Jews were evicted from a few places in Baluty and sent to the Reich. It's not known where they are, or what happened to them. Everywhere people have their bags packed with essentials. Everyone is very nervous.

LODZ, DECEMBER 17, 1939

The Jews are to remain in town till March 1, and then—out! They say that 80 frozen babies from Koluszki were sent to Lodz today. These babies belong to deported Jews.

LODZ, DECEMBER 31, 1939

The last day of 1939, a year that began with tension and ended with war. Let's hope next year will be better, for no one knows what awaits us.

JAKUB POZNANSKI, LODZ GHETTO DIARY

[*The references to events in 1939–1941 were written retrospectively in Poznanski's diaries during 1942 and 1943.*]

FALL 1939

Jews were being grabbed off the streets for forced labor. To improve the situation, the Jewish community leadership bolstered its courage and proposed to the German authorities that it take it upon itself to deliver the required number of workers. After lengthy discussions they agreed on 700 workers at first, and later on 1000 people daily. But even with full [Jewish] contingents, three days later they again began grabbing people off the street—and even worse—pulling people out of their apartments.

Among those negotiating with the German authorities was Mordechai Chaim Rumkowski. Apparently, his grey hair attracted the head of the Civilian Administration, who appointed him the Eldest of the Jews of Lodz. It's said that this was the beginning of the autonomous Jewish authority in our town.

I don't know if it was on his own initiative or on orders from the authorities that Rumkowski created an Advisory Council (the *Beirat*), composed of 31 people, to whom he assigned specific functions. From then on, the German authorities decided that Jews could not address them directly, on any matter. And yet the whole structure of the Elders' organization was still quite weak and imperfect.

GERMAN DOCUMENT

ANNOUNCEMENT

The Eldest of the Jews in the City of Lodz, Rumkowski has been named to implement all orders by the German Civil Administration of the city of Lodz concerning persons of Jewish race.

He is personally responsible to me in this connection.

To implement these tasks, he is entitled to

1. Move freely in the streets at any hour, day and night;
2. Have access to the offices of the German administration;
3. Choose a Council of Elders and to confer with them;
4. Use wall posters to announce his orders;
5. Control the assembly of Jewish labor detachments.

Every person of Jewish race is obliged to absolutely obey all of the Eldest Rumkowski's orders. Opposition to him will be punished by me.

City Commissioner Leister
Lodz, 13 October 1939

THE HISTORY OF THE LITZMANNSTADT GHETTO

[Written by the official ghetto archives staff, these articles were the initial efforts at compiling an "Encyclopedia of the Ghetto," as mentioned in Oskar Rosenfeld's Notebooks.]

PART ONE: FROM THE CITY TO THE GHETTO

THE NOMINATION OF M[ORDECHAI] CH[AIM] RUMKOWSKI

. . . The Jewish Community Board was decimated, and few members of the Council of Elders remained in the city. . . . At this point, in his letters of 13 and 14 October 1939, Mr. Leister, the City President, appointed Mr. Ch[aim]. Rumkowski . . . to be the Eldest of the Jews [or Chairman of the Council].

The Eldest was authorized to supervise the old Jewish Community, to dissolve the Board, the Council and all other agencies, and to organize new offices for which he would take personal responsibility. Penalties were introduced

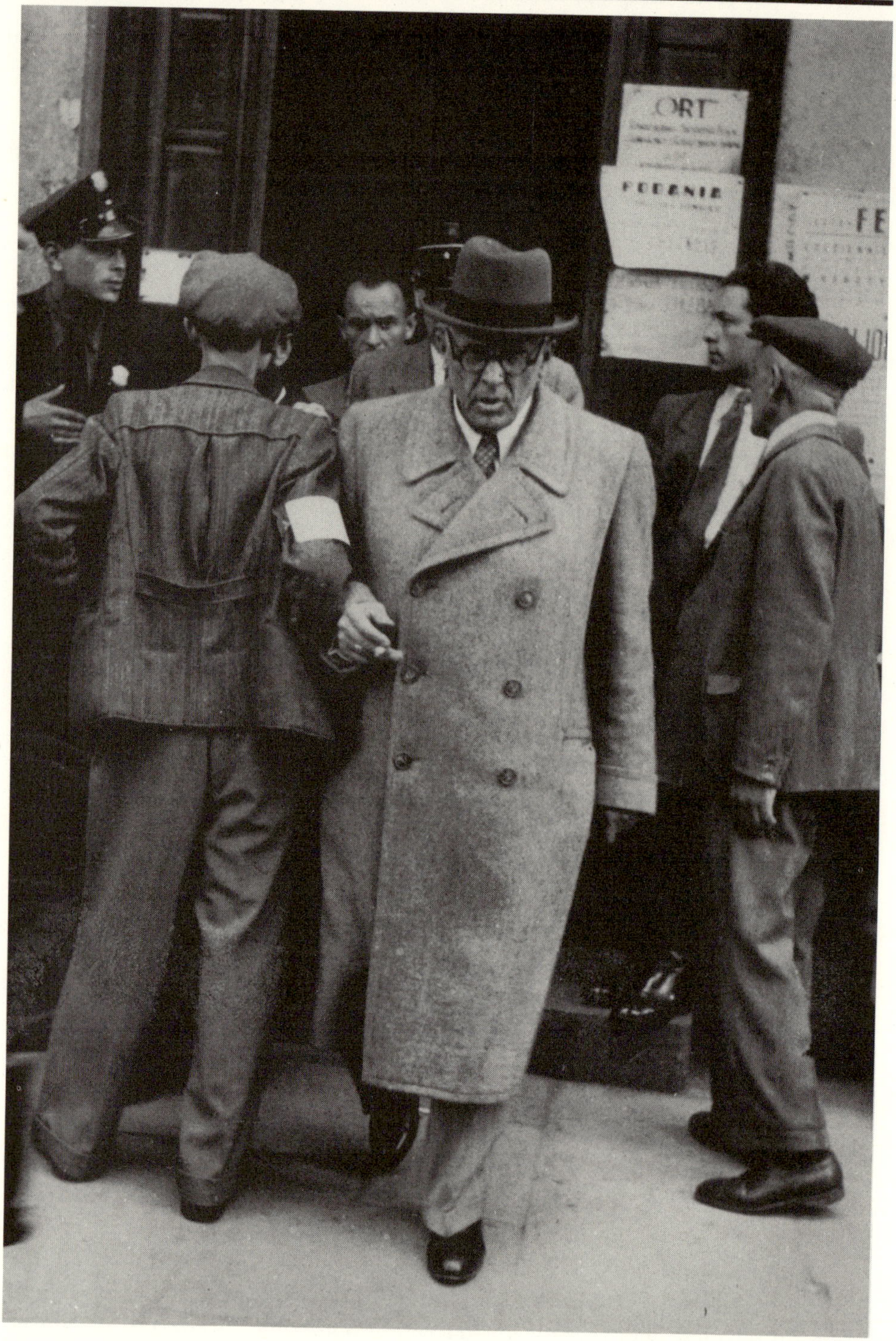

Mordechai Chaim Rumkowski, around the time of his appointment as Eldest of the Jews of the Litzmannstadt Ghetto.

for disregarding his orders. Levies were to be paid by the Jewish population to finance his activities. . . .

The same day, 14 October 1939 . . . the City President wrote to the Eldest of the Jews . . . demanding that Jews immediately return all the goods they had hidden and that they stop practicing usury. He threatened to arrest 200 Jews.

Seemingly uncomplicated, this matter was in truth difficult and dangerous, considering the threat. And it occurred on the very first day, which did not give the Chairman much time to get a grip on the new situation. Nevertheless, true to his usual energy and feeling of responsibility for the Jewish population, the Eldest of the Jews of Lodz answered the call of duty like a soldier. He took cognizance of the situation, grasped the meaning of the new times, saw the magnitude of the work entrusted to him, and decided to do everything possible to fulfill his responsibility.

THE JEWISH SCHOOLS

The separation of Aryan and Jewish children, begun in the first days of the occupation . . . was completed in a short time. . . . The authorities' attitude toward the Jewish schools was clearly negative, so the Chairman's demand that they stay open was perhaps a risky step. Yet children and students in school were so dear to the Chairman that he could not bring himself to yield on this. . . . His arguments were persuasive enough, and in the end he was not just authorized but obliged to open Jewish public schools. . . .

Jewish school buildings were requisitioned for the military and civil authorities, and the high school at Anstadt Avenue for the Gestapo. Thus, children from various schools were placed in one building. . . . Pupils from all sorts of Polish and Jewish schools met at last, brought together by the strange turn of fate. Their attitudes and degrees of knowledge were different, but the Star of David on their breasts and shoulders made them all equal.

THE OFFICE OF LABOR ASSIGNMENTS

Immediately after the German army entered the city, forced labor for Jews was introduced. The purpose was not to achieve anything connected with the war, or to do any sensible work at all, but to humiliate the Jews with all sorts of menial, filthy, and totally useless jobs. People were grabbed in the streets, chased, pulled from streetcars and *droshkies* [horse-drawn wagons], and sent under guard to the so-called "work places." Not only did the authorities (in or out of uniform) engage in this, but also civilians: a janitor or a schoolboy, an urchin, even a nine-year-old child dragged a Jew to work or just pointed him out.

Until the identifying stars were introduced, German soldiers and the civilians who came here from the Reich could not easily recognize a Jew. They

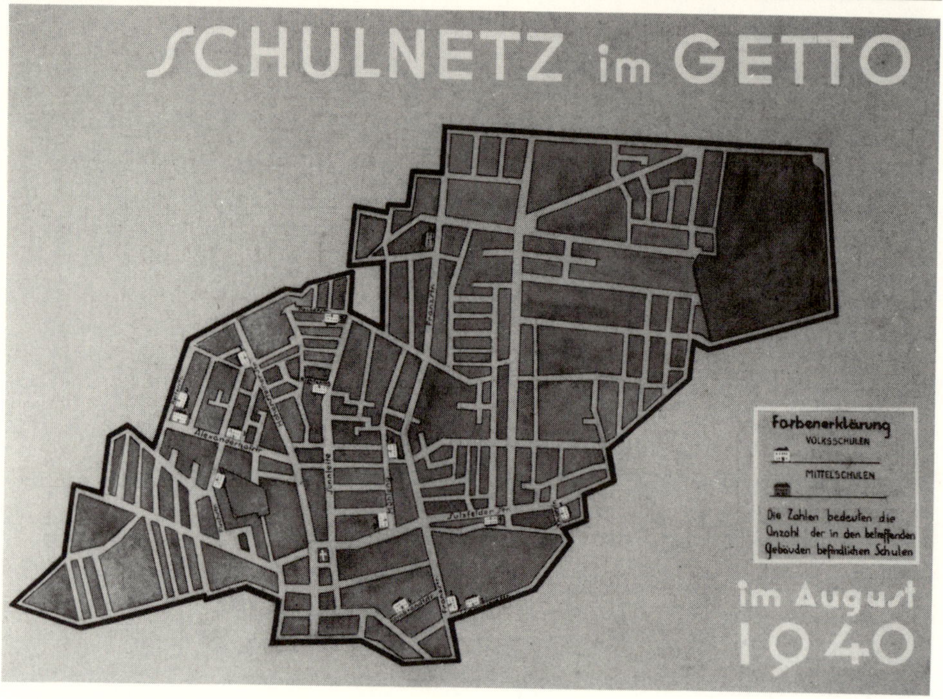

A map of schools in the ghetto during its first year.

were often helped by the local Christian population, who pointed out those Jews who avoided recognition because of their looks. No neighborhood or time of day was safe from this danger. . . . Therefore, Jews avoided the streets. They hid in attics and cellars, sometimes remaining there for days, waiting in fear for the curfew.

Life stopped in its tracks for the Jews of Lodz. They lived in despair and resignation, afraid of dangers which they could not even comprehend. It was not work they were afraid of but the conditions under which the work had to be performed. Everybody heard about beatings, about not being allowed home for days. Only those who had to go out did so, and the streets of the city, whose population was 40% Jewish, became suddenly empty.

The Germans then found another way. They began going into homes to take people for work . . . at first only men but then also women, and even children and old people. Age did not matter; nobody was ever asked about it. Not even the most basic work tools were provided. Laborers were forbidden to use shovels for filling in the air-raid trenches. Even though some had their own tools, with which they could have done the job more quickly and efficiently, they were forced to use their bare hands or empty food cans on stone-hard ground. Cleaning toilets with bare hands, scrubbing floors with fingernails were daily occurrences. Women were told to take off their underwear and use it to clean the floors, the windows, and toilets.

When the problem had reached catastrophic proportions, the Chairman stepped in. A decision was made to voluntarily place a contingent of workers at the authorities' disposal. . . . The authorities accepted this proposal in principle . . . and so the Labor Assignments Office was organized.

GERMAN DOCUMENTS

[*The following appeared in the* Lodscher Zeitung, *14 November 1939.*]

ANNOUNCEMENT

I hereby order all shops in the City of Lodz to immediately place a sign in their windows, at eye level, indicating whether the shopkeeper is German, Polish, or Jewish.

The shape of the signs will be determined by the Industry and Trade Council in Lodz.

Violations will be severely punished.

[Lodz, 11 November 1939 Commissioner, City of Lodz]

[*The following appeared in the* Lodscher Zeitung, *6 December 1939.*]

ANNOUNCEMENT ABOUT JEWISH VEHICLES

It is hereby forbidden for all taxicabs, trucks, or vehicles of any kind to be driven on open roads by Jewish drivers.

[Lodz, 2 December 1939 Chief of Police]

[*memorandum*]

Lodz, 10 December 1939
Confidential!
Strictly secret!

ESTABLISHMENT OF A GHETTO IN THE CITY OF LODZ

I assume there are about 320,000 Jews living in the city of Lodz today. It is impossible to evacuate them at once. A thorough investigation by all relevant

"All shops are to place a sign in their windows indicating whether the shopkeeper is German, Polish, or Jewish."

authorities has shown that a concentration of all the Jews in one closed ghetto is impossible. For the time being, the Jewish question must be solved in the following way:

1) Jews living north of the line formed by Listopada Street, Plac Wolnosci [Independence Square], and Pomorska Street must be placed in a closed ghetto in such a way that, first, the space needed for the creation of a strong German center around Independence Square be cleansed of Jews and, second, that this ghetto include the northern part of the city, which is almost exclusively inhabited by Jews.
2) Jews able to work who live in the remaining part of the city of Lodz must be organized into work details, placed in barracks and kept under guard.

The preparation and implementation of this plan must be undertaken by a staff composed of representatives of the following:

1. NSDAP [National Socialist German Workers Party],
2. The Lodz branch of the Regierungspräsident in Kalisz,
3. The Municipality of the city of Lodz—Offices of Apartments, Building Construction, Health, Food Supply, etc.,
4. Order Police,
5. Security Police,
6. Death's Head Unit [an elite SS unit],
7. Chamber of Industry and Commerce,
8. Finance Office.

Furthermore, the following preliminary steps must be taken:

1) A determination of arrangements for closing streets, barricading entrances and exits of buildings, etc.
2) A determination of arrangements for maintaining a guard along the ghetto boundaries.
3) A supply of the materials necessary for closing off the ghetto, from the Municipality of the city of Lodz.
4) Appropriate steps to ensure the health care for the Jews in the ghetto—with the particular aim of preventing epidemics—by transmitting medicines and medical equipment, from Jewish property. (Health Office)
5) Preparation of future regulations for the disposal of refuse from the ghetto and the transport of corpses to the Jewish cemetery, or the establishment of a cemetery within the ghetto. (Municipality)
6) A supply of the necessary quantities of fuel to the ghetto. (Municipality)

As soon as these preparatory steps are accomplished and a sufficient number of guards is available, I will fix the date on which the ghetto will be suddenly established; i.e., at a set time, the previously defined boundaries of the ghetto will be manned by the guard force, and the streets will be closed off by barbed wire and other blocking devices. Simultaneously, walling up or other arrangements for blocking the fronts of houses will begin, which work will be done by Jewish workers taken from the ghetto. In the ghetto itself, a Jewish self-administration will be immediately established; it will be composed of the Eldest of the Jews and a considerably enlarged *kehillah* [Heb: Jewish community council].*

The Food Supply Office of the city of Lodz will provide the ghetto with food and fuel, which will be transported to fixed ghetto locations and placed at the disposal of the Jewish administration. This must follow the basic principle that the ghetto can pay for food and fuel only with goods, such as textiles, etc. In this way we will succeed in drawing out all the valuables the Jews have accumulated and squirreled away.

The other areas of the city must be combed for Jews unable to work, who will be transferred to the ghetto at the same time as or shortly after its establishment, and for those able to work, who must be organized into work detachments, placed in barracks previously set up by the Municipality and the Security Police, and held under guard. These Jews are destined for labor assignments in secure groups.

Based on the above, the conclusion must be drawn that the first Jews taken for work must be those living outside the ghetto. Those Jews placed in the barracks who are unable to work or who become sick are to be transferred into the ghetto. Those remaining in the ghetto and able to work must carry out the work needed by the ghetto itself. I will decide later whether Jews able to work shall be removed from the ghetto and transferred to the barracks.

It is obvious that the establishment of the ghetto is only a transitional measure. I reserve for myself the decision as to when and how the city of Lodz will be cleansed of Jews. In any case, the final aim must be to burn out entirely this pestilent abscess.

[signed] Übelhoer*

POLICE ORDER

For the Kalisch administrative district,* the following orders have been issued by the police:

1. Jews are to wear a Jewish star, 10 centimeters high, on their right breast and back;
2. Jews are forbidden to leave the town in which they live;
3. Jews are forbidden to use the public transportation system (the tramway);
4. Disobeying any of these orders will be severely punished;
5. This order takes effect upon its publication and supersedes the order of 11 December 1939.

Kalisch, 12 December 1940

The Administrative President
[signed] Übelhoer

OSKAR ROSENFELD'S NOTEBOOKS

[Arriving in the ghetto from Prague in 1941, Rosenfeld recorded the following first-hand account from an unnamed ghetto resident in one of his 1942 notebooks.]

THE FIRST MASS DEPORTATION FROM LODZ

DECEMBER 1939.
"People were torn from their beds one night, taken in two electric trams to Radogoszcz Station.*... From 1 AM until 9 that morning we huddle in a large bay. The doors open. 'All out to the latrines!' shouts the military guard. Everyone races to the toilets. What they find is one long plank as a kind of bench. Everyone is crowded together: an old man next to a young woman, men mixed with women, children with men, and so on. As we sat there answering the call of nature, they photographed us, some from below to show us crouched on the bar. I'll never forget that scene, even though it happened three years ago. What was their purpose: to have 'evidence' of how shameless Jews are, defecating together without distinction as to sex?

"Back in the hall. Guards shout: 'Give your money here! Anyone who doesn't gets shot.' Some had money and gave it up, after which the soldiers took individual men outside, and we could hear shooting. 'Anyone who's got money, gold, and jewelry and doesn't give it up will be shot, just like those out there.' This was repeated a few times. Thrashed and beaten throughout the day. Physicians had to remove dung with their bare hands. After two days of this treatment, 80 people died in cattle cars, at 20 below zero. Frightful scenes in cattle cars—children howling, adults shitting as they stood, some licking at icicles to quench their overwhelming thirst. At some of the stops, Jews brought us food. Cattle cars of doom! Just before getting to Czestochowa we were again hauled out of the cars: 'To the latrines. On your haunches!' The same scene and again the photos. Leaving Cracow, some of us escaped, fleeing back to Lodz."

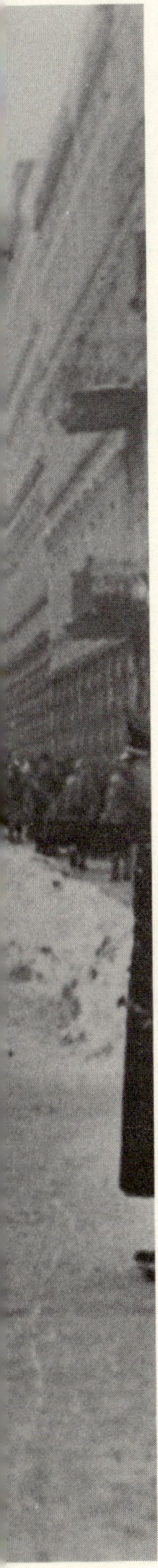

“Every day new throngs of Jews were forced to abandon their apartments and flee to the ghetto.” (Jakub Poznanski)

CHAPTER TWO

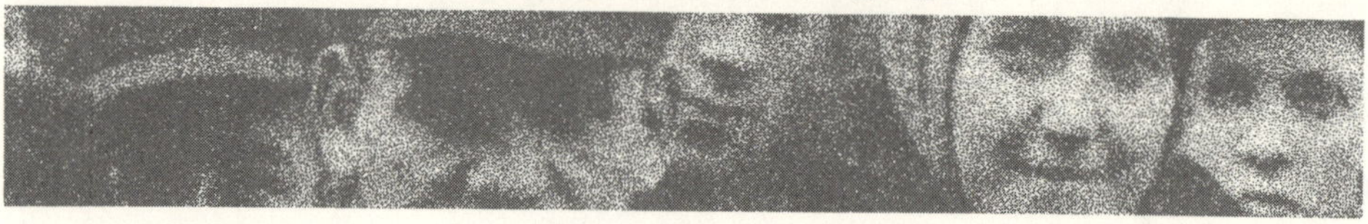

INTO THE GHETTO

1940

LUDWIK LANDAU, THE VIEW FROM WARSAW

11 JANUARY 1940

In Lodz it was announced that the Jewish quarter, i.e., the section of Baluty inhabited by poor Jews, is a "region of epidemic danger." According to an announcement by the police chief, this quarter should be avoided by Germans, and, as much as possible, by Poles. It does not state whether the Jews will experience any difficulties if they want to leave the quarter, but this seems quite probable.

15 JANUARY 1940

Lodz is being Germanized more each day. The Lodz newspaper is thinkjing about changing the city's name and appeals to readers to send in proposals.

2 MARCH 1940

An announcement by the Lodz police chief says that there was a roundup of

Jews from the ghetto who committed the heinous crime of "still circulating between the ghetto and the city."

16 MARCH 1940

There is some concrete news about the pogrom in Lodz. In the big apartment building at 17 Piotrkowska, all Jewish tenants were ordered to leave their apartments and the house within 15 minutes. After 15 minutes, the apartments were searched and anyone found inside was simply shot. About one hundred persons were killed in this way. Such methods are supposed to speed the Jewish exodus from the city to the General Government, or at least from the city to the ghetto.

There are supposedly 115,000 Jews in the ghetto—that would account for a majority of the Jews from Lodz, and is twice as many people as were living in that area before the war. Hence, living conditions are horrendous. Since the Poles and Germans refuse to move out of the quarter, the incoming Jews are given rooms only in the old Jewish houses, so that there is an average of seven or eight people per room. Sanitary conditions are terrible.... In this situation, an epidemic can bring about unheard-of losses.

GERMAN DOCUMENT

[*Decree by the Chief of Police, on 8 February 1940, ordering the establishment of a ghetto, published in the* Lodscher Zeitung.]

POLICE ORDER

REGARDING THE RESIDENCE OF JEWS

Based on the police administration law of 1 June 1931, the following police order is issued:

1.

In order to concentrate all Jews residing in the city of Lodz in one separate quarter, a residential area will be established in the part of the city northward from Deutschland Square.... The exact borderline will be provided by the magistrate of the city of Lodz.

For through traffic by all types of vehicles, Neustadtstr[asse]–Nowomiejska, Hohensteinerstr[asse]–Zgierska, and Alexanderhofstr[asse]–Limanowskiego streets will be open pending further orders. All pedestrian traffic on these streets will be forbidden after a date to be fixed in the future.

2.

All *Volksdeutscher* [ethnic Germans]* and Poles still residing in that area must leave it by 29 February 1940, at the latest, together with their families, furniture, work equipment, and all other portable property.

The *Volksdeutscher* in question will be assigned appropriate apartments within the city of Lodz, on application to the Apartments and Relocation Office of the Magistrate. . . . The Poles will be assigned residences in another part of the city. . . .

3.

The whole relocation will be implemented by streets and areas, according to the pertinent regulations stating on which day and to which new residential section the inhabitants of each block of apartments will be obliged to move. Every house owner and every Polish and Jewish head of household is obliged to accept in his apartment those persons the police or the municipality assign to him.

These regulations will also state which objects the particular group will be permitted to take with them during the relocation.

4.

The persons obliged to move must prepare and keep with them, on the date set for their relocation, a list containing the number of rooms they have owned to date and information about the nature and dimensions of any industrial installations, workshops, or merchandise stores at that place. . . .

6.

Upon application, employers may receive permission to continue to employ Jews who are working in vitally important industries and who cannot be replaced by other persons, provided that the employers make themselves responsible for the upkeep of these Jews and for securing them in closed quarters, without their families, on the employers' premises. In general, the latter must commit themselves to being responsible for these Jews in every way. Further orders of the Security Police may follow.

7.

Disobeying these police orders will be punished by fines up to 150 marks or by arrest.

8.

This order is effective immediately. It will expire on 31 December 1940.

JAKUB POZNANSKI, LODZ GHETTO DIARY

FEBRUARY 23, 1940

Mr. Czopek emptied his apartment, and we moved in with our pitifully modest furniture. Oh, God, how heavy our hearts were! From a recently renovated 5-room apartment to one small room. Nor was it easy getting this place. The Administrator made it difficult, claiming that the building was to be excluded from the ghetto. However, since I'd gotten this apartment with the approval of the Jewish authorities and the German police precinct, I took it by force.

THE END OF FEBRUARY 1940

Every day new throngs of Jews were forced to abandon their homes and flee to the ghetto.

The plan, attached to an ordinance of February 8, 1940, outlined a gradual shift of Jews to the Jewish quarter (Baluty) and Poles to the Polish quarter (past the Gorny Rynek). Every day twice as many Jews were relocated in as Poles and Germans were taken out. The Germans were aiming at a maximum concentration of the Jewish population. Of course, the *Volksdeutsche* were allowed to take all their furniture and belongings with them. Their move gave every indication of being conducted freely. Poles, on the other hand, could take only their bedding and a portion of their furniture. Like the Jews, the Poles had to march in close formation, with the difference that we were stripped of practically all our possessions.

That, however, was not the end. I found out that the German party authorities decided that because the relocation was not occurring fast enough, they'd have to finish removing Jews from the center of the city in 3 days. With this goal, on February 28, some units of German Stormtroopers surrounded the city from Glowna St. at Gorny Rynek, and drove all the Jews living there into the ghetto. They planned to do the same from Glowna St. to Cegielniana and Srodmiejska. The plan for the third day was as far as Polnocna St. This was to be a border for the Jewish quarter.

The accelerated transfer of Jews into the ghetto had its victims. When people were driven out of their apartments at night, a few hundred were killed. In this fashion the NSDAP ordinance was achieved in 3 days. However, even that wasn't enough for the Germans. Because security at the borders was weak, uniformed auxiliary police units surrounded the ghetto and carefully checked everyone entering and leaving. Many Jews who had moved into the ghetto but still went into town, as well as those who had not moved in on time, were caught, beaten up, and put in prison.

And so the tragic history of our quarter began.

MARCH 9, 1940

On Monday morning one of our clients came to see me and we went downstairs to telephone instructions to the factory. Since the telephone was busy, we went to a nearby bakery. On the way back we were both caught, and with some others were taken to a building on 7 Mickiewicza St. where there used to be an elementary school and where Germans from the [Soviet-occupied] Volhynia region were now staying. We were lined up in 2 rows, and were picked for different "jobs." Some of us carried water upstairs from the well to where women were scrubbing floors; others were beating dust out of rugs; still others cleaned toilets with their bare hands.

I was given the pointless job of carrying benches outside and then carrying them back inside. The way to the outside led through a double row of Volhynian Germans with sticks, and they beat us mercilessly with those sticks.

Later I was told to chop ice off the well, but soon I was called into the guardhouse. There I was told that I could have my freedom if I contributed toward the purchase of a new flag. I gave them 10 marks. The Germans started haggling, but seeing that it wouldn't get them far, they allowed me to leave the school building. I informed our client about how to get out, and he bought his freedom for 5 marks.

When we got to the street, we began feeling pain in our backs. After I got home, I stayed in bed for 3 days.

The days went by monotonously. I called the factory a few times a day. Sometimes I travelled there by *droshky,* and sometimes my friends went by to take the money I collected. I was paid every month, regularly. I didn't appreciate the danger we were in—or rather, I preferred not thinking about it.

IRENA LIEBMAN, LODZ GHETTO

[*The original diary, in Polish, was lost and reconstructed later.*]

Thursday night's events were the final signal to abandon our house and move into the ghetto. We rented a cart and dumped our property into it and, carrying knapsacks, we went to our new life, to the ghetto. Starting in the morning, more and more people filled the city streets with knapsacks, suitcases, bundles. Everyone was going in the same direction, rushing toward the same goal, the dirtiest, ugliest quarter of the city, a place with no sewers and paved with cobblestones.

The days were warm and the snow was melting. The mud in the streets of the new Jewish quarter splashed as people walked. They tripped on the uneven pavement, dropping clothes and other possessions into the sticky black mud. Their meager property lay in the street, trampled, crushed, covered with dirt. Waves of people, one after another, were coming. Old people leaning on sticks, cripples sitting in the carts, blind people led by the hand, babies at their mothers' breasts, and older children carrying things. Retarded people with strange eyes and unnatural body movements, sick people riding in *droshkies,* and a great mass of men and women, large and small, attractive and ugly, young and old, bent under the weight of their luggage. Pets of all sizes, brushes, bowls, irons, carpet-beaters, scales, things beyond number. People without faces, their backs curved, their heads hanging low. A caravan of poverty. Grey, weary, miserable.

The ghetto. Tiny, narrow streets. Little houses without conveniences. A well in the backyard. A refuse dump infested with rats. A stinking toilet full of melting snow, impossible to use. A leaking roof, dilapidated walls. One little room and a small kitchen for seven people.

THE HISTORY OF THE LITZMANNSTADT GHETTO

THE SITE OF THE GHETTO

The area where the ghetto is located comprises what were once two completely different sections. Most of it was Baluty, a neglected, deserted spot that until 1916 was not subject to any municipal law or jurisdiction. Houses were built at whim, with no plan beyond their owners' desires, along crooked alleys, following no pattern and submitting to no fire, sanitation, or zoning regulations. Its isolation was evidenced by its having no gutters or street lighting. And it was a breeding ground for disease.

After the area was incorporated into the city of Lodz in 1916, a slow improvement began, although not enough to bring its conditions up to the level of the rest of the city. Its inhabitants were considered the city's outcasts. In recent years, some small houses for civil servants and well-paid workers were constructed, modern homes whose appearance contrasted with their surroundings.

The second part, the Old Town, Lodz's oldest quarter, was until 1861 the Ghetto of Lodz, where in small, cramped spaces the Jews had kept their nests. Until that date, only several Jews were permitted to live outside the ghetto in the city, but thereafter barriers began coming down.

This area, which was now to be inhabited by Jews from the city, had the highest percentage of wooden houses, of decaying houses, of houses in danger of collapsing and begging to be torn down, of houses that had not been repaired in decades, of houses filled with dirt and trash and lacking the slightest comfort. A more descriptive picture than words can provide is offered by the following statistics:

Number of apartments with the following:	
Drains	613
Water pipes and drains	382
Toilet	294
Toilet, drain and bath	49
Lacking these comforts	30,624
Central heating	48
Gas stoves	247

The only thing that distinguished the ghetto from the most isolated provinces was electric lighting, which was present in 42,551 rooms. Of these, 39,317 were living quarters.

For the sake of comparison, we give the following statistics for apartments in Lodz in the year 1931. It must be remembered that the tremendous progress achieved during the last eight years makes the contrast with the ghetto even greater:

1. Plumbing	6.9%
2. Water pipes	14.7%
3. Electric lights	67.1%
4. Gas	10.8%
5. Points 1, 2, and 3 or 4	31.3%
6. Buildings lacking these	14.6%

A view of the ghetto by the artist Hirsch Szylis.

LEON HURWITZ, LIFE IN THE LODZ GHETTO

[*Written in mid-August 1941*]

THE SANITARY STATE OF THE GHETTO

Baluty, the borough of Lodz where the ghetto was established, was known throughout Poland long before the war. Its narrow, crooked, unpaved or badly paved streets were as densely populated as Kercelak in Warsaw or Sukharevka in Moscow. But in its filth, Baluty had no competition. It held the all-time record.

The onset of the war saw Baluty at its filthiest. The garbage containers and excrement pits were overflowing, for the peasants from nearby villages who usually descended in throngs to collect the refuse (which they used for fertilizers) were still busy with their summer work in the fields. In fact, they did not come at all in 1939.

In February 1940 the resettlement of the Jews from the city into the ghetto began. It was supposed to take until May first, but by March they had become impatient and gave us a good push, and we ran for our lives from comfortable homes in the city to the ghetto's filthy, narrow streets. In mid-March the move was complete, and we began putting our make-shift home in order.

It was not only that the garbage dumps and pits were full. The houses and courtyards were in a terrible state as well. The Baluters had never thought much of cleanliness, and for them "hygiene" was an invention of the intelligentsia.

When the shock of resettlement was finally overcome, a clean-up began. The Community administration was then in an embryonic state, the house committees were not yet organized, so the tenants of each building took their own initiative.

The Labor Assignments Office's original task, on German orders, had been to procure Jews for conscripted work outside the ghetto. In time, the authorities demanded fewer Jewish workers for the city, and when this practice stopped altogether in May 1940, the Labor Assignments Office began using workers to clean up the ghetto fields and plots. Soon, in places where, for as long as could be remembered, garbage and refuse had covered the ground and foul air had polluted neighboring streets, patches of green grass sprang up.

GERMAN DOCUMENTS

[*Announcement by the Chief of Police, 19 April 1940, about the possible total isolation of the ghetto. It was published the next day in the* Litzmannstadter Zeitung.]

The creation of the ghetto in the northern part of Litzmannstadt is now so far advanced that its complete closing off has become possible. From 15 April on, *Volksdeutsche* may enter ghetto territory only for moving purposes. In this connection I stress once again that all officials, *Reichsdeutsche* [Ger: German citizens] and *Volksdeutsche,* as well as all soldiers of the *Wehrmacht* [Ger: military], are obliged to assist me in my efforts at regulating conditions in Litzmannstadt. . . .

[*The Chief of Police's fifth and last order regarding the isolation of the ghetto. 7 May 1940*]

Following the final closing off of the ghetto, which was achieved on 1 May 1940, and based on the decrees of 8.II.1940 and 8.IV.1940, I order herewith, and to take effect immediately, that:

Any traffic, including commerce, between the civil population and the Jews is forbidden henceforth. Failure to obey these regulations will be punished by a fine up to 150 marks or by arrest, according to Section 7 of the Police Decree of 8.II.1940.

Chief of Police Litzmannstadt, 10 May 1940

SPECIAL ANNOUNCEMENT

Regarding Trade with the Ghetto

1. Jews are not allowed to leave the ghetto area. This applies to the Eldest of the Jews and the leaders of the Jewish security police and the Jewish secondhand dealers, if they live in the ghetto. Jewish secondhand dealers who still live outside the ghetto are not allowed to enter the ghetto.

2. If Jews are arrested in the ghetto by the criminal police or the state secret police, they are to be taken out of the ghetto through the disinfection station at Baluter Ring. If these Jews are later freed, they are to be delivered by way of the above-named station to the police guard at Baluter Ring, who will then take them into the ghetto.

3. Should Jews be brought in by the Kripo [Criminal Police] or Stapo

Captive workers. From the outset, the Lodz Ghetto was an urban slave camp. The ghetto fence was broken only at guarded gates where goods could enter and leave the Jewish quarter.

[State Police] only for questioning, this is to be done at the Police Precinct at Baluter Ring. They are to be led first through the disinfection station.

. . .

5. Entry into the ghetto by Germans or Poles is forbidden. Exceptions may be authorized by me by an identification card carrying my signature and the police chief's stamp. Also, official Schupo [Local Police], Kripo, and Stapo identification papers permit entry into the ghetto. The official must be disinfected in every case. The official himself will be responsible for this.

JAKUB POZNANSKI, LODZ GHETTO DIARY

1940 in the ghetto was filled with feverish organizational work: the Chairman running around like crazy, screaming, slapping people's faces, throwing them out [of his office].

At the end of February, the Jewish police was established. A certain [Leon] Rozenblat, who worked in the Deposit Bank and who was not known to us, assumed its command. They say he was a captain in the Austrian army during World War I.

Other departments were also established: housing, labor, social welfare, provisions, economics, finance, etc. There was very little money at this time. The community treasury was almost empty.

Everyone was trying to get a job. I talked to Gerszowski and asked him to intercede with Rumkowski on my behalf. The Chairman didn't favor my request very much.

At the end of April I met Rumkowski at a Passover dinner at my friends' house. Since I knew him from before the war, I spoke to him freely, giving my opinion of the ghetto's economic situation. Logically, if the ghetto was to be sealed off and left only with its own resources, the money the Jews had wouldn't last very long. I estimated it to be 20 million [marks]; the Chairman was a bit more conservative and gave half that number. After all, the ghetto had 225,000 inhabitants.

Feeding one person, even minimally, has to cost at least 0.75 mark daily. And so maintaining the ghetto would cost about 4.5–5 million monthly, which means that the available cash would only last 2 to 4 months! And then what?

The only way out of this situation would be to get money from outside, which would be possible only through export. We could export either valuables or work. The latter would depend on getting orders from the German authorities, and payment for orders delivered. Otherwise, we'd be condemned to die of hunger.

Rumkowski informed me that he was just then negotiating such a plan with the German authorities, and that he was assured employment for 35,000 people. Counting the workers' families, this came to about 100,000 or 125,000 souls, or half the ghetto population. The others would support themselves by supplying services for the ghetto population.

On May 3, 1940, our quarter was closed. Only a few Jews remained in town: those who were buying rags and scrap metal, and a handful of Jews requisitioned by factories.

Now the Jewish tragedy began in the strict sense of the word.

Because the Community treasury was quite empty, the Chairman started selling franchises for bread baking, grocery stores, and other enterprises. Every person willing to open a store was to pay between a few hundred and a few thousand marks, supposedly as a down payment for provisions like flour, meat, sugar, groats, beans, etc. In reality, however, these were deposits which were to serve as floating capital for the community administration.

A man who, in my opinion, was completely unfit for the job was made head of the Department of Food Supplies. Officially, the entire food supply was supposed to be handled through Baluter Ring (the seat of the community administration and Rumkowski's residence). However, during those first months of the ghetto's existence, many goods were smuggled in.

It was then that the Chairman, feeling that the community administration had to earn its keep—to pay for administrative costs, electricity, social welfare, etc.—introduced an indirect tax, something like a duty on all goods, which he set according to his own notions. Prices were not based on any kind of calculation but rather on despotic license.

In the first weeks after the ghetto was sealed, private stores—which were controlled by the community administration and which got their goods through its offices—sold their food with no restrictions. But it became apparent (as was to be expected) that these stores were engaging in price gouging and speculation.

A large part of the population was very poor, had no money, and lived on social welfare or from the sale of personal belongings.

The community administration work went on as before. New departments and new work places multiplied. All of it was done chaotically and disconnectedly.

In the middle of May, a Department of Garden Cultivation was created under the auspices of the Department of Economics. Since the organizers knew I was an agricultural engineer, I was asked to join.

Because the people picked to serve were not exactly to my taste, I decided to join only if I could create a *Hachschara* [Heb: training group] for young people willing to learn to work on the soil. I also made it a condition that I be left alone to work independently. At the end of May, we started to work on the project.

THE HISTORY OF THE LITZMANNSTADT GHETTO

THE SEALING OF THE GHETTO

Meanwhile, the construction of the fence around the ghetto proceeded apace, and the day grew near when this patch of land would be totally cut off from the rest of the city. Anticipating possible complications in connection with the fence, the Eldest of the Jews submitted the following request to the Mayor of the City.

In reference to your personal report yesterday, I would like to ask that the following points be taken into consideration:

1. There is a great danger of fire.
2. I must let the feces and garbage containers be taken away at least twice a week in order to prevent illness.
3. When typhus breaks out in a house and the stricken can be transported only on very narrow sidewalks, the danger of contagion is very great. It is impossible to cut through the barbed wire each time and then repair it afterwards.

Considering these factors, I ask respectfully that the fencing-in of the sidewalks in the ghetto be put off for two months, until after April and May, when many cases of illness occur.

In addition, I would like to submit the following:

The original map of the ghetto has been made smaller, and there are now only a few streets in the area with fresh air, which the people desperately need for their health. In spite of this, there remain in the ghetto many islands and large houses not under my control. This makes things very difficult. For instance, on Hanseatenstrasse [Lagiewnicka Street], there is a large building which has room for about 400 beds and into which I could transfer the Poznanski Hospital. I ask that this be considered, so that the following can be kept separate within one hospital: a maternity ward, a pediatrics ward, a ward for internal medicine, a surgery, and a division for prostitutes. In the hospital under my control on Holzstrasse there is room for at most 175 beds, which makes it impossible to separate the different departments.

I therefore respectfully request that the non-Jewish enclaves in the ghetto be reduced, and, if possible, that the houses be made available to me.

Further, I respectfully request an enlargement of the ghetto up to the cemetery, in order to avoid potential strife with the area's other inhabitants.

Hoping that my requests will receive your consideration, I am

Faithfully,
/-/ Ch. Rumkowski
The Eldest of the Jews in the City of Lodz

The territory of the ghetto was enlarged, and clashes with the Christian population along the road to the cemetery were thereby avoided. Blood had frozen in one's veins when one had seen the corpses of dead Jews desecrated and the mourners jeered at and hit with stones. It was the more distressing that this was done by people who had lived here for a long time and who showed, thus, the degree of their barbarism.

Those were difficult and frightening times, so the news about the expansion of the ghetto territory and even the total isolation of the new settlement was greeted with satisfaction by the majority of the population. People realized that the new situation would involve various difficulties, but they were ready to pay the price necessary to live in peace. A warning posted on the large billboards at the entrance to the ghetto stated that no one was allowed to enter the Jewish quarter. Those in the ghetto who did not belong to the Jewish community were told to leave. All German institutions in the ghetto, such as the 6th Police Precinct and the camp for the Volhynian Germans, were liquidated.

The new settlement was perhaps crowded and inconvenient, and also quite dirty, but it was an autonomous settlement, undisturbed by anyone.

This was, in a sense, a small state and required the organization of a work force and its own governing administration—the building of a new life. The Order Service* had been in existence since March 1, 1940, but now its tasks became more complex. The Eldest of the Jews was obliged to enforce the boundaries of the ghetto, but much energy had to be spent cleaning up the ghetto and subjugating the local Balut element. Although contact with people on the other side of the fence was banned, smuggling did not stop; in this respect, the Order Service's task was very difficult. Special administrators were named to organize the management of buildings. Building janitors were given responsibility for cleaning up the ghetto, and little lawns and garden plots soon sprang up. An Address Registration Bureau was organized, as was a department to supervise the ghetto's economy. Rule over all the ghetto's life was concentrated in the hands of the Chairman, whose office was at 4 Plac Koscielna [Pol: Church Square].

The situation slowly stabilized, calm and quiet returned, patches of green began to cover the ghetto's grounds, benches were placed on Lutomierska Street. The rejected community began to look like an island of self-government.

"WORK IS MY GOLD CURRENCY"

The question now arose, how would this community support itself in its sealed-off territory; where would the money, the food come from? There were two alternatives: either the ghetto would provide the authorities with a work force for labor needed in the city or even farther away or, though totally sealed off, it would manufacture goods in exchange for food.

Questioned by the authorities as to how he was going to maintain the ghetto and feed the Jewish population, the Chairman responded that he had in the ghetto a gold currency of the highest caliber—the labor of Jewish hands. After a number of individual conferences, he submitted the following memorandum:

> 5 April 1940
>
> Herewith I take the liberty of approaching you with the following suggestion regarding my plan for the problem of ghetto life:
>
> There are in the ghetto between eight and twenty thousand skilled workers of various specialties: shoe and boot makers (hand and machine workers), saddlers, leather workers, tailors (custom- or mass-production), underwear sewers, hat and cap makers, metal workers, welders, carpenters, bricklayers, painters, bookbinders, upholsterers.
>
> I could organize matters so that these people work for the authorities, who would supply the raw materials and set salaries. The work would be done inside the ghetto, and I would appoint a special department to divide the assignments among the workers.
>
> The workers would turn the finished products over to this department, and cash payment by me and a supply of food (which I would receive for the entire Jewish population) would follow delivery of the goods to the authorities.
>
> I respectfully request that you authorize me to collect rents, though I must draw attention to the fact that a large part of the ghetto population is poor and must be excused from having to pay rent.

Rumkowski's "gold currency." Jewish workers are photographed for identification work cards. The photographer is Henryk Ross.

In order for me to implement all of this without disruption, the authorities would have to free me from allotting workers for forced labor, since Jews are not allowed to leave the ghetto. I would request that an order be issued that no one is entitled to come into the ghetto to take people off the streets for work, for this would cause considerable disturbance.

I hope that, with the appropriate subsidy from the authorities, I and my associates will be permitted to balance the ghetto budget, maintain the Order Service, support the poor and needy, protect the population from disease, and take care of all the other needs of the ghetto's Jewish inhabitants.

In the hope that my proposals will be considered, I sign

Faithfully,
/-/ Ch. Rumkowski
The Eldest of the Jews in the City of Lodz

The authorities accepted this memorandum, and the Chairman received the following letter of 30 April 1940 from the Mayor:

The Oberbürgermeister*
Litzmannstadt, the 30th of April 1940

To:
The Eldest of the Jews
Mr. Rumkowski
Upon the order of the Police Chief on IV.8.40, all residents of the ghetto are forbidden to leave the ghetto, as of 30 April 1940. I make you responsible for the strict enforcement of this prohibition.

Further, with the full power given to me by the Administrative President of Litzmannstadt on 27 April 1940, I give you the task of taking all steps that are necessary or will be necessary for the maintenance of an orderly community life in the Jewish residential area. In particular, you are responsible for an orderly economic life, the supply of food, the division of labor, health care, and welfare. You are entitled to take all steps and use all the authority necessary for this end, with the help of the security police under your command.

I authorize you to arrange registration offices immediately, so that the names of all ghetto residents can be compiled. These lists must identify religious and national backgrounds. Five carbon copies of these lists must be sent to me every week, starting on 13 May 1940.

All dealings with the German authorities will take place only through you, or through a representative from your side named by me, in the administrative offices to be established in the Baluter Ring. Authorization to use other representatives will be established in advance, case by case.

To ensure the nourishment of the ghetto population, you are authorized to confiscate all supplies of food and have them distributed.

Since, in accordance with the laws of the Reich, all Jewish property is considered confiscated, you must list all Jewish possessions of value and, unless they are immediately necessary (e.g., food, clothing, or apartment appurtenances), seize and secure them.

You are further authorized to require that all Jews work without pay.

All important measures require my prior written approval before being implemented.

If a step cannot be postponed and must be taken immediately to avoid pressing danger, my oral approval must be obtained at the time and confirmed in writing afterward.

The authority of the Litzmannstadt Police Chief remains unaffected by this order.

/-/ Schiffer
City Commissioner

On the basis of this authorization, the Chairman issued orders on May 1, 2, and 3 about unconditional obedience to the Order Service, about the establishment of the Address Registration Bureau . . . and about the registration of tailors, dressmakers, seamstresses, etc. for future jobs. 14,850 workers registered. The Chairman immediately informed the authorities and submitted a list of articles that could be manufactured in the ghetto.

The Chairman thus began in this small territory his gigantic task of making the work of Jewish hands a valued commodity. He knew that the job before him was difficult and that he had taken responsibility for the fate of all the Jews of Lodz, but he had faith in himself and was confident that with the labor of Jewish hands he could assure the basic necessities of life for the entire community. Not a few thought it pure fantasy, for everything had to be built from scratch. Workshops had to be organized, raw materials procured, workers trained in mass production, and prospective buyers, who on principle had a negative attitude toward Jewish manufacture, had to be won over.

When the gates of the ghetto closed behind them, people were in a state of panic, believing they could not persevere in this huge task. No one thought it possible that these frightened, cowed Jews could find their voice, could come up with something that would assure their survival.

RUMKOWSKI'S WORK STRATEGY

Six weeks after the ghetto was closed off, the Eldest of the Jews submitted the following report on its conditions and mood to the authorities:

> The complete sealing off of the ghetto on the first of May produced great fear among the Jewish population. The people could not believe it would be possible to survive in the ghetto. Primarily, they were fearful of hunger.
>
> In the first days, there was a noticeable shortage of bread. The situation was exploited by some bakers. It was a difficult and costly battle, but in eight or ten days I was able to settle it and calm the people. I must note here that bread is now the main nourishment for the Jewish population.
>
> Too few bakeries were located in the ghetto's territory, since a large number of Jewish bakeries had been in the city, where production had ceased. Thus, the need was greater than could be met by the number of

bakeries operating. This was exploited by dishonest people and brought on inflation. The shortage also caused people to stand in very long lines in front of the bakeries.

When people have to wait in line a long time, they begin discussing dangerous ideas. In order to prevent this, I was forced to take very harsh measures to stop the rampant profiteering. It took a lot of effort to convince people that through work and organization everything could be made better. In order to provide the necessary quantity of bread, I gave the bakeries large quantities of flour and forced them to turn it all into bread. After the distribution of food to the ghetto population was organized, any fear about hunger was completely set aside.

I employed the severest measures to stop the smuggling that was going on and, thereby, to keep prices from being driven up. It was difficult to catch the small group of smugglers, who operated secretly and were helped by people outside the ghetto, who supplied them with foodstuffs and so on at black market prices. Nevertheless, I was able to control this with the help of the authorities and achieved a normalization of prices.

The workers were further disquieted, since they asked what they were supposed to live on, if they did not work. I can honestly say that the wealthy Jews have fled Litzmannstadt, and the middle class and a large working class remain. The question of work has been, therefore, the principal one for the ghetto population, and the concern about unemployment has been very great. For fourteen days there were disturbances, after which the authorities empowered me to begin work. So, they believed that they would get work [orders for the ghetto]. The work division is still very small, *but I explained to the workers that if they work hard and deliver, many thousands will get jobs.*

In spite of the unemployment, because of which people spend most of their time on the street, I have been able to determine that the politicizing has stopped. Now, the work system and adjustments to the new realities of life in the ghetto are discussed.

Since I publish no newspaper and thus can give the population no explanation of any orders or announcements, I speak publicly, giving the people new ideas and keeping them from politicizing. It greatly calmed the poor that welfare was being taken care of through mass distribution and monetary support. They are particularly satisfied about being freed from paying rent. The poor were afraid that they would have no roof over their heads, since they could not afford to pay rent. Now they can sleep in peace. Of course, the normalization is not yet finished and will not be until the division of labor is established. Complete calm will not reign until then.

The Jewish population could not believe that every person in the ghetto would have a roof over his head. However, I was able, if just barely, to find a place for everyone.

Jewish parents have been satisfied that their children will be taken care of. This is not yet completely implemented, but a large number of children are already affected. Because of this, the parents have been sustained in their view that they too will be taken care of.

Through the hospitals, as well as the outpatient clinics, it is possible to care for the sick, even for those lying at home in bed, and for the rich and poor alike. The poor receive care and medication without charge. In order to prevent an increase in the number of cases of illness, an allocation of the medicine needed would be very desirable.

I have in the ghetto many people whose handiwork is first-class. Should the authorities give me the opportunity to put these people to work in large numbers and to employ a large part of this work force for something the authorities need, I would have a strong basis for payment. And it would permit buying food in large enough quantities to satisfy the population. Then the picture would include what it must, in these circumstances: the confidence and complete calming of the Jewish population.

Six weeks have passed since the ghetto was completely closed off. I must begin to build, from the ground up, the self-administering structure which the ghetto—a small-scale city—demands. I have already organized many things in this regard, and every day something else is completed that provides greater order and a more peaceful life.

In concluding my report, I would like to remark that it would be very desirable to extend the time the Jewish population is allowed outdoors. I ask that it be considered that this is especially needed in the hotter part of the year, particularly for health reasons.

Litzmannstadt Ghetto, the 12th of June 1940
/-/ Ch. Rumkowski
The Eldest of the Jews in Litzmannstadt

And so, the impossible became possible and real. On this little patch of land where conditions were so primitive, 157,955 Jews found shelter. . . . If there had been any workshops here before, they were either removed or destroyed by their former owners, and everything had to be created anew. Rather than surrender to despair, the Chairman began building one workshop after another, until he created those gigantic factories which not only gave food and peace to the ghetto population but also changed how Jewish labor was viewed. The work of Jewish hands was soon well-known and respected throughout the Reich. The Polish Jew gave proof that he need not be a shopkeeper or a speculator but that he can earn his bread through honest, hard work.

THE ELDEST OF THE JEWS

The Eldest of the Jews is the head of the ghetto and, also, the intermediary between the ghetto and the outside world. He had been given absolute power over the ghetto from the very first moment, although at first he was somewhat unaware of it. Every ghetto inhabitant was required to carry out all his programs, orders, and proclamations. He had sole disposition over the wealth of every Jew living in the ghetto. As sole buyer, he received into his hands the entire food supply, which he distributed according to his own notions, having to justify himself to no one. It was within his power to feed someone very well or to press him down to the general level. Subordinate to him were the security service, the postal system, the fire and sanitation departments, contact with the outside world, the execution of justice, and the meting out of punishment. The imposition of the death sentence was the only thing not in his power.

Equally great was his responsibility to the German authorities. As the Germans did not know a single Jew, he was responsible for everything that happened in the ghetto. The slogan "One for all and all for one" was completely valid, since the only one with whom the German authorities dealt was the Eldest. They demanded everything of him. He was the executive organ for all their orders, but he was also the one they held responsible if something failed to meet their wishes.

Although he had received this position by chance, Mordechai Chaim Rumkowski seemed born for it. He was always ready, without discussion, to carry out orders, even those measures with grave consequences. Moreover, his abilities were quite often useful to the position he held. He was smart, and though not exceptionally intelligent, he had an excellent memory and the ability to grasp things rather quickly. At the same time, he was highly ambitious. When he saw that nothing hindered him, he was an autocrat, never forgetting when someone had done him a favor but also not forgetting if someone had opposed him years ago.

He had not been very well educated; his schooling was equivalent to that of the elementary grades. He had been a rich merchant and factory owner who neglected his business for his charitable activities. His rather wide connections let him support himself, with a nice income, as an insurance agent.

In the ghetto, other sides of his character also showed themselves: his

M. C. Rumkowski. "The one hundred percent ruler of the Jewish Ghetto . . . the Jewish King Lear . . . New strength has poured into his old man's body, along with power." (Leon Hurwitz)

intense vitality, admirable in a man of 63; his constant vigilance, day and night, for problems to be averted or overcome; his wish to hold power in his hands at all times, willing to surrender none of it to anyone; his stubborn insistence that all decisions be made by him, even in matters as trivial as employing a cleaning woman for the office; his ability to return on his own to some good advice he had previously rejected. His advisor, whose responsibility it was to support him with counsel and deeds, had to do nothing but listen.

CONTACT WITH THE OUTSIDE WORLD

Since all business with the German authorities had to be conducted through him, in his administrative office at Baluter Ring, the square at Baluter Ring was fenced in, several barracks were constructed and reception and exit desks were created. The business offices of the ghetto's economic and nutrition administration were located there, as were the office of the Eldest of the Jews and those other officers whose responsibilities required contact with the outside world.

As is often the case in border areas, the fenced-off square at Baluter Ring was neutral territory: only Jews with the Eldest's permission and Aryans with the permission of the authorities were granted entry. Aryans were forbidden from entering the ghetto, just as Jews were forbidden from leaving, with rare exceptions. It is no secret that, bad as this segregation was in general, it had a positive side effect, namely, that Jews were no longer sent to work in the city, for the simple reason that they could not leave the ghetto and their persecutors could not enter.

THE POPULATION OF THE GHETTO

On May 1, 1940, when the ghetto was sealed, it numbered about 164,000 souls. The census of July 12, 1940 counted 156,402 inhabitants, but by then the population had already been diminished by death and by legal and illegal emigration. . . .

A statistical analysis indicates that in the ghetto, unlike the general Polish population, there is a decrease in the percentage of people between ages 18 and 36. This is explained by several factors. First, the mobilization of the reserves. Then, the massive, panic-stricken escape, especially of the men, on the night of September 5th–6th, when the authorities left the city. The majority of those who left for these two reasons never returned. Most important was the mobility, energy, and love of life found among the young people, especially the young men without family responsibilities. After the occupation of the city by the German army, most of these refugees went to Russia and the General Govern-

“Born” for the job, Rumkowski “was always ready, without discussion, to carry out orders.”

ment;* a smaller number went to Palestine, North and South America, Australia, and several European countries.

Young women also left, especially in the 20–25 age group, but to a lesser degree, which left a disproportionate number of women in several age groups.

PROFESSIONAL AND SOCIAL STRATIFICATION

According to the Office of Statistics, the percentage of working Jews was disproportionately high in relation to the total population. Among 50,914 men above the age of 15, only 3,979 were unemployed (including 3,600 between the ages of 15 and 19). Therefore, 99% of the age group above 20 was employed.

The same held true for the women. Among the 63,994 above 15 years old, there were 41,678 unemployed, including housewives and house-daughters. Therefore, 30% were employed. Of the 58,742 above the age of 20, 22,316 were employed.

This contradicted the commonly held notion that there was a high percentage of unproductive people among the Jews. A 99% employment rate exists in no other community. Still, we may not accept these figures without qualification.

When the ghetto began, as well as earlier, the idea prevailed that, as a result of anti-Semitic propaganda, so-called "unproductive elements" would be subject to persecution. Everyone, therefore, wanted to be able to have some kind of job, whether or not he could perform it, so as not to be listed as having no profession. For the same reason, many people reclassified themselves in the registration the statistics were based upon. For example, factory owners stated that they were supervisors, merchants that they were administrative or sales employees, and so on. For the most part, this was actually not untrue, since the local factory owners and merchants, all self-made men, had actually worked their way up from these positions. Only the artisans had nothing to worry about, it was thought.

These apprehensions also explain the fact that the typical Jewish professions (rabbis, [kosher] slaughterers, religious teachers) seemed to disappear, as did occupations, such as jeweler, that gave the impression of wealth. It is incomprehensible, however, that no Jewish butchers were listed, since there were several hundred in Lodz before the war.

In a numerical breakdown of individual professions, the following picture develops, with men and women counted together:

Health and Sanitation:	Doctors	128
	Pharmacists	92
	Sanitation personnel	464

	Dentists	61
	Dental technicians	48
		793
Leather:	Tanners	75
	Shoe- & shaftmakers	2460
	Saddlers, strapmakers	74
		2609
Food:	Bakers	987
Clothing:	Dyers	172
	Rag sorters	53
	Operators	84
	Corset makers	248
	Tailors	14,987
	Stocking weavers	4,757
		26,188
Cap and fur:	Cap and hatmakers	790
	Furriers	298
		1,088
Metalwork:	Locksmiths	759
	Plumbers	290
		1049
Paper:	Bookbinders	264
	Printers	283
	Box makers	219
		766
Construction:	Masons	76
	Electricians	329
	Painters	639
	Carpenters	1125
		2169
Commerce:	Merchants	9565
	Commercial employees	8092
	Agents	611
		18,268

What is obvious from this compilation is the tremendous preponderance of clothing workers, especially in tailoring, long a Jewish domain, as well as of merchants and commercial employees. But lacking the appropriate pre-war figures, it is impossible to ascertain how reliable these figures are.

HOUSING

The population moved into the ghetto under the pressure of possible deportation and, later, of life-threatening situations, and therefore it set up quarters wherever it could. For this reason, apartments were so crowded that 15 to 20 people would sleep pressed together in one room, on tables and on the floor, in every which way. This occurred because the area available for the ghetto was quite small and because not all apartments were ready to be moved into. The Aryans had not all been resettled yet and when they did depart, they locked their apartments and kept the keys, in order to get money for them. Since Aryan homes could not be touched, especially if any belongings, valuable or not, had been left behind, they could extort money for making their apartments available. In these dire circumstances, many people preferred renting privately from a Jew, paying up to 50 marks per month for a room, to having the Community assign them an apartment. In time, the Eldest managed to have the authorities open the locked apartments, so that they could be assigned to the needy.

Matters improved only at the end of April, when the Aryans had been completely resettled and the Jews received the Eldest's approval to move into the now empty apartments.

This began on the 3rd of May and provided relief but not quite to the extent that had been hoped, for the Poles, upset about having been moved out, came looking for Jews at night, destroying their furniture and beating up the inhabitants of the apartments they had had to leave. Slowly, as the ghetto became more closely guarded and the Poles were no longer able to enter, things straightened out.

A few charts for the second half of the year 1940 make the picture more complete:

I. Properties and Buildings:	
Gardens	950
Developed properties	2269
Wooden houses	1402
Brick and mixed houses	1959
Single-floor houses	1300
2-story buildings	969
3-story buildings	577
4-story buildings	450
5-story buildings	63
6-story buildings	2
Total	3361

II. Types of Buildings:	
Residential buildings	3340

	Factory buildings	18
	Hospitals	2
	Schoolhouses	1
III.	Apartments:	
	With drains	1338
	With drains and running water	725
	With drains, running water, and toilet	343
	With drains, running water, toilet, and bath	49
	With no facilities	30,624
	Total	31,962 [sic]
IV.	Rooms:	
	Total	50,146
	Residential	48,102
	Space in square meters	
	Of all rooms	706,175
	Of occupied rooms	662,362
	Volume in cubic meters	
	Of all rooms	2,941,469
	Of occupied rooms	2,239,647
	Electric lights	
	All rooms	305
	Occupied rooms	48
V.	Space according to purpose:	
	Residential	48,102
	Stores	1,742
	Hospital rooms	203
	Factory rooms	44
	School rooms	26
	Others	29
	Total	50,146

It would be superfluous to comment on these figures. They are frightening enough in their nakedness. For 160,000 people, there were barely 50,000 rooms available. This meant that there were approximately 3.2 persons per room.

TRAFFIC WITHIN THE GHETTO

Jews were permitted to use the streets only from 8 a.m. to 5 p.m. The exceptions were the Eldest, the Order Service, doctors, medical workers, and administrative employees who had the Eldest's permission. Only the rag pickers and sorters, especially those who were necessary to commercial life, had the right to be on the streets until 19:00. As a result of special efforts, the curfew was later moved back to 19:00 for everybody.

On 4 May 1940, the Eldest addressed another letter to the mayor of Litzmannstadt, asking that the hours of free movement be extended from 7 in the morning until 20:30 at night. This request was granted to the extent that as of May 16th, Jews were permitted to stay on the streets from 7 a.m. until 8 p.m.

The separation of the two parts of the ghetto caused considerable trouble. The ghetto is intersected by two important roads, to Aleksandrow and Zgierz and on towards the north and west. Since it was impossible to re-route this traffic, as was done with the roads to Brzeziny, Strykow, and on to Warsaw, these two streets divided the ghetto into three parts. How to move between these sections was the subject of long discussion. At first, high gates, to be erected at several points and to be moved at different times of the day, were to be used to close off either the ghetto or the through-traffic. Although technical difficulties kept this plan from being implemented, it was consistent with the authorities' obsession with completely segregating Jews from Aryans, for which they used the danger of epidemics as a pretext.

Crossing the blocked streets was torture for the many who were forced to get from one part of the ghetto to the other. The narrow passage, opened only for several minutes, could not accommodate the large number of people, and to keep the congested crowds orderly, the police beat them with bats. The passage was opened at the whim of the guards on duty. On 20 April 1940, a police order set certain hours for the crossing, which proved completely insufficient. . . .

It was not until three bridges were built that traffic between the separate ghetto areas became possible, independent of the guards on duty. The construction costs, approximately 20,000 marks for each bridge, was charged to the Eldest.

ARYANS IN THE GHETTO

When the ghetto was sealed, numerous Christians also stayed behind. They can be divided into two groups: those of Jewish origin and Aryans. Although the first were Christians, they were considered Jews and were forced into the ghetto. They were thought of as fully Jewish, since they concealed their religion, there being no church services in the ghetto. Although Aryans had the opportunity

A ghetto bridge at rush hour. Poles pass on trams below, sealed from contact with the Jews. A Nazi propaganda cameraman films at the right.

of leaving, some remained for various reasons. Many were related to or married to Jews or, like some maids, were so close to Jewish families that they did not want to abandon them, even in disaster.

THE GHETTO'S DEVELOPMENT AFTER MAY 1940

We must alert the reader to one circumstance, namely, that a tremendous lack of data makes it impossible to illustrate various aspects of life properly. We must complain, for example, that—except for a few letters and receipts—the correspondence with the authorities has not been placed in our [the ghetto

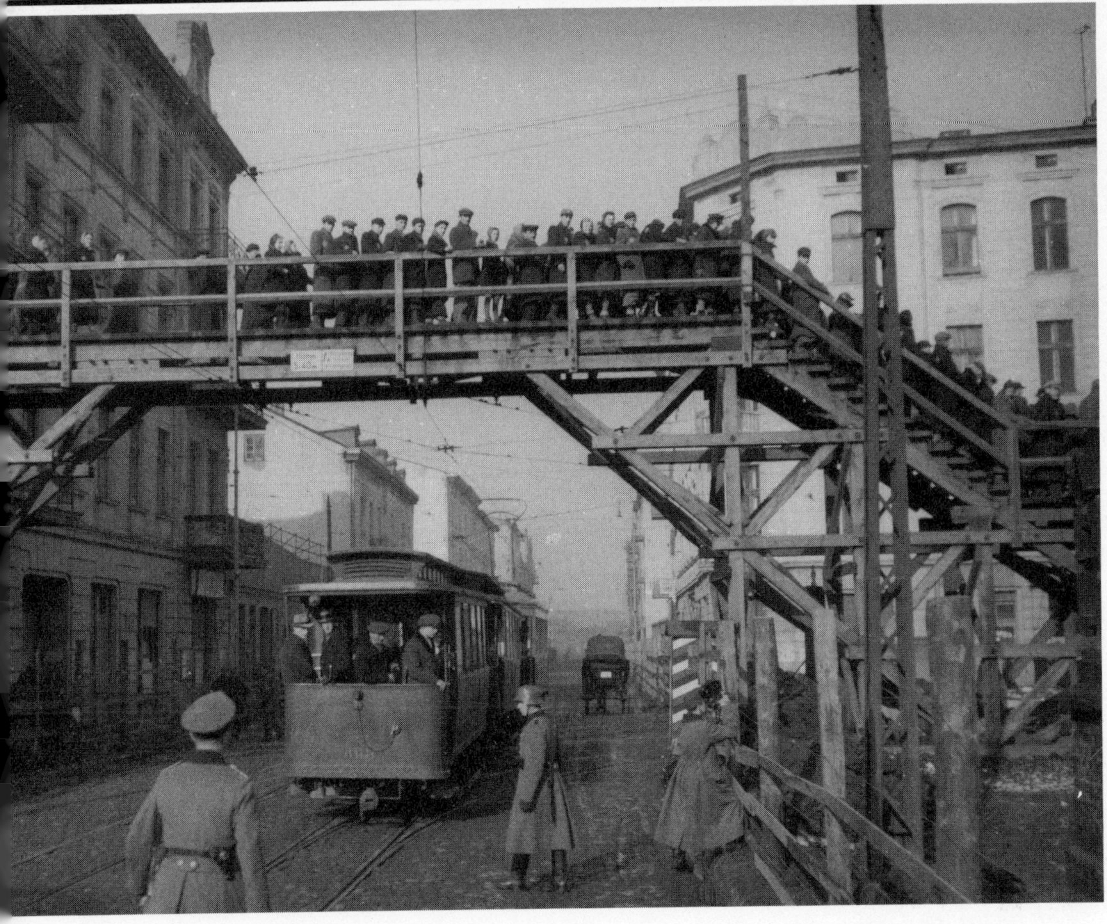

archivists'] hands. Similarly, because there are no minutes of the Eldest's meetings with the authorities, many an order may seem like a *deus ex machina*. In addition, various departments' archives, documents, and books have been destroyed, so that we have only an incomplete, often mistaken, picture.

Nor can the complete truth be determined from what remains, since various people have offered such varying and subjective interpretations. Even data from the Bureau of Statistics cannot always be relied upon, for it includes information which is not accurate or has been carelessly handled. For example, the causes given for death are subject to fashion, since doctors' inclinations change.

JOZEF ZELKOWICZ

"25 LIVE HENS AND ONE DEAD DOCUMENT"

Such an unimportant, trivial document:

> 25 live hens were requisitioned this Saturday on Podrzeczna Street and taken to the headquarters of the HIOD [*Hilfs-Ordnungsdienst,* the Auxiliary Order Service]. As agreed to by [Jewish Police Chief] Rozenblat, the hens were distributed as follows:
> 13 hens were returned.
> 6 were sent to Drewnowska Street
> 1 hen—Rozenblat
> 5 hens, i.e., 20 meals—*Hilfs-Ordnungsdienst.*

Don't throw this paper away, even if it is unsigned, undated and written in pencil.

This dry, insignificant document you've accidentally found among old papers could reveal one of the ghetto's most horrible and tragic stories—if only you knew how to read it.

It's the story of 24 Jews who perished for no reason, none at all.

It's the story of 24 people who lost their lives in the street, like rabid dogs.

This piece of paper you've found by chance in the ghetto archives says nothing about 24 dead Jews. In fact, it speaks only of 25 live hens. But listen to the people, and they'll tell you the story that begins with a Polish ruffian from the city.

A *shaygets* [Yid: Gentile youth] who was born on Zielony Rynek [Green Market], who grew up among Jews and was known by the name Rudy Janek [Red-headed Johnny], decided one day to turn his coat inside out and become a *Volksdeutsch.*

As a *Volksdeutsch* he could grab Jews for forced labor. Some paid him off without a word. Some did not; their pockets were cleaned out by him.

As a *Volksdeutsch* he could enter any Jewish house he wished, and rob Jewish property.

A lowly porter from Zielony Rynek, a sack pusher for the Jews, Rudy Janek was transformed into a lord.

Instead of hanging around the market with a rope on his back, the *Volks-*

deutsch could walk around in his Sunday suit even on a weekday and, just as he used to on Sundays, get dead drunk.

Before, Janek had to carry a 100-kilogram sack on his back for 20 *groschen,* hiding in his pockets the beans he stole for his pigeons from Jewish stores. And now these pockets were filled with 20-Reichsmark notes.

Before, Janek had to beg for those beans, but more often he stole them. From time to time he was caught and got a slap in the face. Now he is given the 20-mark notes with a friendly smile, and those who don't wish to be friendly have their money taken from them and also get a bashing in the face from Janek.

When they slapped him for theft, they did so with justice and pity. The few beans didn't make a difference, but this redheaded lad should learn not to touch them. So he got off with a few well-meaning slaps. He was happy that it was just that, and they were happy, having taught a thief a lesson. But when Janek hits, he knows no justice or pity. Janek likes blood. Lots of blood.

Bravo, Janek! You possess all the attributes of a real German. You've become a true-to-life German. But woe to you, Janek, for just when you trained yourself to be a stray dog, who takes and grabs and lusts for blood, just then they put you on a leash!

Janek, who was no good for anything any more, not even for lifting a sack, who was no more than a stray dog, a mangy dog, was good enough to be a watchman for the German police, a warden of Jewish lives in the ghetto.

Janek, now the German policeman Johann, was posted at the ghetto border to see that Jews didn't slip into the city looking for food.

Janek did not feel comfortable in the uniform they put on him. A dog does not like his muzzle.

The 20-mark banknotes were all gone. Since all the Jews had been driven into the ghetto, there was no way to get new ones. Janek had to live on the modest wages of a police guard. And he had to stand there and watch—like a chained dog.

Janek was not used to it. He was a stray dog. Stray dogs hate having chains around their necks. He was in a state of rebellion but could not rebel openly, for he could get shot. The gall in him rose to his mouth. His life was bitter, his world oppressively small.

Ever since he was put in uniform, Janek had been thirsty for a drink. His tongue felt glued to his palate like a piece of dried liver. And the only taste he had in his mouth was the taste of gall. Gall and liver.

Janek longed for freedom, longed for the 20-mark banknotes. With his stupid mind, with his piggish-blue eyes he began to look for banknotes right there, at the ghetto border.

Standing there one day, his mouth dry and his tongue out like a thirsty dog, Janek spotted Redhead Leyzer.

They hardly recognized each other. The Janek in uniform looked altogether different. Leyzer, who had had a flour store on Zielony Rynek, remembered Janek as a ragged, shabby *shaygets* who wore torn trousers, walked barefoot, and had a face covered with reddish, pig-stiff bristles. On Sundays Janek used to put on his one and only black suit, which he had bought in the Old Town, and his high-heeled red shoes, shave his face, and make the reddish hair cling to his head. But on Sundays Leyzer's business was closed, so Leyzer never saw Janek in his Sunday incarnation. It never crossed Leyzer's mind, therefore, that that scoundrel, that red-headed Polish ragamuffin might be changed into a German soldier with a gun—and that he would be standing right there, guarding him, Leyzer.

On the other hand, in the old days when he owned a store on Zielony Rynek, Redhead Leyzer was a man with a big belly. In the summer he used to wear a shiny alpaca coast, which glittered like a well-cleaned mirror, and light chamois shoes with soft toes. In the winter, a beaver coat with a wide fur collar, boots lined with felt and galoshes. And in every season he had a shiny, reddish, well-trimmed beard. So Janek could not know that this ragged, shabby Jew, with the worn pants around his sunken belly, with a torn, little excuse for a beard, that this pitiful little Jew was Redhead Leyzer from Zielony Rynek.

So they met but did not recognize each other. Yet they'd been looking for each other so long that they finally understood.

"They'd been looking for each other" does not necessarily mean that Redhead Leyzer was looking specifically for Rudy Janek, or that Rudy Janek was eager to see no one but Redhead Leyzer. In fact, Redhead Leyzer was looking for a German guard corrupt enough to want to live well and let others live too, a guard who, as businessmen used to say, would agree to be "poisoned" and would make deals. At the same time, Rudy Janek was looking for Jews who, like in the good times not so long ago, would fill his pockets with 20-mark banknotes.

Thus, facing each other eye to eye—on either side of the ghetto fence—they looked at one another for a long time without speaking. And when they were finally done with the survey—Leyzer of Janek's grandeur and Janek of Leyzer's dejection—Janek took another look around to make sure that nobody was watching—and let Leyzer come closer to the fence.

"How are you, Leyzer? Come, don't be afraid."

Just like that. Feeling a sudden exhilaration over Leyzer's downfall, Janek addressed his erstwhile boss informally.

Leyzer did not appear at all shocked. He even liked this intimacy. A *shaygets,* yes, but our *shaygets.* A servant. And so Leyzer came nearer without fear.

Janek, having grown up among Jews and having earned his keep from them, knew a few Yiddish words, such as *mamele, tatele, a kholere, a kaporeh* [Yid: Mama, Papa, cholera, bad bird (the latter two used as curses)]. Now, to find favor with Leyzer, he embedded these words in the speech he directed at him.

"See, Leyzer. *Di kholere hot gekhapt* [Yid: the devil has taken the lot of] you Jews. Your sacks of flour on Zielony Rynek are now ours. Everything is ours. The whole world will be ours. Me now—Johann, a master. And you Leyzer—a lousy Jew, a servant."

Leyzer saw that if Janek went on like that, he would be unable to begin. Answering with an insult was too dangerous. He had to try diplomacy, a little flattery, and a bit of scolding. So he didn't say a word but sighed deeply instead, meaning: "You are right, Janek, we are in trouble." And then he began:

"Nie boj sie, Janek, tam gdzie woda byla, woda bedzie, a gowniarz gowniarzem zostanie" [Pol: Don't worry, Janek; where there was water, there will always be water, and a shithead will always be a shithead]. In other words, Janek, where there was money, there will be money again, and a swine will remain a swine.

After a bit of this small talk, with hints from Leyzer and punches from Janek, they came to the following agreement: Janek would toss over the fence whatever he could get in the city. Leyzer would sell the merchandise, and they'd share the proceeds.

"You know, Janek—live and let live!"

"That's right, Mister Leyzer: where water was, water will always be; money goes to money. You will have and I, too, will have, as in the old days. Remember, Leyzer?"

These were the first days of the ghetto. People did not yet comprehend the evil which had befallen them. The population was, so to speak, in the honeymoon of ghetto life, and behaved therefore like a young, freewheeling bridegroom, eating well and spending one banknote from his dowry after another.

Everything in the ghetto, therefore, was for sale. Everything that could be procured.

After the turmoil in the city, after the killings inside the homes during the "planned resettlement," after the grabbing of people on the streets for forced labor, after the scare about what was going to happen tomorrow, or even in a few hours, the Jews in the ghetto, among themselves, rejoiced in *dolce far niente* [Ital: sweet frivolity]. Crowds gathered in the street and exchanged good news. Cards were played outdoors, and food was stashed away.

Prices rose by the hour. But the devil had already taken so much, so much Jewish property had been swallowed, the whole wedding was so terribly costly, that these few marks did not matter any more. Thus, exorbitant sums were paid for food, as long as it could be had—which it could, indeed, from the other side of the fence.

These were prosperous times in the ghetto. But it was prosperity turned upside down. People did not earn what they spent. Only a few individuals, who were willing to take the risk and run smuggling operations through the fence, made a profit. The others spent their last money buying everything: soap, sugar, flour, meat, and the greatest of delicacies, live hens! Live hens were capital that increased every day, and there was also the daily bonus—an egg! An egg in the ghetto, God in heaven, it was treasure; two, two and a half marks a day.

Therefore Leyzer urged Janek:

"Janek, by God, remember hens!—not geese, not turkeys, but hens!"

Janek interpreted this in his own way:

"Ha, ha, no more geese and turkeys for them Jews, just hens!"—but since he was "requisitioning" the loot from the peasant woman who brought their merchandise to the city, he was not that strict and sometimes added a rooster to the hens he got for Leyzer.

When the ghetto stores all of a sudden began selling eggs for two and a half marks, and on the streets one could buy a plate of poultry meat for 15 marks a quarter, and live hens were seen in the ghetto, the Jewish police became restless.

How come? Hens in the ghetto? Eggs in the ghetto without their knowledge? Merchandise being smuggled into the ghetto, people becoming rich, and they had no share in it? Jewish *chutzpah* [Yid: nerve]! Such Jews should be taught a lesson!

And who could search better than the Jewish police? So they searched until they found Redhead Leyzer and the twenty-five live hens he had gotten from Rudy Janek.

What happened to the twenty-five hens, we learned from the above document: thirteen hens were returned to Leyzer, and let no one say that the Jewish *Hilfs-Ordnungsdienst* resembles the German police, the Kripo, the Schupo, etc., just because they too made an acronym of their name, the HIOD.

Six hens, according to the document, were sent to Drewnowska Street. Since the recipient is not named, we have to assume that it was the hospital on Drewnowska Street. It's hard to believe, however, that it was the patients who got the hens. It would be closer to the truth that the loot was devoured by the managing personnel.

One hen was given to the commander of the Order Service, the overseer of public order in the ghetto, so as to have approval for the remaining 5 hens given to the HIOD, in the form of 20 meals.

And thus it happened that the principle of "one for all" was finally realized in the ghetto. One Redhead Leyzer was able to satisfy an entire hospital, a whole unit of the Jewish police, and even the commander of the Order Service.

A second part of the "one-for-all" principle was executed by Rudy Janek. Janek was irked, not so much by the loss as by the *chutzpah* of those Jews who, without his permission, used his own method of requisitioning merchandise. He was thinking:

Good. The damn Jews took twelve of his hens away. Well, then, he'd take two Jews for each hen. They decided, "Fifty-fifty"; he responded, "Double—24 Jews for 12 hens. And let the damn Jews know who Janek is!"

Let the ghetto know who Janek is, who—two months and two days after the ghetto was closed off—shot 24 Jews to death, for nothing. Like stray dogs.

On July 2, 1940, he shot a fifteen-year-old girl in the heart.

Three days later, when he was again sent to his post at the ghetto fence, he killed a 29-year-old man and a young woman of 21.

After a pause, on July 10, he shot a 30-year-old woman in the head.

On July 11 a man of 23.

On July 12 he shot the brains out of a 65-year-old man.

On July 16 he hit a 50-year-old woman and a 16-year-old boy.

On July 18 he put a bullet in the heart of a 62-year-old man.

On July 20 he murdered a 20-year-old girl.

With murderous precision he killed five people on one day, July 21: a 17-year-old girl, three young men in their twenties, and a 30-year-old man.

On July 24 two aged women.

On July 26 a 17-year-old boy.

On July 27 a 24-year-old man.

On July 28 his last two victims, a 17-year-old girl and a 50-year-old woman.

A total of thirty-five people were killed by the guards of German justice in the month of July 1940. Rudy Janek killed twenty-four of them. Not one more. Twenty-four—with truly German precision.

But of those twenty-four Jews shot to death, no mention is made in any document. Nor is it mentioned whether the one hen taken by the commander of the Order Service, the guardian of public order in the ghetto, was to his taste or, God forbid, it was not.

IN THE GHETTO, JANUARY 1942

The burning of the Reform Temple on Kosciuszko Boulevard, on the night of November 14, 1939.

SHIMON HUBERBAND, THE DESTRUCTION OF THE SYNAGOGUES IN LODZ

In Lodz there were three large and famous synagogues: the Old Town Synagogue, the Temple, and the Vilker *shul* [Yid: synagogue].

The oldest was the Old Town Synagogue, erected between 1860 and 1863 at 8 Wolborska Street and made of wood. Later on it was moved to 20 Wolborska Street, where it was made of stone. The construction work was carried out by Italian master craftsmen and laborers who were brought to Lodz specifically for this purpose. Poznansky [owner of the largest textile factory in Eastern Europe] donated ten thousand rubles for the decoration of the outer edifice.

The synagogue was very tall and beautiful. It contained two women's galleries. In all, it held fifteen hundred seats. There were thirty-six Torah scrolls in the synagogue and a large amount of silver Torah ornaments, including many antique works of art. All official public ceremonies took place in this synagogue. On national holidays and other official occasions, the provincial governor of Lodz and Polish generals participated in the ceremonies.

The Temple, known as the "German Synagogue," was built in 1888. Its construction cost more than half a million rubles. It was built by "enlightened Jews" known as "Germans," who desired a modern synagogue with an organ, modeled after those in Western Europe. It was constructed by Italian master craftsmen, and was an exact replica of the Königsberg Temple.

Following the style of the Reform temples, its main entrance was headed by the inscription, "For My house will be called a house of prayer until all the nations." The Temple was located in the center of town on Kosciuszko Street.

The Vilker *shul* was attached to a *beys medresh* [Heb: house of study] which contained an extraordinary treasury of Hebrew books. It was the largest place of Torah study in the city. There was a time when study in the *beys medresh* proceeded uninterrupted for twenty-four hours a day. For this purpose, there were special *mishmorim* [Heb: study groups] which alternated periodically, to ensure that the place would not be without Torah study for a single second.

As soon as "they" came into town, they took the keys to all the synagogues from the *ḳehillah* administration.

In early November, 1939, they summoned the representatives of the *kehillah,* returned to them the keys to the Vilker *shul* and ordered them to clean the *shul* and arrange services with a cantor, choir, Torah-reader, and *shofar* [Heb: the ram's horn blown at the New Year's service]-blower. The *kehillah* called upon the Jewish population to attend the service.

The event took place on Tuesday. The *shul* was packed with congregants wearing *taleysim* and *tefillin.* Cantor Winograd and his choir conducted the service. A large number of high-ranking German officers came and filmed the entire course of the service, immortalizing it on film.

Cantor Winograd sang with the choir a number of selections from the Rosh Hashanah and Yom Kippur [Heb: Day of Atonement] prayers. After that, the order was given to take out the Torah scroll and read from it. The Torah scroll was filmed in various poses—with the mantle covering it, with its belt on and off, open and closed. The Torah-reader, a clever Jew, called out in Hebrew before beginning to read the scroll: "Today is Tuesday." This was meant as a statement for posterity that they were forced to read the Torah, since the Torah is usually not read on Tuesdays.

When the *kehillah* representatives were given back the keys, two days after the service, it occurred to some of them to rescue a few Torah scrolls from the *shul.* A number of representatives were reluctant to do so. It was possible, they claimed, that the Germans had counted the scrolls, in which case the rescue of a few scrolls could lead to sad consequences for the greatly suffering Jewish community of Lodz.

The next day, a similar "event" took place in the slaughterhouse. The kosher meat slaughterers, dressed in *yarmulkes* [Yid: skull caps] and *gartlekh* [Yid: silk waistbands or sashes], were ordered to slaughter a number of cattle and recite the blessings, while squeezing their eyes shut and rocking with religious fervor. They were also required to examine the animals' lungs and remove the adhesions to the lungs. All of this was filmed. [Much of this footage survives in *Der Ewige Jude* (Ger: *The Eternal Jew*), a Nazi propaganda film.]

On Wednesday night between November 14 and 15, 1939, the Temple on Kosciuszko Street was set on fire. The firemen were on the scene and prevented the blaze from spreading to private homes.

The thought occurred to a few members of the *kehillah* to pretend that they were unaware who had set the fire, and petition the insurance company for one million zlotys, the amount for which the Temple was insured. Of course, the petition was rejected.

The Temple was completely burned to the ground along with its Torah scrolls and interior fixtures.

On the following night, between the fifteenth and sixteenth of the month, the Old Town Synagogue was burned down in the same manner. The whole synagogue, with all its interior fixtures and Torah scrolls, was completely devoured by fire. All that remained was the western wall, which was shot to pieces by gunfire in April, 1940.

Three days after the fires were set in these two synagogues, a notice appeared in the *Berliner Tagesblatt* saying that, due to the fact that the Jews had destroyed the monument to the Polish freedom fighter, Kosciuszko, the Poles had set fire to the two largest synagogues as an act of revenge.

In the second half of 1940, the Germans set fire to the interior fixtures of the Vilker *shul,* and then dismantled the *shul.* The extraordinary treasury of Hebrew books, including literally thousands of rarities, was burned, and the Torah scrolls were sent off to an unknown destination.

CHRONOLOGY OF THE GHETTO'S INDUSTRY

[*In the following, compiled by Marek Web, the line after the date is taken from the Ghetto Calendar for the year 1942. It is followed by an excerpt from a report in the ghetto archives.*]

1940

April 1. First tailor workshops, 45 Lagiewnicka Street.
The central depot for all tailor workshops is located here. Thousands of pieces of material of all sorts—men's, women's, military, civilian—are brought to this place. Well-lighted sheds overflow with merchandise, and more is expected. In the hall next door, electric cutting machines are installed, so that dozens of suits can be cut out simultaneously, about 14,000 a day. These are distributed to the tailor shops.

June 15. Tailor workshop, 8 Jakuba Street.

July 8. Shoemaking workshop, 45 Lagiewnicka Street. Later moved to 75–79 Brzezinska Street and also to Marysin.

The workshop's activities are varied. At 75 Brzezinska Street, street shoes are made from rags. Materials and labor are entirely provided by the ghetto.

In this case, the ghetto receives all of the profit. There are not only skilled shoemakers working here but also declassé women and girls who earn a few marks a week. At 79 Brzezinska Street new high-quality leather is stored and made into men's and women's shoes (in the latest styles, as seen in magazines) and military boots. The workshop also has a huge number of old shoes, some 40,000 pairs, perhaps from the last war. These have been quite nicely repaired and are said to be used in the POW camps.

July 12. Quilt covers workshop.

July 14. Carpentry workshop.

The carpentry workshop, now employing 700 workers, is located at 12–14 Drukarska Street, though it also occupies neighboring buildings. A carpentry shop this huge was unknown anywhere in Lodz before the war. The first thing we notice is a tremendous storage area for plywood and lumber. This area grows larger all the time, as new orders keep exceeding even the wildest expectations.

We move on to the machine shop and the locksmith, which repairs all of the workshop's equipment. A new dry storage, able to accommodate many carloads of lumber, is being built to replace the old one, which was too small for the mass production typical of this workshop.

We should also mention even larger stocks of old furniture and useless odds and ends, from which beautiful new sets of Chippendale-style furniture are made. To comprehend this transformation, one has to go from one workshop to the next, observing every phase of production.

In November 1940 the workshop employed 407 workers and had 20 machines. At first, raw material was out of the question, so everything was produced from old, unusable junk found in abandoned Jewish homes. Of course, all new furniture in such homes had been promptly appropriated. In May 1941 the workshop was already mass producing on a factory scale.

July 16. Marmalade factory.

July 18. Tailor workshop, 16 Jakuba Street.

With 1200 workers, the shops at 16 Jakuba Street resemble a large factory. The Jewish worker, particularly the Jewish tailor, has never before been part of such a large mass of workers. This is especially true of the old Baluty tailors, who used to work at home for wholesalers. In this concentrated mass, they realize their strength and have become insolent. Walking through the room, we heard various haughty remarks.

August 4. Upholstery workshop, 9 Urzednicza Street.

In the beginning, this workshop employed 100 workers, 90 percent of them professional upholsterers, and was largely involved in taking apart old upholstered pieces for whatever seaweed [used as stuffing], belts, nails, and canvas could be salvaged. In addition to reconditioning old furniture, the workshop produced mattresses. By October it had made 501 mattresses and had separated 5284 kg. of seaweed. It did not have its own equipment; its 8 machines were borrowed from some of its workers.

Today the workshop not only makes mattresses (principally for the military) but also couches, armchairs, and other kinds of upholstered furniture sent here from the carpentry workshop. Materials differ significantly from those used before the war: hay and straw substitute for seaweed, reinforced paper for linen.

August 5. Linen workshop, 5 Mlynarska Street, later moved to 14 Dworska Street and re-named Linen and Clothing Workshop.

Between 12 September and 27 October 1940, the workshop employed only 25 workers and filled civilian orders exclusively.... The number of employees reached 748 in June 1941, at which time the production of white and grey air force shirts began. The workshop received orders for 150,000 pieces. Requirements are extremely precise, and every aspect of each piece must be carefully inspected. Regrettably, the authorities pay very little for the shirts, so that little or no profit is made from this enormous order.... A considerable part of the merchandise is made from our own materials, which accords with the Chairman's goal of selling not only material but also Jewish labor. But many firms entrust the workshop with their own materials.... We are informed that the firms who have had work done, as well as many visitors to the ghetto, are delighted with the work of Jewish hands, which explains the continuous flow of orders.

August 10. Tannery workshop, 5–7 Urzednicza Street.

Twenty people are employed here.... Mr. Topilski, the manager, justifiably calls his workshop an experimental station, because the variety of articles produced here is dazzling. While a pre-war tannery would have specialized in making a certain kind of sole, this workshop makes tops and bottoms for shoes, as well as a number of other leather products for technical as well as personal use.... Thus far, all the raw materials come from the ghetto itself.... The tannery services the shoemaking workshop, the felt shoes workshop, the art works workshop, the hat workshop. Hides are prepared for the saddle workshop and transmission belts for the metal and carpentry workshops.

August 15. Textile factory.

Preparations went on for several months and required a great deal of effort, principally by the Chairman and Dawid Warszawski.* A search for workers and supervisors was necessary, since Jews had not been given jobs in the spinning industry before the war. Luckily, a Mr. Herzog, who had been a foreman in a spinning factory in Germany, was in the ghetto, and he drew up the required plans. Then they began looking for materials, missing parts, and the tools needed to activate the machinery. In the beginning the factory had only 20 people; there were 93 by October.

August 15. Dye workshop.

August 18. Slipper workshop.

The workshop manager is Mr. Sonnabend, who, in fact, came up with the idea for this workshop. In its first months, felt slippers were the main article produced here. By October, 70 workers had made 4,035 slippers.... By June 1941 the number of workers had risen to 127, and production had grown to 16,212 pairs of shoes and 3,244 belts.

Because of the drop in demand for slippers during the summer months, the manager designed a type of sandal with a wooden sole. The clients liked it, and orders began pouring in again. The workshop makes 900 pairs of these sandals daily.

August 20. Tailor workshop, 53 Lagiewnicka Street.

In the tailor shops at 49 and 53 Lagniewnicka Street, uniforms and military coats are finished with the greatest care. Women's overcoats are also made here for the *Reichsarbeitsdienst* [Ger: State Labor Service, required of all able-bodied citizens of the Third Reich]. Working conditions are quite miserable, the workrooms are crowded, and there is no air to breathe. Apprentices work even on the staircase.... Let it be the staircase, so long as there is a job!

August 23. Metal works workshop.

To one degree or another, the establishment of every other ghetto workshop was connected to the Metal Works workshop, which installs electrical wiring, dismantles old equipment, assembles new equipment, and does all kinds of repair work.

The Chairman initially had reservations about this workshop, since he saw it as simply a repair shop and did not think it might also produce goods for export, his main goal. However, the workshop's importance grew in proportion to the growth of the ghetto's industry. By January 1941 it already employed 150 workers. In May there were 301 workers and 53 machines in the workshop. Also, in connection with the Chairman's re-classification program, 180 students were sent to the workshop for vocational training.

At this time, the workshop began receiving orders from the city. Aside from repair and assembly jobs, the workshop has already produced 1700 watering cans, 2240 pails, 1140 gas fixtures.... The number of workers rose to 500 and of trainees to 300. Mr. Chimowicz, the manager, is now energetically exploring export possibilities and has received many new orders from the military and civilian authorities.

In general, the workshop repairs, re-conditions, and makes new products in the following categories of metal work: tinsmithery, casting, blacksmithery, general and precision mechanics.

August 26. Sausage factory.

September 17. Tailor workshop, 2 Mlynarska Street.

September 18. Tailor workshop, 13 Zabia Street.

September 28. Tailor workshop, 10 Dworska Street.

October 1. Central Bureau for the Labor Workshops.

October 8. Fur workshop, 9 Ceglana Street.

At present, 250 workers are employed there. Not that long ago, this kind of workshop seemed an impossible dream, since no one believed that there would be enough material for the production of furs, or that people could be found who knew the work, or that clients willing to buy the products of Jewish labor would come forward.... But professionals like Amzel, Opatowski and others nudged the Chairman and gave him a plan he found interesting.... In the beginning, there were just 18 workers.

The need to enlarge the workshop became acute when the Purchasing Bank was opened on 7 Clesielska Street, because coats of inferior quality, which had been purchased from ghetto residents for a few marks, reached a price of 700 and even 800 marks after workshop workers thoroughly reconditioned them. And coats made from small pieces of fur, which in normal times would have simply been discarded, were similarly assessed. This value, converted into food for the ghetto, was a real gain. Also, very expensive mink coats are made from a variety of collars, muffs, and the like. These are carefully matched, worn patches are removed, and the material is cleaned and dyed.

We were told that if one worker were to piece a coat together from all those little pieces, he would have to work 350 to 500 hours. A work group does this job in just one week. A hefty profit remains, after deducting labor costs, since normally this kind of material would not be used at all.

In addition to using furs from the ghetto, the workshop receives orders in which the client delivers the raw materials for coats. Recently, an order arrived for 300 black horsehide coats [worn mainly by the SS] and for 30 sheepskin coats. All of it was done to the client's great satisfaction.

October 10. Rope making workshop.

October 31. Rubber products factory.

November 1. Knitwear workshop, 50 Brzezinska Street.

At this time, only 15 women work at producing silk lingerie, while 700 workers are busy making epaulettes. The Berlin Military-Uniforms Office has ordered 400,000 pieces! . . .

In a separate workshop, women's dresses are made from wool, and children's wear is patched together from silk remnants and used material. . . . Since nothing can be wasted, any small pieces of material still remaining are sent to the Art Works workshop to be used in making little tapestries and baby dresses.

Working conditions leave much to be desired, especially in winter-time. The workshop is in a burned-out factory building, only one floor of which is in a usable state. There is no central heating. . . . Despite the cold, the workshop worked without interruption during the period of rapid expansion. In November 1940, 68 people worked on 38 machines. In July 1941 there were 750 workers and 350 machines.

November 13. Women's Hat workshop, 7–11 Zgierska Street.

Work began here in November 1940 with 67 employees, who made 1430 hats in 12 days. By June 1941 there were 313 workers. Besides hats, the workshop makes brooches, ornamental belts, leather and felt flowers, etc. One special item very popular with clients is a silk shawl with ornaments attached.

When one realizes that all hats here are made from small pieces and remnants, one understands how much Jewish labor is involved and why so many workers are needed. An exhibit of workshop products, which was organized not long ago, was attended by the German authorities, who, in recognition of the good work being done, arranged for the workshop to receive a modest ration of flour and sugar.

November 15. Rubberized coat factory.

The Chairman announced the establishment of [this] factory on the premises of a former movie theater. Since the plan was to have parts of the coats sent to the ghetto only for gluing and finishing, the Chairman decided that this work would be good for girls and women from the intelligentsia, and he sent in 50 former teachers, kindergarten attendants, and lab technicians but no one who knew anything about gluing parts of coats together. Within a month the factory's work force totalled some 200 women. The German firm sent in an order for 17,000 coats. . . . Since the women had mastered the job, the workshop would have prospered but for the scarcity of synthetic rubber.

December 1. Gloves and hosiery workshop, 7 Koscielna Street.

In these small and narrow rooms, Mr. Radziejowski, a well-known manufacturer in Lodz before the war, is making every effort to achieve maximum production. In its first months, the workshop made 500 dozen gloves, 1907 dozen socks, 226 sweaters, and other articles of knitwear. In July, the workshop employed 400 people, including 200 home-workers.

December 15. Tailor workshop, 49 Lagiewnicka Street.

December 29. Tailor workshop, 28 Nowomiejska Street.

1941

January 25. Leather and saddle workshop, 5 Mlynarska Street.

According to ghetto statistics, there were 35 people working here in March, having 13 sewing machines, one grinder, and one cardboard cutter at their disposal. By July the number of workers had reached 200 and the need for larger facilities became urgent. The workshop was moved to the huge place which had served as a slaughterhouse before the war.

At this point the halls are being repaired in preparation for winter. But there are already piles of parts for knapsacks, for there are orders in the tens of thousands for this article. Work is in full swing, since the orders are mostly from the military, and the deadlines are close. The workshop also makes briefcases from oilcloth, sewing boxes, cigarette cases, suitcases, purses, etc. Leftover pieces are saved for further use.

February 27. Paper products division, 12 Zydowska Street.

The workshop is comprised of three divisions: bindery, box making, and bag making. There is also a paper-ruling shop and, during the summer, a fly-trap shop. The bindery and the paper-ruling shop make all kinds of books, pads, and ledgers for the ghetto's needs. The bindery also fills requests from the German authorities, who are very satisfied with the quality of work.

The managers of the workshop, Messrs. Bajgelman and Ejbuszyc, were at the beginning fully aware that there was not enough equipment and raw material in the ghetto to start a workshop. But they had faith in the good work of the people who knew the job, and in their own inventiveness. They started collecting all the waste paper of the other workshops and succeeded in gathering thousands of kilograms of old paper bags, margarine boxes, etc. These were taken apart, cleaned and glued in various ways. We saw various articles made in this fashion: very attractive, strong file folders, alphabetizers, waste baskets. The workshop recently received a modest supply of paper from the city, but until now everything was produced from ghetto materials. At present the workshop employs 60 workers and 7 trainees.

March 1. Metal works division, 17 Krotka Street.
Carpenters' workshop, 9 Pucka Street.

March 7. Hatters' workshop, 47 Brzezinska Street.

In April 1941 the workshop employed 67 people, who worked on 45 machines. The number of hats produced at that time reached 14,480, which was striking evidence of the workshop's vitality. In June there were 131 workers, who produced 28,180 hats, and in July the number of machines reached 100. At present, the workshop is flooded with army field caps; these, however, are unfinished because the client, despite many reminders, has not yet delivered the accessories.

The workshop recently turned to the production of civilian sport caps, which can be made entirely from materials available in the ghetto. Thus, in accordance with the Chairman's goal of selling as much Jewish labor as possible, materials produced in the Textiles workshop are used here for the production of caps. But here, too, there is no dearth of outside orders. The workshop has already made 40,000 sport caps from the client's materials.

March 26. Art products workshop

May 13. Carved wood products workshop.

May 21. Brush workshop, 21 Urzednicza Street.

The workshop employs 35 brushmakers and helpers and also contracts

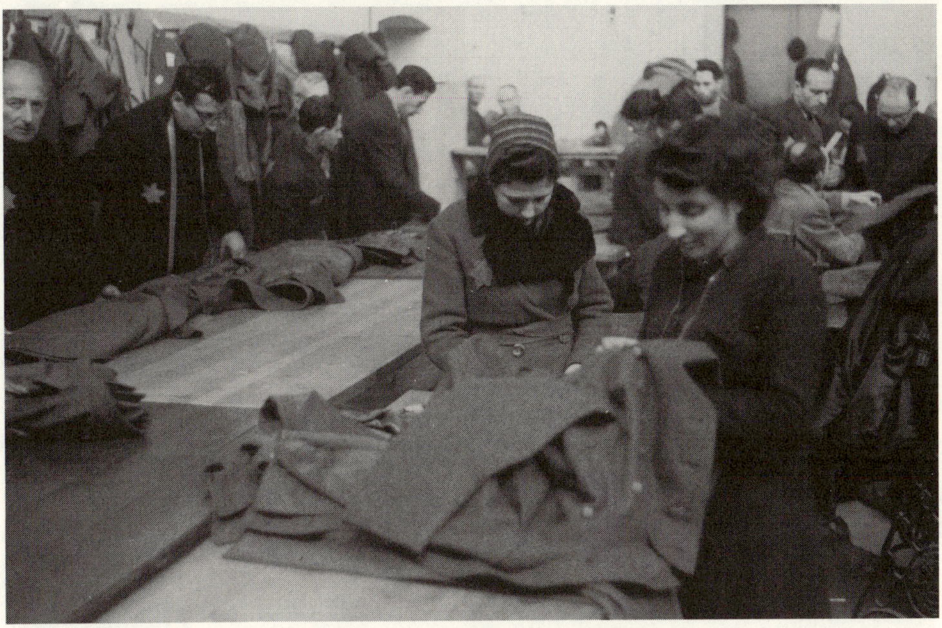

Workers in the ghetto's tailor shop making coats for the German military.

Carpet weavers. Rumkowski's work strategy demanded that people of all ages work for their own survival.

A page from a ghetto album, depicting productivity.

with home-workers. . . . The following raw materials are used: bristles, horse and cow hairs, rice stalks, Hungarian straw, and the like. These materials were requisitioned [i.e., appropriated] by the ghetto, but the source is drying up and there may soon be nothing available for brush production.

The manager, Mr. Ordynans, came up with the idea of using the quills of goose feathers, and he has already received 1000 kg. of such feathers from the Purchasing Office. The German authorities like this type of brush and have placed an order for 6–8,000 pieces, to be made from the ghetto's own materials. The work is more difficult than with the usual materials, but Mr. Ordynans is delighted that he'll be able to keep his workshop working.

June 1. Electrical workshop.

June 20. Brush workshop, 63 Lagiewnicka Street.

June 28. Rug workshops.

August 21. Rubberized coat factory, 36 Limanowski Street.

September 1. Basket workshop.
Cork workshop.
Chemical laundry.

September 27. Straw shoe workshop.

November 10. Chemical waste products factory.

November 16. Corset workshop.

December 1. Sewing machine repair shop.

December 15. Bootmaking workshop.

JAKUB SZULMAN'S NOTEBOOK

(21.3.41) Today is the first day of spring. Who knows if this will be my last spring? My doctor has just told me that I have an incurable heart condition. The main thing is to prevent it from getting worse. Dr. Levy forbade any kind of work requiring movement and said I must take care not to get overly tired or excited and under no circumstances climb stairs. Dr. Shapiro said I might live another twenty years, but only if I lead a normal life and don't strain myself.

I don't wish to be a bad prophet. I'm very curious about life, and I'd like to know what tomorrow will bring. I want to provide for my family—for my wife and for my only son. And finally I want to be able to record for posterity what I have seen. There will be many historians, and a good many of them are now already writing and, at a hundred marks a month, will still be writing later. Others will be writing free "poetry," not being proficient at writing about things that are real.

I've been in contact with original sources for a long time. I know many nuances, many details not known officially. And I deem it my duty to report them, if not in a finished, systematically researched work of history, then at least as source material for the objective historians who will come later.

"Quiet and order now prevail in the ghetto." (Rumkowski) Selected deliberately as "strong-arms," the first members of the ghetto's Order Service had no uniforms but wore arm bands as identification.

The Eldest is planning to go to the Land of Israel right after the war. His opponents are busy trying to foil his efforts. This will surely lead to a struggle over what his role and his deeds were while he was the satrap, while he was the "crazy one" who tended the "golden flame," while he was an Elder in the Litzmannstadt Ghetto, officially appointed by the Germans.

I hope my friends in Israel with any influence over public opinion there will get to know what I manage to jot down. I appeal to my comrades, with whom I spent thirty-five years on the same communal work, to judge my jottings, the words coming from my heart, objectively.

Making use of the [official Ghetto] archives which are now being compiled, I intend to write, in the form of memoirs, a full history of my year-and-a-half's experience as an Elder. I don't know if I'll succeed in this. My notes were lost in Wesola, while we were moving to Drewnowska [from one hospital to another], but I'll try to reproduce them from memory, putting them into the perspective of the present and thus freeing myself from possible subjectivity. I will not lead the reader through narrow alleys strewn with torn-up cobblestones or barricaded with rafters. There was that too. I will omit the feelings of those who have suffered.

And what about the job of the Jewish police in the ghetto, as they understood it, judged it, carried it out according to the orders of their commandant—that I intend to leave to the belletrists and the poets. I will try to tell, with naked objectivity, what my eyes encompassed, for I probably did not *see* everything. Truth need not be adorned, while dishonesty would not be helped by the most original, clearest, most beautiful stories, real or imagined.

In a short time, the people of the ghetto became infused with a new morality, one that might be compared to that of convicted criminals spending their last years in prison. Previously active individuals quickly become demoralized, moved to the side. This is why such individuals did not organize themselves. In an appropriate Jewish atmosphere, they would have again become what they once were. Unfortunately, such an atmosphere has not yet been created. Under ghetto conditions, most people forgot the value of collective welfare. Ill-considered, inappropriate interests emerged in everyone. There were no ideas on a higher plane able to bear immediate fruit. People who couldn't lift themselves up fell ever lower, sank ever deeper.

And those who did not sink lost their influence. Those who rose were the "strong ones," strong because they were unburdened by "simple-minded" sentiments. Things came to such a pass that the expression "a soft heart" acquired a derogatory meaning. In a very short time, words were re-arranged. The new mentality led to theft and other abuses, which the authorities tried to stop with persecution and punishment. But the immorality could not be changed mechanically. There was a need for a new establishment; people who were honest, self-sufficient, independent could not adjust to the existing climate. They either left or stepped aside. Some were rewarded for their accomplishments; others were shunted aside.

Those who were weakest changed most, as it was easier to follow the path of least resistance. At a meeting of the various department heads, the Chairman was reproached for not having found a proper way of fighting the growing dishonesty. His answer was that he had no time for educating people, nor did he have the authority; that he had to fight the abuses which were endangering the very existence of the ghetto; that he had no other means within his authority.

This could have led to polemics, but the Chairman prevented any argument on the question: that was how it had to be, and that was that! Such abuse could not change until those appointed to be prison-heads were teachers, social workers, or others who saw their job as one of rehabilitation.

In our ghetto, however, the task was a much simpler one—to isolate the criminal and punish him. The aim was to instill fear, so that others would not commit abuses or crimes. It is for this reason that, instead of choosing better types, the authorities appointed policemen as prison wardens. The leader of the community ran around in a fog, trying everything: he experimented, looked to his aides to help him, and even tried "setting thieves to catch thieves." But he did not succeed.

Who was he, this Eldest of ours? Before the [First] World War, he was a manufacturer in Lodz, managing a large velvet factory in partnership with another Jew. In debt, and hoping to come to terms with his creditors, he went to England, not knowing English, only an unrefined kind of Yiddish. And he succeeded. Then, during the World War he was in Russia, where he made a fortune. He lost almost all of it in the Revolution, returning to Lodz with the little he was able to save. Having always had a special feeling for children and having been involved in child welfare programs, he took over the management of an orphanage that had been founded during the war and was about to close down. Because he was a Zionist, he managed to place the orphanage under the authority of the Zionist-influenced *kehillah*.

During the war, Dr. [Judah] Magnes, the chancellor of Jerusalem University, came to Lodz. Entrusted by the American Jewish Joint Distribution Committee with forming an industrial council, he had been given the names of three men, including the writer of these lines, as representatives of Jewish labor, and we three put together a slate of about twenty names. The workers were to have seven votes, with the rest allotted to various communal organizations and corporate entities. . . .

In early 1920 the Committee allocated special funds for children's summer camps. I was given responsibility for organizing the camps, and I asked three workers to help me: A. Kagan, the director of the Borochov School, Sh. Y. Ravin, the director of the high school, and M. Ch. Rumkowski, the head of the orphan welfare department, a man with inexhaustible energy. . . . Rumkowski swam about like a fish in water. Possessed of unusual energy, he involved himself in the camps as though it were his livelihood. He achieved a maximum result with a minimal input, and he used the business contacts he had made to strengthen his position as "light to the orphans."

But eating increases one's appetite. The orphanage flourished and moved to larger quarters in Helenowek, a small village outside of Lodz. And here Rumkowski began experimenting. He introduced a farm, where the children were given instruction in agriculture. He built an orangery. He didn't rest for a minute. The orphanage grew more and more well-known, and he won for himself a reputation as a professional *schnorrer* [Yid: beggar; here: fund-raiser], who had *schnorred* 300,000 zlotys but wouldn't let go of even 30 zlotys. Nothing was unattainable for him. Nothing could stop him. He knew everything, and he could do everything. He was an agronomist, an editor, a pedagogue—all in one.

His education had been like that of any other small-town Jewish merchant—he went to *cheder* [Heb: room, for religious instruction], then to the public school; he read several Yiddish newspapers carefully. When he felt he lacked competence in pedagogical matters, he'd go see Janusz Korczak,* a noted authority on childhood education and director of a respected institution. Rumkowski would spend a couple of weeks there, observing the educational method closely.

He won election to the *kehillah* as a candidate on the Zionist slate, and later became a member of its executive board and then one of its leaders. He was cranky. When the budget committee endorsed a project he did not favor, he would take the floor and start a sarcastic monologue, speaking all evening, until the majority, having lost its patience, would adjourn the meeting.

Rumkowski knew everything. He was an editor, having published a newsletter, *The Orphan,* for two years. The publisher of the *Lodzer Tageblatt,* a Zionist daily, was his brother-in-law, and with his usual far-sightedness, he realized that a friendly relationship with the "people's paper" would help consolidate all the social forces of Jewish Lodz around his paper. The competition between the two papers, however, was acute.

Rumkowski's material circumstances were not the best. He had to work very hard to make ends meet, but because he remained a "big innocent," he was forced to curtail his image as a leader.

Helenowek, which had an endowment of over half a million [zlotys], became the most well-known children's home in Lodz and one of the most famous in Poland. To insure it against unforeseen eventualities, Rumkowski formed a membership society, composed of a couple of dozen friends. The executive board, which included some Zionist leaders and some unaffiliated supporters, was not truly a managing body. Meetings were called and resolutions passed, but the board approved only what Rumkowski wanted, and he reported only those facts that were already accomplished.

The Joint Distribution Committee gave lavish support and was always trying to bind together the various welfare agencies. Outwardly, it seemed as though Rumkowski did not oppose such cooperation, but he managed to see that no unification ever took place.

[In the fall of 1939] when a fight broke out in the *kehillah,* and a new executive board was formed, Rumkowski was unanimously elected vice-president. He became deeply involved in the *kehillah*'s business and was the only one of the executive board to take a communal approach in evaluating the situation that developed. The board often met with the mayor of Lodz, the authorized administrator of the *kehillah.*

On October 19 an order came to disband the *kehillah*'s executive board; the Eldest was to step down, and Rumkowski was to be made Eldest in his place. The *kehillah* accepted this news without surprise. It was remarkable! He did not have a friend among the co-workers he had selected to work with him. They worked with him, they carried out his orders, but they treated him with reserve. It wasn't sabotage, but neither was there any warmth to the cooperation. At first he did not react, at least not outwardly, but it was impossible for him not to feel it. When he was held by the Gestapo, none of his personnel, no one in the council, showed the least interest in him. It happened that I was at the *kehillah* office that day, and learning that the Chairman had not yet returned, I demanded that his secretary act. It was only after half a day that a delegate from the three-member council approached the mayor.

From the first day, he began looking for new people. He issued an order that no administrative employee, no worker could be hired without his approval. He tried hiring his old friends, who had similar ideas, but most had left town. He was left on his own, with only a few inexperienced young people whom he could trust. His approach to the whole complex of problems was that of a layman. He made many mistakes, though he did do something. Looking at it now, a year and a half later, especially in light of what happened in Warsaw,* it must be admitted that great things were accomplished by the "tragic, lonely one." And he was certainly alone, without any political experience, without important fellow workers. In the first council there were some individuals with a lot of experience in communal work; in the second council, there were people whose level of accomplishment was, on the whole, not above average.

Lodz had bad luck. Right away, almost everyone fled: the very rich, the community leaders, the intelligentsia, even the important government officials. Whatever the individual motivations, from the community's point of view it looked like desertion. Then others who had remained at their posts began leaving, one after another. The Chairman began looking for other officials, but he avoided working with them. For many months, he was obsessed with an *idée fixe:* that his name should be remembered in history! Even before the ghetto was sealed, he had an inner certainty that his name would be remembered. But he was not sure what "letters" history would use in perpetuating his name. He had been sickly, with a heart condition, and suffered considerably before the war. Now he began to pay a great deal of attention to maintaining his health.

He was lonely, but his ambition drove him. He cared very much about what people said about him, how they accepted his decrees, and (of utmost importance to him) how the common people reacted. He did not see, however, that in the new classless society, which was giving people a new social education, different methods had to be used. His class instinct kept him from taking leftists as co-workers. His mental outlook remained strictly bourgeois. In the new circumstances his views lost their basis, but no one can shed his skin. He publicly declared many times that he had put aside his political sympathies. Whether he really meant this or said it just for effect, his old self often showed itself in his actions.

He conducted zigzag politics, maneuvering ingeniously among the various groupings in the ghetto—those recently formed and those continuing from before the war. One idea he never lost sight of: *divide.* When he felt isolated, when his efforts made enemies, when allies did not materialize or disappointed him, he always returned to his old ambition: *to rule.* And this led him to: *divide.* He was a master in this, giving concessions to the Orthodox, seeking to please the rabbinate and the clergy, making sure he got along with the workers, trying to satisfy a petition, whenever he received one.

When disagreements arose between the workers and the baking contractors during the baking of *matzoh* in the workshops, he decided in favor of the workers, at the expense of consumers. So he won over the workers without losing anyone's respect. He fought strongly against the bakers, the butchers, the merchants, and the wholesalers for exploiting the people. And when these exploiters instigated street disturbances, he created police units to suppress the riots. The people reacted to these demonstrations with jokes and ditties, often bitingly sarcastic.

Many members of the "commando" units were men with criminal records. The first task of these units was to break up demonstrations if they should occur, prevent strikes if they were in the making, weaken the groups who wanted to organize street disturbances when the Chairman made public speeches.

Surrounded by insincere and dishonest associates, he never heard a word of genuine criticism; all his suggestions were accepted, always without reservation. If someone wanted to introduce a project, he would always try to convince him it was his, that is, the Chairman's own idea. Whatever it was, the project would be ascribed to him. And reading in his newspaper about his projects and his ideas, the Eldest believed that, in fact, they were his. He began to believe in his genius, his creativity—that he was sent from Heaven. It impressed him to be the head of everything, to be able to say, and later also to write, *my* report, *my* department, *my* bank, *my, my, my*—.

He also acted on his own in regard to purely Jewish questions, considering them carefully. In 1941, for the High Holy Days, we converted several movie theaters into splendid houses of prayer, down to the smallest details. He came dressed in a white *kitl* [Yid: ceremonial robe] with a woven *keser* [Heb: ornamental collar], white slippers, and a white *yarmulke* embroidered like that of a high priest. He was undecided about being photographed in his outfit. F. [possibly Rabbi Yosif Fajner] advised him to be photographed, but to take the negative away from the photographer—a two-sided *t'shuve* [Heb: response].

In Warsaw half of the population was adrift in difficulties, and the other half was dying of starvation. Here, at least, there was an organization that cared for everyone, as well as for the individual. However insufficient, misguided, and irresponsible it was, its support extended to almost two-thirds of the ghetto population, about 90,000 people, disbursing almost a million marks a month from the three to three and a half million marks it received. The choice was the right one, and the pain that accompanied poverty was lightened. Although the majority of people were unprepared for it, and there was no ready labor, Rumkowski continued to pursue his course. The several minor exceptions he made, mostly of a personal nature, did not alter the basic economic policy, but they did cause considerable resentment and animosity toward him on the part of hundreds of people, including his former associates.

He himself was incorruptible, but he could not control the corruption around him. When he was first chosen as Eldest, Buritsh [possibly Julius Bursche, anti-Nazi bishop of the Evangelical Church] offered him a *droshky*. Since Jews were then forbidden from going into town in a carriage, Rumkowski refused, saying, "How would it look if I rode to town when my brethren must walk?" This was naive, but that's how he was. On the other hand, his sister-in-law, who had been a modest person, could not stand the way things were and decided to have a defiant fling. She became a lady of fashion and caused much bad feeling in the ghetto.

Outraged workers at an early demonstration.

CHAPTER THREE

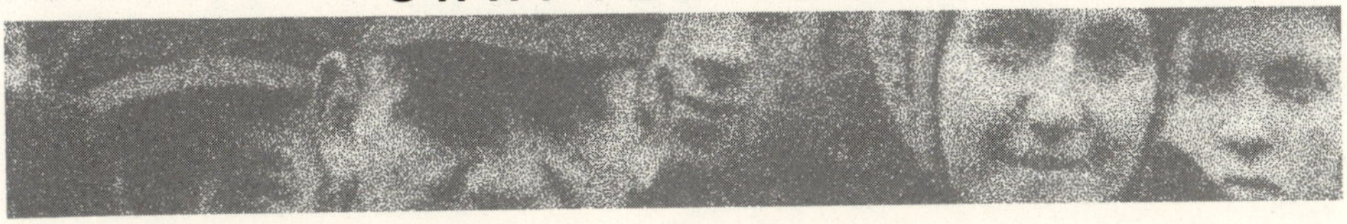

"GIVE UP YOUR SELFISH INTERESTS"

JAKUB POZNANSKI, LODZ GHETTO DIARY

SUMMER 1940

I again turned to the Chairman, asking that the goats be distributed among the people, and received no answer.

It was then that I realized that Rumkowski quite obviously disliked me. To this day I don't understand the reason for it. Was it some baseless denunciation against me, the goat business, or something else?

Since I didn't feel at all guilty, I didn't seek any reconciliation with Rumkowski.

One sunny Sunday I prepared a review of all the *Hachschara* groups, followed by a parade in front of the Chairman. It was a most imposing sight. About 3000 young people marched in close ranks. Commands were given in Hebrew. The boys and girls marched in cadence. The invited guests had tears in their eyes. The young people kept exclaiming: "Long live the prince!"

When I organized the parade I thought that I'd be giving the Chairman the high honor due the head of the Jewish Elders, which he was. However, I think my popularity with the young people—which continues somewhat even today—was among the reasons he disliked me.

The ghetto population began starving during the summer, having lost its old sources of income. Because of the poverty there were even some disturbances in the street, which the German authorities seized upon, using guns to force the demonstrators to keep the peace. There were a few casualties.

This sad episode led the Chairman to create the Department of Relief a few weeks later. This new department allotted 9 marks a month for every member of an unemployed person's family. Children below 14 received 7 marks.

GHETTO DOCUMENT

ANNOUNCEMENT NO. 104

JEWS!

The events of recent days were provoked by irresponsible elements who want to inject chaos into our life.

Those individuals have in mind only their own interest and thus try to prevent the organization of positive and proper assistance for the population.

Soon after the establishment of the ghetto, and with much difficulty, I succeeded in obtaining work from outside the ghetto for some of the tailors, carpenters, shoemakers, upholsterers, and seamstresses; soon I will obtain work for other categories of artisans, as well as for hand weavers.

THE BUDGET OF THE COMMUNITY IS OVERBURDENED!

Care for the sick, children, and the elderly is still our first priority.

Even so, the kitchens will be organized for the old and the young alike.

In addition to the large general kitchens, which will distribute 10,000 meals a day to workers and the unemployed, as well as the kitchens for specific groups, the block committees will continue receiving supplies.

This is our positive plan and should be carried out.

This is not an easy task.

Therefore, I appeal to you:

REMAIN CALM!

Do not let yourselves be misled by irresponsible elements who want to disturb our work and our plans for the future.

JEWS, REMAIN CALM.

I will do everything possible and I will endeavor most energetically to carry out my tasks.

Ch. Rumkowski
The Eldest of the Jews
Litzmannstadt Ghetto, 12 August 1940

GERMAN DOCUMENT

[*Gestapo memo*]

Lodz, 30 August 1940

The office of the Litzmannstadt criminal police has reported the following: On August 25 demonstrations of Jews took place again. The Jews tried to storm Prison I on Franzstrasse. In this prison there were also Polish smugglers serving criminal sentences in the ghetto. Sievers and Mitteldorf, the assistant Kripo chiefs, went to the prison and, due to actions of the Jews, found themselves forced to use firearms. Machine guns were also used. As far as is known at this point, one Jew was fatally wounded and one badly wounded. After the use of weapons, quiet was restored to the ghetto.

LEON HURWITZ, LIFE IN THE LODZ GHETTO

The poverty got much worse. Disillusionment with Rumkowski's rule grew, bursting open during the demonstration at 13 Lutomierska Street. Rumkowski sent his police to disperse the crowd, but the 150 policemen were not enough, and he requested that German riot troops be sent in from the city. The German troops came in trucks, drove up and down Lutomierska Street twice and went back to the city. Casualties weren't that heavy, some ten or twelve people slightly wounded. But before withdrawing, they warned the representative of the Jewish police that next time around they'd really let the Jews have it.

The demonstrations continued the next day with even greater vigor. Who knows how it would have ended if not for several influential individuals who undertook to calm the crowd, on the condition that the police not interfere and that Rumkowski receive a delegation from the demonstrating workers.

Seeing that his back was to the wall, Rumkowski agreed. At the meeting with the delegates, he was very cordial, listened to them, engaged in arguments, treated them to a supper, and in the end promised to open a number of free public kitchens and to meet other demands as well. But at the second meeting the delegates learned he had organized his own riot squad, consisting exclusively of underworld thugs. . . .

Once Rumkowski became the one-hundred-percent ruler of the ghetto Jews, he was no longer the same person. As long as he was unsure of his position, he had heart failure almost every day, and he used to faint whenever a difficulty arose. The stronger his position became, the less heart trouble he had, and now, when he is all-powerful, the problem has vanished altogether. The master has no more need to pretend, the mad actor truly believes that he is the Jewish King Lear. He has also changed externally. Those who remember him as a stooping, sickly, weak man—always worrying, always gloomy, wrapped in a shawl against the cold—would not recognize him now.

New strength has poured into his old man's body, along with power. Looking fit and well-fed, he radiates energy in every direction. He wears new, military-style boots, perfectly tailored trousers and a classy, rather sporty fur coat. He strides proudly from his winter residence to the Balut Market. There, he listens to "political" reports from the police, from secret agents, from regular informers, from all sorts of schemers itching for a position. He revels in the organization he has created in such a short time. And everyone lives in fear of him. . . .

Everybody in the clique Rumkowski has gathered around him sings paeans to his genius and his mission. Once, speaking to an associate about his mission, he declared, "What do you know about power? Power is sweet, power is everything, is life." And with a fanatical gleam in his half-crazed eyes, he finished, "But woe to him who makes the slightest attempt to wrest power from me."

In the fall, cold winds emptied the streets and kept everyone at home. But indoors, too, bitter cold and hunger grew stronger with each day. The ration of coal and wood was so small that it wasn't enough even for one good fire in the stove. In the dark of night, people began stripping wood from fences, sheds, outhouses, wherever they could.

The colder it got, the more widespread the vandalism became. People stopped waiting for the cover of night but descended in throngs on a fence or gate in broad daylight, breaking up the wood within minutes and dragging it away to warm up icy rooms. The police were unable to control this, because it went on in every corner of the ghetto.

Despite all this, people were freezing in their homes. The number of people dead of hypothermia was much higher than the Department of Statistics acknowledged. There were no children in the streets. They were all kept in bed, covered with every possible rag and warming each other with their bodies. Indoors and out, filth began accumulating again. The courtyards, which took on a barren look without fences, were covered with refuse and human excrement. Serious epidemics could be expected in the spring, when the snow and ice would melt. Moreover, the excrement pits were now exposed, since the wooden walls around them had been taken apart.

The Health Department, under the energetic Dr. [Leon] Szykier, recognized the danger and took appropriate action. After a few days' clean-up, the situation was under control. Also, the Construction Department built a number of brick toilets.

GHETTO DOCUMENT

[*Letter to Rumkowski*]

Lodz, November 15, 1940

We have the honor of presenting at the feet of Chairman Rumkowski—the father and guardian of the ghetto's Jews—the following missive:

Delegates chosen by about 300 people were arrested on the night of November 15, 1940. They are (1) Frenkel, (2) Kutas, and (3) Margulis. They were jailed at the Community's headquarters.

We chose the above-named delegates so that they could request employment for each of us. We need employment to save our families from starving to death and from annihilation. This is what the delegation was to tell the Chairman, but, instead, it was arrested.

We wish to ask the venerable Chairman, most respectfully, for a kind and favorable review of this case and for the release of this delegation, our representatives.

GHETTO DOCUMENT

Announcement No. 166

Concerning work outside of the ghetto.

I am hereby announcing that healthy, strong men, age 18 to 40, can get work outside of the ghetto. They will receive salary, accommodation and full board for their work. The costs for board will be deducted from their salary. The rest of the salary they can send to their families in the ghetto. This work program is relief for the unemployed, because 1) they are being offered an opportunity to work and to make money; 2) they will have enough to eat, because they receive full board; 3) they can support their families in the ghetto. They are allowed to let their families in the ghetto have the surplus of their earnings. My account will be credited with the money I will disburse to those whose names the workers give me in writing. Therefore, if a worker wants to have money transferred here for his relatives, he must always specify the person to whom the money should be paid out. According to the negotiations with the authorities, healthy, strong men will be registered, and then examined by a medical commission I will appoint. Afterwards they will be examined again by German doctors, since only men who are physically fit are suitable.

Registration and examination of the workers will begin on Sunday, November 24, 1940 at 4 p.m., at my ambulatory office, Hanseaten St. 36. For the time being, only 600 workers will be accepted.

Personal identity card with photograph, passport, birth certificate, health insurance coupons or ID have to be brought along. Persons who appear without identification will not be accepted.

Ch. Rumkowski
The Eldest of the Jews
in Litzmannstadt

Litzmannstadt, November 19, 1940.

SPEECH BY CHAIM RUMKOWSKI

2 DECEMBER 1940

"ONLY FORCE WILL BE USED"

[Following are the minutes of a meeting Rumkowski had with administrative officials and workshop managers.]

The purpose of the meeting was to find ways to help the population in the present situation. The Chairman promised to distribute coupons worth 20 zlotys with which food could be bought for the winter months. However, because a large part of the 10,000 tons of potatoes the ghetto received was rotten and immediately discarded, only 1,500 tons remain. And since prospects for another fuel delivery are minimal, coal distribution will at best be extremely limited. Necessity requires us to use house and communal kitchens to provide the population with meals. All kitchens should be taken over by the community.

The Chairman also spoke about the hospital strike which began 24 hours ago. He recalled that in the ghetto's first months, when the number of hospitals was small and many nurses were without jobs, he had decided, against the advice of the doctors, to introduce an 8-hour workday and to employ nurses in large numbers. In addition, he had given work to many trainees, even allowing them a nominal wage. But now, when hours must be extended because of the increase in sickness during the winter months, the hospital personnel have gone on strike.

In sharp, forceful language, the Chairman announced that steps would be taken against the strikers and their families, including imprisonment in Radogoszcz. This betrayal of the sick and helpless is harmful in every way, and as the leader of the ghetto, he will eradicate such actions.

Mr. Szper suggested setting up a mediation board, made up of people experienced in labor negotiations, to deal with the strikers. In a sensational speech, Mr. Lederman sharply criticized the means being used to combat the problems of ghetto life, including the recent strike. He insisted that morality be strengthened and that we attempt to persuade the population, instead of threatening it with a policeman's stick and arrests. We should appeal to the conscience of our co-religionists, he explained; everything in the ghetto is public property and everyone should be responsible to his own conscience and history.

Mr. Jacobson favored a compromise regarding the coupons. He would leave consumers the choice between buying food or attending the kitchen. Mr. Minc opposed this, saying that people would buy food and then sell it on the black market, and use the kitchens anyway.

The Chairman responded as follows:

"Everything suggested here has already been tried by me, but the population showed very little appreciation. A while ago I named delegates to make sure that jobs were being distributed fairly, but in the end they gave the jobs not to the experts but to their own people, to party members.

"I suggested that we distribute 40,000 kilograms of potatoes, but the plan was rejected because the delegates didn't like it. They'd rather take away my authority than have the potatoes distributed. They applied the same demagoguery to relief allowances. Justice was not on their minds, so I threw them out and carried it out on my own.

"And now, only force will be used. No one is going to deal with the nurses but me. I will break them. If they had come to me instead of leaving their jobs, I'd have extended my hand."

To Mr. Lederman he responded: "I have no intention of teaching people; I wouldn't want to remain in the ghetto the length of time that would take; in fact, I don't believe such an undertaking could ever succeed. I don't believe in educating the population!" He showed various documents that had been forged and asked what he should do, teach them or use the stick?

"They say that food is spoiling rather than being distributed. This is not true. The disaster began in September, when in two weeks not a single wagon arrived at Balut Market. I curtailed distribution because I wasn't sure I'd receive further supplies. This led to a disastrous limit on the food available. . . . Potatoes were already rotten on delivery. . . . I restricted distribution in order to maintain a reserve.

"What assurance is there that new supplies will become available when we exhaust what we have now? And yet, I gave out potatoes when there was no bread. How should I economize? Should we eat up everything at once, or save it for hard times?"

The Chairman stressed that he now has such a small supply of fuel that he must choose between cooking in the kitchens or heating the schools. Thus, there will be no coal for schools at this time. "I can manage the ghetto's finances, but not the supplies of potatoes and coal because these I do not control!"

GHETTO DOCUMENT

Announcement No. 179

Concerning the purchase of fur coats, fox furs, tippets and fur (pelts) of all kinds.

By order of the authorities, I hereby announce that all women's and men's fur coats, fox furs, tippets and pelts of all kinds must be offered for purchase

until January 1, 1941 at the latest

at my bank, Bleicherweg 7.

The purchase will begin on Sunday, December 22, 1940 at 9 a.m.
After January 1, 1941, all furs that are still in private ownership will be confiscated.

Litzmannstadt Ghetto, December 17, 1940

Ch. Rumkowski
The Eldest of the Jews
in Litzmannstadt

1941

THE CHRONICLE OF THE LODZ GHETTO

SUNDAY, JANUARY 12, 1941

STREET DEMONSTRATIONS

Yesterday's mass demonstrations for an increase in food and fuel rations were repeated this afternoon. It is worth noting that, since the September incidents, there has not been a single instance of the peace being disturbed in the ghetto. It has been determined beyond question that this action was organized by irresponsible individuals intent on disturbing the peace and public order created by the authorities who watch over the law, safety, and food supplies of the ghetto dwellers. A characteristic of this incident is the fact that the individuals inciting the crowd had been recruited from among the workers who enjoy supplemental food allowances and, meanwhile, sell those rations at black market prices. The demonstrations took place in front of the hospital on Lagiewnicka Street [Rumkowski's private apartment was located in Hospital No. 1 at 34–36 Lagiewnicka Street] as well as at several points along Brzezinska Street. Several times, the crowd attempted to steal food that was being transported by wagon, but was thwarted by the hard stance taken by the Order Service. Heavy police patrols have been keeping watch on the ghetto's streets for an entire day now. Peace was completely restored by the afternoon.

Jews fight over wood for heat in a rampage that caused the collapse of a building and the death of a woman.

A SAD CASE OF SAVAGERY

A crowd consisting of a few hundred people has demolished a wooden shed on the property at 67 Brzezinska Street. While the wood was being stolen, the roof of the shed collapsed, crushing several people. In spite of their desperate cries, no one came to their aid and the robbery continued unabated. Thirty-six-year-old Frania Szabnek died as a result of her injuries. Two other persons suffered serious injuries. This lamentable instance of moral savagery, a direct result of agitation by lawless elements, clearly illustrates the necessity for an all-out struggle against the parasites of the underworld.

PARADOXES OF GHETTO LIFE

AN EIGHT-YEAR-OLD INFORMER

Appearing at one of the precincts of the Order Service, an 8-year-old boy filed a report against his own parents, whom he charged with not giving him the bread ration due him. The boy demanded that an investigation be conducted and that the guilty parties be punished. No comment . . .

TUESDAY, JANUARY 14, 1941

SAD BUT TRUE: "LINES" ARE ALSO OBLIGATORY FOR THE DECEASED

"You can't die either these days," complained a woman who had come to arrange formalities in the mortuary office in connection with the death of her mother. There is nothing exaggerated about such complaints if one considers that, with the current increase in the death rate, a minimum of three days' wait to bury the dead, sometimes even ten days, has become an everyday occurrence. The causes of this abnormal state of affairs are worth noting. There are scarcely three horses left in the ghetto to draw the hearses, a totally inadequate number in view of the current increase in the death rate. Several times, there was such a "backlog" in the transporting of bodies to the cemetery that, out of necessity, a sideless hauling wagon had to be pressed into service and loaded with several dozen bodies at the same time. Before the arrival of the current frosts, when the death rate in the ghetto did not exceed 25 to 30 cases per day (before the war the average death rate among the Jewish population of the city amounted to six per day), there were 12 gravediggers employed at the cemetery. Today there are around 200. In spite of such a horrendously large number of gravediggers, no more than 50 graves can be dug per day. The reason: a lack of skilled labor, as well as problems connected with the ground being frozen. And this causes the macabre "line" to grow longer.

GHETTO DOCUMENTS

[*Leaflet*] Lodz, January 1, 1941

Carpenters!

Tomorrow, Sunday, all carpentry workers will report to work. We are demanding that our arrested fellow-workers be freed.

[*Leaflet*] Lodz, 1941

To workers and the general population!

The hospital workers' strike continues. Terror tactics used against us will not break the action we are taking in order that our just demands be met. They are even arresting strikers' family members. Within the last 24 hours, 35 people have been arrested. We demand that the arrested be freed and the persecution cease. We want an 8-hour day in the hospitals!

JOZEF ZELKOWICZ

"NOTES ON THE CARPENTERS' STRIKE"

23 JANUARY 1941

In connection with the announcement about the bread ration for the ghetto population and the simultaneous revocation of the supplemental bread ration for factory workers, the carpenters from the factory at 3 Urzednicza Street stopped working and staged a sit-in strike on the premises. This led to clashes with the police, in which a number on both sides were wounded.

24 JANUARY 1941

Witnesses describe the events at Urzednicza Street as follows:

The carpentry workers had been discontented for quite some time because they earn a flat rate of 30 pfennigs an hour, craftsmen and apprentices alike. In addition, with the introduction of ration cards the daily soup had been discontinued in the workshops, and now the supplemental bread ration, which they received instead of the soup, has also been taken away. Thus, they've issued four demands: (1) a wage increase of 20 pfennigs for craftsmen and 10 pfennigs for apprentices; (2) the receipt of half their wages in kind rather than in cash; (3) the restoration, based on their hard work, of the daily supplemental soup; (4) the restoration of the supplemental bread ration.

The manager of the carpenters' workshop, Mr. Freund, communicated several times with the Chairman regarding these demands. The answer finally came, rejecting the last three points. As for the first, the Chairman promised to approve the increase pending a determination that the carpentry shops actually make a profit.

Yesterday morning the workers of the 1st division of the workshop at 12 Drukarska Street did not start work at the usual time. When the manager informed him of this by phone, the Chairman responded, "Those who want to work should do so, and those who do not should go home."

Mr. Freund repeated these words to the workers, but 200 of them took their tools and moved on to the workshop's 2nd division at 3 Urzednicza in order to hold counsel with the workers there.

The police guards stopped the workers at the door. After a while Mr. Freund arrived and told the guards to let the workers in. Inside, he repeated the Chairman's conditions and requested that they go back to work, especially since the last supplemental bread ration was still due them. Not receiving an answer from the workers, he called in the police.

Police units under Mr. Rozenblat* and Mr. Frenkel were dispatched to the scene. Mr. Rozenblat remained outside, while Mr. Frenkel entered and ordered the workers to leave within five minutes. Those on the ground floor (mainly elderly workers) did so. But the workers on the upper floors ignored the order. The police then began using force to remove them from the premises.

The workers barricaded the front door of the first floor, so that the police had to get in through the rear entrance. Once inside, they again gave their order to leave voluntarily within five minutes. Some workers did leave, but others began throwing their tools and pieces of wood at the police.

After the police cleared the first floor, they found the same situation on the second floor, where the workers had built a barricade both in front of the entrance and behind it. When the police broke the door open, the workers again hurled pieces of wood at them. In the end, the police cleared the entire building.

In connection with these events, the following announcement (in German) was posted at the entrances to ghetto workshops:

"Irresponsible individuals and provocateurs have tried to disrupt work in the factories, and I have been forced to remove workers from one factory. I have information about similar incidents in several other factories.

"I have more than once warned against such disturbances and I have made it clear that the workshops in the ghetto work mainly for the *Wehrmacht*. I am personally responsible for all such acts and for all damages incurred, and I will not tolerate these incidents. I have decided, therefore, to close all factories.

"Wages which were to be paid in the factories today will be mailed by my post office to workers' home addresses. I must stress again that all my efforts at organizing the workshops were so that many people could find employment and live in peace. I will continue to provide food for the ghetto. It should be understood, however, that securing food is not always possible due to weather conditions and transportation difficulties. This situation is being exploited by people of ill will. A number of people have been apprehended, and arrests will continue until peace in the ghetto is restored, in accordance with my duty and my responsibility."

The announcement was signed by Chaim Rumkowski.

26 JANUARY 1941

On Friday, the 24th of January, the following was posted next to the Chairman's announcement:

"Shame to Rumkowski and to his storm troops. We wish to inform the ghetto of the following fact: for several months 600 carpentry workers have been voicing demands which would enable them to continue working. In response to these just demands the Chairman sent in his bullies, who beat up dozens of workers. Thus the Chairman has added one more crime to his list of shameless deeds.

"Fellow workers! Express your protest and bitterness!

—A group of carpenters."

Rumors are heard in the street that one of the injured workers has died and that another remains in a coma.

29 JANUARY 1941

The following announcement (No. 203) was posted on ghetto walls:

"I hereby make it known that all workers in my workshops and factories (but only those now working), house janitors, those employed at public works, firefighters and chimney sweeps will receive special coupons on January 31 for 58 dkg. [decagrams] of meat and 2 kg. of potatoes. Managers of each division will distribute the coupons among their subordinates."

The announcement was signed by the Eldest of the Jews.

That "only those now working" will receive the ration is seen as an attempt to induce workers to go back to their jobs. Certainly, in this time of hunger, such a ration could break even the strongest resistance.

To date there have been no direct negotiations with the workers; all meetings that have taken place so far have involved the Chairman and his shop officials. Rumor has it that at one such conference the Chairman said he would restore the supplemental bread ration if he received the signatures of 100 workers agreeing to cut the bread ration of the entire population by 10 dkg, so that there would be enough with which to increase the workers' ration. With such a document, he would be able to explain the cut to the ghetto population. The workers are said to have rejected this suggestion categorically.

The workers do not want to be left to loiter in the streets. First, doing nothing is hard for someone used to working. Second, someone who doesn't work doesn't get paid and cannot buy even the regular ration, let alone any supplements. Third, it is warmer in the shop than in a worker's home. True, the atmosphere is very depressing and surviving a hard day's work without the supplemental bread ration is extremely difficult, but there seems no other way. Thus the workers are waiting for the shops to reopen so that they can go back. It was decided during a meeting between the shop officials and the workers that the Chairman be urged to re-open the workshops.

But things are not yet quiet in the carpentries. Recently the following appeal was posted on the ghetto walls:

"Comrade carpenters, do not be deceived!!! So as not to collapse from hunger, we demand the following: a wage increase; food instead of cash for up to half our wages; bread and soup in the shop. Our solidarity has not been broken! There is enough work for all, and we will all return to work when our just demands are met.

31 JANUARY 1941

As of yesterday the following divisions of the carpenters' workshop were re-opened: the machine hall, the lacquery, the paint shop. Some 270 out of 650 workers reported to work.

It should be stressed that the workers who returned to the shop did so without pre-conditions, but just resumed working as if nothing had happened.

Yesterday evening the carpentry workers met to discuss the strike situation. It was decided to place pickets in the streets leading to the workshop. The pickets will try to dissuade workers from returning to work. However, if they do not succeed, all workers should return to work by today.

2 FEBRUARY 1941

Today, at another meeting of the carpenters, the decision was taken to return to work and to call off the strike.

SPEECH BY CHAIM RUMKOWSKI

1 FEBRUARY 1941

"GIVE UP YOUR SELFISH INTERESTS"

[*Rumkowski gave this speech at a meeting of workshop managers and the senior officials of the ghetto administration.*]

In all my time as the Eldest of the Jews, I've done everything I could to have the ghetto's area enlarged. Which is why this was such a terrible blow for me. . . .

I made it my goal to normalize life in the ghetto, at any price. We needed, first of all, work for everyone. . . . It was not easy to organize workshops. This task was even more difficult since there were almost no Jewish industrial enterprises within the ghetto's boundaries. I succeeded, nevertheless, in establishing a large number of workshops. Ten thousand workers are already employed in them. About 1000 unskilled laborers have been given employment in public works. And 1800 people have been sent to work outside the ghetto, their wages providing for their families here.

I have to mention something very typical and very unpleasant: namely, that some of the people working outside have given false addresses so that their families can still receive relief allowances. We've had to create a special unit to control this cheating.

Let me also remind you that 5500 individuals are employed in my offices and institutions. I realize that the administrative apparatus may be overcrowded, but it's more important to create a normal existence for these people than have them live on relief.

I can say with a clear conscience that in all my work as the Eldest of the Jews I have never harmed anyone. Applause from the crowds, gratitude, recognition—these have not been my goals. For the sake of our work, my objective has been to clear the air, burn out the ever-growing orgy of fraud, theft, corruption and conniving, as well as the serious crimes sometimes committed by people I personally have known and trusted.

Human language is not rich enough to express the magnitude of the crimes committed everywhere in the ghetto, in every field. So great have been the arrogance and malice of these people that their victims include those who should be dearest to all of us, the children. They have not hesitated to adulterate even the milk for babies. The house committees are another sore point. These institutions, created to help distribute food, have, in fact, been stealing from each gram of food, robbing residents of their meager subsistence rations.

Conniving has extended even to the food coupons physicians prescribe for the sick. There have been cases of doctors signing blank coupons, or of auxiliary personnel bartering these coupons, thereby taking necessities like butter, milk, and oatmeal from the seriously ill. The result is that I must devote all my time and energy to uncovering thieves, instead of attending to my other responsibilities.

Also, a great effort is being made to maintain order and fight anarchy. And who is spreading anarchy? We all remember the bloody excesses of September. Who were the leaders then? Who took the people into the streets? It turned out that the incitement came from the bakers, who fared very well in the ghetto, because they cheated on flour.

Again, irresponsible elements raised their voices at the end of January. This time they were protesting the low bread rations. But nobody knows how

Design for a ghetto postage stamp. Rumkowski was denied the right to issue stamps by the Germans, who did not share his view of the ghetto as a Jewish state.

much effort it took to soften the order and obtain an increase from 27 dkg. to 30 dkg. daily [per person]. The 3-dkg. increase will have to be covered from my own reserves. And doesn't my most recent directive, that everybody in the ghetto, employed or not, is to receive exactly the same bread ration, indicate my concern and my sense of justice?

It's perfectly clear that even if some workers lose their supplementary bread ration, the loss will be made up by members of their families, who will receive 40 dkg. bread each. And yet this occasion was used to place obstacles in my way.

In one of my workshops a sit-in strike was called by provocateurs, supposedly for a return to the old bread rations. Unfortunate incidents took place because the Order Service had to be called in. When I received information that similar excesses were also planned in other workshops, I ordered them closed, thus avoiding unforeseeable consequences, since materials entrusted to us by the authorities were stored in these workshops.

It should be obvious to anyone with common sense that I was in no position to give them the double ration of bread. But the strikers couldn't understand this, having been incited by people up to no good. In their frenzy and total selfishness, they even agreed with my suggestion that their ration be increased by decreasing everyone else's. They almost signed a statement to that effect, though at the last minute they lost their nerve. It's a pity—it would have been a document of unquestionable infamy.

I will not abandon the principle that food must be distributed justly and in the same quantity to everyone.

As for crimes committed by [administration] employees, I've decided to use the most radical measures with them: I will deport all thieves from the ghetto by using them for forced-labor assignments. Their families will be treated as second-class citizens. Only a doctor's diagnosis of a serious medical condition will save a perpetrator from deportation. And exactly the same punishment will be meted out to a delivery boy and a high official, and whether just one potato was stolen or a great deal more.

I will also fight vigorously against laziness. I myself have seen that in many of the 150 food distribution stores employees are late, and often only five people are taken care of in one day, while a crowd stands outside freezing. I'd like to ask the gentlemen who work in the stores how pleasant it was for them to freeze, just a few weeks ago, when they stood on line at my office to get their jobs. It seems that they've already forgotten.

One of my main responsibilities in the ghetto is caring for the children and the sick. The results can be seen in the impressive network of hospitals, dispensaries, emergency stations, and schools, orphanages, day camps, and so on. There has been a place in school for each child; 15,000 children have received breakfast and lunch; 7500 children half-naked and barefoot have been given warm clothing. In the summer the children attended camps and day care, where they were given everything that, in our circumstances, could be had.

All this filled my heart with joy. But, alas, a blow has befallen us. We have to evacuate 540 children from the orphanage in Marysin; we have to give up the schools in order to house the 7000 people who must abandon their homes on Franciszkanska and Brzezinska Streets. This is more important than the schools.

With regard to public welfare, I've succeeded in establishing full relief benefits for 45% of the ghetto population and partial benefits for 25%. As of January 1, 1941 I've used 4,500,000 marks of my modest budget for public welfare. And despite the great burden of spending 50% of the budget on welfare, I was able to balance the budget in the months of November and December. . . .

Help me. You must give up your selfish interests or invite disaster. I do hope that with the assistance of those who understand me and work with me with complete unselfishness, I'll be able to succeed, for the good of us all. Fortunately, there are many people in the ghetto whose work attests to their thinking and acting along these lines. . . .

Only one thing can save us—a collective acceptance of a productive life, in an atmosphere of utter calm. Intensive work and calm: this is the order of the day. There is absolutely no place here for any party whatsoever, except one: Jews of the Ghetto!

I have only one interest, to improve our lot. For this, there must be a clean and healthy atmosphere. I will attack every symptom of corruption with the greatest severity. I will not rest until I succeed, even at the price of my own life.

GHETTO DOCUMENT

BULLETIN

February 20, 1941

SOME REMARKS ABOUT PROVISIONS

Have any of the town's leaders ever stopped to think about how enormous the lines in front of stores are, even with the frost, rain, and mud? People stand about, freezing, hungry, exhausted, ready to faint. Young and old, they stamp their feet, gnash their teeth, get "spiritual satisfaction" out of verbal abuse and noise, keep out of the way of our energetic "guardians of order," and after waiting for hours, finally manage to bring home a few rotten items, along with a couple of broken teeth, black eyes, and broken ribs. Our "guardians of order" have learned quickly, on the heads of the famished masses, how to wield the ghetto's symbol of power—the club!

Especially worth noting are the lines in front of the long-heralded public kitchen at 32 Mlynarska, to publicize which our *Moyshl* [Yid: ruler] organized a caravan, so he could show off his great creative work. But what happened to the tens of thousands of marks invested in the project? After the parades, with all their embellishments and excitement, the kitchen operated only a short while, and then, *dayenu* [Heb: enough]! It had fulfilled its task—it had left its mark—and who needed more?

And who was interested in the whole sea of corruption, in the misuse of the whole economy, in the horribly long lines at the stores? No, not the ruler nor his genial cohorts.

First, the products were received by the committee. Then they were distributed, with the result that all family members suddenly had work—and unemployment in the ghetto was no more! For when someone spends a whole day standing in line, he is not considered a worker!

The 32 existing stores now had to provide food for all residents—this is what caused the chaos! But our ruler rode around in the streets, speechifying, insisting that things were getting better. Maybe he'll parade his wagons in front of the stores and their long lines, to show people how much he has accomplished!

We demand of you, you usurpers and tormentors of the masses—either put an end to the hell of the Provisions Edict or get out of here! Otherwise, the wrath of the masses will boil over and wipe out all of you.

CONGRATULATIONS, MR. BORUCH!

Mr. Boruch,* you are a leader, not only a merchant but an active Zionist, a man whose heart aches for the pain of your Jewish nation! Because of this, therefore, you think you have to hold balls, gorge yourselves and guzzle, carouse and have a good time, enjoying yourselves when the Jewish masses are bleeding.

You, our genial President, who doesn't sleep nights, aren't you interested in where your "assistant king" gets all the goodies for the gluttons he invites to his balls? And whether the hungry masses have to pay for all this? Where did Mr. Boruch get all that money? Answer! We are waiting!

SZMUL ROZENSZTAJN, DAILY NOTES

[*The writer was Rumkowski's personal secretary.*]

FRIDAY, 21 FEBRUARY 1941

It should be said that part of the ghetto population displays uncalled-for behavior toward the Chairman. Dozens of individuals surround him in the street, stopping him on his way, to request work, welfare, etc., ignoring the usual procedure known to everyone. As a result, he tends to show his anger and scold the importunate supplicant right then and there.

The only ones the Chairman does not reprimand for bothering him are the children, in whose presence he forgets everything else. He is friendly with them and shows a true fatherly interest in their lives. The children feel this instinctively and are at ease with him. In fact, one request the Chairman did agree to take with him was handed to him by a five-year-old boy.

There were other exceptions today. For instance, the Chairman noticed how well a house watchwoman removed the ice from the ground in a courtyard. He promised her cash, potatoes, a food coupon for her sick husband, and a place in the Marysin camp for one of her four children.

MONDAY, 24 FEBRUARY

In the morning the Chairman inspected a number of tailor shops. His first visit was to the shop at 49 Lagiewnicka Street. As soon as he entered, some workers began shouting: "Bread, bread!" He immediately ordered the shop shut down, and as a result the workers of the second shift were barred from entering the premises.

In the shop at 10 Dworska Street, the Chairman was met in a friendlier manner, and the workers listened attentively to him. He announced that, from now on, instructors and group leaders are responsible for finished work. Workers who fail in their duty will lose the Chairman's protection.

In answer to questions from workers, he said: "Regrettably, I am not free to go on strike, as you are. But I will do everything so that workers do not go hungry. You all know where I stand: an equal amount of bread for every ghetto inhabitant, 40 dkg. There are no privileged castes. Every newborn child gets the same ration so that his mother has enough milk to feed him." Then he added as a joke: "Maybe those babies will grow up to be decent and honest, not loafers like you" (laughter). Then he appealed for peace and

A food distribution line.

Chairman Rumkowski, thronged on a ghetto street. The woman with him is most likely his secretary, Dora Fuchs.

order in the shops, so that they can earn their wages for themselves and their families.

A similar scene occurred at the tailor shop at 12 Niecala Street. When the Chairman mentioned recent difficulties in getting food supplies, one group of workers sang the same old tune: "Bread!" To this, he answered with a sigh: "If you knew what I know, you'd talk differently. If I had given in to your demands for bread, we'd now be in the situation Warsaw is in, where everyone receives as little as 12 dkg. bread, or Czestochowa or Piotrkow, where they get only 7 1/2 dkg. As for potatoes, better times are coming. In a few weeks, we'll open the mounds and dig out lots of potatoes. In the meantime, my power reaches the tailors but not the Almighty.

"I demand the same amount of bread for everyone in the ghetto. It seems to me that no other state in the world can provide bread for all its citizens, especially in a tiny state like the ghetto. And no other country provides welfare for 46 percent of its population."

Outside their barracks office in Balut Market, Rumkowski and Dora Fuchs meet the chief of the ghetto's German administration, Hans Biebow.

"In all the ghetto offices, pictures of the Eldest, like a king . . ." (Rosenfeld) Here Rumkowski's picture appears above Leon Rozenblat, commander of the ghetto police, and Leon Szykier, first director of the ghetto's Department of Health. To Rumkowski's right is Rabbi Yosif Fajner, the rabbinical council member closest to the center of power in the ghetto.

TUESDAY, 25 FEBRUARY

Today at 10 AM Herr Biebow, the Chief of the Ghetto Administration, visited the Chairman at Balut Market and discussed the ghetto economy with him for more than two hours. Afterward, the Chairman was downcast and irritable.

At 2 PM the Chairman visited the tailor shop at 16 Jakuba Street. About 1400 workers from both shifts gathered in the courtyard to hear the Chairman say: "Just as bad work should be condemned, good work should certainly be hailed." When a worker heckled him, he shouted back: "I don't need the advice of provocateurs who hide in holes!" The workers condemned their colleagues' unseemly behavior.

The Chairman said that he had decided to apportion everyone a bowl of soup per day, as a reward for good work, in addition to the regular food ration. This was greeted with great enthusiasm. He said that each shop worker with a positive attitude toward work will receive such soup. In order to organize the distribution properly, he suggested that six workers be elected—not workers' delegates or party cronies, only honest people.

Today the workers from the tailor shop at 49 Lagiewnicka sent the Chairman a petition with hundreds of signatures, asking that he permit the reopening of their shop. They apologized for a few individuals' tactless behavior and assured him that such incidents would not happen again. Accepting their apology, the "bad" Chairman said the factory would open again tomorrow.

THURSDAY, 27 FEBRUARY

During the inspection of the carpentry workshop today, the Chairman said: "When we organized this factory, I had hopes that you and your comrades would help me in this difficult task. For a short time I let you establish your own *Shulhan Aruk* [Heb: Code of Laws]. But I soon saw that you were going much further—that you were aiming at hegemony and sinecures. At that point I said: Stop! There is not time now for sloganeering and fighting. To do what life demands of us, to create work and turn out production is not as easy as you and your comrades imagine. My motto is: Work! Something that could keep us alive. Politicking and playing the slogan game is all right for normal times.

"On my side, I did everything possible. And you? You didn't want to build but to disrupt. But when you finally got too rowdy I stopped you with a strong hand. In order to save the ghetto, I am forced to act decisively, like a surgeon who cuts a limb so the heart won't stop beating. Believe me, I'd be happy to give you even more than you demand. But I am not that stupid yet. True, in the rabbis' court you probably would have won against me, but don't hold your breath for that."

SATURDAY, 1 MARCH

Today a concert of Jewish music was arranged under the direction of the prominent conductor and composer Dawid Bajgelman. The singer was Miss Ali Dimant. Afterward, the Chairman spoke:

"We all had real pleasure today in hearing at last a concert of Jewish music and song. Our Jewish music is inexhaustible. You, *klezmers* [Yid: minstrels]—and I don't mean this in a derogatory sense, God forbid; on the contrary, this is the true name for a Jewish musician—you are going to give us the spiritual treat, and I'll provide the bread and potatoes. . . .

JOZEF ZELKOWICZ

"DURA LEX SED LEX"

[*March 1941*]

Heavy sins have been committed in the ghetto. The greatest sin has been that people raised in a spirit of civilized decency have been changed, after just half a year of living under inhuman ghetto conditions, into beasts of prey. Overnight they have lost whatever sense of ethics and shame they once had. While many were dying of hunger, while many searched through waste heaps for edible refuse, eating it right there, there were those who stole and robbed at every opportunity and who gorged and devoured.

On March 15, 1941, the following announcement was posted in the ghetto:

"I hereby make known that a Summary Court has been established and that this Court will sit in session beginning March 16, 1941. The Court's task is to prosecute every sort of crime against the vital interests of the ghetto population.

"The Summary Court is entirely independent of the General Court.

"Cases will be heard by two panels, each consisting of a judge and two jurors whom I will appoint.

"Trial before the Court will not be preceded by formal investigation. Prosecutor and defense attorney are excluded from the proceedings.

"Judges will pronounce judgments based on their own conclusions."

Dura lex sed lex. [Lat: Severe law, but law.]

While men and women harnessed themselves to excrement and garbage wagons and dragged their loads, which stank for miles, for fourteen hours a day, those who occupied high offices in the ghetto administration contemplated what else to steal and how to cover up the thefts.

Obviously, such sins had to be eradicated, even by resorting to a Summary Court.

Not so obvious, though, is the fact that when the Summary Court cast its net into the ghetto swamp, in order "to prosecute every sort of crime against the vital interest of the ghetto," only the smallest fish were snared, while big, fat, smelly pikes swam by uncaught.

Not so obvious is why no one in the ghetto ever thought of providing the ghetto's working people with a minimal normal existence, so that they would not have to steal.

Not so obvious is why, along with the culprits, their wives and children were condemned to death by starvation, banned forever from obtaining work and relief benefits.

Not so obvious is why one of the two newly appointed judges is a young fellow lacking in basic knowledge of human emotions and whose intelligence is well below average—and why this impertinent fellow is allowed to render "judgments" that are outright criminal.

Sins that are tried before the Summary Court:

A tailor, who used the sewing machine and tools which were his before the war, put a pair of scissors in his pocket to have them at hand and absent-mindedly left them there. When he was leaving the shop, they were found in the search. He was sent to the Summary Court. His fate, and his family's, was sealed.

A tailor who forgot to put a strand of thread back on the table was a perpetrator.

A tailor who used a scrap of material to patch up his own trousers was a criminal.

A carpenter who cut a strip of wood to fix his table at home was a thief.

Sins which were not tried in the Summary Court:

The managers of food stores who took the best of the produce home with them, concealing the evidence by short-weighing the rations of buyers.

The practitioners of favoritism who took fat bribes for securing lucrative positions for loafers, while so many people with good hands and good minds could not get work and were dying of hunger.

The officials of the Department of Provisions who willfully let thousands of tons of potatoes and vegetables rot, in order to cover up evidence of larceny and shortages in the depots. These people are certainly to blame for the hundreds of wagons of potatoes which have been dumped secretly, under cover of darkness, into the garbage pits.

Although they have hundreds of deaths from starvation on their consciences, none of them has been tried before the Summary Court. In fact, the notorious potato affair did come before the court, perhaps by mistake, but the young fellow took a bribe and let everybody go.

Gedalye had been a tailor since youth. He came to the ghetto when he was given ten minutes to leave his apartment in the city. He brought along his wife, their four children, a thimble and a tailor's tape.

When the ghetto tailor shops began to open, Gedalye had to wait several months until all those who had pull with the shop managers or instructors had been given jobs, even if they had never held a needle in their lives. Only then was Gedalye allowed into the shop, and he began to earn two to three marks for ten to twelve hours of work a day.

Gedalye worked, and he was glad. He was glad, because he worked with his hands, unlike tens of thousands of other ghetto people.

Gedalye was happy with his work and his meager earnings, until one day the man who puts his hands in the workers' pockets, searching them before they go home, found a thread on Gedalye.

It wasn't even hidden, this thread. It was hanging from his shoulder, so he could find it when he needed it. Only this time, Gedalye put his jacket on and forgot about the thread hanging from his shoulder down his shirt.

For this sin, Gedalye was put in jail, and the Summary Court sentenced him to three months hard labor, banning him permanently from working in the ghetto and barring his family from welfare.

And thus the court pronounced Gedalye's doom. *Dura lex sed lex.*

GERMAN DOCUMENTS

[*Criminal Police memorandum*]

14 MARCH 1941

The Secret Service has made a machine gun with 223 rounds available to the Kripo in the ghetto. Months ago, when unrest broke out several times in the ghetto and there was an attempt to free Kripo prisoners from the 1st precinct of the Jewish security police, the machine gun was used three times, and a total of 42 shots were fired into a crowd of several thousand people. Remaining: 181 rounds.

An entrance to the ghetto. The ghetto archives office, where Oskar Rosenfeld, Oskar Singer, and Jozef Zelkowicz worked as official ghetto chroniclers, was housed in the building on which road signs to Warsaw and other cities are posted.

SCHUTZPOLIZEI KOMMANDO

12 APRIL 1941

SPECIAL ORDER

THE NEED FOR FIREARMS BY THE GUARDS OF THE LITZMANNSTADT GHETTO

Pursuant to section 9 of the Police Chief's special order on the entering and leaving the ghetto (V.10.40), every attempt to leave the ghetto without permission is to be met with an immediate use of firearms. With the Police Chief's concurrence, I hereby order the following additions:

1. Wounding of people not participating may easily occur in busy streets but must be avoided.
2. Every person who approaches the ghetto fence in a suspicious manner is to be warned with "Halt." Only after the person does not stop

after the warning of "Halt" or attempts to flee will firearms be used.

3. Every Jew attempting to crawl through the wire of the ghetto fence or over it or to otherwise leave the ghetto without permission will be shot without warning.
4. Every Jew who throws any smuggled goods or money over the fence or who receives goods thrown over the fence will, when caught in the act, be shot without warning.
5. Every Jew going to the fence after the curfew hour (9:00 PM) will be shot without warning. Even inside the ghetto, Jews must have special passes if they are out after 9:00 PM. The Jewish security police has orders to stay 15 meters from the fence. People with special passes need not maintain this 15 meter zone if the entrance to their houses are closer than 15 meters to the fence.
6. Every person caught smuggling goods or money or other things from outside into the ghetto, or receiving them from within the ghetto, will be shot without warning.
7. Every person caught trying to crawl through the ghetto fence or over it from outside will be shot without warning.

All officers on guard duty are to be instructed as above on the use of weapons. A copy of this order is to be posted in the commons rooms of the ghetto guard and their bases.

[signed] Keuck

GHETTO DOCUMENT

Announcement No. 254

REGARDING DISTRIBUTION OF BREAD

I announce hereby that from now on,

ONE LOAF [2 kg] OF BREAD
WILL BE SOLD FOR 5 DAYS

in exchange for one coupon from the bread ration card. [. . .] Large families do not have to pick up all their bread at one time. They are entitled to buy loaves over the entire 5-day period of eligibility.

Litzmannstadt-Ghetto, 21 April, 1941 — Mordechai Chaim Rumkowski
Eldest of the Jews

JOZEF ZELKOWICZ, SKETCHES

"GOD DID NOT ABANDON US"

[*1941*]

(I)

Have you noticed how people in the ghetto are different today? Their faces are radiant, their eyes have a spark of hope, as if they've finally found their way out of the pale.

And what do you think is the reason for this?

Potatoes.

This is what's happened: people who for months vegetated on a daily subsistence of 30 pfennigs, people who could not afford to eat their bread ration because they had to give it to their hungry children, these people were told today that everyone on relief will receive an extra 10 kilograms of potatoes.

So, wherever you go, people are celebrating:

"Don't you see? God did not abandon us!"

"That's right, God is our Father and Rumkowski—our Daddy."

Right, God does not abandon. When all hope was lost, God made Rumkowski to distribute potatoes.

And so, in every house, people are either waiting for the coupon to arrive in the mail, or have already received the coupon and their hearts are now joyfully anticipating the real thing—the potatoes themselves.

"Rumkowski, may he live one hundred years; when he has, he gives."

Poor people. They do not have the strength to blaspheme God, even when he deals them the greatest injustice, and they praise him for the smallest trifle, not realizing that such praise is the biggest blasphemy.

(II)

There must be happy people in this apartment. They've already brought home their potatoes. Beautiful potatoes. Potatoes like apples. Potatoes like fists.

The apartment has two large rooms. Not a typical apartment in Baluty, unless you had the luck to live here before the war or you had enough money to rent such a large apartment when they rushed you here from the city.

The first room is almost empty. A small table. A broken metal bed. A tin pail.

In the second room there are two women. An old, tall woman with a dull

Brother and sister.

expression in her eyes, and a younger one with black beads around her neck.

The women do not look at you. They are totally absorbed in weighing their potatoes on a scale.

Then you notice that a small mirror on the wall is covered with a kerchief. This house is in mourning. That is why you are not greeted at the door. That is why there is no talk of the business that brought you here.

But you still wonder: where are the men of the house? And if there are no men in this house, how do these women know the rites of mourning so well?

How do they know? They've had time and opportunity enough to learn them by heart.

There were seven of them when they came into the ghetto: the father, the mother, their four sons and a daughter-in-law married to the oldest son. In the city they had four rooms and a dry goods store on Geyer Square. They were among the first to move to Baluty during the "planned resettlement." That is why they had enough time to get this apartment for themselves.

The oldest son, the one who was married, was the first to die. He passed away on the Saturday before last Passover.

"He was too gentle to endure this rotten life. His heart gave up . . . "

He at least had a decent burial: a new shroud and a coffin made of good boards.

A few weeks later the father died.

"It took just two days. I paid the doctor, but he came a day late, came after the funeral. But the money was not wasted: I needed the doctor for my second son who was already in bed with dysentery. He never got up again. I spent our last *groschen* on doctors. The shrouds we made from our own shirts.

"Three weeks later my last two sons were dead too. Three weeks. The bench on which I was sitting *shiva* [Heb: the week-long mourning period] for Berish was still warm when I had to sit again for Feivel. This is too much even for a woman like myself who does not cry.

"For those two the house committee had to make a collection to buy shrouds. That's quite an expense, shrouds for two grown men.

"It vexed my mind that I could not afford to bury my two sons as decently as the others, in their own shrouds. And I swore I would do any work to pay the money back to the house committee, but all I had were ten marks a month, the relief payment. And yet, yet, you see—God does not abandon.

"I will not hide what I did because I am not afraid of anyone any more. People can do no worse to me than God has done. I will tell you the whole truth: they sent me coupons for my two dead sons. I don't know, either they made a mistake or they were using a list from the month when my children were still alive. At first I wanted to go and return the coupons, my whole life I did not touch what was not mine. But then I had another thought:

"God must know very well how I suffer over my children being buried in others' shrouds. So He sent me these potatoes. Now I am going to sell them and give the money back to the house committee. They can use the money for a good purpose. Lots of people die nowadays in the ghetto."

You see, God does not abandon . . .

"IN THE LOW-VOLTAGE DIVISION"

[*no date*]

Finally we have come to the mica-splitting shop. Seated in rows around long tables are mostly "by-gone" people—ancient men, old women, people with "obituary" faces. On the table in front of each worker lies a cluster of mica pieces which have to be split into tiny specks, and these, in turn, into the thinnest foil. The tiny speck has to be cut sideways, even if it is so small that the old, weakened eyes can hardly see it, even if it slips between the trembling fingers. One gram of the foil is worth 3 pfennigs. It's quite a pile of foil, this one gram, but the pile grows ever so slowly and the day is almost over. . . .

The hands tremble as they try to cut faster with the sharp and pointed knives. But the sharp edge, instead of hitting the hair-thin speck, finds its way into the hand, or the finger. Sure, the first-aid nurse will dress the wound with a stinking, burning concoction substituting for iodine, and the bandaged hand will again press the knife into the mineral. What else can they do, the old people or those with "obituary" faces? Haul a cart, drag logs, wash floors and windows? They are truly lucky to have this bit of mica, then. They do not have to strain their muscles—just a little patience . . . just to get the bowl of soup and sometimes even a supplement, just to shuffle along and not to sin, to hold on as long as you can to this bit of life in you. . . .

And in fact this sort of work, this splitting of mica is as though specially designed for the ghetto. In prisons all over the world, this job is assigned to criminals. No healthy, normal person would agree to work at it, because the dust from the mineral pierces the lungs, causing them to swell. A perfect job for the ghetto where everyone must be made productive. That is why this work is done by people who are not fit to work at anything else, people with weak eyes, trembling hands, eaten-up lungs, and by children, too, who have the prospect of surviving the war and of then "fixing" their lungs. . . .

With the children, this work is a wholly different matter. Their eyes are good, they do not overlook the smallest piece. Their young hands do not tremble.

Surely and expertly they push the knife into the thickness of *katzengold* [Ger: cat's gold] to make it thinner, to carve out as many foils as is humanly possible. They are not satisfied with just the soup and the supplement, they have bigger expectations. They want to be breadwinners. In the course of their 5-hour workday they must do as much as their grandfathers and grandmothers. . . . And as for the dust, well, they do not understand the dust yet. . . .

FROM "WHO CARES FOR A LITTLE BOY?"

[*1941*]

Enter the room. Around the table sit a number of people, large, small, children, grownups—your eyes count seventeen of them. Your eyes catch sight of three loaves of bread on the table, and you know right away that these people are not one but three different families, each with its own loaf of bread, and that their gathering here in this room is the result of the ghetto's particular circumstances.

Your eyes also notice three beds. Now, how is it possible for three families, seventeen people in all, to live in one room, and how do they share these three beds, which can at most accommodate twelve people, counting two at each end of a bed? And what of the other five human beings, who have no place to lie down?

It works out that there are four people in one family, six in the second and seven in the third. But no, not exactly. Because your eyes missed the far right corner, just near the door, where there is a makeshift bed. A paralyzed old woman lies there. She is the root from which all three families sprang to life. But according to the ghetto's welfare regulations, she is herself a family and as such is entitled to a monthly allowance of 10 marks.

Before Baluty was given to the Jews of Lodz as their latterday Pale of Settlement,* Dvoyra-Khana lived in this house. In those days she was not paralyzed and did not occupy the far right corner near the door. She was 75 years old but looked 50. She lived with her husband, Yosl the weaver, and they had four children, a son and three daughters. When the children got married, they moved to the city, and she, like a good mother, used to visit them on Saturdays. She was then her children's dear guest.

When her old man died, she had but one request of the Almighty: "Do with me what you will, only spare me from having to live with the children."

The Almighty granted her wish: she did not move in with any of her children. But when the war broke out, it was the children who had to move in with her. They had to flee from the city to their mother, who was lucky enough to have her home in Baluty.

First came the middle daughter with her husband and their two children. The mother gave them one of her two beds. Now she and her daughter slept in one bed, and her son-in-law in the other with the children.

A few days later her only daughter-in-law came. Her husband, Dvoyra-Khana's son, had been taken into the Polish army and no trace could be found of the poor man. The mother gave the young woman her spot in the second bed and made a bed for herself on the floor.

Then the other two daughters arrived with their families, and Dvoyra-Khana pushed her bedspreads farther to the corner, near the door. And so there they were now, all together, may the Almighty grant them good health.

And when the daughter-in-law was about to have a baby, and they had to take her in the dead of the night to the hospital from which she was not fated to return, the spot in the second bed became available again, but not for Dvoyra-Khana; after all, there were many other candidates waiting. This was too bad, because as luck would have it, Dvoyra-Khana got a chill in her legs when she went to the funeral, and now she really needed a bed for herself. . . .

A few weeks later the poor little survivor, the newborn baby boy, was sent home from the hospital, strong and healthy despite everything. The paralytic old woman took him to her corner and raised him there.

Little Laybele, a cheerful child, roams around the room, rolls over like a ball, and calls all the men in the room Daddy and all the women Mommy, because that's what he hears the other children calling them.

Thus, Laybele has three fathers and three mothers. But rarely do any of the fathers and mothers give Laybele a piece of bread, for they have hardly enough bread for their own children.

So Laybele has three fathers and three mothers, and a lot of brothers and sisters, but in truth Laybele has no one: not a father, not a mother, brother or sister—he doesn't even have the one and only father of the ghetto, the Eldest of the Jews who doles out welfare allowances. Laybele does not receive support, because he is only a year and half old and cannot wait in the long line to submit a written application at the Department of Relief, and none of the three fathers included him in theirs, because none of them is eager to take responsibility for raising little Laybele with those meager seven marks a month.

Laybl has no one except this old paralyzed grandmother who is confined to the corner floor-bed near the door. But she too, with her three married daughters, with her three living sons-in-law, she too is alone in the world, just like her grandson.

None of her daughters and sons-in-law can afford to share with her their rationed bread because their many children are dying for a piece.

Dvoyra-Khana does not receive support: she cannot get up by herself and go to the Department of Relief to ask for it, and none of her children wants to assume the task of supporting her with the meager ten marks per month.

And so, Dvoyra-Khana has no one but Laybl, and Laybl has no one but Dvoyra-Khana . . . and both have no means of income whatsoever.

Still, the seventeen people who sit around the table, eating their meager supper, envy those two:

"At least they have a place to rest: they are just two, and they have a bed of their own. And if they are hungry, at least they're not sleepy, while we, seventeen people in all, have only three beds, and everyone is hungry, everyone is cold at night, and everyone dreams of sleeping in a place of their own."

"POTATO PEELS, THE ELIXIR OF LIFE"

[*no date*]

The managers of the public kitchens were advised by the Health Department to save all kinds of vegetable peels and to give them only to consumers with a doctor's prescription.

Accordingly, the procedure for distributing potato peels will now be as follows: a doctor will prescribe a certain quantity of potato peels; the patient will present the prescription to the Department of Kitchens, which will then direct him to a particular kitchen to have the prescription filled.

It is not yet known whether the consumer will pay for the total prescription all at once, or for each dose separately.

The logic underlying all this can be explained this way: for several weeks the ghetto has been in the throes of terrible hunger. It has already felled thousands, and many more are expected to perish.

Until death grabs him by the heels, the ordinary ghetto resident must travel a strange road.

Before death takes its victims from this world, it paints sorrowful pictures on their faces. Shadows of what were once called people walk the ghetto's streets, people with sunken black or grey cheeks, with eyes that glare like hungry wolves in the deepest woods during the coldest of winters.

A person like this walks with his eyes glaring, his breathing feverish, his heart pressed down by an enormous weight, and his guts feeling like some beast was constantly gnawing at them.

Such a person does not "walk" but drags along like an accursed specter. When other people see him, their hearts stop. Those glaring eyes, they touch your intestines, and you realize suddenly: "I, too, am terribly hungry. Soon, I, too, will drag along with a glare in my eyes, breathing feverishly like him."

Hundreds, thousands drag along the ghetto streets now. They are driven from their houses into the streets, into the courtyards where the garbage is piled, and they look, they seek:

A piece of a broken pot that can still be licked—

A rag that once wrapped food and can still be gnawed at—

A discarded piece of vegetable—

And they live out their last days up to their necks in piles of garbage.

Sometimes these people drag their bodies into the doctor's office. They show him their flabby stomachs, their sunken breasts, the deep hollow around their necks. They show him their swollen legs. If you stick a finger in such a leg, you leave an impression, a sallow grey spot, as in half-baked bread.

The doctor says: Compellon. Only an injection of this medicine will keep you alive.

And something else he says, the doctor: "Eat well."

And so they search for Compellon, for this miraculous elixir of life, an impossible dream for the ordinary ghetto dweller, as impossible as eating well, as living.

But they are quite inventive, these "Western" doctors. The real essence of life, they say, is hidden in potato peels. And this is how the kitchens became pharmacies where prescriptions are filled.

LEON HURWITZ, LIFE IN THE LODZ GHETTO

THE FIRST ANNIVERSARY, MARCH 1941

We've lived in the ghetto a year, a terrible year of pain, suffering and woe. How much have we gone through in this one year! Is there a single plague in the Haggadah [Heb: the book read at Passover] with which we haven't been punished? But the pain and shame is even greater, for it's been mainly "ours" and those "closest" who have made us suffer.

The Devil only knows where they came from these new "social activists" and ghetto benefactors! People nobody ever heard of or knew about, half-baked intellectuals with no ties to the Jewish masses, no understanding of their problems, and whose Jewish connections went no further than the Grand Cafe or Ziemanska [popular coffee houses in pre-war Lodz]. Now they've become the saviors of the 150,000 distressed, starved and death-tired Jews of the Litzmannstadt Ghetto. They boss people around and, with the dictator, bear responsibility for the terrible physical and spiritual ruin and degradation of the ghetto's Jews.

And woe to us who have the bad luck to live under the rule of the dictator, the sadist, and the gang of impotents who jumped to his service like marionettes. The few material goods the ghetto possessed have been stolen away. Not a day passes without an official being fired in this or that workshop for crimes big and small. The court is overloaded with cases of graft and thievery, and not just individuals but whole units, like the meat provisioning department, are under investigation.

And the dictator organizes concerts so that he can deliver speeches and exposés. An orator, a Demosthenes he's become in his old age! . . . He talks incessantly about the thieves, forgetting that he, the "Chairman" himself, hired them, that he himself bestows posts and jobs, and that he, thus, is responsible for all the thieves. . . . He also forgets that only the small-time thieves are being caught, while those everyone knows to be really guilty are protected by their shield of immunity.

But the ruler does not stop at just preaching against his own employees. He promises mountains of good things to come and, also, threatens repression against the "rebels," who don't want to be Bontche the Silent,* who don't intend to leave this world quietly and modestly, without a protest, without a shout from the depth of their hearts, and without a curse. . . .

We, the people, mark the anniversary of the destruction of the Jewish community of Lodz. Thousands of new graves surround us. With terror we look at the unending tiers of those already bearing the stamp of death. For the ruling clique, however, this is a holiday! They make it a jubilee, with parades, pomp, messages of devotion, albums from "my" institutions, "my" employees, with speeches and group photographs, with large and small gatherings, and with a gala concert on Krawiecka Street,* to top it all off. A holiday for the half-baked bureaucrats, commissars and chiefs, chairmen and managers!

PASSOVER EVE

Tomorrow is the first seder. Stores where *matzoh* is sold are mobbed. Long lines of buyers wait for quite a while. Cries and curses can be heard from afar.

"If I told you everything I know, you would not sleep. This way, I alone cannot sleep. The ghetto, too, is in the war." (Rumkowski, quoted in the diary of Oskar Rosenfeld) A large oil-on-canvas painting now in the Jewish Historical Institute of Warsaw, painted in the ghetto by M. Schwarz in 1942.

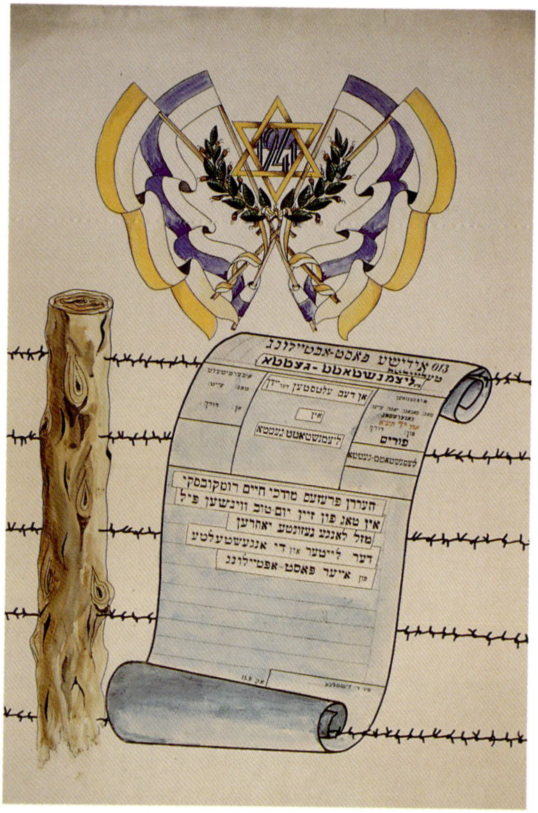

Left: A greeting to Rumkowski on his birthday, wishing him luck and a long, healthy life, from the workers in the Department of Post.

Below: Lodz Ghetto currency, signed by Mordechai Rumkowski and nicknamed "Rumkies" by the ghetto dwellers. *(Photos by Krzysztof Wojchiechowski)*

Rumkowski in his horse-drawn coach. The ghetto's only motor vehicle was a fire truck.

Fecal workers dumping excrement at the outskirts of the ghetto. A gypsy camp adjacent to the ghetto did not have any sanitation system and was quickly wiped out by typhus.

Top: Hans Biebow, the German ghetto overseer, shopping for neckties in the ghetto marketplace.

Above, left to right: Leon Rozenblat, Commander of the Ghetto Order Service; identity unknown; Rumkowski; Aron Jakubowicz, Director of the Central Workshop Bureau, the ghetto's chief of production and closest in contact with the German administration.

Right: "I try mentally to expand the limits of my existence. I idealize myself into the cosmos, an intellectual pursuit which eases me for a while, drives away my despair. I merge with the sun, the moon, the stars, God. Nothing can harm me. I feel the millennia rushing past me. I can read Spinoza, what good fortune. . . ." (Rosenfeld)

Activity on a main street of the ghetto.

Jews arriving in the ghetto from Western Europe, October–November 1941.

The deportation of western Jews, spring 1942.

Above: Leather goods workers.

Right: Carpet weavers.

The few policemen keeping order are hoarse from shouting. "Muscles" are at work every few minutes, ejecting those cutting into the line. The *matzoh* is made of corn flour, and it costs a lot. But never mind that, it's for Passover, and it's the only *matzoh* available.

Eggs are not to be had at all. People are going to be even hungrier than usual, but now, more than ever, the miracle [of liberation] should be retold once again. It's bitter cold outside. Hardly anyone has enough wood to kindle a fire; coffee is fetched from the coffee distribution stores, and watery soup from the public kitchens. At home it's cold and dark, and yet people live with hope. The most fantastic news is communicated from mouth to mouth, a substitute for food and warmth.

But there is no good news today to lighten the mood. Everyone seeks consolation, and no one finds it. General lethargy and boundless pessimism grip the ghetto. Not the mood of Passover, but of Yom Kippur or Tishe B'Av [Heb: the Ninth of Av, a fast day marking the destruction of the Temple in Jerusalem] hovers above.

THE REST HOME IN MARYSIN

For two weeks there's been a shortage of bread in the ghetto. But not everybody goes hungry. There is a small group, a chosen elite, whose wives frequent the meat distribution center at 40 Brzezinska Street every day. They come with empty handbags and baskets and leave smiling, their handbags and baskets full. They also know their way around other divisions of the provisioning department. They feel at home everywhere, these ladies, and they leave everywhere with a load of whatever is to be had. And if this still isn't enough, a smile, a compliment wins them another coupon for nutritional, vitamin-rich products from the dictator.

That's how they live, these celebrities. Their only wisdom is, stay in good health, save your strength until the fence is torn down and life begins anew. And our beloved public provider, whose vision of the post-war order is altogether different from everyone else's, wants very much for this whole gang to remain in good condition until the time when he becomes ruler of all the Jews. And that's why he's established a splendid rest home in the closed territory of Marysin, where his summer residence is.

According to the lucky who go there, you're not only fed very well, but you're also seated comfortably at beautifully prepared tables. The service and the flowers heighten your pleasure. The atmosphere reminds the guests of the good old times, when they had nothing in common with the Yids, the plebeians. Live chickens run around in the garden, and, later on, appear before the dear guests on snow-white porcelain plates. Bread, and especially white bread, begs to be eaten—as much of it as their delicate stomachs can digest.

COAL MINERS IN THE GHETTO

There are no coal mines in the ghetto. But there are coal miners.

In the east, the ghetto is enclosed by desolate plots where the city's garbage was dumped before the war. These dumps border on plots which belonged to a brick factory, now in ruins. These wastelands separate the center of a ghetto from the Jewish cemetery, on one side, and the oasis which is called Marysin, on the other. The chosen few see these bare fields only when they view them from the *droshky* taking them to Rumkowski's royal summer residence in Marysin. Common, unprivileged Jews like myself know these fields more intimately, as we often walk through the mounds of waste and puddles of mud to find a shortcut to the cemetery.

These unfriendly fields, which for years had seen only garbage haulers or sand- and clay-diggers, are suddenly alive with crowds of people. Hundreds of adults and even more children sit there from dawn to dusk and dig into the ground, or rather the waste, using bent iron hooks, small spades and other primitive tools. From a distance you can see only their backs, bent and crooked.

What are they looking for? They are coal mining, and their labor constitutes yet another "branch of industry" in the ghetto. Like many official ghetto industries, it is a parody, a warped image of the real thing. But at least these people have no clever explanation for what they do. They dig in the garbage so that they can buy their soup, their ration card.

Where did this coal come from? Well, there were normal times before the war, when households kept reserves of coal for the winter. The maids in the better-off homes used to throw the small pieces of coal and the coal dust out with the garbage, which travelled to the dumping fields and accumulated over many years.

JOZEF ZELKOWICZ

"THE BREADWINNER"

[*1941*]

Once, at a meeting, a "high official" of the ghetto was explaining how the "ghetto-state" works. He spoke with enthusiasm about our "own" police, our "own" postal service, our "own" factories, and, not least, our "own" currency.

And since the ghetto is a state with its "own" police, its "own" offices occupied by its "own" high, higher and highest officials, and with its "own" borders that are so well-guarded, it must also have its "own" natural resources to back the value of its "own" currency.

The ghetto has yellowish sand which housewives use to hide the squalor of their rotting floors.

The ghetto has clay which serves to plug up the holes and cracks in the walls.

And the ghetto has—coal.

The ghetto "coal mines" are besieged all day long by young and old alike. They dig in the muddy ground, they search, they ransack, they collect piece by piece. The recovered "coals" are later peddled to the better-off homes and sold for forty, fifty, and sometimes even more pfennigs per kilogram, depending on quality, size and, most of all, demand.

The "coals" are dug out in places where once there was a house, a fence

or other structure. The composition of these "coals" varies: they could be burnt pieces of wood, or stones, or rags. These "coals" do not burn, but if you put them on the burning firewood in the stove, the fire goes out quickly and the wood, along with the "coal," smolders for a few hours.

A boy, a girl leave their homes in the morning, a meager slice of bread in one hand, textbooks in the other, but instead of going to school they come to the "coal mine." There, step by step, they learn the "trade" from others, and in time they, too, become enterprising "coal miners." And when this Moishe, Mendel or Chaim comes home at dusk after spending a whole day in the pits and brings along his daily earnings, he becomes in the eyes of his parents an approved breadwinner. Soon he will take his younger and older kin into this business, sometimes even his father who has nothing better to do anyway or his mother who prefers working in dirt to seeing her household starved to the bone.

And once they have become "coal miners," the corruption of their young souls is a certainty. Here in the "coal mine" girls take off the one dress they have to their name before stepping into the pit. It takes only seconds for their naked bodies to get covered in mud. But the nakedness glares through, all the same. The boys of eleven or twelve and the girls of thirteen or fourteen get to know the secrets of their mothers and fathers right there, in the "coal pit." They take care of physiological needs right then and there, in full view. No time for amenities.

There grows in the "coal mines," among the "natural resources" of the ghetto "state," a deformed, crippled generation, which the enemies of the Jewish people are so eager to see, in order to tell the whole world:

"See, we were right, weren't we?"

"Lippa, why don't you go to school?'
"Because I have no shoes."
"But in the summer? Couldn't you walk barefoot?"
"Why should I go barefoot? What would I get there?"
"They teach you to read and write; is this nothing?"
"And if I learn to read and write, will I be less hungry?"
"And if you don't go to school, aren't you hungry?"
"Less than in school. I dig coals."
"How much do you earn?"
"Depends. A mark, a mark and a pfennig, if I'm lucky—"
Lippa, the twelve-year-old breadwinner.

GHETTO DOCUMENT

THE ELDEST OF THE JEWS IN LITZMANNSTADT
DEPARTMENT OF SCHOOLS

May 4, 1941

Dear children!

In the name of our respected Chairman Mr. Rumkowski, whom you esteem and love so much, we turn to you with the following appeal:

We know, children, how precious is the well-being of your parents, brothers, sisters, and others, and how much you want them to be spared any harm. That is why we've told you many times, and are doing so again, that one of the greatest enemies to your and your family's health is dirt and uncleanliness, which can lead to disease and epidemics. Children, keep your bodies and your clothes clean; wash regularly and carefully, especially your hands before and after every meal; do not buy food or sweets from untidy street vendors; clean your clothes often; keep your schoolrooms, your houses, rooms, hallways, stairways, and toilets clean; do not spit on the floor; do not make the walls dirty; do not damage the furniture in school; and listen to your second parents—your teachers. Tell your family, your friends and neighbors to observe cleanliness, to remove garbage from the house, to grow grass wherever possible—and help them with all your might.

Children! In order to give the tired and weak ghetto dwellers some rest and fresh air, and in order to make the ghetto beautiful, public lawns and parks with benches are planned. We must protect these places and keep them beautiful—not damage the benches, walk on the grass, pluck at the plants, break off tree branches, because that would be a disservice to our brothers and sisters and an aggravation for our good father, the Chairman, Mr. Rumkowski. Children! We trust you; don't embarrass us!

And one more thing we want of you: do not loiter outside unnecessarily, especially in crowded and narrow streets. Do not walk near or stand by the ghetto fence. Avoid it entirely. Those who have to walk along the fence should do so without stopping, and should not be curious. The same is true in regard to bridges.

Children! We trust that you will heed our fatherly instructions and that you will urge your relatives to do the same, because this is for our common good, and with God's help we will be able to avoid many troubles.

DAWID SIERAKOWIAK'S DIARY

SUNDAY, APRIL 6, 1941

I start a new notebook, hoping that it will begin a better period in my life than the one recorded in the preceding diary. It's a lost cause, it seems. In spite of a beautiful (and expensive) Passover ration, the situation is as awful as it's been. No hope for any improvement.

Esther Wasser, a ghetto schoolteacher, with her students on August 16, 1941. The photograph was presented to Rumkowski on the Jewish New Year with the traditional greeting: "Let the year be inscribed and sealed, 5702." On the back of the photograph is written: "In gratitude for the fatherly interest of the Honorable Mister Chairman, this picture of what is most beautiful in the ghetto is respectfully presented."

MONDAY, APRIL 7, 1941

The *matzoh* will cost 2 RM [Reichsmark] 25 pf [Pfennig] for 2.5 kilo, the portion alloted for one person for the 8 days of Passover. Of course, we'll take bread instead, since the budget of a menial laborer doesn't allow for *matzoh*. Mother would prefer the *matzoh*, but we need to sell the bread so that we can buy other food.

TUESDAY, APRIL 8, 1941

Jews are hoping that the Balkans will bring us liberation, an idea I do not share. Nothing will come of it.

WEDNESDAY, APRIL 9, 1941

This week I wrote an article for the communist textile workers' newspaper, about the situation of students.

THURSDAY, APRIL 10, 1941

Rysiek Podlaski sent me a note today telling me to report immediately to the tailor shop where his father is the manager. I was given employment for a few days as a 2-marks-a-day laborer, weighing and distributing vegetables to the tailors and other workers. I lift and carry turnips and carrots for weighing. I'll receive an additional worker's dinner (read soup) for 20 pfennigs, every day.

FRIDAY, APRIL 11, 1941

Work is hard but not strenuous. I'm annoyed only at the special privileges extended to office workers and other parasites in the shop by those doing the weighing. The tailors wait on a long line, while an office girl runs out and receives her allotment immediately—taken from better quality stock, with weight added. A policeman's maid (I know her) comes with one coupon; the policeman on duty takes her coupon and orders two portions instead of one. What's to be done? The ghetto functions on bourgeois-bureaucratic foundations, and on these it will fall.

SATURDAY, APRIL 12, 1941

It's the first day of Passover and we're not working because it's Saturday, not because of the holiday, which is not acknowledged. In reality, there is no holiday. The same food as before, and the same hunger.

SUNDAY, APRIL 13, 1941

We no longer cook dinner at home. We eat in a restaurant where we registered for the holidays by using some of our food supply coupons. The restaurant dinners are meager, and we'll join a community kitchen after the holiday, since dinners there are cheaper (15 pfennigs) and better—they're thicker and more plentiful. Dinners in the shops (dinner here and elsewhere means one portion of soup) are also good and plentiful.

WEDNESDAY, APRIL 16, 1941

Last Friday a notice was posted for the voluntary registration of males, 18 to 45, and females, 20 to 30, for work in Germany. On Saturday, all those who had previously registered were notified to report immediately. A few thousand have already left. I think they're the lucky ones, for they get a chance to survive the war, which we in the ghetto do not have. All the letters sent by people shipped out for work assure us that they have plenty of food: "We can eat, eat, and eat some more. . . ."

TUESDAY, APRIL 22, 1941

Rumkowski came up with a brilliant idea for preventing workers in bread stores from eating bread on the job. Starting tomorrow, a loaf will be issued to each person for five days. This way there will be no weighing or slicing of bread and no eating of bread in the stores. The bakery supervisors will be responsible for the honest weight of the loaves.

Also, the private sale of wood is to be forbidden, since it is usually stolen from fences, outhouses and other wooden structures which the authorities haven't gotten around to taking down. The price of wood is now 80 pf. per kilo. We don't know how things will work out, because there has been no distribution of coal for months and wood was distributed back in February. So we'll have to make do on one soup a day from a communal kitchen. Even though our supplementary allotment includes potatoes, kasha and vegetables, there will be nothing to cook them with. If they don't get you one way, they get you another. The inevitability of death by starvation is now growing clearer.

SATURDAY, APRIL 26, 1941

School is at 9 am tomorrow. We'll only get soup, for 10 pf. At any rate, studies are to commence full speed, immediately. We have, at best, five months in which to cover the fourth year. There's an awful lot of material in it.

SUNDAY, APRIL 27, 1941

The trip to school in Marysin is quite long, but the worst of it is the awful mud from the incessant rain. We walk through several fields, so our shoes are in a sorry state. Mine are beginning to go, and there's no chance of repairing them. I may soon have to walk to school barefoot.

The school is in a tiny building where the benches barely fit. There isn't even a blackboard or any other supplies.

Rumkowski came to visit us, with several other ghetto "dignitaries." He looked into the kitchen, tasted the soup (which was simply excellent today, probably on his account), and spoke to the students. He spoke about the difficulties in opening the school and said that he'll try to do more for us. Then he asked that we work diligently, keep clean and behave well. (He's gotten fatter and much younger looking.)

WEDNESDAY, APRIL 30, 1941

Our association's politbureau held a meeting today, after a long period of inactivity. During the winter, we became part of the general ghetto movement, and now we're paticipating in the activities of all the other groups (both youth and adult) with whom we've established contact. Nintek (Nataniel) Radzyner

is well-connected in the leftist movement, and through him we stay in contact with everybody. We've also made progress in our theoretical studies. May we live to use our knowledge.

THURSDAY, MAY 1, 1941
Churchill spoke this week. He admitted that England has suffered major defeats, but he believes that the final victory will be England's. And so one gets the impression that the war, if it ever ends, will go on for many, many years.

FRIDAY, MAY 2, 1941
The meeting today of male groups was very successful. Things look promising for fruitful work. Nintek spoke about the May 1st celebration; I spoke about

organizational matters, and then Nintek gave a lecture on youth in the proletarian revolutionary movement. A lively discussion followed.

SATURDAY, MAY 3, 1941

Large groups of workers are leaving for Germany again. I wonder if there will be further registration.

Today we met with a women's group to discuss the necessity of centralizing the authority of the proletarian government. We were able to fully institute a soviet-type government.

SUNDAY, MAY 4, 1941

All the fields in the ghetto are now parcelled out, plowed and planted by the administration. Not a bad idea, if some good comes of it. Areas around the school are to be cultivated by the students. No free education, but still, it's good to get to know the soil: everything may yet serve a purpose.

MONDAY, MAY 5, 1941

For all the work I did carrying and distributing vegetables, I received only 12 RM. Well, it's something. More important, though, Praszkier* kept the promise he made to me to place Mother in the community kitchen. She's working 14-15 hours a day, and her salary is to be 20-25 RM monthly. The best part is that kitchen workers get two good soups a day, free, without coupons. Now Mother will not starve, and it will be easier at home as well.

THURSDAY, MAY 8, 1941

We had our leadership meeting today. Four of our members were chosen for the all-youth unit of lecturers: Nintek, Jerzyk, me and Szyjo. We'll study Lenin's *State and Revolution* first and then lecture on it to any other youth groups studying it.

FRIDAY, MAY 9, 1941

I've started studying Mehring's *Karl Marx* and find it extremely interesting. I also study economics, intensively.

Today I met one of my former pupils who wants to study his first year of high school with me. I went to his home, but the pay they offered me is awful: 1.50 RM for 6 lessons a week. I want 40 pf. an hour, minimum, for I value my health.

SATURDAY, MAY 10, 1941

I went to a May 1st celebration today, staged (obviously) a bit late. Ziula Krengiel was the main speaker. She talked about the meaning of May 1st, its observance in the Soviet Union, and finally about surviving the ghetto. She spoke wonderfully about readiness for action and was given the usual red bow, which she kept as a souvenir.*

SUNDAY, MAY 11, 1941

It just doesn't want to get warm this year. I feel awful and I look worse all the time. People say it's hard to recognize me.

TUESDAY, MAY 13, 1941

Rumkowski is going to Warsaw to get some doctors, and he is also re-organizing food distribution. The number of stores is increasing. There are now separate vegetable stores, while bakeries and groceries are being combined. The "Spring Program" includes creating new grassy areas and squares, paving and construction around the ghetto, which is marching "in glory, on the road to development and progress."

Yesterday a student in our class died from hunger exhaustion. Because he looked awful, he was allowed to have as much soup in school as he wanted, but it didn't help. He was the third victim of starvation in the class.

WEDNESDAY, MAY 14, 1941

The teachers called a meeting of class delegates from all years. For the first time in my life I had to be a stormy oppositionist and quarrel with the school authorities, namely the superintendent Maria Prentka. A motion was made to give students particularly weakened by hunger double portions of soup. She advised us not to bother about that now but to consider the more important (?) matter of students serving on duty. I protested that feeding students a week before their death is a positive step, and that it was a most important question. Because I had no support from the weaklings who were there, cultivating the soil was discussed instead of feeding people, and because of the late hour the meeting was adjourned. I said that I considered the meeting null and void because of its imposed agenda and procedure. Maria Prentka was furious, and other teachers argued with me. Tomorrow, however, I hope to push my proposal through.

THURSDAY, MAY 15, 1941

I succeeded! In spite of Prentka's fury, the matter of feeding people was discussed and submitted for immediate implementation to the newly organized 7-member committee, which I also joined as leader of the academic section. This committee decided to submit a petition to the soup kitchen department immediately, asking

for an increase in the soup provided. It also organized a student militia and considered the matter or hygiene and collecting money for self-help.

FRIDAY, MAY 16, 1941
A woman doctor examined me and was horrified at how skinny I am. She gave me a note to go for X-rays. Maybe I'll get an extra soup in school, though five soups would be even better. The check-up made me very worried and fearful. Lung disease is raging in the ghetto and mows people down as much as typhus and dysentery.

SATURDAY, MAY 17, 1941
They've asked me to take on the tutoring. I'll get about 1.50 or 1.60 RM for four lessons a week. It will come in handy. If I can only manage it all: school, tutoring, organizational work, theory, languages, books. Strength is most important, yet it won't come from 40 dkg. of bread.

I attended a lecture this afternoon on world literature, specifically positivism and decadence.

SUNDAY, MAY 18, 1941
Nintek's essay about "The Labors of Sisyphus" caused quite a stir, which led to the idea of writing a class newspaper. We'd also like to put out a newspaper for all the communist youth in the ghetto.

MONDAY, MAY 19, 1941
I received 10 RM from Leczycki in Warsaw today. Part of it will go toward repairing my shoes and the rest toward our food allotment. I've begun receiving two soups in school; it does make me feel better.

SPEECH BY CHAIM RUMKOWSKI

15 MAY 1941

"DICTATORSHIP IS NOT A DIRTY WORD"

[*Rumkowski delivered this talk in the Warsaw Ghetto to former residents of Lodz.*]

People from what used to be Lodz, now Litzmannstadt Ghetto, permit me to greet you.

I am to give you a report on my work. Should I say that it was bad at the beginning? What for? But if I said that things are good now, it might sound like a reproach to many of you for deserting your town. Yes, I feel forced to admit, I didn't feel at all capable of assuming the heavy burden of leading the Jews of Lodz. I cried; with tears in my eyes I begged to be released from this business. I argued that neither my health nor my mental faculties, nor my education, equipped me for such matters. But there was no way out. I was forced to accept the responsibility. *Even if you cannot leap over—you must leap over!*

You're now feeling the birth pangs of a new way of life here, just as we did a year ago in Litzmannstadt. But many things can be achieved, much can be done in this place! I warned them many times, saying that all signs indicated Warsaw was on its way to becoming a ghetto. Nobody listened to me. They kept pointing out why it was impossible in Warsaw, and they said this and that. My friends sitting here, fine people, it's truly to be regretted that they are not with us.

When I considered how to combat the problems facing the Jews, I concluded that "work is the best blessing." You know, don't you, my five basic slogans, the ones printed in my *Getto Zeitung* [Yid: ghetto newspaper]. They are 1) Work, 2) Bread, 3) Assistance to the Sick, 4) Care of the Children, 5) Peace in the ghetto.

Overnight I erected factories and created a working town. My *Beirat* only knows how to talk. I have carried out my tasks alone, by force. Dictatorship is not a dirty word. Through dictatorship I earned the Germans' respect for my work. And whenever they say, "Litzmannstadt Ghetto," I answer them, *"Das ist kein Getto sondern eine Arbeitsstadt"* [Ger: "This is not a ghetto but a work-town"]. Initially, I gave workers the right to organize. Each shop used to elect its representatives—and then came colossal disasters. Party rule began. So instead of a tailor, they took into their shop a button sewer, just because he had the right point of view. And the workers also created a *Beirat*. Well, I was thinking. No one likes giving up power. If that *Beirat* does, in fact, work, then everything is okay. If not, then I'll listen to them the same way I do my own *Beirat*.

The workers turned to demonstrations. My ghetto is like a small kingdom, with all the good and the bad. For the price of fifty marks I got reports on all of the workers' top-secret meetings. In the meantime I set up a detention house, and slowly, one by one, I put the leaders inside. They decided to have an Italian [sit-down] strike. This was supposed to happen on a Friday, but the carpenters decided to start on Thursday. And on Friday there was a lock on the door, saying the shop was closed until the issue was settled. The workers themselves helped me with their own devisiveness and conflicting goals.

Then the workers demanded a German commission. When the Germans were sitting in my office, the workers demanded to be heard. I let them in. I let them speak but toward the end I threw them out, in front of the Germans, with a shout of *"heraus Lumpen"* [Ger: "Get out, you rabble"]. The strictest autonomy governs the ghetto; no German would dare touch my prerogatives, and I shall never let any do so.

So, in conclusion, quiet and order prevail in the ghetto. No more politics in factories; no place anymore for smart tricks. I can play the same tricks their factions can. The biggest trick is simply this: that potatoes for the mid-day meal are distributed a half-hour before the faction leaders demand them; a full stomach is the best measure of things.

At present, there are 34 factories operating, twelve of them tailoring shops. All employees of the Jewish Community get lunches in special kitchens. The population gets meat twice a week, and 40 decagrams daily of good quality bread. Each newborn gets a food-card immediately. Children get special food until age three. Bread costs 1 mark a kilo, potatoes 22 pfennig. I distribute subsidies with one hand, while with the other I take from everyone whatever can be taken—for this reflects on the price of bread and potatoes.

DR. ISRAEL MILEJKOWSKI, "THE EVIL OF THE GHETTO"

[*Warsaw, 1942*]

A year ago, the head of the Lodz Ghetto, Rumkowski, came to us in the [Warsaw] Ghetto, and spoke to me about transferring some doctors to the Lodz Ghetto. In this connection, he favored us with a quasi-lecture about Lodz and his views of a Ghetto in general.

Rumkowski's basic premise is that the Ghetto-form enables those in the position of leadership to do something creative for the Jews condemned by fate to live there. He holds that much can be achieved for the Jews. Indeed, they can be transformed into an industrious, productive and creative people. He justifies the Ghetto's existence with its physical and spiritual walls, in that it can be useful for the Jews.

Rumkowski, who loved cigarettes, is conveyed through the Warsaw Ghetto during a "state visit."

My entire being revolts against this position. This is exactly what I cannot come to terms with. The root of all the evil of our sorrowful existence stems precisely from our being confined in a Ghetto—a deteriorating and demoralizing effect. This is the source of our physical and moral breakdown.

The Ghetto and life in the Ghetto has no future because we are confined within its walls against our will, because it came about through brute force which disregarded all human feeling. Therefore we must not pretend even for a single minute that the Ghetto-form can be adapted to our needs, can offer a solution to whatever painful problems there may be in our existence. And what is more, we must avoid and guard against Rumkowski's enthusiasm about any so-called "creativity" in the Ghetto.

The Ghetto for us is nothing but a temporary sojourn which has been forced upon us. It is a *succah*, a roofless booth, devoid of all human living conditions. It is a temporary building, a passing form and the source of all our present-day troubles and hardships. The Ghetto, which struck us so murderously, constitutes the greatest affliction and ruin for both the community and the individual. All our other plagues and tribulations vanish in comparison with the Ghetto.

Indeed, the Ghetto's chief curse lies in the fact that we cannot be creative here. Creative is what we were before the Ghetto, when we created cultural values for ourselves and all mankind, for we are capable of creativity, but only in more or less free conditions. In the Ghetto this is impossible.

Here in the Ghetto we must make every attempt to survive this terrible period of our being. *Endurance and survival* must be our current slogan.

I see this as an exceptionally painful phenomenon in our entire history. We derive no benefit from the Ghetto. On the contrary, the Ghetto brings the confined masses only more and more demoralization and degeneration.

To help clarify my meaning, I will borrow two terms from medicine: endogenous and exogenous. *Internally,* we must do everything possible to permit endurance and survival. But *externally* the oppressor's whip cracks, forcing us to perform tasks and deeds beyond the ability of our frail strength. The oppressor's conduct towards us can be expressed in the words of the officers of the children of Israel to Pharaoh: "There is no straw given unto they servants, and they say to us, make brick. . . . " We are told to perform tasks which we are in no position to execute in Ghetto conditions, precisely because of the difficult conditions themselves.

So I always try—within the realm of my authority—to undermine the control exerted by "them," and with my orders and prescriptions to relieve temporarily the whip lashes. I neither can nor wish to be creative, for it is a wasted effort, not worth the trouble, and impossible.

JAKUB SZULMAN'S NOTEBOOK

When the Chairman came back from Warsaw, he seemed extremely nervous, yet he also became much more sure of himself, and his directives became much sharper. . . . During his week in Warsaw, he had thought things over and decided that his way, that of socializing Jewish property in the ghetto, was the right way, at least for the present situation. From then on he believed in his abilities and saw opposition to any of his decisions as harmful, as an act of sabotage!

GHETTO DOCUMENTS

[*Announcements by Rumkowski*]

May 1941

Right after my return from Warsaw, I received the news that individuals working in my workshops used my absence to try stirring up various kinds of discontent among the workers, in the hope of provoking disturbances.

It is true that this agitation was not taken seriously by the workers, since they have satisfied themselves many times that I never mistreat those who do their work conscientiously and, further, that I have not the least wish to do so.

Therefore, I appeal once again to all workers employed in my factories and workshops, not as the Eldest of the Jews but rather as an older brother, and ask that they keep themselves from being influenced by a few irresponsible troublemakers, who are not concerned with the interest of the workers in whose name they speak.

As for the instigators themselves, I warn them that if necessary, I will treat them in my well-known way—without leniency.

27 May 1941

After irresponsible elements in the tailors' workshop at 12 Halbegasse agitated against work, I immediately closed that workshop.

DAWID SIERAKOWIAK'S DIARY

WEDNESDAY, MAY 21, 1941

Rumkowski came back from Warsaw and brought with him twelve physicians. He announced that air raid defenses would be organized. There are no allotments of food now and the soups in the kitchens are getting thinner. There are no potatoes, kasha, or vegetables in the ghetto.

SUNDAY, MAY 25, 1941

It's May-like, finally. Those who are emaciated and starved (as I am) can't do without warm clothing yet, but overcoats are gone. It's dry everywhere. Marysin smells like spring, and the heart breaks at the memory of pre-war days, when we'd be getting ready for our long-awaited vacation. It would've been an excursion for the graduating class, then camp or the country. Damn it! One could cry at the memory. The hell with it!

MONDAY, MAY 26, 1941

All is okay in school. We're working on Cicero; next week it will be metrics. In math we're doing square roots and soon solid geometry. In other subjects, except for German, we're behind.

I'm organizing a school paper, for which I've submitted a caricature. Maybe one of my Yiddish articles will be accepted this time, though so far none have passed the censor. Even the ghetto has its own bourgeois ideology, distinctly formulated.

Not all is well at home. Mother works from 7 am till 9 pm and father from 8 am to 8 pm. The household chores are done by Nadzia [his sister]. She gets only one soup a day and has 30 dkg. of bread, because she and Mother both give Father 10 dkg. which he doesn't even appreciate. His attitude toward them is bad and shows great egotism.

TUESDAY, MAY 27, 1941

Everyone is eagerly awaiting Roosevelt's speech, promised for today. If I remember correctly, it was on May 27, 1917, that the United States declared war on Germany.*

WEDNESDAY, MAY 28, 1941

Of course, he didn't say anything special. Wait, wait, wait—one can go mad hearing all this jabber. Here there is an unusual increase in cases of tuberculosis in children and young people, the hearse is busy as never before—but over there they wait. Let them go to hell!

MONDAY, JUNE 2, 1941

This afternoon Lolek Dudelczyk and I had an "editorial meeting" of our newspaper. We composed an introductory article, which I translated into Yiddish. My other Yiddish article, together with the caricature, will appear in the first issue. I wrote a mild reminder about the obligation to feed people. There will be time to write critical pieces in the coming issues.

TUESDAY, JUNE 3, 1941

My X-ray shows no change in the lungs, but there is some heart irregularity.

THURSDAY, JUNE 5, 1941

Rumkowski announced that because of gunshots that allegedly came from the ghetto last week, no one will be allowed to leave his apartment Saturday, under threat of extreme penalty. He claims that the ghetto population was in great danger, but that thanks to his intervention the punishment was reduced to house arrest on Saturday. Nobody is inclined to believe this story, but no one can explain the Saturday punishment, either.

SZMUL ROZENSZTAJN, DAILY NOTES

6 JUNE

On June 5, 1941, the Litzmannstadt ghetto was visited for the first time by Chief of the Reich Police Herr Himmler. Chairman Rumkowski began awaiting the guest in the morning, but it was 4:30 PM when the German high officials began assembling. Among them were representatives of the Gestapo in Litzmannstadt.

When Herr Himmler arrived at Balut Market with his entourage, he had the following exchange with Chairman Rumkowski:

"How are you doing here?" asked Herr Himmler.

"We work, and we are building a city of labor here."

"And how is the work here going?"

"Not badly, I think. Hopefully, it will get better. I'm doing everything so that the ghetto will work more and work better. My motto is Work, Peace and Order."

"Then go on working for the benefit of your brethren in the ghetto. It will do you good." Herr Himmler finished the conversation.

Then, accompanied by Chairman Rumkowski, the guests visited the largest tailor shop on 16 Jakuba Street. They expressed their appreciation to Mr. Rumkowski for his work. Afterward, pleased with the visit, the Chairman shared his impressions with his closest associates. He expressed the opinion that Herr Himmler was probably well briefed ahead of time about the ghetto's work.

9 JUNE 1941

During the night of May 27, someone fired shots from inside the ghetto, hitting a spot near the German guard-post but, luckily, hurting no one. Since the sniper's identity remained unknown, the Gestapo, the Police President and the Mayor of Litzmannstadt demanded that 25 Jews be selected by Chairman Rumkowski for summary execution. The Chairman informed only a few of his closest associates and attempted to have the punishment softened. After much effort, he succeeded, but the authorities then demanded a list of 25 Jews for flogging. This, too, the Chairman found unacceptable. When the authorities insisted on going through with this punishment, he declared that he himself was ready to receive the lashing but that he could not provide others.

He then wrote a letter to each of the three above-mentioned authorities, proposing that a curfew be imposed on Saturday, June 7, for all ghetto dwellers, without exception. On Tuesday, June 1, two members of the Litzmannstadt Gestapo appeared at Balut Market, and they and the Chairman went around the ghetto looking for a suitable place for the corporal punishment. Choosing the large square at Bazarna Street, the Gestapo ordered the Chairman to find 25 benches to which the victims would be tied, 25 Jews to carry out the lashing, and iron rods to do it with. At this point, the Chairman presented his plan for a 24-hour curfew and gave the Gestapo men a copy of the letter. They promised to deliver copies of the letter to the Police President and the Mayor, and told him to expect an answer by phone. At 12:30 PM he received a call from the Gestapo that his proposal had been approved. Putting down the receiver, the Chairman fainted.

18 JUNE

Herr Biebow came to Balut Market today at 6 PM. He said that since all the Jews in the smaller towns were going to be deported (that is, the women, children and old people, for the men have already been conscripted for forced labor in Germany), and since their numbers would reach 70,000, a large group will have

"You, whom I love above all." Schoolchildren parade before the Chairman.

to be absorbed by the Litzmannstadt Ghetto. He requested statistical information about the ghetto, from its first day until now.

21 JUNE

Chairman Rumkowski returned from Warsaw on Thursday night, the 19th. The next day he was extremely irritated and asked me, "What rumors are circulating in the ghetto now?" I answered that the biggest rumor related to Herr Biebow's visit. The Chairman suddenly became very serious. "I see that I cannot leave the ghetto even for a day." He said that he had known about the plans to deport the Jewish population in the provincial towns for a long time and had even worked out a plan to help them. His plan was to create a special Jewish district in the vicinity of Tuszyn [a suburb about 10 kilometers south of Lodz] and to establish a triumvirate of himself and two representatives of the deportees. He would select several dozen of his ablest workers and send them to organize the new district.

WEDNESDAY, 9 JULY

Today at 6 AM the Chairman met with representatives of the rabbinate. He declared that he wanted to inform them of a decision he had made before it appeared in the *Getto Zeitung*. So that warm winter clothing could be provided for the ghetto population, which suffered so much last winter, he is forced to request that men (except for rabbis and other religious functionaries) give up wearing long coats. He said that he had in mind an improvement in the general appearance of the population and, most of all, its sanitary conditions, since garments that pile up in small and dirty apartments can spread disease. Besides, remnants from long coats could be used to repair worn clothing.

Questioned by Rabbi Jakubowicz as to whether this was an order of the authorities or his own, the Chairman answered that he had received no such orders. On behalf of the others, Rabbi Laski declared that while the measure might in certain ways be needed, it constituted an assault on the religious feelings of the orthodox, and it would therefore be advisable if the Chairman gave up the whole idea.

The Chairman replied that he had expected that response but was not going to abandon his plan. He also said that in his opinion beards should be shaved off. Long beards and *peyes* [Yid: earlocks] allow germs to grow and spread disease, and this should be fought in every way.

TUESDAY, 22 JULY

Some time ago the Gestapo ordered the Chairman to compile a list of the mentally ill in ghetto hospitals. The list included 53 individuals of both sexes. Many weeks passed and it was assumed that the matter was closed, although during this time 12 more were added to the total. Today at 4 PM, a car with high Gestapo officials arrived at Balut Market. . . . The highest ranking Gestapo officer ordered the Chairman to send a complete list of the mentally ill to the Gestapo by tomorrow, and to send them from the ghetto to the city by Friday. This order had a terrible effect on the Chairman.

SUNDAY, 27 JULY

At 4 PM today, not far from the Chairman's summer residence, there was a parade of all the children from the summer camp, the high schools and elementary schools in Marysin. In all, 3000 children, aged 4 to 17, participated. The Chairman made the following speech:

"I greet you, whom I love above all. It seems to me that I did you no harm when I took you away from your crowded, stuffy homes and brought you here where you can enjoy the fresh air. It was not easy to organize all the schools here. My greatest satisfaction is seeing you here. I demand of you good work, and that you study hard and be obedient students and children. That would reward all my efforts.

"I'm glad to see you happy. Your friends in the city are much worse off. But I care for them, too. Soon they'll be getting supplementary rations in the school kitchens.

"I'm aware how difficult life is for your parents and your families in the city, but what can I do? Not everyone can have it this good. But I will try to save them from hunger. My heart is filled with joy when I see you in good physical and spiritual health. I'll take good care of your older friends who have already finished school. Many of them have been given jobs; others will become good workers in time. I hug you all to my heart, and I say: be well and be strong."

The children presented the Chairman with flowers and gifts, leaving him visibly moved.

TUESDAY, 29 JULY

All efforts by the Chairman to save the mentally ill were of no avail. At 11 AM today, a van arrived at the hospital on 3 Wesola Street to take 58 persons. They had been given [lethal] injections of the sedative scopolamine.

DAWID SIERAKOWIAK'S DIARY

FRIDAY, JUNE 6, 1941

I finally received a letter from Lolek Leczycki in Warsaw; it was a sealed and registered letter, joyful and very important. It's in answer to my postcard acknowledging the 10 RM he sent me. He writes that he'll continue helping me (though I don't see how) and that he'll even send me some underwear soon. He also says that Rumkowski, who was in Warsaw two weeks ago, took along his friend Heniek Landenberg as his secretary, which means he'll have a lot of influence.

SUNDAY, JUNE 8, 1941

After school I went to see this Heniek Landenberg. He is short and well-fed, a guy my own age [17]. He told me that Lolek wrote him about me and that as soon as his position is secure, he'll do all he can for me. Then he did what all the ghetto's "influential people" do, he wrote down my name and address and told me to see him in a week. I managed to get some information about Lolek and the Warsaw ghetto. It's enough to say that a loaf of bread (2 kilo, same as here) costs 60 zlotys (30 RM)! [Bread cost 12 marks per kilo in the Lodz Ghetto on June 26, 1941.]

MONDAY, JUNE 9, 1941

Our school paper *Itonejnu* [Heb: Our Newspaper] came out today, finally. Articles of mine were published for the first time, though they didn't have too many readers, probably because they're in Yiddish. The caricature, though, is very successful. I'm now officially the editor of the Judaic section (Yiddish, Hebrew).

TUESDAY, JUNE 10, 1941

Now we'll study Lenin's *What Is to Be Done* in our group. Work is going full speed: we've gained a few new members and the old ones have made a lot of progress.

The ghetto is getting ready for air-raid defense by naming commandants, messengers, etc., who will, of course, not work at preparing shelters, which is impossible in the ghetto. Rather, it's a chance for them to acquire new titles and honors. It seems that unemployment will continue for a long time, perhaps always.

SATURDAY, JUNE 14, 1941

There was an alarm at night, without an air raid, of course, and everyone slept well (if they had supper). No one in the ghetto fears "enemy" air raids, not even if there were bombing.

SUNDAY, JUNE 15, 1941

Rumkowski, the sadist-moron, is doing terrible things. He dismissed two teachers who are communist: our preceptress Estera Majerowicz and Rykla Laks. The direct reason was their organizing teachers to oppose the installation of Weichselfisz as woman commissioner-director. The indirect reason was their supposed communist activity in school. Even though we knew Majerowicz's views, we never worked with her. We're keeping quiet and, on the advice of the leadership, won't have any meetings for a week or two. There is a threat of a purge among the students and a possible closing of the school.

WEDNESDAY, JUNE 18, 1941

I submitted my first Yiddish poem, *"Der Umet"* [Sadness], to the school paper. Moyshe Wolman, a man of letters and now a Yiddish teacher in our school, looked at it and said it shows talent "obscured by scribbling." It will appear in the second issue, together with my Yiddish editorial.

FRIDAY, JUNE 20, 1941

Rumkowski has a new plan, which he announced today in the ghetto newspaper. Children up to 14 years old will receive an increased ration, bringing it to 12 RM monthly. People 14 to 60 years an increase to 15 RM a month; 60 to 70 years, up to 17 RM; and above 70, to 20 RM monthly. For this allotment, all men 17 to 50 and women 17 to 40 will have to work ten to fourteen days a month, without pay, and will receive one soup at work without coupons. They'll be doing low grade work (such as my father and mother do) in place of all those now doing such jobs, who will be laid off. Women below age 40 with children below age 14 will also be laid off. In this way, thousands will lose their jobs and will accept an allowance while working without pay.

But, according to Rumkowski, the new system will protect the jobs of all office workers who will continue receiving supplements for their wives and children, so that their dependents do not become a burden to them. To put it simply, those who were well off until now will be even better of from now on.

An adult gets 15 RM monthly and a child below age 14 gets 10 RM monthly, which gets added to the salary of the office worker. And that's the clever way in which Mr. Chaim Rumkowski is running things. There is nothing definite as yet about the families of the shop workers, because he has not brought up the subject.

However, Chaimek [Rumkowski] is going after the communists again. We've been told by our leadership that they're especially interested in us and that we should be very careful.

Had it not been for this war, I'd be graduating today.

JUNE 28, 1941

Nintek told me that because all party work in the ghetto has been suspended, an activity center is being secretly established. This is to be made up of people devoted to the cause, body and soul, people for whom nothing else will matter and who will be ready at all times for any kind of party work. I was designated one of five candidates from among school youths, and Nintek asked what I thought. I was so nervous and overwhelmed that I couldn't give him an answer today, putting it off till tomorrow.

At home I came to the following conclusions: even though I'm quite certain of my ideals and convictions, revolutionary activity on a professional level, taken to its ultimate end, is definitely not my life's goal. Also, I'm probably incapable of being in something like a "suicide squad." I decided to answer that I'm prepared to join in a specific action at a critical moment, but that ongoing professional work, precluding all other goals and conducted in circumstances which risk dire consequence, is out of the question.

TUESDAY, JULY 15, 1941

Father is working again, this time as a painter's assistant. Lazy he is not, that's for sure. He'd do anything to earn bread for us. Alas, he hasn't had much luck. Mother's working now, too. Maybe she'll be able to hold onto this job. The thing is not to lose ground, not to be finished off.

WEDNESDAY, JULY 23, 1941

Today our class went to the mandatory bath. It was great! A superb hot and cold shower, a pleasure. It reminded me of the good old days, if only for a little while.

SUNDAY, JULY 27, 1941

We had no classes, because all the students in Marysin had a parade for Rumkowski. What was more important, we had an extra meal—a piece of bread with a slice of sausage. Of course, there was a speech. The old man said that he gives us all he can and, in turn, asks us to study, study hard. A lot of dignitaries and guests came, and of course the entire Rest Home. Rumkowski opened a Rest Home in Marysin for "deserving employees of the Community," where life is said to be better than before the war. This heaven, where the charge per day is 5 RM a person, is populated by doctors, the *Beirat*, etc. Even wines are procured for them. This is such a terrible disgrace that it will never be forgiven.

TUESDAY, AUGUST 5, 1941

It's rumored that there's a plan to establish a summary court that would give death sentences for so-called political crimes (radio listening, spreading "false information," and even for political beliefs). The ghetto, of course, has immediately shut up, and now there's no political gossiping at all. A miraculous remedy, this rumor. The Germans will never find themselves another Rumkowski.

AUGUST 20, 1941

Almost everywhere there are signs of tuberculosis: it's getting worse all the time. Some people arrived this week from Warsaw, and they speak of the horrible

In the ghetto bathhouse.

situation there. Still, none of them has that dreadful pasty tubercular skin seen here. The cadavers walking around the streets give the entire ghetto that pale, musty tubercular look.

SUNDAY, AUGUST 24, 1941

The ghetto is developing grandly. Numerous new shops and factories have been organized, in addition to the ones already existing. All of it is "state property," "of the Eldest of the Jews." Hundreds of people have found jobs and things seem to improve, except for the dying and hunger, the never-ending hunger.

GHETTO DOCUMENTS

BULLETIN

July 20, 1941

THE DANGER OF AN EPIDEMIC IS GREAT

All of us remember the terrible epidemic of last summer—dysentery, typhus, other diseases from which thousands died. We had no way of saving them. Then during the last three months, 3000 Jews died of hunger and cold. Now we are threatened by a new epidemic. This one could be even more terrible than the last one, for people are weakened. They don't have the energy left to withstand its ravages. Our yards and streets are filled with refuse and garbage; the toilets overflow with excrement, and most of them are broken.

The sun is shining. The weather is spring-like, but the air stinks from the piles of garbage. Rumkowski is always boasting that he takes good care of the ghetto. What is he doing to prevent the horrible danger? What are his sanitation and health employees doing?

We Demand

1. A clean-up of yards and streets, as a matter of hygiene;
2. The repair of the toilets;
3. Increased rations for the workers to accomplish their tasks;
4. Free laundry for poor people;
5. Baths and disinfection stations for the people.

If Rumkowski does not provide these, he'll have the lives of another 3000 Jews on his conscience!

GHETTO JUSTICE

On February 16, the Chairman sentenced the two coachmen, Rosenblum and Greenspan, to six months' hard labor in prison. They were allowed a deca of bread and water per day while performing the hard labor. Their crime had been the killing of a horse that could no longer do its work. Did they deserve such a harsh sentence, which almost meant death, in that their weakened bodies could not possibly bear such punishment?

SHOPS ARE CLOSED AGAIN

On Thursday the 13th, notices were posted on tailor shop walls that the shops would be closed indefinitely for reorganization and because workers had neglected their duties. The evening before, Rumkowski called together the tailor instructors and, in his inimitable way, scolded them, threatening them for sabotaging their work, and shouting that he'd make them carry out his orders. Unfortunately, none of the instructors had the courage to protest, to throw the simple truth in his face—that it was not sabotage but a decrease in production due to his hateful ruse to make them—as weak from hunger as they were—even weaker, so that they wouldn't have the strength to fight for better conditions—conditions they needed to remain alive, rather than be destroyed by hard labor. We can truly assure him that he'll never succeed with his bag of tricks, since none of his ruses can satisfy the workers' hunger.

[*Leaflets*]

APPEAL TO THE GHETTO POPULATION

Lodz

Recent events in the ghetto have shown that the current representatives of the Jewish Community were frightened by the reaction of the hungry masses and started distributing meal coupons, with the help of dishonest delegates, as if we were beggars. That's how they hope to console us, to quiet the wronged multitude. They've even started registering workers, including matchmakers.

The masses, however, have gotten wise to our rulers' tricks. The ruling aristocracy wants to compensate the Jewish masses for the blood shed by issuing potatoes. History will eventually deal with today's parasites.

We have as much right to live as Rumkowski and Szczesliwy [the head of the Department of Food Supplies]. We don't want to die of starvation! Victory will be ours!

Here is a list of our demands:

1. Community kitchens—for everybody.

2. Collectivize the bakeries. Flour for the hungry.
3. Abolish office workers' [special] salaries.
4. Prompt and free medical care.

Lodz

To all workers and the general population!
To all the starving in the ghetto!
Enough of poverty, hunger and waiting to be allowed pennies!
We demand:

1. Regularly paid allowances! (Monthly, between the 1st and the 10th of the month.)
2. Lower prices on basic foods, and regular allotments of heating fuel at cost.
3. Those receiving allowances should not have their home expenses reduced.

We have had enough of paper promises!
Our patience is at an end!

APPEAL TO THE GHETTO POPULATION

Lodz

To the workers and the poor!

We've been cheated again. The promised 20-mark food coupons have been withdrawn.

They feed us paper promises, while our children die of starvation and cold.

We demand the promised 20-mark coupons!

We demand fuel for the winter (wood and coal)!

We demand the sale of basic foods at the prices the Community pays.

Our patience is at an end!

We will not look on impassively as our children and relatives starve!

APPEAL FROM THE COMMITTEE TO PROTECT THE JEWISH GHETTO POPULATION FROM HUNGER

Lodz

To all the starving—

Our unwanted representatives want to starve us. The facts are:

1. The allowance (12 marks) was supposed to be given out November 1, but to this day hundreds of people have not yet received it.

2. Potato coupons, which could have saved us from starvation, were withdrawn. Instead, they issued rations. This way they take our last pennies, so that we'll have nothing left with which to buy bread. They will sell the potatoes after they are no longer fit for consumption.

We therefore call on you to report to the intersection of Brzezinska and Mlynarska on December 4 at 11 a.m., to demonstrate that we would rather die by the sword than from hunger.

We call upon you for a decisive battle. Veterans, be there! We call also upon those who yesterday were among the starving and today are policemen.

Remember that the battle forced upon us will be bloody. We will not allow ourselves to be starved. We will not be bullied by work registration, for nothing will result from it. Even if something does come of it, our families will starve to death.

Enough promises!

LEON HURWITZ, LIFE IN THE LODZ GHETTO

. . . At present, in mid-August 1941, sanitary conditions in the ghetto are satisfactory. But winter isn't that far away, and there's no hope of having enough coal and wood. Even the greatest optimists predict that thousands will die this coming winter—if we live to see winter at all.

HIGH HOLY DAYS IN THE GHETTO, 1941

Outwardly, it was difficult to detect any particular sign of the upcoming holidays. Everything was quite "normal." Some people, harnessed in threes, were hauling excrement out of the ghetto. Others were dragging potatoes, cucumbers and other vegetables in the opposite direction. Little boys and girls were selling dubious home-made candies, as usual. "Just look at these sticks, big chunks, a yummy, a sweet, for only a fiver." Lines of varying length formed in front of the cooperatives. From time to time a *droshky* with this or that ghetto dignitary would pass by, like any other day. No sign whatsoever that this was *Erev* [Heb: the Eve of] Rosh Hashanah.

The holiday itself also passed quietly, unnoticed. Some prayed, others stood in line before a public kitchen, waiting for the "better, thicker" soup solemnly promised by the "Chairman" in his newspaper. But the soup was even worse and thinner than usual.

And the Chairman, too, was destined for a bitter disappointment. The ghetto's ruler was in his reception hall, accepting New Year's greetings from "his" workshops and "his" departments. His countenance was radiant, his mood excellent. He was sharing cigarettes, serving cookies and tea, as if he were a real ruler. But the celebration was suddenly cut short by a telephone call from Balut Market [i.e., the German Ghetto Administration], saying that he was to come right away.

He returned all in tears, and everyone understood immediately that a new calamity was about to befall the emaciated ghetto. By evening, when most people had finished eating their potatoes and drinking their black coffee, the news had spread that all the Jews from the Wartheland were to be resettled in our ghetto. Mainly women, children, and old people—because the men had been taken straight from Rosh Hashanah services for forced labor. Fantastic rumors were heard. The number of those who would be moved in was given at twenty, thirty, even fifty thousand.

A "western" Jewish mother arrives in the ghetto with her children.

CHAPTER FOUR

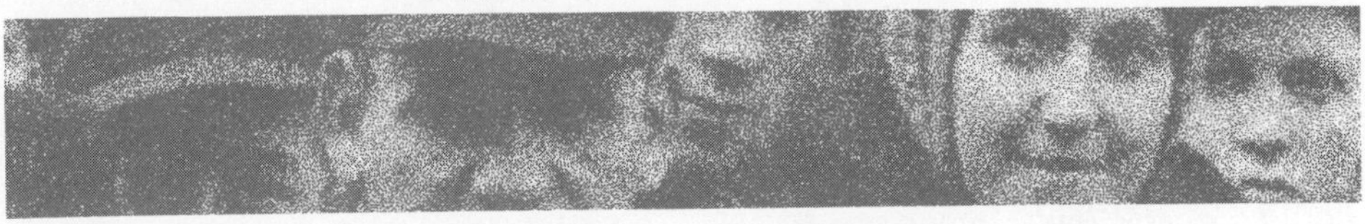

DEPORTATIONS IN

OSKAR ROSENFELD'S NOTEBOOKS

NOTEBOOK A

THE DEPORTATION FROM PRAGUE

...There were already about 50 regulations restricting the lives of Jews, but...then came the Jewish star. This was a decree from Berlin affecting Germany and Czechoslovakia. On Friday, the 18th of September 1941, all Jews appeared on the street with a gold Jewish star on their left breast. Inside the star was the word *Jude,* indeed in a lettering that was made to look like Hebrew, which made it seem even ghastlier, crasser, more Semitic, more provocative. The Czechs, though, did not react as anticipated. On the contrary. Everyone looked the other way, and one could clearly see the good will of the Czech people in their face and gestures.

With the Jewish star on their chests, Jews could not be missed in the crowd. Since thousands of Jews from the provinces were also in Prague, the impression was created that Prague was flooded with Jews, so that the Czechs would find a large-scale "de-Jewing" desirable. The Jews wandered through Prague as though, left over from the Middle Ages, they had the native population's tolerance to thank for their existence but were now ripe for disappearance. People looked at each other without inner sympathy, since all were now in the same position—worse: one made the other responsible for the phantom "Jew."

With Jew easily distinguished from non-Jew, the order was given to report to the Messepalast. No one was exempt. Patients were called out of hospital beds, the elderly out of old age homes; invalids, the blind, the dying all found their way. In the early morning, before dawn, Jews packed themselves onto the electric trams with their suitcases and backpacks. The use of cabs had been long forbidden. Beds were still warm, tables set, china and books remained in cabinets; in foyers and bedrooms there were still clothes, blankets, rugs, pictures—and waiting for it all were the hyenas, the foreigners and natives who had been notified of the Jews' departure.

One still knew nothing about how long the evacuation would endure. When the last transport left at the beginning of November, no one could say for sure what the destination was. This time the participants gave themselves up in the light of day. It was no longer necessary to keep the deportation secret. There was no longer anything unusual about Jews, with their backpacks, suitcases, bags, brass goods, bed linen, pressing into the last trolley car at the station. Among them were people who had already emigrated three times: from Berlin to Vienna, from Vienna to the southern provinces, from there to Prague, each time with the quiet hope of finally finding peace, and satisfied with the smallest little nook.

But they were permitted this little nook only for a short time. They would not be pardoned. The war against the Jews knows no peaceful end. The Jews were shut out of all occupations, violence done to their houses, their bank accounts frozen, their contact with non-Jews broken. They were not allowed to go into any park or garden or theater or cinema or public bath or train station; they could not go into a tavern. And now they themselves, their bodily presence, was to disappear from the city scene. The deportation began. Families were destroyed, marriages torn asunder, friends ripped apart, the strong ties of a lifetime ruined, spiritual life rendered non-existent in one single moment. What effort and love and devotion had assembled in the course of centuries was broken apart with the step of one foot. Collections were reduced to dust, libraries broken up, scientific work dispersed, stately homes left in complete disarray. Dogs, cats and other pets were stroked tenderly—often under the sweet gaze of the officer there to ensure the departure.

It was called taking leave.... Hundreds crouched in their apartments and could not understand "all this," as they called it. Thousands threw themselves into the confusion of packing, cleaning up, choosing things, pretending not to care, being ironic, as if everything was simply going according to the laws of the world, and therefore lamentation or complaint were out of place. More pressing were the practical matters. Since they were told that no one could take more than 50 kilograms with him, including 5 kilograms of food . . . one saw in all of the streets, especially in the Jewish quarter, Jews hunting for light, easy-to-carry bags. The city was in motion. One could feel that something never before considered, something profound, had been set in motion. A new epoch in the treatment of Jews, the solution to the Jewish question had begun. Bit by bit, 5000 Jews in this first round left old, "golden" Prague, their home, where their ancestors had lived, ordered out by the German authorities.

Among the deported were poor Jews and "rich Jews," citizens of every rank and condition, young and old. There was also an "A" group for academics: doctors, lawyers, engineers, scholars, teachers, professors, writers, actors and musicians and other Jews suspected of cultural interest. The de-Jewing of Prague was in gear. The chosen Jews, many quite removed from Judaism, even quite hostile to it, had to find their way to the Messepalast, a building that was empty at the time but which served a few times a year for commercial expositions.

Whoever stepped into this building could say his final farewell to home. The ghetto began here. . . . For three days and three nights, more than a thousand people waited in this drafty, dirty space, cautiously dipping into their provisions. Relationships were established, friendships begun. People with once-impressive names dozed on rags and jackets, happy to rest their limbs somewhere. At times one heard laughing and singing, since there were many young people, and the superficial observer could get the impression that the authorities had decided to send the Jews off with "strength through happiness."

For, it should be stated here clearly, the loss of existence, of possessions, of home, of tranquility, and concern about the next day were not enough to break their spirit. Accustomed to injury and made stronger by it, the Jews were unshakable here in their belief in liberation, in deliverance. One saw no tears, no collapse. And yet one still did not know where this was leading.

Blind, lame, dying people were brought in, the feverish from the hospitals, the elderly from old age homes. They came in, and silently judged the situation. At the same time the officials took care that everything functioned smoothly. Mrs. —— wants to commit suicide, Veronal; the Gestapo demand, "You will ensure that everyone comes through alive." There were no difficulties. All males were shaved bald—out of concern for possible infection (lice, etc.) and looked like prisoners, though it could be said that many would have gladly assumed the role of prisoners had the judge and executioner not been officials of the Third Reich. Siberia or Cayenne did not seem to us as evil an exile, for those places were geographically determined and climatically known, whereas we were going into the unknown.

Just before departure, everyone had to report in conveyor-belt fashion, with his money, papers, and house key. The next-to-last act of the show began. The order was: 1) Give up the house key. One's home was thus given over to the protectorate. One could not discern in any of the departing even a trace of pain at the loss. Take it, you who have taken our honor and possessions and existence and the meaning of our lives. The keys were given to German "purchasers" on the same day, for the most part. 2) Give up all personal documents, certificates with photographs and other identification. 3) Give up all money and gold. 4) Sign a form, the contents of which one was not allowed to read. With one's signature, one gave the Jewish authorities of Prague, i.e., the Gestapo, full power over all property left behind, without restriction. 5) Accept a police statement with the stamp: "Evacuated on. . . ."

With that, the robbery and depersonalization was complete. Nothing was left these "evacuated," except their backpacks and suitcases. Books, musical instruments, objects close to the heart, family heirlooms had to be left behind or given over to the Gestapo. Thus, poor as beggars, stripped of all rights, facing an unknown fate, five times 1000 Jews in the Messepalast went into the room for further processing. No *people* came out, only *deportees*. We marched to some train station. On the way there were the faces of the Czechs in the windows of houses, here and there passing Czechs, sometimes with sad, reflective, disturbed faces.

A railway car stood ready. One tore oneself away, went into the number corresponding to the number marked on one's bag. This was completed quickly. The field officers pushed, bayonets flashed, people pressed forward, but not a sound was heard. The doors were closed, the windows shut, no one was allowed to show himself at a window. A transport of shorn, intimidated sheep—this was the "evacuation" of Jews from Prague. The train rolled into the open. Where to? . . . Further, further. It got to be evening. Everyone was thirsty. When the train stopped in the middle of the night and a Jewish transport leader wanted to bring some water, the field soldiers hit him. There was no water. . . . The night was long. Suddenly a steel-helmet ripped open the door, in one car after another, commanding: Every man must shave and shine his shoes.

SZMUL ROZENSZTAJN, DAILY NOTES

26 SEPTEMBER

At 10 PM the train finally arrived at the Marysin depot. Women, children, and old people slowly began leaving the cars. They were taken immediately to quarters that had been readied for them and given warm meals and drink.

Their belongings were taken to a special storage area. It's worth noting, sad as it is, that a great many policemen used the opportunity to steal bread and even linen from the newcomers' packs.

In the darkness, as they came out of the train, the 920 newcomers made a frightful impression. They didn't know where they were being taken and looked around and up at the cloudy sky, in which there was not even a single star. Everything was blanketed in darkness. Exhausted, they spent their first night sleeping on straw.

DAWID SIERAKOWIAK'S DIARY

SEPTEMBER 25, 1941

Marysin will be taken over by the deportees who will arrive tomorrow. The school year has therefore been shortened.

OCTOBER 4, 1941

Today Rumkowski met with all the teachers in the ghetto. He said that because 20,000 Jews are arriving from all over Germany, he is extending the school recess now, instead of having it during the winter.

I think it's the end of schooling in the ghetto, at least for me, since I don't think I'll be a *lyceum* student, after all.

OCTOBER 9, 1941

This afternoon they read our grades. I have all excellents, except for one good in gym—the best grades of my life and I think in the entire school.

LODZ, OCTOBER 16, 1941

In the afternoon the first group of deportees from Vienna arrived in Marysin. They brought a carload of bread with them, and excellent luggage. They're dressed extremely well. Some have sons fighting on the front. There are rabbis and doctors. There are thousands of them. The same number is to arrive every day, up to 20,000. They'll probably outnumber us completely.

LODZ, OCTOBER 17, 1941

A group of Czech deportees arrived. They too had excellent luggage and carloads of bread. It's said that they asked if it would be possible to get 2-room apartments with running water. Interesting types. These west Europeans will see how people live in the German Reich. Well, the fact that they find themselves in these straits won't help us any. I still can't get work.

LODZ, OCTOBER 19, 1941
German Jews keep arriving—today from Luxembourg. There are many of them in town. They have only one yellow patch on the left breast with the word "*Jude*." They're dressed very well—you can see that they haven't lived in Poland. They're buying out everything in town, and prices have doubled.

LODZ, OCTOBER 20, 1941
We went to visit the Czechs; there are some fine fellows among them, and among the Luxembourgers too. It's great talking to them. Almost all of them know German very well. They've had it so good that they're quite surprised at the filth here.

A new group arrived today, from Vienna or Berlin. Almost all are Zionists (outwardly, anyhow), but there are Reds everywhere. They're intelligent, clean, pleasant and open. It's nice to be among them.

LODZ, OCTOBER 22, 1941
The German Jews are still arriving—from Frankfurt/Main, Cologne, more from Prague and Vienna. All are "big fish," or so they seem.

SPEECH BY CHAIM RUMKOWSKI

TUESDAY, OCTOBER 14, 1941
The purpose of this meeting is to report on the present state of the ghetto. This report will not be complete, but I want witnesses who will know and remember what has been said here. I've never taken the attitude of the street into account, and I do not intend to do so in the future.

I'd like to indicate the danger we were in, what was done about it, and what the situation is now. I know the street will turn my words around and put sentences in my mouth which you are not going to hear from me. They are going to call me murderer and condemn me for accepting this situation.

Regarding the evacuation of Jews from the provinces, I want to say that the matter had been on the agenda for quite a while. I was told to take them into Litzmannstadt Ghetto. In response, I came up with a plan to create a large ghetto near the town of Tuszyn, where some 30,000 Jews would be concentrated, and then to convert it into a labor town. I also declared I was ready to take this ghetto under my protection and to guarantee its budget. I would send my trusted people there, and I myself would go there once or twice a week. After much negotiating, my plan was not accepted.

Not long ago there were discussions about merging Ozorkow [a town on the western outskirts of Lodz] with the Litzmannstadt Ghetto. I would build factories there which would work for the Litzmannstadt Ghetto. I proposed to the Ozorkow Jewish Community that I would have control over their economy and finances. I must stress that this had a good chance, but the Ozorkow Jews spoiled it.

When the matter of the provincial Jews came up, I was against it at first. So I was asked, Do you really refuse your fellow Jews? And I answered, I do want to have them, but you must enlarge the ghetto. All I got back as a result was the orphanage in Marysin. As you know, the first transport of evacuated Jews came from Leslau [Wloclawek], and the later ones from Lubraniec, Brzesc Kujawski, Kowel, and Chodecz—2900 persons altogether, women, children, old people. The order came from above.

And now it's time for the Jews from the old Reich. They are being deported from various places because their homes have been taken and given to Germans whose homes were destroyed by Allied bombings. These homeless Jews will arrive soon; their number is estimated at 20,000.

Second, the Gypsies. We are forced to take about 5000 Gypsies into the ghetto. I've explained that we cannot live together with them. Gypsies are the sort of people who can do anything. First they rob and then they set fire and soon everything is in flames, including your factories and materials. So they began talking about a separate area for the Gypsies, and I agreed to that. . . . Yesterday I received the order to clean up a part of the ghetto where the Gypsies are going to live.

As if this were not enough, I received a third order: to register everyone 15 to 60 years old, listing where each person works, what their earnings are, and how large their families. You should know that there are now about 40,000 people employed in factories. I estimate that we're able to put another ten to fifteen thousand to work. But there are still more able-bodied persons without any sort of employment. I want and I have to protect them from being taken for forced labor.

Because of this problem, I've invited representatives of the ghetto's orthodox circles to this meeting. There are many religious people, young and old, among us—who are jobless and not needed. In addition, there is this danger: studying the Talmud. I'm worried that the orthodox youth, the fanatics, will bring about a calamity with their studying the Talmud. I want you to understand me correctly. I am not against religious instruction. On the contrary, before the war I was among the founders of the *yeshivot* and the *Talmud Torahs* [Heb: religious schools]. But now, when informing on a secret *Talmud Torah* has become the right thing to do, I must stop it at any price, even if only for a short time.

I can easily imagine what might happen if an inspection comes to the *Gerer shtibl* [Yid: house of prayer of the Ger-Chassidim] on Marynarska Street. Look at those fanatics, at their attire, their appearance. I will force them to change this. They absolutely must cut their earlocks and shave off their beards, and shorten their clothes. And I want witnesses among you here, the orthodox, that the "free" Rumkowski is not to blame.

I will find employment for these young people. There is no dearth of projects regarding new factories. We will have to make room for the 23,000 newcomers and for those who have been removed from the area we must give to the Gypsies. I would gladly get rid of several thousand individuals from the underworld. I have detailed lists of these fellows, but to date I haven't done anything about it.

As to the schools, I'll have to declare a school holiday for two months. I do this with pain in my heart. My last consolation, the schools, will close for now. But I will make every effort that this golden thread not be cut off. . . . The school buildings are to become temporary quarters for the new arrivals.

I ask you to tell your relatives and friends that because of the shrinking of the ghetto, it's now in their best interest to take their own kin into their larger apartments. It will be much worse if my Housing Department sends them total strangers to live with. The empty houses will be given to the homeless new arrivals or will be converted into factories.

I demand you tell your friends and others not to loiter in the streets. Do not create the impression that there are too many of us here in the ghetto.

SHLOMO FRANK, FROM A DIARY

19 OCTOBER [1941]

Today 1000 deportees from Vienna arrived in the ghetto. Among the new arrivals are physicians, engineers, professors, famous chemists, dental technicians, once-prominent merchants, several priests from converted families, and twenty Christian women, who have come along with their husbands and children. The Viennese Jews have brought a lot of food and other goods. They said that between Vienna and the Polish border they traveled in second-class railway cars. They were treated well. They say that most of the Viennese population sympathized with them. Some Viennese women cried openly and asked good God to let them see each other again soon. But as soon as they entered Poland, there was a change of guards, and with it good relations ceased. The farther they traveled, the worse their treatment.

21 OCTOBER

Today before noon, 1050 Jews from Prague arrived in the ghetto. They were all in good spirit and replied with a friendly *shalom* to the greetings of the Jewish police at the Marysin station. Some comforted us with quotations from the Prophets, predicting an imminent end to the war.

22 OCTOBER

Today another transport of 1200 Jews from Vienna and its surrounding towns arrived. Most are old people, many of them sick. They looked like they were taken only yesterday from hospitals and old age homes. The transport arrived in the evening. The streets were dark and gloomy, and in this darkness the old, broken Viennese Jews marched step by step, with heavy knapsacks on their arms, dejected and oppressed. One of them, Maurice Kellerbach, told us that among the deportees he saw a Jewish baron from Vienna. Maybe he is already here but has not revealed his identity.

23 OCTOBER

Today a transport of Jews arrived from Frankfurt. At their arrival four men were found missing. The transport list showed 1200 names, but only 1196 were accounted for. Almost all held up well. They greeted us with a bright *"Shalom, Yehudim"* [Heb: Peace, Jews], joked, patted backs, exhorted us to persevere, not to surrender, not to despair. "Courage lost is everything lost." They described dramatic scenes on the eve of the deportation from Frankfurt. German neighbors brought them cookies and other food. Some women cried. Expressions of sympathy were heard at the farewell. Some women prayed to God that he protect the Jews and bring them back to their old home.

24 OCTOBER

Today another 1000 persons arrived from Prague. All deportees were in good shape. Among them are 300 lawyers, 26 physicians, 30 engineers, and many other professionals.

25 OCTOBER

Today 560 Jews from Luxembourg arrived at the Marysin station. They were all beside themselves with bitterness, pain and grief. They spoke of bad experiences during their trip. They rode in guarded and locked cars. Anyone stepping out of the car was immediately punished. There were various kinds of punishment. Some had to run around the train 25 times. Others had to yell *"Heil Hitler"* or *"Verrüchter Jude"* [Ger: accursed Jew]. And others were severely beaten.

While still in Luxembourg, they were treated quite well. The population regretted that the Jews were being deported. People brought Jewish neighbors apples, dried prunes, biscuits, and other food. Some accompanied the deportees to the railroad station with tears in their eyes.

27 OCTOBER

Today 1000 Jews arrived from Berlin. Almost 90 percent of them are old people who can barely stand on their feet. Many were bent over under the weight of their knapsacks. They were allowed to take as much as they could carry. They traveled in first and second class cars up until the Polish border; then they were moved to other cars.

28 OCTOBER

The recent newcomers from Germany have been receiving letters from relatives still at home. The contents of some of these letters are interesting.

A letter from Berlin: "You should know that Uncle is very sick. We expect a catastrophe any day. The curfew hours have changed: Jews may remain outdoors until 5 P.M., Christians until 8 P.M. The situation here has changed very much. Your apartment is still unoccupied."

A letter from Cologne: "It's possible that we will also have to leave our *Heimat* [Ger: homeland]. We expect this any day. The local people envy our being able to leave this hell. They are very sympathetic to us. Don't give up, brothers. In all, we're doing fine."

A letter from Hamburg: "We can't stop thinking of you. Quite possible that we'll see you again soon."

A letter from Vienna: "We have packed our things. We're now waiting for the order. We believe that all Jews will have to leave Vienna, even Community officials. The transports are going to Lublin and Cracow, some to Russia. We envy you. You have a place to live. You know where you are, while we face persecution and terror. We do have enough to eat. Food is no problem. We wish that other problems could be as easily solved."

The writers of these letters are unaware that their relatives here have no place to sit, to rest, to sleep. . . . A small fraction, perhaps only 10%, have found decent accommodations. The rest are in great despair. They live in hunger and poverty and cold. They are plagued by sickness. They are totally unable to adjust to the dirty, overcrowded ghetto. Many are dying, and they are inconsolable. Not a day passes without a suicide.

OSKAR ROSENFELD'S NOTEBOOKS

NOTEBOOK A

The thousand marched, automatically. We were in an unknown country, a foreign landscape. One's heart was not lifted by the looks of these people, the streets, and houses, although everyone knew it was to the benevolence of this place that we were being consigned. People walked as though in a trance.

Suddenly, we stood before a gate that led into a school-like building. People turned and pushed themselves through the narrow entry and up to the school rooms. . . . In each room about 60 people slept, staying there during the day. . . .

The first days went by without trouble. One did not yet think about tomorrow. Each was given 1 loaf of bread for 1 week. In the morning black coffee—that is, warm, brown water. At mid-day, local girls brought tubs of soup from the kitchen: warm water filled with some kind of greens, carrots, and cabbage. The only meal of the day. In the evening came another small cup of coffee, that is, warm brown water. However, since most still had provisions—white bread, jam, dried meat, noodles, chocolate, cookies, etc.—they did not find the shortcomings so crass. Washing was difficult. One had to go down to the courtyard to use the well, since the waterpipes in the hall were inadequate and only for the sick and the children. (Further: going to the latrines in the snow and cold. Toilet paper a rarity.)

Gradually, the provisions came to an end. . . . One began to sell clothing and shoes to the natives: to undersell, that is. For the prices of these things lagged far behind those of food. One pair of shoes = one loaf of bread. The physical and social decline set in. Greedily, people pushed themselves to the mid-day soup.

Children lay siege to the school in which we were housed. Took soup from us. For the stomachs of many of the newcomers could not hold so much water. Children waited for hours in the courtyards and by the windows, let the bowls and pots they brought be filled with the warm soup. One slice of bread was the greatest surprise for them. Dire need cried out from their eyes. Once they had been given such a gift, they always came back. Impossible to get away from. Not an iota of shame left in them. No longer creatures with a soul. They do not speak, just look at you. You cannot withstand this gaze. It gnaws at the pit of your stomach. Your belly growls, your gums cry out to be moistened. You have an appetite. But here in the eyes of these children you see for the first time in your life what had seemed like an empty concept, something you knew only as legend: Hunger.

We read of dire hunger in Russia, of millions starving in China—newspaper headlines, sensations for the spoiled European. Now finally, in its naked, inescapable brutality: Hunger! But the hunger of others. We will save ourselves. Tomorrow will be better. Those there, the Poles, our fellow Jews, have already withstood "this" for two years. They have better nerves. But we must help one another and we will find a way out. How long? The day after tomorrow we'll be out, everything will be fine. So the days went. The nights had a different face.

One hoped to get through the nights as quickly as possible. They frightened the hungry, though morning brought nothing but bustling noises, running back and forth, and the "black coffee." It was not until later, it was only gradually, that one wished for night, long nights, darkness in which one could ponder, wonder, murmur, sigh, and whisper words that no one could understand but the whisperer himself.

THE FIRST HUNGER

Worn out by idleness, tired, the thin lukewarm coffee in their empty stomachs, 1000 people crept onto the hard wooden planks. First they had to put their things somewhere—clothes, suitcases, rags, cooking things—to make room for sleeping. Squeezing together as much as they could, free movement was impossible. Children babbled, cried, whined; the sick people made the noises of their diseases: coughed, wheezed, scratched, moaned, sobbed. The creaking of the boards and animal-like sounds filled the night. The breathing of so many hundreds of people created so much warmth that one did not freeze, even on the coldest winter nights, but one had to go into the courtyard for fresh air.

A little unpleasantness comes over the body. One's belly becomes loose, gradually sinks in. Hesitantly, almost fearfully, one runs one's hand over the restless body, bumps into bones, ribs, runs over one's legs and finds oneself, feels suddenly that one was quite recently fatter, fleshier—and is amazed at how quickly the body deteriorates. . . . With such considerations, the word "ghetto" spread itself above us and laid itself on the brain, forcing one to despair of finding a cure. One had to be careful, parsimonious with oneself. Necessity and the force of the situation gave strength to the weak, thoughtfulness to the rash, a sense of parsimony to the dim-witted. The nights ran, the days walked.

Many Jews from Prague and Vienna were housed in buildings previously used as ghetto schools.

Weakness in the limbs took over. For many it was torture to climb one or two flights. They did not know where the weakness came from. They assumed the monotony of life had made them apathetic, and that it was foolish to use energy for bodily things. It was when they first noticed that their clothes were loosening, their shirts becoming wider around their necks, skirts and blouses ballooning around their bodies, that they began to occupy themselves with this discovery—at first, laughing ironically, warmly, showing each other the missing fat and flesh, even making fun of their deformities.

One still held oneself upright. It was a matter of character to hold out. The children got hollow cheeks, thin legs, rings under their eyes. One pushed crumbs one had saved into their mouths. When there was no other way, one got sick. By lying down one could bring oneself back. One person gave another the advice to "lie down" for a few days. A few days of quiet and then it would get back to normal. But one evening a man broke down on the stairs. People brought him to his place. The doctor came, gave him an injection. It did not help. He died. His legs were swollen, blood clots visible on his arms and ankles. One called this: wasted by hunger. Here it was called: loss of strength.

This case disquieted people, made a few things clearer. One began blaming people and things, actions taken and not taken. The hungry were led to do themselves injustice, each reading his own fate in the eyes of the others, seeing another fall without recognizing himself. People amused themselves with past pleasures . . . and with self-incrimination. You were an idiot not to save yourself in time, not to recognize what threatened you, not to be decisive enough to abandon everything and get away to a place without ghettos and soldiers. But afterward, hunger set in anew and brought all these thoughts about the past to an end. One either had to help oneself or waste away, decay, go under. . . . Thus it was that winter.

DOING NOTHING

One "hungered around" the whole day. . . . There are no books. There are, except for a harmonica, no musical instruments. There are no gramophones, no radios. There are no spaces where one can sit and have a pleasant conversation. Uninterrupted movement. Hurrying, running, pushing, shouting, tears, pushing. Here and there light work, when one removes the muck from in front of the doors, cleans the halls, carries the soup kettle. But a division of the day, an alternation of activities corresponding to the rhythm of one's will, does not exist. One is not out of work or unwilling to work; one stands outside the laws of the cosmos. . . . We vegetate, burdens to ourselves. Idleness has eaten its way into our boundaries and gradually makes us shy away from everything. . . .

Lawyers, engineers, political commentators, teachers, painters, musicians,

cultural workers stand watch in entryways, clean latrines, transport muck, when they do not have the luck to be put to work as doctors, judges, police, ghetto bureaucrats. But whatever the fate of individuals, almost 25,000 people go hungry and lean on the hallway walls and courtyard doors. They wander aimlessly from one plank bed to another, talk into the world—for none of the things one speaks of has real worth; it all hangs in the air. There is no honor, no responsibility, no being held to one's word. There is nothing through which one could become guilty. One word, one concept, one symbol confronts everybody: bread! For bread one would be a hypocrite, a fanatic, a wretch. Give me bread and you are my friend. . . .

At home, doing nothing was associated with relaxing. . . . Here it is nothing but moping around, which does not become a vice because there is no place for vice in the ghetto. One sells one's last shoe, one's last shirt, but one does not debase oneself through crime against those responsible for the ghetto. Even if now and then extreme need seduces one to petty theft, a quick grab into someone else's goods, still the ghetto is free of violence and ostracism. The sabbath finds the poorest of Jews in prayers. On the High Holy Days hungry, collapsing

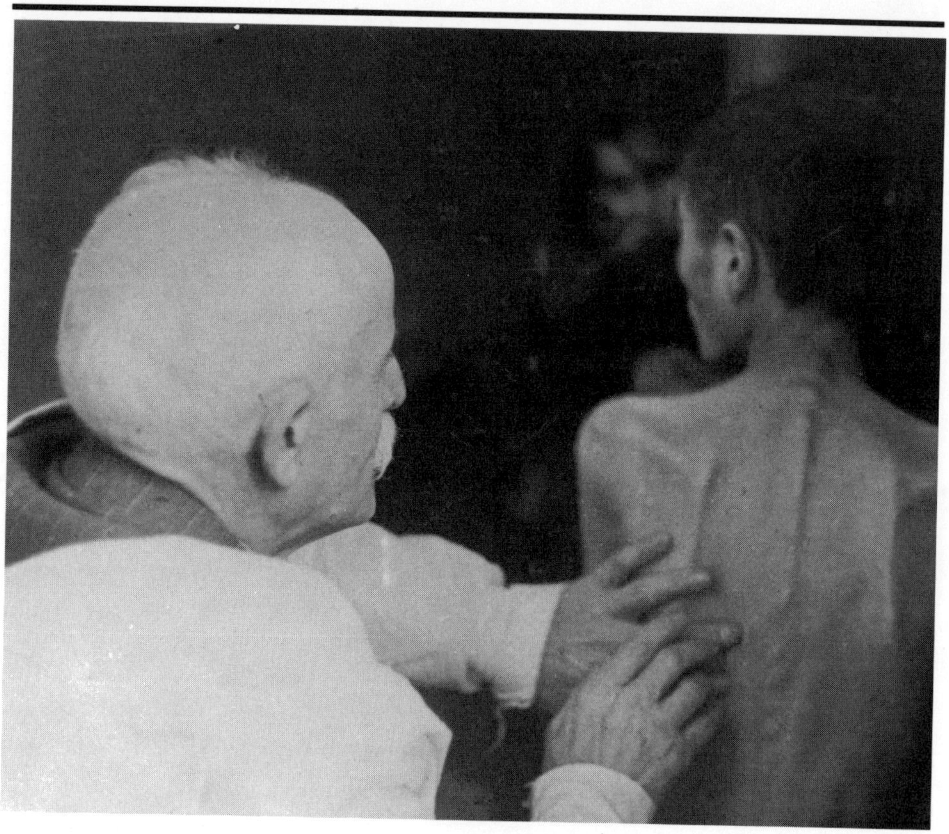

beings, lumped together, press their way into houses of prayer, and the ardor of people praying has not suffered under the pressure of hunger and cold.

UNCLEANLINESS

People had changed in three months of hunger. Almost all had bent backs, shaky legs. Illnesses slipped their way in. Pneumonia even in young people. Thousands tossed on their plank beds, deprived of sleep, since their bones hurt when they lay down, and dreamed of food. . . .

Every day, here and there, someone died. Sometimes it was three, sometimes seven. One did not concern oneself with corpses. Warmth, laughter, humming in pure indifference to fate was unconstrained by a dead or dying neighbor. A pretty young girl shows her displeasure when someone carrying a corpse disturbs her in the moving of her lipstick across her lips. In some all restraint is already gone. The human brute seeks to satisfy its desires. There is still a tiny bit of dignity and self-respect, a residue of respect for the past and for family reputation. Those who were once highly placed retain some sense of proportion and bearing, but these are pressed into decline.

The weather snows and rains. Water cannot be pumped: the well is broken, the latrine flooded. One tries to bring order to things. A woman bumps into the wall of the latrine, spilling her soup. A crippled child, standing nearby, throws himself to the ground and slurps the soup up from the dirty snow. Airplanes thunder above. Suddenly someone crashes into the courtyard, and a few dozen people hope for good news. "The bread ration will be cut back." Two pregnant women fight, uncertain why.

A rag is missing, a rag to wipe up with. One man wants to clean, another dislikes the balls of dust. Both honorable men. Meaningless hate. Both from good Jewish homes. A blind rabbi stands next to them, hears the swearing and the dirty words. He feels his way to the two of them. His whole body shakes.

"Oh, how hunger has brought down my poor people. A piece of bread, a few decagrams of fat could help you. And there father stands against son, brother against brother, friend against friend—because we have distanced ourselves from the commandments? *Ja, ja.* Had we remained the holy people, things would be different for us today. Oh, my beloved Jewish people, how bitterly you have disappointed me."

Behind the rabbi, a woman takes a piece of margarine out of a dirty brown paper, gets a knife and begins to spread it on a slice of bread. It is not time to eat. It is afternoon. An older woman stands next to her. Her stomach growls loudly. At the sight of the margarine, she cries out, staggering. An hysterical attack. She must be calmed down. The doctor is called, gives her a harmless injection. The woman falls asleep from weakness. The beginning of serious hunger. Before starvation no one can sleep. The body is in tumult, the nerves tighten, one is oversensitive to noise. So said a man who was saved just before starving, a rare case.

The Viennese and Frankfurters fell one after another. Those from the Prague deportation held on longer. They were tougher; their constitutions and optimism enabled them to better withstand the circumstances. They understood, too, how to integrate themselves into the tempo and organization of the ghetto. Swarms of Czechs serve as doctors, police, workers. And they find the Slavic terrain more comfortable.

Sicknesses are increasing. We hear of spotted fever, and that quarantines have been instituted. One cannot learn the details. Symptoms of illness abound. After decades of practice, doctors finally have the opportunity to see cases of severe hunger in massive numbers. Three months of undernourishment have put thousands in danger of dying.

"We don't talk about eating," one of the many women going hungry once said. Hungry people who talk themselves into the illusion that they've been eating well often show signs of serious nervous disorders and become quite wild at night. One evening we tell stories of clothes, on another stories of travels, still another of books we've read. We avoid every bodily strain. We must measure every step; otherwise we quickly become tired. The body is no longer up to long walks. There are pains in the shoulder-blades and limbs. Many who cannot sleep use remedies they've brought from home—Shanodoray, Sedomit, Quadronok, Luminal, and Bromoral, here and there even Veronal—but the morning weighs that much heavier on them. They cannot shut out hunger and the sickness that comes with hunger.

NOTEBOOK 11

A few months of this misery have transformed us more than did many years in the past. Not that hidden instincts of an evil nature were immediately exposed and unleashed, but we learned that in order to live, a few spoonsful of thick soup were worth more than all our ideologies and philanthropic feelings and prayers. But there was one thing we did not yet know: calming our nerves is as important as eating.

I enter the hospital. Some man yells, "Oy, Papa, Mama, give me a piece of bread." I lose my temper because I can't sleep. I bellow at him, "If you don't keep quiet, I'll come and throw you into the yard." Next morning, he's dead, having breathed his last. I'm deeply sorry, and ashamed. . . .

Baron Hirsch comes into the hospital. How meaningless everything his forebears created, if he starved to death in the Jewish ghetto. . . .

Gutmann the artist is painting the ghetto as seen from the schoolroom window. He's happy, rapturous over the beauty of the bleak scenery. He's not yet familiar with despair. He still has some provisions (confections, crackers, jam, goose fat, a few other things). Earlier characters come to mind here, showing how our original illusions of "We'll persevere" fell apart.

Victor Deutsch has that vital spark that so many lack. After a couple of days or so with us, he knows where to get the best and cheapest meatballs. Having no money, he sells something, borrows a hot water bottle overnight, exchanges it for a few lumps of sugar, gets a meat ball out of that—and something to smoke. People who never smoked before are doing so now. Croatian cigarettes.

The coffee is often late in coming and therefore cold, so that it's not even fit for washing with, and we'd sooner go into the yard and wash in the fountain.

Some young women also congregate there, loosening their blouses despite the cold weather. Not particularly shy. Everyone is getting hardened to conditions. Nearby is a long plank where people are squatting like birds on telegraph wires, and just past that are the refuse dumps—potato peels, rotting vegetables, fetid pieces of trash, moldy bread. Children search through this trash, crawling and scratching around, fishing something out and sticking it in their pocket or in a pot.

The water closet. *Tanach* [Heb: Scripture] used for the first time, Heine's poems.

The first ghetto diseases: toenail pains, emaciation, inability to sit down, pain in the coccyx. Colossal row because some woman brought in a scrap of bread when it was not mealtime and is eating cheese with it. After the uproar, talk about family. Wife somewhere, son somewhere else, daughter also elsewhere—everything torn apart! They don't know that we are here. Wherever they are, what are they doing? What do they get to eat? "In New York you can get a gigantic sandwich for a nickel: sardines, sauerkraut, cheese, on white bread with olives." The gastric juices begin to stir.

"Stop it, such talk is dangerous!"

NOTEBOOK A

A hellish method for letting people die gradually: giving them worthless cabbage instead of more valuable vegetables. Indeed, posing as well-intended nourishment, a scientific procedure for sapping a whole community of its energy. Along with the cold, having to relieve oneself in open latrines, pulling wagons and carts like animals with powerless arms, sleeping nights on the damp ground, the organism soon has to give up putting its heart into service.

Water and vegetables: the soup stock, the foundation of nourishment! No prison inmate would be satisfied, could long endure, with such a nothing soup. The caricature of a soup—a few grains of barley floating in warm water—appeared as the essence of hunger. One drank, ate, slurped, gurgled the soup and used it to brutally suppress any feeling of hunger. The stomach was filled for a short time, but nourishment did not occur.

The density of people in the living spaces, the lack of soap and water, the impossibility of keeping oneself clean and of changing one's underwear often, the various symptoms of malnourishment and the stubborn indifference of the elderly to caring for the body have given rise to the first skin diseases, mostly due to parasites. The doctors diagnose these as different kinds of eczema, boils, swellings that often lead to gangrene.

NOTEBOOK 11

A bit of sunshine, harbinger of spring. But cold at night, 15 below zero [Centigrade]. During these brief intervals, when one isn't thinking about eating, memories pour in, upsettingly, but finally quiet down as they tire one out and make it easier to fall asleep. One keeps on thinking of one's youth and the mistakes for which one must atone—in the ghetto.

"If my Zionism had been real, I'd be in the Land of Israel now."

"If my Bolshevism had been real, I'd be in Moscow now." And on and on.

These self-reproaches lead nowhere. One no longer belongs to the world.

We are dead to the world. The world has forsaken us. We are lost, but we won't surrender. . . .

On Plac Koscielny, remnants of movie posters printed in German. We endeavor to reconstruct what they say. Names of movie stars—and then quite hidden: "Broadway 1939!" Do we hear jazz, singers, see a revue, the Rockettes? What a dream! How absurd. Will anything like that happen ever again? We talk about it, without using a single "dirty" word. Sex and sensuality have dropped into oblivion. . . .

A young fellow, Professor Hart's nephew, has come into the ghetto from Prague, voluntarily, on account of some pretty young lady. He goes out walking with her, looking for an empty house. There he steals his first kiss since entering the ghetto. . . .

By degrees I look into the depths of the ghetto, not just its face. Here are hundreds, no, a few thousand people who regard their activities in the offices, bakeries, kitchens, storage dumps as normal and legitimate. They are concerned about their professions. It's hard to ascertain whether their innermost hearts are not involved in the things they try to forget. Or have they resigned themselves to their fate? They laugh, plan, and make do for weeks on end.

I try, mentally, to expand the limits of my existence. I idealize myself into the cosmos, an intellectual pursuit which eases me for a while, drives away my despair. I merge with the sun, the moon, the stars, God. Nothing can harm me. I feel the millennia rushing past me. I can read Spinoza, what good fortune, and I discover a pretty Zionist interest.

SZMUL ROZENSZTAJN, DAILY NOTES

SUNDAY, 9 NOVEMBER

This afternoon Chairman Rumkowski visited two shelters for the newcomers from the Old Reich. . . . The Prague I group has the best of the shelters, if only because its premises are sufficiently large and airy. In addition, special plank beds have been installed in all rooms and corridors. It houses 1150 people. Work is being completed on the kitchen, where all residents of this and perhaps also other shelters will receive their meals and coffee. It seems the shelter will stay open for a good while because its occupants are reluctant to leave it and lose all the conveniences they have here. And yet, despite its spaciousness, it is overcrowded, the plank beds are stacked two high, and the aisles are narrow.

Much worse is the shelter for the Jews from Luxembourg, where some 500 people live in four rooms of modest size. There are no plank beds, not even chairs. Everyone sleeps on the floor, together with their few belongings.

. . . After visiting the shelters, the Chairman met with the leaders of the Prague I transport. He spoke as follows:

"My first test with regard to the newcomers from the Old Reich will be made with the Prague I group, and if it proves successful it will be applied to all the other groups.

"First of all, by tomorrow you should submit a detailed list of all the people in the group, giving their age, profession, etc. Since rooms are so overcrowded that it's impossible to move around, I'll try to move out some 150 people, so that the group will not be larger than 1000. That way you'll get two empty rooms where you'll be able to congregate in the evenings, leaving your children and weaker people to sleep in peace. The 150 will be old and infirm people, for whom special quarters are being prepared.

"I know it's very hard to live on bread and soup alone. I will, therefore, include the people in this group in the roster of permanent ghetto inhabitants, so that tomorrow they'll have the same rights as every other Jew in the ghetto. The group will be entitled to the food ration the rest of the population received on November 3.

"I want you to develop a spirit of communal living, according to the principle of 'one for all, all for one.' I have received your money from the authorities at the rate of 100 marks per person. From this sum, I've paid each of you 25 marks, and the balance will be opened for your group, in which I'll keep this balance, plus the wages your people receive at their workplaces, plus whatever money is received from the savings accounts you left behind.

"On the other hand, you will be charged for the food delivered to your kitchen and for supplementary food rations. You'll receive a collective food card for groceries, bread and vegetables. You'll also receive a ration of meat, sausage, butter and margarine. This will mean better nourishment for all of you. You'll be able to have meat three times a week (a weekly ration of 20 decagrams per person), in addition to sausage. . . .

"In regard to your wages, two thirds go to the ghetto treasury and will be credited to your account. The remaining third will go to workers for their private expenses. . . . I will also arrange a milk ration for your children."

At the end, the Chairman told the group leaders that clothes should not be hung on nails in the walls, because lice are brought into the rooms this way, which is absolutely unacceptable.

SPEECH BY CHAIM RUMKOWSKI

20 DECEMBER 1941

"ONLY UNDESIRABLE ELEMENTS WILL LEAVE"

[*Rumkowski made the following remarks after a concert at the House of Culture, to which a select group of ghetto administrators and factory supervisors had been invited.*]

I have not spoken publicly for some time. Lately, there have been few events significant enough to require my comments. But now, while we celebrate Chanukah, black clouds are gathering over the ghetto. It's no wonder that people are becoming highly agitated in anticipation of a new calamity. At the same time not all ghetto residents realize how firm the principle is that "everyone has the right to live." There are still those among us who'd like to abolish this principle and indeed their actions make it impossible for others to live.

Today, as in the past, the issue is one of finding a rational solution to the problems in distributing food. Whenever food is distributed, I try to provide, in the best way possible, for the largest number of people, so that no one in the ghetto goes hungry. Therefore, a reform of the public kitchens is now of the utmost concern. Our experience has been that they have not satisfactorily fulfilled their assignment. For the most part, the managers' primary goal has been profit.

As their [the public kitchens'] use by the community at large became widespread, the importance of the housewife was utterly diminished. Today all rations are supplied to the kitchens, and that is the end of it—the feeding of the family is someone else's worry. It happened in other times, too, among rich and poor alike, that the lady of the house neglected her own kitchen. It's a great social evil. Here in the ghetto, even if the lady of the house does use the public kitchen, she ought to take a stronger interest in her own house, rather than send her husband and children out with a soup bowl.

Since the situation regarding fuel has noticeably improved this year, I've decided to take this propitious moment to convince the ghetto population to cook at home, and for this purpose I am ordering the distribution of a special ration of briquettes. I must emphasize that the food supply is not all that bad. I have definite guarantees that we'll receive large quantities of potatoes.

I would stress, as strongly as possible, that the solution to the most pressing of the ghetto's problems—including having peace—lies in the ghetto's getting work. There are many who laugh at this basic assumption of mine. Legions of

Weighing and serving portions in a public kitchen.

shirkers have ridiculed the need to work. "Why should we work? Isn't it simpler to live from black marketeering and profiteering?"

Some time ago I decided to increase public assistance. I increased relief payments by fifty percent. At the same time I ordered that all who receive such payments and are of appropriate age should work 14 days a month. And what happened? People simply began boycotting this order. Those called to work claimed they were being victimized, forgetting that relief payments are derived from the labor of all the ghetto residents, and that in a large family the recipient gets even more than an important office worker. I introduced work cards because of my conviction that a work card proves one's right to live in the ghetto. A work card is the passport which guarantees your peace.

Now I wish to say a few words to the representatives of the ghetto's new residents. It was not easy to accept another 23,000 people into this incredibly overcrowded ghetto. We weren't interested in what you brought with you. We opened our arms to all of you. We shared all that we had—food and shelter. More, we couldn't give. Unfortunately, not everyone appreciated our good intentions. I don't deny there are many people of good will among the new arrivals, but there is a large percentage of scoundrels, too. Recently, thanks to my censors at the post office, I've learned that certain individuals have money sent to them at the addresses of older ghetto residents, so that they don't have to turn over the two-thirds they would owe to the community institutions which support them. And the newcomers scheme against working.

The community kitchens supplied by the Department of Provisions are famous for cooking the worst meals in the ghetto. I don't know what my friend Neftalin, who is in charge of the newcomers, assigns to them, but I do know that the disbursements are large. I'm also told that the newcomers ignore the requirement that they sell their furs. I will be forced to have my Special Unit apply pressure. There is no getting out of it. Of course, I'd rather be in the position to give every Jew a fur.

Now I must discuss the fight against crime. Neither the ghetto court nor the special court seems to have been up to this task. I myself am at a loss to understand how to get rid of the criminals. Even deportations don't scare them. This rabble multiplies like mushrooms after a rain. I see no other way than to send this undesirable element out of the ghetto. Only in this way will we eradicate this evil for good. Besides, if I don't do it, someone else will. . . . I have the courage to admit this is my position. I argued against deportaions, but my arguments came out rather weak vis-à-vis the deciding factors, who asked me, "Whom do you defend? Bandits, thieves who rob the poor ghetto community?"

On the basis of my authority and the ghetto's autonomy, I received permission to have the selection for deportation done by us alone, and at the same time I was able to have the total number reduced by half, from 20,000 to 10,000. A special commission made up of my most trusted associates is now compiling lists of candidates. I was promised that in exchange for those deported, about 10,000 skilled artisans and workers will be sent here. Should this promise come true, I'll be able to open new enterprises for the new work force. In addition to criminals, I also intend to send out those who received rations but ignored their work assignments. I have reports that out of 100 relief recipients who were called for work, fewer than twenty showed up. These saboteurs will be shipped out! I will also send out the speculators who are buying up the goods brought in by newcomers. I've ordered the arrest of anyone trying to influence the commission on behalf of someone else. That person will share the fate of the one he was trying to protect, and the same fate awaits any member of the commission who allows such interference.

I ask the entire population to understand the difficult requirements of the present time and to remain calm and restrained.

[At this point Rumkowski asked his personal secretary to read the Yiddish translation of the decree, published in the day's *Litzmannstadter Zeitung,* establishing harsh penalties for attempts at sabotage, resistance to authority, and the like. Rumkowski then continued:]

With this new decree, terrible punishment is ordered for stealing even a spool of thread or damaging a machine. I always try to blunt the sharp edge of such decrees but this time everyone will have to be extremely careful. One individual could create a calamity for the whole ghetto. No politicking—the walls have ears. This warning is especially directed at the new arrivals. You talk too much. If our hand is forced, there will be arrests. Not even the title of privy councillor will protect you. All titles are worthless today. A lot of you have a negative attitude toward work. You tell yourselves, why should we work if we can sell things or live off the money we have. I will teach you how to work and how to behave properly. I will cure you of your impudence.

In our hospitals, which we established and in which we take pride, there is a shortage of medicine. Unfortunately, there are cases when patients and even personnel steal drugs and meals. I am going to institute searches at the hospital exits, just as we have in the factories.

I'd give my life for the safety of the decent people who want to work in peace. I will do anything for our youth. A housewife is as important to me as an administrative employee. But I will not tolerate parents who let their children sell cigarettes and candy in the street. Such parents will find themselves and their families on the deportation lists. I will not take pity on those who do harm to the ghetto, because the ghetto can count on no one's sympathy. I am going to teach the Jewish population to have respect for a Jewish administration, which must be respected as seriously as German institutions.

I shall try hard to re-open the schools as soon as possible. My heart bleeds when I see children roaming the streets, without a school to go to. It keeps me from sleeping at night.

Administrators who are hiding goods they're supposed to sell to the community will be removed immediately from their posts, and the goods confiscated. Connections will not help. Let anyone who is hiding anything surrender it immediately, for his own and the ghetto's best interests. The ghetto's expenses keep growing. For example, we have to take care of 4000 old people recently arrived from Germany.

I will do everything possible for the survival of the ghetto, for the well-being of decent people who want to work in peace, and I will give the trouble-makers what they deserve.

THE CHRONICLE OF THE LODZ GHETTO

WHAT THE GHETTO WAS TALKING ABOUT IN DECEMBER [1941]

All local sensations were, in one stroke, reduced to nothing, swept aside, and deprived of all interest, becoming unreal, a sound and fury signifying nothing.... All this was caused by a single sentence composed of a mere five words: *"The Chairman is getting married."*

Probably no wireless telegraph in the world ever functioned as efficiently and swiftly, as intensely and incessantly as the ghetto's "whispering telegraph." The news traveled by word of mouth on the streets, in the lines, in the stores and pastry shops, the market squares, the offices, and the factories; in a matter of seconds it was all over town, from Zagajnikowa to Gnieznienska streets, from Zabia to Wolborska.

In seven-league boots, the news ran through the ghetto's gates, barbed wire, and bridges, electrifying everyone without exception, young and old, the healthy and the sick, and even those who had already become insensitive, apathetic, indifferent to everything....

After the first sensation had subsided, there was a flood of questions: "To whom?," "Who's the lucky woman he's chosen?," "What does she do?," "Is she pretty?," "When's the wedding?" The questions multiplied and touched on the most intimate matters. And answers to those questions multiplied at the same rate and were, for the most part, contradictory and fantastic.... An entire pleiad of the "initiated" went about with enigmatic expressions, smiling their "Pythian" smiles in an attempt to heighten the atmosphere of suspense and mystery in which they were glad to steep themselves....

Everything that had been a topic of interest before—potatoes, soup kitchens, rations, and briquettes—ceased to be of current interest....

The next day curiosity had not only not abated but, quite the contrary, had gained strength and momentum. Facts began to crystallize and emerge from the flood of gossip and talk.

Interest grew.... Just as a voice in a large, vaulted hall reverberates off the ceiling and returns several times in the form of echoes, booming and droning as if trying to smash through the walls and make its way out into wider spaces, so did the news batter up against the barbed wire and the gates, and then, unable to force its way through, return as an echo, magnified many times, and speeding through the ghetto no one knows how many times over.

Rumkowski, with his fiancée, Regina Weinberger (*right*) and his brother's wife, "*Princess*" Helena.

The city already knew beyond doubt that the Chairman's lucky choice was Miss R.W. [Regina Weinberger], that she was a lawyer by profession, that she was young, pretty, and uncommonly wise, that she had already been named legal adviser to the Chairman and been working in the secretariat of the Health Department.

The popularity of the workers in that department increased dramatically. They became the most sought-after people, they were literally chased and inundated with questions. . . .

There were those who expressed their doubts, the born skeptics, people distrustful by nature. . . . They claimed it was all a fairy tale, a fiction. . . . But even those disbelievers had to believe when, on Wednesday evening, the news spread that the lucky woman was sitting in the front row at that Wednesday's concert, that the Chairman had kissed her hand in greeting and, finally, that they had driven off together in a coach which, *nota bene,* had arrived in the ghetto the day before. The unbelievers were dealt the decisive blow on Thursday. The Chairman's carriage stood for an hour in front of the Rabbinate's office on Miodowa Street. And for what purpose? That was no secret. The Chairman was handling the wedding formalities personally. . . . And the Chairman was actually inspecting a coat workshop located in that same building!

A new batch of gossip sprang up. People talked about the fantastic dressing table that had been ordered for the young woman and the apartment they would have, people argued about whether the wedding would be modest or sumptuous, the officials were happy, anticipating their prospective raises, and there was talk of an amnesty for minor criminals. . . .

CHAPTER FIVE

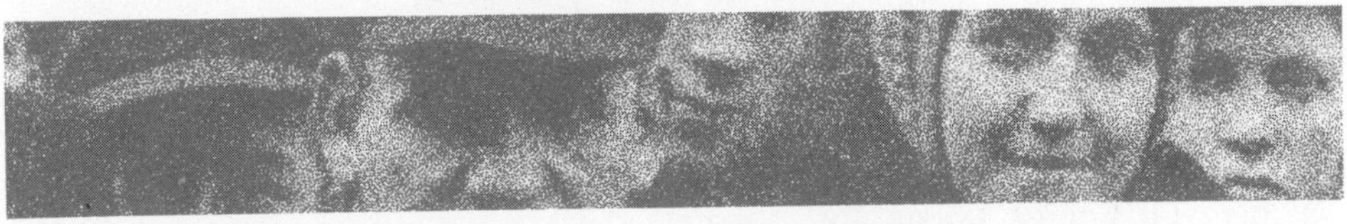

DEPORTATIONS OUT

1942

SPEECH BY CHAIM RUMKOWSKI

3 JANUARY 1942

"NOTHING BAD WILL HAPPEN TO PEOPLE OF GOOD WILL"

[*This was given in the auditorium of the House of Culture to invited representatives of the administration, the workshops, and the newcomers. Rumkowski began by noting that the new year, while not corresponding to the Jewish calendar, offered an occasion for reviewing the year just ended, 1941.*]

I don't know what interests my esteemed audience more, the past, the future, or just plain gossip. We all know that in the course of almost two years in the ghetto we've lived through a great many bad periods. When I think back, I am filled with pride by the record speed in which the ghetto was turned into a place of work. Indeed, from nothing we created enormous institutions of productivity; we've put the most varied enterprises and factories into operation. Today we employ an army of close to 50,000 people. Such a workforce has to be taken seriously by everyone, including, first and foremost, those who make policy. Everyone here should realize that the policy makers I've just mentioned demand categorically that the ghetto be dedicated to work.

Our life in the ghetto would be much more peaceful if Jews were not, as usual, too clever by half. From the beginning I've strived to achieve one goal. That goal is to be able to demonstrate to the authorities that the ghetto is composed exclusively of working people, that every able-bodied ghetto dweller has his own line of work. Unfortunately, a large portion of ghetto society has not wished to understand this, my basic aim. At times, people have even ridiculed my intentions, taking neither my age nor my position into account. In this respect, my efforts have been a complete fiasco. I now have the difficult task of correcting the evils caused by the public's lack of understanding.

The food supply is undoubtedly one of the most difficult problems, the most urgent of problems, not only in the ghetto but everywhere in the country. Last year we struggled with very great difficulties in that area. You'll recall that when we were facing the winter I was far from optimistic on the question of fuel. I made no assurances then, though I was optimistic in regard to food. Fortunately, I succeeded in supplying the ghetto with fuel. And as to the food supply, things could be worse. And yet, prices have risen wildly. Closing stores and increasing penalties have not stopped the orgy of inflation. Profiteering is mushrooming.

I don't mind in the least if someone takes the food from his own mouth to sell it. But I can and will not tolerate the hyenas who act as middlemen, just as I will continue showing no tolerance for the unparalleled exploitation these hyenas practice on the newcomers who are selling off their possessions. As I've stressed many times, the newcomers are leading a life that is simply and unforgivably frivolous. They still suffer from the mistaken belief that the present situation will end and, in that delusion, are living from hand to mouth, selling everything they brought here with them. Unfortunately, the present situation will go on and on. Reason, therefore, suggests the necessity of spending money as cautiously as possible.

It will be a bad day when the newcomers need to receive relief. For me to institute special relief programs for them is out of the question. In fact, they're now receiving relief of every sort in their collectives, while those who have individual dwellings are availing themselves of the same food rations as the rest of the ghetto. Nevertheless, profiteering is flourishing. Before the transports arrived in the ghetto, I had succeeded in eradicating the parasitic trade in food.

I would also remind the newcomers that I will be ruthless in applying strict penalties against those who try to avoid selling their furs, and so on, to the bank.

Last year my monthly balance exceeded 3,000,000 marks and, of that sum, more than a third was absorbed by social welfare. Financially, I am in much better shape than many of Lodz's pre-war manufacturers. It's certain that I'll always have sufficient resources with which to meet my obligations and improve my financial situation. The balanced budget is supported by two pillars—work and requisitions. In any case, if I have any need for credit, I shall receive it without difficulty because I have the best currency in the world at my disposal. That currency is work.

My current concern is to be able to provide work for everyone. At the same time, I will not be discouraged in my efforts to stabilize life in the ghetto. There will be a new registration, which will again employ thousands willing to work. Everyone in the ghetto must have work as his passport. If new work battalions are prepared, I will report to the authorities that my reserves are mobilized and waiting to be employed. In the very near future there will be far-reaching changes in my administration, from the top down.

And now I come to the plague known as gossip. Once again a gang of scoundrels is spreading rumors in the hope of disturbing the peace. Perhaps the authors of these panic-producing stories are lurking even here, in this audience. I would like to murder them!

I don't like wasting words. The stories circulating today are one hundred percent false.* I've recently agreed to accept twenty thousand Jews from the smaller towns, setting as a condition that the ghetto's territory be enlarged. At the present time, only those who, in my opinion, deserve such a fate will be resettled elsewhere. The authorities are filled with admiration for the work that's been done in the ghetto, and it is due to that work that they have confidence in me. Their approval of my request that the number of deportees be reduced from 20,000 to 10,000 is a sign of that confidence. I have complete confidence in the Resettlement Commission,* though, obviously, it too can make mistakes from time to time.

It's to be regretted that officials holding the most important posts engage in unforgivable gossip-mongering. I will give this special attention, with the aid of special undercover agents, and will take an interest in whether people are working or gossiping in the offices. I will treat the guilty without mercy. In our two years in the ghetto you've seen for yourselves what value gossip has had.

In the very near future a newspaper will be appearing again and, among other things, it will contain changes instituted on January first in the regulations

The official ghetto calendar for the year 1942. The text included excerpts from Rumkowski's speeches, and his five slogans: 1. work, 2. bread, 3. care for the sick, 4. supervision for the children, 5. peace in the ghetto.

concerning financial and economic matters: changes in rents, the centralization of the ghetto's entire bookkeeping system, with only auxiliary bookkeeping departments remaining in the individual workshops, and so on.

Bear in mind that at the heart of all my projects is the goal that honest people may sleep in peace. Nothing bad will happen to people of good will. [Thunderous applause.]

It is common for one workshop to inflict damage on another as if it were a competitor. Odd things occur. If one workshop has a machine that another needs, the former is unwilling to consign it to the latter. The creation of mutual impediments is even worse than theft because it strikes directly at the work process. The troubles connected with the attempt to put a dry cleaner into operation, which would provide employment for a few thousand people, were truly grotesque. It could not be put into operation—for lack of a motor.

I appeal to the managers to eliminate these destructive practices and remember that they're not working for the benefit of this or that establishment but for the good of the whole ghetto. The narrow, petty point of view must be entirely overcome; we are a single, united community here in the ghetto. It's one for all here, and all for one.

Comrades, friends. I predicted that hard times, perhaps very hard times, would be coming, but I'm certain that we'll struggle through them if we eradicate the evil in ourselves. You would be very upset if you knew what I have been through lately. And the gossips knew nothing about that, I assure you. Remember the recent repressive rules against Jews and Poles. Had the strike attempts that recently took place here come to the attention of the authorities, the snow would have been red with blood. Using my own tough methods, I put a stop to those attempts in a factory where, comparatively speaking, the workers earn the best wages. Remember, comrades and friends, that my mind is concerned day and night with improving the ghetto's situation, and I am near the breaking point from constant exertion.

I am certain that if the ghetto does its work in earnest and does it well, the authorities will not take repressive steps. I want to be grounded even more firmly in that certainty, and increasing and improving production is the road that leads there. Results in this area depend on you, with the Trade Commission* in the lead. Let's take pains to serve the public good—not me, its servant. Stop dealing in food; stop all the conniving. Remember that when more deportees are demanded, I will put all the parasites on the lists. Exert yourselves in your work, and work together. I will be instituting working papers for everyone. And it's no fantasy that another 10,000 people will very soon find employment.

I give you my word of honor that no evil waits concealed in the wings of the new registration. It's an ordinary precaution against any eventuality, and in case the wind changes direction.

I swear to you that at the present moment I am not on the brink of any new danger. Much has already been saved through foresight. The recent shooting incident was just a regrettable misunderstanding. The assurance obtained from the authorities that innocent people would not be shot is still in force. In that particular case, a passerby, a newcomer from Germany, had not yet learned the lay-out of the streets, and his behavior gave the impression that he was a smuggler. The authorities respect us because we constitute a center of productivity.

I remember the punishment I applied to Community employees who hid articles subject to compulsory sale. People like that will be dismissed from work on the spot. I will deal the same with a shoemaker or a physician; they will lose the right to work here. The loss the ghetto suffers through those who, in extreme selfishness, evade selling articles subject to requisition by my bank can be seen in this: the Kripo has confiscated approximately 1500 fur coats whose monetary equivalent could have been used for the public treasury and whose owners would have been appropriately compensated by me. These assets have been irretrievably lost.

And another abuse has been uncovered. A certain ghetto resident who possessed a significant hidden fortune has availed himself for some time of welfare and special supplements. Necessity requires that we find the goods that have been hidden, and it makes no difference, after all, whether these buried objects are discovered today, tomorrow, or next week. It is far more sensible, therefore, to present them for sale voluntarily and on time. The ghetto's common interest demands this.

At present our workshops have sufficient orders. Isolated problems could not be under more serious scrutiny. I am planning to put new factories into operation. I will again be able to employ a large number of those now without work, which will also relieve some welfare expenses. I repeat, once again, that the ghetto's honest citizens can sleep in complete peace and need not fear anything.

The forced school holiday, extending past the quarter, fills me with the greatest concern for the fate of the children. However, I hope that after the conclusion of the resettlement campaign, I will succeed in having the schools and kindergartens back in operation. Fathers and mothers, believe me, my heart bleeds when I see your children roaming the streets and I cannot open the school doors for them. All the same, it did once make me so happy to see the ghetto's youngest citizens hurrying to school with their little briefcases.

An old people's home for 1500 people is not a fantasy. It is a reality close to realization.

Representatives of the new population, I appeal to you again to finally accept the ghetto's conditions of life. Aren't you ashamed that I've had to use policemen to force you to work? That I had to resort to confining you to your work crews? I wanted to give you the best apartments in the ghetto. Officials of the Housing Department can testify to this.

Representatives of the factory workers, work conscientiously and guard yourselves against dangerous agitation. Remember that I cannot always intervene directly and that the fatal effects of provocation will not be long in coming.

A plan on the threshold of the new year! The plan is work, work, and more work! I will seek with an iron will to find work for everyone in the ghetto. It doesn't matter if it's work in a cooperative or a factory, being a janitor or a tramcar driver. In carrying out the general program, I shall be able to demonstrate, with irrefutable figures, that the Jews of the ghetto constitute a productive element, and that they are, therefore, needed.

Help me discover those who are destructive. This will make it easier for me to carry out my task, and will make it possible for you to lead a more tranquil life. I will devote much of my attention to finding employment for all our young people. I assure workers that I've done everything to secure at least the minimum needed for their survival. I am doing everything possible. I should not be required to do what lies beyond the bounds of possibility.

Brothers and sisters, I insist that without your help I can achieve nothing. But with your help I am certain that I'll succeed in fulfilling my mission: to create conditions which allow us to live through the current period in good health, and to preserve the lives and health of the people of the ghetto and its youth.

GHETTO DOCUMENT

About Evacuation
from the Litzmannstadt Ghetto.

I hereby demand OF ALL PERSONS WHO HAVE BEEN SELECTED FOR EVACUATION, that they

PROMPTLY

report to the assembly center on the indicated day.

"It was said they were to go to Polish villages to work the land." (Rosenfeld)

Opposite: Awaiting deportation, this "western" Jewish mother appears to be dictating a "last letter" to her son.

Those who do not submit voluntarily will be sent out by force. They will be found out. Even if they do not stay in their homes, they will be found out wherever they hide.

At the same time I wish to repeat my Announcement No. 347 of 30 December 1941, and I am warning the ghetto population for the last time that

NO ONE IS TO ALLOW INTO THE HOUSE AND LET STAY OVERNIGHT A PERSON WHO IS NOT REGISTERED AT THEIR ADDRESS.

Should persons who are approved for evacuation hide in the homes of other families, not only those persons but also the families who gave them shelter, as well as the house watchmen, will be sent out by force.

THIS IS MY LAST WARNING!

Litzmannstadt-Ghetto
14 January 1942

Mordechai Chaim Rumkowski
Eldest of the Jews

SPEECH BY CHAIM RUMKOWSKI

17 JANUARY 1942

"ONLY WORK CAN SAVE US"

[*This was delivered at the opening of an exhibit of dresses and undergarments at "Glazer's" factory—Glazer was the manager—located at 14 Dworska Street. The audience consisted of invited guests from Rumkowski's administration and the workers of the factory.*]

Brothers and sisters. Today, in a corner of the ghetto, we celebrate an anniversary which, under present circumstances, is quite an achievement. A certain analogy comes to mind, concerning religious holidays. Every year we celebrate the holiday of Succoth. However, the joy of those days depends entirely on the weather. When the weather is good, the religious Jew occupies his *succah* with pleasure, but during cold and inclement days he is forced to abandon this time-honored tradition. It's the same with today's celebration. We rejoice at our accomplishments of the year, at our having successfully traversed twelve months. But clouding our joy is the fact that the present moment coincides with yet another affliction.

We live today beneath the specter of deportation. Only recently, at tremendous sacrifice, we accepted into our population of 140,000 an additional 23,000 exiles. I am proud to say that these exiles can consider themselves lucky, for the merciless fate which befell them nevertheless extended them some good fortune in bringing them here to our ghetto. It is good fortune in misfortune. However, I cannot remain silent on the subject of the 10,000 people we are now deporting. Unfortunately, I received a most uncompromising order, one I had to carry out so as to prevent others from doing it. Within the bounds of my ability, in this case as in other sad predicaments, I've tried to mitigate the severity as much as possible.

I did so as follows: I assigned for deportation that element of our ghetto which was a festering boil. And so the list of exiles includes members of the underworld and other individuals harmful to the ghetto. I've been criticized many times that smuggling into the ghetto continues. This was irrefutable, and I couldn't deny it. Now, when I am deporting all kinds of connivers and cheats, I do it fully convinced that they asked for this fate.

A commission of my trusted aides determines the list of deportees. This commission guarantees, basically, that it will only designate people for deportation if they deserve it. I realize, of course, that in acting with all deliberate speed the commission might make errors, but the fact remains that there is absolutely no malice on the part of those who decide.

Some people ask others to intervene on their behalf and don't care what crooked means are used. These interventions are to no avail. My expectation, based on authoritative information, is that the deportees' fate will not be as tragic as is expected in the ghetto. They will not be behind wire, and they will work on farms.

A gossip hydra has sprung up on the margins of the deportation procedure. I must condemn, in the strongest terms, the act of disturbing the common peace. I've stated many times that you can build your peace only on work, and the influence of gossip can only undermine this iron foundation which work represents.

Every ghetto citizen should identify himself by means of his work identification card, and that identification card should be without blemish. A work identification card with court remarks on it is worse than no card at all.

We are now on the threshold of very bad times, and everyone needs to be aware of this.

Only work can save us from the worst calamity.

GHETTO DOCUMENT

Announcement No. 356

In accordance with an order, I announce hereby that

FOR
RESISTING
THE POLICE

on Monday, January 19, 1942,

Dr. Ulrich Georg Israel
SCHULZ
from Prague
born on 8 June 1897 in Prague,

was lawfully

SHOT

by the Police

Litzmannstadt-Ghetto, January 19, 1942

Mordechai Chaim Rumkowski
Eldest of the Jews

SPEECH BY CHAIM RUMKOWSKI

1 FEBRUARY 1942

"A SIMPLE JEW FROM LODZ"

[*This was delivered at a meeting of the newcomers' representatives and Rumkowski's personal advisors.*]

Esteemed representatives of the rabbinate and dear guests! On behalf of my wife and myself, I thank you kindly for all your good wishes and your words of appreciation. It's not easy for me, a simple Jew from Lodz, to address such a distinguished audience representing the intellectual elite from the West, as well as the world of finance, politics and mighty commerce. . . . I listened with a heavy heart today to your concerns and to wishes so modest that they could scarcely be considered minimal requirements for existence. I also listened carefully to your words of criticism. Meeting you here today, face to face, in an atmosphere of warmth and mutual respect, makes me glad. Much remains to be done before your life here improves.

One thing you must always remember: that I am no politician but only a work horse in heavy harness, pulling a wagon loaded with 170,000 human lives. I am sorry that I cannot satisfy your minimal daily needs. You ask so little, just enough to survive, but I don't have even that little.

Who would have imagined that bread, the most basic article of daily life, would become unattainable and would obscure all else? There was a time in the city of Litzmannstadt when the daily bread ration was 33 decagrams, while in the ghetto it was 40. That was possible because we had reserve supplies on which we could draw. As times became harder and the supplies diminished, I was compelled to open the granaries so as not to cut these rations. I wish I could still maintain this kind of household, but unfortunately every sack is now counted upon delivery. And so I've had to reduce the daily ration to 28 decagrams. The workers get special supplements, which I can administer on the basis of my autonomous authority.

I am a true believer, and I believe that with God's help and with the cooperation of "my guard," which convenes here with me, I was able to push many things through in very difficult times, to protect our autonomy. You must remember that all manner of politics is to be rejected here in the ghetto, because only work can secure one's existence and gain respect from those whose subordinates we are. My currency is work, and it's a currency better than gold.

The exhibit organized by the underwear factory had positive results, for it properly demonstrated our work. I am sure that the time will yet come when the Jew will demonstrate his productivity under more favorable conditions. Last week, when the authorities visited the exhibit, they advised me to organize an exhibit encompassing the entire spectrum of production in the ghetto.

When I was advised of a new transport of Jews to the ghetto, I decided right away to place them within my own budget, not even asking any support for them. Thanks to me, these newcomers were also spared the unpleasant ordeal of luggage inspection.

The representative from Prague indicated in his speech that he is impressed by the care I've provided for the children and young people here. Your arrival upset some of my plans. Seven hundred teachers, school buildings and other educational structures were placed at your disposal. It is my conviction that a roof over one's head is more important nowadays than education. You must understand my internal conflict: I, who have devoted half my life to the struggle for children's education, had to personally order the closing of schools. I was planning to reopen the schools in December; unfortunately, the buildings are still occupied. This project is always close to my heart, and my mind is forever occupied by it. I am also aware that the newcomers have 1200 children among them, and that they need special care and guidance.

I shall establish two large homes for children, in which children separated from their parents will find the best care and will live in much better conditions than those at home or in community homes. With respect to this collective for children, decisions will have to be made very quickly—there's no time in the ghetto for long debates—and obviously only the children whose parents agree will be placed there.

When I first established the collectives, I anticipated conditions would be much better than what they've, in fact, become. Collectives receive their necessary supplies on account. Meanwhile, their communal kitchens distribute the worst food. There are cases of unsweetened coffee being served, of basic elements of hygiene going unobserved, and so on. These circumstances force me to liquidate the collectives as soon as it gets warmer.

Today, my advisors recommended social welfare projects based on philanthropy. I rejected the idea because philanthropy is a totally alien concept in the ghetto. I will, however, order that the percentage deducted from the money sent to people here be allocated to help the poor. Of the ten percent withheld, two percent is for postal expenses, and the remaining eight percent will go for social welfare. We don't need philanthropic "czars." The funds will strengthen the treasury and will be left for the Resettlement Office* to use. As to the closing of the post office, I must emphasize the fact, well known to everyone, that the ghetto's autonomy ends at the wire border.

Right now, registration of all able-bodied men and women is in progress. Already about half the total ghetto population is working. It's a record number. I shall try my best to increase the number of working people. After the winter, public works will begin inside the ghetto, and the streets will be taken care of. A lot remains to be done. We're proud that nothing in the ghetto goes to waste. Every scrap or useless remnant is made into something worthwhile, which in turn provides money.

Our next project will be the further expansion of the factories. A reserve work force will be in readiness in case we receive new orders. The idea of this reserve work force has practically been accepted by the authorities. It will reduce unemployment significantly. All orders must be 100% filled, without grumbling. The ghetto's older inhabitants, not including the criminal element, understood this a long time ago. I might add that requests to be excused from work, for one reason or another, are futile.

I understand the bitterness of people with higher education who are forced to push wagons through the streets. It cannot be helped. The Lodz worker long ago accepted the fact that the ghetto places all kinds of obligations on its inhabitants, without regard to their former social positions. After all, everything is not done for me but for the good of the whole community.

As to pensions, the subject which was mentioned today, I can state that the central Berlin authority has jurisdiction over them. I assume that this matter will be resolved in a positive way, shortly.

Christian Jews [converts]! You didn't want to come here, and we didn't invite you to come. But since you are here, we consider you our brothers. You have the same rights here that we do. We Jews have always been most tolerant of others' religions. The teaching of religion, which you've requested, cannot be introduced into the schools. It isn't that I don't want to do it for you, but simply because I cannot. Religion has not been taught in ghetto schools, and exceptions cannot be made for Christian students. Remember, what is good for us is also good for you. As far as religious and spiritual matters are concerned, I assure you that I shall help you to the best of my ability, and will do everything so that you can practice your religion freely.

We must strive for better living conditions, and women can play a big part in that. During this month the collectives will be disbanded and the newcomers' children will be selected, as I mentioned before. The parents of such children should have no worries about the fate of their darlings. You don't have to thank me for it. Whatever I've done before, and am doing now, is simply my duty. I'd be less of a *mensch* if I didn't fulfill my responsibility. From the moment the ghetto was closed on May 1, 1940, I have been trying to be an honest and conscientious keeper of the ghetto.

OSKAR ROSENFELD'S NOTEBOOKS

NOTEBOOK B: MEMORIES FOR LATER DAYS
(Loose sketches)

Face of the Ghetto. Mucky paths, half-covered with snow, lead between individual houses set here and there, grim and meaningless. Low trees and bushes spread their sparse, trembling branches against the sky. Gangs of scruffy children, their yellow, wrinkled faces looking aged, walk tiredly through the streets. Sometimes one sees a fleeting smile on their faces, hears singing from their bloodless lips. Sometimes they throw a snowball like children elsewhere.

No one can say what will happen tomorrow. What will happen to all of us. What all this is for? Why the ghetto? Will there be a tomorrow? Is it worth thinking about?

We are lepers, outcasts, common thieves, people without music, without earth, without beds, without a world. There is no other city like this in the world. Come here, people from the outside, from over there where there are normal days and holidays, where there are dreams and desire and resistance. Come quickly. For when it is all over, we will be so thinned out and so miserable that we will no longer be able to enjoy the pleasure of seeing you again.

The snow is dirty, no one knows from what. Soot from the chimneys cannot fly over from there to us. A wagon rolls down the street. Instead of a horse, people are harnessed to it.

Evacuation. Preparation for the evacuation of 10,000 ghetto inhabitants is under way. Whose turn is it? People who have been sentenced, people on welfare, people unwilling to work and other "undesirables." The sentenced are, for the most part, those who were imprisoned a few weeks for having sold rations. This began on December 26th. It was said: they were to go to Polish villages to work the land. But this was only rumor. The only thing the ghetto knew and saw was the expulsion every day of 700 to 800 Jews from their huts and holes and rooms. The police entered the apartments of those who were being deported. Not infrequently they found starved children, old people frozen to death. Fear had seized the ghetto.

At the assembly sites people were wild with hunger before the departure. Those who pushed toward the black coffee were beaten by the police. East winds splintered windowpanes. Giant daws ate the bark off the naked trees. Keys froze in keyholes. Mice lay frozen to death in the middle of rooms, next to shoes and rags they had not been too weak to bite apart.

Day after day it went this way. 1 loaf of bread 100 marks; 1 kilo of margarine 100 marks. That was the end of February 1942. The fear continued. Because the deportations were to continue. No one was safe any longer.... On March 7th 9 people froze to death at the train station, having waited 9 hours for the train to depart. People collapsed from hunger and were dragged into the trains and handed over to the Kripo. Around this time there were already 20,000 candidates for resettlement. Resettlement?—without blankets, without warm clothes, without the hope of a place to sleep at night? Individual Jewish policemen tried to treat the evacuees "humanely." For this, an *Aschkenes* [Heb: German] beat a Jewish policeman, who did not care, happy to have suffered for the Jewish cause....

On the first day of spring, winter returned, like no winter in decades. If the quota of deportees is not met, the Jewish police hunt indiscriminately on the street, driving people into the assembly sites. Many hide in huts and abandoned barns; many spend nights far from their homes. When they are captured, they are carried away, loaded onto carts, and people, people like themselves, pull the carts to the train station. Many of the unlucky did not have the strength to sit up straight and lay on the floor. When one spoke to them, they did not answer. Their eyes were inconsolable. The majority did not even take a bundle with them, fearing that the *Aschkenes* would take it from them at the station....

One heard the words of the Eldest in one's ears: "If I were to tell you everything I know, you would not sleep. So *I alone* am the one who does not sleep." And more of the Eldest's words: "The ghetto, too, is in the war."

The Face of the Ghetto.... And people hurrying, trotting, hungering, barely stepping along. The majority carrying some kind of load, pushing carts, *schlepping* [Yid: dragging] bundles, pails, vats, containers for soup. One scarcely speaks to the other.... Everyone and everything is without sense, like marionettes on a stage. And the more one observes this scene, the more senseless the whole thing seems. For whom? For what? How long? None of these questions can be answered.

Orphans, led by their teachers, sing on the streets, something in Polish. Their daily language is Yiddish, which even in the Jewish ghetto of Lodz seems to be gradually disappearing. The children's faces are rosy, but the doctors know better: the majority suffer from rickets and tuberculosis: the majority are candidates for death.... Yes, the unyielding truth of the words with which the Brauns [the Nazi Brownshirts] described the Lodz Ghetto to us gradually dawns on us: *The death-corner of Europe!*

NOTEBOOK 13

Tliah [Heb: Gallows].* On the twentieth day of February in the forty-second year of the twentieth century, toward evening the skies disclosed the Sabbath of 4 Adar 5702. And God showed me His countenance. The word of God came there to Yekheskiel [Yid: Ezekiel (but also Oskar)] in the Litzmannstadt Ghetto. And he saw and may see . . .

At 6 PM all members of the community were told to be at Fischplatz at 9 o'clock. Rumors: military parade, directives from German headquarters, the Chairman to speak. Sick people were permitted to be absent. Nobody knew what was to happen. Frosty weather. Clear air. Biting wind. Sensing something terrible, many stayed cowering at home.

The victims take their places, men in front, women behind. By 9 o'clock the square is framed by a wall of humanity and the grisly silence of 20,000 people. At last the crowd realized what the game was. A gallows had been erected, put up early that morning by Jewish policemen. At the sight, some of the women fainted; others gave way to convulsive weeping. Those who tried to get away found barriers shutting off the streets.

A small, fairly low dais, three steps up, a rectangular trap door to the left, above the trap door a landing with a horizontal wooden strut and a hemp rope at the top. Horror gripped the onlookers. This was no dream but stark reality. Everyone who was German-speaking knew what was coming.

A few well-fed SS officers in field grey stood there. At the exits from the square, soldiers were stationed with machine guns to keep the crowd in check, making it very clear that leaving would entail the severest consequences.

Almost an hour and a half. The cold getting worse all the time. People falling prostrate, trying to warm themselves with their arms around their knees. Toward 10:30, suddenly dead silence. From the direction of Zgierz, probably from Baluter Ring (Gestapo Headquarters), a hatless man, his grey hair fluttering in the wind, approached slowly, flanked by *Feldgraues*. He caught sight of the gallows. Most of the crowd, especially the women, looked away—though many of them cast furtive glances at the point where the scene was to be enacted. The majority were first-time witnesses to such an affair and had no idea how to behave. They plucked in agitation at their clothes, clenched their fists convulsively, waiting for some sign to show them what to do.

Not a word was spoken. Absolute silence. The victim shivered with cold. The soldiers, clad in fur coats, took off his topcoat. He folded his hands, observed the whole picture, the crowd. He climbed with firm steps to the platform. . . . Then came a moment when the crowd thought something was happening, an announcement or a decision. But nothing happened. A further pause.

"Waiting for some sign to show them what to do." (Rosenfeld)

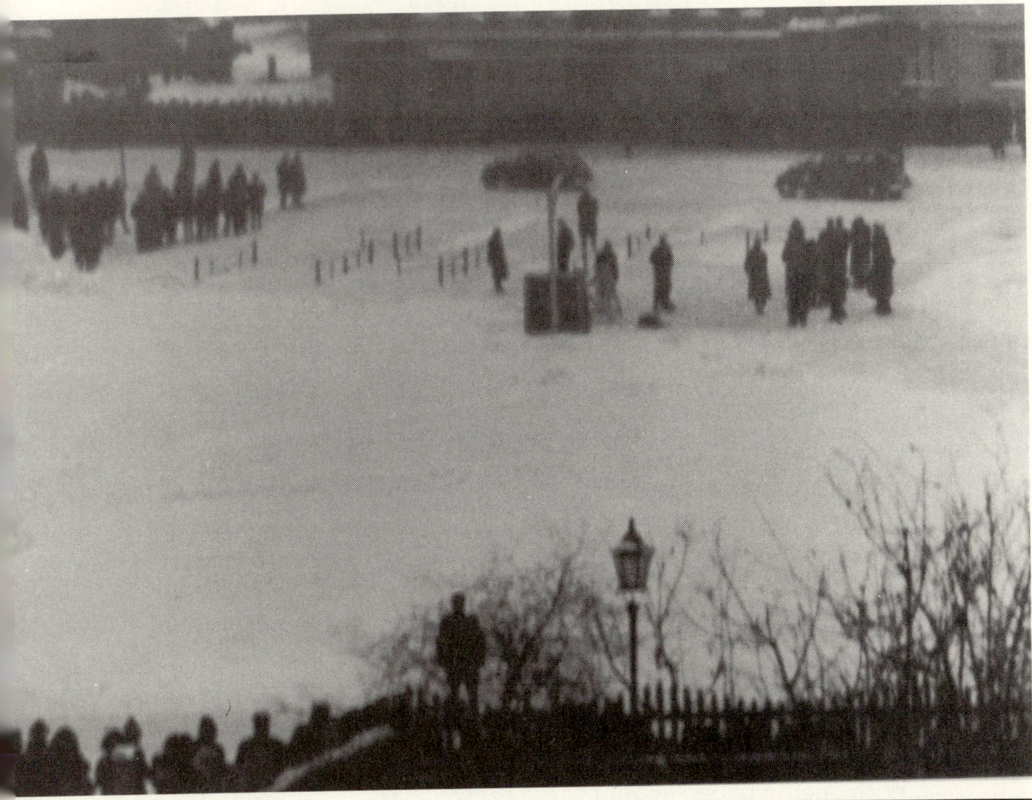

Seeing there would be no reprieve, the man again clasped his hands together and suddenly said, with depths of misery in his voice, "Please let me live. I haven't broken any laws."

Many expected, instead of this appeal, some sort of demonstration from the crowd, a slogan of some kind as his testament. Nothing of the sort. He was no hero in our sense of the term. Now, glances away. A dull thumping of something heavy on wood, and a few seconds later a twitching body, jerking around in the air. . . . The body remained hanging there the whole sabbath. Jews avoided the scene.

At 5 PM on Friday, the building department had received the order for a gallows to be erected on Fischplatz by 7 AM the next morning. Precise specifications were given: wooden beams, heavy iron hooks, bent to a shape just this long and that wide. A man from Germany was entrusted with the job. He worked hard and long, and got it done on time. This worker was, it turned out, an intimate friend of the condemned man. He became melancholic and died of "a broken heart."

Later the gallows was taken away and hired out by the Gestapo. Later still, a gallows for 12 people was ordered, a very fine piece of work, worthy of imitation. All 12 get hanged at one pull.

SIMCHA BUNIM SHAYEVITSH

[*According to the* Lexicon vun der Neier Yiddishe Literature]

LEKH LEKHO

[*The Hebrew title of this Yiddish poem is from Genesis 12:1, in which God tells Abraham to "go forth" from his land.*]

And now, Blimele, dearest child,
Curb your childish joy,
So like a pool of quicksilver—
And let's get ready for the unknown journey.

Do not look at me
With such wonder in your large brown eyes

And don't ask why and for what reason
We must leave our house.

I myself, dearest child, am already
A grown man, am already big,
And I don't know, either, why they're driving
The bird from his nest.

Hold your sweet, gentle
Laughter, so much like the silvery sounds
Of antique snuff boxes—
And get dressed for a second journey.

Put on the pair of warm pants
Which your mother only last night
Mended,
As she sang and laughed.

Not realizing that the house
Listened to her last happy laughter,
Just as the cow lows, unaware
Of the knife sharpened by the slaughterer.

Child, put on your blue dress,
Which, though an edge was burned
While drying on the pipe, will
Warm you in the cold, strange place,

And protect your little lungs,
Keeping them strong and healthy,
For you could catch cold, God forbid,
At any frost, at the slightest wind.

The frost outside burns, sears,
Clutches with an iron fist—
Come, with a red bow
Your mother will braid your hair.

The frost outside burns and stiffens the body,
And the thermometer is at minus 8 degrees—
Come, I have found for you, dearest child,
The golden ribbon with fringes of silk.

Do not stare at me,
With your big brown eyes,

And don't ask why and for what reason
We must leave our home
Departing for far off, far off,
Unknown snow-filled roads,
Where instead of a village, a city,
Fear will meet us.

And we will be like rubbish, or garbage,
Prepared to suffer everything,
And sleep one day here,
Not knowing where the next.

And not know what
Awaits on the long journey—
Whether a warm bed to sleep on
Or a bare floor, cold and hard.

Whether a cup of warm coffee
And a piece of bread with salt,
Or being thrown into a mass grave
And covered alive.

Do not look with such wonder
In your large brown eyes,
That on an ordinary Wednesday
I recite the Friday night blessing.

I am reciting the Sabbath blessing
Over familiar guests,
Saying with joy, "Peace be with you"
To two visiting angels

Who accompany me and, at my side,
Go everywhere with me,
Weeping with me over my sorrow
And rejoicing with my happiness.

The two angelic visitors—who are they?
Come, guess quick as an arrow.
They are you, Blimele, my lovely child,
And your mother, the woman of valor

In whose nature, though her face is careworn,
There always rests the Sabbath,

As the sun rests behind a cloud
When the sky on a rainy day is overcast.

And although our home is in the ghetto
And the frost-spider has spun a silvery snow web
Through our narrow unheated room's thin wooden walls,
Its cold, unworldly glimmer like the white hands of death,

And although hunger and care
Have bent our backs
And fear, like frost,
Has lined our faces like old men,
We are tied to our corner
With thousands of ropes
And fire burns in our heart
And the dream of happiness flickers.

Like the golden kernel
In the little beaks of birds
In our dream we are provided
With a sunny, bronze honey cake,

Which, though we've been fooled
And disappointed more than once,
Has still given us the strength
To wait for better things.

And now, Blimele, my dearest child,
Stop—come, stop fooling around—
Now is not the right time for that—
They can call us at any minute

To leave our poor home,
A poor boat on an island of sand,
And fling us into the middle
Of a naked, raging sea.

There, outside, the first groups
On the journey are already dragging by,
Women, men, old people, heavy bags on their backs,
In their arms—children.

Like drinkers, their covered faces
Are red—from shame and frost;

"In their eyes—their death sentence." (Shayevitsh)

Their steps—faint, tottering;
In their eyes—their death sentence.

But in this torment
Jeremiah is not here to wail lamentations;
He does not go with them into exile to comfort them,
As he did near the waters of Babylon.

And my dearest child, do not ask
With your questioning eyes,
Why only poor people go, and where
On the long journey are those with full stomachs.

My child, the world is always the same,
It's what a famous sage once said.
And I once told you
The story of the Cantonists.[1]

How poor children were snatched
And torn away from their parents.
So why do you wonder, my child,
That the ghetto reminds me of those times?

And we must take in hand
The old walking stick and leave,
Not knowing where our poor
And sick remains will lie.

Whether we shall arrive somewhere
And reach a place of rest,
Where kind words will be extended
With friendly hands.

Or whether like sick birds who die in flight
And lie dead in fields somewhere
We shall expire in the middle of the journey
And not receive a Jewish burial.

And vultures will have feasts
With our bodies,

1. The Cantonists were young Jewish recruits forcibly drafted into the Russian army under Nicholas I. They were often coerced into converting to Christianity.

And when one flock is full,
It will call a second to come.

Do not weep, dearest child, do not weep
Life is really beautiful, and we yearn for it
In the ghetto even more than always,
Even more than everywhere else.

Know, however, that sinful man
Must always be ready
For both a colorful, exciting life
And desolate, sorrowful death.

Here, you see, I am packing the *tallis*
And the white robe for the shroud
And also the little red Scriptures
And Leivick's poems[2] for a moment of comfort.

And you, child, take along a small piece of soap
To wash a shirt for yourself.
You must be clean at home,
And even more in unknown places.
Also, do not forget to take
The fine comb along.
Your mother will comb out your hair
Each evening,

Looking and taking care
That you, God forbid, have no lice,
And she'll sing *"Bibi bibi layzele,"*
Holding you in her lap.

And tell you tales
Of past times like ours,
And she will be like Jeremiah,
Who comforts while his heart bleeds and cries.

And now, Blimele, my dearest child,
Do not make a face,
There has remained only enough time
For us to say goodbye to the house.

2. H. Leivick, the pen name of Leivick Helpern (1886–1962), the Russian-Yiddish poet and dramatist, author of the play *The Golem.*

So let's say farewell
To all that is dear and beloved,
To every small thing we leave behind
And will follow in our thoughts.

With the longing that my lungs breathed in
With each and every thing,
And which jumped like a dog at us,
Everywhere loyal and nimble.

With the unsung songs
That hover here in the house,
That run ahead and go to meet us
To lead us to the grave.

Let's part with each tiny thing,
Just as our old grandmothers did,
When in the twilight they piously
Bade farewell to the holy Sabbath day.

When shadows crawl on walls
And you see weekday stars shining,
The heart gnaws, shivers, becomes sad,
And tears roll down from the eyes.

Here is the table—on the tablecloth
With the blue pattern
Your poor mother
Served her meals.

Although there was sometimes not enough
For her pale hands to prepare,
A happy holiday meal
Always shone from the table.

On the table, too, your father
Poured out his feverish spirit,
The table's wooden heart first heard
The melody of his sad song.

And shuddered with surprise
And began to hum softly along,
Enveloping our humble house
In the sharp scent of wood.

And the wall, moist and warped,
Bent its crooked ear
In wonder, murmuring the song
Of joy, the song of sorrow.

And the garret bowed down
To listen to the strange songs
And the floor responded with ecstasy,
Almost expiring from the sweet song.

Here, lovely child, is the closet—
Two doors, and a mirror in the middle,
Which silently seeing everything,
Sealed the sight in its glass heart.

And carried it in the sun-filled color
Of your rosy new-born body
And the first word of protest
That distorted your sweet little lip.

And like a record disk,
The mirror carries secretly within it
The first song with which you were lulled
To sleep in your coarse straw cradle.

And engraved there is your first laughter,
Which you spurted like sweet chocolate
And also, already, the final grimace
Of the last groan on expiring.

And here, my child, in the closet's right wing
Your mother kept the laundry
That her hand alone washed
And that smelled like lilac.

And she would weep into it
When her hope would dissolve
And her dreams would disappear
Like the evening sun.

But she often laughed when,
Dozing off in the midst of her work,
She would see your fate like a sun
Rising in the blue sky.

And in the left wing of the closet
Lie volumes of books and my writing.
There Isaiah is the companion of Geothe
And Rabbi Yonathan Eibeschutz of Tuwim.[3]

And Yesenin[4] wants to get drunk
And urinate,
But he suddenly sees
Abraham leading Isaac to the sacrifice.

Miriam Ulinover shows off
Her grandmother's precious treasure.[5]
King David flames up at the Psalms
And makes up little dances for them.

And the Rebbe of Kotsk[6] is still standing
And waiting with his clumpy beard and angry roar
For ten young men who will proclaim for the world
That God is the Lord.

But the Vorker rebbe[7] gives him a friendly pat
On the back—the Kotsker rebbe raises his brow—
And says, Don't frown, the Jew is in exile every day
And already fulfills the commandments of martyrdom.

More even, we will take a snifter,
A piece of cheese and say *L'chaim.*[8]
It is time that the Lord of the universe
Also sanctify His holiness.

3. Eibeschutz (1690–1764) is best known for fighting the rising tide of assimilationism. In contrast, the poet and social activist Julian Tuwim (1894–1953), a Jew who was born in Lodz, wrote in Polish.
4. S. A. Yesenin (1895–1944), a Russian poet who befriended Jewish writers, was known for his licentious and bohemian lifestyle.
5. The Yiddish poet Miriam Ulinover (1890–1944) was born in Lodz. She died in Auschwitz. A volume of her poetry was entitled *Grandmother's Treasures.*
6. Menachem Mendel (1787–1859), "the Kotsker Rebbe," was one of the most original Chassidic leaders. Brilliant and sharp-tongued, he insisted on the need for constant tension and militancy in combating egocentricity and conformity.
7. The Vorker Rebbe was a contemporary and a disciple of the same Chassidic movement as the Kotsker, but their temperaments led them in different directions.
8. Heb: To life!

And with humility and with a shiver,
My poems and novels lie there—
They lie and wait with fright,
Like poor people at the threshold of the rich,

And murmur quietly, mumble with entreaties
Until their mumbling is heard by Rashi[9]
And he issues an order to welcome them
And also proud Sholem Asch[10] is friendly to them.

And there is another commotion
In the family. Let's crown him.
Aaron the priest spreads his hands
To bestow the blessing. . . .
Tremble, tremble, holy volumes,
Tremble, dreams of *gaons*[11]—
Some day, in the dawn someone will rise
And in just his pants

Will cut square pieces from you
For toilet paper,
And will grimace, that the writing
May, God forbid, hurt him.

And here is the bed where the power
Of Adam, the first man, was discovered
And which was the witness
Of God's new genesis.

The bed which gently drew us
Into the sweetest, most beautiful dreams
And showed us women—a thousand times
More beautiful than Solomon's thousand wives.
The bed that lifted us
Like a magic rocket
Over all fences and wires
And led us out of the ghetto

9. Rashi, Rabbi Shlomo Yitzchki (1040–1105), the foremost Biblical exegete and commentator.

10. Sholem Asch (1880–1957), the Polish-born Yiddish novelist and dramatist.

11. Heb: geniuses.

And carried us with wings of eagles
Over countries and the most wonderful places—
In nights of despair, pulled us
From the deepest, deepest abysses.

And made us young, and beautiful and fresh—
Placed us in golden castles
And set crowns upon our heads—
Even in the cursed hours.

And told us wonderful tales
Of a thousand and one nights
And brought laughter to our sad spirit
With a thousand charms.

Groan, groan, gracious holy bed—
You will be sold by the kilo.
To cook a ghetto soup
With a flame from your wood is no sin.

And now, Blimele, my dearest child—
See how the second group is already passing
Into exile.
Soon we also will have to go out.

And though, my child, you are a little girl,
And the man who studies Torah with his daughter
Is like someone giving her
Useless silly baubles,

The evil day has arrived.
The evil hour has arrived,
When I must teach you, a little girl,
The terrible *parshe*[12] of *Lekh Lekho.*

But how can we compare it
To the bloody *Lekh Lekho* of today?
And God said unto Abraham,
Go forth from your land,

And from your birthplace and from
Your father's house to the land, which I

12. Heb: Torah portion.

Will show you and there will I
Make a great people of you. . . .

And now the great people must go forth
On the unknown far off road,
Sick and tired—broken boats
Unable to get to any shores.
Who will faint from hunger,
Drop in the snow,
Quietly and painfully
Expiring like injured chicks.

Whose eyes will crawl out from fear
In the middle of the march.
In his heart, suddenly a string will burst
And he'll fall down hard as a stone.

And his shivering child
Will freeze in the fiery frost,
And the mother will carry it yet for a long time,
Thinking that it is still alive.

And fathers will call their children
And mothers will cry out for their children.
Families will get lost
And not find each other again.

For long stretches, they will carry
Large, heavy packs on their shoulders,
And finally throw them away,
And not have a pillow under their heads.

And without strength the invalid
Will remain stuck in the deep snow.
Birds will fly past
And be frightened by the scarecrows.

And women with pregnant bodies
Will kneel in weariness.
Soon they will fall down
And the snow will burn them like fiery coal.

And from their flaming faces
Cold deathly sweat will pour,

And they will bite their lips
From their horrible birth pangs

And vomit and writhe
On the painful snow delivery table,
And cry against the sky, against the sun, against God,
Against all who were causing this.

Over their wombs aborting in the snow,
Fertilizing the field with blood and tears,
White snow burns red,
And the golden wheat will come up red.

And with thousands of agonies
And with thousands of fears, the night will horrify,
Though the moon shines brightly, the starlight
Will chase like fearful rifle bullets.

And ice under the feet will crack,
Exploding like a burst of shrapnel,
And the snow will wink, "Shrouds for everyone!
Shrouds for the young! Shrouds for the old!"

And from each bush and branch
Hands will rise,
Eyes like those of wolves and lions
Will peer from behind each tree.

Somewhere in the wooded desert
That follows your steps
The vapor of your breath will resonate
Like the spurt of your own warm blood.

So, greetings to you, grandfather Abraham—
We are going on your hard journey.
But won't you be ashamed
For your grandchildren's bloody tears?

And now, Blimele, my dearest child,
Put your little coat on and let us go.
The third group is already dragging by,
And we also must be part of them.

But let us not weep, let us not
Moan, and to spite all enemies

Let us smile, only smile, that they
May be amazed at what Jews are capable of

And not understand that in our blood
Flows the power of our forefathers
Who in all generations
Performed all kinds of sacrifices.

That although our step is unsure,
Like the blind man's before a strange door,
The echo of our kinsmen's steps
On the roads of Siberia resonate in us.

That although, like captured animals,
Fright gleams in our eyelashes,
Pride burns in our hot glance,
As in our fathers on the scaffold.

And that although, at any minute
They can torture us and shoot us,
Ah, it is no new thing for us—
Our naked sisters they whipped.

So let us not weep, let us not
Moan, and to spite all enemies,
Let us smile, only smile, that they
May be amazed at what Jews are capable of

And not know that today, the same angels
Accompany us as in the past.
On the right Michael, on the left Gabriel,
In front Uriel, and in the rear Raphael.

And though beneath our steps lies death,
Over our heads is the divine presence of God.
So, child, go forth with a new sacrifice of self
And with the old "*Ekhod,*"[13] the oneness of God.
Shema Yisrael.[14] The Lord is One.

L[odz] G[hetto], February 23, 1942

13. Heb: One.
14. Heb: Hear, O Israel.

SPEECH BY CHAIM RUMKOWSKI

2 MARCH 1942

"WORK PROTECTS US FROM ANNIHILATION"

[This speech was delivered in the House of Culture to an invited audience of administrators, factory managers and Rumkowski's advisers.]

Uncertainty is worse than the bitter truth. Knowing this as well as I do, I've decided to call this meeting, to present the situation to you as it exists and to outline my plan for the immediate future. I stress that I shall speak about the situation as it is today. I cannot, of course, predict how things will develop later on. The explanations which I give today, and which are for the common good, should be repeated with the utmost accuracy throughout the ghetto. I shall be very grateful to you for this.

The legitimacy of my original basic slogan "Work" was confirmed from the minute I first issued it. We've seen many times now that we can have peace only through work. We live here in the ghetto; somehow we've been able to accommodate ourselves to our circumstances, modifying our existence and our behavior accordingly. Just last year I made jobs for all ghetto inhabitants a top priority. I therefore ordered a 15-day work assignment for those receiving welfare. You may remember that I stressed the importance of satisfying this requirement. Experience has made clear that the basic law of our times is: "Work protects us from annihilation." Unfortunately, there were Jews in the ghetto who laughed at this idea, preferring to evade their work obligation by manipulating the welfare system.

In the fall I reduced rations to force the shirkers receiving them to give them up and enter into productive work. But even this didn't help, since those with big families felt it was still to their advantage to remain on relief. And there were other instances of people staying away from work, for one reason or another. I tried other incentives, all in order to ensure peace and a secure tomorrow. Peace of mind is more essential than food. Had my words been given their full due by a wide segment of the population, you and I would have it much easier now.

Cruel fate took over. First we had a shipment of new people into the ghetto, and later a series of deportations. When I received the deportation order, I was able to reduce it by half, that is, to 10,000 people. As everyone knows, I included in that contingent the criminal and other undesirable elements. Unfortunately, that did not end the deportation. Thousands more were requested—this time, in accordance with the agreement that only people who can work can remain in the ghetto. The order must be carried out, or it will be carried out by others.

After painful deliberation and inner struggle, I've decided to deport the people on relief. They too are at fault, if not fully, then partially, in that they stayed outside the ghetto work force. I refer to the obvious disregard of the 15-day per month work schedule. I stressed again and again that I needed a reserve work force, to keep it in readiness for a sudden need to fill orders. People willing to work had to register. It was secondary what kind of work it would be—whether in clothing factories, trolley transportation or public works.

It's not a bluff, and it's easy to see, how a person still unemployed but in the reserve work force can use the indispensible work card for identification. This idea of mine grew out of reality, and I was proved right. But even then there were Jews who laughed at me, and unfortunately they've lived to see this calamity: more and more are being demanded for deportation. I've pointed out many times that a work card guarantees peace.

I'll outline for you the program I've carefully planned, as it relates to my current intentions. Children are always closest to my heart. How my heart rejoiced when I saw the youngsters with their schoolbags on their way to school—the sight gave me hope and inspiration for my work. It was the best breakfast I could have, mornings on Baluty Square. But when there was a need to find housing for newcomers, I decided to close the schools, though it made my heart bleed. It was my hope that in two months the newcomers' housing problems would be solved and that the buildings occupied by them would revert to school use. Unfortunately, that did not come to pass. Even now, when the collectives are being disbanded and the school buildings where they've been located—including the big school building at Franciszkanska Street—are being vacated, new imperatives arise. These buildings have to be used as factories. The only thing that pleases me is that these buildings will enable us to set up large enterprises, in the full sense of the word. Again, my darling children will have to wait for their schools. But in April, with the first breath of spring, we shall take care of them properly.

I point out that the ghetto was assured it would receive orders for a great deal of work. I am implementing some work reform in factories and other enterprises. Many establishments work on a 10-hour or 12-hour day. But with our meager sustenance, a double-digit number of hours per day can have a negative effect on productivity. My reform, therefore, will reduce the hours to eight, which will let us set up three shifts and triple our factory work force.

Every employed person is a productive member of the work force, regardless of the nature of his work: whether he's a laborer, office worker, policeman, or kitchen worker. As I've said, I shall put many new factories into operation, and by increasing the shifts to the maximum, I'll be able to increase our commercial capacity by 20,000 people. Making use of public works, I shall attempt to have ninety percent or more of the population employed. My basic concern is and will be the care of the working class—or to put it another way, everybody who is employed in the ghetto.

Tomorrow I'll open a new office which will be supervised by my most trusted advisors and which will conduct a survey of everyone employed. Each worker will have to supply information about each member of his family. This will enable the new office to assign work to unemployed members of a family: skilled workers to work in their fields of specialization, unskilled in unskilled work or to be re-educated. This is the way I shall solve today's most pressing problem. As far as older people are concerned, working people's parents who are unable to work, I trust that God will not forsake them. Seeking influence with regard to the work assignments will be useless. Everyone will have to be satisfied with the job he gets. Everyone 14 years old and older must work for a living!

My plan is based on sound logic, and my well-founded hope is that once we have the most precise, accurate data, we'll be able to convince the higher authorities and emerge victorious from this difficult situation. I have no doubt that I can achieve this greatly desired goal if the whole ghetto unanimously, in closed ranks, reports to work. Don't be ashamed if many of you have to take jobs which aren't exactly prestigious, jobs which are to be performed in public. Especially you, my sisters who are getting on in years, remember that even if you're sent to sweep the streets or to cart refuse, it's only for your own good. We have a great task to accomplish: we have to find work for 80,000 people. In spite of the immensity of this undertaking, I'm convinced that I'll be able to find a solution. With an 8-hour day in the factory and, subtracting an hour's preparation, closer to a 7-hour day, the odds are that productivity will keep increasing. I am assured that the ghetto will be supplied with sufficient food for all its inhabitants.

I may seem like an eavesdropping child, but I admit that news from "the street" reaches me. Fantastic lies are heard in the street. The latest gossip has it that I and my entire staff plan to flee to Warsaw. This is an ugly, total lie. I consider myself a soldier, staying faithfully at my post. I didn't think of running away at the beginning of the war, when practically all of the community's establishment left Lodz. My conviction that it was my duty to remain at my post didn't waver for a moment. And so it is today; I shall not abandon my post.

I shall try with all my might to realize one hundred percent of the plan

I've described. An atmosphere of calm is necessary, and I urge that everyone maintain it. Remember that this gossip mania makes my job more difficult. Gossip is like a terrible plague, and it's to blame for much of our difficulty.

Returning to the matter of provisions, I want to stress that the powers on which we depend wish to supply us with adequate food and are providing it as best they can. I was assured that when the potato storehouse is opened, the ghetto will be treated fairly. At this point, there is also a potato shortage in the city.

In order to improve the living conditions of the employed, special supplements will be given to this most important group when food is distributed. I had this in mind yesterday when I ordered that meat not be sold to the sick but to workers. I felt bad when I had to telephone yesterday to order the closing of Store R-III, the butcher shop for the sick. We must, alas, do everything to provide for the people who are well and who work. I do what I can, and I can say, with respect to food, that we're approaching a better tomorrow. As soon as it gets warm, my bare cupboards will be filled again.

I always hope and trust. I decided to speak to you because just today a ray of hope appeared, so that it may be possible to prevent the separation of families. That's how things look in a true light. The gossip-mongers, however, are spreading lies that the ghetto will be liquidated.

Managers! I stand before you as a soldier on guard; I ask you to maintain calm and to devote yourselves to your work, and that's how you'll help me realize my important program. See that the questionnaires are fully completed as to the status of family members. It's this kind of paper, this document, presented to the commission that will decide human existence, because the commission will try to match people with jobs.

Nobody should try to avoid work because of poor health or other problems. You can expect nothing from me in this respect, for what can I do? Let's say I could save 10 or 100 people; it's meaningless when you take into consideration the overall numbers. We cannot treat each individual as a special case. That's why I hold all managers personally responsible for the careful completion of questionnaires. If a manager abuses this responsibility, I shall, without hesitating a moment, deport him and his entire family. Managers! You are equally responsible for the regular work in your workshops. If I ascertain the slightest attempt at sabotage, I will deport you without pity. I absolutely will not consider anyone indispensible.

Comrades and friends, I don't have anything more to say. I asked you to come today so I could explain the situation in which we find ourselves. I hope you understood me perfectly. Take pity on yourselves! Work as one man! Do not involve yourselves in politics! Do not shirk work because of sickness!

I shall try to protect first the families of those who have been working a long time. They obviously have priority over those who have just started working. Today in one of the shops a shoemaker asked for a work certificate. He was asked how long he has been working, and he answered, "Since yesterday." This shoemaker is experienced and skilled, and yet he took advantage of the fact that with a family of seven he could remain idle and avail himself of welfare. Surely, individuals like this deserve to be deported. An unskilled person, or one for whom there is no work—that's an entirely different matter.

As of tomorrow and until further notice, I forbid anyone to be hired for any job whatsoever. Hiring can be done only on the recommendation of the commission examining the family situation of workers. This commission will be in existence as of tomorrow and will work with the Labor Department. If you learn of anyone who violates my order, and hires someone on his own, please write to me about this. The only people to whom this order does not apply are those recently laid off because their workshops closed—for example, the workers in the straw-shoe factory. For these, all the doors of my factories are open. They have absolute priority. The work of the Education Department's Retraining Committee remains the same.

I assure you, personally and on behalf of my closest associates, that we'll do everything in our power for the good of the ghetto.

A GIRL'S DIARY: "LIKE BIRDS IN A CAGE"

. . . The community officials nobody deports. There is no justice in this world, and even less in the ghetto. Now they're sending out welfare recipients. There is great panic among the people. And in addition this hunger! . . .

Life is horrible, conditions tragic, no food at all. Our officials are to blame for this. They stole from the provisions everywhere, they left everything to rot so that no one could take an inventory. And we are all at the mercy of fate, waiting to die of starvation. To buy something is simply impossible, we can only watch as death takes away new victims each day. Prices are terribly high; bread costs 70 RM in the street; it's the fault of the deportees from Germany. We receive bread for 6 days, distributions take place twice a week. We get bread and food at 13 Rembrandt Street. At the beginning everything was in perfect order there, but now there's no end to favoritism and chaos. . . . Vegetables are distributed at No. 12 on the same street. . . .

I'm very depressed by the situation—how can one feel nothing over such suffering and remain detached as they take away one's friends, the sick, the old, the children?

FRIDAY, 24 FEBRUARY 1942

Today the new cooking and sugar ration was announced: 1½ kg. of preserved beets, ½ kg. of sauerkraut, 10 dkg. of vegetable salad, 60 dkg. of rye flour, 20 dkg. of noodles, 50 dkg. of sugar, 15 dkg. of margarine, 10 dkg. of [ersatz] coffee. Can anyone live on this for 2 weeks? . . . We cook only once a day, in the evening, and there is not even enough for this, for the beets are all frozen, with lots of ice, but when the ice melts there is only water.

We are a family of five. My mother and brother work in the saddler workshop. Mother works at the sewing machine (1st machinist), and my brother (age 16) is a saddler. My sister (age 17) is also in this workshop. They get [at work] 15 dkg. of bread and 5 dkg. of sausage, and they bring 20 dkg. of bread from home. This is their food for the entire day, and they work very hard. My father works as a painter. The Construction Department gives them soup (water really). He takes 25 dkg. of bread from home. Can a man live on this while working as hard as my father does? He looks terrible, he's lost 30 kg. Mother, brother, and sister are also in bad shape but nothing can be done about it.

I stay at home. . . . I, too, get only 20 dkg. of bread for the entire day. . . . Hunger is terrible; people drop like poisoned flies. Today I got 1 kg. of parsley. Father, brother and I ate it raw. What fate, what irony! Will it ever end? I despise this life, we live like animals. How wretched human life is, a constant struggle.

Impatiently, we wait for March to come. Maybe the weather will warm up and the [underground] stockpiles [of potatoes or beets] will be opened. Maybe we'll get something to eat. As of today, winter persists and deportations continue. Each day 500 people are sent out.

SATURDAY, 28 FEBRUARY 1942

At night there was a thaw; it's very slippery now, but better this than the bitter cold.

Today is Saturday. Everybody works until 2 pm, except my sister, who works until 6 in the evening. At half past twelve, a little girl brought a slip of paper with the following message: "Dear Esterka and Minia, please come immediately, we are being deported, I want to say goodbye to you." It was from my sister's girlfriend. I am very depressed; she suffered so much, her life was always a struggle. What an unfortunate family. Nine months ago she lost her brother, a student in the first year of high school, a genius; he died from throat consumption. Her oldest sister is in the Soviet Union. She herself stayed on with her deaf-mute parents; they were on welfare. This is more like a slow death. A week ago her mother died, and now she is alone with her sick father, without even a shirt to put on her back. . . . I locked the door and left the key with the neighbor. I hurried to her, she lives on Brzezinska Street, 4th floor. . . . Her father was lying totally still on the bed, and a friend of hers, Dorka Cymberknopf, was sewing a knapsack. . . . I helped her pack a few things. At 4 I went back home. . . . She gave me a lot of science books.

SUNDAY, 1 MARCH 1942

March is here at long last! It's warm outside, maybe spring has come. What will this month bring us? Will there be more of this terrible hunger? Will they go on deporting us? Will death devastate us again? . . . All night I saw my sister's friend Hania Huberman and her sick father before my eyes. The day passed quickly. At 4 I started cooking dinner. At 5 my father came back from work. . . . Suddenly the door opened and HH came in. . . . She said that she had submitted an application to be released from deportation, and the medical

Deportation lists, prepared by the ghetto's "Relocation Commission," include dates of birth, occupations, pre-ghetto addresses.

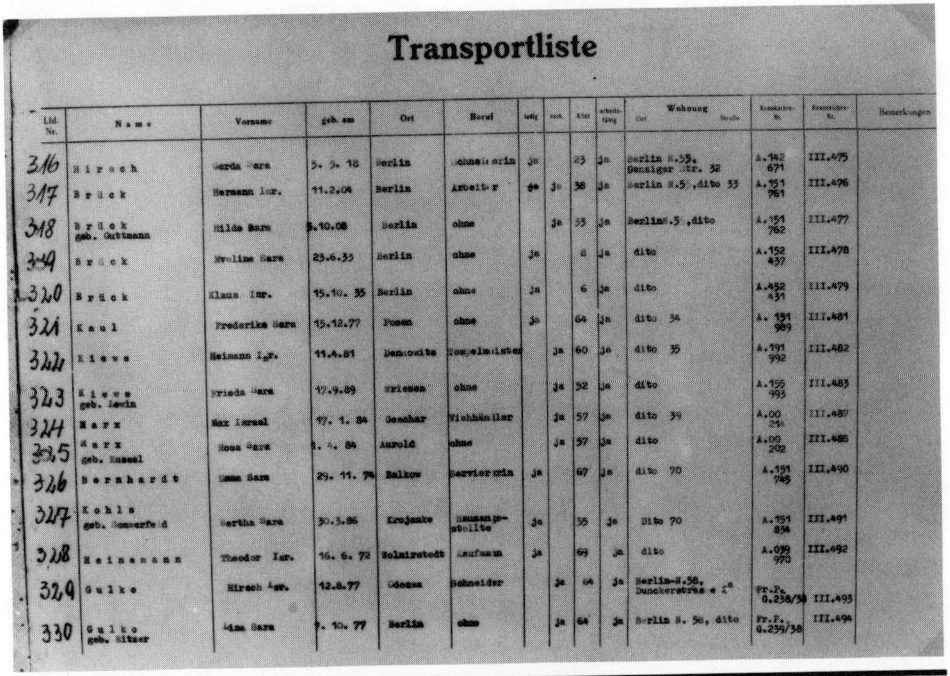

Transportliste

Lfd. Nr.	Name	Vorname	geb. am	Ort	Beruf	ledig	verh.	Alter	arbeitsfähig	Wohnung Ort Straße	Kennkarten-Nr.	Kennzeichen-Nr.	Bemerkungen
316	Hirsch	Gerda Sara	5. 5. 18	Berlin	Schneiderin	ja		23	ja	Berlin N.55, Danziger Str. 32	A.142 671	III.475	
317	Brück	Hermann Isr.	11.2.04	Berlin	Arbeiter		ja	38	ja	Berlin N.55, dito 33	A.151 761	III.476	
318	Brück geb. Guttmann	Hilde Sara	5.10.08	Berlin	ohne		ja	33	ja	Berlin N.55, dito	A.151 762	III.477	
319	Brück	Eveline Sara	23.6.33	Berlin	ohne	ja		8	ja	dito	A.152 437	III.478	
320	Brück	Klaus Isr.	15.10. 35	Berlin	ohne	ja		6	ja	dito	A.452 431	III.479	
321	Kaul	Frederika Sara	15.12.77	Posen	ohne	ja		64	ja	dito 34	A. 151 989	III.481	
322	Kiewe	Heimann Isr.	11.4.81	Demnowitz	Tempeldiener		ja	60	ja	dito 35	A.191 992	III.482	
323	Kiewe geb. Lewin	Frieda Sara	17.9.89	Wriezen	ohne		ja	52	ja	dito	A.155 993	III.483	
324	Marx	Max Israel	17. 1. 84	Geschar	Viehhändler		ja	57	ja	dito 39	A.00 214	III.487	
325	Marx geb. Kussel	Rosa Sara	8. 4. 84	Anrold	ohne		ja	57	ja	dito	A.00 202	III.486	
326	Bernhardt	Emma Sara	29. 11. 74	Balkow	Serviererin	ja		67	ja	dito 70	A.151 745	III.490	
327	Kohls geb. Sommerfeld	Bertha Sara	30.3.86	Krojanke	Hausangestellte	ja		55	ja	Dito 70	A.151 834	III.491	
328	Heinemann	Theodor Isr.	16. 6. 72	Wolmirstedt	Kaufmann	ja		69	ja	dito	A.039 970	III.492	
329	Gulko	Hirsch Isr.	12.8.77	Odessa	Schneider		ja	64	ja	Berlin-N.58, Dunckerstrasse 2a	Fr.P. G.238/38	III.493	
330	Gulko geb. Witzer	Lina Sara	7. 10. 77	Berlin	ohne		ja	64	ja	Berlin N. 58, dito	Fr.P. G.239/38	III.494	

commission had told her to come back tomorrow at 11. I am sure she'll be released on account of her sick father.

MONDAY, 2 MARCH 1942

It's foggy outside. At 12 I went to HH. No answer yet, should be by tomorrow. The day drags on, I am very hungry, there is no food. How I want the night to come! Night is dear to me. Night is my salvation. Oh night, if only you could last forever, during all these hungry days.

TUESDAY, 3 MARCH 1942

Today I got up at 8. I went to the co-op to see if they were giving out any of the food not given out earlier, but no, they weren't. . . . It's a beautiful day today, the sun is shining brightly. In fact, it's Purim today. Before the war there were crowds in the streets, tortes and cakes in the shop windows. Now no one even remembers. . . . Everybody is home already. I am washing some things. The same little girl came to say that Hania H. is leaving. Where will she go with her sick and helpless father, without even a shirt for him and for herself, hungry, exhausted, without money, without food? My mother got out some shirts for them. We ran to her. I started crying, couldn't control myself. I was unable to say even one word of consolation.

WEDNESDAY, 4 MARCH 1942

Deportations continue, hunger gets worse. Luckily my father is painting the [public] kitchen today and I go there for some soup. Mother and brother came back late today. I couldn't wait for supper because I ate just 20 dkg of bread today. . . . Will this hunger never end? The ghetto is in chaos. Some say that everyone will be deported. Others say only the welfare recipients and that an *Arbeitslager* [Ger: labor camp] will be set up here.

THURSDAY, 5 MARCH 1942

Winter again. Deportations are halted for a few days because there are not enough railroad cars. Hunger is tremendous; there is absolutely no hope for a food ration. In the morning I went to the vegetable co-op. I got 3 kg. of beets on my ration book. What beets! Like real dung, with bad odor and vapor coming out. They were frozen several times over. Each family gets 3 kg., whether it's for 5 or 3 or just 1 person. My ration book is No. 21; I am always first. But today they started with the last numbers. There is no food for supper. I tried all day to get something. Finally in the evening I bought ½ kg. of flour for 20 RM. One needs thousands, millions to buy food. No way to live like this.

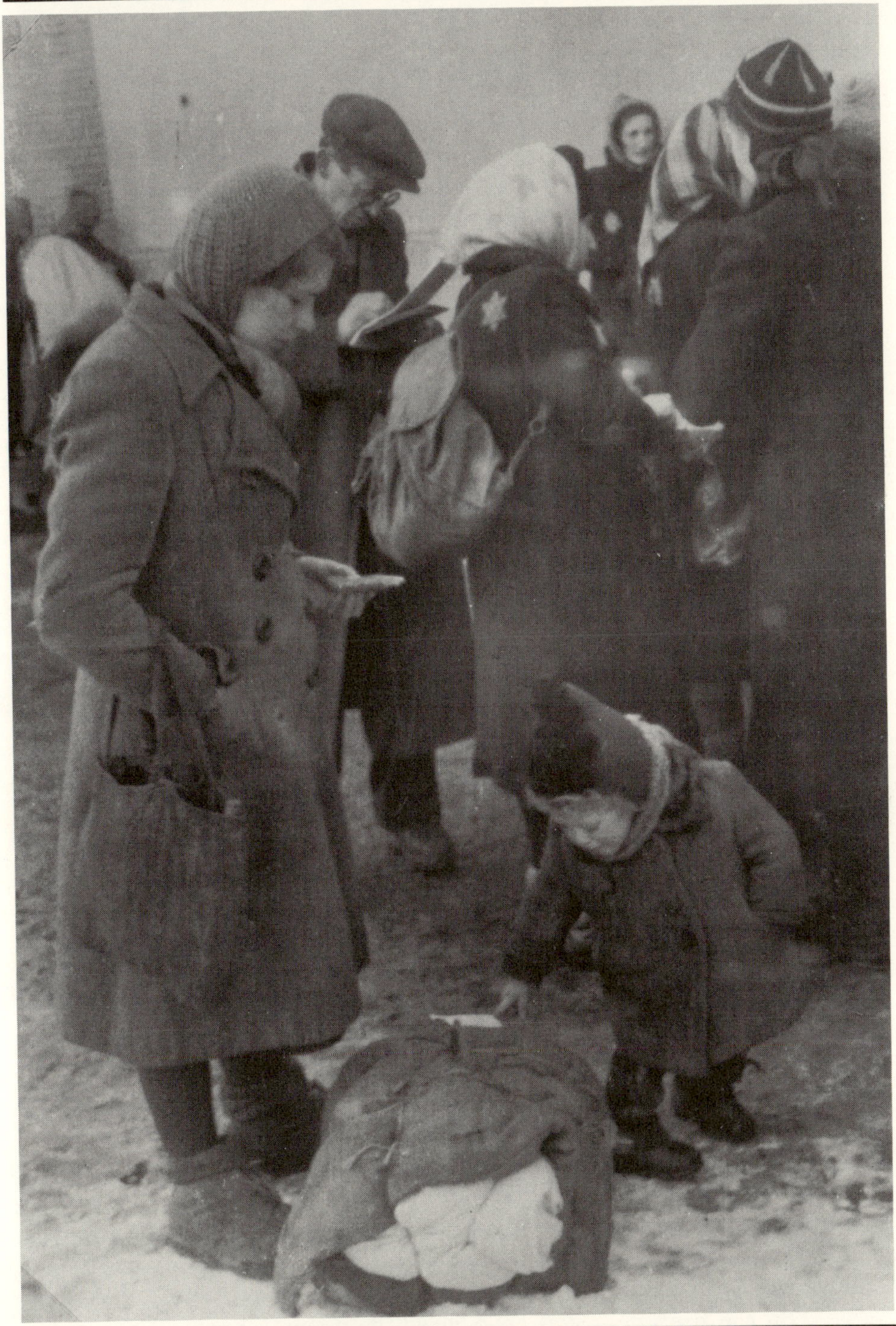

"Deportations continue."

FRIDAY, 6 MARCH 1942

Outside it's freezing. This morning it was [17 degrees Fahrenheit] . . . The heart is heavy when it's cold. Today we have nothing to cook. We are owed 3 breads. As if to spite us, they announced that only 1 bread will be given. I don't know what to do. I bought 3 kg. of beets from a woman. Rotten and stinking. We'll cook half today and half tomorrow. Does this deserve to be called life?

SATURDAY, 7 MARCH 1942

Beautiful, sunny day today. When the sun shines, my mood is lighter. How sad life is. One yearns for a different life, better than this grey and sad one in the ghetto. When we look at the fence separating us from the rest of the world, our souls, like birds in a cage, yearn to be free. . . . How I envy the birds that fly to freedom. Longing breaks my heart, visions of the past come to me. Will I ever live in better times? After the war will I be with my parents and friends? Will I live to eat bread and rye flour until I'm full? Meanwhile, hunger is terrible. Again we have nothing to cook. I bought 1/4 kg. of rye flour for 11 1/2 RM. Everybody wants to live.

SUNDAY, 8 MARCH 1942

The days are more and more beautiful. Sun, it's time for you to really shine for us. Passover is in 4 weeks. . . . I am owed a ration of meat because they were short 1 kg. We're going to have a celebration. Mother divided [the meat] in three portions; today we'll have cutlets. Dad still works in the workshop kitchen at Mlynarska Street. . . . In the evening he tells us what sort of food the staff prepares for itself. And where do they get it? Of course, from our soups. All [administrative] employees steal (they are not deported). . . . It is 5 pm, everybody is back from work. They had virtually a fast day because there was no bread. I got the bread late in the evening. For the whole day they took 5 dkg. bread each; at work they received another 15 dkg. and 5 dkg. of sausage and with this much they survived a day of hard work. My father brought home some soup for me. I was in seventh heaven. My brother was so depressed he cried like a child.

MONDAY, 9 MARCH 1942

The frosts are over, the deportations continue. People are very depressed, the mood is tense. Hunger is unbelievable, people fall off their feet. . . . We have no food for supper. I am owed 1.25 kg. of noodles, 50 dkg. of oil, 75 dkg. of honey, but I didn't get these. What misfortune has befallen our house. My head hurts, I cannot see right, our house is empty, not even a crumb of bread or a bit of coffee. You can drop dead and nobody will help you, a human being means nothing, dozens are of no importance. People are nasty, everyone for himself.... Nothing moves me any more, not even the worst suffering. People have taught me this.... This evening Mother borrowed 20 dkg. of noodles and a piece of bread from a neighbor. We are short on bread.

TUESDAY, 10 MARCH 1942

Mother, brother and sister left for work at 7:30 in the morning, and Father at 8. From my bed I noticed that my sister left her bread. I got up quickly and went to her shop.... I don't understand why I cannot live in peace with my sister; we argue, fight all the time. It causes my parents a great deal of heartache. Sister doesn't look well. I don't really know my sister, she is like a stranger to me. Hunger is terrible. How impatiently I wait each morning for my father to go, then I jump out of bed and eat all the bread my mother has left me for the day. God, what has happened to me? I cannot control myself. Then I go hungry all day long... the whole time drinking cold water and vinegar left from the beets, and this until 7 in the evening. That is why I often have stomach aches. Today bread was distributed. I waited 3 hours on line, got my 3 breads. When I came back I couldn't help it and took a piece. I vowed not to touch another piece at night, although Mother, who else, will give me hers. It is now 4 PM, in 2 hours they'll be home. I could not stay in the house, so I went to the co-op again. I don't know by what miracle I got my back ration.... I made a fire and put on 20 dkg of noodles. Mother came early, brought beets. Luck!... Father came at 7 with 2 men from his work. They put two turnips on the table, divided them in three portions, 70 dkg. each. When the men left, father pulled another piece of turnip from his pocket. The two turnips were stolen from the kitchen by the men, and my father got his piece from women who work at peeling. Though he was hungry, he didn't eat it, because he knew there was nothing to eat at home.... I cannot write, I have tears in my eyes.

WEDNESDAY, 11 MARCH 1942

In the street I heard about the next ration.... We're supposed to start consuming this ration on the 16th. How my heart beat when I read the posters, our life for the coming two weeks depends on this ration.... It is much worse than the last one.... There is nothing to eat, we are going to die of hunger. My teeth ache and I am very hungry, my left leg is frostbitten. I almost finished all the honey. What have I done, how selfish I am, what are they going to say, what will they spread on their bread now?... My mother looks terrible, a shadow of herself. She works very hard. Whenever I wake up at 12, at 1 in the night, she is bent over the sewing machine, and she gets up at 6 in the morning.

I have no heart or pity, I eat everything I can lay my hands on. Today I

"The ration is much worse than the last one . . . we are going to die of hunger."

had an argument with my father, I insulted and even cursed him. And this was because yesterday I weighed 20 dkg of noodles but this morning took a spoonful for myself. When father came back at night, he weighed the noodles again. Of course there was less. He started yelling at me. He was right, of course; I had no right to take for myself the few precious decagrams of noodles Mr. Chairman gives us. I was upset and I cursed him. Father just stood at the window and cried like a child. No stranger ever abused him like I did. Everybody was at home. I went to bed quickly without touching supper. I thought I would die of hunger. . . . I fell asleep but woke up at 12. Mother was still working at the machine. I felt gnawing hunger, so I got up and ate. . . .

THURSDAY, 12 MARCH 1942

Today the new ration was distributed. I wasted 5 hours at the co-op, there were such crowds. People pressed together so much it was difficult to breathe. And lice were crawling everywhere. I tried to stand against the wall so they wouldn't get to me. Coming home I saw a horrible scene: two men dragging an old man who was unable to walk. These sorts of people are being deported now.

Food coupons issued by the Germans.

Young girls of the ghetto were trained to embroider insignia for German uniforms.

A load of bread is hauled to the distribution points. Such shipments were usually accompanied by guards.

FRIDAY, 13 MARCH 1942

Father told me to come and have some soup. Despite everything a father is a father. He is working now at 32 Mlynarska. He gets 2 soups there and he gives one to me. Would another father do that?

MONDAY, 16 MARCH 1942

When I went to the co-op, I heard the news that the bread ration is now for 7 days. I shivered. We stood in line in the bitter cold a long time before we were let in. Finally I got 2 breads. . . . At 3 pm I went to the [coal] depot to get the briquette ration. At the Balut Market,* German workers were repairing the electric wire and were pitching a tent. A woman passed by the tent. One of the workers pushed her to the ground and started beating and kicking her. People ran, scared, in every direction. Nobody said a word. For each word not to their liking, hundreds of Jews could perish. How tragic is our life, how humiliating. We are treated worse than pigs. We Jews of the ghetto, we work so hard, we help them in the war, making beautiful things from rags—military uniforms, rugs, everything a person needs. They treat us worse than slaves. And this is life. Isn't death better? I had to hold back with all my strength so as not to scream insults at them. We have to keep silent, even if our hearts are broken.

WEDNESDAY, 18 MARCH 1942

Business is brisk on our street. German Jews are selling everything they have so they can buy food. Sugar now costs 32 RM for 1 kg. . . . Deportations continue.

JOZEF ZELKOWICZ

BREAD IN THE YEAR 1942

The end of 1941 was marked by the arrival of 20,000 newcomers from the West and by extreme food shortages. The year 1942 began with great hunger and calamity.

The cold was terrible. Heating problems were acute. The Department of Bakeries had to wrestle with this like everyone else. In order to keep the bakeries open, drastic cuts in heating had to be made. These cuts affected first the *cholent*-bakeries. [*Cholent,* a meal consisting of potatoes, vegetables, meat and fat, was left in the ovens overnight.] Closed were Bakeries Nos. 22, 31, 34, and 39. By then, the role of the *cholent*-bakeries had diminished anyway, because people had almost finished their winter ration of vegetables, and there was little left to fill the pot.

The year 1942 was one of the ghetto's blackest and most tragic. . . . Around January 5 people began whispering that the ghetto was about to suffer sacrifices. At the first of the year, the population had reached 162,681, including the "foreign Jews." The authorities in whose hands the fate of the ghetto lies decided that it was technically impossible to feed so many people. Transportation difficulties and so forth were supposedly the reason for halting the delivery of food to the ghetto. Then this became the official explanation for deporting a large part of the ghetto population.

The decree, dry and laconic, numbed people's hearts and minds. Hunger and bitter cold, and now the unknown, the fear about "where" and "why"—all this consumed the last bits of strength on which the ghetto lived.

Meanwhile, the Resettlement Commission began its task. A commission of Jews had to sever limbs and do bloodletting, not knowing which limbs to cut and whose blood to spill, or whether those limbs would ever again be of any use or would be trampled and left to shrivel like broken tree branches. . . .

There was great panic. News and rumors swirled in the air, each more terrible than the other. Even worse was the terror and confusion. One could barely stay home alone with one's thoughts, but it was no better to be with other people. And when the first "wedding invitations," the deportation summonses, were sent out, the machinery of the ghetto simply stopped functioning. There was no work done in the workshops and offices. How could one work when the heart was bleeding? This man's wife was to lose a child; others were to lose a mother, a father, a brother or sister, and even they themselves were not safe. A common fate awaited everyone, if not today, then later, tomorrow, the day after tomorrow.

The ghetto came off its rails. The ghetto lost its "normalcy." Nobody worked, rested, ate, or thought in a "normal" way.

The Resettlement Commission began its work on January 5. In the period between January 6 and January 19, new blood was drawn each day. Fourteen transports left the ghetto—each day a transport of almost a thousand living people who did not know where, why or for what sins.

Ten thousand and three persons were deported in those fourteen days. The food shortage kept step with the deportations. The price of bread rose on January 6, with the first "wedding invitations." Those receiving the summonses, to report to the Central Prison from where they'd be sent away, began liquidating their pitiful households, selling their last belongings, and spending their

"Rumkies" on food and first of all on bread, for which they paid exorbitant prices. Taking the "Rumkies" with them did not make sense.

The hunger psychosis and the fear of dying from starvation was so great then that money was of no importance, especially for the deportees, who had nothing more to lose but the ghetto money, which was worthless outside, anyway. Thus we note that the price of a loaf of bread was 20 to 22 marks in the first half of January but rose to 30, 32 and even 35 marks in the second half of the month, when the deportations began in earnest.

A certain relaxation of the tension could be felt between January 29 and February 15, when no new transports left the ghetto and it seemed that the deportations had stopped. The ghetto slowly got back to "normal." People, who just a short while ago were mourning their deported relatives, were now going back to their "normal" occupations. But the price of bread did not normalize. It fell a little to 25 marks, but when rumors began circulating in the second half of February about impending new deportations, the price immediately jumped to 35 marks.

For those who were not registered in the public kitchens, the food ration for the period February 1–15 included the following for cooking: 50 dkg. of flour, 20 dkg. of *farfel* [Yid: noodle dough in the form of small pellets], 7.5 kg. of vegetables, excluding potatoes. From this ration, the citizen of the ghetto could prepare one meal a day consisting of 5 dkg. of solid food and 53 dkg. of vegetables (not excluding peels and rotten or frozen items), and he would use 3 g. of oil. The oil ration for the 14 days was 5 dkg. Meat was not distributed in February at all, except for a single 30 dkg. ration for workers. A small, hardly noticeable improvement in the food situation came on February 5, when a supplemental ration was announced. This ration consisted of 20 dkg. of corn meal, 5 dkg. of *farfel,* 10 dkg. of oil and 50 dkg. of preserved beets.

The situation was much worse for those receiving their meals in the public kitchens. They depended on the kitchen's one daily soup, a substance without content, and except for the above-mentioned supplemental ration, they received nothing else in February. They had nothing to sell or exchange, except perhaps for the slice of bread, while others could exchange sugar, flour or oil for frozen or rotten vegetables.

On February 22 a new series of deportations began. Simultaneously, deliveries of food to the ghetto decreased daily in volume. Vegetables were not to be had at all. Kitchens had no produce with which to make soup. The ration for the second part of February . . . was reduced by 7.5 kg. of vegetables. The ghetto was facing not just hunger but total catastrophe.

The Department of Bakeries was charged with maintaining the balance between hunger and despair and had to work more intensively than ever. Bread was now the ghetto's ultimate fate.

The kitchens had no food to cook, workers were passing out, and therefore the Department of Bakeries had to do all it could to make enough so that workers could be given 15 dkg. of bread every day, instead of soup. The population was starving; vegetables were not available. The bread ration had to be increased from seven to six days, and the bakeries had to increase their production.

As already mentioned, the new deportations began on February 22, and they lasted without interruption until April 2. Transports left the ghetto each day during these 40 days, sending away 34,073 Jews.

In March a slight improvement in provisions could be noticed. Those who cooked meals at home received the following ration: 60 dkg. of flour, 25 dkg. of *farfel,* 50 dkg. of sugar and 15 dkg. of margarine. Beginning on March 7, workshop workers and office employees regularly received a separate food supplement. Despite all this, the price of bread was such that it was absolutely impossible to keep up with it. Having gone from 35 to 40 marks, it now began rising every hour.

But the real jump in the price of bread came on March 16, when the bread ration was again cut back. The same ration now had to suffice for a seven-day period, instead of for six days. And the price jumped from 50 to 60 marks, and two days later it reached 100 marks.

The reduced bread ration was felt in the ghetto as yet another calamity. People could not accept the cutback as something natural, and it was explained in various ways. There were optimists who believed and kept assuring others that the reduction was temporary, "that the ghetto was, God forbid, not yet in such bad shape that it needed to skimp on bread rations. It just happened that, with everyone preoccupied with real problems, with the deportations and so on, somebody cut a slice off the bread ration." Others went further, explaining the reduction as a result of the deportations: "Because the deportees were buying out all the bread and the price had jumped so high, the ration was reduced so that there would be no surplus bread to sell . . . but the minute the deportations stop, the ration will return to its old level." The pessimists foresaw further reductions in the ration, which, they predicted, would soon have to last eight, and maybe even ten days.

We should emphasize again that the reduced bread ration was not the only reason the price rose. The main reason was the deportations. People who received the "wedding invitations" were ready to buy bread at any price. Here lies the whole tragicomic situation of those times: within just three square kilometers, the price of bread on the same day would be different in different parts of the ghetto. In the center, that is, in the vicinity of the "market," or Jona Pilcer Square, where the whole sorry business of selling bread was concentrated, the price was lower than at the ghetto's borders, where no bread was to be had. Bread was most expensive near the Central Prison, where the deportees were held. There, the only sellers were the police or those who paid them a "commission." The price of one loaf there could reach 200 marks.

There was a respite with the arrival of Passover. The deportations stopped on April 2, and at the same time the ghetto was suddenly flooded with potatoes. People had not seen a potato since January but now received 2.5 kg. of potatoes and one kg. of vegetables each. In addition, workers received another 2 kg. of potatoes and one kg. of red beet leaves. This, in turn, caused the price of bread to slide to 70 marks.

During April, the price of bread was generally very shaky and underwent many fluctuations.

On April 1, bread cost 160 marks. On April 2, it fell to 70 marks. Two days later it cost only 50 marks, with the demand quite weak. On April 12 it was announced that the new ration for those cooking at home contained 7.5 kg. of potatoes but that this included the month of May, and no further potatoes were to be distributed until the end of April. Thus, any illusions about an improvement in provisions or an increment in the bread ration were shattered, and the price of bread jumped again to 100–110 marks. On April 17 the distribution of the "May" potatoes began, and with these potatoes safely in their hands, everyone felt more secure, which caused bread to lose a bit of its spell and its price to fall by 30 marks a loaf. On April 18 there appeared the well-known Announcement No. 374, about "stamping" all non-working individuals and which caused so much fear in the ghetto. Even if no one knew what it really meant, the scare alone was enough to increase the price of bread by 30 marks, and this price persisted until April 25.

The notice did not indicate why medical examinations were being given to the non-working population. People reasoned that those who were examined and found unfit for work would be deported from the ghetto, which seemed confirmed by the various stamps affixed to the bodies of those examined. This in itself should have been sufficient to raise the price of bread to new heights, as happened during previous deportations. That the price did not go up for an entire week was, therefore, not normal. Yet those who observed the mood in the ghetto streets understood it very well:

The ghetto had lost its head. Almost every family in the ghetto had been hit by the stamping decree. Everyone was now trying to find a way out of getting stamped and being deported. There was only one thing they could do: find employment—or at least have their names appear on an employment list—

anywhere in the ghetto. Day and night thousands of people besieged the Work Assignments Office. All trading stopped. Nobody bought or sold anything. A week later, when the population had somehow calmed down, business slowly picked up and the price of bread increased to 115 marks, and from there it went up steadily each day. Finally on April 30 rumors about an impending deportation began to circulate, and the price of bread shot up in the black market to 160 marks.

SIMCHA BUNIM SHAYEVITSH

SPRING 1942

1.
And in an hour of good fortune
Spring is here again—
Heigh, Heaven—rejoice, rejoice—
You are newly reborn.
You lie in a blue and golden cradle
And the mild wind rocks you.
The swallows sing to you
And you play with a large bear-like cloud
That has strayed into your lap.
You wake at dawn
With a dreamy violet smile,
With the shimmer of the rainbow.
And twilight lulls you to sleep
With the most beautiful children's stories
And the colorful fires of sunset.

2.
And in an hour of good fortune
Spring is here again—
The tree will send another root
Deeper into the earth,
And the birds will build
New cozy nests.

Only my ghetto brothers
Still must leave their homes,
With their gold-spun dreams
In herds—in dozens,
In hundreds—to trudge
Day after day, night after night
Down to the gathering place
To receive the blessing of expulsion.
Tired and sick, their steps
Totter, reel like drunkards.
But they are not drunk from wine
Or whiskey but from anguish and agony,
From despair and bitterness.
Half-numb, their hands—which
Can hardly move—are like sick birds' wings.
Their glances—abysmal, black—
Like those of sheep being led to slaughter.
And in their hearts fear strikes,
Like clumps of earth falling on graves.

3.
And in an hour of good fortune
Spring—God be praised—is here again.
Night blows on the silvery horn
Of the young moon
And learns a new tune
In honor of Spring, which this year
Came as a very late guest.
But like a camel a mother is hunched
With a pack on her back,
Her five children dragging behind her,
One smaller than the next,
Clad in rags
And torn shoes
Tied with string,
With heavy sacks
Like beggars' bags
Hung on them.
They are tired and can walk no further.
The mother spreads her arms like a hen.

The oldest she leaves unattended,
The second she scolds,
The third she pushes ahead,
The fourth she pleads with,
And the fifth she takes in her arms.
But soon she stands still, breathless
Like a dead fish,
With staring eyes
And open mouth,
And the pack on her back and the child in her arms
Rock cumbrously—
On the mother's scale—
Down and up
Back and forth,
Up and down
Back and forth.

4.
And in an hour of good fortune
The miracle of rebirth occurs
And Spring is here again.
But for us in the ghetto
No one any longer cares about hunger
Which cries out from every limb.
And everyone has forgotten
Death which visits everyone personally
And does not skip a house.
And like a desolate, trembling sheep,
One shivers and trembles
At the order for deportation
Into an unknown land.
One trembles and quakes
At Belshazzar's cryptic writing:[1]
—Life or Death.
An old woman sees the hearses drive by;
Her eyes gleam with envy:
—Yes, yes, the man was lucky.
And the young man lowers his head:

1. In the Book of Daniel, it was Belshazzar who saw the writing on the wall.

—No, no, everything is hell anyway.
And the young girl spits three times:
—Tfu, tfu, tfu, let the Angel of Death be my bridegroom, already.
And even the child trudges on the march,
Stammering with a plaintive weeping:
—Mamele dear, Oh I don't have any more strength;
Oh, put me up there on the black wagon.

5.
And in an hour of good fortune
Spring—an honored guest—
Is here again.
The buds fill up with nectar
And young hearts with new blood.
But in the ghetto, in a garret somewhere,
For ten days in a row,
A seventeen-year-old girl lies alone,
With a smile on her clayey lips,
With corroded lungs,
And waits for the wagon
To come for her—
They took her father and mother immediately
And were supposed to come for her
Within an hour.
Before leaving, her mother said:
"Itkele, my jewel, I'll wait there for you;
In the meantime, take a piece of sugar.
Eat a slice of bread.
And dress warmly when you go."
And her father added:
"What's so bad about going out
For a breath of fresh air?"
But at dawn they sent her father and mother away
From the assembly point.
Her mother tore her hair:
"And where is my Itkele?
Where did you murderers leave my child?"
And the father, his eyes blank
And his lips trembling stood around awkwardly,
Tearing out a hair

From his shaggy beard.
And at home the seventeen-year-old girl
Waits and waits, waits and waits.
A day passes, a night comes;
A dawn laughs wildly
And a sunset whispers piously;
The first part of the night passes in seriousness,
And the last part is like a cat-and-mouse game:
The young moon peers out through a crack,
And a cloud catches it in its plush paw.
But no one comes for her.
She has no more bread left.
On the second day a neighbor brings her
A hot cup of bitter coffee
With sniffling comfort:
"Perhaps they'll come soon;
The world, after all, is not wanton."
A night passes, a day follows.
An evening reddens—drunkenly reels—
And a sunrise mournfully, bitingly follows.
A frost covers the windowpane
And the sun licks it up with its golden tongue.
The little piece of sugar is also gone.
She lies with froth on her yellow lips.
On the fourth day a woman brings a cup of soup, sighing heavily:
"It's unfortunate. There's such hunger now—
They'll surely come for you tonight."
A day changes into night,
A night into day—two loyal watchmen
Guarding her empty, desolate, sick life.
Her hands search the chair—
Perhaps some kind of crumb
Can be found to take into her mouth—
And they tremble and tremble.
Her glance scans the emptiness
And her ears are alert.
But there is no friendly mouse
To gladden her
With a familiar grating sound of life.
Just steps running on the stairs

Up and down, down and up
Avoiding her door, and avoiding her door.
On the fifth day she reels.
At the sixth twilight, she sips a drop of soup.
On the seventh dawn, she dreams.
On the eighth, she knows nothing.
On the ninth, a string bursts in her head,
She falls back on her pillow,
And her hands are like two hard rocks.
On the tenth night, she dreams again—
Shadows swim move run—
Now they're coming for her—
Now they're knocking at the door.
On her clayey lips
Green foam bubbles and boils
And her yellow smile beams:
—Tatele, Mamele, it took you so long?!
Through the crack in the cloud
The moon spits out:
—It's a holiday today, ha? So shine, shine
Oh, it's my wedding night, my wedding n-i-g-h-t!
But everything suddenly becomes dark
And her head flies falls drops
Sinks into the abyss:
—Tatele, Ma-mele
M-a-m-e-l-e, m-a . . .

6.

And in an hour of good fortune
Spring is here again.
They will lead the stallion to the mare,
The bull to the cow,
And the snow will melt, disappear,
And the grass will soon become green.
But the farmer plowing his field
Will come upon the bodies
Of those who found death in the middle of the road
And will see the last gaping, distorted mouth
And the shock in the open eyes:
—Ha, little daughter, where are you leaving me?

The farmer will look and see
Footsteps that trail weakly away
And circle zigzaggingly back
And are as if deliriously alive:
—Tatele dear, a slice of bread,
A little bag of sugar
And the rest—
He who over us is—
But the farmer notices
That the dead man's muddy hand
Clutches a piece of bread.
He stands and wonders and does not know:
Should it be regarded as a good sign—
Here is bread—
Or is it a bad sign—
Nearby lies death . . .

7.

And in an hour of good fortune
Ha, ha, ha, Spring is here again.
The grass, the trees will dress
Themselves in dew, as though with pearls,
And the sun will again present the world
With her gold, squandering it extravagantly.
But why do a branch, a bush
Crack and break when you step on it?
And poor cursed heart of mine,
Do you not break from the pain
When your brothers are driven like dogs?!
Whorish, benumbed heart,
Why don't you die?
Why don't you take leave of your mind
And dance in the middle of the street
And do somersaults—with your head upside down.
With your feet to the sky.
With your fists clenched on your breast.
With your fists clenched toward Him above.
And you bang your head on the wall
And sing a holiday song.
And bite off a piece of your hand,

While tears flow from your eyes,
Pailsful, pailsful.
You poor, cursed heart,
Why don't you burst from pain?

8.
And in an hour of good fortune
Life turns over
Like pages of a book
And Spring is here again.
But where is the great ghetto Jew,
Where is Don Isaac Abrabanel,[2]
Who should be a pillar for us
As he once was in Spain?
I do not have the strength for it,
Nor do you, friend,
So what will be?
What will be with the thousands
Of poor ghetto Jews?
Who will comfort them in their terrible tragedy?
Who will ease their agony
On their horrible unknown road?
Who will heal the sick,
Who will bind the wounds,
Who will lift up the fallen,
Who will feed the weak,
Who will quench the thirsty,
Who will bury the dead
And still the crying of the child?
Alas and woe—where is the great ghetto Jew,
Where can we get Isaac Abrabanel?!
But how could such a one help us today?
In the ghetto he himself would walk
With a bent, aching back
And would consider the whole Spanish expulsion
And all the bitter edicts that followed
Child's play, when compared to today.

2. Don Isaac Abrabanel (1437–1508) was prominent in fifteenth-century Spain just prior to the expulsion of the Jews.

9.
And in an hour of good fortune
May no Evil Eye befall us, Spring is here again.
Even graves will be covered in green.
So rise up, great poet,
Master of the "City of Slaughter,"[3]
From your green-laureled grave.
I invite you to walk with me.
In our ghetto you will be quickly satisfied.
Although we are exposed here to ridicule and shame,
No wife's husband—even the most pious—will run to the rabbi
To ask if he may continue living together with his wife.
In our ghetto you will be satisfied.
Not like there in the other "City,"
Where they decreed a fast
And gathered together in the synagogues
"With wild horrible cries
With a burning sea of tears."
I doubt, great poet, if today you will find
Anywhere in a ghetto synagogue a *minyan*[4] to recite the *Kaddish*.[5]
One trudges quietly on the desolate march
And even more quietly one expires
And the bridegroom leaves his weeping bride
And the lover does not know of his bride's remains
And the child is torn in rage from her mother's arms
And the gun pursues her further
With cries: "Shoot—shoot—."
But forgive them, great and wrathful poet.
Although we still have no fist
And the great thunder still does not echo
Vengeance for all "generations"
And although you mocked and ridiculed
Such innocent victims and martyrs,
You will bow your head three times to the ghetto Jew

3. "City of Slaughter," a well-known poem by Chaim Nachman Bialik (1873–1934), concerns the Kishinev pogroms. Shayevitsh's debt to this poem is suggested by the often-quoted line: "The sun shines, the acacia blossoms and the slaughterer slaughters."
4. Heb: prayer group, requiring ten or more men.
5. Heb: the prayer for the dead.

And murmur with ecstasy, "Holy, Holy, Holy."
God with a mild hand
Also presented us with twins,
A death expulsion and a Spring.
The garden blooms, the sun shines
And the slaughterer . . . slaughters.
And yet we do not demand acknowledgment,
For when a man is slaughtered
They also slaughter his God.
But do you know, poet of wrath and vengeance,
What I require of you?
I ask that you wake from their sleep
Our mother Rachel,
And the Saint of Berdichev[6]
And that the three of you go together before God.
You will thunder and demand.
Rachel will weep and plead,
And Levi Yitzhak will argue his lawsuit, proclaiming:
—If, Lord of the Universe, You will not be the Savior
Of Living Jews,
You will, God forbid, be the Savior of Corpses.

10.
And in an hour of good fortune
The circling wheel turns
Round and around
And Erev Pesach,[7]
Blessed be His name, is here again.
So let us sit down
To the poor holy *seder*.[8]
Matzoh is here.
There will be four goblets of wine:
Of our tears
And *Morer*[9] and the *Charoyses*[10]

6. The Chassidic leader Levi Yitzchak of Berdichev is especially well known for enacting symbolic little dramas to "argue the case of the Jewish people before the Heavenly court."
7. Heb: Passover eve.
8. Heb: Passover service, including ceremonial meal.
9. Heb: bitter herbs.
10. Heb: mixed fruit, wine, and nuts.

Are also here—
Our dismal anguish
And the dark, sad, wrinkled faces.
Now, Blimele, my child,
Ask the question:
"Ma"—Why is this night
No different from every other night:
Every night people leave their homes—
"Halaylo haze"—And this night of Passover—also.
"Ma"—Why did miracles occur each time
And today we are so wretched?
And, my lovely child, you should know
That I do not have an answer for you.
Just this one—
Let Mother—
Our dear and beloved friend—
Open the door
And with my father's holy melody
Translating it, as was his custom,
Into plain Yiddish:
—*Shfoykh hamoskho al hagoyim*—
Pour out Your wrath on the nations
—*Asher lo yedsukho*—
Who do not wish to know You
—*Ki akhol as Yaakov*—
Because they devour Jacob
—*Veos navehu heshamu*—
And destroy his home.
Tirdof beaf
Vetashmidem mitakhas shmay adonoy
Chase them in anger
And destroy them from the heaven of God . . .

EREV PESACH 1942

Frantic trading in household goods as those ordered deported attempt to convert their last possessions into currency for food on the journey "into the unknown."

"In barely half a year, they have been stripped of all their European finery, and now must make another journey, into the unknown." (*The Chronicle of the Lodz Ghetto*)

GHETTO DOCUMENT

Announcement No. 380

Concerning the evacuation of Jews who came from the Old Reich, Luxembourg, Vienna and Prague and who were settled in the ghetto of Litzmannstadt. I am hereby announcing that by order of the authorities the evacuation of the Jews who had come from the Old Reich, Luxembourg, Vienna and Prague and who were sent to the ghetto of Litzmannstadt is taking place starting Monday, May 4, 1942.

The following persons are exempted from this order:

1) bearers of the Iron Cross
2) bearers of a badge awarded to a wounded soldier
3) employed persons

   Persons referred to under no. 1 and 2 must furnish documentary proof of the possession of their decoration at the Department for Persons Resettled in Lodz, at Fischstr. 8.

Only 12 1/2 kilograms of luggage per person may be taken along. Persons who are ordered to evacuate, and who might still own objects that must be left behind, can offer these objects for sale at the purchasing center, Kirchplatz 4, and at my bank, Bleicherweg 7.
The evacuation office is situated at Fischstr. 8.
All information regarding this matter is given there, and all requests and reclamations are accepted at this office.

Ch. Rumkowski
The Eldest of the Jews
in Litzmannstadt

Litzmannstadt ghetto, April 29, 1942.

Fecal workers heave and haul an excrement wagon toward the outskirts of the ghetto. Such a work assignment was usually a death sentence, the fecalists soon contracting typhus.

CHAPTER SIX

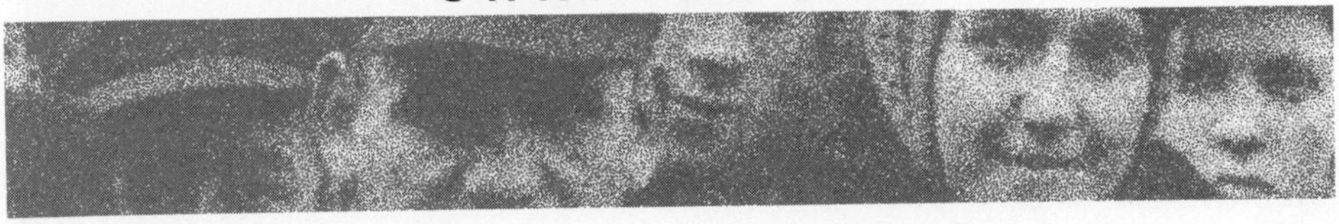

"LIFE IS NARROW"

DAWID SIERAKOWIAK'S DIARY

MARCH 21, 1942
This evening there was suddenly news that another 15,000 are to be deported immediately, in groups of a thousand a day. Everyone is saying that now all the ghetto's inhabitants will go.

MARCH 25, 1942
I feel very sick. I read but can't study at all, so I'm working on English vocabulary. Among other things, I was studying Schopenhauer. Philosophy and hunger, some combination.

MARCH 26, 1942
Again, total confusion. The deportations are continuing, while at the same time the shops are receiving huge orders and there's enough work for a few months.

MARCH 28, 1942
Today we bought an étagère (my pre-war dream) and a kitchen table with drawers from our neighbors who are being deported. These—and some other household items—all for two packs of local cigarettes.

MARCH 30, 1942

Aside from the deported, a number of people have left in the last few days, taken out by relatives (for big money).

APRIL 9, 1942

Rumkowski made a long speech today but said nothing of importance. It's the demagoguery of a megalomaniac.

APRIL 19, 1942

Mother cried when I came home today. She's the only one in our family who [as unemployed] is in danger. Father, whose rage intensifies all the time, revealed his true nature today. He wants to get rid of Mother, as he has not even lifted a finger to do anything for her. All he does is scream at her and annoy her on purpose.

Oh, if only things with Mother were different: the poor, weak, beloved, broken, unhappy being! As if she didn't have enough trouble, she has to put up with these noisy quarrels (which according to Father are due to my "indifference" toward the family, or rather toward him). If we could only save her! We'll settle with Father after the war.

Since Mother isn't feeling well, she's decided to give my father only 25 dkg. of bread from her loaf (rather than the 50 dkg. she used to). He doesn't like it, but he's probably figured out that if she were not around he'd have even less.

APRIL 20, 1942

The ghetto is going crazy. Thousands of those at risk are struggling every which way to get jobs, mostly through influence. Meanwhile, the German commission started its work. All those examined by the commission get an indelible letter stamped on their chests, a letter whose significance nobody knows.

APRIL 23, 1942

Last night the police went through apartments. Those who have not reported to the commission and could offer no excuse had to give up their bread and food ration cards. Today there were round-ups in the streets. There's talk that soon the entire population of the ghetto will be stamped.

Another group of people left today by bus, to join relatives in Warsaw. They say that things in Warsaw are wonderful. The ghetto is open, and one can buy anything for money; work is paid for, and it's easy to get. Meanwhile, we perish here.

APRIL 24, 1942
A commission came to our shop today, and they stopped by our room. These people come from another world—these rulers, these masters of life and death. Their look doesn't in the least suggest a quick end to the war.

APRIL 29, 1942
Again I have no desire, actually no strength to study. Time is passing, as is my youth, my energy and enthusiasm. The devil knows what will be rescued from this pogrom. I'm gradually losing hope that I shall come back to life, or be able to hold on to the one I am now living.

MAY 7, 1942
Things in the ghetto are ever more scandalous, but we are now in such a state of exhausion that I truly understand what it means to lack the strength to complain, let alone protest.

MAY 18, 1942
In the last few days, with frightening speed, my legs have become weak. I almost cannot walk because it tires me so. Still I can't avoid it, since my unit works on the third floor.

MAY 21, 1942
Again, life has been extended for a time: on, from day to day, from one food ration to the next, more deportations and more new arrivals into the ghetto, until . . .

SATURDAY, MAY 30, 1942
Our situation at home is again getting extremely tense and awful. Father, who for the last two weeks was relatively peaceful and divided his bread into equal daily portions, lost his self-control again on Thursday and ate my entire loaf yesterday and today finished the extra half kilo of bread he gets from Mother and Nadzia. He also stole another 10 dkg. from them when he weighed the bread. I don't know why he hoards all the money, or why he takes Mother's and Nadzia's wages. He doesn't want to give us any money to buy rations. Today he went to get the sausage ration and ate over 5 dkg. on the street (Nadzia saw him), so that we were all short-changed. He has also managed to borrow 10 dkg. of bread from Nadzia. (Foolish girl!) I took tomorrow's portion of bread and half of Monday's with me to the shop. I'll do so every day from now on.

Father bought meat today, and with the liter of whey he got for the whole family, he cooked and guzzled it all up. Now there is nothing left for us, so we'll go to bed without supper. Mother looks like a cadaver, and the worrying is finishing her off.

MAY 31, 1942

In the evening when I returned from the shop I was missing a few teaspoons of honey (which we received instead of marmalade), and Mother was missing even more honey.

JUNE 11, 1942

The days pass imperceptibly, and no change is visible. The food supply has improved; however, the specter of next winter is confronting everybody. Everyone realizes all too well that he won't last through the winter (I'm not talking about those who gorge themselves, of course)—and pessimism is getting worse all around. "Either the war will end before the winter, or we will." It's true: we're pushing on with our last strength.

JUNE 26, 1942

Today I heard that two people went to Warsaw. Apparently, one of them ate so much the day he got there that he was in bed with a high fever for a week. At least he felt full, something I haven't experienced in two years.

MONDAY, JULY 14, 1942

It seems that last year Rumkowski said that he couldn't save everyone and, therefore, instead of having the entire population die a slow death, he would save "the top ten thousand."

JULY 27, 1942

Apparently, they're deporting a huge number of Jews (ten thousand a day) from Warsaw. Accompanying this, of course, were pogroms, and those being deported were shot. The Eldest there committed suicide. However, they didn't go through the kind of extreme suffering we have had, and there is no end for us yet.

OSKAR ROSENFELD'S NOTEBOOKS

NOTEBOOK B:

Passover 1942 31 March. The Kripo has taken the Torah scrolls. Preparations for *seders* in the home.

1 April. One prepares. Finally. The Eldest sends wine, 4 bottles. Rabbi Krakauer conducts the *seder,* holds forth. Festive atmosphere. Wonderful, the strength to believe in the Messiah in the midst of this misery. He will lead us out. "This is the bread of misery that we eat." *Matzoh* out of dark flour, so hard it cannot be chewed. Speech about *Eretz Israel* [Heb: Land of Israel], where we will all end up.

The next day a few older Jews look on as some boys pull carts. One boy remembers the Haggadah reading and says without changing the expression on his face: "Not one stood up against us, but rather in every generation they have raised themselves against us in order to annihilate us, and each time He has saved us from their hand."

One of the older Jews, a redhead, says: "If he had left us in *Mizraim* [Heb: Egypt], we'd be sitting in a hotel in Cairo today, drinking a Turkish coffee." He laughs; his neighbor too. Then a gray-haired man says: "*Moshe* [Heb: Moses] knew what he was doing. If we had stayed in *Mizraim,* we would not have had the honor of being given the Torah."

"And what have we learned from the Torah? I have never occupied myself with the flesh-pots of Egypt, so I don't miss them today. Hunger? One goes hungry. Beatings? One is beaten. We are the only *Am S'gulo* [Heb: chosen people]. There's nothing we can do about it. We are chosen, have taken the responsibility upon ourselves. When the time comes for fighting, we will fight. For the time being that won't work. For the time being, the call is not upon us."

"With what should we fight? With our *pinkeln* [Yid: pinkies]? With our weak arms? And where is the strong arm, the strong hand, to lead us? I do not see it?"

"Take a look at the boys, how patiently they pull their carts. No one wants to give up what he's gotten from birth. If one were told he could be transformed into another people, he would respond: No! He holds tight to the *briss* [Heb: covenant]! For the Eternal has sealed the covenant not only with our forefathers, but with us as well, and with the coming generations until the end of time. Do you want to exclude yourself? Do we want to be cleverer than our ancestors?

They let themselves be burnt. For us, for us, that we can live today. And our children here will not want to be cleverer than us. So it will go on from generation to generation."

Gardens. On March 22nd the Eldest posted a notice regarding ground to be leased for farming. Seeds were to be officially obtained. Cultivation of small plots, wedges of land, little gardens, began on 17 April. Mostly radishes, chives, onions, and various kinds of lettuce were planted. One planted not knowing if one would enjoy the fruits of one's labor.

In front of the houses, alongside the sidewalks, right next to the puddles, young and old worked together. The sun warmed the ghetto air, but the people, not trusting the spring, were still packed like mummies in their winter rags. Jews from Lodz, Frankfurt, Vienna, Prague—speaking German, Polish, Yiddish—petty bourgeois, children, youths from the *cheder* and the bar, doctors, piano virtuosi, scholars—they all plough, while airplanes steer their way over them to the east.

Cemetery. A long field with a high wall, first built in Autumn 1941, behind the Marysin cottages. There, where one expects to find only quiet, there in the villa section, at the end of the ghetto, far from the actual ghetto city, lies the

" 'When the time comes for fighting, we will fight.' " (Rosenfeld)

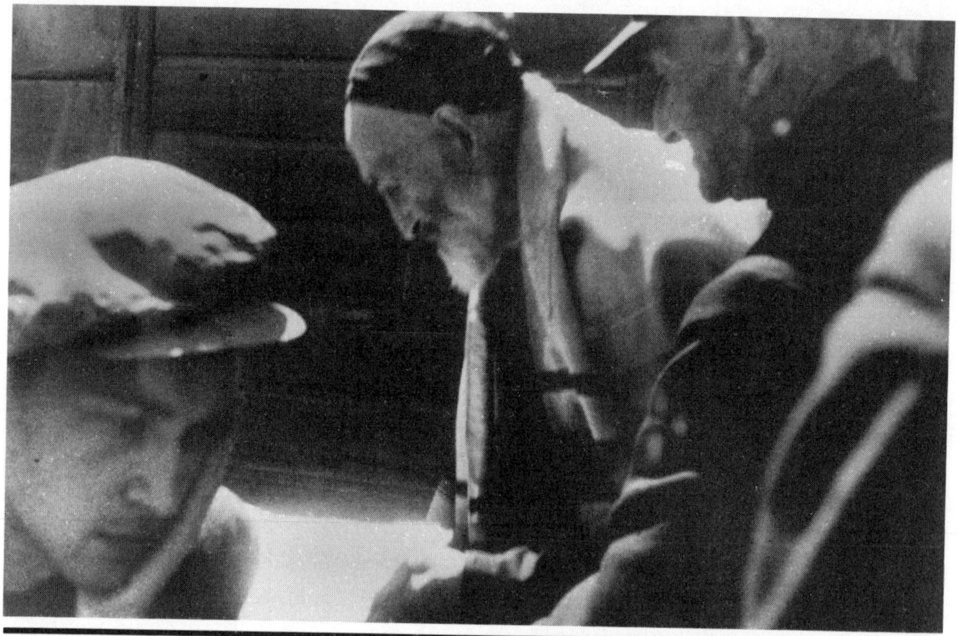

"green grass" for the dead. No green grass. Brown, slimy earth, on which thousands of gravestones are already standing.

The dead are brought from the mortuary without stop, to all parts of the cemetery. Every day there are the same several dozen burials. The graves are about 60 centimeters wide, even narrower than the wooden planks in the barracks. The ritual washing of the corpse is forbidden by the *Aschkenes.* There are no coffins. The corpse lies between two boards, packed in old scraps of paper. It is held, like a dead fish, in a net that is carried on two slats and let go over the grave. Sobbing and moaning here and there. The sheet-metal wagons keep delivering the dead into the hall, the nets keep taking them out of the hall. The earth fills itself with the dead. These are the people who came to the Lodz Ghetto, sentenced to a quick death. Starved, frozen, damned, suicides. As numerous as grains of sand in the ocean, stars in the heavens. From the Frankfurt transport, 18 percent died in the six months since October 1941.

How much spirit of sacrifice with all the corpses! In the homes, mothers save bites from their food for their sons, sisters for sisters, indeed for distant relations. For his wife, the husband with hunger cramps pretends to be full, and vice versa.

10 May. Wire. Between the oppressed city of Lodz and the artificially created ghetto the victors have stretched barbed wire. On the Lodz side *Feldgraues* always stand guard. Whoever stands near the wire for a few minutes attracts these guards. Every gesture, every attempt to make oneself understood is useless. Even if a ghetto Jew lives right next to the wire, he must be careful, duck and run toward his door. The guards aim, fire—done. No one concerns himself with the dead. Bullets are as cheap as beans. On November 17 a young girl, unhappy in love, decided to go to the wire. There she stayed with her lost dreams, paid no attention to the guard's warning, acted as if it did not matter to her. The guard shot, the girl fell. It was the first suicide by an "evacuee" in the ghetto. But the benefactor wire comes to the aid of many unhappy people. The natives, already accustomed to the ghetto for two years, do not make use of it; their hardness and their religious belief do not allow for such giving up of oneself. Others, however, do. "I am going to the wire" has become a familiar saying.

The Uniqueness of the Ghetto. Every living thing breathes, blooms, creates, wants to grow. The ghetto is the exception. People locked in decaying houses with just enough air to vegetate. They do not grow corn, do not have cattle, poultry, vegatables, fish, milk, fat or bread that they make themselves. There is no fabric, no leather, no metal. You cannot produce. When your suit falls apart, you must go in rags. When your shoes are torn apart, you wrap them in rags so that water, snow and *dreck* [Yid and Ger: filth] cannot get in. The bolts rust, the colors stay the same. The shops have no wares, in the sense of there being any choice. There are no cameras, no radios, no books, no paints, no watches.... Pretty prayer books, Polish, Yiddish, German, Russian novels are sold as scrap paper. Everything falls apart.

And unemployed, people go hungry here: engineers, chemists, mathematicians, botanists, zoologists, pharmacists, doctors, builders, teachers, writers, actors, directors, musicians, linguists, administrators, bank people, electricians, wood workers, carpenters, metal workers, tapestry makers, house painters, furriers, tailors, shoemakers, underwear makers, lathe turners, watchmakers. The talents are at hand. Give them the means and they will build you houses, villas, apartments, streets, canals, water pipes, train stations, railroad tracks; they will clear a forest, saw boards, establish institutes, hospitals, universities, libraries, schools, observatories, kitchens, laundries, workshops. They will build you cities and colonies with all kinds of possible growth and beauty.

Thus, things which could be of value to humanity are squelched, crushed. But what is "humanity" now? Human nerves are destroyed, their sense of life lost. No philosophy can help here. Every week more of them are undone.... University professors who gave lectures from rostrums walk around here with their pots ready for a little soup; famous singers push a coal wagon; important chemists and actors wait in front of decayed barracks for the call to go into one workshop or another.

NOTEBOOK C: REMEMBRANCES, PRIVATE DIARY 3

In all the ghetto offices, pictures of the Eldest, like a *Melech* [Heb: king], even on calendars.

12 May 1942. When completely destroyed in the soul, people dream. Thousands lie on plank-beds and dream. One recounts: my father appeared in a dream and told me about something good. Thus: the danger of further deportation is past. I can feel it, I know.

13 May. For one's own birthday...

Ghetto has become practically Polish, since all the Germans [i.e., Western Jews] have gone. Prof. Baerwald (University of Prague), most important mathematician in Prague, and his wife died end of April 1942, starved. Prof. Otto Stein (Indologist), Buddhism, 2nd Prague transport—

NOTEBOOK E

Moving out of those who were moved in. Before being transported out to the train station, those people leaving (each day about 1000 men, women and children) were brought to the Central Prison where they had to stay for 2 days and 2 nights. The Jewish police drove them together like sheep. Often they appeared at night where the unlucky were living, forcing them to come away immediately. Many were taken directly from bed to train station without ceremony—night—always at night. It seemed to them like the suitable time for the horror of deportation. And then they came on their own, with the summonses in their pockets. All around the Central Prison the crowds pushed forward, looking like a procession of the damned, those selected for torture, those who have to enter Inferno.

On May 2nd the Central Prison was filled for the first time with the people given these summonses. They got soup from the ghetto and bread. On May 4th they were taken to the train station. Rainy, cool. There the German Kripo officiated. The Kripo took away people's backpacks and bread sacks. Whatever food they had was taken away. Blankets, cushions, warm things. Indecision. What to do? Hopeless. At the same time those who could not move fast enough thrashed with whip[s]. Threats of shooting! Hands up! No one is to carry anything. Hand over wedding rings. Watches. So, complete beggars.

This was reported everywhere. The result? People began selling their belongings. Wild trade in the alleyways, in the courtyards. Food prices went up. Bread, 700; margarine, 1000; 2 pieces sugar, 1 mark; 3 strings of chives, 1 mark. The Jewish police took away non-essentials, even in the collection centers, sometimes for their own pockets. One sees wagons of baggage driving back into the ghetto.

At the same time hundreds report of their own free will. It can't be worse "there," supposedly Kolo, 90 kilometers away.* Perhaps even more bread and potatoes, if working on a farm.... We would gladly eat from a pig's trough, just to get out of the ghetto.... People from Vienna, Berlin, Cologne are the first sacrifice.

On May 10th a transport left with baptized people, not Mosaic Jews. Further evacuation, further sales, soup 28 marks, potato peels 14 marks, potatoes 90 marks. One sells allotments of workshop soup for 30 marks, a pair of shoes for 125 marks. Women sit and sew sacks for inside [of clothing]. Touching sympathy, a piece of heart goes with each person leaving. Growing nervousness, since it is not clear if more will follow the initial 10,000. Then suddenly another 2000! Driven together in the alleyways, some individuals break down; no one looks after them.

350 people evacuated from the old age home, over 80 years old, and just as the blind, lame, dying, trembling elderly were brought into the ghetto, so now they go on from the ghetto. The 13th and 14th of May go by in horror. Anxiety when the letter carrier appears. Does he bring an order to report to

In the ghetto's Central Prison, Jews await transport "into the unknown."

the authorities? 15th of May, last transport out. And now more natives [Polish Jews] are supposed to arrive . . . from surrounding villages.

Morale. The tragedy is gigantic. Those in the ghetto do not comprehend it. For it brings out no great people as in the Middle Ages. This tragedy has no heroes. And why tragedy? Because the pain does not touch upon something human, on another's heart, but rather is something incomprehensible, linked with the cosmos, a natural phenomenon like the creation of the world. One must begin again with the Creation, with *B'raishit* [Heb: In the Beginning]. In the beginning, God created the ghetto.

NOTEBOOK C

14 May. Clarinetist Leo Birkenfeld (Vienna), skin and bones starved, ripped out of hospital bed in the night, transport, dragged along.

17 May. Evacuation! But what then? What afterwards? What have the arrangers of this imagined? Without a profession, idle for years, aged, without clothes and underwear, without instruments, without pencil or pen, without the

slightest possibility of pursuing an occupation, with ripped backpacks and bundles, without bedding and without blanket, a street beggar without the hardened quality, stripped of one's worth and outlawed. What then? Where will we go? Who has given thought to this! What tomorrow? How is this to end? And other members of the family? Spread around the world. Without contact. For half a year cut off from human community.

Jews from nearby brought in, actually only parents—children stay there. Whimpering children ripped from their mothers' breasts—horrible. One asks, for what? No one can give an answer.

19 May. Unusual beings among those coming in, like teachers, young girls, some in short lambskins—à la kaftan—without any sort of baggage—driven out, not evacuated, the picture of the [two words in English:] Wandering Jew, of the fleeing, chased, hunted Jew. . . . Not to be forgotten: all this is the solution to the Jewish question. Hold tightly in memory, think about it, and set it into specific episodes.

22 May. What happened to the small children of Brzeziny? . . . A *shaygets* threw child like puppet to window. *Yeled* [Heb: child] a mess [in English].

Ardent desire: each for something else: for children, for unseen grandchildren, for foods, for landscapes, for books, for something very nebulous; in the end, desire itself. The object is lost: the senses cannot grasp the object of desire in the fog of hunger.

For chapter on dying: "He went to the fathers . . ." is now a jumble: the son goes before the father, the grandfather along with the grandson. Absurd, illogical—mean. Death has lost its other-worldly beauty, its wonderful, holy feeling of something secret. The mystery of death is desecrated by the brutality of the earthly cause—hunger—daily.

24 May. Noise in Marysin and cries of the new arrivals from Brzeziny. From the 1000 evacuated as "German," nothing has been heard. Days fly by. Always only 2 questions: 1) Will we not starve? 2) Will *Geulah* [Heb: liberation] come in time?

25 May. New symptoms of hunger: pain in the nails and the toes for no apparent reason; inflammation of the nasal passages; pain in the shoulder blades, in the limbs.

Soup. On the street 5 women sit on a stone step with bowls and eat soup, red soup. Eat? No, they slurp, suck, drink, tip the bowl in order to lap up the last drop. Near them sit other women, one of them once a well-known Viennese opera singer. [Sitting] on the wall young men and old men drink soup in pots. On the ground, among weeds and field flowers, children slurp soup.

The schools are closed. Thousands of young people are not occupied intellectually, contrary to the Jewish requirement for reading and study. *Im ejn*

Torah, ejn Kemach! [Heb: Without Torah, no flour (i.e., sustenance); a reversal of a well-known saying, "If there is no flour, there is no Torah."]

26 May. a) Into the ghetto, b) Nuremberg, Cracow, c) Germans in, d) Poles out, e) Germans out, f) neighboring Poles in, g) the same, partially out, h) Poles out again. In the process of this upheaval, thousands are destroyed. . . .

The wealth of the Lodz Jews—who made textiles—is visible in the gravestones and family tombs in the cemetery.

Control of the ghetto: the appeal to "My brothers and sisters" and then the raising of the whip.

Backside of the ghetto: The Eldest's women demand that the residents of the Marysin home keep away from the front section and that they not use the reclining chairs near the Eldest's villa.

1 June. Face of the ghetto, May 1942. Re novella, "He looks for the secret of the ghetto." Faces fallen, hollowed, so that bones [show] everywhere, skulls grotesquely visible. Temples sunken in, ears standing out, unshaven, beard stubble, so that one looks like a prisoner released from jail. With the bundle already on one's back, the Wandering Jew is complete.

Lending library. Rare old books, otherwise not to be found: Thackeray (*Vanity Fair*), Seneca, Gorki, Dickens, Disraeli, Bellamy, *Salammbô* (Flaubert), old Yiddish books, Polish, even Russian.

Blessing. First Bk of Moses. 22.16.17 "I have sworn . . . that I will bless your seed and increase it like the stars in heaven and like the sand on the shores of the sea."

Job. I. 21 "I came naked from my mother, and naked will I be taken back. The Lord has given, the Lord has taken away; blessed be the name of the Lord."

Song of Solomon "My child, do not throw away the Lord's teaching and do not be impatient with any punishment."

JOZEF ZELKOWICZ

"LAG B'OMER IN THE GHETTO"

MAY 1942

Lag b'Omer: the traditional Jewish arbor day. On this day children are given a holiday from their studies and taken to the fields and forests to see the world in its greenery.

Lag b'Omer: how does it look in the ghetto? It's wrapped in clouds and rain. The skies are angry and send a cold wind—and snow. *Lag b'Omer,* and it snows!

And you, son of the earth, where will you send your children? Where will you find fresh, free air for them to breathe? And anyhow, where do you find children in the ghetto? This species dies out before it even reaches the stage of development recognized as childhood. And if such a creature is lucky enough not to die, he immediately turns into an old Jew.

There are no children in the ghetto. Little Jews do not go to work before the age of ten, but they stand in line at kitchens, bread stores. . . . Jews eleven years old and older already go to work. Their faces are not covered with beards, they have no wives, but they go to work, all right.

The children of the ghetto are workers. They earn ten pfennig an hour, eighty pfennig a day. Their wages are small, and their jobs are hard, too hard. For eight hours a day they're locked between the walls of a factory or workshop, which sometimes lacks even the most basic sanitary conditions. They must report, like soldiers, at seven in the morning. For each lateness 50 pfennig are deducted

Ghetto boys build a model train with cattle cars.

from their wages. And to be at work by seven, a little Jew must be up at six. And the more hours he is awake, the more hours in the day he is hungry. He often gets nothing to eat at home in the morning, and he has to work several hours before they give him a watery soup for his 50 pfennig, and 5 dkg of sausage, which many times weighs only 4 dkg.

It's hard for a child who works the morning shift, from seven A.M. till 2:30 P.M. But it's even harder for those who work the evening shift, from 2:30 to 11:30. Often these children fast until they get to work, where they still have to wait until seven in the evening to finally get their soup.

If working is hard for a child on the evening shift, going home from work is even harder. Since people are permitted on the ghetto streets until only 9 P.M., there is not a soul around when the little Jew returns from his job. Walking along the ghetto fence, he is often stopped by: *"Wohin?"* [Ger: "Where to?"]

Children have to work in the ghetto, or they may be taken from their parents and sent away somewhere. On the other hand, if they work they are citizens of the ghetto, useful and protected. Little, 11-year-old *Schützjuden* [Ger: Protected Jews, like those who lived under the special protection of pre-eighteenth-century German rulers].

Instead of running in the fields, or going to the warm forest to play with wooden swords and bows and arrows, ghetto children go to work. *Lag b'Omer* or not, the work machine sucks in their tender little bodies and grinds them into scrap. Just as it did with their parents. Even if their legs are not yet swollen from hunger, their backs will become bent and their breasts sunken, and their eyes will look as distant and as cold and grey as today's sky.

THE CHRONICLE OF THE LODZ GHETTO

THURSDAY, MAY 7, 1942

A FOOTNOTE TO THE RESETTLEMENT OF THE HAMBURG TRANSPORT

BARELY HALF A YEAR...

Barely half a year has passed since they arrived in the ghetto. At that time they arrived here in long lines, festively-attired people whose appearance contrasted so sharply with our native squalor. We were struck by their elegant sports clothes, their exquisite footwear, their furs, the many variously colored capes the women wore. They often gave the impression of being people on some sort of vacation or, rather, engaged in winter sports, for the majority of them wore ski clothes. You couldn't tell there was a war on, the way those people dressed; and the fact that, during the bitter cold spells, they strolled about in front of the gates to their "transports," and about the "city" as well, demonstrated most eloquently that their layers of fat afforded them excellent protection from the cold.

Their attitude toward the extremely unsanitary conditions in which they were quartered was one of unusual disgust, though perhaps that was not without justification; they shouted, they were indignant, and beyond the reach of any argument. At that time they were not concerned that the ghetto's entire meager transportation system had been paralyzed as a result of their arrival, which also caused the entire winter allocation of vegetables to freeze at Marysin. They could not see that quartering 20,000 newcomers in the ghetto's meager terrain could only be done at the cost of reducing the area inhabited by the old population. It is true that this problem was not solved at once as it should have been and became a great sore spot, but, in all fairness, one must admit that to solve that problem would have required a certain amount of time, even under the best of conditions. However, they were very impatient and swore a blue streak!

Somewhere along the line they had been misled. . . . They had not been informed of where they were going and what would happen to them. They had heard that they were traveling to some industrial center where each of them would find suitable employment, which was why they were disappointed when they found themselves in a situation that was entirely different from what they had expected. Some of them even asked if they mightn't reside in a hotel of some sort. There were, indeed, some arrogant and ill-mannered people among them, but, at bottom, losing their bearings had made them feel small and helpless. Upon their departure, they had been allowed to take along only 50 kilograms of baggage (things were not the same everywhere!) but they rarely observed the rule, and that is why the Department of Transportation was busy for six weeks transporting their luggage.

Nearly all of them brought extra food with them, but those who, for whatever reason, were unable to do so, found considerable amounts of bread, margarine, and other products offered for sale by the old population. New customers, a wealthy market which absorbed everything on sale each day. Prices shot up from one hour to the next, and in a short time the price of a loaf of bread had risen to 25 marks, whereas in previous conditions a price of 10 marks would have seemed sky high.

The newcomers could see the poverty of the local population; they knew that, due to their own financial advantage, they could tear the last bite of bread

"Like a stone in water, they disappeared. 45,000 deported from the ghetto." From an "underground" album made in the ghetto. (Yad Vashem archives)

A family's room following their deportation from the ghetto.

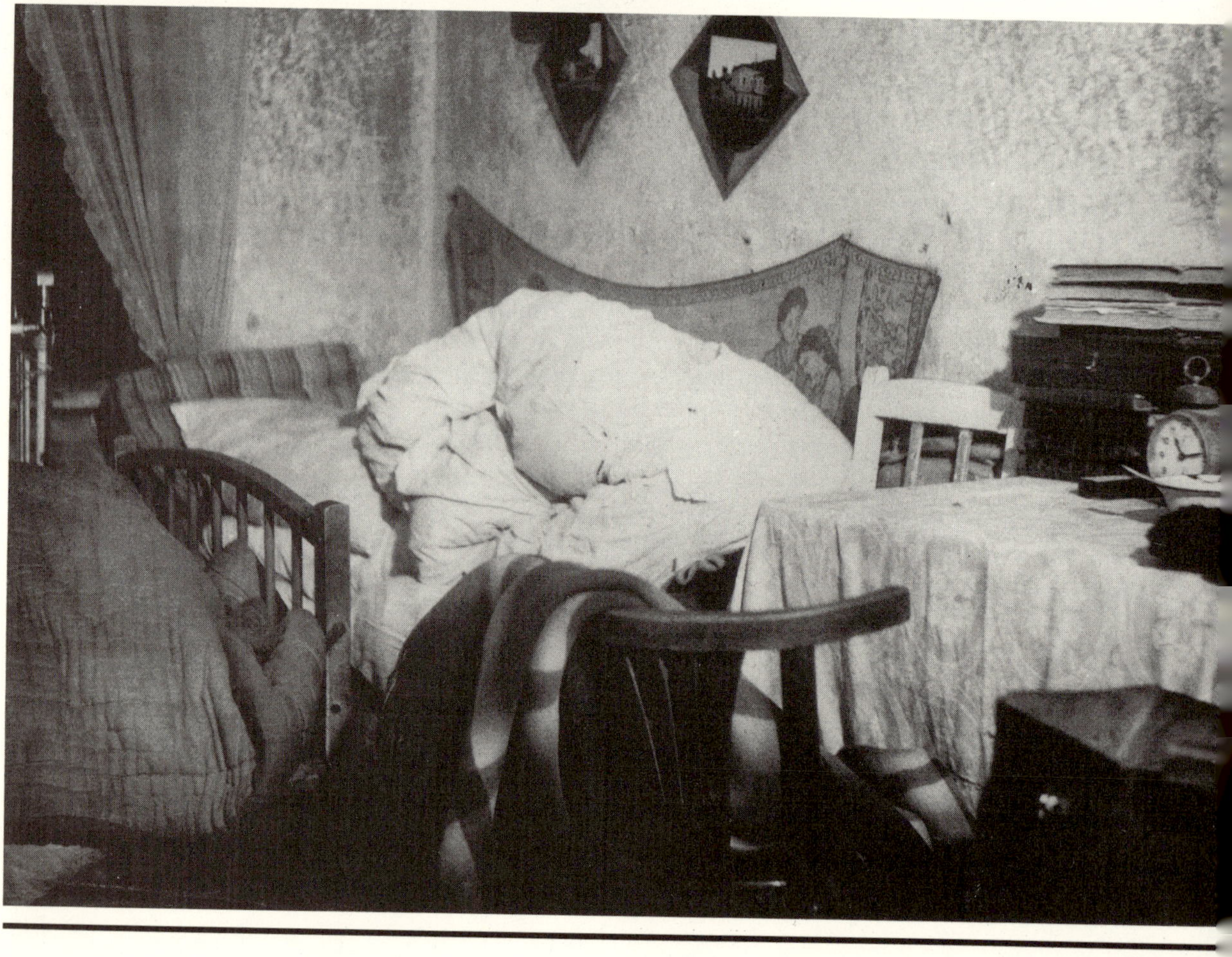

from the mouths of their brothers from the East, but that did not faze them. Large numbers of people in front of butchers' stalls sold them their rations for next to nothing, initially for some thirty-odd pfennigs. They looked with disgust at the soups served to them, and it was rare for any of the newcomers—at least in the beginning—to be seen eating a meal in any of the Community's soup kitchens. They would give away their soup to our local paupers in exchange for various favors and services.

Part of the Hamburg transport was quartered in the building where the Bajka Cinema was formerly located, at 33 Franciszkanska Street. This took place on Thursday evening, the 20th of November, and on Friday morning the Chairman arrived to greet his guests. They were spread out on the floor, sleeping on their bundles, the old people and the women sitting in chairs lining the walls.

They rose to his greeting and the Chairman delivered a short speech, perhaps the shortest speech in the history of the ghetto. It contained but a few sentences, but it was so warm and sincere that not only the women but many dignified men wiped tears of emotion from their eyes. It was a genuine brotherly greeting, as well as an assurance that he would share his humble roof and his bread with them.

That evening, the newcomers from Hamburg arranged a Friday service. Dressed in their best clothes, with many candles lit, they said their first prayer to God with uncanny calm and in a mood of exaltation. Those who had left Judaism a long time before, even those whose fathers had broken any connection with their forefathers, stood there that day, festively attired, in a sort of grave and exalted mood, seeking consolation and salvation in prayer. When their prayers were concluded, they went out into the lobby, the same words on all their lips: "Now we see that we are all equal, all sons of the same people, all brothers." This was either mere flattery or, perhaps, a genuine compliment to the old population—or perhaps a premonition of the not-too-distant future.

Events outpaced time, people changed visibly, at first outwardly, then physically, and finally, if they had not vanished altogether, they moved through the ghetto like ghosts. . . .

The rutabagas and beets they [the newcomers] had at first disdained, they now bought at high prices, and the soups they had scorned became the height of their dreams. Once it had been others, but then it was they who prowled the "city" with a cup or a canteen on a chain to *shnorn* [Yid: beg] a little soup.

Conditions changed enormously in that short span of time, and a soup kitchen meal became a luxury; the price of such soup had reached 15 marks, and no one was in any hurry to sell his soup, even though it bore no resemblance to the soup available six months before. They sold off the last of their possessions to secure themselves food of any sort, which they now saw as their last salvation from doom.

And indeed, it was only half a year, only six months, that had proven to be an eternity for them! Some of the metamorphoses could not be imagined, even in a dream. . . . Ghosts, skeletons with swollen faces and extremities, ragged and impoverished, they now left for a further journey on which they were not even allowed to take a knapsack.

They had been stripped of all their European finery, and only the Eternal Jew was left. . . .

[Jozef] Kl[ementynowski]

JOZEF ZELKOWICZ

"HOLD ON TO YOUR BOWL"

[*This was written on 2 June 1942, the day after a reorganization of the meal distribution system was announced.*]

A painting by a ghetto artist will surely end up as kitsch and trash if the artist leaves out—the soup bowl. Kitsch, because the painting would not be true to life; trash, because it would not be true art.

Neither the bridges, nor the barbed wire, nor the gate are symbols of the ghetto. These are just props, accessories, signs on the outside. The real symbols of the ghetto are—the bowl, and, well, perhaps the wooden sandal, too.

Not so much the wooden sandal, though. Not everyone who walks or drags his feet in the ghetto is yet wearing sandals. One can still see people who walk around in shoes. For instance, the managers wear boots as a sign of their grandeur. On the other hand, no one is without a bowl, neither the higher-ups nor ordinary people, from the lowliest garbage or excrement hauler to the highest, most important manager.

An administrator returns home from his office in the evening, and he presses against his tired body the briefcase signifying his officialdom, and the bowl.

A worker goes home from his job late at night, and on the way his bowl swings along with his tools.

Six, eight or perhaps ten women are pulling a cart with waste, and as many bowls are banging against the cart.

Four men are dragging a cart with excrement, and they have the bowls hanging from their curved backsides. And the bowls get entangled in the barbed wire. They might even, God forbid, damage the ghetto.

A woman goes for an ordinary walk, and even if she has washed her hair in her last drops of vinegar and made up her face with her last bit of cream (there are still such women in the ghetto), she takes not only her purse or handbag, but the bowl as well—to be prepared for the unforeseen.

A child is dispatched to the cooperative, to check if something is being distributed, and he is told to take the bowl, just in case.

When thousands of Jews were deported from the ghetto, the one thing they could take along without anyone objecting—was the bowl.

Not the wire. Not the bridges. Not the gate. Not even the yellow [Star of David] patch. None of them are symbols of the ghetto. All are merely markers, set decorations. The symbol of the ghetto is—the bowl.

Therefore, an artist who is going to paint the ghetto Jew, even if he paints him all in yellow, even if he wraps him in a *tallis,* if he does not put a bowl in the Jew's hand or hang it at his side, he would expose himself as a botcher. The first requisite for an artist is to observe, and if he does not see the bowl, he must be blind and cannot call himself an artist.

But there are no more bowls in the ghetto! Since yesterday, the workshop kitchens are empty. Since yesterday, the teeth and stomachs of the kitchens' people are idle, and along with them the bowls remain idle, standing like orphans, forgotten by God and mankind.

These bowls, which only yesterday were shining in every tint and color in the streets, which even had the *chutzpah* to brush against the ghetto wire, which were the *sine qua non* of human survival in the ghetto, which symbolized the ghetto and human dejection—today these bowls stand still, in their own hollow emptiness.

GERMAN DOCUMENTS

To: The State Criminal Police
Litzmannstadt

III.16.1942

Re: Seizure of Jewish goods in the District of Litzmannstadt.
Reference: Your memo of III.10.42

Concerning the above, the director of the Head Trustee Office (East), Vice-president Dr. Moser, and the Ghetto Administration have agreed that:

1. All goods and valuables seized from Jews in the residential area are to go to the Ghetto Administration for assessment.
2. Goods and valuables seized through the mediation of the ghetto office of the Criminal Police inside the city of Litzmannstadt can, after their value is estimated, be transferred to the Ghetto Administration.

In the end, the Ghetto Administration is a division of the H.T.O.,* since upon the dissolution of the ghetto all valuables—for example, textiles, machinery, factory equipment, money, etc.—will still be in the possession of the German Reich and thereby go to the H.T.O., like property remaining in the Ghetto Administration. The required estimates of value for the goods seized inside the ghetto are an internal matter before the H.T.O. and the Ghetto Administration; therefore, no offices other than these need be unnecessarily encumbered by it.

On behalf of:
/B/ Biebow

To: The Reich Governor in Warthegau
Treuhandstelle [Trustee Office], Posen
Litzmannstadt

III.26.1942

Re: Goods confiscated by the Ghetto Administration from the Jews
Reference: Your letter of II.28.1942

Response to your letter of the above date is made today, since intensive consideration was given to how the questions posed might be answered in a way that meets your goals.

Despite the greatest effort, I am unable to provide you with precise information, since the structure of the ghetto and of the Ghetto Administration simply do not allow it.

You request in your first point: "What have the Ghetto Administration or offices working under its control or its orders (the Criminal Police, the Secret State Police, etc.) confiscated, secured, assessed, or used in the area of the ghetto itself, in the way of portable property of any kind, including goods, raw materials, semi- and fully finished products, machinery, money, precious metals, furs? To what estates did the confiscated goods belong; what kinds of goods were they, and what amount was expected in their sale?"

Normally, almost all confiscated goods in the ghetto are treated as so-called ownerless property. Semi-finished and raw materials, insofar as they are not direly needed by the Jews themselves, are finished and sent on to the German market. For example, ready-made suits or dresses were made from the material that was found, and the Litzmannstadt Trade Association was given them in exchange for point-checks. On the advice of the Reich office, valuable metals were sent to the refinery. Everything is done to extract the highest possible benefit for the German Reich.

By my estimate, approximately 2,000,000 RM have been secured in goods of all kinds and cash. A settlement of accounts has generally taken place through the account of the Eldest of the Jews, particularly since the condition in which the goods were found was such that they had to be reworked and reconditioned in the ghetto workshops and factories. Everything that was taken was once possessed by Jews.

Your second point reads: "What Polish or Jewish enterprises (handiwork, trade, and industry) existed when the ghetto was sealed? What of value was found in the ghetto workplaces? What has since happened with the workplaces?"

The Polish and Jewish businesses found in the residential area of the Jews upon the closing of the ghetto were transferred to the H.T.O. *All* things of value stored in these businesses were given to the Eldest of the Jews in trusteeship before the transfer of the building, thus neither left to the Jews nor brought to the Ghetto Administration for the purpose of transfer. The machines found in the businesses were in part disposed of through the trusteeship and sent out; the remaining machines were all put back into operation and lent to the Jewish community with the injunction that they be handled most carefully.

The machine depot (including shoe machines, locksmith machines, furrier machines, tailor's machines, laundry machines, and so on) has been considerably expanded. The machines have, in part, been bought by the Ghetto Administration in the Old Reich; the necessary expense was covered by the money made by the Jews. All in all, after the dissolution of the ghetto, especially in regard to the machine depot, you will realize a substantial profit, since everything restored to working order or built anew, at great cost, will be yours in the end.

After the sealing of the ghetto, the Ghetto Administration was not required to keep track of every operation. Thus, what you have requested is not now possible, after almost two years. Thus, I must provisionally restrict myself to the already-mentioned estimates. An audit of the Ghetto Administration was made by the accounting office of the German Reich. If you should want it, I will make a copy of the report available to you; it will show that the accounting office agrees in all areas with the Ghetto Administration's procedures.

On behalf of:
[Biebow]
Director

THE CHRONICLE OF THE LODZ GHETTO

WEDNESDAY AND THURSDAY, MAY 20 AND 21, 1942

LARGE ORDERS

are constantly being placed here in the ghetto. I have learned from reliable sources that the dry cleaners have received consecutive consignments of 300 train cars of dirty underclothes for cleaning and, thus, are assured of work for a very long time (many months). The woodwork factory, apart from its current orders, is to produce a million pairs of clogs. 800 people work there in three shifts. The metal workshop is supposed to have work enough for two years. The straw-shoe workshop has been manufacturing straw boots for the army since Tuesday. Its location at the outskirts of the ghetto presents a serious problem to its workers, who are recruited from among the women and the elderly. The long walk exhausts the workers, who are not exactly radiant with excess strength and health these days. Further orders are expected for other workshops.

B[ernard] O[strowski]

THE MOOD OF THE GHETTO

has changed completely since Sunday. Reports of resettlements from the provinces have had a depressing effect on the entire populace. Nothing could be more shocking than to visit the site at 22 Masarska Street, where over a thousand (1,082) women from Pabianice have been quartered. In every room, in every corner, one sees mothers, sisters, grandmothers, shaken by sobs, quietly lamenting for their little children. All children up to age 10 were sent off to parts unknown. Some have lost three, four, even six children. Their quiet despair is profoundly penetrating, so different from the loud laments we are accustomed to hearing at deaths and funerals, but all the more real and sincere for that. It is no surprise that anyone with small children or old parents awaits the days to come with trepidation. The greatest optimists have lost hope. Until now, people had thought that work would maintain the ghetto and the majority of its people without any breakup of families. Now it is clear that even this was an illusion. There were plenty of orders [for new work] in Pabianice and Brzeziny, but that did not protect those Jews against wholesale deportation. Fear for our ghetto's fate is keeping everyone up at night. Our last hope is our Chairman; people believe that he will succeed, if not totally, then at least in part, in averting the calamities that now loom ahead.

RESETTLEMENT

Talk of further resettlement becomes increasingly definite. It is said that it will begin on Friday, and other stories say not until Sunday. The Chairman is supposed to have said that he will make an effort to keep the suffering of local people to a minimum. The first to be resettled are the most recent arrivals, that is, those from Pabianice and Brzeziny, followed by the "Germans" [i.e., Jews from the West]. Insofar as necessary to fill the quota, people from Lodz will go in the following order: those who hid from the last resettlement and then those who were stamped at the medical commission's examinations. As for the residents of the Old People's Home and children under 10 in the Orphanage, the Chairman is making assurances that he will spare no efforts to keep them here. This information is supposed to have originated from the most authoritative sources.

B[ernard] O[strowski]

SATURDAY AND SUNDAY, MAY 30 AND 31, 1942

LARGE SHIPMENTS OF BAGGAGE

have been sent to the ghetto since May 25. The people of the ghetto are tremendously puzzled by the arrival of these shipments, which contain clothes of all sorts and other things and which are transported here each day by trucks, including five-ton vehicles. The Department of Used Articles has been ordered to store all this material. The department has assigned some enormous warehouses for that purpose, namely those at 75 Brzezinska Street, 20 Marynarska Street, 93 Franciszkanska Street, and 32 Dolna Street. What is it that these large trucks are carrying? It would be difficult to enumerate the contents. One reason is the tonnage involved, which, in every case, exceeds 100,000 kilograms and is perhaps even higher. Among their contents, the things most frequently encountered are improvised sacks made from rugs, blankets, sheets, and so on. This type of bundle indicates that they were not packed by their owners but by other hands. These bundles for the most part contain clothing, linen, and bedding. This latter has passed through disinfection. Among other frequently encountered items are shirts and slips rolled together, three or four at a time, and also two pairs of pants rolled up with a few pairs of unmentionables. Nearly all the jackets and coats bear traces of having been ripped along their seams. . . . There are also a great many *taleysim*. There are no knapsacks or suitcases to be seen. Documents—letters, papers, ID cards, and so on that had been issued in Western European cities—often fall out of the bundles, but there

Prayer shawls confiscated from the deportees, stored in the ghetto.

Right: Feather beds left by the deported Jews are sorted and stored in the Church of the Most Blessed Virgin Mary.

are also a great many from Wloclawek, and often there are papers that were drawn up in this ghetto as well.

A very significant percentage of the items are brand new. For the time being, these things have been placed in storage; they will be distributed to the deportees from the surrounding areas, to the residents of the Old People's Home and orphanage, and perhaps even to the Clothing Department.

GERMAN DOCUMENTS

[*Gestapo document*]
Lubien, 2 June 1942
On the first of June 1942, around 5 pm, the Jew Lejb Zelkowicz, born on 20.9.1919 in Lipno, was taken prisoner by Meister d. Gend. Rapude in Parcelle Janowo, community of Lubien.

On 2 June, when he was supposed to be transported to the office of the Secret Police in Leslau, for the purpose of verifying personal papers, Lejb Zelkowicz was shot while trying to escape. A 7.65 mm pistol was used.

According to the information given by Lejb Zelkowicz, he had been in the Litzmannstadt Ghetto since June 1940. He apparently fled the ghetto in July 1941 and stayed on various Polish farms in the county of Gostynin until 28.5.1942. From 28.5 he wandered around the town of Lubien, county of Leslau.

[*Lodz Gestapo memo*]
Lodz, 9 June 1942
Since the Jews of the province naturally found out about the evacuation, they tried—by moving property, fleeing into the General Government, and absolutely refusing to follow the orders of the authorities—to disturb the evacuation. For this reason, the RSHA [the Secret Service]* were ordered from here to take the sharpest measures against the Jews, and multiple executions were ordered by RF-SS. Thus, a total of 95 Jews have so far been publicly hanged. The consequence has been that the Jew recognizes the strong measures taken here and for the most part now follows all orders quietly.

GHETTO DOCUMENT

Announcement No. 387
concerning the obligation to salute in the ghetto.

Lately it has been noted repeatedly that the previously ordered obligation to salute all German officials is not being carried out.
I am warning you again that all German officials—in uniform and in plain clothes—are to be greeted by the residents of the ghetto. This obligation to salute also applies to cars that are passing through.
Members of the organization for the maintenance of public order and fire fighters are to carry out this obligation to salute by standing at attention, and all others by taking off their headgear.
Women as well as persons without headgear will greet by bowing their heads.
Failure to observe this order will entail severest punishment.

Ch. Rumkowski
The Eldest of the Jews
in Litzmannstadt

Litzmannstadt Ghetto, June 27, 1942

OSKAR ROSENFELD'S NOTEBOOK

NOTEBOOK 12
[CULTURE]

The dynamic spirit of the Jewish people could not be broken. Social necessity of every kind directed cultural life inward. With no possibility of response from the world outside the ghetto, all artistic and theatrical aspiration had to occur intellectually. The largest Jewish rallying points, such as London (Whitechapel, *The Jewish Times–Die Zeit*), New York (the East Side, the Bronx, *The Forward, Der Tag, The Jewish Morning Journal*), Vienna (Leopoldstadt, *Die Neue Welt, Die Stimme*), Lvov, Riga, Krosno (East Galicia), even nearby Warsaw (its press and literary journals), and significant beachheads like Vilna and Kovno suddenly fell away. The Lodz Ghetto stood alone. That meant surviving with its existing human and intellectual resources, adapting these to prevailing conditions, and organizing them to prepare for future tasks.

The House of Culture is in Marysin—a kind of hamlet of children's, orphans', and old age homes cheek to jowl with dainty summer cottages inhabited by ghetto personnel in need of a holiday. It is a very long, one-story building with plain, unadorned walls and wide windows, and a flat, light green roof. The entrance is on the side, hard by a garden hedge, an open gutter and rubble—with the waste and bleakness of the ghetto on every side.

Inside the entrance is a hand-lettered placard in Yiddish and German announcing the program. The price of seats cannot support the cost of individual programs. However, we do have an office and checkroom, to say nothing of the spacious lobby, which, with its tall windows and gardens, provides a metropolitan ambience—especially during intermissions, when good-humored smokers of both sexes discuss in Yiddish, Polish, German and even English the music they've just heard.

The hall resembles a theater auditorium. The 25 rows of seats and the two dozen upholstered alcoves accommodate an audience of about 400 people and are occasionally fully sold out.

A few minutes after 6 PM, the members of the orchestra come on stage, serious and silent, wearing soberly dark street clothes. Most of them, of course, work throughout the day in some officially assigned job—maybe making straw shoes or sorting filthy, stinking old clothes, cementing rubber soles or some other necessary wizardry.

Concerts: Beethoven Recital, May–June 1942

The Ghetto Symphony Orchestra has performed Beethoven three times in succession, namely May 26, June 2 and 7. The three full houses testify to the ghetto dwellers' need for uplifting classical music. This is not to be made little of. What intellectual and mental appetite remains after these last two years of privation is not to be thoughtlessly given up. These concerts must, therefore, be fashioned with the greatest care.

. . .The first movement of the Fifth Symphony was the main piece. The demonic blows with which Fate batters on our doors are common knowledge. Here was a momentous theme that became more gripping the more deeply one became absorbed in it. . . .

The small orchestra (almost exclusively strings) performed brilliantly. The saying that Jews have a special talent for the fiddle was confirmed. Theodore Ryder conducted with devotion. The yellow *Mogen David* [Heb: Star of David] on his right shoulder quivered in sympathy when Ryder swayed emotionally to the music. The audience—mostly Lodz natives—felt magnetized.

. . . Rudolf Bandler from Prague sang arias from Italian opera. . . . When he sings Loewe's ballads or Schubert's *lieder,* people—even those born here—feel at home.

Symphony Concert, July 1, 1942

The individual movements of the Fifth Symphony heard during the recitals of June 2 and 7 were now performed in their entirety for the first time. The impression on the audience was, of course, more profound and impressive than before. The emotional thrill here in the ghetto was greater than was ever felt in the concert halls of any European metropolis. Even the fugue, that pleasant thematic treatment in the third movement, was greatly appreciated. The deliverance motif thundered majestically throughout the hall, and conductor Ryder seemed to be carried away in this finale. In that instant, future salvation could almost be experienced.

Jewish Life. Public schools: The Eldest introduced a sabbath of rest and religious instruction. Many Hebrew teachers were engaged, and in 1940 children were zealously learning Hebrew. Later the Chairman ordered the use of Yiddish in primary schools. That change of language created an element of chaos, which continued until all the schools were closed on German orders. Talmudic instruction was strictly forbidden.

The public celebration of Jewish holidays was discontinued; religious life and private tutoring was suppressed. A ban on *shechita* [Heb: ritual slaughter] made keeping kosher impossible. Work put an end to the traditional sabbath. Hebrew books were neither printed nor allowed into the ghetto.

The Eldest organized seven *dayonim* (scholars in the administration of justice, Talmudic law, and certain rituals) as a rabbinate that would hold sessions in an apartment and indirectly supervise the ghetto's religious life. Orthodox circles brought their queries to these *dayonim* and accepted their verdicts as legal. Divorce, marriage and funeral rites were all banned. At a burial, only the recital of *Kaddish* is permitted; orthodox interment, the washing of the dead, has been forbidden.

Torahs were confiscated and torn to pieces, though some were rescued and hidden in private quarters. The orthodox speak Yiddish; the orthodox young people also speak Polish. (Lodz was predominantly orthodox.) Hebrew is fostered mainly by the Zionists. The rabbinate corresponds in Hebrew.

On Friday nights there is practically no sabbath mood, except for a few candles here and there. No going to *shul*. At work, however, one does get greeted with "Good Shabbos." Most of the men have their sabbath *siddur* [Heb: prayer book] with them and study the *Tanach* even as they work. Certain passages of the Talmud are discussed.

Rumkowski at a concert in the ghetto's House of Culture. To his right, his secretary, Dora Fuchs. To his left, the commander of the Order Service, Leon Rozenblat.

Eventually, books in all languages were used as toilet paper, even old copies of the Talmud (*chillul hashem* [Heb: desecration of God's Name]).

NOTEBOOK 11

Religious Life: There's been no official worship since *Yamin Noraim* [Heb: the Days of Penitence (preceding Yom Kippur)] 1941. Circumcision is performed unofficially. *Succahs* are not permitted. No *Metaher* [Heb: individual who performs the ritual purification of a corpse]. *Mikvas* [Heb: ritual baths] not permitted. There were still *matzohs* available for Passover 1942. *Shilechlach* [Yid: little shuls, i.e., services] still in private homes. The rabbinate is non-existent. Marriage ceremonies by the Eldest. No official *bar mitzvah*. No *Bes Midrash*. Children up to ten are supervised by female teachers; after ten they work in administration departments. The tailoring and carpentry departments have sections for youths learning those trades. Unofficial teachers give mathematical instruction in Yiddish. Torah no longer taught; children grow up with no religious or traditional

Jewish life. Fathers go looking for Hebrew instruction for their boys, but there are no teachers, since money has no value. Several Torah experts ask for [food] coupons for themselves or their children as a fee.

NOTEBOOK 12

Language. Encyclopedia of the Ghetto

Nowhere else in the world has there been a society like that of the ghetto, and the change in all social, mental and economic functions required a corresponding change in thought. Concepts which previously had a straightforward meaning for all Europeans underwent a complete transformation. New words had to be constructed; old words had to take on new meaning. The fact that the ghetto was trilingual—Yiddish, Polish, and German—enlarged the possibilities for new constructions, as well as for indicating nuances.

Yiddish words, especially, multiplied their meanings. Words associated with the religious tradition became imprinted with a contemporary meaning. Words for things in daily life—in particular, getting food—quickly dominated. But even on this thin strip of mental activity, fantasy and humor grew. Serious terms took on ironic flavor; everyday expressions were raised to a higher sphere.

A collection of the ghetto's linguistic properties and words is part of its cultural history. In a later epoch—the epoch to which the investigation of the ghetto belongs—such a collection, such an encyclopedia, will be able to make clear what a simple outline of the circumstances cannot. Language is a more reliable source of truth than other, more material memorials: this is a thesis supported by a long academic tradition.

GERMAN DOCUMENT

Ghetto Administration

To the Eldest of the Jews
Re: Reports to the Registry Office

The Registry Office is complaining that in recent death notices the cause of death has been given as hunger, starvation, or swelling from hunger. I want to bring to your attention that such references have to stop and that the general term "malnutrition" must be used in such cases.

Ghetto burial.

Also, the Registry Office again points out that in birth and death notices, the first and last names of parents and spouses are often missing.

Care must be taken that the requirements of the Registry Office are always met.

On behalf of:
Biebow

OSKAR SINGER, SKETCHES

LITZMANNSTADT DEATH

Litzmannstadt Death has been unknown in Europe. Perhaps our early ancestors experienced similar events, but human beings have not known death like this.

In a very brief span of time, life has veered off its usual course, and death has changed its face. This has taken place with a speed not even the wildest imagination could have predicted. Life has become strange, and death, therefore, has also. The surviving world will have only the barest idea of what it was like here. Repeatedly, one hears the muted question: Will there be anyone able to tell the world how we lived and died here?

This is, indeed, a horror that challenges the creative hands of the poets. I do not know if among those living here there is a poet who could master the task, and if so, whether he will survive. Not everything that happens here can be explained by war. We have witnessed war and know that life takes on a different face when cannons speak. The basic forms, though—the elements of daily life—stay the same. Morality cracks, but ethics remain. The rules of social life are not abolished; at most, they are altered. The family, the pillar of domestic life, does not collapse. There is an evolution of thought during war, which we see among the young.

It is different here in the ghetto. Everything is upside-down, and yet we are far removed from the war itself. The ghetto developed without a period of transition, which created an unbridgeable gulf between us and the rest of the world. This cannot be explained entirely by the strict separation. For us Jews, the ghetto is a basic catastrophe.

We can no longer die as other people do. We no longer have the possibility of a noble end. Litzmannstadt Death is an alien, ugly death. I will draw it as it is—with no fictitious stories. He shall parade past us unadorned by literary device.

Mordche K. works in the carpentry workshop. Skilled furniture-maker that he is, he once had a good shop in Lodz, lived in a four-room apartment, and ran a respectable bourgeois household. A good, hard-working wife stood by his side, and they had two good-looking, well-built young lads. Naturally, the world changed for him in the ghetto. Now he lives in a small house very near the barbed wire at the edge of the ghetto. His wife, 19-year-old Icek, and 13-year-old Chajmek work in different factories.

Mordche K. is a sincerely good man who works honestly. But winter was rough and early spring cruel. He complains of being tired, of general weakness. His feet, especially his feet, do not want to do their duty. They have become very heavy, and the knee joints have become strangely stiff. But that will pass.

It looks very desperate in his apartment. But who should make it neat? The most his wife can do is make the beds; to dust or scrub the floor is impossible. Her strength does not extend that far. It must be accepted this way. One cannot afford to waste the slightest amount of energy not directed at acquiring food. Only now does she understand what she could never grasp before: the hopeless dirt in the apartments of the very poor. All her thoughts circle around only one thing: the dinner soup.

Where does one get some vegetables, carrots, a spoonful of flour for a soup? To hell with cleanliness. Dirt does not kill as fast as hunger.

Mordche feels his feet getting even heavier. Is this because of his worn-out shoes with the holes in the soles and the slanting heels? Does one walk with so much difficulty because of that? He must freshen up his feet; a hot bath might help. He just does not want to think about the swelling in his joints. It is not necessarily caused by hunger. Feet also swell for other reasons. You stand at the machines too long, and the long walk to work . . . no, it can't be hunger, as it is with so many ghetto people.

Mordche tries to ignore the water in his feet. He can only drag himself about, for this is no longer walking. Suddenly he realizes that his tools no longer rest as securely in his grip as they once did. His hands tremble. Very often, the hammer or the screwdriver falls. What the hell is this? Such weakness at only 45 years of age? He studies his hands. They are not that skinny. On the contrary, the right one has grown heavier. The fingers have heavy padding. This is strange: a hand like this should be able to work. Mordche would like to ignore the water in his hands. He knows that his hands are swollen, really swollen. But hands can also swell up for other reasons. For example, from being overworked. From being injured. The last injury caused an inflammation that has probably gone into the fingers. You must bathe the hands warmly; that helps with inflammations. But water is water! It will not be driven from the flesh by warm water.

Mordche explains to his frightened wife that he has burnt his hands with acid and now they're swollen. His wife knows better. Also his feet are not swollen from exhaustion. She knows that what's going on is hunger. She does not say anything. Why should she frighten him? And if he does know, why should she unmask his fiction?

Now when she handles the little weights—28 decagrams per day, 14 in the morning, 14 in the evening—she must cheat slightly. Her husband must not notice that his slice has become thicker. Naturally, it is not the children who can be deprived. Women need less, she has often heard, they can take it more easily. A few deca will not be a great loss to her, and they might help him.

And, in fact, it does go better. A few deca of bread make a difference. And he notices how it is happening. But should he do anything about it? Scared, he watches his wife, in case the same symptoms now show up in her. It is not from egoism but for his family's sake that he wants to live. Better times are bound to come. One day this war must end, and then he'll be able to give the boys a good start and his wife an easier life. One day. Till then one must sustain oneself.

This goes on for two weeks. The slice of bread is still as thick, and now the margarine is spread more heavily. Why the margarine? Mordche is not blind. The bundle in the shopping bag did not escape his eyes. His heart stopped at this discovery. Mother sells a quarter loaf to get the margarine on his slice. He doesn't say a word. Isn't that horrible? The few deca for me already equal more than a quarter. What is left for her, then? This is going too far. At night Mordche tells her he will not put up with it. He tells her he feels much better, it is not necessary any more. But she denies it. Not a trace of bread has been sold; he is making a mistake. Mordche likes so much to be put at ease.

But the swelling returns. He goes to a hard-working doctor he knows from the old days in town. The doctor shrugs his shoulders, cannot prescribe anything. No injection, no medication. Perhaps K. can get a few ampules of Campellon in some clandestine way—that would help. It can be had, but it costs a fortune. That much money doesn't even exist—100 marks for four ampules, and there would be no sense in getting less. He cannot tell his wife. God only knows what she would sell of her ration to get these ampules. The doctor also prescribes yeast. But where does one get yeast? The drugstore does not distribute it anymore. From private hands, one can get some at three marks a deca. How often can one buy that, if one only earns three marks a day? Even so, he will have to buy yeast. He buys, and the swelling goes down a bit again. Or is it just his imagination? It doesn't matter. Objectively or subjectively, better is better.

After two weeks he can stop the yeast. But Mordche is out of luck. A boil on his hand hinders his work. But he cannot call in sick. Anxiety about [missing] the designated day for rations forces him to keep struggling. The hand gets worse. Off to the emergency room. The doctor can do nothing. To cut is a possibility, but in the ghetto boils are not lanced, because then they never heal. The body lacks immunity. Take yeast! All right, he takes yeast again. He must tell his wife: his last few pfennigs are used up. Mrs. K. gets yeast. We don't even want to ask what she has sold, our heart would break. That her feet are swelling, we already know, but we are not concerned with her at the moment. She is one of the many unknown soldiers of the ghetto. Her heroism belongs on a different page.

The boil gets larger. Mordche is in terrible pain. Finally, it opens, and he is relieved. But immediately another appears. The next day a third, and soon his entire body is covered. A very bad case, the doctor reports. Only yeast, over and over again yeast. Now, thank God, getting it is not such a problem. Large amounts of it have come into the ghetto for therapeutic needs, and each week 5 deca can be had. That is affordable. Mordche eats yeast, raw and prepared. He is sick of it, but it's rich in vitamins. The boils heal, but his body is swollen even more. The sleepless nights have ravaged his strength. The money spent on yeast has not been spent on food.

Mrs. K. wears down her tired feet trying to get food for her husband, and finally, Mordche eats well for a couple of days. He is really satisfied, but his stomach and bowels are not used to it, and they rebel. He becomes sick with diarrhea. The doctor cannot prescribe the usual diet in these cases, as the organism cannot afford to go without food even for a day. Not in the ghetto. Eat, eat at all costs. The patient forces himself to take nutrition, and every hour his bowels force him to leave his bed. He falls down like a stick. His feet are merely bones covered with skin.

The swelling in his face has gone, but the skin on his forehead is now like tough leather. The intervals become shorter and shorter; soon he must go out every 15 minutes. A European normally has everything at his disposal in such a case, but here there is only a pail in the middle of the room, one pail for four people. In the past, K. carried the pail out himself. Now he has to leave this to his wife. He is too weak.

She wants to force into him what she can come up with that is edible. K., in fact, does want to eat. He knows too well that this is the only way to keep himself strong. But an alarming loss of appetite settles in. Perhaps a delicacy—fried potatoes—could still taste good. But potatoes are not to be had.

He would like to rest for just one hour without interruption, but his body refuses to obey. Every ten minutes he must get up. Mother K. finally gets a bowl. At first he rejects this convenience. A man cannot expect his wife to do this. Finally, she teaches him, and he permits her.

He asks for sleeping pills. Perhaps sleep will calm the body; that could be the answer. The pharmacy no longer has sleeping powders. She tracks down acquaintances who have brought some with them from Berlin. He takes the medication with the hope of a believer.

No, the illness stubbornly remains, but now K. lies in semiconsciousness during the small breaks his suffering permits him. Now, he cannot be made to eat anything. Here and there, a sip of coffee, that's all. Incomprehensible, where his body gets all the fluid from, since nothing goes into his stomach anymore.

Mrs. K. checks anxiously: perhaps this is dysentery. No, there is no blood to be seen. The doctor finally comes to the house again. He comes, knowing he is superfluous. He cannot prescribe anything. There are medications that might help, strong opiates, for example. But such things do not come into the ghetto. What for?—we are supposed to die.

Mordche can hardly speak anymore. He can only give tired signs with his finger. He wants to tell the doctor something but can't. Yet one must be careful.

He hears everything. Outside, the doctor says it could take hours, perhaps a day.

Mordche's strength makes it for two days. Then he dozes off.

People die this way in great numbers, a result of the so-called Ghetto Disease, diarrhea. The doctor fills out the death certificate. "Cause of death: heart failure!" Nobody in the ghetto is allowed to die of hunger.

—27 July 1942

AT THE HATMAKERS

"Have you ever visited our factory? Our hat factory will definitely interest you. Well, to tell the truth, its interest is not exactly great, because, really, who needs hats in the ghetto? We know that hats were made in former days, and it's not likely that they'll be made any differently in the ghetto. And what's produced is plainly visible on the heads of the many in the ghetto who wear hats."

But the director said this with a certain hint of pride, suggesting that he might have more to show than would be expected. And why not pay a visit to the hatmakers? It was worth it. We got to see much more than we could have possibly guessed. The Lodz hatmakers are making a contribution to history, inscribing themselves into the book of this war.

Mr. David Rosenthal did not make hats before the war. But who in the ghetto does now what they used to do? Before the war he was a master weaver and a clothing manufacturer—and now he just happens to make hats. There is no reason why this should not be so. With skilled workers, some organizational talent and a sense of responsibility and order, you can manufacture whatever the war demands. From Rosenthal the war happens to need hats. Ergo Rosenthal makes hats, and he makes them superbly.

We arrive at the factory exactly at lunch time. A workshift is just fetching the soup, and it strikes me that they do so without a sound, which is rarely the case in the ghetto. That alone indicates something of this factory's prevailing spirit. We step into the office and find the director, along with his office staff, eating the seasonal cabbage soup. He hurries to finish his frugal meal so that he can show us around.

The first floor of an old and very rundown former residence houses the workshops. As we leave the office we notice something resembling a pot. Upon closer inspection we recognize it as the felt helmet of a tank regiment. There are boxes and sacks with metal badges indicating rank and insignias for hats. So here too they're working for the army. Puzzled, we examine the gunner's helmet, this flat pot with rows of air holes. How is it possible that such work is done here? Well, the director explains, the helmets cannot be manufactured here because we don't have the necessary machines; they arrive already made, but we'll show you what we do with them.

In the first workshop on this floor, we see a group of workers producing flying caps for the summer. Made of sturdy material and with a soft silk lining and easy-to-handle leather buckles, the caps look very elegant and are work to be proud of. They're fitted onto beautifully carved wooden heads.

As soon as we enter the next workshop, the secret of the tankers' helmets and how they get their winter furs is revealed. Fur, already cut, is supplied by the Eldest's furriers [after confiscation], and here, in this workshop, they are mounted on a foundation. A hodgepodge of all kinds of fur is used for this. Skilled workers sit at machines in groups of ten or twelve and are supervised by a foreman.

The next, somewhat larger room is used for the remounting of service caps. It's a kind of sanatorium for ailing caps, the famous flat caps of the German army and the SS. Damaged and discolored pieces are replaced here. The supplier provides only half of the material. The department head has to manage with that and yet supply the necessary quota of new caps. He must, therefore, use extreme economy with both old and new material. It's up to his instructors to show the workers what kind of material may be sewn into the hats and what is completely beyond use. Seeing what condition the old hats are in and comparing them to the newly repaired hats in the storeroom, one realizes how dire necessity can break iron, or rather, turn old into new. This is what Mr. Rosenthal is particularly proud of. One of the ghetto's greatest achievements is the creation of much from nothing. The finished pieces in the hat storeroom look brand new.

Finally, we go into the room where the tank gunners' helmets, with their winter furs, are stacked. A woman would be delighted by so many furry animals, or rather their coats. The helmets' air holes have been filled with cork made for this purpose—as air is not in great demand in the winter. There they sit, not resembling helmets any longer but Siberian fur hats: nutria and skunk, beaver and lamb, opossum, fox, and soft rabbit, all here in their most charming shades. Who would suspect the variety of furs now on their way to the front, packed neatly into boxes labeled: Berlin Clothing Office, lot number such-and-such.

Many thousands of hats have already left the factory and many thousands more will follow. The department was founded in March of 1941, and 67 workers using 45 machines had produced 14,490 hats by April. By May there were 93 workers and 85 machines. Now, in July 1942, 120 machines are whirring and 230 workers are employed here, including 30 youths. At first there were only ten youths, who had to work without pay. Then the workers gave them some of their own wages. And now it is somewhat better, since the boys make their own money. Also, in addition to the skilled workers, there are just under 30 laborers.

The director points out, not without pride, that his workers earn relatively good money: a foreman makes about 40 marks a week, the leading machinist about 25 to 30 marks, a laborer at full employment, 18 marks. Compared to other departments, this is pretty good. The work week is seven eight-hour days, and wages come to an average of 3000 marks a week.

It's a quiet department and doesn't make much of a fuss about its efficiency, but it's a very remarkable factory.

—28 July 1942

THE GHETTO SALAD

The far-too-active hustle and bustle in front of the dairies of the Eldest of the Jews tempts the reporter to look behind the scene. Just that there is something like a regular creamery in the ghetto, in this town without farmland, cattle breeding, or fodder, is interesting enough. Actually, there was a Cattle Breeding Department, but it was finally renamed, more appropriately, the Transportation Department. The few scrawny cart horses in the ghetto, the few cows and goats that may be counted on the fingers of one hand, and the handful of four-legged oxen were a caricature of cattle breeding and hardly the basis of dairy farming for a town of some 100,000 inhabitants. And since every inch of soil has been planted with vegetables, cows or sheep—even were they to exist in greater numbers—could not find as much as a modest breakfast on the meager pasture this side of the barbed wire. And yet, there is actually a Dairy Department which not only distributes products but processes them as well.

The source of the white stream flowing into the languishing ghetto—the cottage cheese, whey, skimmed milk, and the famous ghetto salad—is located "At The Spring." (The name derives from the well which, from time immemorial, provided Lodz with supposedly the best water imaginable, though nobody uses it now. Water vendors used to get the "most superior tea water" there, carrying it to the center of the city in buckets.) On our arrival there, we find that the dairy department, one of the ghetto's most important provisioning departments, consists of four buildings at ground level, connected by yards and the typical ghetto vegetable gardens, which give it a thoroughly neat and rural impression. In between are several primitive wood sheds. The smell of sour milk comes surging toward us.

We're greeted by the director, Israel Gurin, a rather good-looking, energetic man of about thirty. He gladly takes it upon himself to guide us through the empire he himself founded.

"This seems to be your line of expertise," we say.

"I'm a specialist, yes—but from the metal trade," he smiles wickedly. This is typical in the ghetto, and we ask Gurin about his career. His parents used to own a large hardware store in the city. When the ghetto was established, the young man worked in his father's store. The family still owned some property then and lived waiting for things to change. The situation could not last forever (so he thought) and returning merrily to the paternal store was just a matter of time. But the situation lasted longer than optimism could possibly fathom, while the young man's money declined rapidly. What does a young man from a good family do if he is short of money and has a head on his shoulders? He goes into business. In the beginning with great success. But gradually the Chairman monopolized all business in the ghetto, taking over all the stock. And Gurin found himself with shoulders that could not quite carry his head any longer. He needed to find a more stable income, preferably a permanent post.

He went to the Order Service, becoming one of the Chairman's policemen and in a very visible position: the central prison, the empire of Commander Hercberg.* The two men, Gurin and Hercberg—one the son of a good family, the other from the gutters of Baluty—did not get along well. Gurin had no talent for brutality, which the notorious prison warden could not do without. Gurin knew he couldn't have much of a career under such a boss. He wanted to get out of that hell, but in the ghetto only chance or the Chairman can help—or isn't that the same thing?

During a visit the Chairman saw him. "What, you're here?—This is not for you!" And things changed right there. Gurin became a bread and dairy store inspector of the Eldest. Here he developed his talents and made a career. From a small inspector he rose to become a director. One day, in the course of a reorganization, he was entrusted with the dairy department. In those days, regular (non-skimmed) milk was still available, though in modest quantities. Then when it failed to arrive at all one day, he was left with a department without goods, without work. The plant employees pressed him to do something to save their livelihood. But how do you make milk? Jews can do anything—but making milk is a bit too much. That Gurin could not do.

But he wanted to remain a director. So he had to find something to direct. One day he became aware of the waste in the vegetable yard. He had his idea:

Waste in the ghetto? That simply can't be. The ghetto cannot afford it. Everything must be utilized. And when it comes to recycling waste, saving money and creating something edible in the process, the Chairman cannot refuse.

The plan was approved, and with the help of a specialist, a vegetable salad made of scraps, the "ghetto salad," was born. Production started in ridiculously small quantities. The product even tasted like herring salad. (How the palate can fantasize when the stomach is hungry.) Finally, milk arrived again—skimmed milk but better than nothing. The resourceful young man thought of turning part of this milk into cottage cheese, and he had specialists for that, too. And so, Gurin soon had a regular dairy plant. Sixteen stores now distribute his products.

Gurin introduces us to the department supervisor, Gertler, formerly a store owner, who introduces us to the salad production. In the yard we're greeted by a strange smell, or, to put it more honestly, a stench. Vegetables have just arrived on the well-known hand carts. Vegetables? Withered things, like the red-beet leaves strewn about the Vegetable Department's yards. These leaves are not left to die a natural death; they must still make a detour through the ghetto's intestines.

Several women sort the miserable scraps. Being withered is not the end of the world; only the truly rotten parts are discarded. What remains is carefully soaked in barrels of water. Dust, dirt and soil fall off. The leaves, which are soaked three times, come back to life, become fresh again. Cured, the leaves then go to the kitchen.

"But what stinks so much?" we have to ask.

Grinning, the vegetable artists point to the ground, which is covered with a dirty, slimy mass. "It's the potatoes."

We're speechless. This reeking garbage is supposed to go into the salad? And yet they *are* potatoes, newly arrived in this state, so-called "second-grade." We shudder to think what third-grade might be. The magicians who conjure new life from this rot sit by the door in the peeling room. Every woman has in front of her a pile of this garbage that's been dried in the sun. She picks out the more solid pieces, peeling the healthy core from a stinking skin. And even these healthy pieces still smell. They have to be soaked in barrels for hours and continually stirred, until—a ghetto miracle—they no longer really smell.

The percentage of potatoes saved this way must be very small, but if one of these women peels out just half a kilogram a day, she produces a multiple of her wages. For what do potatoes cost at present? About 30 to 40 marks per kilo. The worker earns only two marks a day. A situation like this could be found only in Lodz's hunger town, in the ghetto.

We leave this scene shaking our heads and turn to the actual production process. This takes place immediately next door, in the salad factory. A chef boils the refurbished vegetables. Right next to him an electric grinder rattles away. And bread is soaking in some of the barrels. The ghetto's precious gold for these greens? Well, don't think for a minute that this is regular bread from bakeries. Nothing *but* scraps come here, but is there waste bread in the ghetto? We start exploring the phenomenon: Some bread gets moldy while being stored in the bakeries, due to low-quality flour. The moldy parts are used as fodder in the "cattle breeding" or transportation department; the good pieces go into the salad.

The salad chef shows us the pan with real butter and lets us smell it. Yes, they do provide real butter, and it really does go into the salad. And now the other ingredients: caraway, paprika, salt, tartar—vinegar is too scarce, but the Chairman would permit all the spices of Arabia just to tame the salad's ghetto aroma.

Every day 1400 to 1500 kilos of salad are produced this way, and twice a month a worker may hope to get a coupon for some decas of this ghetto *salatka*. Today it's green like cabbage leaves and almost-rotting beet leaves. Tomorrow it will be red perhaps, when *buraczki,* the red beet itself—of course, of the lowest grade—is among the leftovers. Thus the *salatka* changes its colors with the seasons, just as we changed color looking at its raw ingredients.

—2 August 1942

LUDWIK ASZ

"AT THE CEMETERY"

It's cold. A bitter wind is driving a mass of jagged clouds, as a drizzle begins. The cemetery is dark, although a distant lantern illuminates some of the broken marble tombstones. On the left, in the unused section directly under the wall, newly dug graves stand out, dark smudges against the light earth surrounding them. These are for future use. Several people steal along the narrow, overgrown path. They are three women, two men and two boys. All of them are dressed for cold weather and are wearing hobnailed shoes, or so it sounds as they walk. Where are they going? For a while they disappear among the shadows of the taller tombstones, but then suddenly they're at the wall. They move ahead, crouched over, almost on all fours. A muffled whistle. They stop as if rooted to the ground, and listen.

From one of the empty graves a man emerges. "It's you! Okay, let's go, there's no time to waste. Thank God."

The wall is high and has barbed wire along the top. The guide drags some wooden boards nailed together. "It will be easier for the ladies. Let's begin, because in an hour there'll be a change."

There is some hesitation. Who'll go first? One of the men volunteers. "Let's go," says the guide. He climbs nimbly up the wall, in an instant placing himself on the edge. He cautiously lifts his head and looks around. On the other side, obscured by darkness, stands the guard's booth, its contours barely visible. He lifts his leg over the wire and catches his trouser cuff. It's nothing, everything is fine. The thud of a falling body is heard, and he is on the other side. A moment of anxious expectation.

"Next! Hurry up!" The voice from behind the wall is trembling and strange. Two minutes later a second shadow falls with a thud next to the guide. "Is everything okay?" Good, that's the second man. Now it's the turn of the women. This is much more difficult. Two pairs of hands lift a trembling body and push it to the top. She is on the barbed wire and is trying to swing over to the other side. Suddenly, a sharp beam of light hits the wall and almost instantly a gunshot is heard. The woman screams in fright from atop the wire. A second shot is heard, and after it a third.

One of the forms huddled under the wall emits a quiet moan and becomes motionless. The second form picks itself up and runs but after a few steps is confronted by a silhouette with a rifle. Another shot, and it seems that the form has been swallowed by the earth. All this has taken less than a minute, and already sharp beams of light search the terrain. No, there is nobody else here. Two corpses on the ground and one woman mortally wounded and caught in the barbed wire, three meters above ground. They approach her. They place the gun barrel almost at her temple and shoot. The woman hangs suspended as before, only now her head is bent backward and her bared teeth are visible. One eye stares vacantly into space.

A hunt through the cemetery ensues. Several searchlights probe under bushes and into every crevice. There has to be somebody here. They search. A shot is heard, and then three shots in a row. There is one more person hiding in an empty grave, head pressed tightly into the soil. The lights find him, and he has no chance to make a move. He remains in his grave.

Under an overturned marble tombstone a boy is huddling. He is curled up, close to the ground and out of sight. He holds his breath, watching the beams of light as they cut across the darkness. He hears shots and sees silhouettes moving. They're still here. It's cold and the ground is damp, but he cannot move. He's found himself this place by chance. Seized by uncontrollable fear, he ran across the tombstone, stumbled, fell and hit his head. A sharp pain restored him to consciousness, and in an instant he was in his hideout. Now they are approaching. Through a crack he can see three pairs of legs in leather boots and a searchlight. Fast, strong steps and those hateful voices. They are almost here. Bright beams fall everywhere, lighting every inch of ground. They are thorough. His heart beats faster; a spasm grips his throat. The bright searchlight moves on, and his sharp, inquiring eyes follow. Maybe he will not be found? Yes, they are leaving, for their silhouettes and the searchlight are now further away. So are their voices. What relief! Except now his nerves let go. His body trembles and tears fill his eyes. He stifles his sobbing, and to keep from making a sound, he bites his lips until they bleed. He carefully lifts his head and looks around. Silence and darkness. They are gone.

—JULY 11, 1942

OSKAR ROSENFELD'S NOTEBOOK

NOTEBOOK B

Memories for later days (loose sketches)

FACE OF THE GHETTO, JUNE, 1942
Girls already sit by the open windows at sewing machines or sewing by hand. . . . Other girls go through the alleys like prostitutes, paint their lips using the dirty window panes as mirrors—pretty figures among the garbage of the street and the crumpled beggars, blonde, blue-eyed in racy outfits, with coquettish hats, coiffured, manicured, pedicured—one could see the colored toes in the open summer sandals; and if one follows them, then one comes in a few moments upon a vegetable plot in which radishes, lettuce and other things grow, even right next to the open latrine; an appealing little garden, cared for by hands that until now never touched a thing in nature.

NOTEBOOK D: MEMORIES

9 June. At the edges of the ghetto, across the wire from the old age home, one hears unusual noises: roosters crow, hens cluck, gramophones, radio music, clocks striking—like a dream within a dream.

[Paragraph in English:] I am sure the Jewish people will be eternal, but not like the Wandering Jew, nor a singular appearance in the history of humanity. The atrocities of the ghetto cannot break the resistance of Jewish souls. We can truly say: the future belongs to us, although at present we are tired and weary of hunger, cold and beatings.

12 June. II Book M[oses]. Chap 17.14 And the Lord spoke to Moses: Write this for memory into a book and lay it in the ears of Joshua, for I will exterminate Amalek [the enemy of the Hebrews] from beneath the heavens, that one no longer thinks of him.

Isaiah. Chap 14. Prophesy against *Aschkenes!*

Jewish Police. Partisans of the Eldest, brutal, in the mold of *Aschkenes,* Gestapo. Numerous, since bodyguards for Chaim.

Hunger (Deportation) People apply of their own free will for German deportation, because of insane hunger. Before leaving, they get a bowl of soup and a loaf of bread.

15 June. Death. Many report the people who die on Monday and Thursday a day late, so that they can bring home their bread rations on those days.

Kripo—Vanya [in Greek letters]: The German [in Greek letters]: What do you have for us? Vanya [Code: Russia]: How can I help you?

21 June. Schools, teaching forbidden. The children are growing up without any learning. Even private instruction is forbidden. Without schooling, even technical schooling, a wild, primitive Jewish life.

22 June. One suddenly discovers in the summer—when the sun shines down and the sky surrounds the roofs with blue and white clouds—that the streets are long and wide enough to support normal city traffic. But the sidewalks are uneven, full of potholes and broken up by the gutters—which come out of the houses completely uncovered—so that one is in danger at every moment of stepping into the flowing urine.

23 June. New hope for an end to the *Milchome* [Heb: war], in that Vanya's [Russia's] *Schituvim* [Heb: allies] work *mi maala* [Heb: from above] and make *churban* [Heb: destruction] out of the *aschkenes Irim* [Heb: German cities].

1 July. This part of the town developed vegetatively rather than by plan. For all that, however, a tolerant observer could find a kind of harmony in the confused jumble of houses and barracks. The streets resemble those of Central European or Balkan cities, such as Belgrade, Bucharest or Sofia. Buildings are not usually more than three stories high, with tiny iron balconies, on which laundry is hung to dry. Doors and gates, as well as shop windows, are locked tight with iron bars. The stores are closed, their signs destroyed. Here and there one sees a sign in a dirty window: "Jewish Shoemaker," "Doll Clinic," "Paper Store," "Hair Dresser"—all written in odd orthography or in Yiddish. Vestiges of Polish nameplates and inscriptions can still be seen.

Down these streets—once inhabited by gangsters, denizens of the underworld, poor and middle-class Polish tradesmen—people from Vienna, Prague, Berlin, Frankfurt, Hamburg, Danzig, Munich, and Luxembourg came, slinking in tolerably fashionable clothing, like tourists among the natives, the deportees from Lodz, who have lived in the ghetto of Poland from time immemorial, and with whom assimilation can be achieved only very, very slowly.

The "population transfer" in May 1942, the uprooting of some 11,000 Jews from the West, simplified the problem. After this "resettlement," a deportation assured of a lethal ending, the "German element" in the ghetto vanished. The small number remaining could no longer alter the character of the ghetto. Once more, the men passing by wear only skullcaps on their heads and the women scarves, except for a few flirtatious eccentrics. Everything wobbles and jostles, lumbering through and over the cobblestones of the filthy alleys. The noise of the street urchins echoes shrilly in one's ears. Dust rises in the air. The clouds float dreary and damp. Gusts of wind beat round every corner, and July comes in cool and almost cold.

NOTEBOOK E:

NOTES AS MEMORY.
THE MOST IMPORTANT QUESTIONS.

Wire. Before 7 AM no one is allowed to cross the bridge near the wire. Young man wants to report that his father is sick and cannot work. Goes over the bridge in the grey dawn of early morning and is shot by a steel-helmet.

3 July. On top of the bridge, one sees the trucks of *Aschkenes* driving through Hohensteinerstrasse, between the fence and the barbed wire. One can look down into the open wagon: the most beautiful radishes, lettuce, cabbage, carrots, fruit.

5 July 1942. Today a good day. It is true there were 105 who died, but some births that came out well. Interruption of pregnancy (induced abortion) is allowed—because of the difficulty finding nourishment for the infant.

Noise from over there: factory whistles, smoking chimneys, singing, automobile horns, fire brigades . . .

For chapter on relocation, as marginal note, *Lekh lekho* [Heb: Go forth], see Moses I [Genesis] 12.1 ff. Abraham.

. . . The melancholy of the ghetto takes on, in concert, a religious character.

. . . Ghetto Litzmannstadt is the *Golem* [Jewish folklore: an artificially created human being] of the world's cities. Important to sketch a figure who goes through the ghetto and also carries in itself all the ghetto's characteristics. The eternal Jew, Christ, *Golem,* Police, *Feldgrau,* and so on.

For chapter on relocation. Brzeziny 18 kilometers from Lodz. 17,000 inhabitants, 5750 Jews. Ghetto: Eldest of the Jews Felix Ikka, since two years ago. Primarily tailors (also before the war) for military. . . . Evacuation: Friday, the 15th of May, afternoon. Jewish police take women and their children in pouring rain into empty houses. Terrible crying. Sleep on naked earth. 3 o'clock in the morning Gestapo from Lodz, with whips, smash their way in. The women stay, the children thrown into trucks. 8 o'clock in the morning the women brought back to the ghetto. Shouts, crying. . . .

On Saturday, the Jewish police went into the houses and demanded that all Jews be at this or that place in the market, in each alleyway with backpack and bread sack. . . . At the marketplace women, children [over 10 years old], and men were separated. The older men, the older women, and the children were taken out in groups in wagons, the baggage separately, and were brought to Galkuwek [near Lodz]. Here they were driven into railroad cars, the cars sealed, the windows shut. The train stood in the station the whole night. 6 am to Lodz.

Arrived in Lodz, taken over by the Jewish police. Put up in barracks, some of them in space left empty by those who had been moved on. In all about 4500 people, among them older men and women incapable of working (of these 1200 sent on immediately; 360 men to some place for forced labor).

Dreams. The dreams build on hunger, the path to the cemetery, the passageway near the ghetto courthouse, that is, daydreams. One must always be reminded of the *Golem*-like.

a) Tasty tidbits, land of milk and honey, goes over into the erotic, repeats itself, oranges over and over, going into lemons, breasts.

b) When dream of father, then pleasant surprise.

c) A rich man passes out loaves of bread—etc., brawl, thrashing, police.

d) 700 million Jews running over country roads between potato fields. Bombed from airplanes, then machine-gun fire, then gas, then clothes sent back with bloody holes to the workshops, where the dreamer must clean them and recognizes his father's suit.

e) He is still a clinical professor, in white smock, is supposed to bury people alive, since the white smock is like the robe of death. Suddenly Jewish police force him into wagon, move him out, put a doctor's cap on him. He is happy, wakes, has knocked over black coffee that he prepared for brushing his teeth.

f) Beggar goes through the street: unusual picture, Rembrandt. This beggar walks slowly (describe path), into the Polish/German lending library—prompts reflection on Socrates, then Faust (describe in all detail).

g) The whole ghetto working: *y'ledim* [Heb: children] and *S'kanim* [Heb: elderly]. People with weak character working along with others, giving orders, debasing their brothers and sisters into slaving for an allotment, for 5 dkg butter, for a can of sardines, for 4 dkg sausage.

One will ask one day: Did *Sakune* [Heb: Elder] Chaim Mordechai do right? Will someone demand righteousness from him? Was he the clever one? The *Shofet* [Heb: judge]?

[*Transcriber's notes*—Above a sketch: *Mogen David* with inscription "The Secret of the Ghetto." Underneath: a *menorah* (Heb: candelabra). On both sides the flat hands held high as in a blessing and words: "Who will uncover it? Later generations."]

Capital and labor. One does not know these categories in the ghetto. One does not see capitalists or workers, faceless capital or the private individual, the exploiter or the proletarian. We live in a commune. Of 104,000 inhabitants in July 1942, about 100,000 are all at one level. The remaining 4000 live somewhat better, with larger food rations and better hygienic conditions. That is all.

11 July. Vegetables in the grocery store, indeed beets and carrots. . . . A wagon pulled by human slaves. Green leaves and tiny bulbs of red and yellow.

Pushing in front of the entrance. A few children push their way skillfully through the crowd: nets, baskets, sacks, string, even pots and cartons. Doorman keeps people out. Crowd pushes more furiously. Suddenly, everywhere, police caps. One sees sticks swinging. The police thrash, beat their way in. The people take the blows, noise louder. Wild faces, swollen arteries, tempestuous eyes—uncertain faces. Finally, the door is broken down. One is in the store. Police go in. Wild greed.

13 July. Hunger again. Prices rise. One remembers January 1941. Then 1500 people died, no briquettes—hunger and cold. Lie down in the evening, in the morning frozen. Whole family, excepting only one boy, whose leg had to be amputated. Why not us? We are guilty, *all* of us, that we may live while others, in contrast, are ——. We, all, in the ghetto are guilty, that it is so.

14 July Dying. Women lie on the large bridge. Police officer walks up to them. Female doctor comes, continues on. Police officer nods at doctor. Doctor shrugs shoulders, examines the women, goes away. No one going over the bridge does anything about this picture. Dead, simple, done. The Jewish problem resolved in installments.

In the official offices, posters: "What can yet be built?"

19 July. Half-starved near-corpses flank the street, right and left, outside the hospital. Too late. Pitiful sight. Rumor that 15,000 Praguers from Theresienstadt are coming here!

22 July. Hebrew teacher from Vienna sells rations in order to buy books—already has 300 books.

23 July. *Tishe B'Av*. No one feels it. In the hospital a few Chassidim read the *Kinaw*. [Heb: poems expressing mourning, pain, sorrow].

24 July. Discussions about places. Spain (*Marranos* [Spanish and Portuguese Jews who had been forcibly converted to Christianity]). What *Insel* [Ger: island; Code for England] wants. The strength of Vanya. Secret meeting between Insel and Horowitz. A *Mabul* [Heb: flood] will come. Destruction of the world. Another apocalypse.

25 July. Neighbor has green cucumbers from his own garden. Big sensation. Everyone sees them, is astonished by them. Miracle. "Not the person, the *Rebojne schel Ojlem hat a grosse Gewure*." [Yid: the Almighty has great power.]

27 July. Rumor that Jews are to be evacuated from Warsaw. At the same time rumor that potatoes will be in the next kitchen ration. In fact, 10,000 Jews evacuated daily from Warsaw with guns and shooting. Not evacuated but driven out, as from Lodz into Litzmannstadt Ghetto. Eldest of the Jews in Warsaw—suicide. None of it strategic but a matter of Jews.

4 August. Talkie. Talkie encompasses ever more. Three parts: plot, speaking, music. Music: a) street noise, b) the sewage wagons, the transport of the

dead, c) *Ausufern* [Ger: overflow] on the street, d) *Nigun* [Heb: tune] in the Chassidic *shul,* e) singing in the workshops, f) revue at house of culture, g) folk songs, h) choir of *Feldgrau Aschkenes* sounding above. Begin *[Ha]tikvah* [Heb: "Hope," the Zionist anthem].

5 August. No one sees what the Jews have contributed to the economy of Poland: manufacturing, ready-made clothes, export. All stolen by *Aschkenes.* Partly destroyed, partly in use.

Fear in the ghetto. Trenches everywhere since the time the air-raid defense was prepared. Watch over the trenches. Why? "Who knows why trenches are still protected! Maybe they'll murder us and throw us into the ditches, or even throw us in alive at the end. Similar ditches were used to throw masses of soldiers in on top of one another." One looks, silent and horribly sad, at the other.

8 August. Hospital is supposed to be liquidated and transformed into a workshop. German commission already inspected; thus preparations in gear. Has central heating, while the other tracts do not.

Acquaintance of Dr. Vogel, Prague, tells of his brother's death. Confused, made remarks against *Aschkenes,* in Litzmannstadt prison, in a so-called court trial, and shot.

Fear of not surviving. "On our bones Palestine must be built, the only hope still left."

10 August. While 100,000 go hungry, a few gluttons: they have strawberry jam, condensed milk, wine, liqueurs, fine cigarettes, etc.

15 August. I weigh 47 kg. [103 pounds]. Since Prague lost 10 kg [22 pounds].

18 August. *Milchome* [Heb: war] critical stage.

Sister comes to bed of the patient: "Oh, life is hard and narrow." *Life is narrow!* Finally the word is found.

21 August. Heard again that a few weeks ago Horowitz-*Hanoar* [Heb: youth; Code: Hitler Youth?] wanted to come into the ghetto, but *Aschkenes* ghetto administration prevented it, since it wants quiet and order.

Alarm. It is said that Vanya and west of us bombed. No further details known.

23 August. About Warsaw, told that machine guns set up there, shot at *Iwri* [Heb: Jews] and hunted them down.

24 August. Statue of Mary in front of Catholic church in Kirchplatz moved away. In spite of that, many Poles going by tip their hats.

26 August. Ghetto illnesses. "Protect yourself from typhus of the stomach! No unboiled (!) water; no unboiled (!) vegetables." Neither the possibility of boiling nor of getting warm water easily. Cleaning of the [water] closet, where there are only open latrines. Flies! No flypaper. Massive deaths from dysentery!

27 August. Village 40 kilometers from Lodz, Zdunska Wola: *Yeladim*

separated from older people and parents, ordered *Yeladim* with *rosch* [Heb: head] down, then shot with revolver. Mothers must bury their own children. Adults come into the ghetto. Of these, the older people immediately deported to unknown destination; only working people left here.

Rumor of differences between Vanya and *Insel*. *Aschkenes* foreign minister said to be at Vanya. Atmosphere depressed.

GERMAN DOCUMENTS

To: The Eldest of the Jews
Litzmannstadt Ghetto

VII.16.1942

Re: Machines in the ghetto.
I request that you immediately investigate whether there is a

Bone Grinder

in the ghetto, either with a motor or hand-driven. The special command in Kulmhof [Ger: Chelmno] is interested in such a grinder.

on behalf of
F W Ribbe
Assistant Director,
Ghetto Administration

[*Gestapo memo*]

August 15, 1942

It is increasingly clear on the faces of the ghetto residents that the Jews of Europe will not survive this war. One thing that occasions this is the evacuations, especially of those from whom no news is ever received. It should not be overlooked that rumor mongers are at work, and that lasting and substantial disquiet would disturb discipline and order in the ghetto and, in particular, disrupt its productivity.

Because a number of Jews, particularly in the rural districts, have left their living areas illegally, wandering around the countryside like vagrants, in the month of July a total of 13 Jews were publicly executed on the RSHA's orders, as a scare tactic. There were 9 in Warta Krs. Schieratz [Sieradz], 2 in the county of Lask, and 2 in the Litzmannstadt Ghetto who refused to work.

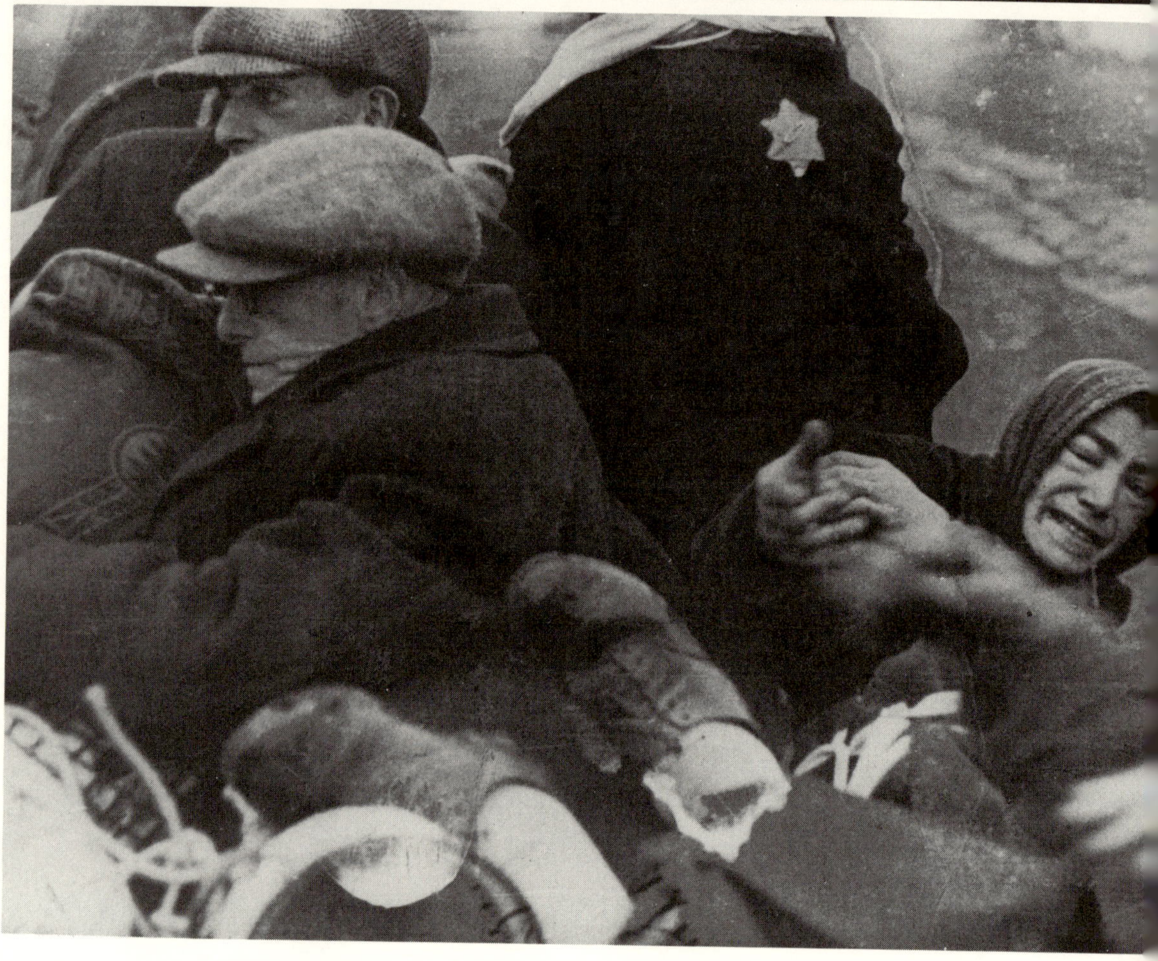

Wagon to the trains.

CHAPTER SEVEN

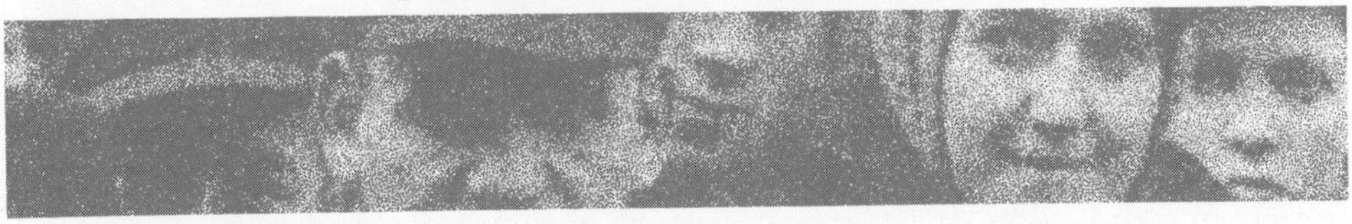

"NIGHTMARISH DAYS"

DAWID SIERAKOWIAK'S DIARY

TUESDAY, SEPTEMBER 1

The first day in this new, fourth year of the war has brought the terrible news that the Germans have emptied all the ghetto's hospitals.

In the morning, the areas around the hospitals were surrounded by guards. All the sick, without exception, were loaded on trucks and taken out of the ghetto. There was a terrible panic, because it's no secret, thanks to people who've recently come from the provinces, how the Germans "take care" of such evacuees. Hellish scenes occurred during the moving of the sick. People knew that they were going to their death! They fought the Germans, and were thrown onto the trucks by force. In the meantime, a good many of the sick escaped from the hospitals which the Germans got to a little later. It's said that even the sick in the Marysin preventorium were shipped out. In our office nobody could think about work (I'm now in an office which distributes payments to the families of people working in Germany). It seems no work was done in other offices and factories, either. People are fearing for their children and for the elderly who aren't working.

WEDNESDAY, SEPTEMBER 2

Having discovered that many of the sick escaped, the Germans are demanding they be brought back. On the basis of hospital records, the homes of the escapees' relatives have been searched and the sick captured. On this occasion, the Jewish police committed a crime unlike anything, it seems to me, committed previously in the ghetto.

The Germans demanded a full complement of all those on the hospital registers. The police found a novel way of doing the job, following instructions from people with influence to spare any of their relatives who escaped. They went to the homes of other sick people, namely those already deported, and asked where the sick could be found. When the unfortunate families answered that the sick were most probably deported, since they had never come back, the police detained some of these relatives as hostages, until the "escapees" were turned in. And when the Germans sent in vehicles today to fetch the rest of the sick, some of these hostages were included among them, as substitutes for sick people with influential relatives.

The mood is still panicky, though things progress their normal way. It feels as though something is hanging in the air.

THURSDAY, SEPTEMBER 3

It seems the Germans have asked that all children up to the age of 10 be delivered, most probably to be murdered. The situation resembles what happened in all the surrounding small towns prior to deportations and differs only in the precision and subtlety which prevails here. There, everything was sudden and unexpected.

JOZEF ZELKOWICZ, IN THESE NIGHTMARISH DAYS

[In These Nightmarish Days, *a manuscript of 345 pages in Yiddish, is the longest monograph which has survived from the ghetto.*]

Son of man, go out into the streets. Soak in the unconscious terror of the newborn babies about to be slaughtered. Be strong. Keep your heart from breaking, so you'll be able to describe, carefully and clearly, what happened in the ghetto during the first days of September in the year one thousand, nine hundred and forty-two.

Mothers run through the streets, only one shoe on, hair barely combed, shawls dragging on the ground. They still keep their children at their sides. They can clasp them even more tightly to their emaciated breasts. They can still pour kisses onto the bright little faces, the dear eyes.

But what will happen tomorrow?

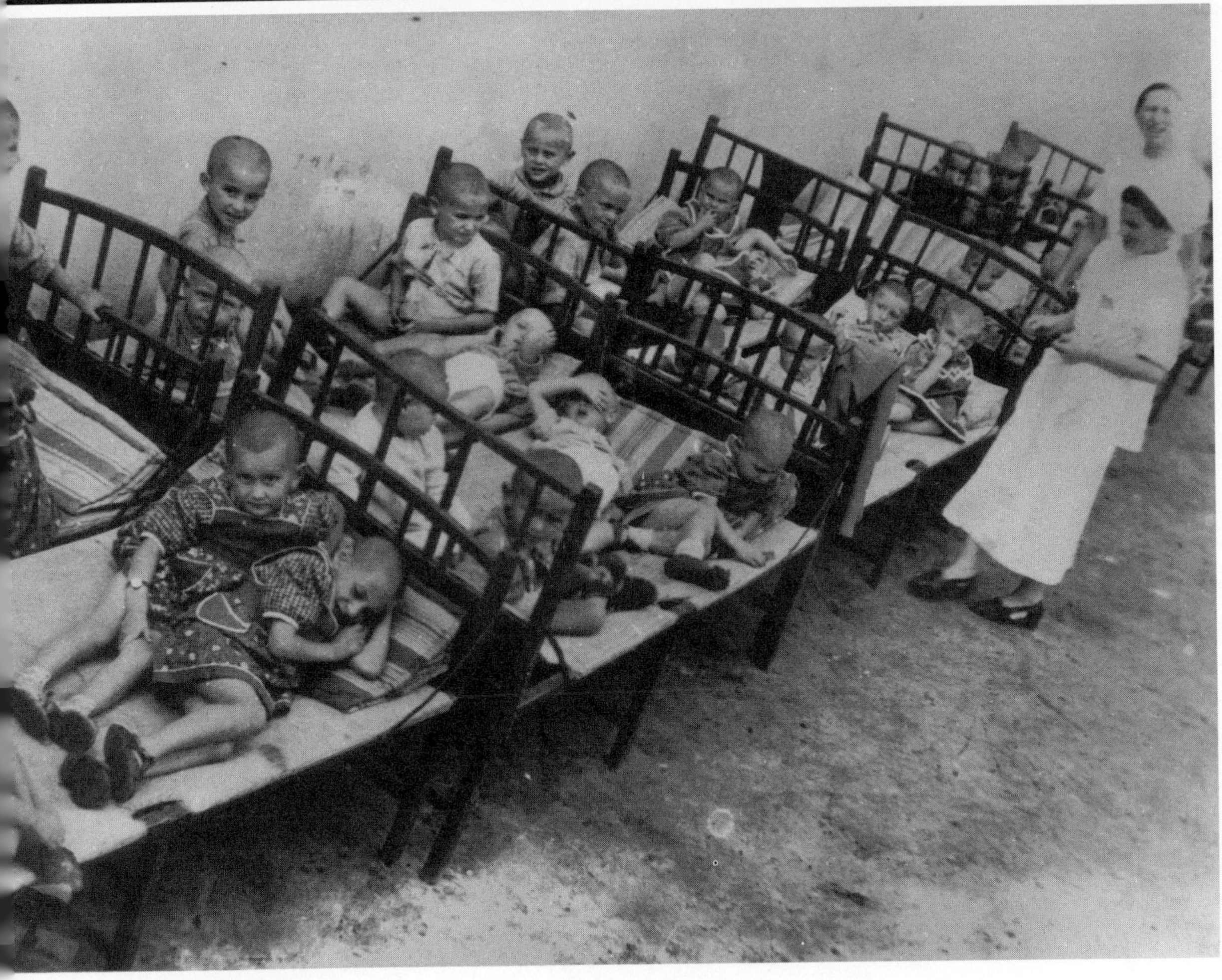

Children in a ghetto hospital.

TUESDAY, 1 SEPTEMBER 1942

The hospitals are emptied.

The morning of the third anniversary of the war struck like a bolt of lightning. At seven o'clock sharp, trucks drove up in front of the ghetto hospitals on Lagiewnicka Street, Wesola Street and Drewnowska Street, and began loading the patients who were in these hospitals onto them.

At first the crowd was disoriented. There had been talk that the hospital buildings would be evacuated—the ghetto cannot afford the luxury of housing patients in buildings that could be converted into workshops. There were even rumors that the barracks being built on Krawiecka Street were the buildings into which the sick from the hospitals would be moved. So, when the trucks drove up and the patients began being loaded onto them, the crowd did not take it unduly to heart.

But onlookers gathered in front of the hospital—as usual, for no reason or purpose, paying attention only to what was happening right before their eyes on this beautiful, bright morning. More and more onlookers gathered, and the Jewish police began to chase them away. As moment succeeded moment, their gawking eyes widened and their gazes froze. Questions began pouring from their hungry mouths:

"What does this mean? Suddenly, to help the Jews, they're using military trucks?"

"What does this mean? Why are the patients thrown up on the trucks like slabs of *treyf* [Yid: unkosher] meat?"

"Where will they be taken? To which barracks? The barracks on Krawiecka Street are obviously far from ready?!"

The blood froze in everyone's veins. The answer was self-evident. And it forced itself upon each person like a blunt iron to the brain:

The Jewish hospitals had already been "evacuated" and emptied twice: the first time, in March 1940, it had been the neurology section of Poznanski's hospital, which was still in the city [before the ghetto was sealed off in May 1940], and the second time, on the 17th of July 1941, when the hospital for the mentally ill on Wesola Street was emptied. To this day, no news of the evacuees from either hospital has reached any of the ghetto inhabitants. And not a month passes in which those incidents do not disturb everyone's consciousness:

"They're still purging! . . ." In the ghetto there is no place for the sick and for those who eat gratis [on welfare]. In the ghetto only those who can work can live. All who cannot work are thrown to the scrapheap.

The morning of the third anniversay of the war was soaked in tears that could not rinse the dust and blood from the ghetto streets.

The news—"The sick are being taken from the hospitals"—spread like wildfire across the ghetto. Fearful pandemonium began. Who in the ghetto did not have someone in the hospital? Who did not have a wife, a child, a father, a mother, a relative or a friend there?

No one walked through the streets—everyone ran. And who had the strength or the time to run—No one at all!—So we took to the air. It is not known how we flew. Our wings were clipped at their roots, and yet we flew. . . . Our feet were swollen, but we moved—we took shortcuts—houses and streets disappeared. . . . Everyone, large and small, the entire ghetto was aware of only one direction, and—

This was not the way to the food cooperative, the butcher shop, the sausage store, or even the place where potatoes are distributed. —Today the ghetto is perilously and fearfully sick—today it knows only a single direction—to the hospital.

Why run? Everyone wants to be there. Everyone wants to see his sick relatives with his own eyes one more time. Maybe it will be easier for them, maybe it will be easier for us to calm down and . . . Maybe it will be possible to save someone.

But the streets around the hospitals, the thoroughfares and the approaches are blocked. Hundreds of Jewish policemen stand guard; the executioners can do their work in peace. No one will hinder them. Cries from the distance will hardly reach them. But cries only reach human hearts. Animals are merely provoked, agitated by crying and shouting . . . Now all who come running find their wings truly clipped. Their feet now are heavy, unable to budge. They can only flail their arms. Therefore they stop, wringing their hands, and their throats issue such strange, crude, entirely non-human sounds that their eyes, as if on command, overflow with, pour forth tears. It is incomprehensible how so many tears can come from weakened and exhausted people who haven't the strength to breathe.

Among the bedridden sick, who cannot even move—those who have an arm or leg in a cast, who are generally weakened, and who lie inert in a high fever—there is a fearful panic. They are cast upon the roads like calves driven to slaughter. Among the sick who are mobile, a feverish activity rules—they make attempts to save themselves, jumping from the upper stories, leaping over fences, hiding themselves in cellars, impersonating hospital attendants. Many of those who could conquer their nerves and maintain their equilibrium succeeded.

WHAT IS SAID AND WHAT IS TOLD

Various versions sprang up, as around every event in the ghetto. According to one, the Eldest of the Jews knew about this evil decree, signed over Jewish blood and had even dropped hints about it; in the preceding days, during his visits to several workshops he is reported to have definitely said something about "black clouds hanging over Jewish heads."

According to a second version, he not only knew about this evil decree, he was its initiator. Having received orders to evacuate old people and children, it was his decision to sacrifice the former in order to save the latter.

In a third version, the evacuation of the patients was almost as much a surprise to the Eldest of the Jews as it was to the whole ghetto population; his advice had not been sought, his authority had not been consulted and the proceedings had gone forward without him. For too long, too many Jews had

Jewish police catch Jews trying to flee through windows at the rear of the ghetto hospital.

been "resting comfortably" in the ghetto, and today, on the third anniversary of the start of the war, something had to be demonstrated, so that minds would not grow dull and hands not sit idle....

Fearful rumors spread that the present events were merely a prelude to the tragedy to come, the inevitable deportation of the elderly and the children. It is covertly reported that the Eldest of the Jews has already met with the Jewish Deportation Commission. Although this information has not yet received official confirmation, the crowd would not be mollified, and, as in a riot, one rumor proved more terrifying than the next.

WEDNESDAY, 2 SEPTEMBER 1942

NOT ONLY FROM THE HOSPITALS

Meanwhile, the Jewish police sweep through Jewish houses and round up the sick who, by some miracle, had extracted themselves from the hospital the day before. Terror-stricken, heart-breaking scenes are played out. There is crying and pleading, there is kissing of hands. But can anything help them? If we knew that Moloch [in the Scriptures, a god of the Ammonites to whom children were sacrificed by burning] would be satisfied with these sacrifices, our tears could be wiped away, our hearts could turn to stone and we could resign ourselves to their fate as to the fate of all the dead.... Indeed, nearly three years in the ghetto have schooled the people well. They have learned to feel so at home with death that death has become more obvious and more ordinary than life. But the question "Will it end with this?" is profoundly vexing. It permeates every mind, turning blood to water. This water freezes in the veins, where it is kept chilled by outrage.

"Will it end with this?" The provincial Jews who have recently come to the ghetto laugh gallingly at the naiveté of the question. They have experience. They know. But they do not want to bring it to their lips. Everywhere in the provinces it began like this: At first "stigmatized persons" went. Later the sick were taken from the hospitals, and after them, children and the elderly. Then the rest were sent off—shot, murdered, turned to ash—scattered and spread across the seven seas, wives pried loose from husbands, parents from children—killed several times over, as though a single death per person were not enough to ask. The Jews from the small towns know this pattern all too well; everywhere the tragedy is staged the same way. So they don't answer that question, they are afraid, they tremble to bring the words to their lips. But they laugh gallingly. It is the laughter of people who have nothing to lose. But the local Jew who until now has lived together with his family, with his near and dear—he doesn't laugh. At the galling laughter of the provincial Jews, his blood stops in his veins.

The patients who escaped from the hospital and hid in their homes or with their relatives, and who were ferreted out by the Jewish police and then held in the Central Prison—were loaded onto trucks early this morning and sent away.

THE ELDEST OF THE JEWS DID NOT KNOW

It has become clear that the Eldest of the Jews did not know of the evil decree to evacuate the patients. One of the hospitals held his father-in-law and his brother-in-law. The father-in-law was rescued at the last minute. The brother-in-law died of fear. That part of the ghetto populace touched by this evil decree envies the Eldest: At least his brother-in-law died in a bed, among human beings, and the fate of his bones is known. . . . But who will ever know what happened to the sick who were poor and friendless, who were loaded half-dead onto the trucks and sent away yesterday.

THURSDAY, 3 SEPTEMBER 1942

TERRIFYING CONFUSION

This unbelievable day brought absolutely no relief to the mood of the ghetto. Exactly the opposite, for the longer the day lasted, the more the panic grew. The night passed in sleeplessness. Dawn brought frightened swallows into the ghetto, fluttering in terror. The children who were staying in the hostels in Marysin, in relatively better conditions than the other children, relinquished their "privilege" and came running into the ghetto under the protection of their relatives. Only the children with nowhere else to stay—orphans who were utterly alone and had absolutely no relatives in the ghetto—remained in the hostels.

"BITTER AND SIMPLE WORDS"

The logical thinkers and optimists misled us. The deportation is a fact. Various rumors are circulating that they may be in the process of making it *Judenrein* [Ger: Jew-clean] here, as they did in Pabianice and other Wartheland cities. About 2 PM announcements appeared on ghetto walls. "At 3:30 in Firemen's Square, the Chairmen and others will speak about the deportation."

As if on Judgment Day, the sun stabbed like needles. The heat was unbearable. The sky was like a leaden cover. It was not mere curiosity that brought the people here today. Curiosity alone would not have torn them from the lines at the potato stores and the food distribution points.

The people gathered here have come to hear their sentence—whether they are to live or, God forbid, they are to die. Mothers and fathers have come to hear the judgment on their children's heads. Old people have come with their last strength, leaning on thin sticks or on the wasted arms of their children, to learn what is wanted of them. The majority are old people, their sunken heads leaning over their canes, or young people clutching babies in their arms, or children standing alone.

The 1500 people gathered here in the square are like a great tribe that has been condemned to death and is now in its last minutes. They stand, they wait, they fry in the sun. With all his crudeness, Kaufmann, the commander of the firemen, treats the crowd as if they are a herd of cattle in front of the slaughter house, instead of people with heavy hearts. He cannot bear that they push closer and closer to the stage and to the left, where there is shade. At his command, the crowd is pushed to the right several times and away from the stage again and again. He seems detached, unconcerned. It must be true, what people say, that the families of the firemen and Order Service are safe. It would not be possible, otherwise, to have such iron nerves, to boss people around so tactlessly at a moment like this.

At a quarter to five, the Chairman appears in the company of Dawid Warszawski and Stanislaw Jakobson.* The immense changes which have taken place in this man in the last several days or hours are immediately obvious. His head is bowed as if he can't hold it above his shoulders. His eyes are without life. He is an old man, barely standing on his feet, barely dragging himself on his feet, an old man like all the other old men here on the square. His face is no longer fuller, less gaunt than theirs. His body is no longer dressed in proper and beautiful garments, unlike their rags. In the disarray of his white hair, it can be seen that he has had a dreadful time in the last few hours. In the pursing of his lips, it can be seen that his mouth contains not a single word of comfort for the assembled crowd. They will find no joy today.

The Chairman drags himself up to the stage.

Gall does not have to be drunk from a beautiful vessel. The people came to hear the truth, and Dawid Warszawski [Director of the Tailors' Central Office] tells it in bitter and simple words: We all know the Chairman, how many years of his life, how much of his strength, how much work and health he sacrificed in educating Jewish children, and it is precisely from his hands that the sacrifice is being demanded, precisely from the one who has raised more children than are in today's decree. It is done and over, it is a decree which is impossible to have rescinded, the sacrifices are demanded and the victims must be provided.

"We understand and feel the pain, and there is nothing to hide from you. All of the children up to age ten and all of the old people must be surrendered.

The decree will not be revoked. It can only perhaps be slightly lessened by our carrying it out calmly and quietly. There was a decree like this in Warsaw as well. We all know, it is no secret to anyone, how the decree was carried out there. It happened that way because not the community but the authorities carried out the decree. We have undertaken to carry it out ourselves because we don't want that."

SPEECH BY CHAIM RUMKOWSKI

4 SEPTEMBER 1942

"GIVE ME YOUR CHILDREN!"

A grievous blow has struck the ghetto. They are asking us to give up the best we possess—the children and the elderly. I was unworthy of having a child of my own, so I gave the best years of my life to children. I've lived and breathed with children. I never imagined I would be forced to deliver this sacrifice to the altar with my own hands. In my old age I must stretch out my hands and beg: Brothers and sisters, hand them over to me! Fathers and mothers, give me your children!

[*Transcriber's note*—Horrible, terrifying wailing among the assembled crowd.]

I had a suspicion something was about to befall us. I anticipated "something" and was always like a watchman on guard to prevent it. But I was unsuccessful because I did not know what was threatening us. I did not know the nature of the danger. The taking of the sick from the hospitals caught me completely by surprise. And I give you the best proof there is of this: I had my own nearest and dearest among them, and I could do nothing for them.

I thought that that would be the end of it, that after that they'd leave us in peace, the peace for which I long so much, for which I've always worked, which has been my goal. But something else, it turned out, was destined for us. Such is the fate of the Jews: always more suffering and always worse suffering, especially in times of war.

Yesterday afternoon, they gave me the order to send more than 20,000 Jews out of the ghetto, and if not—"We will do it!" So, the question became: "Should we take it upon ourselves, do it ourselves, or leave it for others to do?" Well, we—that is, I and my closest associates—thought first not about "How many will perish?" but "How many is it possible to save?" And we reached the conclusion that, however hard it would be for us, we should take the implementation of this order into our own hands.

I must perform this difficult and bloody operation—I must cut off limbs in order to save the body itself!—I must take children because, if not, others may be taken as well, God forbid.

[Horrible wailing.]

I have no thought of consoling you today. Nor do I wish to calm you. I must lay bare your full anguish and pain. I come to you like a bandit, to take from you what you treasure most in your hearts! I have tried, using every possible means, to get the order revoked. I tried—when that proved to be impossible—to soften the order. Just yesterday I ordered a list of children aged nine—I wanted, at least, to save this one age group, the nine- to ten-year-olds. But I was not granted this concession. On only one point did I succeed, in saving the ten-year-olds and up. Let this be a consolation in our profound grief.

There are, in the ghetto, many patients who can expect to live only a few days more, maybe a few weeks. I don't know if the idea is diabolical or not, but I must say it: "Give me the sick. In their place, we can save the healthy." I know how dear the sick are to any family, and particularly to Jews. However, when cruel demands are made, one has to weigh and measure: who shall, can and may be saved? And common sense dictates that the saved must be those who can be saved and those who have a chance of being rescued, not those who cannot be saved in any case.

We live in the ghetto, mind you. We live with so much restriction that we do not have enough even for the healthy, let alone for the sick. Each of us feeds the sick at the expense of our own heath: we give our bread to the sick. We give them our meager ration of sugar, our little piece of meat. And what's the result? Not enough to cure the sick, and we ourselves become ill. Of course, such sacrifices are the most beautiful and noble. But there are times when one has to choose: sacrifice the sick, who haven't the slightest chance of recovery and who also may make others ill, or rescue the healthy.

I could not deliberate over this problem for long; I had to resolve it in favor of the healthy. In this spirit, I gave the appropriate instructions to the doctors, and they will be expected to deliver all incurable patients, so that the healthy, who want and are able to live, will be saved in their place.

[Horrible weeping.]

I understand you, mothers; I see your tears, all right. I also feel what you feel in your hearts, you fathers who will have to go to work the morning after your children have been taken from you, when just yesterday you were playing

Rumkowski speaks in a square in front of the ghetto firehouse.

with your dear little ones. All this I know and feel. Since four o'clock yesterday, when I first found out about the order, I have been utterly broken. I share your pain. I suffer because of your anguish, and I don't know how I'll survive this—where I'll find the strength to do so.

I must tell you a secret: they requested 24,000 victims, 3000 a day for eight days. I succeeded in reducing the number to 20,000, but only on the condition that these would be children below the age of ten. Children ten and older are safe. Since the children and the aged together equal only some 13,000 souls, the gap will have to be filled with the sick.

I can barely speak. I am exhausted; I only want to tell you what I am asking of you: Help me carry out this action! I am trembling. I am afraid that others, God forbid, will do it themselves....

A broken Jew stands before you. Do not envy me. This is the most difficult of all the orders I've ever had to carry out at any time. I reach out to you with my broken, trembling hands and I beg: Give into my hands the victims, so that we can avoid having further victims, and a population of a hundred thousand Jews can be preserved. So they promised me: if we deliver our victims by ourselves, there will be peace....

[Shouts: "We all will go!" "Mr. Chairman, an only child should not be taken; children should be taken from families with several children!"]

These are empty phrases! I don't have the strength to argue with you! If the authorities were to arrive, none of you would shout.

I understand what it means to tear off a part of the body. Yesterday I begged on my knees, but it didn't work. From small villages with Jewish populations of seven to eight thousand, barely a thousand arrived here. So which is better? What do you want: that eighty to ninety thousand Jews remain, or, God forbid, that the whole population be annihilated?

You may judge as you please; my duty is to preserve the Jews who remain. I do not speak to hotheads. I speak to your reason and conscience. I have done and will continue doing everything possible to keep arms from appearing in the streets and blood from being shed. The order could not be undone; it could only be reduced.

One needs the heart of a bandit to ask from you what I am asking. But put yourself in my place, think logically, and you'll reach the conclusion that I cannot proceed any other way. The part that can be saved is much larger than the part that must be given away.

DAWID SIERAKOWIAK'S DIARY

FRIDAY, SEPTEMBER 4

There is terrible panic. No work is being done anywhere. Everyone is trying to get jobs for those not working. Parents are trying everything possible to save their children. The registrar's office was sealed after the lists were completed. Now any attempt at falsifying birth certificates, registry books or other documents is for naught. Today in our office job assignments were given out in great haste, even though there is talk that they're meaningless, because there will be orders confining everyone indoors. That way medical teams can decide who is fit for work.

As an office worker, I was able, despite great difficulty, to get a job in the furniture factory for my mother. In spite of this, I'm terribly worried about her, because she is emaciated and weak. She's not sick though and has worked in the vegetable gardens on the outskirts of the ghetto all along, and she cooks, cleans and does laundry at home.

In the morning, children between 8 and 10 were registered at the school office for work, but at 12 o'clock it was announced that these registration lists would be void. At 2 o'clock our office was closed, and we were all told to go home until further notice. All factories, offices and agencies were closed, except for food supply, sanitation wagons, police, firemen and various guards. Panic is increasing by the minute.

At 4 o'clock Rumkowski and Warszawski, the head of many factories, spoke at 13 Lutomierska. They said: Sacrificing the children and the elderly is necessary, since nothing can be done to prevent it. Therefore, please do not hinder our effort to carry out this action of deporting them from here.

It's easy for them, since they're able to get the Germans to agree not to take the children of factory heads, firemen, police, doctors, instructors, bureaucrats, and the devil knows who else. All kinds of favoritism will also be set in motion, and the Germans will get entirely different people than the 25,000 they've demanded, people who are fit for work but who'll be sacrificed for the elderly and children with pull.

In the evening, my father's cousin came to us with her 3-year-old girl, trying to save her. We agreed they could stay and later took in her whole family as well, because they're afraid to stay home, in case they're taken as hostages for the child.

Later there was an air raid; a few bombs were dropped, producing sounds that were bliss for every Jew in the ghetto.

SATURDAY, SEPTEMBER 5

My saintly, beloved, worn-out, blessed MOTHER has fallen prey to the bloodthirsty Nazi beast!!!!

In the morning fright enveloped the town, as news spread that last night some children and elderly were taken from their homes and placed in empty hospitals, from which they'll be deported beginning Monday, at a rate of 3,000 a day.

After 2 pm, vehicles with medical examiners, police, firemen and nurses drove into our street, and the raid began. The house across from us was surrounded and after an hour and a half three children were brought out. The cries, screams and struggles of the mothers and everybody else on our street was indescribable. The children's parents were completely frantic.

While all of this was going on, two doctors, two nurses, a few firemen and policemen quite unexpectedly came to our house. They had a list of the tenants in every apartment. The doctors, sour and angry, from Prague, began examining everyone very thoroughly, despite objections from the police and nurses. They fished out many "sick and unfit" people, as well as those they described as "reserve." My unlucky, dearest mother was among the latter, which is no consolation, since they were all taken together to the hospital at 34 Lagiewnicka.

Our neighbor, 70-year-old Mr. Miller, the uncle of the ghetto's chief doctor, was spared, and my healthy though exhausted mother took his place!! The doctor who examined her, an old geezer, looked and looked for some ailment, and when he was surprised he couldn't find any, said to his companion, in Czech, "Very weak, very weak." He wrote down those two wretched words, despite protests from the police and nurses present. These doctors apparently didn't know what they were doing, because they also took David Hammer, a 20-year-old who has never been sick in his life. Thanks to his cousin, who's an official, he was re-examined and released, and the two doctors were denounced to the Chairman and not allowed to examine anyone else. but what good is this to me? My mother fell into the trap, and I very much doubt anything will save her.

After my mother's examination and while she was frantically running around the house, begging the doctors to save her life, my father was eating soup. True, he was a bit bewildered and approached the police and the doctors, but he didn't run outside to beg people he knew in power to intercede on her behalf. In short, he was glad to be rid of a wife with whom life was lately getting too hard, a fact which Mother had to struggle with. I swear on all that is holy that if I knew Mother would not be sent to her death, that she'd survive after all, I'd be very pleased with things the way they are.

My little, exhausted mother, who has suffered so much misfortune and whose life has been one long sacrifice for family and others, would probably not have been taken because of weakness had she not been robbed of food by my father and Nadzia. My poor mother, who always believed in God and accepted everything that came her way, kept her clarity of mind even now, in spite of her great agitation. With a certain resignation and a heart-rending logic, she spoke to us about her fate. She agreed when I said that she'd given her life by lending and giving away so much food, but she said it in such a way that I knew she had no regrets, for even though she loved life dearly, there were things to value greater than life itself—such as God and family. She kissed each one of us goodbye, took a bag with some bread and potatoes in it, because I forced her to, and left quickly to meet her terrible fate.

I could not muster the strength to look at her through the window, or to cry. I was like a stone. Every now and then nervous spasms gripped my heart, my mouth and my hands. I thought my heart would break, but it did not. It allowed me to eat, think, talk and go to bed.

Up till now I've considered myself an egoist where life was concerned. However, I'm not sure that it would make that much difference to me if I went to death together with my mother.

It exceeds human endurance to have heard the words Mother said before she was taken and to know that she is an innocent victim. It's true she was designated for the reserve contingent, but our officials will give away the healthiest reserve for the infirm whom they protect. Cursed capitalistic world!

Hala Wolman came to see us in the evening. She works as a nurse in the hospital Mother was taken to. She consoles us that Mother is scheduled for a re-examination and that she'll be released. But nothing can make me happy now, because I know what it means when thousands of condemned have pull—and reserve victims are put in their place.

Nadzia cried, screamed and carried on, but that hardly moves anyone now. I am silent and near insanity.

SUNDAY, SEPTEMBER 6

Yesterday afternoon notices were posted that from 5 PM until further notice no one may leave his apartment without a pass from the police. Excepting, of course, these, those, the others, and so on! Apparently, there is going to be a serious raid. At night a great many people were taken in other neighborhoods, but ours was relatively quiet. So far, all this is being done without the Germans and without slaughter—the one thing everyone fears. But let it happen—if only Mother could be returned to me!

Today, at 6:30 I went to Hala Wolman and took a towel, some soap and clean underwear for Mother—articles she requested yesterday through Hala, who promised she'll do everything she can to have Mother re-examined and released. Father, apparently moved by his conscience overnight, went to two or three acquaintances in the morning, seeking help—to no avail, of course.

Tonight there was no air raid and little said about miracles coming to us from the outside.

The heat is still extraordinary. In spite of the ban, people are running around the streets, everyone seeking help in his adversity. Now there is talk that the Germans are accompanying the medical teams, and they are deciding who should go and who should stay. All children previously exempted have now been told to report to one hospital, and though Rumkowski insists that the children's registers are iron-clad, no one believes him. Even policemen, instructors and managers are despairing. The cries, mad screaming and wailing are now so common that not much attention is paid to them. Why should I be moved by some other mother's cries, when they've taken my own mother away? No revenge would be enough for this deed!

On Bazarna Street huge gallows have been erected to hang some people from Pabianice who ran away before it was cleared of Jews. The devil knows why they need these gallows.

People who are hiding children in attics, lavatories and other holes are losing their heads in despair. Our street, which is very near the hospital, is filled all day with the wails of passing funeral processions, which follow the wagons of victims.

In the evening my father was able to get to Mother. He said the hospital is real hell—everyone is in terrible condition, everything is confused. Mother, apparently, is changed beyond recognition, which narrows her slim chance for release.

At times I get such jitters and heart spasms that I think I'm going insane or entering delirium. In spite of this, I cannot stop thinking of Mother, and suddenly I find myself, as though I were split in two, inside her mind and body. The hour of her deportation is approaching with no rescue in sight.

It rained a bit this evening, with some thunder and lightning, which did not lessen our suffering any. Even a torrential rain could not renew a torn heart.

In Central Prison, awaiting deportation.

JOZEF ZELKOWICZ, IN THESE NIGHTMARISH DAYS

SATURDAY, SEPTEMBER 5, 1942

It has begun.

It's a few minutes after 7 A.M. Everyone, nearly the entire ghetto is on the street. Whose nerves don't force them out? Who can sit at home? Who has peace of mind? No one!

So the ghetto streets are busier than ever. And how peculiar this bustling is. A silent, dead busyness. People don't talk; it's as though everyone has left his tongue at home or forgotten how to speak. Friends don't greet one another, as though they are embarrassed. Everyone stiff in their movements, stiff in the

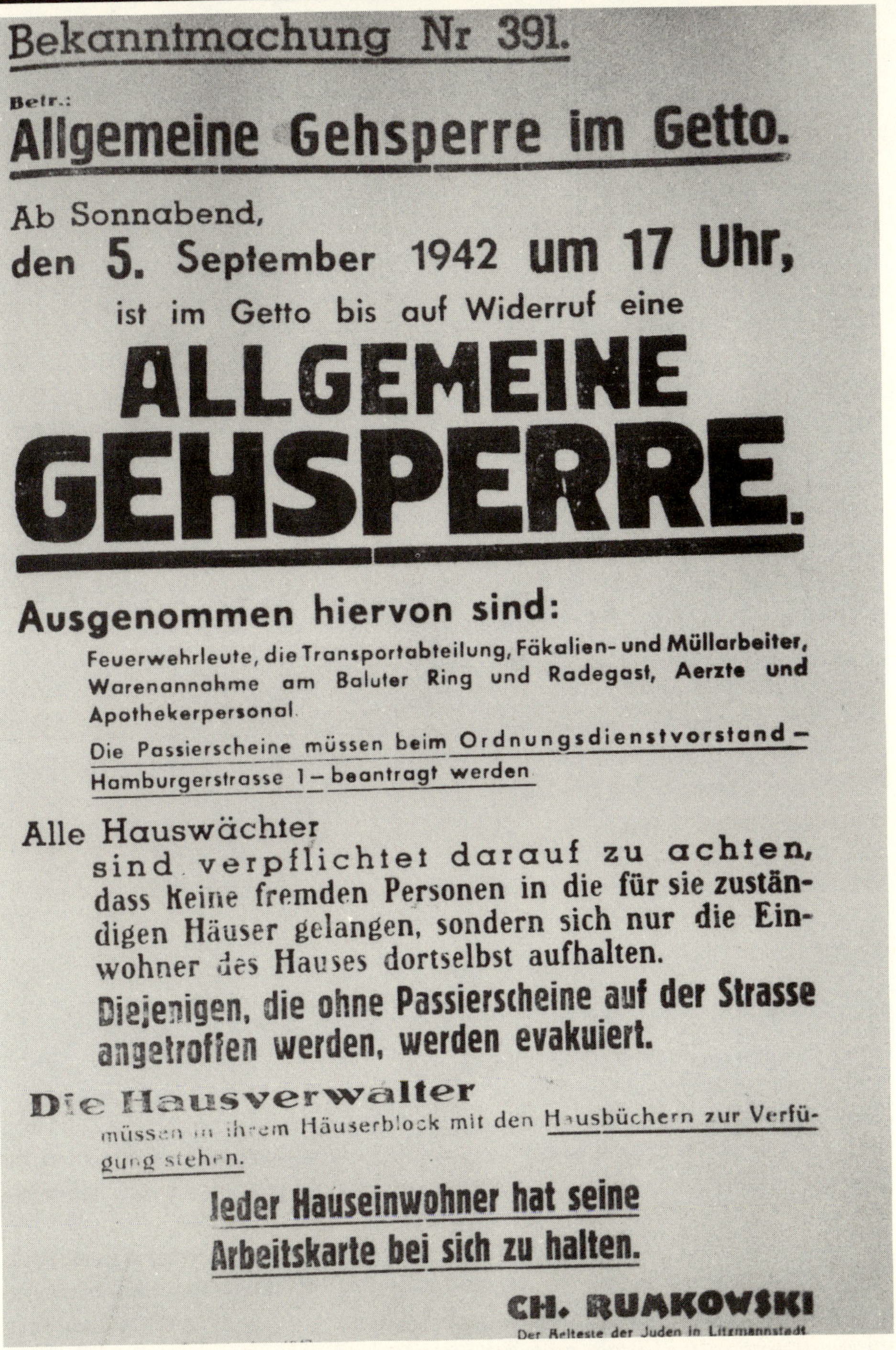

Bekanntmachung Nr 391.

Betr.:

Allgemeine Gehsperre im Getto.

Ab Sonnabend,
den 5. September 1942 **um 17 Uhr,**
ist im Getto bis auf Widerruf eine

ALLGEMEINE GEHSPERRE.

Ausgenommen hiervon sind:

Feuerwehrleute, die Transportabteilung, Fäkalien- und Müllarbeiter, Warenannahme am Baluter Ring und Radegast, Aerzte und Apothekerpersonal.

Die Passierscheine müssen beim Ordnungsdienstvorstand – Hamburgerstrasse 1 – beantragt werden.

Alle Hauswächter
sind verpflichtet darauf zu achten, dass keine fremden Personen in die für sie zuständigen Häuser gelangen, sondern sich nur die Einwohner des Hauses dortselbst aufhalten.

Diejenigen, die ohne Passierscheine auf der Strasse angetroffen werden, werden evakuiert.

Die Hausverwalter
müssen in ihrem Häuserblock mit den Hausbüchern zur Verfügung stehen.

Jeder Hauseinwohner hat seine Arbeitskarte bei sich zu halten.

CH. RUMKOWSKI
Der Aelteste der Juden in Litzmannstadt

GENERAL CURFEW. This announcement began the eight "nightmarish days" during which the ghetto's children, elderly, and sickly were taken.

distribution lines. A dead silence hangs over the ghetto. No one even sighs or groans. Great, heavy stones press on the ghetto residents' hearts.

People run through the streets like unleashed spirits, like the restless souls of sinners, with that same persistent silence on their set lips, that same fear in their eyes. They stand in line like condemned prisoners, stand and wait their turn at the gallows. Rigidity, terror, collapse, dread—there are no words to describe the feelings that well in the frozen hearts that cannot cry, cannot even scream. There is no ear that can hear the silent scream that deafens with its hardness and hardens with its deafening silence.

They run over the three ghetto bridges like a herd of hundred-headed serpents surging back and forth, forward and back. People hurrying, rushing. The air laden with oppression; morbid tidings in its weight. The sky constantly swelling and welling, soon to burst and spill out utter horror and utter reality.

It has begun!

No one knows what, where, how. If everyone is silent, if no one looks at anyone, if everyone keeps clear of everyone else, the way thieves avoid their pursuers, then who was it who first uttered the dreaded words: "It has begun!"

No one spoke them. No one uttered those evil tidings. Only the skies broke open, spilling the words: "It has begun!"

Begun where?

People say, "Already they're forcing the residents out of the old age home on Dworska Street."

People say, "They're on Rybna Street; there's a truck, they're loading it with the elderly, and children."

Pity. The stories are all true. They're taking them here, there, and everywhere. They're already loading on Rybna Street.

It has begun.

First the Jewish Police began. They wanted to practice their work against the least resistance. The old age home. It was easy there. They were waiting to be taken. The people there are being taken *en masse,* no selection or rejection. They're all old, all headed for the scrap heap. Who would waste words standing up for them, old people who for weeks have been living on the welfare of the community council. So the old people are thrown up on wagons like calves for slaughter.

On Rybna Street the police have to take people out of their apartments. There they are encountering resistance. There they rip babies from their mothers' breasts, drag grown children from under their parents' wings. There they tear husband from wife. People who have lived together for forty or fifty years, in

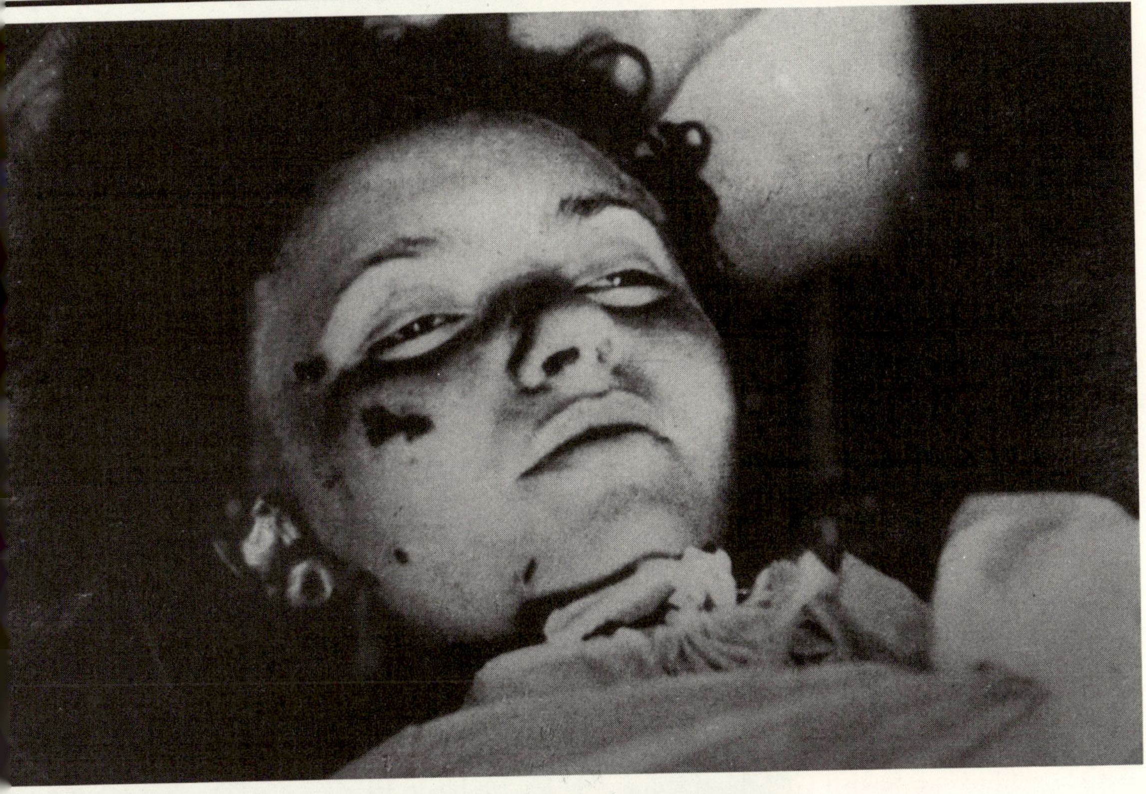

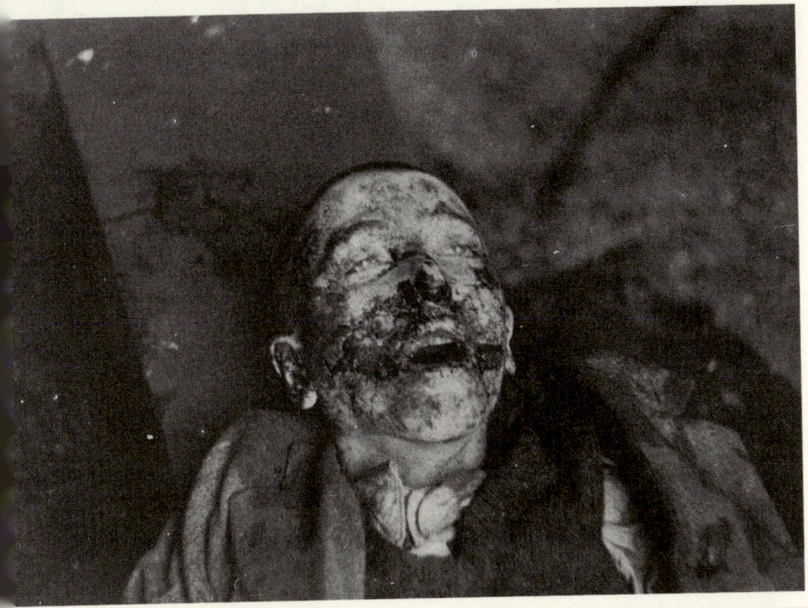

"On Rybna Street the police are encountering resistance."

joy and suffering, people who have had children together, who have reared them and lost them together—forty or fifty years together so that now they are practically the same person.

The Jewish Police have been bought. They've been made drunk; they've been drugged with hashish: their own children have been exempted from the order. The police have been given one and a half kilograms of bread a day for their bloody piece of work—gorged with bread, and given an extra portion of sausage and sugar.

They have worked for the sake of a concept: "When we pull the molar with our own, Jewish hands, amputate the limb, cut the body in half, then perhaps it is less painful than were strange, harsh hands to do it."

There is no reason to envy the Jewish Police.

On the bloody pages of this history should be written in black letters the names of the so-called White Guard, the porters from Balut Market and the Department of Food Supply. This gang, fearing they would lose their soup rations during the curfew period, the *Szpera* [Yid: curfew],* volunteered their services in the raid—on the condition that they be given the same rewards the police were promised: bread, sausage, and protection for their families. Their offer was accepted; they've taken part in the *aktion* voluntarily.

THE ROUND-UP

Oh God, Jewish God, how vulnerable Jewish blood is!

Oh God, Almighty God, how vulnerable human blood is!

Blood flows in the streets. Blood flows through the courtyards. Blood flows in the buildings, the apartments, the rooms. Not red, healthy blood. There is no blood like that in the ghetto. Three years of war, two and a half years of ghetto life have squeezed the red corpuscles out. Just pus and running bile are to be found in the ghetto.

And how can such blood satisfy the beasts? It only whets their appetites, no more.

It is no longer just a rumor, it is a certainty. The chief of the German Ghetto Administration, Biebow, the man who is least concerned with the survival of the ghetto, he himself has taken the lead in this raid. He himself is directing the resettlement.

When the Jewish Police take, they take with mercy, following orders: children up to the age of ten, old people over sixty-five, and sick people who, in the doctors' judgment, have no prospects of recovering.

It is possible to talk to the Jewish Police, to throw rocks of various sorts at their consciences. It is possible to weep in front of them, to try to avert the evil.

They are taking people. This is how it's done:

The Jewish Police show up—a whole army of police caps, firemen's caps and porters' caps. The house is surrounded, the entrances blocked—the house where you have lived all this time and have felt on your own home ground, now suddenly turned into a prison. "Everyone must be in his own apartment!"—that's the order which is shouted from the courtyard. So the people are chased like mice into mousetraps. The world becomes narrow. The room becomes narrow. The eye sockets become too narrow for eyes. The chest too narrow for the heart. The throat swells in torment and wants to burst.

The Jewish Police have addresses. The Jewish Police have a superintendent, and the super has a record book. The entries say, in such and such an apartment is a child who was born at such and such a time. The list tells, in such and such an apartment an old person can be found of such and such an age. A doctor enters the apartment. He examines the occupants, sees who is healthy and who is only trying to appear healthy. He can tell at a glance. He has had all too much practice already in the ghetto.

It is to no avail that a child clutches its mother's neck with its two small hands. It is to no avail that the father throws himself in front of the doorway like a slaughtered ox: "Only over my dead body will you take my child." It is to no avail that the old man clings to the cold walls with his gnarled hands and begs, "Let me die here in peace." It is to no avail that the old woman falls on her knees, kissing their boots, and begs: "I have grown-up grandchildren who are like you." To no avail does the sick man bury his feverish head in the sweat-covered pillow and sob away his last tears. . . .

It is all to no avail. The police must fill their quota. . . . If they don't take, others will.

IT LOOKS COMPLETELY DIFFERENT WHEN OTHERS TAKE

They come into the courtyard and immediately there is a revolver shot. Next comes a harsh order, shouted loudly, and repeated by the Jewish Police: "In two minutes, everyone must be in the courtyard. No one may stay indoors. Apartments must be left open!"

Who has the power to describe the insane, wild rush of frozen corpses hurrying to carry out the command? No one.

Old, twisted legs, sclerotic and rheumatic, stumble over crooked steps and jagged stones. Young, deer-like legs fly with a bird's speed. The clumsy, doubting legs of invalids chased from their beds bend back like bagels as they run. Swollen legs of starving people shuffle along, groping blindly. All run, hurry, race to the courtyard.

Woe to the latecomer. He will never walk that last short stretch of path—

he will have to swim it in his own blood. Woe to the one who stumbles on the way and falls—he will never stand again. Woe to the child who wants to call out *Mama!* He will get out *Ma* and never finish. The second *Ma* will twirl and fall back into his heart like a bird killed in flight. Our last two hours have demonstrated this with utter clarity.

The Jewish Police take, they take whomever they can. Whoever is there. If someone has hidden and cannot be found, he remains free. But *they,* when *they* take, take the one who is there and the one who is not. In place of someone not found, they take someone else, and if the person in hiding is found, he will no longer have to be led away. He will have to be carried.

It is five o'clock. The *Szpera* has begun.

The sun settles bloodily in the west, the entire west, swimming in blood. It would be foolish to think the sky is reflecting the blood shed in the ghetto today. The sky is too far from the earth. Nor have the cries and moans of the ghetto reached it. The lamentations were all in vain; the tears were shed and lost for nothing. No one saw them. No one heard them.

What iron strength today had. It dragged on like Jewish suffering. It was as tough as Jewish woe. And what great strength ghetto people have. After three years of hunger, after three years of bitter enslavement, they still endure such days as this one. Like inanimate creatures, they bear everything silently. Like rocks in sand, they just lay there.

SUNDAY, SEPTEMBER 6, 1942

"THE TRUTH OF HIS FANTASIES"

She was called Blimele, the six-, seven- or even eight-year-old girl. Her father was a Yiddish writer. Her mother was the quiet wife of a Yiddish writer. Blimele had golden locks, blue eyes and white teeth. Her father's most beautiful songs were inspired by his daughter. The fresh sap of his song and the fresh dew of his talent were spent on her beautiful limbs. A small girl—a poem. A child—a song. She was called Blimele.

Her sister had as yet no name. Now at 10:00 A.M., she is just 33 hours old. The fears of Friday morning must have brought this younger sister prematurely into the world. She was born only a few days into the ninth month. A girl—a mere dot with two little fists, which had already found their way to her little mouth. Two quiet, closed, inexpressive eyes. The little girl had no name—none as yet.

The new mother was weak and trembling, but happy tears gleamed in her eyes and gathered around the corners of her dry mouth. Just a few hours after childbirth, the trembling new father was sitting near her bed, chasing the nagging ghetto flies from her face.

He chased the flies away and the wolves came. Yesterday, Saturday evening, the police barged in, Jewish police. They took away Blimele, the most beautiful of his songs. His Song of Songs they brutally and cynically profaned. The mother was weak with postpartum fever. She lay there, and near her lay the infant without a name. The mother was weak and the father helpless. Blimele was taken away, and only the new-born infant reacted by screaming.

The infant was screaming, half dead. The mother became weaker and more feverish, and the father, the Yiddish writer, had to become the hero. Not one muscle of his wizened and strained face could ripple. For the mother was not to look at his wrinkled face and thereby become weaker and more feverish. His eyes must not lose one tear, certainly not now. He, the writer, who took even fantasy for truth, now had to deny the naked, the bitter truth.

He had to console the new mother with words that pierced him, each of them, with their falsity: "They won't send Blimele away . . . overnight, or maybe the next day . . . maybe she'll be held a few days . . . but she'll be returned . . . Jewish police would hold on to the child of a Jewish writer. Because, he says it quite seriously, he is a Jew. . . . She is supposed to see how calm he is, how relaxed about Blimele's fate . . . and how much he loves her. She knows him after all. Had he the slightest suspicion, the slightest doubt, could he sit so calmly?

The feverish new mother was weak. She lay in a half dream. It was twilight. The lamp could not be turned on. Therefore, the new mother could not see how the literary forehead of her husband gleamed with moisture. She could not notice how every hair of his disheveled head was soaked in water. She could not feel how his entire body was bathed in anxieties, how his soul was more feverish than her weakened body. He covered his eyes with the stones of his heart. His tears found no outlet through them—so they streamed through his forehead, so they soaked his hair and streamed through every pore of his body.

Every drop of his wasted blood cried out. Every word he used to console the new weak mother was false. False, but a beautiful fiction, because the literary fantasy made it true. He repeated the falsehood so many times, he reassured her so earnestly and with his strongest oaths, he argued so logically and rationally, until his reason began to believe his own made-up logic.

So the Yiddish writer believed the truth of his fantasies an entire night. He believed in them today for three and a half hours, until 9:30 A.M. At half past nine the German commission came and routed the writer from his bed and the sick and feverish wife and the new-born infant, who was only 33 hours old and who did not even have a name.

Above: The "White Guard," teamsters of the ghetto. Zelkowicz's condemnation was general, but the individuals pictured, if they survived, have their own stories.

Right, above: A chart prepared in the ghetto of the ranks and insignia of the ghetto police force.

Right, below: A unit of the ghetto police. While nearly all members of the Order Service participated in the actions of the *Gehsperre,* there is no way to know how these eight men might have performed their duties.

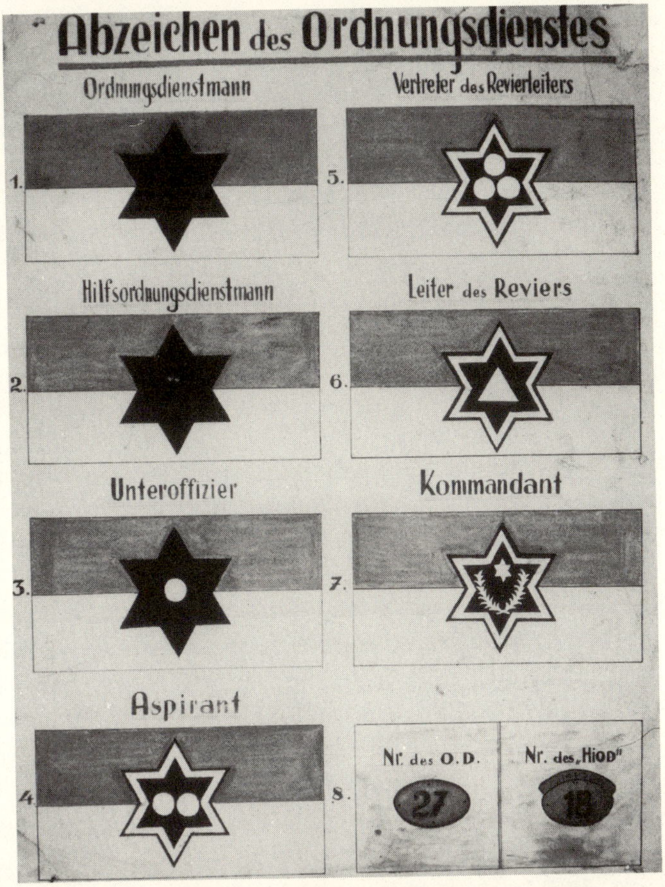
Abzeichen des Ordnungsdienstes
Ordnungsdienstmann
Vertreter des Revierleiters
1.
5.
Hilfsordnungsdienstmann
Leiter des Reviers
2.
6.
Unteroffizier
Kommandant
3.
7.
Aspirant
4.
8.
Nr. des O.D.
Nr. des „HIOD“
27

This is one hundred percent true. But the writer of these lines will think no one unjust who doubts it, just as he does not expect to be believed when he adds that the father, the Yiddish writer, wanders with his extraordinary woe in his heart, compelled to believe that he will once again see his weak and feverish wife, who will bring back his most beautiful song—Blimele—and his beautiful, tremulous little infant—the new-born who will then have a name.

SAD NEWS FROM THE STREET

Listen and believe this, even though it happened here, even though it seems so old, so distant, and so strange.

At number seven Zytnia Street lived the wife of Doctor Tzamber. "The doctor's wife," as the neighbors called her. She was not a doctor herself, only her husband was. He had tried to escape from Dachau and was shot. That's what she was told officially.

She was sent to the ghetto from a small town together with her small, four-year-old girl, a little blond angel with mystical blue eyes.

Together with her child, she was taken from her apartment out into the courtyard for the "selection."

She held the child by the hand. They smiled to one another. The child was happy that her mother had taken her out to the yard. It was so bright today in God's world, such a delightful sun. And the mother, the mother also had to smile, to show a courageous face, that she was healthy, capable of working, that she didn't yet necessarily have to go into the caldron.

The freshness, the blond and milky pinkness of the girl caught his eye. As a good party man, he wasn't permitted to appreciate the beauty of a Jewish child. As a good party man who is only born to eradicate everything Jewish, he had to rule thus:

—THE SUCKLING MUST BE TAKEN AWAY.

But she, she was just a mother and . . .

—No, she won't give away the child. As long as she lives, she won't let the child be torn away from her.

And she smiled on. What was she to do? Perhaps move him with her tears? Make a mirror of her heart? A show of her heart, gratis, for his sake, and display that on her face?

She smiled, and she wouldn't give up the child.

He screwed himself up into a mocking grimace.

—Really? Truly? She really, seriously intends to resist?

Yes, she may in fact be smiling, but that in no way stops her from being a serious, dedicated mother. SHE WILL NOT GIVE UP HER CHILD, and let him do what he wants.

He was too well bred. In his chivalrous Prussian military school he had been taught, it had been beaten into his brains—Be polite to women. He just didn't know whether the basic rules of politeness also applied to Jewish women. He continued smiling, and smiling, he took her, together with the girl, out of the row. The good schooling won out. He gave her a three minute stay . . .

Three minutes, by the clock.

Their neighbors were seized with convulsions. Neighbors who stood in the central row and stole glances with their weeping eyes at the two, set off by themselves, who stood and smiled at each other. The child from the satisfaction of still being with her mother, and that her mother was still holding her hand. And the mother from satisfaction that she still had her child with her and in her.

Just three minutes. Not a second less nor a moment more.

—WELL, HOW IS IT? WHAT DID YOU DECIDE?

She had nothing to decide. Nothing had changed for her during the three minutes. She would not relinquish her child's hand as long as she lived. Nothing had changed for her during those three minutes—not even the smile.

Only his smile grew darker, perhaps more cowardly, and perhaps that was the reason why he forgot the rules of politeness concerning women. HE PRACTICALLY SHRIEKED HIS ORDER.

—TURN TO THE WALL!

With the same smile as before, she turned to the wall. It's true, she did hold the child's hand more convulsively and perhaps that was the reason why the child lifted up her head to her mother. The child probably wanted to complain about the slight pain that the hard pressure on her hand caused. But the change was internal, a secret only between mother and daughter.

Externally nothing could be seen about the mother while it could be seen clearly how the smile on his twisted face trembled. He gathered his forces to keep smiling.

And later, after he had laid both the mother and daughter low with two shots from his little revolver, he didn't even need to waste that energy. The smile was already frozen on his twisted face by then, and if someone had asked him the reason for the smile, whether it expressed cowardliness, bestiality, insanity, perhaps he would not have known at all that he was smiling. Perhaps he would not have known at all that it was true, he had just now, so calmly, so politely and freely, murdered two people. A young, vivacious mother with her four-year-old child, hand in hand.

The clock says twelve noon. It's a bright summer day. You sit at home, casting furtive glances at your wife, who has aged dozens of years in the last two days. You look at your beautiful son, see his dark, hollow face and the mortal fear lurking in his eyes. All the terror around you makes you fear for yourself, makes you fear for your wife, makes you fear for your trembling child.

All of you are candidates!

A FATHER'S LAMENT

[An anonymous remnant, written in Yiddish on the back of four pages of soup kitchen records:]

WEDNESDAY, SEPTEMBER 8, 1942

A calamity suddenly befell the ghetto. Last week the authorities surrounded the hospitals, detained all patients and took them away. It didn't matter who was seriously ill and who wasn't, who had a contagious disease and who didn't—all were taken. Three days later the bomb exploded. The authorities demanded 20,000 children and old people. A rush began to change dates of birth or to get a waiver. The Jewish police, for the price of having their children exempted, were ordered to carry out the deportation. When they started the action on Limanowski Street, there was dreadful wailing, and people put up resistance. The next day the Gestapo came, and now the police worked with the Gestapo. This was how it looked: the police with one or two Germans came into a courtyard. All tenants had to come down. People were selected at whim, with no inspection, then loaded onto a wagon and taken to a detention center (the hospital on Drewnowska Street or the Market); from there they were taken to the vans. Of course, there was a chance to get away. I suffered a loss, due to my own stupidity. I walked off with Anya but Mookha [. . . illegible] was left behind. At the last minute I hid her in the basket and she, poor thing, began crying. If I had stayed with her, she would have been saved—I myself killed the child. In just one hour they were all gone from the hospital . . . What will I do, how will I atone for this guilt, how . . .

WEDNESDAY, SEPTEMBER 8, 1942

Yesterday I lost Mookha, my sweet little daughter. I lost her through my own fault, cowardice, stupidity and passivity. I gave her up, defenseless. I deserted her, I left the 5-year-old child, did not save her, and I could have done it so easily. I killed her myself because I didn't have the least bit of courage. I have blood on my hands, the guilt is mine because I did nothing to rescue her. The Germans were deporting, it was chaotic, like work round-ups, it was so easy to get away. I went to the courtyard, all the tenants had to come down, they were making the selection. Of course, they were taking away the children. But it was possible to hide them, it was easy to do. I walked off with Anya, but I left Mookha behind. Instead of hiding with her in the cellar or in the toilet, I put her in a clothes basket and she gave herself away with crying. Naked, barefoot, miserable—my dear child, it's me, your father, who betrayed you, it's me, driven by selfishness, who did nothing for your salvation, it's me who spilled your blood. When I came to the hospital and [. . . illegible] I deserted her. I, her father, did not protect her, I deserted her because I feared for my own life—I killed . . . I can't write—I deserve to be punished—I am the one who killed her. What punishment awaits me for killing my own daughter? There was no need to do anything heroic in order to save her, protect her. On the contrary, I made this offering myself, without being asked. I killed the child with my own hands. Ola, too [. . . illegible]. She, too, lost her courage and jumped off the wagon in front of the hospital, leaving child and brother at the mercy of fate. I can't concentrate and describe it all chronologically. I am broken, I feel guilty, I am a murderer and I must atone, because I won't find peace. I killed my child with my own hands, I killed Mookha, I am a killer, because how can it be that a father deserts his own child and runs away? How can he run away and not save his own child? God, if you are watching, please punish me. In what name did Mookha lose her life? Why did she have to perish?

[*Author shifts to Hebrew, a variation on part of* Yizkor, *the prayer for the dead:*]

Merciful God in Heaven, grant perfect repose to the soul of my daughter Miriam, who was slaughtered in the deportation of September 8, 1942, and who has passed to her eternal resting place. May she be under thy divine wings among the holy and pure who shine as brightly as the sky. May her place of rest be in paradise. O Merciful One, keep her soul forever alive under thy protective wings. As the Lord is her heritage, may she rest in peace, and let us say Amen.

IRENA LIEBMAN, LODZ GHETTO

The Jewish police surround our house. They search one apartment after another, bringing out the old, the children and the sick, whom they load onto horse-drawn wagons. Suddenly we hear screams coming from the stairway. It's the wife of the policeman. She screams horribly, hysterically: "Murderer! Murderer! You're sending Jewish children to their death! You, with your dirty, bloody hands!" Quietly, he tries to free himself from her grip, and slowly, soothingly, he speaks to her: "You know perfectly well we're forced to do this. We never use force; we never search thoroughly. If someone is well hidden, good for him. But if the Germans do it, it will be a hundred times worse. You know that." But the woman can't calm down. She tears her hair out; she has white foam on her lips. And she screams as her husband goes downstairs: "Murderer! Murderer of Jewish children!"

This evening my sister comes home totally shattered. Our police did not handle their assignment well enough, so starting tomorrow the Germans are going to continue the action themselves. Luckily, our street has already been through it. We just have to keep quiet. The action has gone on to other streets.

All week long we hear the distant barking of dogs, gunshots and shouts in German: *Alle Juden raus!* [All Jews out!] My sister tells of thousands of people, not just the children and the old, who are brought on the wagons to the hospitals, from where they're taken in trucks to the unknown.

Today is the 11th of September. We get up at 6 in the morning, as always. We drink boiled water with saccharine. Sister leaves for work. This is the last day of the deportations. Most likely this evening they'll say that everything is returning to normal. There is nothing further to fear.

Suddenly we hear gunshots outside. Orders are given for all Jews to come out. What is it? What's happened? Why did they come back? No time to think. Shouts are louder now. Rifle butts bang against the door. Mother grabs my arm. Maybe we can hide somewhere? Father is ready to leave. He tries to calm us, telling us softly what should be done: rub your cheeks and bite your lips several times so they look flushed, straighten up, and walk with a smile wherever fate takes us. Surely, my sister will come back soon and get us out of this. We go calmly into the street and join a long single line of people. I am first, my mother is behind me, my father is the last. Father is 56 years old, but he looks fine. His face, swollen from hunger, looks round and full, his well-rubbed cheeks have a normal color, and there are no grey hairs on his balding head. On the other hand, Mother is thin, very thin; her face is drawn, her hair is all white. But she is only 42 and her shining eyes have a beautiful young smile.

We begin moving slowly toward the selection commission. I stand as tall as I can, holding my head straight. I'm told to go to the right, and suddenly I find myself surrounded by a group of people standing in dead silence. I wait. I cannot feel my own heart beat. My whole body is now a petrified bundle of taut muscles and nerves. Other people approach, but they're not my parents. I suppress a scream in my throat: why aren't they here? And suddenly, as though an electric current is running through my body, I feel a shock of recognition: this time fate has struck me. I have nothing to lose. I elbow my way through the crowd of people and start running toward the Germans. I see a hand raised, and in a split second recognize our neighbor's face. My mind drowns in darkness. When I re-open my eyes, I realize I'm standing among the same people, who are trying to hide me. I don't know how long we stood there. It seemed an eternity. Finally, there was another burst of fire, and wagons loaded with people and with armed Germans started rolling. Our group began walking slowly toward the house.

I saw my sister in front of our door. She rushed home when she heard about the action. She looked at me and understood everything. "Don't leave home until I come back. I'm going to look for them," she shouted and ran downstairs. Through the window I saw her white uniform, and I felt the beat of her fluttering heart. Then I noticed that my classmate Fryda was standing at the door. Her parents also did not return from the street. We sat in mute silence at the top of the staircase. All of a sudden we heard cries of joy in the courtyard. A man whom the Germans took came back home with hopeful news. The quota for deportees had been filled. Some people were being sent back home. It was again permitted to walk outside. Everything returned to normal. We ran into the street, hoping to hear more news. But those who were coming back could not tell us much. They all hurried home, to their bowl of watery soup, to their diseases and their lice, to hunger and to cold, to everything they call life.

At home my sister was already there. She looked at me in silence. Then she burst out: "Yes, I was late. Shitty luck. They didn't bring them to the hospital this time. Straight from the wagons to the trucks, and then they were gone. It was the last transport."

. . . A new day began, after all. A terrible loneliness descended upon me after my sister left for work, and with it an uncontrollable hatred of all those who hid and were now coming out of their holes. It's because of them that my dearest were taken away! I go outside and rush to work. Suddenly I notice a macabre figure of a swollen woman, who literally crawls along the wall. I immediately recognize the terrifying mask of this semiconscious, half-alive creature. It's Roza, a close friend of my mother, a lonely spinster. A suffocating hatred tightens my throat. Why not her? She has only a few days left, anyway. Maybe they took my mother in her place? I walk past Roza, and though I feel her eyes boring into my face, I do not stop.

OSKAR ROSENFELD'S NOTEBOOKS

NOTEBOOK E [continued]

4 September. Friday night. Sobbing, screaming in the neighborhood. Children of the Jewish Police taken away [for protection]. Air-raid alarm, bombs. Stifling night. No one can sleep. It feels like before the end of the world.

Saturday, 5 September. Quiet morning. It becomes hot again, thunderstorm expected. The Registration Office is working for the deportation. Scenes: Mother running out of the house, to prevent the police from entering; police driving people away from entrances. Terrible heat. At 2:30 yellow poster: "Notice: General *Gehsperre* from 5 PM until further notice. Exceptions: Doctors, police, firemen, and people with legitimate reason. Those not complying will be evacuated." Food stores empty, street peddlers selling food have disappeared. People who believe in God toy with suicide. The human brain cannot comprehend it. Anyone surviving this will lose all memory of it, will not believe it himself.

Hunger catastrophic: with the workshops closed, no mid-day soup.

Sunday, 6 September. 4 o'clock in the morning: the children. Screams of misery in the neighbors' house, no human sound but the howling and whistling of animals. The children themselves are quiet, only whimpering.

A man and wife: "If only we could go together." Someone else: "The ghetto's questions *Why* and *How much longer?* have become *Where? Where are they sending us?*"

The Eldest gave numbers: 13,000 elderly, 8,000 children, a total of 21,000. That's 20% of the ghetto in order to save 80%. Even the children of the *Beirat* members and the doctors and others must go; only the policemen's children are exempt.

Henuschi. Think of her constantly.

Ghetto within the ghetto. Cut off from the world: no mail, no newspaper, no radio, no telephone, no gramophone. Total curfew. The horror goes on.

There is fear the Germans will take over the action if the Jewish police don't do it. I have never before felt as I do this day.

Jeremiah 31:15 ff. So saith the Lord: "One hears a voice complaining and a bitter crying on high. Rachel cries over her children, for it is over with them."

7 September. Stormy night. Daybreak is cool. Police surround houses, take children. Wagons in front of houses. Suddenly screaming women appear, girls, old women, up into the wagon, children thrown on like packages. In front, a *Feldgrau* with whip, soldiers with rifles, revolvers, steel helmets. Window must be shut. Pressing of faces to the window.

8 September. Eaten nothing since early morning. What is to happen? No news, not even rumors. Already 3 days' house arrest. Everything staged for maximum effect. Rumor that people are being taken at whim, even among the "protected." The question *Where to?* is no longer asked at all. Where are the children? Have the transports already left? Questions!! Fear of the night. In the courtyard, residents pace back and forth.

Intermezzo. [in English:] 2x a week an *Aschkenes* travels with the *Eleck* [the electric trolley] across Zgierska to see his wife from afar. He disappears like he comes and sends money to her with Jewish workers engaged in the city. A gallant gentleman.

9 September. Because of the curfew, no one can report deaths. Police are aware of this and let wagons through to collect corpses, direct to the cemetery. The corpses are already decaying, dry, yellow, blue, swollen, stinking.

The neighborhood houses have been surrounded since yesterday. Now at 6 AM: Get dressed, come down! Everybody double- and triple-dressed, suddenly cold. Two dozen people walk into the courtyard. A *Feldgrau* with a whip: Where do you work? Where is your wife? Your daughter? How old are you? He wants to take me with him. A Jewish commandant whispers something. Saved. The old people come with us. Blind Rabbi Krakauer and his wife conduct themselves heroically.

The afternoon is quiet. Old people who'd hidden themselves suddenly come back, weak; since they haven't eaten for days, held by relatives so they don't fall over. Apparently the quota of 21,000 has been passed, so further evacuation is not expected.

Gloomy rain. Alone in the apartment, since rabbi and his wife were taken. Perhaps they will come back.

In the courtyard a woman jumps at me: "What do I have in life? My 12-year-old boy was shot today, my girls, six and fourteen, were sent away." She sobs. Her husband comes, a figure from Chagall, silent. Suddenly another woman: "My sister!" Moving scene. A young fellow cries with them.

People in the house congratulate me. "Why didn't you color your mustache?" one asks (to look older). Dusk comes. In spite of deep depression, hope for *nezuchon bituchon* [Heb: victory].

Henuschi is awake. What is she doing now? Is she working, thinking? How does she live? Has she heard from Wilma and Erich?

10 September. Still terrified by every noise at the door. Can't sleep. Many jumped from the wagons and were saved; the police closed an eye to it.

Since the fall of last year, the ghetto has dropped from 160,000 to 90,000. Of these, 20,000 died and 50,000 were deported (first 30,000 natives, then 10,000 Westerners, now 10,000 mixed).

Suddenly sun. Another night lying alone, unable to sleep. The fate of Rabbi Krakauer difficult to bear. . . . They say the Chairman wanted to commit suicide.

11 September. *Aschkenes* said to go through streets shooting at groups of people. A second search is expected. Terrible fear. I myself am very concerned, have chills despite the sun. Have already cleaned toilet, cleaned garbage pail, brought it down, cooked, washed, ironed. Stomach cramps, fits of diarrhea; smoke a lot.

Train cars like prison wagons: small window, full of people. Fear and worry, because of *Erev Shabbat* [Heb: Sabbath eve] and *Erev Rosh Hashana* [Heb: Rosh Hashana eve]. Have read a lot of *Tanach* [Scriptures], especially *D'vorim* (commandments, blessings, and curses). Rabbi Krakauer, alas, is lost.

Could it have been avoided? No, because the order came from Berlin. Voices are heard, "Pay a ransom! Liquidate the treasury! The Eldest's bank has enough jewelry and gold, carpets and furs." Rumor: There are negotiations on this subject. Rumor: The children will be released at the last moment.

Today is the sixth day of *Szperre* [Ger: curfew]. No sign of change. The streets are devoid of people. A few shy faces watch from windows. Everything is like after a pogrom. One does not comprehend it all.

12 September. Henuschi. More and more worried. At 5 AM a search. I get dressed, stand with the others in ranks in the courtyard, march to the Old Market. *Aschkenes* pull people out, onto the wagons; I am pushed to the side, saved.

I have dyed my beard and hair brown with coffee. . . . Rabbi Krakauer's fate? All 7 of the Lodz rabbis arrested and sent away, as well as the kosher butchers and slaughterers. Considered superfluous. Ghetto will be called *Arbeitslager,* a change perhaps for the better. Everyone waits for 6 o'clock, the start of Rosh Hashanah.

Two notices: curfew lifted at 6:00. Announcement from the Ghetto Administration, signed by Biebow (the first from this official), that normal work will resume on the 14th, since the evacuation is ended.

The nightmare over, people walk in the streets. Timidity, but movement again.

13 September. Thousands in front of the stores to fetch their rations after 7 days of hunger. People greet one another, wish each other well for the new year, like after an earthquake or shipwreck. Did you get through? Who was taken? My brother. My mother. My parents. My children.

Talkie. Child is torn away from a young woman by a *Feldgrau.* "Let me have my child or shoot me." *Feldgrau* pulls out revolver. "I will ask you three times if I should shoot." He asks three times. The reply is always *yes,* and he shoots the woman down.

Today is Sunday. Along Zgierska, wagons with *Feldgraues* and families, on little Sunday outings. People who are safe, who came out of hiding, feel like they are newly born.

14 September. Episodes for Talkie. Polish workers at the wire, to Jewish police who loaded the children: "Aren't you ashamed to have given up your brothers like that? The same will happen to you."

Woman, forgetful, goes to work in the potato field early in morning. Is shot.

Feldgrau at deportation, to western Jew staring at him for a long time: "Do you know me?" Yes! "From Vienna?" Yes, from Vienna; you were a boxer. "Lie, I was never in Vienna, but you come with the others."

Girl speaks often with a soldier at the barbed wire, a 19-year-old boy. Someone the girl knows crawls through the wire, past the German guards, enters the other part of the ghetto. Soldier notices, lets it happen.

Friend wants to give bread to someone being taken away: "Not necessary, they'll be taken care of."

After the deportation, no outbreak of feeling, since it has never been experienced before, no reflex for such an event.

People fear knocking at acquaintances' doors. Are you there?

16 September. [*Ordnungsdienst,* the Jewish Order Service] Commander Rozenblat has come to live with us, because one of his house-mates has stomach typhus.

Talkie. The Jewish police robbed during the deportation but also enabled many to escape.

19 September. Nothing is heard from the Eldest. Suddenly there is cold weather.

20 September. Air-raid alarms for a few days. Many mothers who hid

Left and below: Captives, awaiting the wagon which will take them to the train.

Opposite: Under the age of ten, this boy was separated from his mother and brothers, who have come to say goodbye.

Wagons deport children from the ghetto, September 1942.

Ghetto children being paraded to the deportation trucks.

their children were taken; now the fate of these children is being considered. Rumors that tomorrow, Monday, Yom Kippur, all rabbis will go to the *Tliyah* [Heb: gallows].

21 September. Yom Kippur. Terrible. Diarrhea all day. Worked all day. *Cholent* instead of soup for the first time, but did not eat it because of stomach. Cold night, first frost, feel wretched despite [in English:] very good news.

Henuschi: what is she doing today?

THE CHRONICLE OF THE LODZ GHETTO

WEDNESDAY, SEPTEMBER 23, 1942

PEOPLE ARE SAYING . . .

A rumor spread through the ghetto today that fifty children who have returned here are saying that all the children who have been resettled are now in the garden of Helenow[ek]. This report is pure fantasy.

OSCAR ROSENFELD'S NOTEBOOKS

FROM NOTEBOOK 11:

Fall has come. A September resettlement with all its horror. A chapter to itself. If something like that was possible, what else is likely? Why a war? Why starvation? Why does the world go on?

There's little more to say: what comes after is merely memory, echo, nervous twitch. After that experience, our existence, always on the verge of death, took a very simple form, limited to the barest essentials.

We are alive—some say—because we've adjusted ourselves to primitive conditions. We're still alive—say others—because our feeling for what is great and right and hereafter is to be eternally guarded by us.

Still in store for us: the firing squad, typhoid fever, hanging, death.

Small boys haul provision sacks.

CHAPTER EIGHT

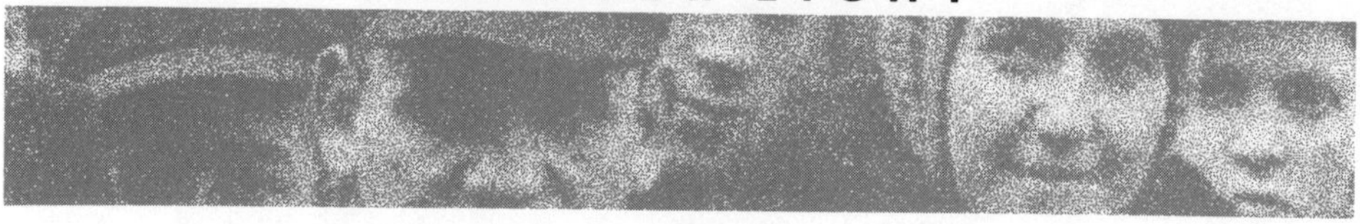

"ADAPTING TO CIRCUMSTANCES"

OSKAR ROSENFELD'S NOTEBOOKS

NOTEBOOK F

Sketch for a *Cultural History of the Ghetto.* During the [First] World War, the Germans made efforts to understand Eastern Judaism, to conserve it, to preserve its traditions, in that they left Jews their freedom. But now they use, wipe out, destroy, reshape, deface, cripple, represent them to the world as hateful parasites who need to be taught German ideas about work.

Workshops. There is a lack of tradition, no freedom for the person carrying out the work, no satisfaction with work, no ambition. Workers do not see the point of their work. They have no relationship with their product. Everything is governed by the fear of not finishing, the desire for a job, the wish to get one's needs met. The one concern: what will the soup be like?

23 September. Thinking of Zurich 4 years ago, the return to Prague. Henuschi shocked: the evil began then.

24 September. Lots of Polish workers suddenly come into ghetto. What for?

25 September. Masses of potatoes, 5 kg vegetables (4 kg cabbage and 1 kg radishes) extra per person. Extra allotment for butter, sago, noodles, zwieback. Terrible diarrhea, ghetto illness for the second time. Prices go down.

Tomorrow, Saturday, I will give a public reading of my novella, *The Secret of the Ghetto,* that is, Prague to Lodz. I'm pleased about this.

The Chairman goes through the streets on foot, crowds gape at the man with the high boots—he chases them away, loudly—painful scene.

26 September. Sabbath and Succoth. For October, 13 kg potatoes. Sigh of relief. We will hold out. No more fear, even of the winter: 6 kg briquettes and 4 kg peat.

29 September. Ghetto made smaller. The Franciszkanska area is sectioned off for the *Aschkenes'* benefit. A new evacuation of thousands in 24 hours. Great tumult. Also, vacating quarters for the construction of a new workshop. The Jewish police, brutal, criminal, a category unto themselves—with the spirit of torturers. "*Wos stajt ihr du, ganowen, gayt awek, gayt ahejm* [Yid: What are you standing here for, thieves, go away, go home]"—so someone calls out to the men loitering in front of the potato and briquette warehouses.

Face of the Ghetto, September 1942. In the morning, when people hurry over the bridge and through the streets to work, the observer does not feel himself among provincial or proletarian Jews of the East or the Balkans. The wide-swinging gestures, the loud voices are missing. Everything is subdued, only once in a while coming loose. Nothing of Goethe's "feelingful Jewish language," for feeling has disappeared completely from life. The greatest desire: to eat more soup. The faces are dull. Nothing to be read in them, not even suffering. Slavic types predominate. The "Eastern Jew" of Yiddish literature and art (Chagall, etc.) not at hand. Earlocks, beard, caftan, velour hat, skull cap missing, the *tzitzis* [Heb: prayer fringes] not visible. Since there is no devoutness, no Torah and Talmud learning, there is also no shimmer in the eyes, no fervor and reverie. The brooding boy, the elderly teacher—only in secret. A *succah* was set up for a dozen Chassidim: otherwise no trace of Succoth.

30 September. Secret of Ghetto. Group of Jews across from where potatoes are distributed: boy with missing teeth, lying on the ground grinning; old man, bald, traces of *peyes* visible; women with heads covered, flour carriers, coal haulers, loitering figures. The corpse wagon drives by. The old man asks, "Who are you coming to pick up?" Answer: We'll find someone; we have enough corpses in the ghetto. "And who will pick you up, driver?" No one has to pick me up. I'll let my mare bring me to Marysin. She knows the way. And she is the best at bearing suffering.

3 October. Tragic that in Yiddish Jews dragged along the German jargon of the Middle Ages. Bad luck: German education, inclination to *Aschkenes* culture. Spinoza, Goethe.

5 October. Yesterday Simchas Torah and I was a guest at the Praszkiers'. Beautiful religious service with *Chasen* [Heb: cantor], called to Torah, 3 To-

The corpse wagon had a removable coffin with a hinged cover.

rahs around the table like back home. The meal: schnapps, *cholent* (barley, peas, potatoes, meat), pickled meat, chopped with beets, coffee with gingerbread, Yiddish and Polish songs. No end to Judaism. Thought much about Henuschi.

9 October. Horrible news: 600,000 are supposed to be deported from Warsaw. Agitation, since the same is feared here despite the ghetto's productivity. We've lived in the shadow of death for three years. Uninterruptedly threatened. Thousands hunted down, shot, starved, whipped to death. New sacrificial victims

Unmarked ghetto graves in the old cemetery, the second-largest Jewish burial ground in Europe.

every day. The nearer the end, the greater the danger. An announcement from Biebow: "Warning: The strongest measures will be taken against the smallest thefts, whether against the war production or from the food division."

12 October. Face of the Ghetto. Cold autumn. Wooden shoes, goat skins but also summer skirts. Puddles, streams of waste, muck. One expects further horror. The faces of last winter reappear: pale, yellow, mummies in rags.

13 October. What is Henuschi thinking now? I will move to Zgierska 24/4 soon, in a kitchen with gas. Friend Natan and wife coming along.

15 October. A ghetto law: what is not taken care of immediately will never be taken care of. Read Schiller, am caught up in this blinding storyteller.

18 October. Marysin fenced in. Wooden planking with barbed wire, very thick, electric current running through it, cut off from the rest of the ghetto. Do not show myself on the street. Chills. Think of Henuschi, Wilma, Erich constantly. When will the end come? Everything trembles.

Kitchen living is agony—sleeping, cooking, eating, cleaning, studying, writing, storing potatoes, etc.

19 October. Even the Poles driving through Zgierska are very poorly clothed, their faces serious. Some give a melancholy look at the people behind the fence. It is said of Warsaw: in the course of one week 500,000 Jews evacuated. There are now 8000 people working in the straw shoe workshop (straw insulation for military boots)—winter advance against Vanya. Greatest hurry. Air-raid drills.

NOTEBOOK G:

NOTES FOR MEMOIRS

24 October. The Eldest. Two profiles. One: well-mannered, clean, calm, benevolent, religious, a traditional Jew; the other: deep, ironic, cunning, spiteful, treacherous, *gaslonisch* [Yid: predatory].

25 October. After the September evacuation, the closest relatives of the evacuees dove into their bread, sometimes without tears. Best friends feel no pain. Terrible hardening and brutalization of the spirit. People do not answer questions.

Three times as many men are dying as women, since the women were already accustomed to eating less. We defy the laws of medical science, in that we're still alive on this nourishment.

27 October. Did not sleep because of concern about apartment. For the time being intervention not possible. The Eldest deeply pre-occupied, broken, not to be spoken to.

2 November. The electric [tram] brings sacks of potatoes for the privileged. Almost everyone has already consumed the November and December potatoes, I as well. —The Ghetto Administration (Biebow) gradually takes over the administration of the most important workshops. The Eldest's signs disappear. Instead of gold and black, white and blue. Anxiety as a result. . . . Beautiful day, warm and sunny, what foliage, like at home.

3 November. The Eldest. "In the ghetto no one must go hungry." (Speech, IX.19.40) "I will be the proper guardian of the ghetto." (IV.30.40) "The problems

of the ghetto rule my entire being." "I will not stray a hair's breadth from my program." Other points worth noting: Chairman recounts assassination attempts against him, even with the knife—but does not loosen things. Children run behind him: baa, baa.

4 November. There is no clock. The clock in the tower of the church always reads 5:00. No mid-day bells, no time.

Reading in the ghetto: Albrecht and Joachim Prinz, Spinoza, Pinsker, Haeckel, Rousseau, 5-volume history of art, Turgenev and Gorki, 5 Books of Moses. Schiller, Heine. Something about Lodz. Sholem Aleichem's autobiography. . . . Bergelson. . . . Blume: Freud's lectures.

5 November. Henuschi. Gave Dr. Oskar Singer and Dr. B. Heilig* a kind of will. In case. Feel weak in the heart, cold in the feet, shivering fits, giant hunger. Stabbing pains like angina pectoris. Again the first grey-black crows in the gloomy sky, fall and winter mixed.

7 November. There is no sabbath, no day of rest. Open latrines in offices:

Rumkowski. "Deeply pre-occupied . . . not to be spoken to." (Rosenfeld)

on one side a man crouching, on the other, women crouching, next to them men pissing, all without shame.

For 11 months no mail. First snow, 12 noon. Cold. I sit in unheated office with stiffened fingers.

18 November. Of the second Prague transport, 187 have died as of yesterday, about 500 evacuated. A loss of 50%.

20 November. Enter Marysin home. Mornings bathe, then stand for a long while in the open air.

21 November. Gigantic moon over the cemetery in Marysin. Discussed with the Eldest idea of living in the home.

85,000 people eat the same thing every day: potatoes, cabbage and radish. A few hundred have some meat, beets, flour mixed with potatoes. Not a drop of milk or cheese has come into the ghetto for a week. Have swollen feet. What next? Despite Marysin, hungry, have sugar with me. At the next table constant discussion of the specialities of well-known restaurants in Vienna, Berlin, Warsaw, London, Paris, Copenhagen, etc. Sense of hunger increased.

27 November. Leave Marysin—am without a place to live. Am without bread, without potatoes. Have never been so forsaken. Henuschi. What is she thinking? Does she know, the poor thing? Is she thinking of the 28th of November 1937? Of the chicken and the poppy torte? My golden child. Will I ever see her again?

Kripo go through the streets. If two Jews chat with each other, Kripo slams their heads together, saying: "Good news, huh? Good news?" This on days when there is good news from outside. Much fear that *Aschkenes* will massacre when retreating.

The evacuated leave everything behind, except themselves, when they are taken away. Jewish police are sent into villages, take everything with them into the ghetto. The good things go to Litzmannstadt, the rest given to the needy in the ghetto, with the permission of Biebow. Thereby, a slightly better clothing situation.

30 November. On the next to last day of the September evacuation, the rabbis brought to the Central Prison. Taken out, they prayed, consigned themselves to God.

After terrible snow, the ghetto is white and dirty-white. The sewage wagon keeps returning, pulled by wrapped-up beings with mummy faces. The dazzling snow makes them even more ghastly. Freezing people wait in the food distribution lines. Pushing, fighting, hitting, swearing. Woe to him who challenges the person in front of him.

"The ghetto is dirty white . . . wrapped-up beings with mummy faces . . ." (Rosenfeld)

"Freezing people wait in the food distribution lines . . . Woe to him who challenges the person in front of him." (Rosenfeld)

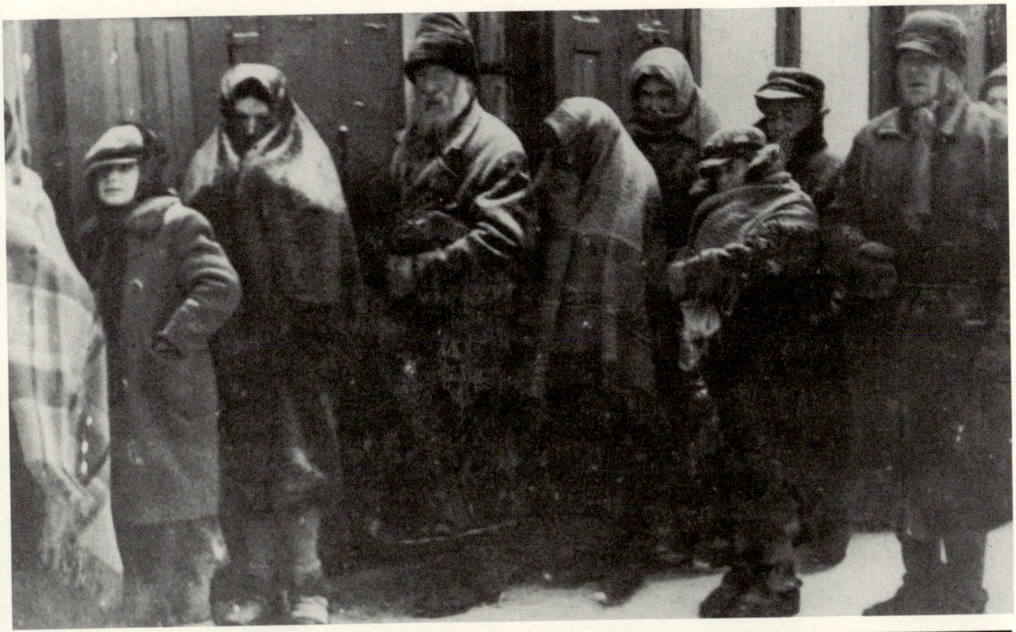

SPEECH BY CHAIM RUMKOWSKI

7 NOVEMBER 1942

"HERE IN THE GHETTO WE ARE ALL EQUAL"

[Transcriber's notes—*Most of the ghetto's Jewish administration was present for this speech, which Rumkowski delivered after a concert in the House of Culture. His tone of voice was calm, which put the audience at ease.*]

I have not spoken to you for a number of weeks. Now, once more, we will be having our regularly scheduled concerts, and my speeches will be more frequent as well. A lot has developed in the last few weeks, but one cannot and should not speak about everything.

In the first place, I wish to sincerely thank all those who agreed with my idea about caring for orphaned children, and who acted upon it. God will reward them for it. It's a very important and very difficult task. It would help if people in the ghetto finally stopped twisting my words and spreading gossip and panic. Unfortunately, I have to conclude that this is a disease that cannot be cured.

The most important problem at this moment is that of the children. In the future, it will be imperative that little children be kept from running around everywhere by themselves. The population is probably aware of the prevailing conditions, and of the need to adapt to them. Almost everyone in the ghetto is working, and the children remain home alone, unsupervised. This is dangerous, because they spend most of their time in the streets.

In connection with this situation, an effort has been organized to select one or two places in each large building, and one common room in small houses, for all children whose parents are working. This way parents will be able to work in peace and not worry about their children. For the sake of complete order in this regard, I've decided to establish a female police force whose members—girls with a Matura [four years of *Gymnasium* (high school)] education—will supervise the children.

I'm addressing parents so that they will understand, finally, that it's dangerous for children to roam the streets. Everyone probably understands why. The policewomen will get the children off the streets and make the parents pay a fine if their child is found again in the streets. Ghetto residents who see policewomen confronting a child in the street should not view it negatively but as an expression of care for the child.

Anyone who understands this matter should see to it that children below the age of ten are placed in designated community centers, as children ages 11 and 12 are my co-workers and are employed in factories. I shall be rigorous in demanding honest work from the new female police force. The order of the hour is: Children must no longer remain unsupervised.

Illnesses: Rumors about supposed plans to deport the sick, as well as totally unfounded news that a 4 PM curfew is to be instituted, are completely untrue—and have resulted in many cases of infectious disease going unreported, since the sick are afraid of the hospital. This is why I've given the doctors strict orders to report every case and to place the sick in the hospital. A doctor who does not satisfy this responsibility will lose his right to practice his profession, and his name will be placed on a special list.

For the sick who stay at home, nurses will be sent around to visit them free of charge. We'll see to it that the sick have enough money to buy their rations. Isolating those with contagious diseases is of primary importance, as everyone will appreciate, if they understand how illness spreads. Again, people have to realize that adapting to the ghetto's situation is a necessity.

Work: Regarding work in the factories, I have to admit that lately it's been quite a mess, since many working hours were used in getting potatoes. Fortunately, this has now come to an end. Strict control over punctuality is about to be instituted and will be supervised by a special commission, and I'll also be personally interested in this matter.

For my part, I shall also see to it that workers receive sufficient compensation for their work for the purchase of all allotted rations. For those workers unable to earn enough, we'll create opportunities for them to do so. However, people who do not want to work will be forced to.

Each of my workers has to earn enough for himself and his family to live on. I have therefore ordered that apprentices must earn 50% of the cost of their allotment and that their parents should cover the rest. It's obvious that if a worker cannot fulfill his quota for reasons he cannot control—such as lack of work—he will receive compensation.

I ask every manager to keep an honest attendance record, and to make sure that the number of workers listed agrees in all respects with the number of soup rations issued. The Commission for Regulating the Professions, on which I assume my most honest people serve, will take care of departmental problems, while the craftsmen in the factories must not forget their responsibilities.

Provisions: I've heard all kinds of jokes referring to potato consumption. This is not a proper topic for jokes. We've received and distributed potatoes

Children selling sweets. Rumkowski threatened to deport parents who let their children be street peddlers.

for the period ending April first. If people eat their potatoes earlier, there will be hunger—and that's not a joke! In the city, too, potatoes were issued in advance, till August first, on credit. Considering my population, I could not afford such long-range credit.

Trading in potatoes has to stop. Apparently, they've already reached a price of 7 marks. A special commission will check on the careful management of potato allotments and will apply sanctions accordingly. Inferior potatoes should be eaten first, and the better ones saved for later. Everyone knows how good Jewish humor is, but this is not the time nor the place for jokes. It's a dangerous game. The allotments I issue must last.

The coupons given to the sick were very helpful, but now, because of the very difficult food situation, I cannot afford them. I can only give them to those with typhus or jaundice, but it is out of the question for people suffering from the swelling caused by hunger to get them. That sickness threatens everyone who eats his potatoes ahead of time. Only fools and the nearsighted leave worrying about tomorrow to God.

Clothing and coal distribution: The distribution of coal for the winter will begin in a few days. Along with the clothing distribution now in progress, this is a matter of great importance because its primary goal is to prevent the children who work from catching cold.

I shall do everything to improve the workers' existence. I have organized free medical care for all who work; therefore, if an assigned physician does not visit a patient the same day he is called, please report it at Balut Market. I will deliver that physician.

There must finally be an end to private trading, trading in one's own blood! The watchword of my workers should be: "Here in the ghetto we are all workers, we are all equal!"

JOZEF ZELKOWICZ

CHILD LABOR IN THE TAILOR WORKSHOP AT LAGIEWNICKA STREET

DECEMBER 1942

Among hundreds of adult workers one notices many adolescents, 300 of whom are employed in this workshop. Most of them can hardly eke out a living. Many are orphans or the children of deported parents. Because their meager wages are too small, they must sell a part of their ration. (Thus, sugar, soup, meat and sausage coupons are bartered here.) And their working hours make their lives even more miserable. Working from eight in the morning till four in the afternoon, they go home to clean house, light the fire in the oven, cook supper, and often have to get their ration at the distribution store when the lines are longest.

Particularly moving are the stories of the orphaned children. Left entirely on their own, they usually stay with distant relatives or with total strangers. In most cases such children are helpless, ideal objects of exploitation. For instance, 13-year-old Meyer, whose mother died and whose father was taken to Germany for forced labor, says that he has not even tasted sugar in weeks because the woman at whose house he stays gave all of it, first, to her consumptive husband and, when he died, to her little daughter. Keeping their food rations separate was impossible. Then there is Rafael, who describes how long he has to wait until they let him put his supper on the stove to cook, how they steal from his food, even from what's already in the pot cooking.

The time the children spend in the workshop is only partly a respite from their painful experiences at home. For eight hours they stay in large, brightly lit halls which are kept warm by central heating. Unfortunately, the attitude toward them in the workshop is far from proper. The workshop management shows a total lack of concern for the conditions and needs of the children. Complaints are heard all the time that there are too many of them here, that loitering is all they do, that their work is of low quality. Many instructors and workers are of the opinion that beatings are the answer—and quite often make use of them.

The attitude toward the adolescents varies according to the number of orders. When there's enough work, their help is very much appreciated and sought, but when there are few orders, there is no end to the complaining.

An apprentice receives a weekly wage of 8 marks, but from this amount charges for soup, tax, rent, and vegetables are deducted, leaving them a net sum last week of 3.20 marks. Lateness is punished by a fine of 1 mark. Each day of absence is deducted from the pay. And the little errand boys who sometimes carry a heavy load of military overcoats are expected to pay for every coat that is damaged, or even crumpled.

DAWID SIERAKOWIAK'S DIARY

NOVEMBER 12, 1942

Father picked up his potatoes but did nothing to get a job. Meanwhile, he rules the household, but I don't protest. Damn it!

NOVEMBER 13, 1942

Father's lying and cheating ways are re-emerging, and I still can't restrain myself.

NOVEMBER 17, 1942

Father is still in bed and the situation is getting more irritating. When Nadzia and I are away, he cooks a lot of potatoes for himself and uses a lot of briquettes. He has no intention of getting a job. His old thievery has re-emerged, and he steals from our food.

NOVEMBER 21, 1942

Tension is mounting at home, and sudden outbursts between Father and me are growing more frequent. In spite of all his dirty tricks, he tries to get along with me, but I can't control myself enough to remain detached. The office is now like paradise for me, and going home fills me with fear and loathing.

JANUARY 14, 1943

Nadzia went to see Father in the hospital today. He keeps asking for food, so she gave him the 25 dkg. of bread she always did. We can't give him any of our watery vegetable soup. He is not the kind of father for whom it pays to sacrifice one's own health, as our unhappy mother did. My saintly, beloved mother, whom I cannot forget even for one minute, day or night.

MARCH 6, 1943

My unhappy father, once so powerful, died today at 4 pm. He became so weak during the night that he could hardly move in the morning. It was increasingly difficult for him to breathe. He spoke very little, although he was totally conscious and aware of everything.

About 3:55 pm he suddenly asked me to straighten his pillow. I did, and Father bent his head, lying quite still and breathing imperceptibly. I kept looking at him constantly, from my bed, and all of a sudden he stopped breathing. I didn't believe it and was numb with fear. I called Anka to get a neighbor. A lady came and tried to move his head. Terrified, she had to say that Father was dead.

OSKAR ROSENFELD'S NOTEBOOKS

NOTEBOOK G

4 December. Yesterday, beautiful Chanukah evening at Jakob Schipper's. The lighting of the *menorah,* a *bruche* [Heb: blessing], speeches, Yiddish and Hebrew songs, a memory of Herzl.* Wonderful winter evening, thought a lot about Henuschi.

5 December. 87,949 Jews in ghetto. 22 non-Jews, female, including two ethnic Germans. The rest Polish. All these women in workshops. A loss of 75,000 in one year. Am hardened myself.

9 December. Rumors because of Cervantes [Spain?]. Disruption. If true, increased duration of *milchome*. Still no apartment. Sweets have disappeared from street sales.

17 December. Rumor that † [the Pope?] is coming to Poland. Thick morning fog, like in London at Henuschi's. Good *psires* [Heb: news] from abroad, but not verifiable.

20 December. A deaf mute fell after his mother and sibling were buried in Marysin, could not make himself understood, froze. A doctor takes patients who are expected to die within 24 hours, takes away food and bread cards. A mother and daughter die. Their neighbors, who let them go to ruin, break into their room, steal bread, sugar, oats, bed covers, throw rags over the two corpses—the dead daughter holds dead mother in her arms. The Eldest speaks bluntly to the people in the Culture House after a concert or a revue, about the authorities' power over potatoes, cleanliness, bathing facilities, laundry. *Geserah* [Heb: evil decree] not to be feared.

21 December. Four years ago Henuschi left Prague. She is crying! Golden child! Am alone in my pain, see her before me constantly. In spite of good *psires,* terrible depression inside the ghetto. I have lost patience.

1943

1 January 1943. Have hope of seeing Henuschi again. Fire in a clothing workshop. Jewish women designing patterns for *Aschkenes*. Unheard of, that Jewish taste should create fashions for the *Aschkenes*. Living outside the world—and yet. Fashion: pleated skirts.

Face of the ghetto. Women with kerchiefs on their heads, long socks à la ski—strong dirty linen fixed to their shoes, those in rags. Sometimes with men's caps, men's jackets. Men: sheepskin without sleeves, sleeves made of dirty shirt material, socks from scraps of fabric, old galoshes on their feet. Heads bent forward, faces covered with earlaps that go across the cheeks.

New Year's celebration: a large crowd at Miss Fuchs's. [Dora Fuchs—Rumkowski's personal secretary] As much as elsewhere, women with their hair waved, in evening dresses, etc. Alcohol.

4 January. New Year's Eve celebration at a dignitary's. Two kinds of meat, two kinds of fish, schnapps, wine, baked goods. People are talking about it. The same night, 40 people (petty thieves) were taken out of the Central Prison without warm clothing and sent to Posen to work.

A Jew, who, until this point, had lived disguised in Litzmannstadt, is brought into the ghetto—without punishment.

7 January. In Marysin again. Leizerowicz* tells of *Aschkenes* who get tears in their eyes when the fate of the Jews is brought up. Rare case. All *Aschkenes* on the Baluter Ring happy, singing. One does not know why.

8 January. Stories that gold, jewelry, diamonds, dollars, pounds have been found in the shoes of the evacuated; the Special Unit* take these, giving them to the Ghetto Administration. Also from the evacuated: 10,000 *tefillin*—the leather used.

12 January. Rumors of a pogrom in Vilna against Poles and Jews. How true is this? Is it a result of the front?

17 January. Henuschi—birthday—hurts!

18 January. Women without periods, complete death of the erotic, especially among the Western Jews. Thus, no marriages.

21 January. Fifty Jewish workers from Berlin have come here. Tell of apparently terrible bombing of Berlin. Also, 40 *tliahs* in Litzmannstadt for *Aschkenes,* Communists from Wolhynia. Heard that I'm to get an apartment.

22 January. September evacuation. Jewish police throw infants through windows into the horse-drawn wagons. From the children not a sound.

27 January. Night air raid alarm. What's going on? Vanya presses on. *Aschkenes* weaken, so one is told.

2 February. Danger of death as the Reich receives bad news. How much longer will this go on? Haven't they also had enough?

3 February. Rumor: [In English] Asia Minor in the war! Lively company in the home. Accordion and loud singing next to the cemetery wall, above which one can see the caps of the hearse drivers passing by.

5 February. Yesterday, an amusing conversation with the Chairman in Yiddish. Have hope of being protected until the end, if no evacuation.

8 February. New posters: Reading a newspaper in a group will be punished by death.

12 February. Jews brought from Lublin and Bialystok to the Central Prison, an evacuation and pogrom. Perhaps in connection with the front.

13 February. Miss Rosenblum in the personnel division owns *Magic Mountain* in original German.

14 February. In Bialystock there are German posters which say: "This will happen to you, if you do not win!" Two Germans are harnessed to a wagon, a Pole holds the reins, a Jew drives with a whip. Snow drifts. Completely without news from the outside world. What are Henuschi, Wilma, Ernst, Erich doing?

18 February. Marked change of mood among *Aschkenes* here. Individual *Aschkenes* workers at the train-station speak in a friendly manner, say they have found many good, respectable people among the Jews. As one was departing for the front, a Jew wished him good luck. He covered his face, sobbing. Even they want an end.

23 February. So-called dignitaries have left their wives and strut around now with their sweethearts. This is completely shameless and open, especially among young police officers.

Aschkenes spy, go through the ghetto wearing *Mogen David,* eavesdrop and report. Dangerous! But we have no interest in political conversation, since we cannot change anything under present conditions. Besides, there is no sympathy for England, which terribly deceived us about Palestine.

24 February. We see ourselves as three Jewish holidays: we eat as on Yom Kippur, live as during Succoth, and look like we do on Purim.* Rumor that in a discussion outside, the butchering of all Jews was asserted. Cannot be verified.

27 February. The Poles. On the track between the barbed wires, two young Poles go sledding, show their behinds to the Jews: "You can——us." Others shovel snow and throw it under the wire onto the ghetto sidewalk. Going by on the electric trolley, they stick their tongues out at the Jews. They have no understanding of the fact that England has allied itself with the Poles. Woe, when a servant becomes a master! On May 3rd, the Polish national holiday, signs with "Kill the Jews!" Vile actions of the Polish police against the Jews.

2 March. What is Henuschi doing? Is she as grey as I?

5 March. Starting today a new life for me in the ghetto. I will leave the home and stay in Ch. Praszkier's house, installing myself in a room. Am surprised and touched by the goodness of the Praszkier family.

Latrines. The toilet facilities in Plac Koscielny, above the courtyard, are open sitting boards, since the doors do not shut, because the people's muck blocks them. In the entrance and in the room itself, piles of feces and puddles of urine. A well-cared-for woman's hand holds the door, in case one mistakenly tries to open it. The hand belongs to a pretty young woman I come in contact with in the office. Even she crouches on the board without shame. Of course, the room, in which there are 8 sitting places, is fairly dark. Everything is congested with *dreck*. Used toilet paper sticks to one's shoes and is carried into the courtyard—where, in one corner or another, someone relieves himself in broad daylight.

NOTEBOOK 11

April. Where's X? Where's Y? Dead! Dead! Dead! and buried. We no longer feel emotion. Thieves go scrounging around the corpses, grabbing crockery, scraps of bread, shoes, pocket knives—especially when there are no bereaved relatives.

No inheritance rights: everything belongs to the ghetto. That started in the fall of 1942. The nearest relative or close friend may claim a few trifles.

Life is dreadfully depressing. People are pitiless, dissociated, stone-hearted. Unresponsive.

Suddenly all the Polish Jews are hostile to me. Is there a real opposition between East and West, between Ashkenazi [Western Jews] and Sephardi [Eastern Jews]? One's opinion about that changes according to one's latest experience. . . .

Suddenly: I must get away, out of the ghetto. I think about fleeing. Off with the yellow star. I am embittered.

Voices approach. Somebody calls out to me: "Sir, you don't have the *Mogen David*." It's a Jewish policeman. My blood turns cold. He takes the star and pins it on me. "Take care," he says. "If an *Aschkenes* sees you, you're done for."

I feel happier. Suddenly I belong to all of them, the so-called Polish Jews. We have the same fear of the *Aschkenes,* of the hardness of life, of the fate awaiting us. Those few words saved me.

NOTEBOOK 13

Ghetto philosophy. We struggle every day, says a woman of the workshop. What for? Do we know if we'll live to see freedom? Death doesn't bother us anymore. I lost my father here, nothing. My son I haven't seen for three years.

I don't even long for him anymore. Even desire is dead, like the other feelings. No one notices, since the desire for food outweighs all else.

Face of the street. Everything old, mummylike, the people, houses, trees, memories. Even fresh vegetables wither when they're brought into the ghetto. Everything is a used-goods shop, stinking like old *tefillin* and *tallisim*.

The nights in the ghetto. Except for people working in certain workshops (laundry, cleaning, dyeing for the *Aschkenes* military), everyone goes to bed at 9 o'clock. The women have already cooked, washed, ironed, mended. Family life no longer exists.

Everything is chaotic. Son does not see father, man does not see wife, because most work different hours. Children lie in the streets, courtyards, latrines, gutters, go through the garbage, are street sellers.

The neglect of children extends further and further. They do not study. They have no books, discipline, order. They learn no languages or prayers. There are already many uncircumcised. Their language is a chaos of Polish, Yiddish, German.

Popular sayings. The best lie is the *Emess* [Heb: truth]. The best *chochme* [Yid: wisdom] is *shtil* [Yid: silence]! A piece of wood cannot burn by itself; one person can not resist.

SPEECH BY CHAIM RUMKOWSKI

13 MARCH 1943

WE TOO MUST MOBILIZE

[*In an address to a crowded meeting of department and workshop delegates, Rumkowski outlined the need to reorganize the work force to satisfy the Germans' demands.*]

. . . At one time, we had autonomy. But step by step, that autonomy was curtailed, so that today only a few paltry remnants of it are left. As you know, my brothers and sisters, orders from the authorities are not subject to discussion. There is a war on and there is a total mobilization in the Reich; new factories must be created, for which additional workers must be found. Where will these workers come from? The problem can be solved only by reorganization, and it is better that we face the inevitable fact soberly and undertake the necessary steps ourselves in order to prevent chaos.

What is the real issue here? Is it a tragedy if today we reassign young people, most of whom have been sitting in offices for the last three years, that is, for as long as the ghetto has been in existence, while people aged 50 and over have been utterly worn down by hard physical labor. It's not a tragedy to move people around and allow older people a bit of rest. We're a labor camp, yet it's possible for us to regulate things in our own sphere. Don't make this difficult for me. Put yourselves in my place and you'll see that it's better to tell me what your occupation was before the war, so that I won't assign workers with skills to the wrong jobs.

In these difficult times, when our productivity is essential, it's a sin against society for experienced, skilled workers to hide in offices instead of using their skills for the good of all. We too must begin a total mobilization. Of course, this can't be done overnight. We must first get some idea of the workers available to us. They are, so to speak, our reserves. As soon as the factories open, this human resource will be put to work. Office staffs will become smaller, or older people will replace the young. I'm aware that in many cases the change will be very difficult, particularly with respect to actual living conditions. But we've coped with greater difficulty, and we'll also surmount this problem—which can be solved only by changes in the budget. With a monthly budget of 5.5 million marks, we will definitely find a solution. Trust me!

But also bear in mind that mobilizing people up to the age of 40 is not the end of this. We don't know how things will develop or whether other age groups will also have to be mobilized in the near future. And, above all, don't think that this move is limited to the departments. We will have to restaff the offices in the factories as well. Yes, if need be, I'll even take a secretary away from a director, whether or not he sheds tears over the loss of his trusted right hand. And "diplomatic" illnesses will also be of no avail. We have to be firm, for everything is at stake here. For the time being, we have a three-month plan. What happens after that remains to be seen. Don't try pulling strings. Don't provide false information, for here, as everywhere, honesty is the best policy.

JAKUB POZNANSKI, LODZ GHETTO DIARY

APRIL 25, 1943

There is talk, lately, of an uprising in Warsaw.* Apparently, armed Jews and Poles resisted a plan to transfer people out. A factory was set on fire. To subdue the revolt, the Germans had to use machine guns, tanks, and even bombers. Only after the war will we find out how much truth there is to this.

GERMAN DOCUMENTS

SECRET MATTERS OF STATE

Lodz, 5 May 1943

Telex To: Research Office A 3 MZA. Lodz No. 384
Re: Warsaw and Lodz ghettos
Event: Stapo [State Police] conference

In the course of a long conversation on 5 May, about the riots in the Warsaw ghetto, one of the senior executive officers, Dr. Rosse, remarked to Deputy Fstl. [unintelligible] that presumably a large number of German deserters were in the Warsaw ghetto, and that enemy parachuters had found cover there as well.

In reply to the question whether such riots were also possible in the Lodz ghetto, Dr. Rosse said that such events would always have to be expected. But since informers—probably Jewish spies—had been employed, it was assumed that information regarding any such intentions would be obtained on time. If, however, serious riots should break out one day, Dr. Rosse continued, a critical situation would arise, as the surveillance of the ghetto had to be deemed inadequate, considering the quite substantial number of inhabitants. The Jews might succeed in overpowering the guards, particularly if riots were to break out in the Polish part of the Lodz population.

SECRET MATTERS OF STATE

Lodz, 8 May 1943

Telex To: Research Office 5 A 3 MZA. Lodz No. 383
Re: Execution of army commissions in the Lodz ghetto

As reported by NL 7500, of 5-7-43, Ribbe of the Ghetto Administration in Lodz informed Biebow in Bremen on 5-6- that he had reassured Major General von Stein, the post senior officer in Lodz, that events similar to the ones in Warsaw were totally impossible in the Lodz ghetto. Delivering the above-mentioned report to the Stapo, the senior executive officer, Dr. Bradfisch, added that Major General v. Stein had probably inquired whether the orderly execution of army commissions could be guaranteed in the local ghetto or if riots might also be expected there.

OSKAR ROSENFELD'S NOTEBOOKS

NOTEBOOK 11

Marriage. Some people marry out of need, others from having extra. In either case, the social situation in the ghetto motivates the union. A young man, working alone in his department from early morning until 5, returns to an empty apartment to prepare himself a meal. He looks around for a female companion, a helpmate. Two weak people together can become strong: their rations are equal, and the double measure of coal and firewood expands their possibilities.

A manager has food coupons, extra rations, special allocations. Compared to others, he is living in luxury. He has a yen to make some ghetto girl happy. And what about her? She feels lucky, thinks she's been rescued from a prison-like existence.

But why not a pure and simple union untrammeled by social circumstance? Consider that lovemaking has on the whole withered away. As the finer, more tender aspects of life—music, literature, springtime, flowers, and the rest—have vanished, so too has love.

How much is religious ceremony maintained? By the *hassen* [Heb: groom] placing the ring on the finger of the *kallah* [Heb: bride], as he utters the traditional blessing. The father is the witness, along with another Jew. The Eldest officiates at the House of Culture. The marriage is just as valid as rabbinical marriage and satisfies current authority. Young people for the most part, about ten couples a week. Natives.

"SEEK IN THE ASHES," PAPERS FOUND IN AUSCHWITZ

[*Excerpt from an Anonymous Diary*]

When I observe the street from my window, I see the human beings entrusted to the care of the Eldest. I watch how their faces change by the minute, their bodies bent and spineless, their legs hardly able to move along. When I see workers who give all their strength and energy and talent; when I observe the testimony their crippled look gives about the attitude of the Eldest towards them, I can't help thinking: "God Almighty, in what hands did you leave these unfortunate people!"

Rumkowski performs a wedding ceremony after the rabbinate was abolished.

JOZEF ZELKOWICZ

[*6 August 1943*]

"NIGHT LIFE IN THE GHETTO"

Life is no romance, not in the ghetto, anyway. The eye is unable to notice the rich nuances of black and grey. An ear cannot distinguish among hundreds and thousands of voices crying out silently. Mere human language is too weak to relay what we see and hear. Thus, no matter how much we write and tell, in the end we come up with but a pale reflection of reality.

Although much is already written, said, sung, even painted about the ghetto in daylight, no one has ever tried to describe ghetto life at night. Let the following lines, then, count as a modest beginning.

Even if most days in the ghetto are grey or black, there is still an extraordinary variety within the limits of these colors. Ghetto nights, however, have no tincture at all, none that the human eye can comprehend.

While the ghetto's daily life is concentrated in the workshops and offices during working hours, and after that in the distribution stores, night life is centered in the courtyards and around garbage dumps.

Ghetto apartments are not surrounded by the quiet, cozy, intimate walls of yesteryear. Such walls bred domestic feeling. Ghetto walls are permeated by cold and frost in the winter and by hunger in the spring. Their recesses are filled in the summer by bedbugs, and with mildew in the fall. One wants to run away from such walls. One cannot live, cannot breathe between such walls.

Thus, at about 9 PM, after 15 hours of exhausting work (a worker in the ghetto must rise at 6 AM at the latest), the ghetto dweller finally begins his night life, racing away from the bedbugs.

Men, women, children, like hapless beings visited by otherworldly spirits, look for a spot where they can rest the bodies which tired, weakened legs can no longer carry. The wooden stairs groan, the unoiled doors shriek and grate. Deformed legs shuffle along; dry, shrunken lungs breathe heavily; hoarse throats make wheezing sounds: the ghetto's people are in search of fresh air for their trembling, damaged bodies.

As the bedbugs crawl over the dirty, cracked walls in the abandoned apartments, the human mass creeps into the courtyard. If there is a well, it is surrounded by those looking for a place to sit on its wooden frame. Bodies fall heavily on the wet boards, tired legs dangle with pleasure and worn-out breasts give sighs of relief that sound like saws scratching on tin.

Lucky are the ones who come early enough to find a place to sit. They can stretch their legs. They can even slip their worn leather shoes or wooden sandals from their feet. They can start a conversation about their work in the shop, tell of their dreams about "supplements," or fantasize about a food ration that may be imminent, because that's what was heard from someone who learned it from his good friend who works in Provisioning. And they are happy with anticipation.

Those who did not find a seat around the well must find a clean enough spot on the ground. The earth cools off the flushed body, but swollen legs cannot be stretched, unless the spot is near the well and one can lean against it. The spot on the ground is not as good as the spot on the well casing, but it's not all that bad: you can prop up your body so that your rebelling legs do not have to drag it around.

Then there are those whose stoves produced more smoke than heat and so were late preparing their lean meals. For them there is not even a free spot on the ground. They are doomed to stand or walk around. They form what looks from afar like clusters of people leaning against each other; should someone move from his spot, the cluster would fall apart like a house without walls.

The darkness thickens; the black clusters in the courtyard swell larger and larger, until they become one thick dark mass. As darkness envelopes the courtyard, the mass becomes darker and exudes more life. Tongues begin to loosen. Someone makes a discovery in the sky: a wagon.

"Really, a wagon. Just look—four wheels and a crooked pole. So what does it mean?"

"The *Moshiah* will come on that wagon," jokes a comedian.

The Messiah is, of course, a favorite topic of the children of Israel. Never before have the children of Israel needed the Messiah as much as they need him now. And so the Messiah-theme is pursued with stories, wonderful legends that let fantasy fly high, allowing them to tear away reality, to forget that they are crowded here in the courtyard not for pleasure but to get away from the bedbugs. Everyone has a story to tell, everyone knows something about the Messiah and lives in a fantasy of his own. Everyone knows what they will do when redemption comes.

"When *Moshiah* comes, we'll eat all the bread we can . . . and all the young potatoes . . . and we'll cook the potatoes with young onions . . . and we'll spare no butter."

SS Reichsführer Heinrich Himmler is greeted on his arrival in the ghetto by Rumkowski, June 7, 1941.

Women making sandals from scrap leather, sometimes gathered from the phylacteries of deported Jews.

Jewish police were assigned to oversee the large ghetto workshops, keeping order and preventing workers from taking any materials.

In the leather workshop.

Special machines were provided to the ghetto by the German armaments commission for the production of bullet casings.

Left: "The ghetto advertises its slavery." (Rosenfeld) These displays were prepared as showcases for visiting German officials. Rumkowski, Jakubowicz, and Biebow worked to attract German military and consumer production contracts for the ghetto.

Below: Ghetto youths use grommet machines to produce ammunition bags and knapsacks for the German military.

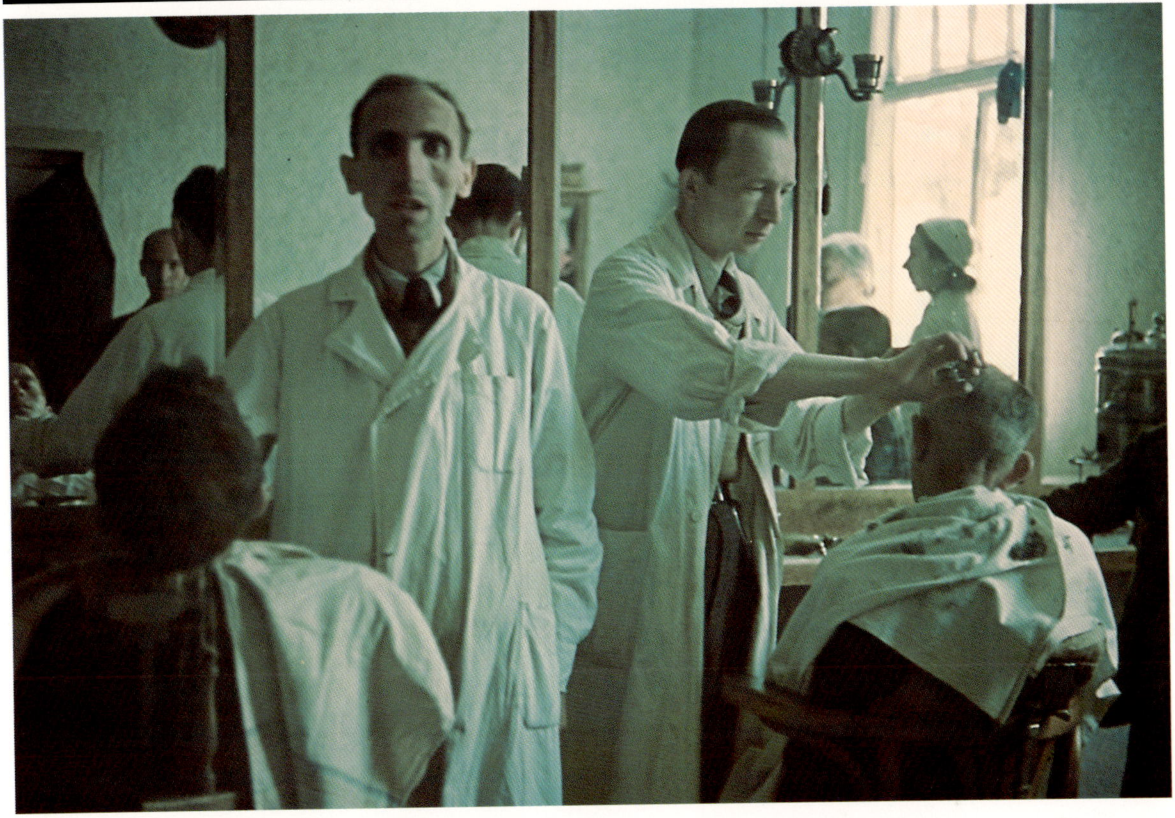

Above: Tatarka's barbershop, where secret newspapers were available and sometimes read aloud.

Left: A clandestine radio used in the ghetto, now at the Ghetto Fighters' House in northern Israel.

JUDEN

26
VII
DR
1933
44

Above: After a Deportation, painted in the ghetto by the artist Hirsch Szylis.

Left, top: A view of the ghetto by Hirsch Szylis.

Left, bottom: A bracelet made in the ghetto, depicting a well pump, a Nazi guard at the ghetto gate, the ghetto bridge, and the fecal workers. The bracelet is at Yad Vashem. *(Photo by Zvi Reiter)*

A ghetto man operates a semimechanized weaving loom.

Straw boots were ordered by the Germans to protect their foot soldiers on the Russian front.

The courtyard surges, the crowd hums and buzzes as if in a beehive, and saliva runs from wide-open mouths. Children of Israel rejoice in the wisdom of mind; children of Israel enjoy the rotten air that the warm wind blows from the garbage pails.

Those that sit around the well have it really good. When the exhausted bodies tire of talking and listening, they can lean against the well and close their eyes. Enough, enough already of this all-too-real ghetto day. Now, when all the talk dies down, now it's time for a nap, and maybe dreams will take them to those lands of their fantasy.

Those whose backs press against the courtyard walls can also close their eyes, have a nap, and at the same time celebrate their revenge on the bedbugs. No human blood for them tonight; tonight the bedbugs will fast.

The worst is the lot of those who have to stand. As long as the talking lasts, the bodies linger in a state of inertia. Talk about the ration, about the Messiah, about the wagon in the sky standing there like a ghetto dignitary's *droshky*. But now the swollen legs have had enough. How many hours has it been since they last rested—sixteen, seventeen?

But before they leave, the bodies line up at the walls as if in a mysterious ritual, and they relieve themselves of all the waters they guzzled during the day: kitchen soups, cabbage, all sorts of vegetables. Puddles form in the night, and their stench bears witness to stomachs ruined on the ghetto diet; to bodies of sinful flesh which are unconscionably, inhumanly tried and maltreated; to weak, emaciated, but nonetheless stubborn bodies which seem to have sworn not to give in, not to fall apart, but to carry on, to survive.

And then blankets, pillows, quilts are brought from the dark rooms and spread on the ground—wherever there is an unoccupied spot—and the tired bodies are finally relieved to be prostrate.

The hours of the ghetto night drag on like lazy mice in an empty garbage pail. The stones in the ground press harder into the wasted bodies. Cold pierces the skin. The wait begins for the day to come and bring a warm sun, a soup from the workshop kitchen, and maybe even a brand-new ration—which will give them the strength to live through another day and another night and then through many more such summer nights.

JAKUB POZNANSKI, LODZ GHETTO DIARY

SEPTEMBER 27, 1943

There are constant rumors in the ghetto concerning the liquidation of ghettos in all kinds of towns in Poland. I think people are exaggerating, as usual. Even if there were such excesses, in certain towns, it's impossible to believe that a mass murder of Jews will take place.

I personally, at any rate, exclude the possibility.

POLISH DOCUMENT

[*From a situation report, October 1943, sent to the Polish government-in-exile by its representative in Poland*]

Jews. In the Lodz ghetto there are still some 70,000 Jews, mainly foreign. Mostly they work for the military. The liquidation of the Warsaw Ghetto created panic among them, but despite dire predictions, certain improvements in their situation have been noted. The rash of massacres has altogether stopped, people have been given more freedom of movement, and meals consisting of soup are now distributed in the factories.

SPEECH BY CHAIM RUMKOWSKI

17 OCTOBER 1943

"I WILL REMOVE THE TROUBLEMAKERS"

[*Addressing the pressers of the tailors' workshop, Rumkowski spoke of the need to resist agitation.*]

Friends, ghetto workers! I greet you who have appeared in such large numbers, demonstrating your sound instincts. I bear no grudge against those who haven't appeared because they weren't invited, or against ailing workers who, unfortunately, couldn't come, or even against those who let themselves be foolishly misled into not coming. Perhaps you're suspicious because I'm here alone, without your managers! I wish to speak to you alone, frankly and honestly, as is Rumkowski's way—to speak clearly, in the simple style that's customary here.

First, a preliminary remark: It's a principle of mine not to speak before a hungry audience—first a bite to eat, then the discussion. This time, however, it had to be the other way around. It's not my fault but the cauldron's. I can't, however, impose a penalty on a cauldron. The kitchen tells me that the food will be ready soon. We'll have a bite and then resume our meeting. Meanwhile, I'd like to make one thing clear. I am not, God forbid, your enemy, but your friend, and a friend must, above all, be understood, or at least trusted.

[At this point, there was a break for an unusually substantial meal. Rumkowski then continued.]

I know that the pressers do hard manual labor. But I also know that they're hard to deal with. Jews, in general, are a hard people to deal with, but pressers are the hardest of the hard. The pressers have always considered themselves the elite, as if they were the only craftsmen in their department. This was so in the past. Today it is no longer the case. In the past, I myself supervised the workshops and, if anything went wrong, well—after all, I'm a sly Jew—I simply turned a blind eye. Today the workshops are not supervised by me, but by a different agency. Every workshop has to turn in a production report. I am responsible only for seeing to it that production quotas are met.

The fact of the matter is, no one works ten hours a day anymore, but only eight. It was very hard to push this reform through. But I believe that I've thereby eased the lives of the ghetto's workers, thus fulfilling my duties and keeping my promise to the ghetto. Even any appearance of sabotage must be avoided, for I needn't elaborate on the consequences of such an accusation. You all know that in the Jewish quarter I am no liar or speechifier and so I tell you candidly: I will not permit even the slightest irregularity in the workshops that can be interpreted as sabotage. And in this matter I'll do anything I must do. Your so-called leaders, who make you believe that they're your friends, are in reality misleading you, and I will be forced to put them out of business. I am not a private entrepreneur intent on exploiting you. This is your enterprise as much as it is mine and that of all the ghetto's Jews, who want to live just as much as the pressers do. In order to sustain the ghetto and protect it from disaster, I will—let me say this openly—show no consideration for particular individuals or groups of workers! I will remove the troublemakers and agitators from the ghetto, not because I tremble for my life, but because I fear for you all. You have to be protected. As for me, my hair is white as snow, I walk with a stoop—my life is already behind me!

I appeal to you again, brothers! Look upon me not as an entrepreneur, but as a man who knows the particulars of the ghetto's life. I keep my finger on the ghetto's pulse at all times, and I will continue to do so. I have guaranteed with my life that the ghetto will work and that order will be maintained. I shall be forced to eliminate any individuals who stir up trouble. The purpose of our meeting today was for me to tell you this frankly. Further negotiations will not alter my resolve, and I have no time for frivolity or empty talk.

You are angry with me for doing away with the CP and B III coupons* and replacing them with special-nutrition meals. If you took a proper look at the facts of the matter, you'd certainly drop your objections. As workers performing heavy physical tasks, you were granted coupons. Now you receive the special-nutrition meals instead. Granted, these are meant only for yourselves, while the coupons could be used by your families as well. But the Jewish sense of community, the Jewish concern for your family is not applicable here. At stake is the collective fate, not the fates of individuals.

Let me give you an example. I gave a lot of thought to the hardships endured by those who had no teeth or very bad teeth, and I created a clinic for false teeth. Now I'm besieged by the entire ghetto; everyone needs dentures. But I don't have anything like the amount of material that would be needed. I have shown my good will often enough, but when something or other goes wrong, it is in fact your fault and not mine.

It is possible that I don't have the right people around me, but it's too late to do anything about that.

Another example, which just occurred before your very eyes. I received a written request from one of your group, then a second and a third. I read these on the spot and tried to deal with them. Suddenly, however, I was inundated with requests, making it impossible for me to deal with them. So I stuffed them in my pockets—for later attention. I will certainly do whatever I can, but I can't attend to everything and everyone.

Please understand this. I appeal to you as human beings and Jews! Please accept that you must show consideration for the ghetto as a whole and subordinate your personal interests to the collective interest. Do not force me to use methods I would rather not. We've already received enough blows, and the wounds have been slow in healing. I will therefore not permit those who are unqualified to interfere in the administration of workshops.

[At this point, several pressers gave voice to a number of complaints, including their view that the coupons were of greater value to them than the special-nutrition meals. Rumkowski then replied.]

Life in the ghetto is not easy. There will always be people who are dissatisfied and disappointed. Today you request special meals; tomorrow it will be the metal workers, carpenters, saddlers, and so on, making the same demand. My answer is to the point and not merely rhetoric.

In good times the coupon entitled you to 300 grams of meat; in times that weren't so good, to 200 grams of sausage. For three coupons you could, therefore, get 900 grams of meat or 600 grams of sausage a month. Today, in the special-nutrition kitchens, you get 100 grams of meat daily for two weeks—a total of 1400 grams of meat, and corresponding amounts of potatoes and grains. These figures tell the story. I'd be happy indeed if I could give equally generous meals to all the Jews in the ghetto.

I've conferred with medical experts, who say that the special-nutrition meal is indeed sufficient to provide workers with energy and to improve their health. The coupons, which you shared with your families, lasted for only a few days in any case, while now you go empty-handed for only 14 days a month. And as for the children, I always do my best to take care of them separately, as you yourselves well know. Four thousand children have been lodged in special hostels where they receive good soup twice a day.

I ask you to bear in mind that I am dependent on the unique circumstances of the ghetto, with which I am fully familiar. Once again: we will get nowhere with demagogic slogans. My actions are limited by the range of my options.

I will not introduce a system that grants exceptions to a specific group of workers. I can only promise you that I'll do everything within my power for the ghetto, just as I've always done. I also hope that it will be possible for me to provide the ghetto with coal, so that it doesn't freeze. I regret I cannot extend the special-nutrition meals from 14 to 28 days a month. When the overall situation improves, everyone will benefit, not just the pressers.

JAKUB POZNANSKI, LODZ GHETTO DIARY

NOVEMBER 9, 1943

Today marks the 25th anniversary of the German revolution, which ended the rule and license of Kaiser Wilhelm II. Could this day, possibly, bring some happy announcement to tortured humanity?

Yesterday, the factory managers were invited to our directors' office. Mr. Bajgelman, who attended the conference, gave a full account. The purpose was to inform those attending of the reasons for cancelling Allotment "B." Rumkowski said that he considers it appropriate to suspend the additional allowance because of the catastrophic shortage of food supplies, especially potatoes. The German authorities promised to supply potatoes in quantities which would cover weekly rations of 7 kilos for each ghetto inhabitant. Now the senior ghetto officials have been notified that this ration is to be cut in half. However, even this reduced allotment has, so far, been delivered in inadequate quantities. What's worse, 15% of the potatoes are unfit for consumption. Thus, there is no alternative but to cancel the supplement soups and with them Allotment "B"—"because of the mood of the workers." Altogether, about 800 families, 160 doctors, and 97 pharmacists have been granted this privilege.

The Chairman sighed heavily at this point, and a long silence ensued. After this "psychological pause," Rumkowski stated that as "head of the government" he had certain "discretionary" rights, on the basis of which he would keep the special allotments for 40 families. Therefore, he was asking those present to help him make an appropriate list of people.

A discussion followed the Chairman's speech—an event quite extraordinary in this fortunate circle! Bajgelman divided the group into two categories: the demagogues and those dealing with pure facts. Pathetically, the demagogues demanded abolishing all special privileges and distributing the food supplies equally among the entire ghetto population. The others proposed leaving Allotment "B" for a certain number of people, limiting it, however, according to the availability of supplies.

The next day, without delay, the Chairman's message was posted on building walls. Rumkowski most probably is trying to gain some cheap popularity by asserting that supply privileges are being abolished. Is it possible that this sly fox is all that naive?

Szczesliwy and Reingold, the two supply directors, notified the authorities

With a bayonet, a German guards a ghetto gate.

today that if no potato shipment is received this week, it will be necessary to open the reserves. There are over 2000 tons of potatoes and 500 tons of vegetables in those bins. Now that the food allotments are cut in half, the supply should last about 8 weeks.

NOVEMBER 26, 1943
Postcards from Jews from different cities in the Reich have recently arrived from Theresienstadt (in the vicinity of Prague). One could conclude from these cards that a type of Lodz Ghetto has been created there.

People are working in different shops. It's not known if they're fed better, but at least they can use the mail, which we cannot. It is really a most inhuman punishment. Unfortunately, however, we've gotten used to it. For the last two years, we've received no news from our loved ones.

IRENA LIEBMAN, LODZ GHETTO

A commission headed by the lawyer Neftalin came to our shop. The Germans want him to organize an office where hundreds of thousands of index cards would be filled out, for use in distributing coal to all the Poles and Germans [in the Wartheland]. All girls were invited to apply for the job. This time I did not hesitate for a moment.

There are some 30 of us young people working in the new office. The rest are 40 to 60 years old, remnants of the ghetto intelligentsia, mainly German and Czech. Most of them have higher education, and titles like doctor and professor resound in the gloomy corridors. We, the few younger workers, bear the brunt of the assignment. We organize the work, control the quality, correct mistakes. They sit in their coats and caps, with their gloves on, their bodies bent, their minds set on the bowl of soup and the slice of bread. They talk constantly about all the dishes they've ever had, and they fill out the cards without enthusiasm, at a snail's pace. We explain the same problem to them countless times, advise, cross out, correct. We try to find a way into their dazed brains, and get back the smallest amount of good will.

Here, then: each Pole with two pigs is entitled to this much coal. A German with two pigs gets more coal by a certain percentage. They make an effort to understand and remember. But how can you understand something as strange as a pig getting a coal ration. A pig is a pig. Her meat is red and juicy, and its place is in a boiling pot. Suddenly, a gorgeous, heavenly flavor rises from all these cards and papers, a vision of schnitzel, bacon, and a slice of bread with lots of pig fat.

There is among them a music professor who used to lecture in our school. We always listened intently to him, admiring the way he handled his subject, his ability to hold our attention, to fire us up. And now? Poor curled-up figure of a lonely old man with glassy eyes and shaking hands. He listens carefully to my instructions and strokes my hand. "Dear girl," he says, "could you ask them to give me some more soup?" I am deeply ashamed to see his drawn face and wretched gaze begging for help.

THE CHRONICLE OF THE LODZ GHETTO

TUESDAY DECEMBER 14, 1943

NEWS OF THE DAY

A day of extreme agitation in the ghetto. The ghetto has not known such a grave hour since the days of the curfew [*Gehsperre*] in September of last year. Toward 11:30 A.M., a rumor spread through the ghetto like wildfire: the Chairman had been taken to the city by members of the Secret State Police [Gestapo]. The incident occurred as follows. Toward 9:30 A.M., an automobile of the Secret State Police arrived at Balut Market from Poznan. Two men, one plainclothesman, the other in uniform, entered the Chairman's outer office and had themselves announced.

"Are you the Eldest of the Jews? . . . What is your name?"

The Chairman gave them his name, whereupon the men entered his office and said: "Let's talk in private." The two men who happened to be with the Chairman at the time, Mosze Karo and [Eliasz] Tabaksblat, immediately took their leave.

The meeting between the two officers and the Chairman lasted approximately two hours, with interruptions. The men also spent some time at the offices of the Ghetto Administration, and while they were gone Miss [Dora] Fuchs had to prepare certain statistical data. They also demanded population statistics from [Henryk] Neftalin, the attorney. Likewise, inquiries were made at the office of Kinstler ([Department of Food Supply,] Balut Market). At 11:30 A.M., the Chairman left the ghetto in the direction of the city with the two men from the Secret State Police.

At first the ghetto did not quite grasp the meaning of this episode. It was only when the Chairman had still not returned by 7 P.M. that the ghetto hearts began to pound. Groups formed everywhere; people clustered in the offices, heatedly discussing the events. The ghetto's chief officials gathered at Balut Market to wait for news. As always, the Chairman's *droshky* stood at Balut Market and remained there until late at night, but still there was no report. Many were convinced that the Chairman had been taken to Poznan.

When leaving Balut Market the Chairman just barely managed to say to Dr. [Wiktor] Miller, who happened to be present: "If anything happens, you should know that this concerns food supply problems, only supply problems." The Chairman was very composed. This incident, as everyone without exception realized, concerned the father of the ghetto. Fear was in everyone's bones, and never before had people felt so deeply the undeniable fact that "Rumkowski is the ghetto." Those who were particularly anxious foresaw disaster and said that the ghetto was in imminent danger. Hardly anyone slept peacefully tonight. People waited for the Chairman's return until 11 o'clock, but he did not appear. Further alarm was occasioned by the fact that the *Amtsleiter* was also summoned to the city and that there was no word from him either, even by late evening. Under the circumstances, it is assumed that the Chairman has indeed been taken to Poznan. All one can do is wait.

WEDNESDAY DECEMBER 15, 1943

NEWS OF THE DAY

The Chairman returned to the ghetto from Litzmannstadt last night at 10:30. He came to Balut Market by tram. The few people who learned of his arrival spread the news as fast as they could. In some buildings people ran from door to door, knocking and calling to the occupants: "The Chairman's back!" In the morning, when the whole ghetto knew that the Chairman had returned, everyone breathed a sigh of relief.

The Chairman was already at Balut Market by 7 A.M. [He was] clearly tired and weary—he had, after all, gone to the city [the day before] without breakfast and had not eaten anything until late in the evening. Most of all, he had missed his beloved cigarettes, for he is a heavy smoker. During the morning, friends and associates visited him at Balut Market to congratulate him on his return.

He refuses to discuss the purpose of the investigation. He only repeated his assurances that it had to do with food supply problems. He did relate a few details. When he was brought before the deputy chief of the [local] Secret State Police, the Chairman promptly identified himself as the Eldest of the Jews in Litzmannstadt. The official replied that since he had been brought in [for

"Rumkowski is the ghetto."

Rumkowski meets a commission from the German military command.

questioning], he did not have to identify himself as though he had come voluntarily. Rumkowski answered: "Well, since I *am* here, I have most obediently identified myself." With his characteristic resiliency he succeeded in improving the atmosphere by remarking in jest that this was his first day off from work in years. He was said to have been treated correctly; he was told that he bore full responsibility for everything that went on in the ghetto. Nothing more could be gotten out of the Chairman.

The ghetto has breathed a sigh of relief, particularly on account of the Chairman's reassuring statements. Whether he was simply putting minds at ease or further investigations are, in fact, to follow cannot be determined.

[The Chroniclers had no way of knowing why M. C. Rumkowski was suddenly summoned to the city, and Rumkowski was either himself unaware of the reason or preferred to keep it a secret, sharing it only with those closest to him. In fact, he was summoned in connection with the plans that the *SS-Ostindustrie GmbH (Osti)* had for the Lodz Ghetto. Whether Eichmann and Horn were present when Rumkowski was questioned is not known. However, together with Bradfisch, the mayor, and the chief of the Lodz Gestapo, they visited many workshops during the next two days, the 15th and 16th of December, with the ghetto's Department of Vital Statistics supplying them with information of every sort.]

J.B.A. [JERAKHMIL BRYMAN], "THE NATURE OF GHETTO PRAYER SERVICES"

Prayer services were maintained in the ghetto and adapted to its particular conditions and circumstances.

Minyans were in existence as soon as the ghetto was established. A whole series of small prayer rooms were added to those that had been in the Balut Market area from before the war. There were a few synagogues. The Bajka Cinema was transformed into a nice-looking one. The Star of David decorations there had special meaning, and around the prayer platform there was a Star of David outlined with electric lights. There were still some synagogues with women's balconies on Brzezinska, Zgierska and Mlynarska Streets. Services were held publicly and were led on *Shabbos* [Heb: the Sabbath] by a cantor. Rosh Hashana prayers in the Bajka synagogue were conducted with great pomp and even with representatives of the authorities present.

The situation changed after the children and old people were deported in 1942. On Rosh Hashana (one day after this deportation), all the *minyans* stopped functioning. Even behind closed doors, in the privacy of their homes, people were afraid to pray. Their fears that the sound of the *shofar* might be heard recalled a discussion in the Talmud about the individual [in hiding] who must blow the *shofar* in a well or wine barrel.

Only a few individuals got together to pray in an attic somewhere or on the fourth floor of some building. People would get up at dawn and, leaving out all the special liturgical poems, would blow the *shofar,* trembling in fear. In many *minyans,* the *shofar* was blown only once [instead of the 100 sounds usually mandatory on Rosh Hashana] and a blessing said. In some *minyans,* only those first *shofar* sounds were blown which precede the *Amida* [Heb: the silent prayer said standing] of the *Mussaf* [Heb: the special service said on the sabbath and holidays].

On Yom Kippur [eight days later], when the initial panic had subsided, a great many *minyans* met in the courtyards. In some of these, prayers began only with the memorial services for the dead.*

In the winter of 1942–43, when the work hours went from 7 a.m. to 5 p.m., the *minyans* became very small in size and number. At night it was easier to catch a *minyan,* because of the hundreds of *Kaddish* sayers interested in attending services. There were a lot of *minyans* on *Shabbos.* They were even held in many workshops.

For a long period of time, there was at 15 Stodolniana Street a *"Shomrim* [Heb: Watchmen's] *minyan,"* so called because its members were firemen, policemen, and others who didn't work the regular shift, as well as some young people who didn't work a full day. This *minyan* had the character of a society, with by-laws, meetings and even lectures on religious subjects, since many of its congregants were elderly Torah scholars. When the organizer of this *minyan* was arrested by the authorities, it was discontinued.

Rosh Hashana, 1943, occupies a special chapter in the history of the ghetto's religious Jews. Services were organized in almost all the workshops, and prayers were recited with great fervor and spontaneous outbursts of religious feeling.

That event, as well as Yom Kippur a week later, when prayer services were held in almost open fashion, contributed to the reopening of many houses of prayer. In the winter of 1943–44 a rumor spread that *minyans* were prohibited. Many stopped, although some changed their meeting places and continued.

The following are the various types of *minyans:*

1. Chassidic groups, such as the Aleksandrer Chassidim (Brzezinska Street), Gerer Chassidim (Podrzeczna Street and also on Zgierska Street), Kozhenitser Chassidim (Lagiewnicka Street), Chabad Chassidim (Mlynarska and other places), and Bratslaver Chassidim (Wolborska).*
2. Inter-party groups, such as the one on Pieprzowa.
3. Groups affiliated with political parties, such as Mizrachi (Limanowski Street), Agudath Israel (Brzezinska, Zydowska and Dolna Streets), Chashmonoim (Franciszkanska) and others.
4. At the homes of important personalities, such as rabbis and yeshiva teachers, and places where the *cheders* are located.
5. At the homes of mourners who are observing their year of mourning.
6. In the workshops, many of which regularly organize *minyans* on *Shabbos.*

These *minyans* have a deplorable appearance. There are few chairs and tables. Many prayer shawls lie about, those of people who have died or been deported. For a certain payment, they can be borrowed by those wishing to catch a quick *Kaddish.* There are many Torah scrolls, mostly from provincial synagogues that were vandalized. The books consist mostly of Psalms, prayer books, and volumes of Mishna. There are only a few copies of other works, such as commentaries or books of Jewish law.

It must be emphasized that, as much as possible, the managers of the above-mentioned workshops provide the *minyans* with assistance and supplies. Also, the Housing Department is careful not to assign a displaced family to an apartment occupied by a functioning *minyan.* Regarding supplies, there are silk robes hanging in some *minyans,* to be used by a prayer leader or by a learned man who comes in for *Shabbos* prayers on a break from work.

The so-called *cheders* are held in the houses of prayer. Young children sit around tables with a *rebbe* and learn. There is also a *Mishnayos* [a Mishna study group], and its teacher or leader receives a certain payment from the mourners.

The weekly congregants are mostly mourners observing their year of bereavement. On *Shabbos* and *Yom-tov* [Yid: holidays], there is a large crowd of congregants. Hardly anywhere is a women's section to be found. During memorial services, women who have gathered to say the prayer for the dead stand at the window or in the courtyard.

Rarely do you see a *yarmulke*. Almost everybody prays in their winter hat. Ritual sashes [worn usually by Chassidim around the waist] are also rare. There are many married men who pray without prayer shawls [which traditionally were not worn by single men]. But the prayer leader must wear a *gartel* and a *yarmulke*. The *gabaim* [Heb: sextons] conduct their responsibilities with a firm hand. Some of them do a pretty good business, charging people for going up to the prayer platform. The price is determined by the appearance and position of the mourner or the person who is observing *yartzeit* [Yid: the anniversary of a relative's death]. The minimum fee for being prayer leader for a day is 10 marks.

The *minyan* keeps a teacher or a *magid* [Heb: commentator] who gives lessons, delivers sermons from the platform, listens to everyone's worries and confidences of the heart, and says *Kaddish* for those who die without survivors. Sometimes he receives a little material reimbursement from a respectable congregant.

The holy books in the houses of prayer bear the following kinds of inscription: "In memory of——, son of——, who was taken from the ghetto on——. May G-d have mercy upon him wherever he may be." We found this on a holy book: "——who was taken with his whole family to an unknown place. May G-d send his holy assistance." And: "In memory of the terrible day that my son Hainik——was taken from the hospital. May G-d avenge his blood."

The *minyan*'s door serves as the only religious bulletin board and means of communication among the congregants. Some examples:

A. Attention: anyone needing a proper *Kaddish* to be recited every day during public prayers should contact——, address——.

B. Taking home holy books or prayer shawls, which were contributed and which belonged to people now deceased or deported, is strictly forbidden. It is in one's interest to heed this.

C. Because of the strictness of the prohibition against eating *chometz* [Heb: food not kosher for Passover], dishes can be made kosher for *Pesach,*

Yom Kippur, 1940. A prayer service in a ghetto courtyard.

free of charge, at——, from 5 o'clock after work until 10 o'clock at night.

D. Today, in honor of *Yom-tov,* baths will be available at very low prices at Wolborska Street, from four p.m.

There are also business announcements, including some about the sale of books and *mezuzahs* [Heb: the small piece of parchment inscribed with Scriptural quotations and affixed, in a container, to the door frame of a Jewish home], even one for a scribe. There are also announcements such as this one: "I write requests to the Chairman."

Psalms are of principal importance in the various ghetto prayers. Every day between *Mincha* [Heb: afternoon services] and *Maariv* [Heb: evening services], ten chapters of Psalms are said together aloud. At the end, Psalms 79 and 83 are said. According to informants, this follows a ruling by the Gerer Rebbe.

Every day, except *Shabbos* and *Yom-tov,* the prayer "*Avinu Malkenu*" [Heb: "Our Father, Our King] is said during *Shacharis* [Heb: morning services] and *Mincha.* Instead of "Inscribe us in the Book of Life," they say, "Remember us for the Book of Life," which is the version said during public fasts. The Bratslaver Chassidim say the Psalm: "May the L-rd Answer You in Your Day of Trouble," as well as a prayer attributed to Rabbi Nachman to be said in times of trouble. There are also those who say a special prayer authored by a resident of the ghetto.

Kaddish is the most important prayer today. Most congregants say *Kaddish,* and in many prayer rooms the text of the prayer is written on a board hanging on the wall. Little *Kaddish* tablets, with German, Latin, and Czech transliterations, are sold to deportees from other places. Many children, lined up in rows, come from their schools to say *Kaddish.*

During the memorial services for the dead, the courtyards where there are prayer rooms are crowded with women. Many women whose husbands or children were deported come and stand around grieving, not knowing what to do. When the rabbis are questioned on this matter, they answer vehemently that the women are not permitted to say *Kaddish* [since they may not assume that their relatives have died]. So, what do they do? They say the *"Av Harachamim"* [Heb: "Merciful Father"] prayer. In almost all *minyans,* a memorial prayer for the martyrs is said. In some *minyans,* the *"Mi Shebayrach,"* the special blessing for the leader of the community, is said for the Chairman.

In some *minyans* a little tablet with the *Gomel* blessing [Heb: special prayer said when one is saved from great danger] lies on the reader's stand. This blessing is said very often, almost at every second reading. Also said is the prayer for sick people who have recovered and, in most *minyans,* the blessing for those who have been released from imprisonment. In some places, people listen in silence when this is said; no one asks any questions but eyes glisten.

Various *Halachic* [Heb: religious law] questions come up regarding matters of prayer, because of the work schedule. For example, is one allowed to put on *tefillin* between sunset and the appearance of the stars? The answer is that during the *Mincha* service, the *Shema* and *Kaddish* are said, *tefillin* are donned and nothing more is said. On *Shabbos* during the summer, there are places where the Torah is read between six and seven in the evening. *Mussaf* and *Mincha* are said together.

Morning prayers are said by many observant people while on the way to work. Because of this, there is often no response to a "Good Morning," because the person is in the middle of a passage during which he is not permitted to speak.

In the church on Plac Koscielny, you can find a worker praying in his *tallis* and *tefillin* beneath a Christian religious painting or a cross. When I expressed my surprise, I was told that a rabbi had ordained that it was permitted to pray here but with closed eyes.

We could not be objective if we did not mention the religious Catholics of Jewish origin in the ghetto. For several years their leader, a one-time *Yeshiva* student and later a missionary, has had a little church where they have gathered every Sunday for prayers.

In the ghetto's final liquidation, 5,000 Jews a day were sent out.

CHAPTER NINE

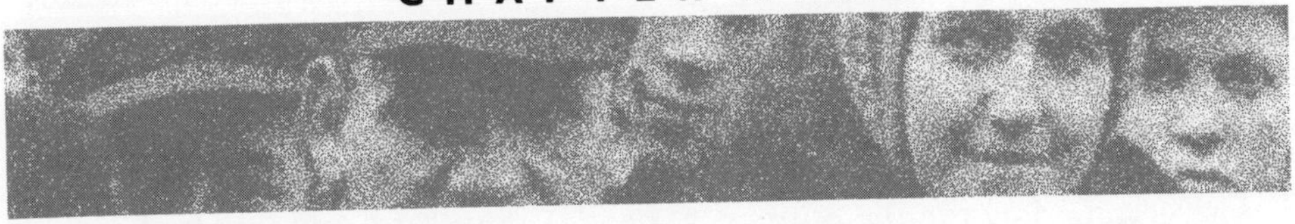

THE FINAL STAGE

1944

JAKUB POZNANSKI, LODZ GHETTO DIARY

FEBRUARY 3, 1944

There has been talk in the ghetto lately of a philanthropic institution being established in the United States for the purpose of rescuing the remnants of European Jewry. Supposedly, we are to receive food supplies and clothing from them. I'm curious when this help will arrive and who will distribute it. Most probably, not the present directors of our "ship of state."

FEBRUARY 11, 1944

From a camp in Poniatowa, near Lublin, 6 freight cars arrived with machine tooling equipment. An oppressive question arises: what happened to the Jews who worked in that camp?

SPEECH BY CHAIM RUMKOWSKI

13 FEBRUARY 1944

"MEN HAVE GONE INTO HIDING"

[At a gathering of factory and department heads, Rumkowski reported that although the Germans had demanded 1500 healthy men for labor outside the ghetto, the men had gone into hiding.]

Before getting down to the business at hand, I must say a few words about the critical issue of the day. I must ask you to understand my remarks correctly and to give an undistorted account of them to others. I find it very hard to speak on this subject.

The issue is the 1500 men who are to depart for labor outside the ghetto. The situation is that we have to hand over 1500 healthy men, and we are not allowed to touch the factory work force. This time, however, one can say with certainty that these men are in no danger. Well, the order *has* come, and the question is, who will carry it out, I—or another authority?

I have said that I'll need about 4600 people for new production projects, and that I'll have to draw them from the internal administration. But now I am losing 1500 men who were, so to speak, my labor reserve. When the day I need them comes, I don't quite know how I'll solve the problem. At the moment, however, that is not the issue.

I intended to carry out the entire operation very quietly. But this has not succeeded, because the men have gone into hiding. Now the fact is that when one is assigned to carry out an order, one must also bear the responsibility. If we do not produce these men, you know very well what may happen. This should be borne in mind by those who are helping others to hide. We're faced with the dangerous possibility that the authorities will demand the names of those who failed to obey the enlistment order. I've called off the arrests for tonight, and tomorrow I will have to report on the present situation. At the moment, I cannot predict what might happen to those who haven't reported.

I warn the factory managers: I'm aware that people are hiding in workshops. I cannot say who has acted more sensibly: those who have reported as ordered or those who have gone into hiding. But in any case, the authorities ask me, "What's the meaning of this? Why haven't these people responded to your order? We'll find ways of flushing them out!"

Of course, it's very fine that a family stints on provisions and soup in order to feed a son or husband in hiding. But such families are also in danger, and I must make this explicit, for—hard as it is for me—I have no choice. After all, I cannot endanger the entire ghetto for the sake of 1500 men. This is no time for mercy. And I must avoid creating a precedent. Tell this to your people!

Circumstances change in the ghetto every day, and we have to adjust to every new situation. The current problem is that there are too many people in the streets! That is the most serious problem of the day. Commissions can be expected at any time, and we will not always have enough prior notice. A commission might enter the ghetto without calling first at Balut Market. Therefore, I've decided on the following:

1. To begin with, distribution points will remain closed during working hours, that is, from 7 AM to 5 PM. The same will hold for the outpatient clinics and other institutions and offices dealing with the public.
2. The factories will remain hermetically sealed from 7 AM to 5 PM. No one will be permitted to leave his plant. All persons on a plant's official roster must in fact be there.
3. I regret that I, a 67-year-old-man, must give the ladies an order concerning cosmetics. But I exhort them: Get rid of your makeup, powder, and lipstick!
4. I order those working at home to remain there and work continuously under all circumstances. Loitering in the street, on whatever pretext, must stop.
5. I order a regular inspection of apartments. A campaign against the filth in apartments! I know how hard life is in the ghetto. The father works, and so do the mother and children, each in a different place, and it isn't easy to manage the housework under these circumstances. But it must be done.
6. From now on, no one will be able to leave his job site, factory, or office during working hours without a pass. Every manager will appoint someone to take responsibility for this, along with the gatekeeper, who is to let no one out. Passes will be administered in such a way that it will be easy to know to whom and how often a pass has been issued. Anyone found in the street will have to show his papers. Furthermore, the work card will indicate the worker's shift. If he works at night, there is no reason why he cannot be outdoors during the day.

During the recess I overheard some of the managers' conversations, and I think you completely misunderstand the situation. You greatly underestimate the problem. If a commission simply drops in on one of your factories and we haven't been able to notify you in time, then you won't know which way the wind is blowing. A random inspection can easily create an extremely dangerous situation. Not only those who are absent but also those in charge will be called to account. I'm resolved therefore that the measures I've announced here will be effective as of tomorrow, Monday. Furthermore, I order that a slate be displayed in each factory with the names of absent workers.

Now I invite you to ask me questions of a practical nature, to which I'll respond immediately and as fully as possible.

GHETTO DOCUMENTS

Read with Greatest Attention,

Announcement No. 410

about the DUTY TO GREET ALL UNIFORMED PERSONNEL AND [civilian] GERMAN OFFICIALS

By order of the authorities I draw attention FOR THE LAST TIME TO THE MOST RIGOROUS DUTY

to greet all uniformed personnel and German [civilian] officials.

Members of the Order Service and the Firefighters Brigade should salute by straightening the body; all others by straightening the body and taking off the hat.

While performing the duty of greeting, hands should be removed from the pockets, and cigarette taken from the mouth.

WOMEN GREET BY BOWING THEIR HEADS.

Most severe punishment will be meted out for disobeying this order.

Mordechai Chaim Rumkowski
Eldest of the Jews
Litzmannstadt-Ghetto, 16 February, 1944.

Announcement No. 414

WARNING

regarding sending workers
out of the ghetto

In view of the fact that despite my repeated warnings certain persons failed until now to report to the Central Prison, I demand FOR THE LAST TIME that they unconditionally

REPORT TO THE CENTRAL PRISON
IMMEDIATELY AFTER THEY HAVE READ THIS
ANNOUNCEMENT.

Those who still remain in hiding are sorely mistaken to think that when the transports with the workers are gone, all food ration cards will be reinstated.

THIS BELIEF IS TOTALLY FALSE

Even after the transports are gone, the persons in question as well as their families nevertheless will have to report to the Central Prison.

If they make an attempt to have their ration cards reinstated, they will be arrested, interned in the Central Prison, and interrogated as to:

Where they were hiding all this time,
Who assisted them, and
Who provided them with food.

So that the other persons will also be brought before justice. UNTIL THAT TIME no food ration cards will be reinstated.

Those who report to the Central Prison immediately, as well as their families, will not be subject to the above mentioned measures.

Mordechai Chaim Rumkowski
Eldest of the Jews   Litzmannstadt-Ghetto, 3 March 1944

SPEECH BY CHAIM RUMKOWSKI

15 MAY 1944

"I'M JUST A SERVANT OF THE AUTHORITIES"

[*The following account appeared in the Chronicle.*]

Metal Plant II has had another soup strike. As in the other workshops, it is primarily the juvenile workers, the adolescents not burdened by the problems of the ghetto, who strike when the soup doesn't suit them. Do they imagine that anyone else is satisfied with this soup? We have described this scene often enough: the Chairman appears, immediately induces the boys to accept their soup, and only a group of four rebels wishing to prove their heroism at any cost refuses to go along. The Chairman has to discipline them and sends them out to do demolition work. He addresses the boys in a calm, forbearing tone, saying:

"These soup strikes are senseless. I can't put any more into the soup than I have. Who is this demonstration against? Against me? I'm just a servant of the authorities. I have to bow my head and do as I'm told. No strike of yours can force me to make thicker soup, for I have nothing. Do you intend to strike against the [German] Ghetto Administration? Do you believe that they will be intimidated by you? The Jewish authorities are definitely doing all that can be done. I do what I can, wherever possible. I hope that the situation will improve in the near future."

JEWISH UNDERGROUND DOCUMENT

[*A report sent on 24 May 1944 by the Jewish National Committee, a clandestine leadership group in the Warsaw Ghetto, via the Polish underground, to Ignacy Schwartzbard* et al. *of the Polish National Council in London.*]

. . . And what is the present situation outside Warsaw? Lodz still remains the only "legal" Jewish center. In December 1943 and January 1944 tens of thousands were deported from there to their deaths. Most recently, several thousand were sent to the camps in Skarzysko, Kielce, and Czestochowa. At present there are still 80,000 Jews in Lodz. Polish Jews are only part of this population; significant numbers of Jews were brought there from all over Europe. The Lodz Ghetto is still hermetically sealed. Despite our many efforts to make contact with the Lodz Jews . . . we have failed to make our way into the ghetto. It is an island, totally cut off from the rest of the world.

All other cities in this country are already "Judenrein."

ALBERT SPEER, INFILTRATION

On October 22, 1943, the war diary of the Posen Armaments Inspection said: "Discussion by ghetto administration in Lodz and production manager in . . . Berlin on the monthly manufacture of 20 million steel cores for infantry munitions. There was also discussion of taking over the manufacture of 500,000 moldings for 2 cm explosive shells with tracer path. The Supreme Command is prepared to make the special machines available to the ghetto for manufacturing both items, in order to use the exceptionally large manpower there."

[At the end of October 1943, Government Director Weissker, representing the Supreme Directorate of the Wartheland, commented:] "Changes in the populace of the Lodz Ghetto are expected. However, the clearing of the ghetto seems momentarily to be postponed for the sake of armaments manufacturing. Government Director Weissker will put in a good word with the Gauleiter [Greiser] so that the Wehrmacht manufacturing in the ghetto will not be imperiled."

This remark shows that there was still a danger of implementation for the extermination goals that Himmler had announced 24 days earlier. One month later, . . . the situation got worse. . . . "The directive for clearing the Lodz Ghetto does not appear to be rescindable," goes the Armaments Commission's report of November 30, 1943. "The evacuation deadline is not yet set. New manufacturing orders are no longer being taken by the ghetto." However, the chairman of the Armaments Commission, who was in charge of the matter, parenthetically added: "A stoppage of Wehrmacht orders is not known. . . ."

He was right. . . . On December 10, 1943, the war diary of the Armaments Inspection . . . had the following entry: "Discussion with ghetto administration of Litzmannstadt about manufacturing pouches for infantry spades." On February 13, 1944, while visiting Posen, Himmler stated that production must continue. Greiser wrote to Pohl the next day: "The ghetto of Lodz will be reduced to a minimum population and will keep only the number of Jews that must absolutely be preserved for the sake of the armaments industry." He added, "The ghetto will not be transformed into a concentration camp." To be sure, Himmler's measure was only temporary, to protect armaments interests. Without giving a specific date, Himmler unswervingly stuck to the Final Solution, for Greiser's report continues: "After the removal of all Jews from the ghetto and the dissolution of the same, its entire property is to become the property of the city of Litzmannstadt." . . .

Himmler's . . . tolerance of important armaments manufacturing in Lodz lasted only four months. Then my Berlin Central Office of the Armaments Inspector was informed of the imminent evacuation of the Lodz Ghetto. Evidently it had thereupon issued orders which induced Gauleiter Greiser to inform Himmler on June 9, 1944:

"Reichsführer: The Armaments Inspection has undertaken considerable counterthrusts against your order to clear the ghetto in Litzmannstadt. In the night of June 5, Reich Minister Speer requested, through the officer on duty in the Armaments Inspection, the number of people employed in the various manufactures in the ghetto, their weekly work time, as well as the weekly output in the various branches of production, allegedly in order to present these figures to the Führer. Since I have finished the preparations for clearing the ghetto and have undertaken the first evacuations of the same, I duly inform you of this thrust to thwart your order. Heil Hitler. Greiser."

Himmler replied the next day: "Dear Greiser. Many thanks for your telegram of 6/9. I ask you to carry the matter out as before."

Greiser . . . knew that Germany was heading toward disaster. He was smart enough to see the advantages that our war effort had from the employment of the Jews. Even if the Lodz production was not considerable when compared with the overall capacity of the armaments industry, he must have realized that in our crisis, any fraction of production counted, especially since in this spring, it was still relatively safe from aerial attack in Poland. His telegram indicated that any demonstration of the considerable achievements of the Jews was undesirable, yet he had to warn Himmler that such reports were in the making. This points to a truly bizarre situation, utterly eccentric in its tragedy. Greiser's fanatical anti-Semitism, his hatred and his obedience outweighed any rational consideration. He accepted the execution of production together with the execution of the Jews.

On June 7, two days after this nocturnal call to the armaments inspector of Lodz, I had a long discussion with Hitler. Although the minutes do not mention the Lodz matter, there is reason to assume that I made Hitler aware of the production losses that could be expected. At any rate, Himmler's order was not carried out.

JAKUB POZNANSKI, LODZ GHETTO DIARY

MAY 12, 1944

For the last two days there has been postal service in the ghetto. We can write postcards to the Reich, Czechoslovakia, Moravia, and the General Government. We're also allowed to receive letters and packages from those places.

There are all kinds of rumors about why the German authorities reactivated the postal service after a two-year hiatus. Some refer to the International Red Cross. People will hear about their dear ones, and many family tragedies will now make themselves known. Many a Jew, fearing horrible news, will try to avoid receiving mail.

MAY 19, 1944
The letters, to be written in German, may be sent to relatives. One is not allowed to ask for packages or money. Letters to Warsaw, Vilna, and Lvov are not accepted, apparently because those cities are *Judenfrei* [Ger: free of Jews]: in other words, those ghettos no longer exist.

JUNE 6, 1944
The postal service has lately delivered a lot of mail sent in response to the postcards sent out from the ghetto. There are even food packages from Rumania, Czechoslovakia and even Portugal. However, the Special Unit removes all wrappers and does not disclose the names of senders.

Postal workers censoring letters written by ghetto dwellers.

JUNE 10, 1944

Lately, a lot of answers to postcards and packages from all over the world have come in. These packages are addressed and distributed to more and more people. Unfortunately, we're still waiting for news from Czestochowa and Radom.

JUNE 25, 1944

It turns out that Friday's transport was sent to Munich. According to some people, the German authorities did not mistreat the people removed from the ghetto. Each freight car had a big pot of hot coffee, and a floor covered with straw. Families were not allowed to be separated. Before the train left, some Gestapo officer made a speech in which he assured the Jews that they were being transported to Munich to clean up the rubble left after the bombing of the city, and that they would be treated well.

THE CHRONICLE OF THE LODZ GHETTO

SATURDAY, JUNE 24, 1944

NEWS OF THE DAY

A MINOR PANIC

The ghetto is agitated because the railroad cars that carried off yesterday's transport are already back at Radogoszcz station. People infer that the transport traveled only a short distance, and a wave of terror is spreading through the ghetto. People recall the frequent shuttle of transport cars and trains during the period of the great resettlements [of 1942] and the alarming rumors of that time.

Reportedly, a note was found in one freight car indicating that the train went only as far as Kutno [Kolo County, near Chelmno], where the travelers were transferred to passenger cars. This information has not been confirmed. No one has actually seen the note; so no conclusions can be drawn about the quick return of the cars. Perhaps further transportation is being staged in Kutno. It is hoped that we will soon learn what is happening with these people.

SUNDAY, JUNE 25, 1944

SKETCHES OF GHETTO LIFE: IN EARNEST

Reality has completely stemmed the tide of rumors. Ghetto dwellers are now being shipped out of the ghetto to perform manual labor. One transport has already gone off; the second will leave the ghetto tomorrow. Today is Sunday, June 25. A Sunday of sunshine and drifting clouds, of calm and storm and rain showers. The streets leading to Central Prison are unusually lively. People of various ages and of both sexes, as well as children and the aged, are hauling suitcases, knapsacks, and tightly packed bundles on their shoulders. Many valises bear German personal and place names. They belong to the Jews who were resettled to the Litzmannstadt Ghetto in the autumn of 1941 and have now received departure orders. There is also a good deal of colorful baggage to be seen: striped pillows and garish blankets—the bedding for future sleeping quarters.

People go their own way. Some pass by holding flowers, hedge blossoms and peonies, jasmine and other June flowers. People chat, stroll. The *dzialkas* [Pol: small gardens] are full of ghetto dwellers at work. Crowds throng outside the stores. Life as usual.

And yet there is a pall over the ghetto. Twenty-five transports have been announced. Everyone knows that the situation is serious, that the existence of the ghetto is in jeopardy. No one can deny that such fears are justified. The argument that not even "this resettlement" can imperil the survival of the ghetto now falls on deaf ears. For nearly every ghetto dweller is affected this time. Everyone is losing a relative, a friend, a roommate, a colleague.

And yet—Jewish faith in a justice that will ultimately triumph does not permit extreme pessimism. People try to console themselves, deceive themselves in some way. But nearly everyone says to himself, and to others:

"God only knows who will be better off: the person who stays here or the person who leaves!"

O[skar] R[osenfeld]

MONDAY, JUNE 26, 1944

NEWS OF THE DAY

LABOR OUTSIDE THE GHETTO

Today, Transport II, with 912 persons, left the ghetto (accompanying physician: Dr. Adolf Wittenberg, Berlin). The same train as last time was used under the same circumstances. Once again Gestapo commissioner [Günter] Fuchs said a few words. This transport included a large contingent of young people, several of them volunteers, leaving the ghetto in high spirits. On the other hand, there were also a great many feeble and sickly people. Reportedly, the next transport, which is to leave on Wednesday the 28th, will be smaller.

LISTS POSTED

In accordance with the instructions of the Inter-workshop Committee, which is already operating at full speed, the lists have been posted in all workshops. Inter-workshop Committee is being flooded with intercessions and petitions.

Anyone who plays even a minor role in the ghetto is now besieged by people hoping to pull strings. The workshop corridors are crowded with lines of workers trying to submit their petitions for exemption to the managers. There is a petition for every name on the list. Similar scenes are enacted in physician's offices. During consultation hours they are mobbed by patients who claim to be sicker than they are and by healthy people who want to be sick at any price. We observe only in passing that doctors are now raking in enormous sums.

Shady deals that involve human lives are negotiated behind the scenes, among the workshop managers. By the time the Inter-workshop Committee completes the clearing procedure, the managers have come to terms. You cross out my Jew and I'll cross out yours; if you list my Jew, then I'll list yours. Personal intrigues and vendettas are rampant.

It's a mystery how the workshops can still function. The streets are teeming with people looking for friends in high places.

Today, the Inter-workshop Committee issued orders to the workshops and departments; they concern mainly the regulation of quotas.

PEOPLE ARE SELLING THEMSELVES

Once again people are selling themselves—people who have either nothing to lose or who are reckless or desperate or believe that they are drawing accurate conclusions about the general situation are volunteering as substitutes. They sell themselves. This time the price is fairly uniform: a human being is worth three loaves of bread, a half-kilogram of margarine, one pound of sugar. Plus, perhaps, shoes and other items of clothing.

SKETCHES OF GHETTO LIFE: THE FINAL STAGE

Those about to depart bring their belongings to the purchasing agency in order to raise money for food for the journey: a few grams of sugar or bread or some kind of grain. On the basis of the appraisals, they receive a voucher made out for ghetto marks and Reich marks; the ghetto marks are paid out at the Main Treasury, the Reich marks, at Central Prison.

Thus do people bid farewell to the last of their goods and chattels. No tear is shed, no harsh word spoken. Fatalism prevails. People think: "It's the final stage. Now nothing more can be taken from us. We are as poor as when God created us. The clothes on our bodies and a few remaining necessities—

A last farewell.

this will suffice until *then.*" *Then* is the moment when fate chooses between life and death.

O[skar] R[osenfeld]

LES VRAIS RICHES

[*A young man's diary, written in four languages in the margins of a French novel entitled* The Truly Rich.]

5/5/1944 LITZMANNSTADT-GHETTO [WRITTEN IN ENGLISH]
I have decided to write a diary, though it is a little too late. To recapitulate past events is quite impossible so I'll begin with the present. This week I committed

an act which best illustrates the degree of "dehumanization" to which we have been reduced. I finished my loaf of bread in three days, that is to say, on Sunday, so I had to wait till next Saturday for a new one. I was terribly hungry, I had the prospect of living only on the workshop soups, which consist of three little potato pieces and two dkg. of flour. Monday morning I was lying quite dejectedly in my bed, and there was my darling sister's half loaf of bread "present" with me. To cut a long story short: I could not resist the temptation and ate it up totally. After having done this—at present a terrible crime—I was overcome by terrible remorse of conscience and by a still greater care for what my little one would eat the next 5 days.

I felt like a miserable helpless criminal, but I was delivered from the terrible situation by the reception of a B-Allotment. I suffer terribly, feigning that I don't know where the bread has gone and I have to tell people that it was stolen by a supposed reckless and pitiless thief. And to keep up appearance, I have to utter curses and condemnations on the imaginary thief. "I would hang him with my own hands if I come across him" and other angry phrases. Indeed, I am too nervous, too exhausted for literary exertions at the present moment. All I can say is that I shall always suffer on remembering this "noble" deed of mine. And that I shall always condemn myself for being able to become so unblushingly impudent—that I shall for evermore despise this part of "mankind" who could inflict such infernal woes on their "co"-human beings.

15/5/1944 [WRITTEN IN ENGLISH]

Many times I resolved, many times I began writing memoirs, diaries, but after a few entries I dropped it—it is the total lack of mental and physical energy which accounts for it. All I should like to have in life, at the present moment, is plenty to eat. I have been saying lately that the inhuman state of mind we are in may be best proved by the sad fact that a Ghettoman, when deprived of half a loaf of bread, suffers more terribly than if his own parents had died. Was ever a human being reduced to such tragic callowness, to such a state of mere beastly craving for food? Nay, it is only German artistry in sadism which enables this, which makes it possible. Nobody who didn't experience it will be able to believe it. I really feel too poor, too miserable even to attempt describing it.

In this infernal condition into which I am plunged I trouble my mind and cannot decide if—o fool that I am!—I should go to Palestine or remain where I am. I want to go, socialist cosmopolist, and yet I have many misgivings as to the best way of realizing the World United States. Dear old Hebrew and ancient Palestine have an irresistible fascination for me—although in my terrible wrath against nationalism caused by the barbaric German exaggeration—I rebuke myself as being a "particularist," a "parochialist"—but after all I scarcely believe that, let us say, the Poles would overnight forget their age-long hate toward the group of people named Jews because of the "sobriety" which should be brought about by recent history.

31/V/1944 [WRITTEN IN ENGLISH]
We are exasperated, despairing, dejected and losing hope. Our hunger grows stronger continually; our suffering is unimaginable, indescribable; to describe what we pass through is a task equal to that of drinking up the ocean or embracing the universe! The question arises if, after all that is now happening, any hope is left for humanity. I am still uncertain in my mind if in case of survival I shall go to Palestine, or remain here—how ridiculous—for to go, to do, to accomplish, one must live—and how can one be sure of life in L.G. when everyone is almost certain of his death?

6/6/1944 [D-DAY; WRITTEN IN ENGLISH]
Today the news of the . . . penetrated into the Ghetto. Who knows?

7/6/1944 [WRITTEN IN ENGLISH]
It is true, the fact has been accomplished, but will we survive? Is it possible to come out of such unimaginable depths, of such an unfathomable abyss?

We are quite at sea about what is taking place, only rumoring and canarding.

I am very hungry. I have to go 5 days without the bread ration because I finished what I usually do in 3 days. God be in our help.

12/6/1944 [WRITTEN IN YIDDISH]
I dream of being able to tell the world, as much as this is possible, of my suffering. In fact, I should call it our suffering. For never before was suffering so collectively shared as it is for us in the ghetto. After all this writing in many languages, I turn again to my own language, to Yiddish, to our graceful mother tongue, because only in Yiddish will I be able to express my true self, directly and without artificial embellishment. I'm ashamed to think how I've neglected Yiddish, because like it or not, it is my language, and the language of our fathers and grandfathers, mothers and grandmothers. So I shall love Yiddish, because it is mine.

16/6/1944 [WRITTEN IN POLISH]
We are suffering so much. The Eldest has been abused in a barbaric manner by Biebow, so that he had to be taken to the hospital. Again they are getting

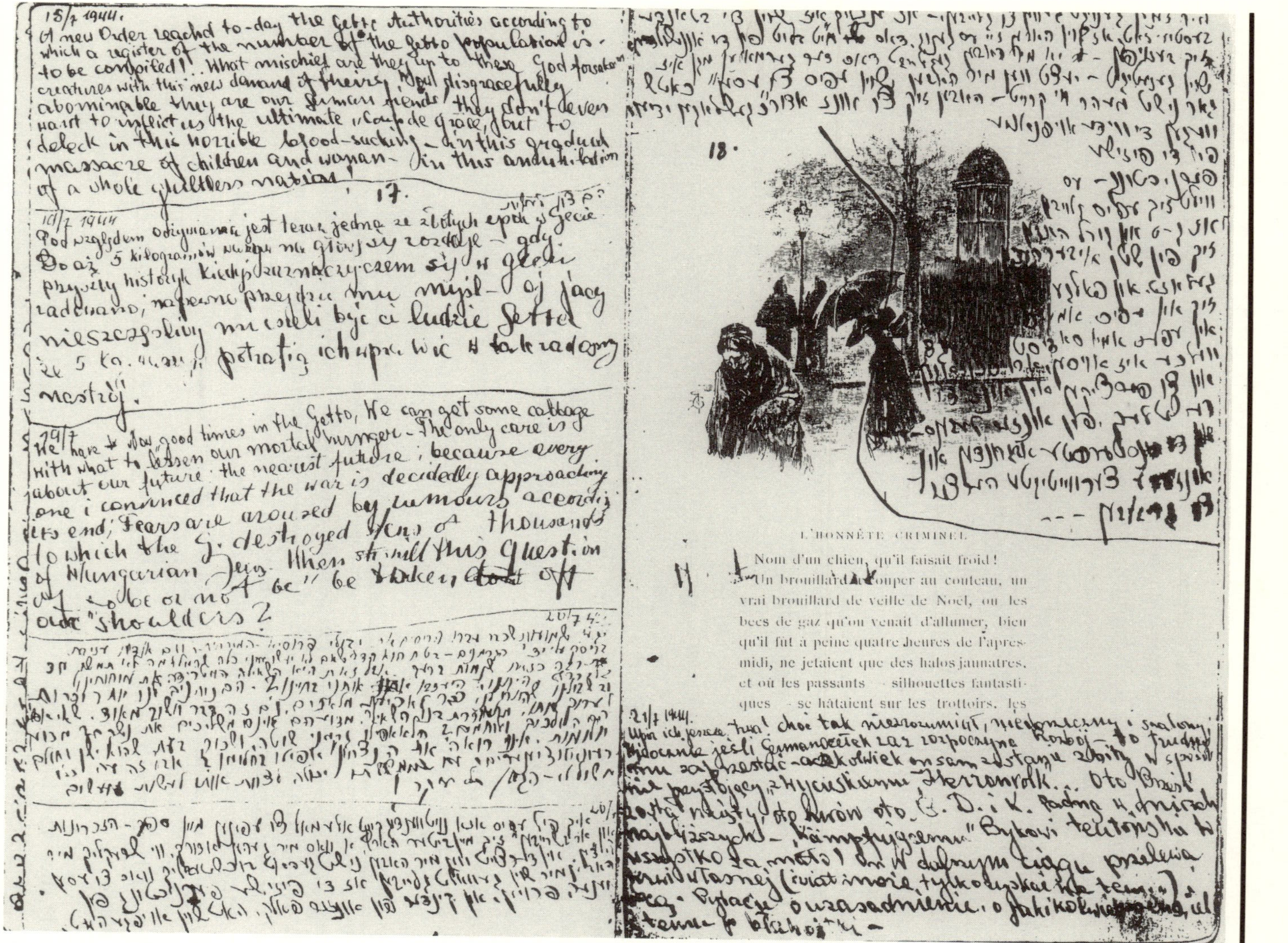

18/7 1944. A new Order reached to-day the Getto Authorities according to which a register of the number of the Getto population is to be compiled!! What mischief are they up to these God forsaken creatures with this new demand of theirs, How disgracefully abominable they are our German fiends they don't even want to inflict us the ultimate "coup de grace," but to delect in this horrible blood-sucking – in this gradual massacre of children and women – in this annihilation of a whole guiltless nation!

17.

19/7 We have now good times in the Getto, We can get some cabbage with what to lessen our mortal hunger – The only care is about our future: the nearest future; because every one i convinced that the war is decidedly approaching its end; Fears are aroused by rumours according to which the G. destroyed tens of thousands of Hungarian Jews. When still this question "to be or not to be" be taken off our shoulders?

18.

L'HONNÊTE CRIMINEL

Nom d'un chien, qu'il faisait froid! Un brouillard à couper au couteau, un vrai brouillard de veille de Noël, où les becs de gaz qu'on venait d'allumer, bien qu'il fût à peine quatre heures de l'après-midi, ne jetaient que des halos jaunâtres, et où les passants – silhouettes fantastiques – se hâtaient sur les trottoirs, les

Two pages from the unknown boy's diary, written in four languages in the margins and on the endpapers of a French novel. The volume was found at Auschwitz and is now in the Yad Vashem archives.

500 people ready to be sent out of the ghetto. Again uncertainty overtakes us. Oh! Was all our suffering in vain? If they annihilate us now in their usual manner, why didn't we die in the early days of the war?! My little sister complains that she has lost all will to live—how tragic this is! Why, she is only 12 years old. Will there be no end to our suffering? If so, how? Oh God, oh humanity, where are you?

16/6/1944 [WRITTEN IN ENGLISH]
Today was a sad day, for people once again lost their belief in any possibility of survival—on account of the barbarous hounding of the Eldest by Biebow, and also because of the new batch of 500 people to be sent away. We are so tired of "life." I was talking with my sister of twelve, and she told me, "I am very tired of this life; a quick death would be a relief for us." Oh world, world, what have these innocent children done to be treated like this? Really, humanity has not yet progressed very much from the cave of the wild beast!

18/6/1944 [WRITTEN IN ENGLISH]
Curse those who are able to cause such agony—as I suffer now—for their fellow creatures. I write and I don't know if tomorrow I shall be able to read this, because our disgustingly untiring oppressors "want" a thousand unhappy Ghettonians to be sent for "work." How one must understand "work" in its Teutonic interpretation we already know! Oh heaven! How much longer will this senseless cruelty be continued? What am I guilty or accused of? My little poor sister of 12! It is already more than 4 years since you've been toiling in the most unimaginable manner, since you've been working harder, suffering more than a Napoleonic soldier! Will all this horror, trouble, agony, tears and beastly fears have been in vain? Ah, if it is to turn out that way, why didn't we die 5 years ago?

18/6/1944 [WRITTEN IN ENGLISH]
Truly it is difficult to believe that we shall escape! Fiends like these relish annihilating their victims to the end! Why have we been born in this beastly generation? This most conscienceless generation of all?

19/6/1944 [WRITTEN IN YIDDISH]
We're now going through a hard time. Thousands are receiving notices about being sent away to do labor. People know how to read these and are frightened, but they console themselves that perhaps they really are being taken for work. They'd be happy if it's nothing other than work. And so they hope. Besides, everyone feels numb, since we are all so dead tired and exhausted.

25/6/1944 [WRITTEN IN ENGLISH]
Is any hope left for us? Thousands are once again being led away, resettled, and taken away from their ghetto "homes." Countless rumours are current: "They have not drunk their coffee"; "10 hours after they departed the train came back quite empty"; etc. etc. No living soul is able to imagine what terrible anguish all these rumours cause us. Can our enemies ever be surfeited? Are they *Nimmersatts* [Ger: gluttons] when it comes to the blood of their innocent Jewish victims? Even my sister of 12 must help herself with the fatalistic philosophy that "really life is not worth living," that "so or so [i.e., no matter what], one must die," and that "death will be our liberation" and "Father died by starvation, so why should we live?" Really if the world had a face, how it would blush that such philosophy is the only escape from its horrors, even by little children!

26/6/44 [WRITTEN IN HEBREW]
How horrible that a child of 12, my sister, has to judge life and death. I am writing in a terrible mental state. From the 25,000 remaining in the ghetto, 500 are expelled every day. We'd be happy if we knew they were being sent to work or to be slaves. Even though they promise that they're sending them to work, we hope they don't do with them what they've done with so many others. It's said that a train came back after 11 hours. Some say one thing, others another. Every day a few hundred leave the ghetto. The hunger is getting worse.

[WRITTEN IN ENGLISH] They are the torpedo with which the devil is torpedoing the ship of humanity.

27/6. [WRITTEN IN POLISH]
The situation is getting more and more critical. As I write these words, I do not know if I'll ever read them again. Will anyone ever read them? There were searches done at the Eldest's, at Jakubowicz's, Gierszowski's,* etc. Dawid Warszawski was arrested and taken away with his whole family. These are events which arouse certain ideas, events which—may my words not come true!—are very sinister and sad. I am incapable of describing my present emotional condition. I'm angry and extremely bitter about this eternal enemy of mankind, about the whole human race, my people, the world, the universe. That should cover it, I suppose. For I'm quite sure by now, alas, that humanity (as much of it, without exception, as I can see and also the rest of it) is an abject crowd of greedy beasts devoid of any pity or mercy. I firmly believe that man is only able to do good when he has plenty of the best the earth produces; only then, wanting to flatter himself, he wants to be thought of as good. When he is deprived,

when the wish to be considered good is forced into the background, man becomes more vicious and more abject than the lowest species of animal. Damned nationalism, at that point, is only a vent for man's hideous egoism and self-love.

What kind of world is this and what kind of people are these who are able to inflict such unbelievable and impossible suffering on living beings?

Our nearest ones have been murdered, some by starvation, some by deportations (modern civilian death). In a manner unheard of in history, we've been crippled physically, spiritually, emotionally—in our whole personality. We vegetate in the most horrible misery and need; we are slaves who, deprived of our own will, feel happy when we're being trodden upon, begging only that we not be trodden to death. I don't exaggerate: we are the most wretched beings the sun has ever seen—and all this is not enough for the "strong man": they continue deporting and tearing our hearts to pieces—while we'd be happy to live even as enslaved, wretched insects, as abject, creeping reptiles—only to live . . . live . . . Really, we merit all these surnames, because we ourselves do not end our shameful suffering but clutch desperately to this base existence on this wretched earth. Even a fatalistic philosophy does not help bring a single minute's peace of mind in the Litzmannstadt Ghetto. We're not human beings any more, nor have we become animals; we are just some strange psycho-physical product "made in Germany." Hasn't modern humanity definitely contradicted some original idea in the creation of the universe? What intelligence possessed of goodwill and foresight could create something so monstrous?

When I watch my little sister in her suffering, in her modest and heroic efforts; when I watch the struggle this 12-year-old orphan leads continuously, permanently—terror overcomes me that she too might be deported. . . . Woe is me . . . Then I feel my heart break into pieces and I wish that the sun were extinguished immediately and our earth thoroughly pulverized!

1/7/1944, 12 o'clock [WRITTEN IN POLISH]
I haven't had breakfast and don't want to live anymore; I don't have the guts to commit suicide, but if I could in some painless manner cease to exist, if I could do it—I surely would not hesitate.

1/7/1944, 12 at noon [WRITTEN IN ENGLISH]
I write these lines in the greatest disturbance of mind, because our fate has turned so decidedly bad. It is sure they will drive us from our wretched home, and even if they deal with us immediately in their "human" way, we are exposed to mortal danger because of our utter physical exhaustion, so that they in their "mercy" might "help" us to die.

Registers are being made without stop of those to be sent away; everybody is anxious to not find his name on the *Liste,* because this means expulsion, terrible *Strapazen* [Ger: fatiguing toil], etc. etc. (impossible to enumerate).

2/7/1944 [WRITTEN IN ENGLISH]
Time passes and our suffering seems never to end. The cursed devilish foe is further annihilating the last remnant of our unhappy nation. They are afraid of the approach of the Russian front and therefore they begin to resettle again. Spirits terribly low. God be in our mercy and destroy them who seem never to be satiated with human blood and tears.

3/7/1944 2 pm [WRITTEN IN POLISH]
The situation gets more and more uncertain. New lists are being compiled in all workshops. Again thousands of victims are being prepared. It seemed that a respite had occurred yesterday, but unfortunately it was only an illusion, and the preparations for the deportation continue without stop. Oh, how sad our situation is! I am so unhappy about my little sister, who has suffered so much—more than one of Napoleon's old soldiers! The child is utterly deprived—of a mother's warm heart, of clothing from a dress to stockings—to say nothing of her permanent hunger. She always has to make do with "Ersatz"—instead of shoes, some wooden contrivances; instead of stockings, some rags sewn together; instead of food, hunger; instead of a mother's love, the hard reality of lining up and learning ghetto cooking. Nor do I deny that I too have caused her quite a lot of suffering, because my nerves are in such extreme disarray! Oh God! Will all this be in vain, senseless, purposeless? How horrible, how heartbreaking! Oh God, how can you, how are you able to watch all this as if you were a neutral spectator?

3/7/1944 3 pm [WRITTEN IN POLISH]
I am sitting and dreaming—dreaming and floating in the clouds. I am overtaken by an indescribable longing for life, life as I conceive it, full of beautiful things, of intellectual interests, a passion for books, theater, movies, radio, oh! (it is not fair to sigh)—and yet I am trapped in such a swamp.

4/7/1944 [WRITTEN IN ENGLISH]
Insecurity increasing steadily because of the fresh demands for victims besides the 25 thousand. Another 3000 are needed. They seem to enjoy the fun, our hideous enemies; otherwise it is not to be understood how they are not satiated. Even German "thoroughness" could already have been surfeited. Curious if anybody could explain this madness of theirs. I just finished my breakfast

consisting of some ersatz coffee-cakes, a terrible meal even for insatiables as we are.

Politically there is rejoicing news, but who knows if we shall live long enough for this. I cannot but always repeat that my after all human heart is cut into pieces when I perceive how terribly my little one is tormented by literally everything—no stockings, no clothes wherewith to cover her nakedness, no food, no tenderness. Oh you poor orphan! And what you have to suffer by my unjust treatment, because of my shattered nerves! When I read about the suffering of young children before the war, I think how foolish people were to imagine suffering when there was none. God seems to have abandoned us totally and left us entirely to the mercy of the heartless fiends. Almighty God, how can you do this? How can you, in the face of such unheard of horrors (to speak with modern language) maintain such unhesitating neutrality?

4/7/1944 [WRITTEN IN ENGLISH]
When I write these lines I am quite certain that they will not allow us to stay. Who knows if all our plans were not in vain. I am already getting gradually accustomed to imminent death, or rather wanton assassination. I keep repeating the proverb: that when dead, one is equal to Napoleon—Alexander the Great—Caesar. A nice philosophy, is it not? But one cannot do otherwise in a world which is killing its sucklings!

5/7/1944 [WRITTEN IN HEBREW]
I write these lines in anxiety and grief—who knows what the next several days will bring us? Thousands have already been deported, tens of thousands more will be sent away. In our present situation, too exhausted for walking on our feet—in the strictest sense of the word—deportation is obviously a mortal danger for us, for even if they don't kill us outright, we will surely die from the hardships along the way, and from starvation.

5/7/1944 [WRITTEN IN HEBREW]
7 o'clock in the evening.

Our life is full of anxiety and fear. Rabbi Silman told me yesterday that when Dr. Ley* gave a speech that not a single Jew would remain alive if Germany is defeated, people instantly linked this threat with the deportations—though afterwards this was seen to be mistaken. Yet this doesn't help us, since we are in awful distress—epidemics and hard labor and hunger are destroying us, we who are the last remaining. This is the time of preparing lists, lists for deportation. Those who aren't friends of his are sent out; a nice girl whose laugh captures his heart escapes death. How terrible is man's tyranny over his neighbor.

6/7/1944 [WRITTEN IN HEBREW]
Impossible to measure our suffering at present; the terrible uncertainty shakes our bodies and spirits. The wicked madmen (were they not mad, they would not fight, kill innocent people), the accursed continue to do their job; the poor remnant continues to collapse. There is not one house untouched. One can say positively that there is not a single family left intact in the Jewish diaspora all over Europe.

7/7/1944 [WRITTEN IN HEBREW]
The thought of those 7000 Jews sent out of the ghetto in the last few days is killing me. I was sure that they would not dare at the very last minute, but who can fathom the depths of those knaves' minds (have they any minds at all?). There is joy because the *wysiedlenie* [Pol: resettlement] has stopped. There is joy because all ghetto inhabitants have received 1½ kg vegetables. If [the future historian] of the ghetto deliberates over what moved the ghetto inmates to feel happy, he will surely say: woe to them, to these human beings that such a thing moved them. Woe to them, to these people that this was their joy.

7/7/1944 [WRITTEN IN POLISH]
I'm filled with sorrow because of the absurd quarrel I had with my little sister. When I see how much pain is in her poor little face, I am overcome by a suffering beyond all imagination.

8/7/1944 [WRITTEN IN POLISH]
Everybody and everything makes one believe that this diabolic game is definitely coming to an end, for they're getting hit on their heads as never before. But this is of no help to us, since deportation lists continue to be compiled. Even if—in the best case—these deportations are for labor, there is the greatest threat to life, as I witnessed with my own eyes yesterday, when I saw a group of "volunteers" returning from labor, having been taken there some weeks ago. They made an awful impression on me. They were terribly tormented, swollen, and entirely exhausted—all this after only a few weeks of labor.

For some time, all distribution of rations has been stopped, which worries me enormously—because death from starvation, although "rational" (caused by eating only one's "rations"), is the worst kind, accompanied by the most horrible suffering, beyond imagining. We are now—how to put it—full of hope and despair, full of stoical resignation and, at the same time, full of trusting expectation. One thing is certain: we have stayed alive this far, to see the "black end" of our enemies, although there is still an extremely dangerous road to go before liberation.

9/7/1944 [WRITTEN IN HEBREW]
Now everything for us depends on the news which reaches us. It's said that they're leaving Warsaw, but it's hard to know how much truth is mixed with lies; we don't know what to believe and what not. Our food supplies get worse and worse. In the future, people will wonder how human beings could live on so little food. It's true, we are at last seeing their defeat, but our liberation, our salvation—not yet.

10/7/1944 [WRITTEN IN YIDDISH]
I am exhausted, I've lost all patience and my nerves are off. What I do have is an indescribable disgust with the world and people, with groups and individuals, with theories and dogmas. I do not believe, I do not believe in any change in the world, no! Anyone able to sink to the depths that contemporary man has can be nothing more than an unsuccessful experiment of Nature, which surely regrets it!

10/7/1944, evening [WRITTEN IN YIDDISH]
Tonight the Germanic lice with truly sadistic joy made sleep all but impossible. I remembered my friend Zikhronovitch [*zikhroynes* in Yiddish means "memoirs."] and here I am writing to him in my usual neurotic manner, on one foot.

There is news of a crushing defeat for our enemies, which seems to have finished them for good. No music for them this time. I've tried to figure out the Germans many times, to find an explanation, a logical reason why they continue this, the most senseless war of all times. Their madness defies all logic. Everyone who is normal or even half-normal can understand madness. But their sort of madness is so Germanic, Teutonic, Wotanic, Führerish—madness without goal or meaning, thoughtless, soulless, fed on a mystical faith in Führer and Fatherland—that now when his faith is a bit shattered, this German creature's mental decay has gone too far to let his ears listen to what is dawning somewhere in the dark depths of his bestial mind. Indeed, the puzzle of the suicidal German murderers will baffle generations of humanity, not counting the Germans themselves, for whom war and killing will forever remain their greatest pleasure. Their militarism will always be dear to them, and the will to die stupidly but heroically will stay with them forever!

The accursed Bolsheviks make bitter jokes, the impertinent Cossacks are tramping on holy German soil. Brest fell, Lvov fell—in a word, the horrible drama is coming rapidly to its end. The beast lies in an agony of despair, humanity and the world await its death—it won't be long now. And we are now facing the terrible question of our fate, of our survival. We know that every Jew yet living makes his heart heavier, that he still lusts for our blood. The men, women, children killed, executed, buried alive are still not enough for his insatiable murderous stomach. Now, in his final moments, he's got hold of Hungarian Jewry, solving the problem his way.

What then will happen to us?! Can he accept the thought of a few broken Jews—just skulls—still alive? Even though no longer much of a human, ravaged by tuberculosis, terribly crippled physically and mentally, one still wants to live, one yearns to be "present," so much so it is difficult to imagine. We all know that after death there is no revenge—and in all of us there burns such hate for the Germans, such yearning for revenge—that we must *live on!!!*

11/7/1944. [WRITTEN IN ENGLISH]
It is 3 o'clock AM. I am nearly devoured by "my" (the only property allowed Jews under Ger. "law") bugs. They obviously have also undertaken an invasion: they besiege, destroy, occupy, penetrate into the most hidden places of my body and nerves. They resemble awfully their Berlin brethren, who are even more lacking in sense than my bedbugs. I curse them both, the first I want to have sent to Verkhoyansk or Yakutsk [in Siberia], the latter to Hamburg—but it is worth nothing: they don't obey.

11/7/1944 [WRITTEN IN HEBREW]
Today, early in the morning, I had one more of those many adventures I've already gone through. The cruel, evil Kripo arrived with a lot of noise and threats in every direction. Right away they "examined" Rabbi Silman who was in the middle of prayer. He instantly knew with whom he had the honor, and bowed to them very carefully. They asked him if his little son wore a *tallis-katan* [Heb: ritual fringes]. He answered that, to the best of his knowledge, the little boy would not commit such a sin, and scolded him (oh, what a bitter irony of fate!) to take the dishonorable thing off immediately. They asked him if the numerous books in the house were his property, and he answered that his apartment previously served as a place for prayer and the books have remained and are only a burden and a nuisance for him. Woe to us that our souls have weakened to such a degree, and that our human dignity has fallen so low.

11/7. [WRITTEN IN ENGLISH]
We suffer terribly as usual. This morning we had a visit of the so-called "Kripo" (criminal police), the most brutal beasts humanity has ever seen. They came to

look for "their" jewels; they made noise, beat, threatened. An old man was seriously wounded by the "gentlemen." He was told to depart by way of the window (a German invention). We all felt we were looking into the proverbial eyes of death. The friends stayed more than an hour; they robbed some trifles and went away.

11/7/1944 [WRITTEN IN ENGLISH]
Litzmannstadt-Ghetto, 10 o'clock in the evening

I could not resist the temptation of reading my little sister's introduction to her diary. It touched the deepest chords of my soul. I wondered how it was possible that such a mere child could write so philosophically and wisely about her suffering. It runs as follows:

[WRITTEN IN POLISH]

> "Many times I intended to begin to write memoirs, but certain circumstances kept me from this activity which lightens the burden on one's soul. Dear days of my childhood—now, I only dream of you. You were so short-lived, since happiness on earth is short! To begin with those days when defeat and suffering were unknown to me, I must go far back in my memory, because the present moment is entirely devoid of what was so abundant in the days of my childhood."

12/7/1944 [WRITTEN IN HEBREW]
I long for a Jewish life in a Jewish state. I think that if the Jewish people had had no history but that of the last five years, it would be enough to justify a special entity, one which would not be mixed, since I doubt that even Jews will be able to understand all that has happened to us, let alone other nations. The hunt for our brethren grows stronger and stronger.

[WRITTEN IN YIDDISH]
If being Jewish is so strong, so "personal" and specific, if its difference from everyone else is so special, enough to provoke so much hate, hostility, sympathy, antipathy, then it must be a strong power *an und für sich* [in and of itself].

12/7/1944 [WRITTEN IN YIDDISH]
One wants to shout to God, to humanity: Woe, woe! What's going on here? After all, we are all human beings. How is it possible to torture living people so much? What philosophy, religion, theory can explain this? Oh God Almighty, once and for all destroy the world whose principal creature, man, performs

sadistic vivisections on his fellow humans, which have become his main pleasure! Oh God! Take back the oath you swore: No other flood on the beautiful world with its ugly creatures!!! Oh, God, leave no more Noahs behind; Noah's children have become devils, Noah's children have made this war! A deluge is necessary, but no Noahs; destruction must be thorough, precise, and total.

12/7/1944 [WRITTEN IN ENGLISH]
I have been in my only recreation place in the ghetto, the old-books shop. A woman came in to buy a buckle for her rucksack, which she was preparing for her exile. She was displeased with the pattern she was shown by the seller and went away without concluding the purchase. Then the merchant uttered a few words which made me shiver and shudder all over: "She will not have to carry her rucksack very long, because those who go to heaven have no need for such." To say that is unimaginable, undescribable, unspeakable, un . . . un . . . un . . . etc., etc. is to have said nothing. Such a terrible barrage on the poor walls of the human heart can only be experienced in modern ghettos. (There is no proper plural indicated in non-Hitlerite grammars.) I remember my dying father uttered in a scarcely audible voice, "Oh! How is it possible to torment living creatures in such a way? Oh! Woe to us!" Now I also agonizingly repeat it. Oh! Is it possible to be so tormented? How is it possible to suffer this?

If a Ghettonian should get power over the universe, he undoubtedly would not hesitate for a moment and would have it destroyed, and indeed he would have done the only right thing.

15/7/1944 [WRITTEN IN POLISH]
I am writing these words at ten o'clock in the morning. Everywhere, only moaning and sighing is heard from the tormented, tortured, starving—and all the same, nobody commits suicide, nobody decides to put an end to this inhuman suffering with his own hands.

Good news arrives. I have said that we already have managed to live long enough for their defeat, although not yet for our liberation. Future generations will deliberate over that peculiar creature, deprived of any sense, the German!

15/7/44 [WRITTEN IN HEBREW]
There is word that the deportations have stopped. Everyone is overcome with joy. People kiss one other. Jews drink in their imaginations, having nothing to drink in reality. It's hard to believe these rumors, we've been disappointed so many times.

16/7/1944 [WRITTEN IN HEBREW]
The deportation has stopped. Rumors have reached the ghetto that the Jews of Hungary, numbering 400,000, were brought to Poland and annihilated. Woe to us, impossible to describe the feelings which arise in us when we hear this news.

16/7/1944 [WRITTEN IN ENGLISH]
It is almost certain that those 7000 of our brethren deported in the last month have also been "treated" in the "well-known way" . . . A letter was found in a wagon being cleaned in the ghetto after its trip, a letter whose contents made us shudder. It stated that the deported were approaching Kolo, the place of the abattoir for the Jews.

18/7/1944 [WRITTEN IN POLISH]
What do these disgusting men want from us? Why didn't they kill us on the first day of the war? Why don't they grant us, at least now, the *coup de grâce?* How can they find so much delight in murdering innocent people? Can the Germanthropoid really find no other pleasures than nonsensical killing? They have again ordered that a list be compiled of inhabitants. What are they aiming at? Whom would they murder [when there are no more Jews]? Probably their own children! It would do the world only good. The German brat is a warrior and murderer.

19/7/1944 [WRITTEN IN POLISH]
Regarding the food supply, this is one of the golden periods in the ghetto. We are getting as much as 5 kg of vegetables per person. When the future historian notes what the food in the ghetto was, he will certainly think: Oh, how wretched they were, if 5 kg of vegetables could stir them to such a joy.

20/7/1944 [WRITTEN IN YIDDISH]
I feel such a need to open my memory book at every moment and to lighten my bitter heart by writing. We were inclined to believe that, at last, the blond beast was sated, that he had had enough to drink of the blood of the innocent—yes, we believed that the German stomach was now satiated. But now, when we finally have something to eat, even though it is nothing more than cabbage, news has reached us that physical annihilation has resumed. One is inclined to believe that God and fate have let themselves be persuaded by Satan—and have given themselves up to the pleasure of some kind of hunt, a sort of sadistic

pursuit whose aim is to drive out of us and stifle within us what remains of our will to live, and to dig into the deepest abysses of our tortured hearts.

21/7/1944 [WRITTEN IN POLISH]
Nobody is able, like the Germanohyena, to suck blood with such delight, with such conviction. I think that these . . . how am I to find a fitting term?—handled those 7000 wretched Jews in the same way, expelling them in a cowardly way from Lodz (sorry, Litzmannstadt). At the present, mixed feelings possess us; at one moment we are full of hope, in another we are seized by that so well-founded resignation, to the point of feeling choked. Because, can one suppose that they would let us live? After all, these gentlemen were not ashamed of murdering hundreds of thousands of children in a manner unknown to humanity; they destroyed half our nation under their grip. All the same, it is difficult to foresee what the next days have in store for us! And the mortally wounded hyena is able to feel its head reeling: it will want to [continue killing] but will not be able to—it will be forced to deal with its own agony!

21/7/1944 [WRITTEN IN POLISH]
Half an hour later the news came about the coup against Hitler. It's said that it succeeded only partially. According to the German newspaper: only injured. At the present moment, I am unable to fully grasp the importance of this major event; I only regret—along with all of humanity—that he is still alive. However, it grows clear that they are becoming fed up, that they have had enough of it, that they are surfeited with the *stolze Trauer* [Ger: proud suffering] and the "pleasure" of sacrificing their lives to the Führer.

22/7/1944 [WRITTEN IN POLISH]
Unfortunately, it is not yet certain what happened to him, Enemy of Mankind Number One. Rumor has it that he is severely wounded. What satanic power guards him, takes care of him? Yesterday, I had a sad and yet joyful day: sad because if he had been killed it would have meant the end of the war, since clearly he is the "life" of the war and of all these horrors as a whole. I was glad too, as these are obviously signs of what must occur in the very near future, what not even the murderous determination of the Führer will be able to prevent. Something has gone wrong in the satanic kingdom; it begins to seethe and must inevitably explode! If the world had consented to subjugation and then assassination, so be it. But the unruly world was not obedient: it took up arms and now threatens the "*Vaterland*" in an *unerhörte Weise* [Ger: unheard-of way], so that even the dull-witted Hitlerite generals have had enough.

That is why we are so glad—perhaps too early—because we know perfectly well that he and we—well, it's best not to get too far ahead in our thoughts—There's a joke that Adolf Hitler swore to his mother that he'd annihilate the German people down to the very last person, but in a different, more dignified manner than the Jewish people. Otherwise, really, one can hardly explain why they don't stop and capitulate. No mysticism, no *Führung* [Ger: leadership] will rescue them; events are against them and stick their tongue out at *Führer und Vaterland,* so that they're left with no way out but unconditional surrender—if they have the least bit of common sense left in their *nordische Schädel* [Ger: Nordic skull]! What will be with us? Won't this madman decide to do us wrong before power definitely falls from his hands? Who can tell? In any case, it is very easy to guess that our changes have improved considerably. As soon as this satanic madman disappears, nothing further will threaten our lives. There won't be another Führer, even if any of his favorites take over. "Heil Goering" or "Heil Himmler" doesn't have the proper ring. So, we've lived to see their twilight; now we need only survive till our new dawn and all of humanity's!!!

23/7/1944 [WRITTEN IN YIDDISH]
In a conversation with Rabbi Silman we recalled certain details of the *Szperre.* I remembered how terrible it was when the murderers came to our homes and how, inhumanly terrified, we tried to find hiding places! No, I am unable to write any further—because this belongs to the indescribable!

23/7/44 [WRITTEN IN HEBREW]
There are rumors that make us happy and encourage us. General Keitel, head of the general staff, resigned. The Russians are approaching Warsaw. The opposition inside Germany is growing in strength and numbers. There are many towns where the Gestapo is no longer in control. There are rumors that are difficult to believe. The war is at an end. I talked with Rabbi Silman about liberation. I tremble when I remember how my little sister and I tried to hide from the beasts, and my old father was overcome by an inhuman fear. Who will avenge us?

25/7/44 [WRITTEN IN HEBREW]
Two hours past midnight.

I can't sleep because of the bedbugs and my own agitation. For five years I kept my patience, and now it's suddenly gone. One can feel the coming liberation in the air. The Russians have captured Lublin. In Germany there was an attempt on Hitler's life. They want to end a war they definitely oppose. Even in their view, the war is no longer a thing of pleasure. The end is knocking on our doors. Another moment and, if they let us alone, we'll be free. Just the idea makes me cry. It seems they will let us go before the liberation. Hitler's power has weakened. The opposition within Germany keeps growing. The whole awful world can no longer see the point. Though the war is coming to an end, people are still being killed. One does not believe they'll harm us, yet we're still fearful. Who knows what will enter their minds? We're full of hope and impatience.

?/7/1944 [WRITTEN IN POLISH]
On the whole the present day has brought us nothing particular. Thank God for this, since we only gain time. There are rumors going around—one more fantastic than the other. For example, Warsaw is under artillery fire; Gora Kalwaria, Radzymin, and Garwolin are taken. But I don't believe these. Maybe they'll come true in a few days. Allegedly, before they left Vilna, the crazy Germans perpetrated another of their "choice" slaughters of the civilian population. This is how far this German beast goes and how short-sighted he is. In the last days I've entirely lost the patience I'd maintained during the whole of the war. I want so much to be on the other side of the barrier that I get sick at the thought. As to the food supply, the situation in the ghetto is not bad now: we get enough cabbage, which seems like extremely good luck to us, whose desires are so reduced. Impossible to tell what the next days will bring us, but one feels that they'll present events of decisive importance. We assume more than ever that they'll let us remain alive—but every one of us knows that one cannot be sure, for one can scarcely expect logic from beasts of prey. Can one negotiate with a tiger? My days pass in utter tension and excitement. Everybody tries to guess the future and—even if only in imagination—find a solution to our insoluble situation. There are rumors about a speedy departure by the *Reichsdeutsche* from Litzmannstadt. May the next hours bring us liberation from our inhuman bondage!

28/7/1944 [WRITTEN IN POLISH]
Can anyone imagine a convict in his gruesome cell hearing quite clearly the blows of a hammer on his prison walls? We are now able to hear these blows. Every night there are air raid sirens. No wonder, they themselves admit that the fighting is taking place in *Ost-Warschau* [Ger: East Warsaw]. What magic words!

?/7/1944 [WRITTEN IN ENGLISH]
Litzmannstadt-Ghetto (once Lodz)

I am in a state of terrible excitement mixed with disbelief and fear. Who of us subjected to such suffering could believe that we should get out, that we should be among those who survive! Oh! If I were a poet, I should say that my heart is like the stormy ocean, my brains a bursting volcano, my soul like . . . Forgiveness, I am no poet. Imagine a Jew of Litzmannstadt-Ghetto not wholly deprived of imagination when he is told the few magic words of the O.K.W. [*Oberkommando der Wehrmacht,* the Supreme Army Command] which run as follows: "*Am Rande der Stadt Warschau (!!!) kam es zu erbittern Kämpfen* [Ger: Bitter fighting has reached the borders of Warsaw]." At last it is not in Asia, not in Africa . . . but in Europe, in Poland, in Warschau [Warsaw] . . . If we lived this long, perhaps we shall live until the moment of our dreams. If we live to see our capital taken, it is nearly certain that we'll also see Litzmannstadt delivered. Meanwhile, I am like a lunatic, feverish with impatient expectation, full of hope and fear, I should like to become a few weeks older and still be alive!

29/7/1944 [WRITTEN IN HEBREW]
Litzmannstadt-Ghetto

How well I now understand the [Hebrew] words "From the abyss I called thee" [Psalm 130]. In our poverty and degradation we cannot believe; till the very last moment we will not believe that this really is coming true and we are still living. Can anyone imagine the feelings of a ghetto Jew hearing about the capture of Warsaw? I tremble all over. We are seeing the realization of our dreams. If only the wicked do not do anything to us . . . But I suppose that they have worries now of their own, to the extent that they won't be able to carry out what they intended to do to us.

I joked with Mr. B. that I don't know what "transgressions," what "sins" helped us survive, to be passed over. Because all the honest, innocent, righteous people are gone, all of them—my honest, warm, wise father, a real man.

People say that if we survive, the Jews must settle only in Palestine. Beyond any doubt, the nations of the world which give us their condolences and encourage us to our faces, will forget what was done to us—and there may even be some of them who will be pleased. This "do not forget," we can find full solace only in a Hebrew state. Because all our words, every utterance out of our mouths will be devoted to our suffering, to the pain of European Jews under Hitler's rule. Others, outsiders will not be interested in these problems; they will each turn to their own business and think about their own losses.

31/7/1944 [WRITTEN IN HEBREW]
If we come through this and are still alive, and no longer have to worry only about how to fill our stomachs, then surely the memory of our holy martyrs

will be foremost in our minds: those pure people, the many heroes who died a guiltless martyr's death. We will remember our fathers, relatives, acquaintances who were murdered, starved to death, made to suffer beyond imagining. We will remember those who were buried and burnt alive. We will remember our brethren who were cut into pieces, hanged, roasted, crucified, thrown into water. The Jewish people will remember its heroes, its martyrs who suffered as never have any living creatures on earth. Our only fear now is that they may do with us what they usually do. Because every Jew is a yoke and a burden on their defiled hearts, since they know the joy with which we'd celebrate our second Purim. But maybe they'll be forced to leave our city in panic and confusion, and therefore be unable to do us harm. Yes! These are great and awesome days we pass through now—days in which the wicked are being destroyed, days of ruin, shame, and defeat for the enemy of humanity.

Even though I write poor and dubious Hebrew, I cannot but write in this language because Hebrew is the language of the future, and because in Hebrew we will be proud Jews in *Eretz Israel.*

3/8/1944 [WRITTEN IN ENGLISH]

I write these lines in a terrible state of mind. All of us have to leave Litzmannstadt-Ghetto within a few days. When I first heard this, I was sure that it meant the end of our unheard-of martyrdom equatanously [simultaneously] with our lives, for we were sure that we should be *vernichtet* [Ger: destroyed] in the well-known way of theirs. What for to have suffered 5 years of *Ausrottungkampf* [Ger: annihilation war]? Couldn't they give us the *coup de grâce* at the very beginning? But evidently pressure on the part of the victorious allies must have had some effect on the brigands and they became more lenient. And Biebow, the German Ghetto-Chief gave a speech to the Jews, the essence of which was that this time they should not be afraid of being dealt with in the same way all the other deported have been—because of a change in war conditions, "*und damit [das] Grossdeutsche Reich den Krieg gewinnt, hat unser Führer befohlen, jede Arbeitshand auszunützen* [Ger: and the Führer has ordered that every worker is to be used in the war effort]." Evidently, the only right which entitles us to live under the same sky with Germans, though to live as the lowest slaves, is the privilege of working for their victory, working much and eating nothing! Really, they are even more abominable in their diabolic cruelty than any human mind could follow. He further said, "*Wenn Zwang angewendet werden muss, dann überlebt niemand!* [Ger: If compulsion has to be used, no one will live!]" He asked the crowd if they are ready to work faithfully for the Reich and everyone answered, *"Jawohl"* [Ger: Yes, indeed]. I thought about the abjectedness of such a situation. What sort of people are the Germans that they managed to transform us into such low, crawling creatures who say *"Jawohl"*? Is life really worth it? Isn't it better not to live in a world where there are 80 millions of Germans? Is it not a shame to be a man on the same earth as the German? Oh! Shabby miserable human, your meanness will always surpass your importance!

When I look at my little sister, my heart is melting. Hasn't the child suffered her part? She who fought so heroically the last five years? When I look on our cozy little room, tidied up by the young intelligent poor being, I am getting saddened by the thought that soon she and I will have to leave our last particle of home. When I come across trifling objects which had a narrow escape all the time, I am sad at the thought of parting with them, for they, the companions of our misery, became dear to me.

Now that we have to leave our homes, what will they do with our sick? With our old? With our young? Oh God in heaven, why didst thou create Germans to destroy humanity? I don't even know if I shall be allowed to be together with my sister! I cannot write more, I am terribly resigned and black-spirited!

[NO DATE, WRITTEN IN HEBREW]
My God, why do you let them say that you are neutral? Why do you not punish, with all your anger, those who are destroying us? Are we the sinners and they the righteous? Is it so? Is this the truth? Surely you are intelligent enough to understand that we are not the sinners and they the Messiah!

20/8/1944 [WRITTEN IN HEBREW]
Days come and go. There are rumors that we won't have much longer to wait. The Germans admit they've retreated from Lublin, Bialystok, Brisk [Brest Litovsk], Dinanburg and other places. But for the stubbornness of their leader, it would all be over. I worry terribly, because despite everything the situation is still unclear. Who can predict our future? Maybe they won't kill us. How I would like the privilege of going to *Eretz Israel.* There are no Jews in the Diaspora. Who can console us in our grief—Poles, Hungarians, Rumanians? Only a Jewish heart can feel the depth of our pain. If God helps us, we will live and console ourselves.

[NO DATE, WRITTEN IN YIDDISH]
It is now five full years that we have been tortured in the most terrible way. Describing all our pain is as possible as drinking all the ocean's water or lifting the earth. I don't know if we'll ever be believed.

GHETTO DOCUMENTS

STEPS WHICH THE POPULATION SHOULD TAKE DURING AN AIR RAID

In the resorts. Stop the machines. Extinguish fire in the irons, smitheries etc. Leave the work halls calmly and in orderly fashion. Go to the previously assigned field, lay flat on the earth, avoid crowding, use all natural opportunities for cover.

In residential homes. Turn off electricity and gas. Extinguish fire in the kitchen stove. Fasten the windows. Take with you solid food, do not lock the front door.

Go to a square or a field, find a spot away from walls. Lay flat on the earth calmly.

Ch. Rumkowski
The Eldest of the Jews

Litzmannstadt-Ghetto, July 1944.

Announcement No. 417

On the instruction of the Oberbürgermeister [mayor] of Litzmannstadt, the ghetto will be evacuated.

The workshop crews will go as units, together with their families

THE FIRST TRANSPORT DEPARTS
ON 3 AUGUST 1944

5000 PERSONS
MUST REPORT DAILY

Luggage is not to exceed 20 kg per person.

The first transport includes:

Plant No. 1 of the Tailors' Division, 45 Lagiewnicka Street, and Plant No. 2, tailor shop, 36 Lagiewnicka Street

The families of the evacuees will go with the same transport so that no family will be torn apart.

Other plants will be informed separately about their departure.

The evacuees are to report at the Radogoszcz station.

The first transport leaves at 8 AM. Therefore the evacuees are to report to the station at 7 AM at the latest.

(—)Mordechai Chaim Rumkowski
The Eldest of the Jews

Litzmannstadt-ghetto, August 2, 1944

GERMAN DOCUMENT

ADDRESS BY AMTSLEITER BIEBOW ON 7 AUGUST 1944, 4:45 PM, TO THE WORKERS IN THE TAILORS' WORKSHOPS

The Chairman (Rumkowski) makes some introductory remarks and says that H[ans] B[iebow] will speak on the transfer of the ghetto. Biebow says:

Workers of the Ghetto:

I have spoken on various occasions and hope that you've taken to heart what I have said. The situation in Litzmannstadt has changed again, and as of noon today, even more so. There will be a total evacuation of women and children, on the part of the German population. That means that all ethnic Germans have to leave. Those who believe that the ghetto is not facing total dissolution are badly mistaken. Every last person must leave and will leave. Bombs have already fallen near Litzmannstadt, and had they fallen on the ghetto, not a stone would have been left unturned.

The transfer of the ghetto will be conducted in a calm, orderly, and considerate way, and it is insanity for Plants I and II to fail to report and, as a consequence, to make coercive measures necessary. Four and a half years of working together . . . always trying to do the best one can . . .

I assure you that we'll make every effort to continue doing our best, and—by transferring the ghetto—save your lives.

In this war, in which Germany is fighting for its life, it's necessary to transfer workers to lands from which, at Himmler's orders, thousands of Germans have been taken and sent to the front; they have to be replaced. I am telling you this for your own best interests and assume that Plants III and IV will report to the railroad station in full force.

They will be followed by Mühlgasse and 8 Neustadt. According to the Eldest, this involves a thousand people, and counting family members, at least two thousand. So, if a woman is working in the tailoring shop, and her husband is in the carpet workshop, he goes with her. Families go as a unit to the various camps, which will be newly constructed—and factories will be built. Baubles like those here, carpet weaving, etc., are finished, for good.

Siemens, A.G. Union, Schuckert, every place where munitions are made, need workers. In Czenstochau [Czestochowa], where workers are employed in munitions plants, they're very satisified, and the Gestapo is also very satisfied with their work. After all, you want to live and eat, and you will have that. I'm not going to stand here like some stupid oaf, making speeches and have no one show up. If you force us to use coercion, there will be dead and wounded.

We will see to it that the railroad cars are supplied with food. The trip will take about ten to sixteen hours. You will take about 20 kg. of baggage with you. Anyone who is working in a tailoring shop going later and wants to go along now, I have no objection. But the sloppiness and carelessness have to end, that I can tell you. I am no itinerant orator, storming through the ghetto. If you don't act sensibly, the Ghetto Administration will resign and strong measures will be taken [by others]. I therefore ask you to be reasonable, to pay heed to my words and obey. I have nothing to add to this. This morning the people from the Central Prison had to be stuffed into the railroad cars. Machines are standing idle, with no workers to operate them.

In the camps you will be paid in Reichsmarks. The heads of the enterprises are Germans. The foremen and instructors are going with you; they have to report first. Tomorrow after 12 noon at the Central Prison, and if there is too little room, at Schneider Street or whatever the names of the places.

There is enough room in the cars. Enough machines have been shipped. Come with your families; take along pots and pans, drinking and eating utensils. We don't have these in Germany because they've been distributed to air-raid victims. I assure you once again that you will be taken care of. Pack and report. If you don't and measures have to be taken, I will no longer be able to help.

JAKUB POZNANSKI, LODZ GHETTO DIARY

AUGUST 2, 1944

Yesterday a new "bomb" burst. Early in the morning Rumkowski, Kligier,* and Jakubowicz were called to the Sixth Police Precinct, in Balut Market. The police chief, who is also responsible for the security of the ghetto's borders, informed our dignitaries that on Thursday, August 3, Lodz and the ghetto will be evacuated.

The evacuation of the ghetto is to comprise 5000 people daily. People are to leave with factory machines and goods. For this purpose, a detailed plan is to be worked out and presented to the German authorities for approval, as soon as possible. Rumkowski's answer to this proposal is supposed to have been that, while he's scrupulously carried out all of the authorities' orders until now, he will not undertake the implementation of this plan. The police chief did not discuss the matter further. He stated briefly that the plan will be presented to the Jewish Elders, the very same day, in the afternoon. And so it was.

This unexpected news hit like a bolt of lightning. The factories emptied instantly. People ran about in a frenzy. After a while, some composure returned and common sense took over. People realized that with the front so near, it would be impossible to evacuate such a large city in a few days. In their hysteria, the crowds veered toward the other extreme: laughing and making jokes about evacuating "quick as lightning," alluding to the Nazis' notorious Blitzkrieg.

In spite of everything, Rumkowski convened a conference at 6 PM, with the managers of factories and 3-person delegations from various crews—or, as he is supposed to have expressed it, "people with heads on their shoulders." When he told them the nature of his conversation with the German authorities, they all understood that a final decision has not been made, that the date of the evacuation has not been set, that we are in the war zone (apparently 120 kilometers from the front!), and that unforeseen events might yet occur, including liberation.

At 7 PM news spread about a possible postponement of the evacuation for 20 days. Later I heard that only machinery and goods are to be sent out, and that the people are to remain in the ghetto.

In my view, this whole affair will end up, as the proverb has it, "light rain from a huge cloud." Mass evacuation under present circumstances is not feasible. But aside from that, carrying it out will depend not on the Germans, or the Jews. The last word in this matter will come from the Red Army.

In our factory the management lost its head. Only some of the workers reported to work. I have the impression that some of them are hiding, just in case.

I think Rumkowski highly exaggerated the situation in presenting it in such black colors. It is, after all, his usual tactic. A notice posted yesterday regarding procedures to be followed in the event of an air-raid was printed in German, Yiddish, and Polish—a language not used in three years for official notices. The clock of history is at five to twelve.

AUGUST 4, 1944

There's been indescribable panic here the last three days. On August 2nd, at 1 PM, all managers of the metal and tailor shops were called to Hans Biebow's office. Representing the Germans were the head of the Lodz Gestapo, Czarnulla from the Ghetto Administration, and a young man who said he represented the Reich's Armaments Division and who made a long speech echoing Goebbels.

He said that because of the war situation, the metal and tailor shops must be moved away from the front and into the Reich. The first two transports would leave the next day, Thursday, the 3rd, and the daily contingent of evacuees would be 5000 people. Only electrical machinery is to be taken; all hand- and foot-operated workshops are to remain. The other tailor shops are to leave on Friday and Saturday, and, with a break on Sunday, the metal shops will follow.

Biebow said he'd submit a general evacuation plan. The print shop got paper ready and waited for the text of an announcement. At 7:30 PM, a notice arrived, signed by Rumkowski, that the main tailor shop would leave Thursday. There was no mention of further plans or of sanctions if people failed to report.

The idea to evacuate probably comes from Biebow and his supporters. Not wishing to die for their Führer, they prefer to relocate their enterprise far from the front. My rough estimate is that 100 railway cars would be needed within a few days, just to transport people, not to mention machinery and goods. Where will they get this many cars in the present situation, on the eve of defeat?

Wednesday, after the mid-day meal, our shop was asked to prepare a sufficient quantity of paper for wrapping the machinery to be dismantled by the sewing machine repair shop.

On Thursday morning, fewer than 100 people appeared at the Radogoszcz Station, but even they couldn't leave, since there were no trains. The day before, at a public meeting in the metal shop, Biebow made a fervent request for everyone to listen to him and leave for the Reich. His voice was especially sweet when he said, "*Meine Juden* [Ger: My Jews]." He stressed that the evacuation was for the good of the ghetto population, because the front was moving toward us and the Russians would be cruel to all those who had worked for the German army.

His entire speech was devoid of harshness and was rather a kind of pleading. For the first time in a very, very long while, the Jews could feel some sense of triumph.

At noon on Thursday, Chairman Rumkowski spoke right after the representatives of the Ghetto Administration, advising people to heed the German authorities. Bradfisch* spoke next and, in a lyrical voice, advised the Jews to leave voluntarily. Biebow spoke in a few shops, growing sentimental over the fate of people whose stubbornness would keep them inside the war zone. He assured everyone that the authorities were motivated by their honest desire to save the Jews from "certain annihilation."

AUGUST 8, 1944

Nothing changed on Saturday or Sunday. Acting like a Jewish tribune, Biebow kept trying to persuade workers from different shops to leave. He had little success, and the evacuation idea is being resisted.

On Saturday night the Jewish police entered some apartments. It's not clear why certain people were pulled out of bed, since they were employed in various shops, even in the fur shop and the corset shop. Most likely, they were on lists prepared by the shops a few weeks ago.

Food supplies reaching the ghetto are inadequate and very irregular. Yesterday, instead of a "normal ration," 5 kilos of potatoes and the same amount of cabbage were issued per person. We received no marmalade, flour, fat, or groceries. Instead, we were given 50 dkg. of rye cereal per family member.

Early yesterday morning, Hans Biebow made another speech, saying that the situation had changed drastically and that within the next 48 hours everyone, including ethnic Germans, would have to leave Lodz. He advised the Jews to leave Litzmannstadt Ghetto voluntarily: the advancing front will bring nothing good. These appeals were harsher and conveyed a very definite threat.

Again last night people were pulled out of their beds. About 250 were taken.

There's panic in the ghetto. I'm still sure that Biebow's satanic plan cannot be accomplished. Even Rozenblat, the head of the Jewish police, told Bradfisch outright that he cannot be responsible for delivering people, since the Jews have lost their confidence in the German authorities. I'm not convinced that the notorious "general" of our security forces did, in fact, use these words. Frankly, I've never suspected him of such courage.

Reingold, the manager of food supplies, has not abandoned his way of gaining influence. He still sends extra food to dignitaries, just in case; it's significant that some of them have refused to accept these gifts.

AUGUST 9, 1944

In spite of all Biebow's urging, only several people reported for yesterday's transport. People don't want to leave even the worst holes in the ghetto.

The Ghetto Administration began a round-up around 11 AM. At about the same time, German firemen entered our sector with rifles in hand and surrounded a quadrangle bounded by Lagiewnicka, Zawisza Czarny, Mlynarska, and Brzezinska Streets. Each house was then searched by the Jewish police, and its occupants brought downstairs. The thoroughness with which premises were searched depended on the position held by their occupants.

In this fashion about 2000 people were brought to the square at 1-3 Lagiewnicka Street and then transported to the movie theater at Marysin. It's said that more than 700 people escaped en route. Apparently, some of the remaining 1300 were sent away yesterday—destination unknown.

Some people say that if the tailors continue defying the Ghetto Administration's orders, we can expect another round-up in the next few hours.

Such is the situation. My wife and daughter went this morning to the Record Office and I went to my shop. When I arrived, I found our dignitaries there, together with their families and possessions. There was word that there will be another "action" today. The Jewish police are at maximum readiness. It will be dawn in a few hours.

AUGUST 10, 1944

It's 10 AM. We can hear rifle shots nearby. One, two, three, four, then more frequently. A new round-up has started, this time in the area where our paper shop is located. I'm watching its entire progress from our third-floor window.

I have to commend Ejbuszyc's energy and posture, for he kept the police from entering the factory by insisting, "There is work going on here." I noticed Biebow and Czarnulla on the street near our shop.

The action takes place as follows: the German police or firemen scare people by firing a few shots. Then come the Jewish police, assisted by the ghetto firemen and chimney sweeps. This group calls the occupants of the various buildings to come down, and after a few minutes a search of apartments ensues. Often the fate of an entire family depends on the whim of a fireman or policeman; influence and the jingle of money play a big part.

After the occupants are searched and sent to the assembly area, the apartments are searched again by the German authorities. All of it is accompanied by terrible crying and screaming. A veritable manhunt. This is how the white man once hunted the black man. Now, the Jew is the slave.

About 2 PM, the area was finally "cleaned out" and the operation was transferred to the other side of the bridge, where it lasted till late in the evening.

GHETTO DOCUMENT

ATTENTION!

This is to announce that a new assembly center for the evacuees has been opened

ON 3 KRAWIECKA STREET

Persons under consideration may report there with their luggage.

(—) Mordechai Chaim Rumkowski
Eldest of the Jews

Litzmannstadt-Ghetto, 10 August 1944

JAKUB POZNANSKI, LODZ GHETTO DIARY

AUGUST 12, 1944

[Friday] We've had some terrible days. I've been so preoccupied with events that I've had no time to write.

On Wednesday, about 9 PM, we learned that the print shop was working on new notices from the authorities, pertaining to the closing of all shops and the compulsory transfer of the population from the western side of the ghetto to the eastern side. People who knew about it were moving *en masse* to our side. For our part, we'd prepared some knapsacks ahead of time so that we could elude the evacuation by escaping to the shop.

At 5 AM I went outside. There was great activity and an incredible tumult. People were running in every direction, while at the same time residents from the other side were moving into our streets in great panic. In a word: indescribable chaos. The ghetto is like a huge insane asylum.

I took some things to the shop the first thing in the morning. I found quite a number of people there with their families, and after half an hour my wife and daughter arrived. I went back to our house several more times, trying to save what I could, mainly bedding, underwear, and the most indispensable clothing. At 7 o'clock we received word that the action had started.

We saw how they grabbed people who were coming from the other side of the ghetto. With no questions asked, they were taken by trolley to the Radogoszcz station and shipped in an unknown direction. They apparently traveled in conditions much worse than those in which the tailors went. About 1 PM the round-up stopped for lunch.

After lunch the "action" resumed, and before evening it was declared finished. People began emerging from hiding places. Cabbage rations were issued. The ghetto was coming back to life.

And so Thursday passed. Tired from not sleeping at night, exhausted from our experiences during the day, we finally rested about 10 PM. We made a make-shift bed in the factory loft, using benches and bundles. We slept soundly till 5 AM.

Our shop looks like an inn now. The management is treating the strangers who sought shelter here with great tolerance.

At 6 o'clock we heard that the action had started again. We also discovered that we were sheep without a shepherd. Our supervisors have disappeared, apparently finding a more secure roof over their heads in a shop at 36 Lagiewnicka Street.

GHETTO DOCUMENTS

Announcement No. 425

Regarding the clean-up
of the western part of the ghetto

TODAY THE WESTERN PART OF THE GHETTO MUST BE ENTIRELY CLEANED OUT.

Tomorrow, Monday the 14th of August 1944, the western part will be totally closed off, so that no traffic in and out of this part will be possible.

Instructions regarding workers who are quartered in the plants there will be issued separately.

(—)Mordechai Chaim Rumkowski
Litzmannstadt-Ghetto, 13 August 1944 Eldest of the Jews

Announcement No. 426

JEWS OF THE GHETTO,
COME TO YOUR SENSES!!!
VOLUNTEER FOR THE TRANSPORTS!
You will make your own departure easier

ONLY THOSE WHO REPORT VOLUNTARILY HAVE THE ASSURANCE THAT THEY WILL GO WITH THEIR FAMILIES AND WILL BE ABLE TO TAKE ALONG LUGGAGE.

I advise you to report TONIGHT to the Central Prison or at the assembly center on 3 Krawiecka Street.

(—)Mordechai Chaim Rumkowski
Litzmannstadt-Ghetto, 15 August 1944. Eldest of the Jews

ATTENTION!

AN ORDER TO THE REMAINING TAILORS FROM ALL RESORTS

Tailors, I, the Eldest of the Jews, and your undersigned colleagues turn to you again and we demand that you promptly, for your own good, report voluntarily

TODAY, SATURDAY THE 19TH OF AUGUST 1944

AT 19 KRAWIECKA STREET

Together with your family members and with the luggage for tomorrow's transport.

You may report all day until 12 midnight. Thus you will avoid being taken by force from your homes, without any luggage.

If you come voluntarily to the assembly center, you will immediately be issued

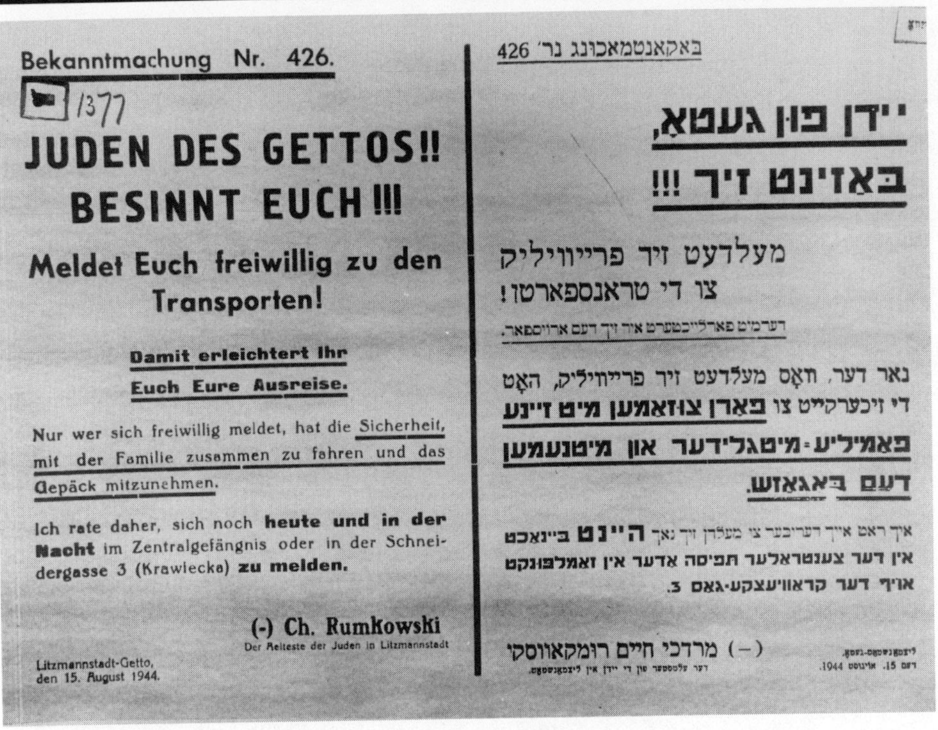

Bekanntmachung Nr. 426.

1377

JUDEN DES GETTOS!! BESINNT EUCH!!!

Meldet Euch freiwillig zu den Transporten!

Damit erleichtert Ihr Euch Eure Ausreise.

Nur wer sich freiwillig meldet, hat die Sicherheit, mit der Familie zusammen zu fahren und das Gepäck mitzunehmen.

Ich rate daher, sich noch **heute und in der Nacht** im Zentralgefängnis oder in der Schneidergasse 3 (Krawiecka) **zu melden.**

(-) Ch. Rumkowski
Der Aelteste der Juden in Litzmannstadt

Litzmannstadt-Getto,
den 15. August 1944.

באקאנטמאכונג נר׳ 426

יידן פון געטאָ, באַזינט זיך !!!

מעלדעט זיך פרייוויליק
צו די טראנספארטן!

דערמיט פארלייכטערט איר זיך דעם ארויספאר.

נאר דער, וואָס מעלדעט זיך פרייוויליק, האָט די זיכערקייט צו **פאָרן צוזאמען מיט זיינע פאמיליע-מיטגלידער און מיטנעמען דעם באַגאַזש.**

איך ראט אייך דעריבער צו מעלדן זיך נאך **היינט בײנאכט אין דער צענטראלער תפיסה אדער אין זאמלפונקט אויף דער קראוויעצקע-גאס 3.**

(–) מרדכי חיים רומקאווסקי
דער עלטסטער פון די יידן אין ליצמאנשטאט.

ליצמאנשטאט-געטא,
דעם 15. אויגוסט 1944.

your food ration and you will go together with your family members and with your luggage, and together with other tailors(. . .)

(—)Mordechai Chaim Rumkowski
Eldest of the Jews

Zysman, Israel
Group Leader of the Tailors' Transport

Kuczynski, Abraham
Tailor Resort Instructor

Lajbusiewicz, Leizer
Tailor Resort Instructor

Litzmannstadt-Ghetto, 19 August 1944.

"They were uncertain if we'd survive here and wondered if we wouldn't follow in their footsteps at the last moment." (Poznanski)

CHAPTER TEN

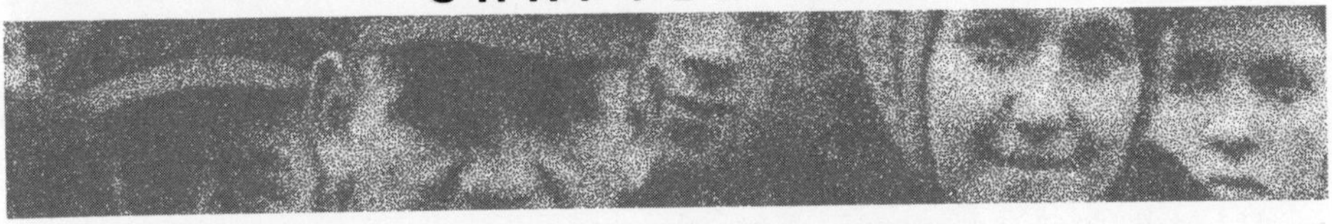

IN HIDING

JAKUB POZNANSKI, LODZ GHETTO DIARY

AUGUST 20, 1944

Yesterday (Saturday) went by quietly. There was no "action" in the ghetto. On Zydowska Street, which now is excluded from the quarter and onto which the windows of our hiding place look out, there was a lot of movement most of the day. People were going to their apartments to get their possessions, to the vegetable place or the shop where potatoes were distributed. At twelve noon a horse-drawn cart with rubber tires appeared to pick up the sick.

We eat only twice a day to make our provisions last longer. Since getting water is also a problem, we literally count every drop. Our hiding place is in an attic. It's very hot and humid here. We do have electricity and can cook on a hot plate.

Around midnight I went to visit my co-worker, and was not noticed on the way. My friend complained of feeling ill and stayed in bed while we talked. Although his situation has yet to be settled, yesterday the superintendent and the office head came to tell him to definitely leave the shop, together with his family. His wife's sister, her husband, and their little daughter are also in hiding with them. Today we'll meet again, this time in my place.

Inactivity is killing me. All day long different thoughts run through my head, and my nervous tension is aggravated by the lack of news from the front. We can observe things easily from our hiding place's little windows. There are still people in many buildings, and I think that they have no intention of leaving.

Today, at dawn, we were awakened by commotion in the street. People were taking cabbage and potatoes from the vegetable store at 8 Zydowska Street.

The friend I visited yesterday arrived around noon, and told me that his name had been crossed off the register of people officially housed. There was even a fight over him, between Bajgelman and Ejbuszyc, but in the end Ejbuszyc gave in.

I've learned that others are hiding in the shop, besides me and my family. The house superintendent and the office head were told (on orders "from above") to remove these people, but it seems they're delaying carrying out the orders. Someone told them of our presence, but for the time being no one bothers us.

AUGUST 21, 1944

Today is the fourth day of our voluntary imprisonment. This morning we could hear Jewish police and firemen yelling, as well as the sound of axes, crowbars, and hammers knocking doors and windows down. After a while, two German policemen came by and casually inspected a few ground-floor apartments. After they left, the Jewish "stormers" stopped inspecting the vacant apartments.

The "action" in our area is coming to an end. The entire day was relatively quiet. Only a few people arrived from the other side of the ghetto. I don't know if compulsory recruitment for departure is still going on in the other areas. The ghetto population not officially housed receives no provisions, not even bread.

Apparently, the electrical workers left today, directly for Berlin, but under better conditions, because they could take a lot of luggage and were to travel in passenger trains. Encouraged by their example, mechanics and other skilled workers joined them. I don't trust this "trip to the Reich's capital."

Last night the shop supervisor came to us on an "official" visit, and "in the name of all those officially housed" asked us to leave the shop. When I told him I had the boss's permission to remain, he asked me politely to straighten out the matter with the office head. I did so without delay. The matter is not definitely settled, but the prospects are good.

Our hiding place is a roomy attic. All day long the heat is unbearable, and sweat drips from all of us. Our daughter has difficulty tolerating the heat and is running a fever. We sleep on "beds" made of boxes on which we spread blankets. Turned-over trash cans serve as our chairs, and the only stool is our table.

On the window side the attic is about 140 centimeters high; on the opposite side over two meters. It served as an apartment before the war, for there are

Final deportations, August 1944.

still *mezuzahs* [signs of the covenant] affixed to the door frame. Stairs end a floor below; the entrance to our place is camouflaged and the ladder hidden behind a secret place filled with rubbish.

There was a skilled worker by the name of Koplenicz in our shop. Wanting to avoid deportation, he too came to stay in our work place. The hiding place was not yet ready, so his wife and small child kept walking around the factory rooms. Suddenly the Germans arrived. All those hiding in the shop ran down to the cellar. Fearing that the child might give them away by crying, the parents gave it a little poppy seed brew. Unfortunately, the dose proved too strong. After the child's death, the Kopleniczes broke completely and, giving up their hiding place, left voluntarily with the first transport.

AUGUST 23, 1944

In the afternoon there was a round-up. Yesterday it was on Brzezinska, Franciszkanska, Dworska—today it took place on Koscielny Square, Zgierska, Balut Market, and Lagiewnicka. This area was supposed to have been separated from the Jewish sector a long time ago, but it's evidently still inhabited.

We have a meager supply of food. We are now eating half, or rather a third, of what we used to. Our daily nourishment consists of 7–8 dkg. of stale bread (which means 1/8 of a loaf for 3 people!) and about 30 dkg. potatoes. From time to time this is supplemented with a microscopic piece of "babka," made of flour and ersatz coffee, or a few beets. We do have some real coffee and tea, but we're saving it, in case of sickness. I received these delicacies at one point from my brother in Portugal.

We've figured out that our supplies will last 25–26 days, during which time the war will probably end, and with it our torment.

Last night there was a rain storm. A lot of water came through the holes in the roof, into our hideout. We had to rescue our "beds," food, supplies, and clothing. Although we were very frightened, we didn't suffer much damage.

During the day it's quiet in the street. Movement starts only toward evening, when the sidewalks begin to fill with people. I'm intrigued by the sight of certain people carrying small bags. What is in those bags?

Lately, the neighboring houses at 14, 16, and 18 Zydowska Street and 3, 5, and 7 Brzezinska have been designated "residences" for feces removers and garbage collectors. The Nazi system: throw people out, bring others in!

Several similar residences have been established. In them are grouped transport workers, policemen, firemen, the so-called "white guard" (the porters of the Department of Food Supplies), Jakubowicz's "army" (the supply guards from Balut Market), and people from certain shops and departments. Also, "assembly camps" have been established for people from the workplaces designated for transport. Doctors, pharmacists, bakers, etc. are housed at 36 and 63 Lagiewnicka Street. However, these groups have no intention of leaving, at least not yet.

AUGUST 26, 1944

Saturday, the ninth day of our voluntary imprisonment. Roundups and deportations continue.

Some of the registered shop workers have already left the ghetto, among them also Metallurgy I. Since the transport conditions seemed tolerable, some influential people and a few dignitaries from the Meat Distribution Center joined the mechanics, lathe workers, and locksmiths for the transport.

I also heard that transport workers had their knapsacks with food and clothing taken away, without explanation, at the last minute before being transported out of the ghetto.

The biggest problem of our "cave" existence is bringing in water and removing waste. All this has to be done at night, and the nights are dark now. Unfortunately, the electric motor broke, and pumping water manually takes a long time and requires great effort because of the well's depth.

The day before yesterday we heard that the German army has been crushed in France, that Paris has been captured, and that Rumania has surrendered.

On Friday, in our usual way, we ate a portion of stale bread about 10 am; then "dinner" was divided into two parts—to be eaten at 1 pm and 4 pm.

We were just getting ready for our first dinner—this time beet soup with potatoes—when we heard a commotion in the street. We looked out and saw people running toward Wolborska Street and returning with loaves of bread. Some people were carrying sacks full!

We couldn't budge because some Germans were supposed to come to the shop that day to pick up merchandise for a company in Hamburg. Suddenly, I heard someone call me. In the doorway stood the shop supervisor, Lichtenstein. He handed me two loaves of bread, saying: "Eat your fill today!"

Imagine my wife's and daughter's surprise. After a short discussion we decided to eat double portions, and a real holiday mood set in. The happiest was our daughter, who confessed that all this time she's been experiencing intolerable hunger.

An hour later a friend came by with the news that the bakeries had been abandoned by their workers and that people were carrying off anything they could. We spent a long time considering whether we should show ourselves in the daytime. Arguments for the stomach won out, for we realized that such an opportunity would not present itself again. The three of us decided that I would go downstairs and try my luck.

Unfortunately, I arrived at the bakery too late. The bread had run out, but there was still a supply of flour. I took about 10 kilos and ran back to the shop. At the entrance I met some German chauffeurs, who were just leaving. They looked at me but said nothing. Once I had put the flour in a safe place, I debated whether to go back for more, since the truck from Hamburg was still in the courtyard. I decided to do it and took a pillow case with me.

The bakery at Wolborksa Street was completely empty by then, so I ran to 4 Jakuba Street and found some leftover flour there. I was able to take about 15 kilo and returned to the shop. I did not go out a third time, because the sinister vehicle was still in the courtyard. Meanwhile, my wife and daughter baked some rolls and a babka—our first filling supper in a few years.

It's clear that many people are hiding in apartments that have been closed off. Since we had betrayed our presence in the shop, it no longer made any sense to hide that fact from people housed officially. These officially registered friends almost all came down with stomach sickness, probably due to overeating.

About 10 PM I was invited into Bajgelman's private apartment, where a meeting was held to decide about leaving on a transport. Because an order for the deportation of the shop's workers was expected, we had to decide who would go and who planned to stay in hiding. Bajgelman assured all those present that there would be a safe place for all 40 people now officially housed. No one present gave a definite yes or no answer. Staying at the shop would depend on certain conditions. Finally, it was decided that at 4 AM today certain hiding places would be furnished with tables, chairs, and bedding.

Today another German truck came to pick up merchandise, at about 8 AM. Then about 9 AM a horse-drawn wagon from 36 Lagiewnicka Street came into the courtyard, and from it emerged Ejbuszyc, Orbach the bookbinder, and Kligier's son. They're planning to set up a new paper shop in Szamotuly [about 130 miles northwest of Lodz], where there are already about 600 people. They're collecting raw materials and supplies from different concerns. Apparently, construction workers from the building shop also went to Szamotuly, where they promised to restore an apartment for Czarnulla. High time! Most of them have been busy till now dismantling the barracks near the Radogoszcz station.

I heard today that the Jewish police, the Special Unit, and the bakers are to leave the ghetto—destination unknown.

AUGUST 28, 1944

Monday. I went outside on Saturday evening. The ghetto looked terribly strange. The streets were dead. Here and there one saw lone individuals stealing toward the Department of Supplies. These are either people housed officially or those who receive nothing officially but who sometimes can beg for food coupons.

Nor did Mr. Szczesliwy refuse me rations, either. After 10 days "officially" without food, I was given an allotment for three people, one loaf of bread, a half kilo of sugar, and 15 dkg. of rice. I asked him for some jam and oil also, but he didn't give me any. Sugar and rice constitute our iron reserve.

After I got back, my wife and daughter went to our apartment on Wolborska Street to bring back some things. Even though the doors had been very securely locked, the apartment had been ransacked. All the better things were gone, lost without a trace.

Sunday started with an "action" on Plac Koscielny. A group of soldiers, accompanied by the "white guard" from Balut Market, passed our street.

In the afternoon a Gestapo notice was posted on ghetto walls. According to new regulations, all ghetto inhabitants—officially and unofficially housed—must report by Monday at 6 PM to the assembly point at Krawiecka Street or at Czarneckiego Street, from where they'll be sent out of the Jewish sector.

The last transport will be leaving on Tuesday, August 29, 1944. Whoever is in the ghetto beyond that date will face capital punishment!

Everyone who was planning to hide with us in the shop building has been frightened by the notice and has decided to report for relocation. Eight of us will remain here—the three in my family, plus the Bajgelmans.

I went outside again in the evening. There is intense activity. People are hurrying to get ready for tomorrow's transport. Everyone wants to be first. No one wants to get on the train last. I heard, however, that there will be about 500 people left in the ghetto, together with our Chairman, of course. They'll have the honor of "cleaning up" our sector.

The Food Distribution Department is closed. I came home empty-handed. We've begun in earnest to prepare a new hiding place, together with the Bajgelman family.

AUGUST 31, 1944

Thursday, the third day in our new hideout.

On Monday, starting early in the morning, our friends began getting ready for the trip. They were all very upset, and the least sound rattled them. They looked at us with pity. They admired our courage, perhaps even envied it, but they were uncertain if we'd survive here and wondered if we wouldn't follow in their footsteps at the last moment.

They are apparently going to Vienna. They'll make the trip in the company of Rumkowski, who was stripped of the dignity of his title as head of the Jewish Elders. Better late than never! His position was given to the technical director of the tannery, Karmiol.

On Monday all those who are to remain in the ghetto were inspected. Hans Biebow conducted a ruthless selection, refusing, among others, the request of the pharmacy inspectors to remain. He picked Dr. Eliasberg and Dr. Mazur among the physicians, so that the total of the "chosen" is about 500 people. All of them were housed in a building at 16 Jakuba Street.

Monday evening we transferred the rest of our belongings to the new place and ate our supper there. Though we share this new apartment with the Bajgelmans, they only spend daylight hours with us. In the evening they go back to their own apartment. Not one ray of sunlight reaches our hideout and we depend on one tiny electric light.

For the time being we can't complain of a lack of food. We have enough bread, flour, and potatoes. We also have some beets which were left behind by our former neighbors, as well as dry foodstuffs, such as soup mixes, paprika, caraway seeds, etc. Our ladies dream up new specialties all the time.

Tuesday went by peacefully. At 5 AM we woke everyone because water had to be brought in from the neighboring area. We have a problem with water. While pumping it, one has to be extremely careful because the pump makes a grinding noise. So far, so good. Let's hope we'll be able to carry on like this until the end.

Around 8 PM we go out into the courtyard to get a breath of fresh air. Then we go to bed and get up at dawn. That's our schedule every day.

From time to time we hear someone walking inside the shop. They are most probably collecting the remaining goods. Still, who knows? Each such "visit" makes us extremely nervous. This afternoon we had quite a scare. Suddenly, we heard very distinct footsteps in a workshop adjoining our hiding place. The steps came near our door. Someone was trying to open it. We were paralyzed, and our hearts stopped beating. Suddenly a familiar voice was heard: "It's me, Blachowski. . . ." What a relief!

Blachowski is our friend from the shop and is officially housed at 36 Lagiewnicka Street. He came to get paper. He told us that not all shops have had their people sent out. The transport of metal workers (Metal II) left only yesterday.

Germany is expected to surrender any day now. He promised to visit us again tomorrow.

Apparently the "clean up" of our sector is starting from the other side of the bridge, the west side of the ghetto.

IRENA LIEBMAN, LODZ GHETTO

The ghetto is being reduced. Everything on the other side of the bridges is now cut off and becomes Aryan territory. We have 48 hours to move into the reduced ghetto and find new living quarters. The cage is tightening.

All workshops are concentrating their employees in designated buildings. The Germans come to the factories and shops to explain that the workshops, together with workers and their families, are to be relocated to other cities, where living conditions and job opportunities will be better. They tell us to take part of our households along, so that we can settle down as soon as we reach our destination. Every day, another workshop is liquidated and more people taken to the train station.

We leave our little room with a feeling that this time we'll be gone from here forever. We take along only the most important things and some clothes in bags and knapsacks. I wrap my parents' portraits carefully, and my father's *tallis* and *tefillin.* We don't lock up, leaving the door wide open.

My sister takes me to an apartment near her hospital which is occupied by the nurses. She gives me a white nurse's uniform and a cap in case the Germans run into me and ask what I'm doing here. They leave me some bread and water and forbid me to go out. But the noose is getting tighter. I hear clearly the rumble of passing bulletproof cars, shouts in German, and rifle butts banging on the door. My new place is not safe anymore. At night I'm taken to the hospital, which is not yet scheduled for deportation. Here I hide in a room where two nurses live. Their lives will be in danger if I'm discovered, but they don't care. I myself don't know anymore what it is I want. I live in tension all the time, like a hunted animal. During the day I lie on a straw mat behind the closet; at night I sleep in bed, since no searches have yet been made during the night hours.

After a long discussion with Saul and Dr. Lewin, a good friend of my mother, it was decided to take me to the ward as a patient. Since I've already had typhoid fever, there's no danger of catching it again. Thus, I can stay in the same room with the sick, as long as the Germans leave the hospital alone. To be on the safe side, they leave me with the nurse's uniform. And so, I remain in the ward for several days, healthy among the sick, but like them restless and miserable.

Until today, the personnel tried keeping the truth from the patients, but now everything has become cruelly clear. Those patients able to walk are leaving the hospital to join their families. Others, who cannot leave their beds, are hoarding food. There are no limits on getting bread now, and sugar is available. All storage rooms are being emptied.

On the 26th of August the hospital receives an order to reduce its staff by 50 persons. My sister is on the list. I leave my bed and dress up. We take along some bread, sugar, soap, a few photographs, writing paper, and a fountain pen. My sister has luminal and veronal in her bag, enough for the two of us.

We arrive at the train station. A sea of heads and bodies. In front of us there are freight cars standing wide open. In each car, there are small windows with heavy bars, just below the ceiling. . . . It's our turn now. Forty-seven, forty-eight, forty-nine, fifty. Enough! Shut the door! They don't care if a family is separated. Fifty is the norm. Fifty human beings in one car, with no air to breathe. The car has been sealed. Two armed German soldiers ride inside the cars to watch us. More watchmen are on the car rooftops. There is one pail in the car to be used as a toilet for all fifty people.

Again shouts, whistles, and the train starts rolling. The cage with people inside is set in motion.

I do not know how long we've been riding. I've lost my sense of time. Outside, dusk falls. One German stands at the door; the other is asleep. It looks like we're coming to a stop at some station, because we hear voices shouting and talking. The train slows down. It's probably changing tracks. Suddenly I hear someone speaking in Polish, as if from under the floor of the car. Ignoring the danger, I put my head down as much as possible and whisper: "Man, friend, tell me, where they're taking us?" The German did not hear me. He looked around with a glassy gaze. Then, through the squeaking of the train, we hear clearly spoken words: "Bad, very bad. Your cars are going to Oswiecim [Auschwitz]." The train picks up speed and returns to its monotonous rhythm.

ABRAM KAJZER, "BEHIND THE WIRES OF DEATH"

We board the train. I say to my wife, maybe it's better that we've finally left the Lodz Ghetto. It was obvious that the ghetto wouldn't survive until the end of the war, and constant worry, deportation, and hunger were poisoning every minute of our lives. What is fated to happen will happen anyway. The tension was simply too much for us.

Where are we going now? To Germany probably, as laborers. We'll see. Unbearable stench inside the car. Everyone has diarrhea. I listen to what my comrades in distress are saying. They think it was a waste of time to have hidden out that long, that they should have joined the deportation much earlier. Now, at least, bullets don't fly over our heads and no one is hunted like a wild animal by the Schupo and the Gestapo. At long last our first quiet night.

Although our destination is unknown and no one believes anything good will happen to us, our nerves are not pulled so taut any more. We feel safe in this locked car. Besides, there is hope that the near future is not going to be all that bad. It may be true, after all, that we are going to do work, because all the equipment, the tools, tables, benches, everything from the workshop is being transported along with us.

It is now high noon. The train stops dead. We look out through the cracks in the door. I see a lot of barracks surrounded by barbed wire. Somebody whispers:

"Oswiecim . . . Oswiecim."

My wife asks, "What is Oswiecim?"

"A town in Upper Silesia," I say, still not realizing where we really are.

"And what about the wire? Look how many women, they all have their heads shaven, and I don't see any children. Tell me, what does it all mean? Do you know? Tell me!"

"These women are probably at work here," I say. "And the children are staying home with the old people. Don't you see that there are no old women here?"

My anxiety grows with each minute. The car doors open with a grating sound. Men in striped uniforms tell us:

"Come out, fast. Leave everything here, take only something to eat! Fast! Fast!"

They are Jews. They don't look bad. A thought occurs: "It must be better here than in the ghetto. In the ghetto nobody looks that well."

Sentries have been posted along the train at each car. The SS men direct everybody to one side. People go obediently, no signs of resistance. On the way, the SS officer waves his hand and orders: "Women to the right! Men to the left!"

I hold my son's hand tightly and walk as if hypnotized. I see hardly anything. All my attention is concentrated on the SS man, and more specifically on his power-wielding hand, which nonchalantly segregates people, sending them to the right or to the left. Patches of dark move before my eyes and a terrible noise rings in my ears. He tears the boy away from me: "Children go with the women."

I look dumfounded after my son, until he vanishes into the crowd. Utter despair. Total darkness. I realize now that once again we have been shamelessly deceived.

They order us to go. We enter the camp. I ask a man in a striped tunic, "Where are we going?"

"You will see," he says. "To heaven."

I cannot think straight anymore. All my senses are dulled. I move automatically along. It seems to me that time has stopped and that we are marching in place. At last we come to a halt. They tell us to line up, we are to go to the showers. We are ordered to give up all valuables and money. A pile of watches, gold rings, bracelets, chains, medallions, fountain pens, and other items grows before our eyes. Those who are finished can go to the showers. We go in and undress. Again comes the SS officer. This time he surveys our bodies. He separates from us the thin or handicapped: they are led away. We move on to where barbers are waiting with shearing tools, which are anything but sharp. They shave all hair, wherever it grows.

The photographer, Mendel Grossman, kept his Leica camera hidden in the briefcase and often worked jointly with photographer Henryk Ross. These deportation pictures were taken at risk to the photographers' lives.

After the barber and the shower we receive prison uniforms and we come outside. I am overwhelmed by terrible fright. Now I see how entirely grim and helpless our situation is.

Shaved heads, striped uniforms, and barbed wire everywhere destroy our last hope. Especially upsetting is the fact that our co-religionists, Jews like us who have evidently been here for some time, are no less vile than the SS men. They would not utter a single word of hope or sympathy.

After the shower we are taken to a camp, one of many in this complex. As far as one can see, there is only the sky and rows of barracks stretching in every direction. The barracks are surrounded by barbed wire, through which electricity flows. A sign says: *Achtung! Hochspannung!* [Warning! High Voltage!]

JAKUB POZNANSKI, LODZ GHETTO DIARY

SEPTEMBER 2, 1944

Saturday. Yesterday marked five years since the outbreak of the war, and the start of the sixth year of the worst slaughter in the history of the world. People in the assembly place at 36 Lagiewnicka have not left yet, and the workers among them are still filling orders. They even come to our shop and make sacks for cement. It's not known how long they'll be employed filling these orders.

We do know that aside from the 500 people left to clean up the ghetto, there are still some small groups around. Engineer Weinberg and a small crew was left in Balut Market. Thanks to the crew's legal status, some people in hiding crept out into the open and are moving about freely.

Ejbuszyc and Blachowski told us about something horrible that happened at 36 Lagiewnicka Street. Dr. Sima Mandels, a pediatrician, was there with her engineer husband and her two children. The tragedy occurred when Hans Biebow noticed their beautiful 16-year-old daughter. One evening when he was drunk, he grabbed her in the hallway, dragged her into his office, and tried to rape her. The girl tried to defend herself and started screaming. It was then that "the master of life and death" shot her in the eye. The mother started crying in despair. In order to silence her, Biebow ordered the entire family shipped out immediately. The same happened to the chief physician, Dr. Miller, who spoke up for the Mandels family. He was deported with his wife and little son.

There are horrible rumors, namely that all the transports supposedly going to Vienna or to inside the Third Reich are actually going to a horrible camp in Auschwitz. Even the once-omnipotent Rumkowsi was sent out with one of the latest transports. In a severe heat wave he was placed in a closed car, with more than eighty other people.

That's how Hans Biebow fixed him up!

What made the German authorities liquidate the Chairman and his coterie so quickly? It could not have been the situation at the front, in which case Lodz would have been evacuated. I suspect that personal matters played their part here. It could have been the fear of serious abuses being discovered, especially since the [German] Ghetto Administration officials took a great many goods from Jewish enterprises for themselves.

Money has completely stopped circulating in the ghetto. Every worker housed officially gets an allotment of food for the work he does. Had they used this system from the beginning, many injustices and much harm would have been avoided.

No changes have occurred in our personal lives. We get up early and go to bed around 8 PM. Our food is still the same: potatoes and flour, flour and potatoes, and some bread. This poor nutrition has damaged our health. We often have stomach problems.

They say that the ghetto "clean-up" means getting all apartments ready for use. Beds are even being made up, and tables covered with tablecloths. The rooms have a lived-in look. For whom are they preparing these apartments?

SEPTEMBER 4, 1944

Monday. Our friends Blachowski and Ejbuszyc came to visit us yesterday. They brought us soup, which they received at the camp at 36 Lagiewnicka Street. A delicious, thick potato soup.

They gave us the latest news. A new Council of Elders was created, composed of seven members: Dr. Eliasberg, Dr. Mazur, Engineer Weinberg, Karmiol, Mozelsio, and Dancyger (a former group leader of the so-called "yellow guard" in Balut Market). Karmiol was named head of the Council, with the title Eldest of the Jews.

It's said that Biebow is abusing Rumkowski's supporters and forcing them to do the heaviest labor.

So far the camp at 36 Lagiewnicka is staying where it is and performing the same work assignments as the camp at 16 Jakuba. The men are loading machinery onto trains at Radogoszcz Station, and a group of women is cleaning abandoned apartments.

We also learned something of Rumkowski's unexpected departure. Biebow included in that transport Rumkowski's brother Jozef and his wife, who for some time was referred to as "Princess Helena" or "the Princess of Kent." The Chairman went to the Ghetto Administration, asking that they not deport his immediate family. Biebow refused, but he added, "If you wish, you can accompany them." Rumkowski accepted this half-facetious offer.

Biebow drove him to the station himself, assigned him a separate car on the train and placed only twelve of Rumkowski's closest people with him. He said goodbye to him, most sincerely. As soon as he turned around, however, the Schupo standing guard—probably on Biebow's instructions—began assigning the deportees just arriving at the station to that very car. And so there were finally over eighty people in Rumkowski's car. As they say in the trade, it was a record-breaking crowd.

SEPTEMBER 6, 1944

Our friends visit us every day. Yesterday we heard a full report about what happened the day before at the camp at Lagiewnicka Street. Biebow found out by chance that one of the women from a cleaning crew took something from an apartment she was cleaning. Boiling over in Teutonic anger, he ordered everyone to assemble, picked out ten women and ordered them to walk around the courtyard in front of the other women, yelling, *"Wir haben geplündert!"* [Ger: "We have robbed!"] He then gave a speech about honesty, and finally in moving tones expressed his regret at the liquidation of the ghetto, saying, "What do I need all this for, when the war is ending anyhow?"

Yesterday our shop was visited by a Ghetto Administration functionary, a certain Lemcke. During his unofficial visit, he spoke to Ejbuszyc, assessing the Nazi situation with great pessimism. According to him, the entire "party," as he put it, might last another two or three weeks. The Allies have taken Belgium and Holland. The Finns have surrendered. In other words: *"Führer kaputt!"* He should only be right!

Lemcke is an old Lodz citizen. Though German by origin, he spent his whole life in Jewish firms, which is why he gives his views openly on current developments. Apparently, these views are not all that rare on the other side of the barbed wire.

Our friends brought us a few bars of soap, some jam and onions today. We are all well. We miss only air, fat, and protein. And of course freedom, freedom! . . .

SEPTEMBER 9, 1944

Dr. Eliasberg was given Karmiol's position, with the theoretical title of Head of the Jewish Elders. In my opinion, this job does not suit him. Why did the Germans, at the last moment, thrust this kind of position on one of the most decent of people?

The day before yesterday Biebow personally discovered three people hiding in a house on Stary Rynek. He beat them till they bled, then had them stripped to their underwear and sent to the camp at 16 Jakuba Street, where he ordered them to register.

The barbed wire on the other side of the bridge was moved from Podrzeczna Street to Lutomierska Street, thereby excluding the following areas from the ghetto: Podrzeczna, Zgierska, and Lutomierska Streets up to the hospital on Drewnowska Street.

Biebow is leaving Lodz for a week, so the transport out of 36 Lagiewnicka Street will probably be delayed until he returns. This is something of a consolation for us.

Our life in the cell goes on without change. We eat and sleep, we sleep and eat. This enforced rest does not agree with us. Our faces are becoming more drawn and paper thin. We need air—we breathe fresh air only a few minutes every 24 hours—and our food is monotonous (potatoes and flour, flour and potatoes).

Certain institutions are already dividing the loot, that is, what remains of Jewish possessions. In this connection, there was even an argument between the Ghetto Administration and the Municipal Gas Works over the gas stoves in our sector.

The German authorities not only named a Chairman of the Elders, they've designated a Jew from Wielun, by the name of Bruder, as chief of police. He came to us with a transport in August 1942, and a month later was employed by the Special Unit. A few months ago he was assigned to Radogoszcz, as director of a shop manufacturing pre-fabricated barracks parts for bombed-out towns. Now he has climbed even higher.

SEPTEMBER 10, 1944

Today, for the first time in many days, no one has visited our hiding place. Is it chance, or is it because it's Sunday? Or maybe our friends have already left? We don't know. Many possibilities come to mind. The fact is, however, that we have lost contact with the world and don't know what is happening. We also have other worries. For example, we've noticed that most of our extra loaves of bread are getting moldy. What are we to use in place of bread, and how long will our supply of flour last?

SEPTEMBER 12, 1944

Fortunately, our worries about the camp at 36 Lagiewnicka Street proved premature. Our friends visited us yesterday and brought all kinds of news.

Biebow is taking revenge on Rumkowski's followers. For example, Dr. Mazur is now transporting human excrement.

Supposedly, somewhere near the Stary Rynek, not far from us, a few hundred people are in a huge hiding place. Our friends guess that there are about two thousand in hiding. Not long ago, the Germans stated that according to their figures about four thousand people have disappeared. That number must be highly exaggerated.

It's almost certain that all the destination points given by the Germans were pure fraud. All transports go to Auschwitz. There is a huge camp there, a relocation center that can hold a quarter of a million people at one time and which is run like a prison. New arrivals are stripped naked, bathed, shaven, and told to wear some kind of rags and wooden clogs.

According to our friends, the civilian population here cannot use the railroads, as of this morning. It's probably due to the situation at the front and to military transportation. Sirens went off yesterday at 11 AM. The alert lasted close to an hour, but we didn't hear any explosions that would indicate that the city or suburbs were being bombed.

Today, around dinner time, the lights went off in the shop and in our hideout. Our neighbors panicked and started guessing all kinds of things. They even wanted to warn our friends at 36 Lagiewnicka Street. I forced them to stay calm, though my own nerves were quivering. Common sense indicates that as long as shops are operating, the ghetto will not be kept dark. Indeed, the lights came back on two hours later.

It's hard to describe what we went through in that short span of time. Electricity not only lights our cell but enables us to get water and cook meals.

SEPTEMBER 13, 1944

Yesterday's electric failure was caused by some city electricians working on the transformer in the ruins of the synagogue.

The camp at 36 Lagiewnicka has sent out, so far, 70 train cars with all kinds of machines and barracks parts manufactured in the Auxiliary House Construction shop. Yesterday there was no train at the station, which is how the news of the railway curfew was confirmed.

We have no news, direct or indirect, about the camp at 16 Jakuba. We received some sugar from there not long ago. Someone even promised to visit us. We have no idea why the visit did not materialize.

Lemcke came to the shop again today and spoke with Ejbuszyc about politics. He said the Ghetto Administraiton will be liquidated in the next few days and that all the property of the Jewish sector will be taken over by the municipal Department of Economy. For us, it's not a change for the better.

I read yesterday's paper, which is now in a smaller format and has only four pages. Apparently, there's a paper shortage in the Reich, just as in the occupied countries. New fighting has begun on the eastern front, including an offensive by the Soviet Union directed toward Warsaw and, therefore, Lodz.

In the west, the German army is suffering defeat after defeat. It's no longer a strategic retreat but panic and confusion. The Allies, having liberated France and Belgium, have reached the borders of the Old Reich, on one side, and, on the other, Italy, where units of the *Wehrmacht* have already been crushed. In Yugoslavia the partisans are at the German's heels.

A Finnish peace delegation is in Moscow. There's been a radical change in Bulgaria, which has declared war on the Third Reich and where the soldiers turned their guns on the hated "friends." In Germany some prominent NSDAP leaders were killed for taking part in an attempt to assassinate Hitler. The conspiracy was discovered, but what didn't succeed today could well occur tomorrow. May it happen at top speed!

SEPTEMBER 14, 1944

We had an unpleasant surprise today. Yesterday there were suspicious noises coming from the locksmith shop. Today at dinner time we heard them again but only for a few minutes. We were sure that it was an acoustical illusion. One of our ladies was careless enough to go into the shop and came upon a worker from Ejbuszyc's group by the name of Riesenberg. When he saw her, he was speechless. Let's hope this has no repercussions.

The camp at 36 Lagiewnicka is still sending out raw materials, finished goods, and machinery. They filled seven cars yesterday.

SEPTEMBER 16, 1944

We got a newspaper again yesterday. It's clear that fighting is going on in Praga, a suburb of Warsaw. The Anglo-American army has crossed the Reich's borders at many points. They've taken all of France, Belgium, and Holland. Rumania has signed an armistice with the Soviet Union, leaving the Nazi coalition and sending at least 12 divisions against the Germans.

Lemcke came to our shop this morning. He said that the war will be ended by an internal revolution, which has to take place soon. News from the city indicates that the Germans are very nervous: they're literally sitting on their suitcases. The antagonism between the Reich Germans and our ethnic Germans is becoming quite obvious, as the latter have nowhere to run.

Also, our dignitaries are preparing hiding places, so that they can detach themselves from their subjects and remain here, in case of a transport. Biebow came back but has not shown himself either at 36 Lagiewnicka or 16 Jakuba. This German, a shrewd Bremen businessman with a degree, knows which way the wind is blowing!

Our friends Blachowski and Ejbuszyc supplied us with 8 liters of oil and about 5 kilos of jam yesterday, which were brought in on the truck that came to fetch the goods from the shop.

SEPTEMBER 17, 1944

Sunday. Last night we heard some steps and noises under our window, which is covered with bales of paper. It sounded as if someone were trying to get into the cellar, since the cellar doors are right under the window.

The other day, about 8 pm, when our ladies went to fetch water from the well, which is quite far from here, two people appeared near them in the darkness, one carrying a large sack. There was mutual consternation and embarrassment, interrupted by a pleasant young voice which assured the ladies that they'd "be bothered pumping water" only a few more days. Our ladies were frightened and ran quickly from the courtyard.

The camp at 36 Lagiewnicka Street is supervised by a "command" composed of Lewin (former boss of the straw workshop), Feiner (former boss of the tailor shop), and Kligier (former boss of the *Sonderkommando*). Everyone officially housed is under the jurisdiction of these three, regardless of their former position.

Yesterday afternoon the former owner of this building (a plant producing carbonated drinking water before the war) came to visit our shop with Dr. Leider. They plan to set up a hiding place for 20 people and looked over the cellar below our windows.

SEPTEMBER 18, 1944

Today is the Jewish New Year, 5705. According to the Hebrew calendar, this is the seventh year of the present war.

Two alarms sounded this afternoon, one after another. We didn't hear any explosions or detect the kind of shock connected with bombing.

Our friends came, as they do every day. They were unable to get out of work, and plans for holding holiday services at 36 Lagiewnicka came to naught. The "command," afraid of a visit from Schwind [Heinrich, a deputy to Biebow], ordered an earlier roll call and an immediate march to work. At 6:30 there was no one left in camp. It's encouraging that talk of transports has stopped completely.

Ten trainloads of soldiers came through the Radogoszcz station yesterday. The soldiers greeted the workers along the rails with a communist gesture, that is, a raised fist. If this report is true, then the disintegration of the Nazi army is certain.

SEPTEMBER 19, 1944

Only one of our friends came today. The other remained in camp where, this time, he was able to conduct a short service. The "command" was at a loss as to what to do, since tradition proved stronger than fear of an unannounced inspection by the Ghetto Administration.

Today we distinctly heard some explosions. Unfortunately, in our cell, we couldn't tell if they were caused by bombing, artillery fire, or just the demolition of certain structures. In any case, we see it as a sign that the liberating Red Army is approaching our town.

We're in a state of complete nervous exhaustion, and it feels sometimes as if we're on the edge of madness. Tomorrow will be six weeks since we moved to the shop. For six weeks we've slept on beds improvised from boxes, packages, and bales of paper. Two weeks of starvation, then scant monotonous food which the stomach can't digest. Is it any wonder our psychological state is what it is? The least murmur so upsets us that we've become watchful, frightened animals. When will we be human again?

SEPTEMBER 21, 1944

Yesterday a hiding place in Marysin was uncovered. Eight people were caught, one got away. It was a well-camouflaged shelter on the border of the ghetto. They gave themselves away by singing New Year's prayers. A Schupo policeman, passing by on the other side of the barbed wire, heard them and notified the station at Balut Market. All eight were put in Kripo cells. In the evening they all went to the camp at 16 Jakuba Street.

Some confidential news was received yesterday that out of the entire transport of workers from Metal I, some 800 people, only 50 arrived in Szamotuly. The rest remained in Auschwitz. Many of the "privileged" went with that transport. Were they also kept in that camp about which such horror stories are told?

An office worker from the Ghetto Administration came to our shop and told us that 200 Anglo-American fighter planes and bombers were flying ammunition and food supplies to the insurrectionists in Warsaw. So Warsaw is fighting after all!

SEPTEMBER 23, 1944

Another Jew was sent to the camp at 16 Jakuba after he was caught leaving his hiding place because of hunger.

Yesterday our ladies ventured out in search of some bread and potatoes. All we have left is one loaf of bread. Instead of going into neighboring apartments, they chanced upon some little garden plots and brought back a few kilos of tomatoes and beets, seven big pumpkins, and nine melons. The expedition took not quite an hour. They walked back along the fences surrounding the courtyards. At one point, they thought that someone saw them. It could well have been so, for each such undertaking is a gamble.

I found out that Jozef Sachs and a certain Pick from Zdunska Wola, on Biebow's recommendation, are selling machinery and goods from the ghetto on Balut Market. The buyer goes to the Ghetto Administration office in town, gets the proper paper and takes it to Balut Market, where he establishes the price and terms of purchase with the two Jews.

Lemcke said goodbye to our shop yesterday. Even though he is 50, he has to report to his military unit no later than October 2. Before he does so, he'll visit his badly wounded son in the hospital. His second son disappeared somewhere on the front.

SEPTEMBER 25, 1944

Today, a new Ghetto Administration functionary, the one who has taken Lemcke's place, came to visit us. In our first conversation, on the first day, this new representative of the authorities switched unceremoniously from German to Polish. He told Ejbuszyc many interesting things, including that the Ghetto Administration has a large supply of straw shoes for sale. The military supplier refuses to buy them, indicating without doubt that the leadership is not thinking about a winter campaign.

It's the end of September. We think of the coming winter with horror, since most probably none of us will survive it.

SEPTEMBER 28, 1944

Hitler's army has not as yet received the mortal blow which all humanity awaits impatiently.

Our friends still visit us. According to their reports, every few days a curfew is set for the cemetery, which means that Jews are not to go there, under threat of death. There are all kinds of rumors. Some claim that the cemetery has become a place for executions; others that graves are being dug there for future victims. In any event, such orders bode us no good.

SEPTEMBER 29, 1944

Friday. Today's events were so memorable that we'll probably remember them the rest of our lives.

About 8 AM, one of our friends came to warn us to be extremely quiet because the Germans were in the shop. We found out later that two Germans—one from the Department of Economy—came with two Jews from Balut Market, in order to buy the shop's machinery. They went from building to building, finally coming to the one where we're hiding and where Bajgelman has his apartment.

Since the apartment door was locked, they asked for keys, and when there were no keys to be had, they broke down the door. When they went in, one of the Germans noticed that water had been spilled on the floor recently, that there were fresh melon rinds in the trash can, that a nightgown was on the bed. Our friends tried to explain it all away but to no avail. What was there to say! Next the Germans went into the engine room adjacent to our hideout, where they found something valuable, a carbonator for soda water.

It's hard to describe what we went through in that hour! When our friend who'd taken them around came to us later, he was still so pale and frightened that he could not accurately report on the unexpected visit. He only said: "The Germans are convinced that there are secret hideouts in the shop and plan to go to Balut Market and from there to the Kripo to get police dogs."

We realized that our lives now hang by a thread and that our fate depends on the Germans' zeal or laziness. Visions of the last five years appeared before my eyes, as in a macabre kaleidoscope. Will our hopes for survival be destroyed just as the Red Army and the Allies are on the verge of victory? How slow these terrible hours of waiting are!

Around 5 PM we heard steps in the courtyard. Someone was going to the engine room. We heard bits of conversation in German. We disconnected the electric hot plate and remained motionless. Next to us a lively discussion went on about the positive and negative features of the carbonator. Finally, the conversation stopped and the steps became more distant. We all breathed sighs of relief. It's hard to describe the nervous tension of the twenty minutes during which our lives hung in the balance.

OCTOBER 1, 1944

Our friends visited us only in the morning, after we had given a pre-arranged signal that we were all safe inside. It turns out that one of the Germans hurried to the Ghetto Administration office and told Schwind, second in command to Biebow, that someone is hiding in our shop. Schwind, however, said that he knew all about it, since "a woman and a child were apprehended near that building." And so, by coincidence, the danger was temporarily averted.

We still have to be extremely careful, since the carbonator is to be dismantled within a few days, and therefore we can expect an unwelcome visit at any time.

We finished all the bread. Our ladies now bake "rolls" made of rye flour and grated raw potatoes. That little hot plate is a real blessing!

Our friends reported that the Soviet Union has entered Hungary and is approaching Budapest. When will they approach Lodz, so that we can get out of this hole?

OCTOBER 4, 1944

I want to explain why we changed our place in the attic for this "hole." The attic's windows, which faced Zydowska Street, were covered by the masks and puppets left over from the shows in the shop. They gave the attic a nightmarish look. From morning to night, queerly painted pusses stared at us. Of course, we wouldn't even go near the windows or open them. It was hard breathing the hot, humid air.

These disadvantages were compensated for by how well camouflaged the entrance was. The attic was on the second floor. The outside stairs ended on the first floor, where there was a small porch leading into a paper warehouse. The ladder to the attic was hidden behind a kind of wall.

But more important, we realized, were the difficulties in bringing in water and the fire hazard. Since the stairs and attic were all wood, one fire bomb or artillery shell would mean, inevitably, dying in flames.

We decided to find something more suitable in the cellar. In the paper workshop there had been a soda water factory before the war and an ice storage area 12 meters deep. That hole was very cold and damp, not suited for habitation, even for a short time. Still, we couldn't spend time thinking about it. We brought in some tables, benches, and bedding and then camouflaged the entrance. In front of the door we placed a trash bin, which we filled with so much paper waste that it became impossible to get close enough to the wall to find an entrance or window. We kept the cellar as a refuge of last resort and picked the storage area above it as our hideout.

The most important task after we moved in was camouflaging the entrance doors connecting this part of the cell with a store leading onto the street. On the store's back wall, something resembling a closet was built out of the door leading into the hideout. A few rows of shelves were nailed over the door, and on those shelves heaps of locksmith's tools were placed. The bottom shelf, situated very close to the floor, has no door behind it but rather some plywood covered with rags. It's very difficult to get through the small opening, and one has to lie flat on one's stomach and slide in.

Our friends reported that the order for them to leave the camp on October 5 was not withdrawn. It's now almost certain that they'll leave tomorrow at dawn. They're apparently going to Königswursterhausen, by way of Sachsenhausen concentration camp. When they left us, our friends said goodbye with great feeling. I don't quite believe that they're going. Their departure has been announced so many times, and so many times called off.

OCTOBER 5, 1944

The camp at 36 Lagiewnicka did not leave. Early in the morning our friend arrived with his group in the shop area, and he hurried over to tell us the good news.

The camp made feverish preparations till late at night. When everything was packed, around midnight, Jakubowicz went to Balut Market to get Biebow's final instructions. Biebow and Bradfisch were then in a meeting that was probably conducted with a generous supply of alcohol, because Biebow was drunk afterward, when he received Jakubowicz. Unsteady on his feet, he quickly announced that the camp was not leaving and that he'd provide further details the next day. That was all Jakubowicz wanted to hear, and he went back to camp with the good news.

In the event that the camp at 36 Lagiewnicka does leave, the authorities have said that Szmulewicz the dentist and all shoemakers and tailors are to remain in the ghetto and to transfer to 16 Jakuba Street. Apparently, the Germans want their services till the end.

OCTOBER 7, 1944

Jews all over the world are celebrating Succoth. Here, our friends have made a *succah* within the shop area, where with some religious friends they eat their meager meal. It's hard to believe the sacrifices Jews make to keep up age-old traditions. They erect a *succah* within the vanquished ghetto, where even the presence of "unofficially housed" Jews is punished by death.

For a few days now, our shop has been haunted by all kinds of Germans who come to look over the engines and machinery.

An air raid is going on at this moment. We can hear loud explosions, though it's hard to know what's causing them.

OCTOBER 8, 1944

According to our friends, yesterday's explosions were the result of the first Soviet air raids on Lodz and its environs.

About 1 AM we were awakened by fire engines racing down Zydowska Street. When we dared look outside, we saw a huge glow over Wolborska Street. Today we learned that a few houses burned to the ground.

Our situation has become a little better, especially in regard to food. Our courageous women have made a few excursions into the immediate neighborhood, where the people collecting scrap metal, waste paper, refuse, and feces were housed for a short time. In practically every apartment there were potatoes, flour, cereals, lard, ground coffee, and other staples. So there was food in the ghetto, while the population went hungry.

OCTOBER 11, 1944

Wednesday. For the last few days we've had our own observation post. Since we want to know who is coming into the shop and at what time, we keep watch, lying flat on the balcony of Bajgelman's apartment, lifting only our heads above the wall. We rotate every hour and a half.

This morning, at 7 AM, our scheduled "guard" suddenly rushed down the stairs. We were about to turn the lights off when we heard his happy cry: "They're here." That meant that our friends and a group of workers had arrived at the shop. We found out later that the people at 36 Lagiewnicka had gone through a lot during the last two days.

On Monday, right after dinner, Jakubowicz made a long speech, saying that they'd almost certainly leave Tuesday morning. Every worker should prepare a bundle with one work outfit, one pair of shoes, bedding, and three changes of underwear. Then there was a "voluntary" surrender of valuables, such as watches, wedding bands, rings, silver cigarette cases, and all kinds of currency. Even fountain pens, leather suitcases, and briefcases were collected. Many people think this is a kind of ransom for postponing the enforced departure, and that they'll never again see the things they packed in the bundles.

A new communiqué was issued every few hours. It was torture. But eventually people got used to these tactics, and since it was *Simchas Torah,* they drank and were merry. By late that night there had still been no final decision. Only this morning the different groups were ordered to report to their workplaces.

As to the front, all we know is that the Soviet offensive in East Prussia is progressing well. The workers from 36 Lagiewnicka who work at the Radogoszcz railroad station meet police and soldiers there. The Germans often express regret that the attempt on Hitler's life on July 20th did not succeed. "Had it succeeded, we'd be free by now, along with you."

OCTOBER 13, 1944

The Jews who are officially housed in the ghetto are experiencing swelling from hunger, due to a lack of protein in their food. We've also noticed that kind of swelling on our legs and faces.

Because the bedding the people at 36 Lagiewnicka packed in bundles was taken from them, they have nothing to use for sleeping and have to search for pillows and blankets in nearby houses. It sometimes happens that they find a totally decomposed body under a blanket.

It was relatively quiet yesterday. Only Weinberg, an engineer, came to visit. He asked in a caring way if we needed anything. What a courageous, helpful man! Thanks to him there is electricity in the ghetto, the most indispensable commodity.

Today, though, there was a lot of activity. Early in the morning a sergeant came with two soldiers asking to be given the "L.S. Wart" pumps for extinguishing fires during air raids. They had hardly left when a paper buyer arrived and asked to see the merchandise for the second time. After him came the buyer of electric motors, which were priced at 90 marks. Then a representative of a German firm came to get bags. Two Germans from Balut Market took away the dismantled machine.

About 3 PM one of our friends came and told us that he is working in a group which moves the posts surrounding the ghetto. After Jewish apartments are "cleaned out," a special commission inspects the houses, marking some of them with a circle and others with a cross. Some will be demolished; others will remain untouched. Our friend's group follows them, and by moving the posts, excludes those buildings from the ghetto area.

When we went outside at 5 PM, we heard single gunshots, then many, accompanied by loud screaming from women and children. This lasted until 6 PM. There is no doubt that there were executions at the cemetery.

OCTOBER 18, 1944

We read today's newspaper and gathered that the Allies are steadily advancing from the east, west, and south, and that the Germans are on the defensive everywhere. In addition, Horthy, the Hungarian regent, gave up his position, and a Committee for a Free Germany with General Seydlitz at its helm was formed in the Soviet Union.

According to our friends, there is a serious possibility that the camp at 36 Lagiewnicka will be deported next Saturday. Their belongings are still being kept at the Radogoszcz station.

OCTOBER 19, 1944

Our friends brought us sad news today. Everything now indicates that the hour of departure is approaching. Yesterday, bags and bundles were loaded onto a train car. Only 300 pieces fit inside, or less than half of the total! The car was marked "Oranienburg," but the bill of lading was made out for Königswursterhausen. Why? A layover at Oranienburg concentration camp is very dangerous, and I suppose that not everyone will be let out of there. Most probably the overwhelming majority will find themselves behind barbed wire again.

There is an outbreak of scarlet fever among the children at the camp. Sick youngsters and their parents are transferring to 16 Jakuba St.

OCTOBER 21

Saturday. We waited in vain for our friends today. They did not come. Instead, a certain Pick—one of a few workers left at Balut Market—came by and told us that the Lagiewnicka inmates left at noon. The railway cars had been on a siding at Radogoszcz station since early morning. At first I couldn't believe it. Unfortunately, the news was fully confirmed.

People from 16 Jakuba worked in the shop today. A few Germans accompanied them, and we had a big scare. Fortunately, the eight of us were able to get to "secure places." Even Bajgelman made it to the hiding place, despite his disability.

I'm worried about my wife's health. Her legs swell more every day. Nor has the swelling of my face gone down.

After the camp's "inmates" had left Lagiewnicka Street, there remained a lot of food and a crate of "voluntarily" surrendered watches, which Jakubowicz had not had time to give to the Ghetto Administration. They were taken by some Germans who were there by chance. This is what results from tactics taken over from Chairman Rumkowski.

The transport conditions were fair: 37 persons per railway car. Biebow took them to the station and waved goodbye. He even kissed Jakubowicz.

OCTOBER 23, 1944

Today our new friend Pick sent us radio receivers and now, for the first time in five months, we've heard German and foreign bulletins. The Nazi Army is retreating all over, and Dzialdowo and Gabin were surrendered to the "enemy."

OCTOBER 25, 1944

The Germans came by twice today to get paper and a machine. We had to maintain absolute silence and even disconnect our hot plates.

We hear that a treasure was found in the garden at 36 Lagiewnicka Street:

3 jewel cases with jewelry, a few crates with finished men's suits, a lot of fabric of the best quality, etc.

Today we learned that instead of going to Oranienburg, the people from 36 Lagiewnicka went to Auschwitz. It's hard to ascertain which of these two hells is worse.

OCTOBER 30, 1944

It's nine weeks since we moved to this hiding place. Our nerves are shattered, but we're not sorry we didn't listen to the Germans or our disposers from Balut Market. We're alive, and we'll probably live to see the end of this butchery.

OCTOBER 31, 1944

This morning we took care of a most urgent task: concealing the place where we keep our potatoes and flour, because of the constant, unexpected intrusions into our shop. We did it using paper waste.

Relative quiet reigned until 9 o'clock. Then there was a heavy explosion, as if from a heavy caliber bomb. Our hiding place shook all over. Plates clanged on the make-shift shelves. Ten minutes later, there was another explosion, this time a lighter one.

The bombing didn't scare us, but at 10 o'clock we heard hurried steps and someone speaking German. Someone ran into the tool room, came up to the concealed door and stopped in front of the shelves. All eight of us were paralyzed with fear. A few minutes later, we heard someone say in Polish: "There are tools here." This one sentence in our native tongue calmed us. We went back to "normal." In the evening we found out that two Germans had been looking for gas meters. All kinds of people are robbing what they can, on the eve of the German Reich's downfall.

NOVEMBER 1, 1944

Pick sent a new "contact" to visit us. He told us that 60 older people were deported from 16 Jakuba St., of which 45 were sent to Uniejow, and all the sick to Kolo.

The explosions we heard a few days ago were not bombs. A few buildings on Wolborska Street were dynamited, and it's possible that the building where we were living was demolished.

NOVEMBER 9, 1944

The peace was disturbed very early yesterday by a visit from the well-informed Pick, who hurriedly and very excitedly told us to double and triple our guard because of "extreme danger"—and then off he went.

GERMAN DOCUMENT

Lodz, 6/XI/1944

The Jew Bruder reported he had determined that some Jews were hiding in the area of Metal Division I on Hanseatenstrasse.

The undersigned and work leader Schwind proceeded with two Jews to the spot, in order to take the Jews and deliver them to the Kripo. There was also supposed to be a large quantity of food stored there, which was confirmed upon search.

Below a cellar trap door we found one Jew, who left with Mr. Schwind and swore that no one else was in the cellar. Biebow then told Mr. Schwind that he should guard the three Jews by the door. Biebow and a Jew then started to search the cellar, where six other Jews were hiding. At the moment the Jews came out of hiding and were in the entrance hall, a Jew cried out that Mr. Schwind was being killed. Biebow ran outside immediately, saw Mr. Schwind streaming with blood, and jumped on the main perpetrator, a certain Dr. Weiskopf (Doctor of Medicine) who possessed colossal physical power. There ensued a difficult struggle on the ground between the undersigned, Mr. Schwind, and three Jews who hurried to our aid. Finally, the Jews who had hidden themselves were overpowered.

The ringleader, Weiskopf, took 5 shots. It is to be assumed that his wounds killed him quickly. Oberltnt. [Ger: First Lieut.] Schulz from the 6th police precinct was of assistance. Two of the shots were fired by Oberltnt. Schulz, three by Biebow.

JAKUB POZNANSKI, LODZ GHETTO DIARY

NOVEMBER 19, 1944

I have not opened this notebook for the last ten days. Our situation has taken an unexpected turn. For the last ten days we've been housed at 16 Jakuba Street.

On Thursday, November 9th, around 6 PM, we heard an agreed-upon signal: three heavy knocks on our shutters to warn us of immediate danger.

Two of our trusted informants from Balut Market brought us the news that our hiding place had been revealed and that Bruder, the chief of Jewish police, intended to visit us the next day with Kripo agents.

We were told that this was not the first time that a hideout had been identified. Five such places in cellars were liquidated this week alone, and in one of them a dramatic struggle took place with a physician, Dr. Daniel Wajskopf. His brother-in-law and nephew had earlier been caught and sent to 16 Jakuba Street but managed to run away from there. When Hans Biebow found out, he was furious and (together with Schwind, Bruder, and a certain Krajn) went to the place he was told the physician and his family were hiding.

In spite of a broken leg, Dr. Wajskopf went out to meet them and heroically protected the entrance to the cellar. His sisters and nephews joined him. As a result, Biebow, Schwind, Bruder, and Krajn were badly beaten up. Obviously, the final victory belonged to the "courageous" Germans and Judases. They were able, eventually, to get Dr. Wajskopf, but his desperate defense allowed some members of his family to escape. Biebow and Schwind, who had no guns with them, ran to Balut Market. They came back quickly and with four shots from their pistols killed a wonderful human being, who had dared lift his hand against a representative of the "master race." It was this incident that started the liquidation of a number of hiding places in the ghetto.

But getting back to our case. Our contacts were barely out the door when another representative from Balut Market presented himself and asked us, in Bruder's name, if we wanted to report voluntarily to camp. If so, then he would come with some Kripo agents to get us the next day. Nothing would threaten us. After they interrogate and register us, we'd be sent to take baths and be disinfected, and then to camp. We asked for an hour to think it over. After lengthy deliberations, we agreed that if our hole was already discovered, they'd take us away anyhow. We accepted Bruder's proposal with a heavy heart and spent our last night in the dungeon.

Friday morning we packed our belongings. We were barely ready, when we heard calls from the courtyard: "Bajgelman! Bajgelman!" We looked outside. There were two Kripo agents waiting with Bruder and Krajn, and a cart for transporting our possessions. They told us to get dressed and bring out all our bundles and the dungeon's "furniture."

From the shop we went to the Kripo building at Koscielna Street, where they wrote up our personal data and asked routine questions about currency and valuables. We were then sent to be disinfected and to have baths on Balut Market, from where we went to 16 Jakuba by trolley car.

NOVEMBER 24, 1944

We have already "settled in" at the camp. I work at 63 Lagiewnicka Street, cleaning feathers and down, and my wife and daughter work in the paper shop.

Today two trucks brought over furs and suitcases, which belonged to the German Jews deported to Kolo in 1942. That camp was liquidated not long ago.

For the last few days, apparently on orders from the Kripo, lists are being drawn up, which in addition to first and last names have one other entry—age. A few days ago they burned the birth and death records. We saved some of them by undertaking, with my wife, a very dangerous night expedition to the Office of Records.

Our work at 63 Lagiewnicka is not limited to feathers and down, which are sent to Germany. Along with the bedding, all kinds of personal belongings from "cleaned" Jewish homes reach us, such as men's clothing, dresses, outerwear, underwear. All of it has to be thoroughly sorted for use by refugees from the bombed-out cities in the Third Reich. Yesterday, Czarnulla told us to prepare 500 sets of clothing and underwear and as many pots, pans, and dishes, as quickly as possible, for Dresden.

I was offered a change of job: a position in the German office on Balut Market. I refused. I would not, for anything in the world, collaborate with the executioners of my country and my people!

NOVEMBER 26, 1944

I was shaken yesterday when I found Dr. Wajskopf's clothing and green hat among the things given to me for sorting.

DECEMBER 3, 1944

Sunday. I can write in my notebook only once a week now. I work very hard till about 3 PM every day. I come home very tired and then have to stand in line for bread, get some soup, find out what's happening, and get some kind of newspaper. I'm so tired at night that I can't even hold a pen in my hand.

I'm told that after much discussion at Balut Market, the actual and legal leadership of the few hundred people of the ghetto "population" was assumed by Bruder—instead of Dr. Eliasberg, who is responsible only for sanitary conditions.

The building at 36 Lagiewnicka, which once housed the tailor shop, was excluded from the ghetto area. A German military hospital will be established there. Every day the poles and barbed wire are moved again.

Last week two hiding places were uncovered on Zydowska Street. A lot of food was found but no people. Most likely, everyone was able to escape.

DECEMBER 10, 1944

Sunday. Again a week has passed.

We didn't work as hard as usual today, since our German supervisors had *"Volkssturm"* exercises* and didn't come to the ghetto. We were assigned to the so-called *Räumungskommando* [Ger: clean-up unit]—in other words, to "cleaning out" the apartments in Stary Rynek. We found a lot of watches, sewing machines, washers and wringers, candlesticks, etc.

Yesterday at exactly 7:30 AM, Hans Biebow arrived by car with Neuman, the Kripo boss. As usual, he started dispatching various groups for work. When we came out into the street, we noticed that the trolley cars were standing empty. We saw a few Kripo faces we knew and a number of new people talking to each other in Ukrainian.

At 2 PM we heard a whistle blow and the *Gruppenführer* [Ger: unit leader] ordered everyone to fall in. A German made a short speech punctuated by heavy name-calling. He had been made responsible for contraband by Hans Biebow and recommended the surrender of watches, cigarette cases, fountain pens, and similar valuables. Whoever disobeyed would receive the severest punishment, possibly death. After this juicy speech, the *Gruppenführer* began a personal search of men and women. We realized that those condemned to die are treated this way. However, that was not it.

DECEMBER 17, 1944

Biebow is not letting up. In these days which will decide our "to be or not to be," he would take the last shirt from our backs. Today he called the leadership to Balut Market and demanded, categorically, that we give up all hidden wealth. For a change he was sober, and allowed us two hours to do the searching. When he was brought some not very valuable, everyday objects, he let out a barrage of curses at the "*verfluchter Juden* [cursed Jews]."

Even Solomon could not pour anything from an empty vessel, but appetite grows with eating: Last Sunday a canteen containing some 200 gold and platinum ladies' watches was dug out on Lagiewnicka Street.

On Thursday, the so-called "Rumkowski archives" were unearthed in a garden adjacent to the cemetery. They contained a number of documents that would have been important to a future historian of the ghetto. Unfortunately, they were immediately destroyed. [Included was one of the copies of the official Chronicle of the Lodz Ghetto.]

On Friday three Gestapo men from the Poznan region arrived. With a sketch in hand, they searched two areas in our section, but their excavation work yielded nothing.

DECEMBER 25, 1944

Monday. Christmas. We were promised a day off from work, but 26 railway cars arrived last night at Radogoszcz station and we had to load them with down and feathers early in the morning.

Of course, no German came to the roll call. Our people were not too eager to work, and some disappeared, even though they knew the consequences. Those who remained, including myself, had to sweat it out. Where did our proverbial solidarity go?

1945

JANUARY 14, 1945

Sunday. The New Year has passed and nothing has changed. I have not looked at these notes for 3 weeks now. There's no reason to hide the fact that fear overtakes me every time. All kinds of uniformed people circulate in the camp, and there are also many informers serving the gentlemen from Balut Market.

On the Tuesday following the New Year, Biebow came to us and, during roll call, made a speech which, more or less, was as follows: "Our" year has started, and even though "you" have your own calendar, living among us has gotten you used to our date. Then he began naming a litany of sins, offenses, and transgressions, such as looting apartments, "stealing" things (Jewish possessions) slated for shipment to the Reich, concealing valuables, etc. Finally, he enumerated a "decalogue" of punishments we faced, starting with flogging and ending with the gallows.

A week ago there was alarming talk that 300 people will be shipped out, beginning with the "cave dwellers" who had left their cellar hideouts voluntarily. We lived through a few nightmarish days. Fortunately, the danger was temporarily averted.

On Friday, January 5th, when Schwind came for the roll call at 8:10 AM, he found only 200 people outside and had to wait a good 15 minutes before everyone appeared. Because of that, he ordered a 7:30 roll call for the next day.

He arrived exactly on time on Saturday, with Neuman, the Kripo commander, who was wearing an SS uniform. Neuman accused us of not working well and of looting the wealth of the ghetto, which belongs to German authorities. Bruder came forth and mentioned two individuals in whose possession "stolen" goods were found. Then Dancyger mentioned the names of four Jews who were sabotaging work. Neuman ordered the six "dishonest" people to step forward, and handed them over to the Kripo. Our unlucky comrades were killed in the late evening.

JANUARY 15, 1945
We were able to get a newspaper yesterday. The Soviet Army has begun a wide offensive on the Eastern Front. Fierce battles are underway near Warsaw, and our fate is being decided on the banks of the Vistula River.

Today we had the usual roll call. Although a certain uneasiness was apparent among the Germans, they issued the usual orders. Our group was assigned to loading straw shoes. Do the Germans anticipate a possible winter campaign?

Otherwise, the day went quietly. At night, a few daredevils listened to the radio by hiding, covered with blankets, in the cellar of a neighboring house. They reported that the Russians are advancing in our direction from the south and the east.

JANUARY 16, 1945
Today we were regrouped. Because there are no railroad cars available, we cannot load the straw shoes. Instead, they had us sort ribbons, buttons, and other odds and ends. There is confusion and chaos among the Germans. One order cancels another.

There was an air raid in the morning, and a few bombs fell on the city. All day long there were reports of the Russian offensive. Just before evening, we heard an explosion and ran outside. It was as bright as noon. Three rockets had lit up half the horizon. We continually heard bombs exploding and the sound of anti-aircraft guns. A fire bomb exploded in the field across from our camp, part of it falling on a neighboring roof. The camp firemen put it out immediately.

Otherwise, the night was quiet.

JANUARY 17, 1945
There were some Germans at the roll call this morning, but most of our overseers had notices to report to the so-called *"Volkssturm."* Still, our groups were sent to work.

There were two air raids during the day. The representatives of the *Herrenvolk* [Ger: master race] walk around pale, depressed, and fidgety. They keep going to town and coming back. They're probably packing.

Commander Bruder arrived in camp around 6 PM and announced that on order of the authorities there will be a general roll call tomorrow. Attendance is absolutely compulsory, not only for the camp's inhabitants but also the telephone operators and teamsters outside the camp.

We gathered from this that something ominous was brewing. After an hour people started leaving the camp en masse, and we followed their example, obeying common sense and our instinct for self-preservation. The experience of these past few months has shown that he who hides, survives.

We are hiding in a cellar at 10 Zydowska Street. Our new dungeon is 12 meters deep. A single bulb provides light. This is the shelter we planned to use last August, before we decided to find a place in the paper shop.

We have a group of more than 40 people with us. Our teeth chatter—from fear and cold—even though we all have at least two sets of underwear and outer clothes on. We know that the Germans plan to slaughter us before they leave Lodz.

There is deathly silence in our dungeon. We take turns sleeping.

Night. It's 10 PM.

JANUARY 18, 1945

We sat all day on top of a suitcase we brought to the dungeon back in November, just before we moved to the camp.

We have a supply of water, about 600 liters, and we decided that each of us will get three glasses of water per day. We've also pooled all the fat we had—oil, butter, and margarine. In the morning we distribute the "food rations" for the entire day.

Our nervousness exceeds the limits of human endurance. We think constantly the Germans are in the courtyard, looking for us.

Of course, we have our own reconnaissance: a few nimble lads. They set out at dawn for 16 Jakuba Street and carried back 18 loaves of bread.

Water drips from the dungeon walls. There's a lack of oxygen, a lighted match goes out immediately. How long will we last here?!

The boys have just arrived and are quite scared. They went to the camp a second time and saw trucks arriving. They had come for us. The boys heard the Germans talking. They are to transport us to the Jewish cemetery where, a week ago, they ordered nine large graves to be dug—each for a hundred people. Any minute now the search will begin.

If they find our hiding place, I will leave these notebooks in the dungeon. They might be our last trace.

JANUARY 19, 1945

Today, at 11 AM the long-awaited moment arrived: WE ARE FREE!

JANUARY 20, 1945

Saturday. Yesterday somebody suddenly lifted the cover hiding our dungeon, and we heard a joyful cry: "Gentlemen! Long live Poland!"

We couldn't believe our ears. The skeptics cried that it was a trick. Yet some of us were called by name. We overcame our fear and used the ladder to climb out—just the men. The women stayed in the cellar.

Daylight blinded us, but we were immediately deliriously happy, hugging and kissing even strangers. We ran through Franciszkanska Street; the ghetto gate was wide open.

Suddenly we heard: "They're coming, they're coming!" At the end of Smugowa Street was a Soviet tank. It moved slowly and was greeted by the population with great enthusiasm. After a few minutes, two army cars, a mounted unit, and a group of foot soldiers appeared. Then a limousine arrived, stopping at the corner. I approached, since I speak Russian fluently and could serve as an interpreter.

The general in the car made a short speech saying that the Polish Commonwealth now has an independent democratic government, in which all factions are represented and with President Bierut at its head. I translated his words into Polish. Everyone applauded and cried, "Hurrah! Long life!" The Poles gathered around us, asking how we had survived, if we had food, etc.

About 2 PM my wife and daughter and I went to our old apartment on Andrzeja Street. We found it almost empty. The furniture had been shipped to Germany. Only some old dilapidated pieces remained in the corner.

We spent the night in camp at 16 Jakuba Street. For supper we ate almost all of our food from the cellar, and for the first time in five years we ate until we had enough.

Of the entire population of the ghetto, more than 200,000 Jews, probably about 800 remain, some of them still wearing the Star of David on their chests. Their pale, emaciated faces are very conspicuous.

The Germans did not have time to transport even a single Jew to the cemetery. Nine open graves remained waiting.

JANUARY 21, 1945

After breakfast today, I walked over to Siedlecka Street, to Haessler's factory. I met a few older workers, who welcomed me with genuine warmth. The Germans had not had time to destroy the factory or dismantle the machinery. Some machines were taken apart, but the parts remained in place. We decided to guard them, keeping a sharp eye on them.

In spite of the physical exhaustion, I feel a new surge of energy. There is a lot of work waiting for us.

NOTES ON RUMKOWSKI

Hypotheticals abound in considering Mordechai Chaim Rumkowski's culpability in the deaths of the ghetto Jews, and also in assessing how many lives he may have preserved.

¶ Had Stalin not held up his troops on the east side of the Vistula River, outside Warsaw, through the summer and fall of 1944—waiting while Polish national fervor subsided after the Warsaw uprising—most of the 80,000 Jews in Lodz in May of 1944 would have been saved.

¶ What would the Jews of Lodz have done if they had known the truth about the awaiting death camps?

¶ Would any resistance have been possible?

¶ Was it just as well they did not have to suffer the knowledge that they were going to their deaths?

Isaiah Trunk, in his acclaimed study *Judenrat,* concluded that the outcome was the same for all the Jews of Europe, regardless of their leadership. Nearly all perished.

THE VIEW OF THE TORAH

In July 1942, Adam Czerniakow, the Nazi-appointed Eldest of the Jews of the Warsaw Ghetto, took poison rather than carry out German orders to deliver his ghetto's children and elderly. And immediately in the wake of that loss of leadership, the most intensive deportations in the history of the Holocaust occurred: within three months some 310,000 Jews were sent from Warsaw to die in Treblinka.

Rumkowski knew this when similar orders came to him just following the evacuation of the Warsaw Ghetto, in September 1942: hand over your Jewish children, elderly, and sickly—20,000 Jews considered unproductive.

Rumkowski asked the Council of Rabbis to participate in the deportation selection process, but they declined. Repeatedly he told Jews in the ghetto that when the war was over he would stand before a Jewish tribunal; he insisted that his policies would be vindicated.

It seems beyond question that the consensus of a rabbinic court on *Dat Torah,* the Torah's Law, would view Rumkowski's participation in the deportations, and their enforcement through his police, as murder, *if he knew the fate of those being sent out.*

The Talmud, in San Hedrin 74, states simply: "Who tells you that your blood is redder?"

The great rabbi and philosopher Maimonides (1135–1204), in his organization of oral Jewish law, the *Mishna*, confronts the question of what should be done when a group of Jews is confined and told to hand over individuals in order to save their own lives. And in his *Yessoday Ha Torah*, The Basic Precepts of the Torah, he considers such situations in the context of pogroms. Citing *Mishna Trumot* 12/8, he writes: "If they should say, 'Give us one of you and we will kill him, and if not we will kill all of you,' the Jews should allow themselves to be killed and not hand over a single Jewish life."

But the Germans did not tell Rumkowski they intended to kill his Jews. Or did they? We can use documents in this volume to better assess what Rumkowski knew about what awaited the Jews he was sending "into the unknown."

WHAT RUMKOWSKI KNEW

During the summer of 1942, a Jew relocated into the Lodz Ghetto brought with him this letter, written by Jakub Szulman, a rabbi in the town of Grabow, northwest of Lodz:

> My Dearest Ones:
> I have not answered your letters until now because I did not know exactly about things that were being rumored. Now, to our great misfortune, we know it all. An eyewitness who by chance was able to escape from hell has been to see me . . . I learned everything from him. The place where everyone is being put to death is called Chelmno, not far from Dabie; and

they are all buried in the nearby forest of Lochow. People are killed in one of two ways: either they are shot or gassed. This is what happened to the towns of Dabie, Izbica Kujawska, Klodo Wava and others. Recently, thousands of gypsies have been brought there from the so-called gypsy camp in Lodz. And for the past few days, they have been bringing thousands of Jews from Lodz there, and doing the same to them.

Do not think that a madman is writing; unfortunately, this is the cruel and tragic truth (Good God!) O Man, throw off your rags, sprinkle your head with ashes, or run through the streets and dance in madness . . . I am so wearied by the sufferings of Israel, my pen can write no more. My heart is breaking. But perhaps the Almighty will take pity and save the last remnants of our People.

Help us, O Creator of the universe!

Grabow, 1/19/42 Jakub Szulman

(The letter writer is not to be confused with the physician of the same name whose diary is excerpted in this volume.)

Jacob Nirenberg, in a Yiddish history of the ghetto published in New York in 1949, states that the letter was brought to Bundists in the ghetto. They turned it over to one of their leaders, Israel Tabaksblat, charging him with presenting the letter to Rumkowski—an undeniable warning to the Eldest of the Jews of the consequences of deporting Jews from the ghetto.

Nirenberg reports that Rumkowski acknowledged to Tabaksblat that he had known the facts about Chelmno for some time.

But Israel Tabaksblat in his own history of the ghetto obscures whether or not Rumkowski actually saw the Grabow rabbi's letter. He confirms that the letter was brought into the ghetto; then, without mention of Rumkowski or himself, he says it was sent out again to warn the Jews in Warsaw. (At this time there was some traffic between the ghettos.)

Two previously unrecognized bits of information appear in this volume which weigh heavily in assessing what Rumkowski knew, and when.

Oskar Rosenfeld recorded this cryptic acknowledgment from Rumkowski:

> One heard the words of the Eldest in one's ears:
>
> "If I were to tell you everything I know, you would not sleep. So I alone am the one who does not sleep. . . . The ghetto, too, is in the war."

Dating is intermittent in Rosenfeld's notebooks. This appears to have been written between February and April of 1942.

But even closer to the issue is a memorandum which has remained unnoticed these past forty-four years among the documents from the Lodz Ghetto's German administration. Frederick W. Ribbe, second in command over the Jews, wrote to Rumkowski on May 16, 1942, during the first waves of deportation from the ghetto:

> I request that you immediately investigate whether there is a
> Bone Grinder
> in the ghetto, either with a motor or hand-driven. The special commando in Kulmhof [German for Chelmno] is interested in such a grinder.

Was this inquiry simply passed procedurally on to Rumkowski as Ribbe followed up on a requisition from the Chelmno asphyxiation operation? Or was Ribbe leaving for history an almost undeniable piece of evidence, forced in front of Rumkowski, to end any question about his complicity?

Rumkowski faced the most effectively destructive force in the history of mankind. There are many who say that only a man uncompromised by moral compunctions could have done so.

Felicia Weingarten, a survivor of the ghetto who now lives in St. Paul, Minnesota, recently wrote to us in response to the film made from these documents:

> Rumkowski, although temperamental, power greedy, lecherous, was not a collaborator. He wanted to save at least a remnant. Whether he had the right to decide who was to live, to save some at the cost of many, is a very good question.
>
> He was courageous. It took all he had to face the Nazis every day, and he did care about the Jewish people. In the end he died in the gas chamber although he could have stayed in the ghetto. He played God and I don't believe that it is permitted to do so.

One can read and reread his astounding "Give Me Your Children" speech to understand the contradictions Rumkowski attempted to reconcile through the exercise of his power, and the morbid awareness he clearly had of his own tragic role in history.

A man whose life immediately before the war had been devoted to the care of orphans, who had visited with Janusz Korczak in Warsaw to discuss educational theory and child care, who might well have even heard that his colleague Korczak had chosen to go with his orphans into the gas chamber—Rumkowski must well have meant it when he stood before the thousands of ghetto Jews in the Fire Brigade Square on September 4, 1942, and said: "I never imagined I would be forced to deliver this sacrifice to the altar with my own hands."

RUMKOWSKI'S DEATH

We lose sight of Rumkowski in this volume with Poznanski's description in the last chapter of Rumkowski's own voluntary deportation in August 1944, to accompany his brother Jozef. In 1979, *Commentary* magazine published an extended debate among supposed eyewitnesses about how Rumkowski died. That the train he boarded went to Auschwitz is undisputed. Nor does anyone challenge that the Eldest of the Jews of Lodz perished there. But three versions of how Rumkowski died have emerged, each told by people who claim to have been there.

¶ In one widely accepted account, Rumkowski was beaten to death by Jews from the ghetto who were awaiting his arrival. His body was then thrown into an open pit where bodies were burned.

¶ A second account describes Rumkowski's arrival at Auschwitz with his young wife and their adopted son. He presented a letter of introduction provided to him in Lodz by Hans Biebow, the ghetto's German overseer. The letter allegedly *transferred* Rumkowski to Auschwitz, commending his administrative ability. By this account, Rumkowski was duly met and welcomed on the platform at the death camp, told he had been expected and would be given a tour of the facility with his family. The wagon brought them to a crematorium. They were burned alive without being gassed.

¶ The least sensational version has Rumkowski arriving at Auschwitz, separated for his age from those who could work, and put to death in due course.

There is no well-researched figure for how many survived the Lodz Ghetto. The best estimates seem to be about ten thousand Jews. Some had the good fortune to actually be sent to work camps—always the Nazis' deportation claim. The remainder of those who survived arrived at Auschwitz in the summer of 1944, when the death camp was overflowing with humanity and when many were being sent on to other camps. Some of those who survive believe Rumkowski saved them by keeping them protected in the ghetto for so long. Survivors commonly assert that more Jews are alive today from the Lodz Ghetto than from any other concentration of Jews under Nazi rule. I have not seen this documented, but believe it should be reported.

The numbers of those lost are more concrete. Sixty thousand people died in the ghetto, whether from starvation, freezing, disease, hanging, or suicide. From the ghetto, 130,000 who were deported died either in the exhaust vans at Chelmno or the gas chambers of Auschwitz.

The Nazis killed these Jews. Rumkowski did not will their deaths. But again, a hypothetical: If it had not been for Rumkowski's deceitful or misinformed assurances of their safety, and his constant restraint of those truth-telling "rumor mongerers" who warned of the Nazi genocide, would so many of those people have willingly boarded the trains?

—Alan Adelson

NOTES ON THE WRITERS AND MANUSCRIPTS

[We have not made the writing more literary than it was originally, nor have we rendered it into smoothly idiomatic English. Our goal was to be true to the flavor of the original Yiddish, Polish, German, and Hebrew. Those passages written originally in English have, for the most part, gone unaltered, their occasional awkwardnesses retained. In general, the different languages' variant spellings of names and foreign words have also been retained.]

THE CAST OF INDIVIDUAL VOICES

ANONYMOUS: A GIRL'S DIARY

The text indicates only that this girl's first name was either Esterka or Minia; her fragment of a diary was written in Polish during the winter and spring of 1942.

ANONYMOUS: *LES VRAIS RICHES*

This young man's diary, in Polish, English, Yiddish, and Hebrew, was written in the margins of the French novel *The Truly Rich,* in the very last months of the ghetto's existence. The writing recalls Anne Frank's noble humanity, although without her innocence and hope, for this young man's vulnerability is racked with pain, his goodness outraged. And yet as deeply as his fate may upset the reader, there is pleasure to be taken in his dignity, as well as in his talent for languages and literature.

The book was found at Auschwitz after the war and is now in the Yad Vashem Archives.

ANONYMOUS: "SEEK IN THE ASHES"

Written in Polish by a man deported from the ghetto in August 1944, this diary was found at Auschwitz, half-burned. It was published in *Szukajcie w popiolach: Papiery znalezione w Ozwiecimiu* [Seek in the Ashes: Papers found in Auschwitz], Janusz Gumkowski and Adam Rutkowski, editors, Wydawnictwo Lodzkie, Lodz, 1965.

Ludwik Asz wrote in Polish. His manuscript "At the Cemetery" is in private hands. Asz was recently described by Felicia Karo-Weingarten, a survivor of the Lodz Ghetto now living in St. Paul, Minnesota:

> Lutek, as we called him, was born in Lodz, in 1925. He lived at Magistracka Street 16, in the apartment building next to ours. His mother was a dentist, his father had a fine position in an export and import company. They were educated, comfortably situated people. They did not give their only child any Jewish religious education, as they were rather assimilated.
>
> Lutek attended a Polish gymnasium until 1939, completing three years. He attended school in the ghetto two more years and was one year short of finishing. He was a very bright, intelligent boy. He was especially good in languages and loved literature. He was tall and broad-shouldered and had a very pleasant open face. Since we were friends, he occasionally read to me the poetry he wrote.
>
> After the war, as I traveled throughout West Germany to visit many DP camps, I often asked about Ludwik Asz, as I was desperate to find any relatives and friends. I know he was deported with his parents to Auschwitz in either August or September of 1944. I believe he perished, because no one whom I could question had seen him in the camps.

Hans Biebow, far more than other Germans, realized how profitable the Lodz Ghetto would be if converted into a work complex based on virtual slave labor. As part of his effort to become head of the *Gettoverwaltung,* the German Ghetto Administration, he submitted the following *curriculum vitae* on 10 May 1940:

> I was born December 18, 1902, in Bremen, the son of Julius Biebow, an insurance company director. After graduating from secondary school, I

> entered my father's company—the district branch of the Stuttgart Insurance Company—as an apprentice, planning on eventually assuming my father's post. I received thorough training, remaining there an additional year as an employee. Since the insurance business had come almost completely to a standstill during the inflation, I then gave up my position to join the cereal and foodstuff bank in Bremen as a trainee. From there I went into the cereal business and stayed in this trade until I was 22. I should mention that I managed a large branch of an Eichsfeld cereal company in Göttingen for half a year. When the inflation ended, I became particularly interested in the reviving coffee trade. After a short training period with a business friend of my father's, I opened my own business with very little capital, building it, in the course of 18 years, into one of the largest such companies in Germany. At the end I employed about 250 workers and office personnel.

A ruthless administrator, he was concerned primarily with the ghetto's productivity and his own personal gain. He was directly responsible for starving the population beyond the limits of endurance, and he assisted the Gestapo in rounding up Jews during deportations. He probably hoped to eliminate all surviving witnesses to the role he had played, for in the days just before the Red Army's liberation of Lodz, he had large burial pits dug in the cemetery, intending that the Gestapo execute the 877 Jews who remained in the ghetto as part of a clean-up crew. Apprehended in Bremen after the war, he was tried before a Polish court in Lodz and hanged in 1947.

The text of his address, in German, to the ghetto tailors on August 7, 1944, is preserved in the Zonabend Collection at the YIVO Archives.

Jerakhmil Bryman was on the staff of the Ghetto Archives and wrote for the *Chronicle*. He was trained as a theologian and wrote extensively on the ghetto's religious life, signing his articles "JBA." Not many of his manuscripts have survived, but his report, in Yiddish, on the ghetto's religious services is in the Yad Vashem Archives.

Shlomo Frank was, according to some sources, a journalist before the war. In the ghetto he was a member of the Order Service, the Jewish police, and also of the semiclandestine Zionist-Revisionists. Deported from the ghetto, he was incarcerated in several concentration camps and survived the war.

Having hidden his diary "somewhere in a ghetto hole," Frank recovered it after the war, giving it to the Jewish Historical Commission in Lodz, a predecessor of the Jewish Historical Institute in Warsaw. Written in Yiddish, the diary was published as a book: Shlomo Frank, *Togbukh fun lodzer geto* [A Diary of the Lodz Ghetto], Buenos Aires, 1958.

Shimon Huberband was born in 1909 in Checiny, Poland. A rabbi and scholar, he moved to Warsaw in 1940 and there joined the *Oyneg shabbos* [Yid: Joy of the Sabbath] group, under which name the Warsaw Ghetto Underground Archive was known. To this archive, which was founded and directed by Emanuel Ringelblum, Huberband contributed a large number of notes and essays on the religious life of Polish Jews under the Nazi occupation. He died in a death camp on August 18, 1942.

His notes were preserved in the Ringelblum Archive, which was recovered after the war in the ruins of the Warsaw Ghetto. The bulk of this Archive is now deposited in the Jewish Historical Institute in Warsaw. The English translation of Huberband's notes on the destruction of the Lodz synagogues was published in: Shimon Huberband, *Kiddush Hashem: Jewish Religious and Cultural Life in Poland during the Holocaust,* David E. Fishman, translator, Jeffrey S. Gurock and Robert S. Hirt, editors, Ktav Publishing House/Yeshiva University Press, Hoboken, New Jersey, 1987.

Leon Hurwitz was trained as an engineer. In Lodz before the war, he was an active member of the Folkists, a Jewish populist party, and in the ghetto he was bitterly critical of Rumkowski. His diary was written in Yiddish. In a section not included in this volume, he wrote: "The ghetto's internal life is similar to the feudal system of the Middle Ages."

Before his deportation to Auschwitz in August 1944, Hurwitz and a friend hid his diary. The friend survived the war, retrieved the diary after liberation, and deposited it in the Jewish Historical Institute, Warsaw.

Abram Kajzer, a worker, and his wife and son were deported from the ghetto to Auschwitz in August 1944. Surviving the selection process that sent his wife and son to the gas chamber, Kajzer kept a secret diary in Auschwitz and the other camps to which he was subsequently moved. A Polish translation of his diary, which was originally written in Yiddish, was published as: Abram Kajzer, *Za drutami smierci* [Behind the Wires of Death], Wydawnictwo Lodzkie, Lodz, 1962.

Ludwik Landau was born in 1901 in Tomaszow Mazowiecki. A renowned Polish statistician and economist, he made his home in Warsaw. Under the Nazis, he continued his scholarly activities, compiling surveys of the economic situation for the Polish underground. When the Warsaw Ghetto was established, he remained on the Aryan side.

Writing in Polish, Landau kept copious daily notes, which were based mainly on his extensive reading. When he failed to return home on February 29, 1944, his wife suspected the worst and gave the notes to a neighbor. She and her daughter took poison when the police came the next day to arrest them. The notes were published as: Ludwik Landau, *Kronika lat wojny i okupacji* [Chronicle of the Years of War and Occupation], 3 volumes, Panstwowe Wydawnictwo Naukowe, Warsaw, 1962.

Irena Liebman was deported from the ghetto to Auschwitz in August 1944. She survived the war and reconstructed her entire diary from memory. Now living in Israel, she is the one Lodz diarist still alive. Her Polish manuscript and her Hebrew translation are in Yad Vashem. The following is a statement she prepared for this volume:

> I was born Irena Aronowicz in Lodz, Poland, in the year 1925. I began to write when we moved to the ghetto. I didn't write a day-by-day diary, but blitz pictures of our life there, in a kaleidoscopic form, when I could find a quiet corner in our little room. Often I wrote while standing with the open copybook on the wall. Later (after September 1942) when only my sister and I stayed in our empty room, I had more opportunity to write, but then it was harder for me to do it, and I wrote and erased, wrote and erased . . . and cried.
>
> I took my four full copybooks in my knapsack when, with my sister, I went to Auschwitz in August 1944. I left them with my knapsack on the train. After the American troops liberated Mauthausen on May 5, 1945, when I found enough strength to let my legs go and my brain think, I knew that I had to re-write my ghetto memoir. I started my project by finding a few pieces of paper and my first pencil and then a real pen. I wrote in Polish. Very interesting is the fact that I couldn't write about the last nine months of the war—my time in the concentration camps: Birkenau, Freiberg (a little labor camp in Germany, between Chemnitz and Dresden), Mauthausen (Austria)—but I wrote about my "journey" to Auschwitz.
>
> I lived for more than a year in U.N.R.R.A. camps for displaced persons in Italy. I never went back to Poland again, because I had nothing to find there, only graves and ashes. In August 1946 I went to Palestine via Naples and Port Said, posing as the wife of a Palestinian soldier (Jewish Brigade Group in the British Army) and started my new life (a very hard one) in

our Jewish Homeland. I worked in industry factories, saved money and bought Hebrew study books and lexicons. I knew that I had to continue my writing in my new language, Hebrew.

In 1949 I married Joseph Liebman. He had escaped in 1939 from the Polish Army, arriving in Palestine in 1941 (via Russia, Japan, South Africa), where he volunteered for the Jewish Brigade. We built a new home together and had two sons, Samson and Abraham (Rami). After my husband died in 1965, I worked as a technical librarian for our Air Industry.

Between 1965 and now, twelve books of mine, written in Hebrew, have been published. In 1956 I gave my ghetto memoir, with my Hebrew translation, to Yad Vashem in Jerusalem. The first of my published books describes the first months after our liberation from Mauthausen; the second, the life of a 12-year-old Jewish girl in Poland in the months before the war. I have written three books for children, with stories about Jewish children in the Holocaust, and another one (a very good one) about a 15-year-old girl in the ghetto. I received a literature prize in 1977 for *Piki Is Me,* a book about an Israeli boy who grows up without a father. A recent book, *See Naples and Live,* is a novel for adults and describes a group of Jews in Italy after the liberation.

I live alone now in an apartment in a very nice place, Givataim. I have seven grandchildren (6 girls and a boy). My sons live with their families in other parts of Israel, and we are very close to one another.

Israel Milejkowski was born in Warsaw in 1877. A physician, he was active in Jewish health-care organizations and was an official in the Warsaw Ghetto's Sanitation and Health Departments. Deported in January 1943 to the Treblinka death camp, he committed suicide in the transport car by swallowing cyanide.

His statement on the evils of the ghetto was given in response to a questionnaire developed by the Warsaw Ghetto Underground Archive now in the Jewish Historical Institute in Warsaw. The English translation of Milejkowski's statement was published in *To Live with Honor and Die with Honor! . . . Selected Documents from the Warsaw Ghetto Underground Archives,* Joseph Kermish, editor, Yad Vashem, Jerusalem, 1986.

Jakub Poznanski held university degrees in agronomy and chemistry. In the ghetto's first months, he supervised the youth *kibbutzim* [Heb: collectives] in Marysin and, after these were liquidated later in 1940, held various jobs, the last of which was in the paper products workshop. As his diary reveals, his self-possession, a kind of skeptical pragmatism, alienated him from Rumkowski but was responsible for his surviving the war. He died in Lodz in 1959.

Writing in Polish, Poznanski began his diary in 1942. His many references to events of 1939, 1940, and 1941 were written retrospectively, in small print. The entire diary was published as Jakub Poznanski, *Pamietnik z getta Lodzkiego* [A Diary from the Lodz Ghetto], Wydawnictwo Lodzkie, Lodz, 1960.

Oskar Rosenfeld was born on May 13, 1884, in Korycany, Moravia. He attended the University of Vienna and remained in that city for some years, working with Theodor Herzl in the Zionist movement there, helping to found its first Jewish theater, and editing the Zionist weekly *Die Neue Welt.* After Germany annexed Austria in 1938, he moved to Prague, where he was a correspondent for *The Jewish Chronicle* of London. In October 1941 he was deported from Prague to the Lodz Ghetto, where he joined the staff of the Ghetto Archives and wrote for the Ghetto *Chronicle*. He was included in the final deportation from the ghetto to Auschwitz in August 1944.

Rosenfeld was the author of many books, including *Philipp Otto Runge in der Romantik, Die vierte Galerie* [Phillip Otto Runge in the Romantic Era, the Fourth Gallery] (Vienna, 1910) and *Mendl Ruhig* (Heidelberg, 1914). He also translated into German works by Sholom Aleichem, Isaac Leib Peretz, H. Leivik, I. J. Singer, and other Yiddish writers. As his notebooks make abundantly clear, he was a man of highly developed culture and sophistication, possessed of extraordinary consciousness and sensibility.

Written in German (with occasional words and passages in Hebrew, Yiddish, English, and his own private code), these notebooks contain Rosenfeld's working notes, a superb chapter of a never-finished novel, and a running diary; they render the face of the ghetto and its deeper reality in wonderful detail. Rosenfeld noted how he and other Western Jews, when they first arrived, walked among the impoverished natives like fashionably dressed tourists—and how the dignity they'd earlier maintained in the face of the Nazis' abuse was gradually torn away by the squalor of the ghetto, the horror of the deportations, the unavoidable obsession with food. He thought of the ghetto as the golem of cities, and yet in describing its subjective life—its cultural activity, its religious practice, what people were actually saying, his own wide-ranging thoughts—he underscored the ghetto's humanity.

This volume publishes large sections of these notebooks for the first time. The original manuscripts are now in Yad Vashem.

Szmul Rozensztajn was born in Lodz in 1895. Before the war, he had a career as a journalist and was the Lodz correspondent for *Haynt* [Today], the Yiddish daily published in Warsaw. In the ghetto he was Rumkowski's press secretary, the manager of the ghetto's printshop, and the editor of the *Geto-tsaytung,* the

Ghetto writers Oskar Rosenfeld (LEFT) and Oskar Singer (RIGHT), in conversation with a clandestine radio listener named Weksler.

Dawid Sierakowiak. The only known photograph of the young diarist, an enlargement from his ghetto high-school class picture.

The photographer Mendel Grossman.

Left: The cover of one of Dawid Sierakowiak's diary notebooks. *Right:* Two pages of Dawid Sierakowiak's notebook, now owned by Konrad Turowski, who took the photograph.

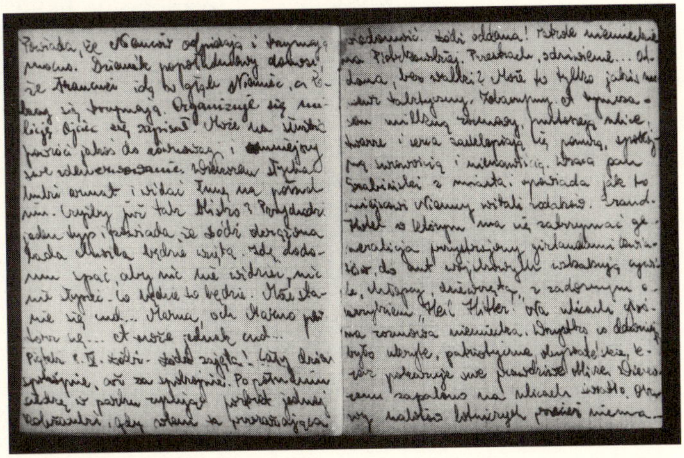

Ghetto Gazette, which ran for eighteen issues between March 7 and September 21, 1941. He survived until August 1944.

Rozensztajn's daily notes, in which are recorded Rumkowski's actions, decrees, and speeches, have a sycophantic character and present the Eldest of the Jews in the most favorable light. The manuscript of these notes is now in the Jewish Historical Institute, Warsaw, and a typewritten copy is in the Yad Vashem Archives, Jerusalem.

Mordechai Chaim Rumkowski was born on March 27, 1877, in the village of Illino, Byelorussia. He received only a minimal formal education. He was a partner in a large velvet factory in Lodz before the First World War but failed in this and a subsequent business venture; however, he found that communal work, particularly child welfare, more successfully channeled his great energy and boundless ambition. He organized the well-known orphanage in Helenowek, near Lodz, and was its director until 1939. From 1931 on, he served on the board of the Lodz *kehillah,* the Jewish community council, leading its Zionist faction. After the German occupation of Lodz, the *kehillah* was replaced by a Council of Elders, and Rumkowski was ordered to become its chairman, the Eldest of the Jews. When the Lodz Ghetto was established, he became its virtual ruler. On August 20, 1944, he and his family were deported from the ghetto to Auschwitz.

Rumkowski's speeches, in Yiddish, to the ghetto population and to ghetto administrators were transcribed by the staff of the Ghetto Archives and by Szmul Rozensztajn, his press secretary. These transcripts, today preserved in several archives, are in Yiddish, Polish, and German.

Simcha Bunim Shayevitsh was born in 1907 in Lenschitz, Poland. The son of very poor parents, he was mostly self-educated, and in Lodz he earned a living making mittens. His poems reflect the influence of the Haskelah movement, in that they make reference to secular and religious learning, modern and ancient culture; they were published in literary journals as early as 1933. A storyteller as well as a poet, Shayevitsh survived until 1944.

The two poems in this volume were published, in Yiddish, in 1946, in Lodz by the Central Jewish Historical Commission.

Dawid Sierakowiak was born in Lodz on July 25, 1924, and graduated from the ghetto's *Gymnasium* [high school] in 1941. Weakened by malnutrition, he contracted tuberculosis and died in the ghetto on August 8, 1943, at the age of nineteen. His diary suggests that he was a remarkable young man: possessed of strong character, talented as a writer and a caricaturist, he was personally exuberant, intellectually ambitious, and socially conscious. He was an active Communist and a member of the ghetto's political underground.

The entries in his diary for the summer of 1939 indicate the fullness of his life on the eve of the war. In July, on holiday with other students, he went mountain climbing, swam in the Danube, practiced reading in English, acted as the master of ceremonies at an evening around the campfire, and, on the eve of Tishe B'Av, gave a little talk in Hebrew on the meaning of the holiday. Returning to Lodz at the end of the month, he describes his joy at being back home with friends and family. In August many of his entries concern the political situation and the possibility of Hitler's starting a war. He notes that he is writing a paper entitled "Semitia," dealing with the future of the Jews and suggesting a program of cooperation with the Arabs.

On August 24 there was a general mobilization but "no sign of defeatism." Reporting for civil defense duties two days later, he notes, "Jews—old, young, women, Chasidim—like other citizens (except for Germans) are volunteering."

Writing in Polish, Sierakowiak made entries in his diary every day. The entries between April 6, 1941, and September 6, 1942, were published as *Dziennik Dawida Sierakowiaka* [The Diary of Dawid Sierakowiak], Iskry Publishing House, Warsaw, 1960. The present selection includes both previously published and unpublished fragments; the latter appear in this volume with the kind permission of Konrad Turowski.

Oskar Singer was born in 1883. Like Rosenfeld, he earned a doctorate, had an active literary career, was deported from Prague to the Lodz Ghetto in October 1941, joined the staff of the Archives and the *Chronicle,* and survived until 1944.

He was a writer of some accomplishment before the war, working as a publicist, contributing to a number of general and Jewish journals, and writing the anti-Nazi play *Herren der Welt: Zeitstück in 3 Akten* [Gentlemen of the World: A Topical Drama in 3 Acts] (Refta-Verlag, Prague-Vienna-Zurich, 1935).

His earlier efforts as a publicist may have influenced the sketches of ghetto workshops he wrote for the *Chronicle,* for these, unlike his grimmer pieces, have a cheerful public-relations quality to them. Typed copies of his sketches, written in German, are in the YIVO Archives.

Albert Speer (1905–81) was an adviser to Hitler from 1933 to 1945. During the war he was the Nazis' Minister of Armaments. Convicted as a war criminal for using slave labor, he spent twenty years in prison. His memoir, *Infiltration,* was published in New York by Macmillan in 1981.

Jakub Szulman was born in 1890. A physician, community activist, and journalist, he was a founder and leading member of the Labor Zionist Party in Poland, a contributor to the Yiddish journal *Naie Folksaytung* (New People's Daily) and to other Jewish publications, and a founding member of the Vilna branch of YIVO. Given responsibility in 1920 for organizing children's summer camps, he requested the help of M. C. Rumkowski, then in charge of orphan welfare.

When he died, in early 1942, the *Chronicle* carried the following obituary:

> On January 2, Jakub Szulman, aged 52, well-known in Jewish society as a socially active and indefatigable civic leader in Lodz's Jewish life, departed this world in the prime of his life. Szulman, of blessed memory, enjoyed the same trust and universal respect in the ghetto as he had in pre-war Lodz. Until the last moments of his life he held the important position of chief of Hospital No. 2 on Drewnowska Street. Due to his uncommon abilities and selfless perseverance, the deceased distinguished himself in organizing life in the ghetto, which earned him the fullest appreciation of the ghetto's leader and of everyone who worked along with him. Among other things, the ghetto owes the creation of the building superintendents' system and successes in the field of hospital management to the initiatives of the deceased. Szulman, of blessed memory, was one of those rare people of whom all, without exception, can speak only in superlatives. Ghetto society has lost an extremely useful, righteous, and noble man of great merit. The funeral took place on Sunday, proceeding from the mortuary to the cemetery. Hundreds of people from all walks of life, as well as Chairman Rumkowski, took part in the funeral ceremony. The deceased is survived by his wife and son.

His memoir, begun as soon as he learned that he had an incurable heart condition, was an effort "to record for posterity what I have seen." Written in Yiddish with notes in Russian, it was found on the site of the ghetto after the war and eventually deposited in the Archives of Beit Lohamei Hagetaot [the Ghetto Fighters House] in Israel.

Jozef Zelkowicz was born in 1897 in Konstantynow, near Lodz. He received a religious education and was ordained a rabbi but never practiced this vocation. He continued his education at a Normal School and, on graduation, obtained a teacher's license. He served in the Polish army and saw military action during the Soviet-Polish war of 1920.

Coming to understand that his main interests were history and ethnography, he began devoting himself to research and writing, first in Polish but then almost exclusively in Yiddish. He published his work in a wide variety of Yiddish journals in Poland, as well as in the United States. He was secretary of the Lodz Society of Friends of the Jewish Research Institute YIVO of Vilna. While with YIVO, he wrote and published two major scholarly works, one on death in Jewish ethnography and folklore and the other on the image of Jewish social life in a mid-nineteenth-century Polish shtetl.

On the staff of the Ghetto Archives and the *Chronicle,* Zelkowicz also contributed to the unfinished "Encyclopedia of the Ghetto." The essays he undertook on his own are often characterized by biting irony and implicit criticism of the ghetto leadership. His great work is *In yene koshmarne teq* [Yid: In These Nightmarish Days], a harrowing account of the events of September 1942.

Zelkowicz died in Auschwitz in 1944. Many of his manuscripts were lost in the ghetto, including two monographs on the Jewish communities of Konstantynow and Lutomiersk. A great number of those that survived are now part of the Zonabend Collection in the YIVO Archives.

OTHER SOURCES

The circumstances of the Jewish community's life and death in Nazi-occupied Lodz are represented in an extraordinarily comprehensive body of documentation. Over a period of more than four years, two bureaucracies—the German *Gettoverwaltung* and the Jewish ghetto administration—produced large quantities of correspondence, memoranda, reports, statistics, photographs, publicity albums, and works of art. The German administrative records were paralleled by the wealth of historical materials compiled by the Jewish workers of the official Ghetto Archives in their effort to record for future generations the story of their besieged community. They wrote the monumental *Daily Chronicle,* the unfinished and fragmentary "Encyclopedia of the Ghetto," and a multitude of essays, monographs, reports, and literary works.

All of this, as well as the private writings of individuals, would have been obliterated, as was the case with hundreds of Jewish communities east of Lodz, had the Germans not been forced into sudden retreat by the swift military advance of the Soviet and Polish forces in January 1945.

This volume presents materials from a variety of sources, the largest of which, the records of the Eldest of the Jews in Litzmannstadt, generally known as the Rumkowski Archives, contain all the extant documentation of the Jewish ghetto administration. Not all these records survived. In August and September 1944, during the final deportations from the ghetto, the staff of the Ghetto Archives buried one part of the records in the ghetto cemetery and another part in the courtyard of the ghetto's fire brigade at 13 Lutomierska Street. The Germans succeeded in discovering and destroying the documents in the cemetery but not the rest. These were unearthed and secured by the workers of the Central Jewish Historical Commission in Lodz in 1946.

A third, smaller group of materials belonging to the Jewish ghetto administration was rescued through the effort of Nachman Zonabend, one of the 877 ghetto inmates assigned by the Germans to clean up after the final deportations. One day in October 1944, he ventured into the rooms previously occupied by the Ghetto Archives at Koscielny Square, where he found packed suitcases the archivists had not had time to hide. Zonabend took them to the courtyard and dropped them into a dry well, covering them with quilt covers and pillows. When the ghetto was liberated in January 1945, he returned to pull the suitcases from the well and carried them away.

Another vast archive, the records of the *Gettoverwaltung,* were found almost intact in the offices of this agency on Cegielniana Street, outside the ghetto area.

A few years after the war, the Rumkowski Archive and the records of the *Gettoverwaltung* were transferred to the Jewish Historical Institute in Warsaw. However, during the anti-Jewish campaign in 1968 these records were removed from the Institute and sent back to Lodz, where they have remained in the custody of the Lodz State Archives.

Nachman Zonabend took the documents he had safeguarded with him to Sweden, when he settled there in 1947. In 1948 he donated much of the collection to the YIVO Institute for Jewish Research in New York, where they are now registered as the Nachman Zonabend Collection.

The bulk of this rich documentation is largely unknown to the general public. Only selected materials have been made available to interested readers in several published source books. Certain documents from those publications have been reissued in this volume as original English translations. The following should be mentioned here:

Arthur Eisenbach, ed., *Dokumenty i materialy do dziejow okupacji hitlerowsskiej w Polsce, Tom III: Getto lodzkie* [Documents and Materials in the History of the Nazi Occupation of Poland, Vol. 3, the Lodz Ghetto], Central Jewish Historical Commission, Warsaw-Lodz-Cracow, 1946. This volume includes documents from the *Gettoverwaltung* archive on the establishment, exploitation, and destruction of the ghetto by the Nazis.

Isaiah Trunk, *Lodzher geto: a historishe un sotsyologishe shtudye* [The Lodz Ghetto: A Historical and Sociological Study], YIVO–Yad Vashem, New York, 1962, Yiddish. The author appended to this monograph a selection of documents from both German and Jewish sources.

Danuta Dabrowska and Lucjan Dobroszycki, *Kronika getta lodzkiego,* vols. 1–2, Wydawnictwo Lodzkie, Lodz 1965–66; and Lucjan Dobroszycki, *The Chronicle of the Lodz Ghetto,* Yale University Press, New Haven, 1984. While discomfited by his own limited education, Mordechai Chaim Rumkowski so respected the intellectuals in the ghetto, and so wished to preserve for posterity a detailed record of the era of his Jewish domain, he assigned more than fifteen writers to full-time positions as ghetto archivists. Central to their work was the compilation of this official day-to-day account of ghetto life. Several of the appointed Chroniclers, including Oskar Rosenfeld, Oskar Singer, Jozef Zelkowicz, and Jerakhmil Bryman, wrote their own personal accounts, published here in *Lodz Ghetto,* which could not be contained in the remarkable community-sponsored chronicle.

It is not evident whether Rumkowski ever actually read or corrected the *Chronicle* typescripts, but they are generally faithful to his administration. At one point, however, the *Chronicle* speaks out to criticize Rumkowski's personal violence in beating people who displeased him, and the way this behavior was being emulated by the ghetto police and workshop managers.

The *Chronicle* was originally to be published in Poland in a comprehensive five-volume edition prepared over many years by Dabrowska and Dobroszycki. But in 1968, with only the first two volumes published, the project was abruptly discontinued by the Polish government during the anti-Jewish campaign that followed the Six-Day War. The plates of the remaining three volumes were destroyed.

Lucjan Dobroszycki then emigrated to New York and proceeded to edit the material down to the English-language edition, one-fourth the length of the entire *Chronicle,* which came to publication some sixteen years later.

The Lodz Ghetto also left for posterity a staggering quantity of pictorial documentation. Ghetto photographers were officially employed by the ghetto administration and also worked on their own. The greatest among them were Mendel Grossman, and Henryk Ross, whose hundreds of photographs were unmatched in their powerful depiction of ghetto life. There was also a group of officially employed artists, and their works, too, vividly illustrate ghetto reality. Of the photographs, large numbers of early-generation prints made in the ghetto are now in Yad Vashem, YIVO, the (Warsaw) Jewish Historical Institute, and Beit Lohamei Haghetaot. The latter two institutions also hold most of the works of art created in the ghetto.

—Alan Adelson,
Robert Lapides,
and Marek Web

AFTERWORD

Reading this book is a haunting experience. It is as if we had an open line right into the ghetto. By careful choosing, the editors bring us voices crying from the archive rather than documents buried in it. A whole community becomes present to us, from the Eldest of the Jews with his proud yet pathetic speeches, to the anger and self-pity of a young girl demanding a life denied to her. The one hundred and twenty-eight substantial excerpts are full of astonishing humor and self-criticism: nothing escapes observation. There is no need for me to describe how these voices, arranged by the compilers' art of chronological montage, compel us to deeper and deeper levels of sympathy, as we follow them in their variousness, querulousness, vacillation, wit, outrage, human perplexity. Unlike the traditional Remembrance Book, however, which can include events and stories from pre-Holocaust days, this anthology limits itself strictly to the five years and four months of the Occupation, during which time, as Ringelblum observed of his own community (he organized "Oneg Shabbes," a secret project preserving the story of the Warsaw Ghetto), the Jews were forced back into medieval conditions and a world (world?) no one from the outside could enter.

The internal perspective of these stories about life and death in the Lodz Ghetto, culled exclusively from eyewitnesses, creates plot, drama, tension, tragic irony. The drama and tension have to do with hopes of outliving the war, and the deteriorating conditions of a community kept on starvation rations and ravaged by disease. The tragic irony comes from the fact that we know what the inhabitants could not know: their hope of surviving was a false hope. There are vivid sketches of daily life that do not spare the inhabitants, pungent caricatures of the *Yekes* (German Jews), descriptions of a landscape of death more eloquent than any photo, scenes of family life with sacrificing women, and dramas centering on half a slice of bread. The plight of the sick and the children is inscribed everywhere. The record of this individual and communal effort to survive is overwhelming. One becomes ashamed of one's own voice, and wishes to do exactly what the compilers of this book have done: to quote, and avoid commentary.

Fifty years after the beginning of Lodz's agony there are questions that trouble us. What does this book commemorate? What can we learn from such comfortless stories? Can anything in our increasingly documented and detailed knowledge of the Holocaust redeem what happened? Of course, even should we be unable to find a redemptive meaning, it would still be our duty to remember. But the burden is shifting from historian to reader. We are at the point where the historical and memorial activity, while it must continue (for there is still much to be done), may not neglect the issue of interpretation: of how to say more, after reading this, than *never forget.*

The collective memory, which preserves the traumatic event in a bearable way, is not concerned with troubling moral questions but with reviving the community's faith in itself. Our rituals, too, the commemorative services we hold, aim at that result: they emphasize survival and bind up the wounds of loss. Yet, to ritual and to research a third, more personal response should be added. It would allow us to discuss the *shame* (Primo Levi's word) that afflicts us when we read these materials. It is a shame afflicting our image of human nature and does not spare anyone. It chastens the redemptive drive of the collective memory.

The self-administration of the ghetto under Rumkowski resulted inevitably in Jews oppressing Jews, with a Jewish police that did its job only too well. Where else do we find, on such a massive scale, Jews doing the work of the Nazis in the hope that the ghetto would outlast the war and that a portion of its people—the strongest, or those most favored by the Rumkowski administration—might survive? The entire scheme of self-administration appears demonic in retrospect: the Germans compelled Jews to act as their agents and execute soul-searing, soul-besmirching orders. They threatened worse if there was no compliance, and raised Rumkowski's hope that each deportation would be the last. His speech on September 4, 1942, when the Nazis have once more betrayed his hopes and demanded the delivery of 20,000 Jews (bargained down from 24,000, he tells us, and limited to children below the age of ten, but a quota that will fall mainly on the children and the sick) is an astonishing piece of rhetoric. "In my old age I must stretch out my hands and beg: Brothers and sisters, hand them over to me! Fathers and mothers, give me your children!" The end of his speech reveals that he still believes, despite this catastrophe, in the rationality of his plan.

> One needs the heart of a bandit to ask from you what I am asking. But put yourself in my place, think logically, and you'll reach the conclusion that I cannot proceed any other way. The part that can be saved is much larger than the part that must be given away.

It is hard to see how Rumkowski's desperate gamble was less catastrophic than if cooperation with the Germans had been refused or resisted. There were deeply divided attitudes in the ghetto toward this man who felt obliged to lead his people *into* slavery. He is reviled as a corrupt administrator and exalted as a father of his people; his reputation, as is reported here, can shift with the availability of potatoes. But at the moral center something else emerges, more frightening by far than doubts about a dictator installed by the Nazis and trying to manage. The naked truth is that Rumkowski's plan, unless the war ended quickly and the Nazis were removed, was bound to result in the death of the sick and of children below working age. A clinging to life remained in the ghetto but there was not enough moral oxygen to breathe. In this *huis clos,* this man-made hell created by the Nazis, most choices were not choices—whatever was done would cause death, injury, humiliation. Even acts of "spiritual resistance," as they tend now to be called, such as cultural activities kept up in these surroundings—performances of Beethoven, religious worship, schooling, the writing of the Chronicles—are morally dubious if they instilled a deceptive hope that weakened other kinds of resistance. By 1942 the Jews of Lodz were all death-bound: the Final Solution had been set in motion. The "logic" to which Rumkowski appeals at the end of his speech is no longer there, if it ever was.

There are many negative lessons, then, which can be the subject of painful moral debate. A single phrase in those bureaucratic German documents also assembled here makes the heart freeze as we realize the world it stands for. How is confiscated property from the ghetto to be legally classified? It belongs to the state because it is "ownerless." Legally the ghetto's Jews were dead persons to the Nazi administration. They just did not exist as human beings. One wonders again what forces of coldness, what inhumanity, what propaganda, could bring the Nazi administrators and their followers to this point.

After a while, among the victims too, the heart grows cold. There is the phenomenon of the *Muselmänner,* who go about like zombies, no longer feeling, no longer caring. Even those who cling to life notice a deterioration. To see, day after day, starving children, to know that the sick are ripped out of hospital beds in the night. . . . So many dead, everywhere. "There are no coffins. The corpse lies between two boards, packed in old scraps of paper. It is held, like a dead fish, in a net that is carried on two slates and let go over the grave. . . . The sheet-metal wagons keep delivering the dead into the hall, the nets keep taking them out of the hall. The earth fills itself with dead. . . . As numerous as grains of sand in the ocean, stars in the heavens."

In the same mortal year 1942, Oskar Singer invents the category of *Litzmannstadt death.* "Morality cracks," he writes in his notebook, "but ethics remains." Certain institutions like the family do not collapse, though they are severely altered; death, too, is altered. "We can no longer die as other people do. We no longer have the possiblity of a noble end. Litzmannstadt death is an alien, ugly death."

The moral and descriptive power of these impressions, even when they parody Scripture, as in the comment on the dead "as numerous as grains of sand" (which mocks God's promise to His Chosen People) begins to answer my question: What comfort can we take from this record of desolation? In the "foreign land" of this ghetto world, the writer does not lay down his pen. He cannot praise God or most of his fellow Jews, but he can still describe what he sees and perceives—holding to a standard provided by the tradition, even if he quotes it against itself.

There is an incredible resilience in these testimonies, which comes only partly from a respect for life under any conditions. The private notebooks are sensitive to the slightest sign of normalcy and open up to a beautiful day or a picturesque detail. So great is the discontinuity, the departure from normalcy, the separation of the ghetto from the world—also, incongruously, from the war, for this War against the Jews has superseded the other—that any sign of constancy is greeted. That is why the journals abound in marvelous caricature of different types and groups. *Something* has remained unchanged. But this discovery is often mingled with the opposite mood: How could the outside world (insofar as the ghetto has an outside) remain the same? How could God Himself remain the same? (He rarely enters this book, however, except in the form of Bible quotation.) The conflicting moods meet in Shayevitch's poem *Lekh Lekho* ("Go forth," Genesis 12:1), in which the poet identifies with Abraham as he prepares his own daughter Bimile for "the unknown journey" of deportation:

The evil hour has arrived,
When I must teach you, a little girl,
The terrible *parshe* of *Lekh Lekho.*
But how can we compare it
To the bloody *Lekh Lekho* of today?

There is a sort of comfort in that bitter, homiletic application: a traditional paradigm is maintained. But the poet's mood turns, as he images in a passage both blasphemous and humorous the desecration of his own writings, so full of holy paradigms:

Tremble, tremble, holy volumes . . .
Someday, in the dawn, someone will rise
And in just his pants
Will cut square pieces from you
For toilet paper,
And will grimace, that the writing
May, God forbid, hurt him.

The witnesses—private diarists, official chroniclers, experienced artists—intend their voices to survive, even if they and the community perish. Despite a temptation like Job's to "blaspheme God and die," they exercise restraint and remain *observant.* It is the reader who may feel like drawing up a dossier against God: they have no use for such fictional and self-indulgent exercises. We commemorate them, their testimony, their clarity of voice and mind. I wish I could say more, for instance that we confront here a great and purifying tragedy, one that could make us respond with woe and wonder. But though the totally ghettoized perspective of the eyewitnesses creates a concentrated picture, a place and action as unified as the neoclassical stage, and though that stage is as crowded as a Shakespearean play, the tragedy here is that there is no tragedy. We do not have heroes to identify with. Rumkowski has a touch of madness and pathos but he does not represent the community. Nor can the Holocaust ever be the subject of tragedy without shame's being added to the root emotions of pity and terror. Primo Levi has said that this shame can never be purged, that there is no catharsis. I end by quoting Oskar Rosenfeld, whose notebook suggests a different understanding of the tragic that should be set against mine. It points to God, even to a gnostic insight, yet avoids accusation:

> This tragedy has no heroes. And why [call it] tragedy? Because the pain does not touch upon something human, on another's heart, but rather is something incomprehensible, linked with the cosmos, a natural phenomenon like the creation of the world. One must begin again with the Creation, with *B'raishit* [the first word of the Bible]. In the beginning, God created the ghetto.
>
> —Geoffrey Hartman

GLOSSARY

ARBEITSLAGER: Work camp [German]
ASCHKENES: Germans [Hebrew]
BEIRAT: Council [German]
CHEDER: Room for study or prayer [Hebrew]
CHOLENT: a meal consisting of potatoes, vegetables, meat and fat
DRECK: filth [Yiddish]
DROSHKY: open, horse-drawn wagon [originally Russian]
ERETZ ISRAEL: Land of Israel [Hebrew]
FELDGRAU: field-gray [German], of soldiers' uniforms
GEHSPERRE: curfew [German], sometimes shortened to *Sperre* or *Szperre*
HACHSHARAH: training group [Hebrew]
KADDISH: prayer for the dead [Hebrew]
KRIPO: short for Criminal Police [German]
MILCHOME: war [Hebrew]
MINYAN: quorum of ten men needed for a prayer service [Hebrew]
REICHSDEUTSCHE: German citizens [German]
RUMKIES: slang for the ghetto currency, after Rumkowski, whose signature appeared on it
SCHUPO: short for Schutzpolizei, the local police [German]
SEDER: the Passover meal [Hebrew]
SHAYGETZ: Gentile youth [Yiddish]
SHUL: synagogue [Yiddish]
STAPO: the secret state police, short for Geheime Staatspolizei, the Gestapo [German]

SUCCAH: booth [Hebrew], in which meals are taken during Succoth.
SUCCOTH: The holiday commemorating a temporary shelter Jews found in the wilderness [Hebrew]
TALLIS: prayer shawl [Hebrew]
TEFILLIN: prayer vestments [Hebrew]
VANYA: Oskar Rosenfeld's code word for the Soviet Union
VOLKSDEUTSCHE: ethnic Germans [German]
YARMULKE: skullcap [Yiddish]

NOTES ON THE TEXT

CHAPTER ONE: THE INITIAL TERROR

[p. 9] At the Battle of Warsaw, in 1920, the Polish forces defeated the Red Army against great odds; in the Battle of the Marne, in 1914, the French turned back the German advance on Paris.

[p. 13] Great Britain governed Palestine under a 1919 League of Nations mandate.

[p. 16] The Germans treated failure to pay rent as sabotage.

[p. 16] Z.U.S. stood for *Zaklad Ubezpieczen Spolecznych* [Pol: Office of Social Security].

[p. 16] After the partition of Czechoslovakia in March 1939, the Nazis referred to the territories of Bohemia and Moravia as the Protectorate.

[p. 25] The council's official name was the *Aeltestenrat* [Ger: Council of Elders].

[p. 26] *SS-Brigadenführer* Friedrich Übelhoer, the author of this memorandum, was chief of police and president [*Regierungpräsident*] of the Kalisz regency.

[p. 26] Wartheland, the part of Poland annexed to the Third Reich, was divided into three regencies. At first Lodz belonged to the Kalisz regency, but later the regency seat was moved from Kalisz to Lodz.

[p. 27] Radogoszcz was a northern suburb of Lodz, adjoining the ghetto. The railroad station there became the depot for transporting the ghetto's goods and supplies and for deportations.

CHAPTER TWO: INTO THE GHETTO

[p. 32] *Reichsdeutsche* referred to German nationals living within the pre-1939 boundaries of the Third Reich. *Volksdeutsche* were ethnic Germans, that is, people of German origin whose families had lived outside Germany for generations.

[p. 44] The Order Service [Ger: *Ordnungsdienst*] was the official name of the Jewish police in the ghetto.

[p. 47] *Oberbürgermeister,* abbreviated OBM, is the German equivalent of mayor.

[p. 55] The General Government was the Nazis' official designation for that part of Poland they occupied but did not incorporate into the Third Reich.

[p. 74] Dawid Warszawski was a high ghetto official and the head of the clothing industry.

[p. 85] Janusz Korczak (Henryk Goldszmidt, 1878?–1942), a physician and educator, was the author of popular books for young people, novels on social issues, and works on child psychology and education. He was the founder and director of the Jewish orphanage in Warsaw. Refusing an offer to be rescued during the deportations from the Warsaw Ghetto in 1942, he went with the children from his orphanage to Treblinka and died with them.

[p. 87] Szulman probably refers to the general situation in the Warsaw Ghetto, which was depicted by Rumkowski as incomparably worse than in Lodz. Rumkowski visited the Warsaw ghetto in 1941.

CHAPTER THREE: "GIVE UP YOUR SELFISH INTERESTS"

[p. 103] Leon Rozenblat was commander of the Order Service.

[p. 110] Boruch (Bernard) Praszkier was Rumkowski's "Special Assignments" chief.

[p. 126] The Pale of Settlement was that part of Czarist Russia where the Jews were permitted to live.

[p. 130] Bontche Shvayg was the Y. L. Peretz character who kept silent in the face of even the greatest injustice done him.

[p. 130] Krawiecka Street was the location of the House of Culture, in whose auditorium symphonic concerts were performed. During the final deportations in 1944, the house was converted into an assembly point for deportees.

[p. 142] Praszkier (see note for p. 110) directed the Department of Kitchens, which managed the ghetto's network of public kitchens.

[p. 143] Ziula Krengiel (Rachela Krengiel-Pacanowska), a teacher and Communist activist, was a co-founder of the ghetto's underground leftist organization. In 1942 she was deported to Chelmno, where she died.

[p. 151] In fact, the declaration of war had been on April 6, 1917.

CHAPTER FIVE: "DEPORTATIONS OUT"

[p. 199] On the day of the speech, there was a persistent rumor that the entire ghetto population was to be deported.

[p. 199] The Resettlement Commission, established by Rumkowski on January 5, 1942, prepared lists of those to be deported.

[p. 201] Rumkowski's reference was to the Trade and Control Office, a supervisory authority of the ghetto industry.

[p. 210] The Resettlement Office, established in 1941 to deal with the influx of deportees to the ghetto, was headed by Henryk Neftalin.

[p. 214] This account describes the public execution of Max Hertz, a deportee from Cologne who attempted to return to that city after slipping out of the ghetto. The execution took place on February 21, 1942, a Saturday; all deportees from Germany were ordered to attend.

[p. 245] The Gestapo office was located in the Balut Market [Ger: *Baluter Ring*].

CHAPTER SIX: "LIFE IS NARROW"

[p. 275] The destination of the transports was Chelmno, a village near Kolo. The Jews deported there were asphyxiated in specially designated vans which pumped the engine's exhaust into the sealed rear compartment. This occurred while the trucks drove from the loading point, a small church in the center of the village, to a nearby woods, where the bodies were dumped and burned.

[p. 286] H.T.O., the *Haupttreuhandstelle-Ost* [Ger: Main Trustee Office, East], was in charge of confiscated property in German-occupied territories.

[p. 292] RSHA stood for the *Reichsicherheithauptamt* [Ger: State Security Main Office], of which the Gestapo was part.

[p. 307] Szlomo Hercberg, a Gestapo confidant, was chief of the *Sonderkommando* [Ger: Special Unit] and later commandant of the ghetto's Central Prison. He was arrested on charges of profiteering and deported to Chelmno in March 1942.

CHAPTER SEVEN: "NIGHTMARISH DAYS"

[p. 327] Stanislaw Jakobson, a lawyer, was chairman of the Ghetto Court.

[p. 340] A general curfew [Ger: *Ansgehsperre* or *Gehsperre*, Yid: *Szpera*] was imposed on the ghetto from the fifth to the twelfth of September.

CHAPTER EIGHT: "ADAPTING TO CIRCUMSTANCES"

[p. 367] Dr. Bernard Heilig, a historian of Czech Jewry, was deported from Prague to the Lodz Ghetto in October 1941. On the staff of the Ghetto Archives, he died in 1943.

[p. 376] Rosenfeld worked during his youth with Theodor Herzl, the founder of Zionism.

[p. 377] Israel Leizerowicz (1902–44) was a painter, poet, and essayist. He produced paintings in the ghetto on apocalyptic themes and wrote verses satirizing ghetto notables. He died in Auschwitz.

[p. 377] The Special Unit [Ger: *Sonderabteilung* or *Sonderkommando*], a unit of the Order Service, was in charge of expropriations, operations against the black market, and political espionage.

[p. 378] One fasts on *Yom Kippur,* lives in a shanty during *Succoth,* and wears odd clothing on *Purim.*

[p. 382] The uprising in the Warsaw Ghetto began on April 19.

[p. 390] Food coupons CP and B III entitled workers in the ghetto industry to supplemental rations. They were canceled on September 29, 1943, and replaced by "special nutrition mid-day meals."

[p. 399] Soon after the *Gehsperre,* the Rabbinate was dissolved, and *Shabbos* and holidays were declared regular working days. However, religious practices were not officially forbidden and religious life continued to be conducted, although on a modest scale.

[p. 401] The Chassidic movement is composed of numerous groups. For the most part, these groups are called after the towns where their founders resided. Thus, Aleksandrer refers to Aleksandrow Lodzki, Gerer to Gora Kalwaria.

CHAPTER NINE: THE FINAL STAGE

[p. 424] Aron Jakubowicz was head of the ghetto industries and Rumkowski's deputy. Pinchas Gierszowski was the director of the ghetto bank; his ties to Rumkowski dated back to the 1920s, when Gierszowski founded the Jewish children's home in Helenowek, of which Rumkowski became director.

[p. 427] The Nazi Robert Ley was head of the German Labor Front; he committed suicide in 1945, while on trial for war crimes.

[p. 442] Mark Kligier headed the ghetto's Special Unit.

[p. 444] Otto Bradfisch was chief of the Gestapo in Lodz.

CHAPTER TEN: IN HIDING

[p. 483] The German home guard, the *Volkssturm* [Ger: People's Army] was raised as a last defense in the winter of 1944–45. Service was mandatory for all able-bodied Germans not in the military.

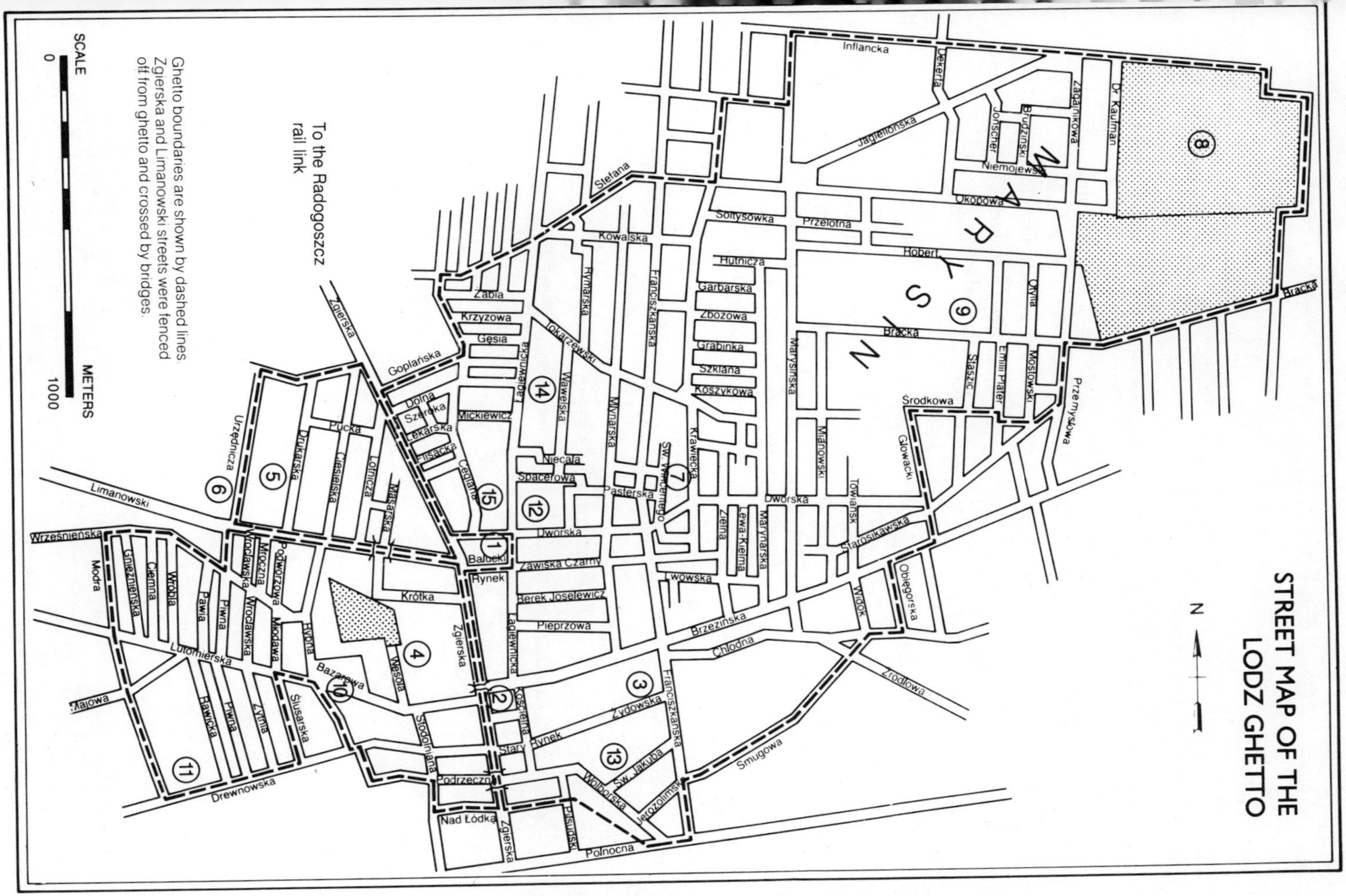

KEY TO APPROXIMATE LOCATIONS CITED IN THE TEXT

1. Balut Market, site of the Jewish and German administration offices. 2. Plac Koscielny, the church square. At Number 4 was the ghetto archives office, where Rosenfeld, Zelkowicz, and Singer did much of their writing. 3. Number 10 Zydowska Street, site of the ice cellar where Poznanski hid with his family until the liberation. 4. Hospital at Wesola Street, brutally evacuated by the Nazis in September 1942. 5, 6. Two primary carpenters' workshops, sites of early labor unrest. 7. The House of Culture, where concerts by the ghetto orchestra, musical reviews, literary readings, and speeches by Rumkowski were given. The building on Krawiecka Street was designated as an assembly point during the final liquidation of the ghetto in the summer of 1944. 8. The old Jewish Cemetery. The area to the south holds the "ghetto field," where tens of thousands of ghetto dwellers were buried in graves marked only with temporary placards. 9. Marysin, the "rural" region of the ghetto, which contained the "villas" of the ghetto elite, the old-age home, the ghetto orphanage, the major school buildings, and many communal gardens. 10. Number 17 Lutomierska, the Fire Brigade Square, where Rumkowski delivered many speeches, including the "Give Me Your Children" exhortation of September 4, 1942. 11. Drewnowska Street hospital, also used as a deportation site. 12, 13. Two primary tailors' workshops. 14. Home of Dawid Sierakowiak, Number 9 Wawelska Street. 15. Hospital at Numbers 34–36 Lagiewnicka Street, evacuated in the September 1942 "Nightmarish Days"; Rumkowski had his apartment on the second floor of one of the side buildings.

INDEX BY AUTHORS

TRANSLATORS

Stanley Bergman (Polish, Hebrew), Jonathan Boyarin (Yiddish), Danuta Dabrowska (Polish, Yiddish, German), Regina Gelb (Polish), Miriam Halberstam (German), David Kallick (German), Fruma Mohrer (Yiddish), Chana Mlotek (Yiddish), Mary Schulman (Yiddish), Michael Skakun (Yiddish), Renate Stein (German), Charles Stern (German), Marek Web (Polish, Yiddish)

PHOTOGRAPH REPRODUCTION

Director: Mary Bachmann. Assistants: Lisa Adelson, Lori Barbagallo, Elizabeth Ellner, Nancy Huddleston, Yitzchak Mais, Zvi Reiter, Krzysztof Wojchiechowski